MODERN
Accounting Practice
A modular approach

REVISED EDITION

MODERN
Accounting Practice
A modular approach

REVISED EDITION

SHEILA BURDEN and HELEN DUNLOP

JOHN WILEY & SONS
BRISBANE • NEW YORK • CHICHESTER • WEINHEIM • SINGAPORE • TORONTO

Revised edition published 1998 by
JACARANDA WILEY LTD
33 Park Road, Milton, Qld 4064

Offices also in Sydney and Melbourne

Typeset in 11/12.5 New Baskerville

First edition 1997

© S. Burden, H. Dunlop 1997, 1998

National Library of Australia
Cataloguing-in-Publication data

Burden, Sheila.
 Modern accounting practice: a modular
 approach.

 Rev. ed.
 Includes index.
 ISBN 0 471 34118 5.

 1. Accounting. I. Dunlop, Helen. II. Title.

657.044

All rights reserved. With the exception of the
masters on pages 539–573, no part of this
publication may be reproduced, stored in a retrieval
system, or transmitted in any form or by any means,
electronic, mechanical, photocopying, recording,
or otherwise, without the prior permission of
the publisher.

Cover illustration by Kate Barry

Printed in Singapore

10 9 8 7 6 5 4 3 2 1

CONTENTS

Preface   xiii
Acknowledgements   xv

CHAPTER 1   THE ACCOUNTING ENVIRONMENT   1

What is accounting?   2
What is bookkeeping?   2
  Role of the bookkeeper   2
  Objectives of bookkeeping   2
  Rules in keeping a manual set of books   3
Function of accounting   3
  Management accounting   3
  Financial accounting   3
  Public accounting   3
  Auditing   4
  Public sector accounting   4
Accounting conceptual framework   4
  Accounting entity convention   4
  Continuity of activity convention   4
  Historical cost convention   4
  Accounting period convention   5
  Accounting monetary convention   5
  Accounting equation convention   5
Accounting Standards and concept statements   5
Accounting Standards   5
  Statements of Accounting Concepts   6
Accounting entity versus legal entity   6
Accounting concepts and terms   6
Main types of business ownership   9
  Sole trader (or sole proprietor)   9
  Partnership   9
  Company   9
  Cooperative   10
  Franchise   10
The account   11
  Assets   11
  Liabilities   12
  Owner's equity   12
The accounting equation   12
  Transactions and the accounting equation   14
  Balancing the accounting equation   16

Transaction analysis chart   18
Owner's equity and the capital account   19
Profit and loss statement   24
Balance sheet   25
Recording transactions   34
    Recording increases and decreases in the accounts   34
    Format of ledger accounts   34
    The double-entry system   36
    Debit entry   36
    Credit entry   37
Analysing transactions   37
Keeping a record of transactions   48
    Financial source documents   49
    Journals   49
    Ledgers   49
    Trial balance   52
    Profit and loss statement   52
    Balance sheet   52

> **NOS322: Bookkeeping — General Ledger**
> *Learning outcome 1*
> Describe accounting concepts and terms.
>
> **NOS124: Accounting to Trial Balance**
> *Learning outcome 1*
> Describe accounting concepts and terms.

CHAPTER 2   FINANCIAL SOURCE DOCUMENTS   53

Types of business document   54
    Purchase requisition   57
    Purchase order   58
    Invoice   60
    Delivery docket   63
    Credit note   64
    Cheque   65
    Remittance advice   68
    Petty cash   69
    Receipt   70
    Statement of account   72
    Records of cash sales   73
    Credit card sales voucher   75
    Credit card credit voucher   75
    Credit card merchant summary   76
    Bank deposit slip   79
Validity of source documents   81

Internal controls and security   84
   Administrative controls   84
   Accounting controls   85
   Security of financial source documents   86
Accountability of source documents   86
Batching of source documents   86
   Accounts receivable   89
   Accounts payable   89
Electronic reporting systems   93
   Speed   93
   Output   93
   Posting   93
   Error protection   93
   Reports   93
   Printing source documents   94
   Automatic adjustments   94

NOS134: Financial Source Documents
Learning outcome 1
Identify and prepare business source documents according to organisational procedures.

NOS124: Accounting to Trial Balance
Learning outcome 2.1
Complete the following source documents:
- receipt
- sales invoice
- credit note
- cheque
- purchase order
- bank deposit form
- petty cash docket.

CHAPTER 3   PREPARATION OF JOURNALS   96

What are journals?   97
   General journal   98
Accounts payable journals   104
   Credit application   105
   Entering details from source documents into journals   106
   Purchases journal   107
   Purchases returns and allowances journal   112

Putting it together   115

   Cash payments journal   117

Putting it together   121

Accounts receivable journals   126
   Entering details of source documents   127
   Sales journal   127
   Sales returns and allowances journal   132

Putting it together   135
   Cash receipts journal   138
Putting it together   144
General journal miscellaneous entries   149
   Purchase and sale of non-current assets on credit   149
   Inventory (stock) drawings by owner   151
   Interest expense charged by creditors on overdue accounts   152
   Interest revenue (interest charged on overdue debtors' accounts)   153
   Bad debts written off   154
   Correction of errors   157
   General journal miscellaneous entries   161
Putting it together   163

NOS240: Bookkeeping — Accounts Payable
Learning outcome 1
Prepare journals from source documents and information supplied.

NOS241: Bookkeeping — Accounts Receivable
Learning outcome 1
Prepare journals from source documents and information supplied.

NOS124: Accounting to Trial Balance
Learning outcome 2
Prepare journals from source documents and information supplied.

CHAPTER 4   POSTING TO THE LEDGERS   166

Section 1: The general ledger   168
   Subsidiary ledgers   168
   Posting to the general ledger   169
   Posting from the general journal   170
   Posting from the accounts payable journals to the general ledger   182
   Posting from the accounts receivable journals   189
   Extracting a trial balance   201
   Reconciling with subsidiary ledgers   205

NOS322: Bookkeeping — General Ledger
Learning outcome 2
Post journal entries to the general ledger and extract a trial balance maintaining the accounting equation.

NOS124: Accounting to Trial Balance
Learning outcome 3
Post journal entries to the general ledger and extract a trial balance maintaining the accounting equation.

Section 2: The accounts payable ledger   205
    Posting to the accounts payable ledger   205
    Schedule of creditors' balances   214
    Reconciling invoices for payment to creditors   228

NOS240: Bookkeeping — Accounts Payable
Learning outcome 2
Explain the purpose of the accounts payable subsidiary ledger and post journals to the accounts payable subsidiary ledger and prepare a schedule of creditors' balances.

Learning outcome 3
Reconcile invoices for payment to creditors.

NOS124: Accounting to Trial Balance
Learning outcome 4
Explain the purpose of subsidiary ledgers and post entries from journals to the accounts payable subsidiary ledger and prepare a schedule of creditors' balances.

Section 3: The accounts receivable ledger   237
    Posting to the accounts receivable ledger   237
    Schedule of debtors' balances   247
    Preparing statements for debtors   258
Putting it together   267

NOS241: Bookkeeping — Accounts Receivable
Learning outcome 2
Explain the purpose of the accounts receivable subsidiary ledger and post journal entries from journals to the accounts receivable subsidiary ledger and prepare a schedule of debtors' balances.

Learning outcome 3
Prepare statements for debtors.

NOS124: Accounting to Trial Balance
Learning outcome 4
Explain the purpose of subsidiary ledgers and post entries from journals to the accounts receivable subsidiary ledger and prepare a schedule of debtors' balances.

Section 4: Bank reconciliation procedures   286
    Reconciling the cash records   286
    Preparing a bank reconciliation statement   291
    Reconciling over two consecutive periods   325

NOS124: Accounting to Trial Balance
Learning outcome 5
Reconcile bank statements with cash records.

CHAPTER 5 CASH RECORDS 338

Receiving and documenting payments/takings 339
　Cash sales 339
　Credit card sales 342
　Payment by cheque 344
　Issuing receipts 345
Verifying the day's takings 346
　Security of cash 346
　Ethics and accountability 347
Maintaining a cash book 348
　Format of a cash book 349
　Recording receipts and payments in a cash book 350
　Recording dishonoured cheques 354
　Balancing the cash book 356
　Checking the accuracy of the cash book 358
　Different types of cash books 358
Reconciling the cash records 367
　Overdraft 369
Preparing a bank reconciliation statement 369

Putting it together 398

> **NOS229: Cash Records**
> *Learning outcome 1*
> Receive and document payments/takings.
>
> *Learning outcome 2*
> Use source documents to complete a cash book.
>
> *Learning outcome 3*
> Reconcile cash records and prepare a bank reconciliation statement.

CHAPTER 6 CASH CONTROL 408

Maintaining a petty cash system 409
　What is petty cash? 409
　The imprest petty cash system 409
　Recording petty cash transactions 413
　Petty cash book 414
　Balancing the petty cash book 415
　Manual versus computerised petty cash systems 420
　Checking petty cash records 435
　Dealing with errors and irregularities 435
　Security of petty cash 436

Preparing and validating documents for banking   440
　　Record of takings   440
　　Sorting cash ready for banking   446
　　Organising and counting cheques for banking   449
　　Organising credit card sales for banking   449
　　Preparing the bank deposit   451
Balancing and validating cash receipts — a summary   457
　　Cash   457
　　Cheques   457
　　Validating bank deposits   458
Electronic banking processes   458
　　Electronic transfer of funds   458
　　Automatic teller machine (ATM) transactions   458
　　Electronic funds transfer at point of sale (EFTPOS)   459
　　Telephone banking   459

> **NOS122: Cash Control**
> *Learning outcome 1*
> Record and balance petty cash transactions for financial records according to organisational procedures.
>
> *Learning outcome 2*
> Prepare and validate documents for banking.
>
> **NOS124: Accounting to Trial Balance**
> *Learning outcome 6*
> Record and balance petty cash transactions for financial records, using an imprest system.

CHAPTER 7   PAYROLL   461

Internal control   462
Organisational policies and procedures   463
Payment for labour   464
Salaries and wages   464
Payroll systems   465
　　Commercial payroll systems   465
Deductions   471
　　Income tax deductions   471
　　Deductions authorised by the employee   471
　　Allowances and payments   471
　　Medicare Levy   476
　　Superannuation Guarantee   476
　　Tax File Number   476
　　Employment Declaration form   476
Prepare a manual payroll register   481

Employee earnings record   483
Group certificate   483
Preparation of wage envelopes (pay packets)   485
   Cash analysis sheet   486
Completing pay slips   487
Leave   488
   Paid leave   488
   Unpaid leave   489
Calculating holiday pay   489
Recording payroll transactions in the accounting system   512
   Gross wages   512
   Net wages   512
   Deductions   512
   Journal entries   512
   General ledger entries   515
Remitting deductions   520

Putting it together   526

NOS135: Payroll
Learning outcome 1
Maintain an established manual payroll system under supervision.

NOS124: Accounting to Trial Balance
Learning outcome 7
Prepare a manual payroll and record payroll details into the accounting records.

Masters   539

Glossary   575

Index   589

PREFACE

When I hear I forget
When I see I remember,
When I do I understand.

In *Modern Accounting Practice* we have endeavoured to remain faithful to those principles laid down in our previous text, Modern Bookkeeping Practice:
- step-by-step instruction on each topic
- adequate practice exercises
- presentation of exercises in simulated documents format
- provision of consolidation exercises to reinforce learning.

This text was written to meet the objectives of the National Office Skills modules. It adopts a modular approach and has been structured to meet the requirements of the following modules:
- NOS322 — Bookkeeping: General Ledger
- NOS124 — Accounting to Trial Balance
- NOS134 — Financial Source Documents
- NOS240 — Bookkeeping: Accounts Payable
- NOS241 — Bookkeeping: Accounts Receivable
- NOS229 — Cash Records
- NOS122 — Cash Control
- NOS135 — Payroll.

For ease of use, the Table of Contents provides information on which modules are covered in each chapter.

In addressing the requirements of NOS124 — Accounting to Trial Balance, care has been taken to ensure that the sequence of accounting procedures has been maintained and that bookkeeping principles are presented in a logical format.

Another feature of this text is that, within each section, the accounts payable and accounts receivable modules are self-contained and may be taught in any order to achieve the same result. Each topic may be taught in isolation, but there are linking exercises common to all.

The text assumes no prior accounting knowledge. A demonstration exercise continues throughout the bookkeeping modules, with each step fully explained, illustrated and integrated with the next step. In this way, the journalising of source documents, the subsequent posting of the journals to the ledgers and the extraction of trial balance and schedules of debtors' and creditors' balances is shown in full to provide a handy source of reference for students working the exercises which follow.

Exercises are presented at the end of each topic, and it is recommended that students complete these exercises before moving on to the next topic.

As each topic is learned it is integrated with the previous work to constantly reinforce the earlier learning. Photocopiable masters of all the journals, ledgers and forms needed to complete the exercises are included at the back of the book. A glossary of important terms is also included at the back of the book for easy reference.

We are very grateful for the tremendous amount of feedback we have received from our former colleagues, especially those who gave their precious spare time to review the manuscript. Where possible, their suggestions and comments have been incorporated. However, for any text to continue to meet the needs of both teachers and students, it must constantly re-invent itself. To this end, comments and suggestions are always welcome and may be passed on to us through the publishers, or by completing the feedback sheet included in the text.

Sheila Burden and Helen Dunlop

ACKNOWLEDGEMENTS

The authors and publisher would like to thank the following copyright holders, organisations and individuals for their assistance and permission to reproduce material in this book:

Commonwealth data included in this publication is copyright and reproduced by permission. Apart from any use as permitted under the *Copyright Act 1968*, no part may be reproduced by any process without prior written permission from the Australian Government Publishing Service. Requests and inquiries concerning reproduction and rights should be directed to the Manager, Commonwealth Information Services, Australian Government Publishing Service, GPO Box 84, Canberra ACT 2601; Westpac Banking Corporation — Merchant Services for permission to reproduce the credit voucher, sales voucher and merchant summary; Westpac Banking Corporation — Personal Transaction Accounts for permission to reproduce the cheque form with butt, bank deposit slip, bank statement and bank deposit book; Jenny Mowatt, Woolworths Supermarkets for the general overview of point-of-sale procedures, duties involved in cash and credit card transactions, cash handling procedures, accountability and security; Sue Bolton, Education Section, Independent Commission Against Corruption for the outline of basic strategies for implementing ethics and accountability in the workplace; Lucy Russell, Maggie Saldais, Tony Zadravec and others at Jacaranda Wiley for their help and support.

Every effort has been made to trace the ownership of copyright material. Holders of information that will enable the publisher to rectify any error or omission in subsequent editions will be welcome to contact the Permissions Department of Jacaranda Wiley. In these instances, the publisher will be happy to pay the usual permissions fee to the copyright holder.

CHAPTER 1

The accounting environment

WHEN you have studied this chapter and completed the exercises, you should be competent in the following skills. Tick each skill when you have completed the relevant section.

LEARNING OUTCOMES

1. Outline the main types of business ownership.

2. Explain the following concepts and terms:
   - accounting entity
   - legal entity
   - reporting entity
   - reporting period
   - balance date
   - owner's equity for a sole trader
   - revenue and revenue recognition
   - expense and expense recognition
   - accounting equation
   - double entry
   - chart of accounts.

3. Analyse transactions and apply rules of debit and credit in terms of the accounting equation.

WHAT IS ACCOUNTING?

Accounting is the process of recording, classifying and summarising financial information collected by bookkeepers for analysis and interpretation. It provides guidance in making business decisions and provides useful economic information to interested parties and users who depend on these results.

WHAT IS BOOKKEEPING?

Bookkeeping is the detailed and accurate recording of all **transactions** which take place in a business. It is necessary to record the date, nature and value (in money terms) of the transaction. Bookkeeping records provide the information from which financial accounts are prepared.

Role of the bookkeeper

Source documents arise as a result of transactions. It is the task of the bookkeeper to convert financial data gathered from source documents into useful economic information. This is done by:
- identifying source documents resulting from the transactions
- recording and summarising details in journals
- classifying the information from the journals in the ledger.

Once the information has been collected, recorded and arranged in a meaningful way by the bookkeeper, it is used by the accountant to prepare accounting reports. These reports assist management in planning for and controlling an organisation and are also communicated to outside users such as shareholders and potential investors to assist with economic decision-making.

Objectives of bookkeeping

Bookkeeping is the process of maintaining a clear, concise and permanent record of all transactions as they occur, to assist the owner/s of the business to ascertain:
- amounts owing to the business by **debtors**
- amounts owed to **creditors**
- amounts of losses and gains in a particular accounting period and the reasons for these
- flow of **cash** and goods, both into and out of the business
- nature and amount of what the business owns or what is owed to the business (assets)
- nature and amount of what the business owes (liabilities)
- the amount of owner's equity (**capital**, **proprietorship**) that the owner has invested in the business
- the overall financial standing of the business at a given date.

Rules in keeping a manual set of books

- Writing must be in permanent ink and be neat and legible. Figures are expecially important. They must be clearly formed to avoid any confusion.
- If an incorrect figure is written, it must be neatly ruled out and the correct figure written in. Write the new figure in pencil until the accuracy of the amount is checked. Then write it in ink.
- Erasures and correction fluid alterations are not permitted, as this could indicate falsification of entries.
- When entering figures, keep them in strict alignment to make additions and checking easier.
- All lines in all books of entry must be neatly ruled, using a ruler.
- Follow formats set out by your teacher. Although formats may vary, standards do not. Your work must always be clean, neat and well presented.

FUNCTION OF ACCOUNTING

Accounting is concerned with providing information relating to economic activities. In our personal lives we keep records of our economic activities. Most of us like to control our finances to ascertain that we have spent wisely in the past and to plan how to spend in the future.

Similarly, accounting is concerned with the economic activities of a business. Accounting involves gathering information, processing it and reporting on it to management and other interested users. This information is used to evaluate past economic events, control current economic activities and make economic decisions and plans for the future.

Over the years, accounting has developed into specialised areas such as management accounting, financial accounting, public accounting, auditing and public sector accounting.

Management accounting

Management accounting provides management with information to help make decisions about the overall planning and control of the business. As well as accounting reports, managers need detailed information about many other aspects of the business from many different sources.

Financial accounting

Financial accounting is concerned with measuring and reporting economic events for the reporting period in order to determine operating results and the overall financial position. It also entails the preparation and presentation of the accounting reports (financial statements) of an organisation.

Public accounting

This area of accounting is concerned with those accountants who practise within the community. They offer services to the public and are involved in the preparation of accounts, taxation returns and financial advice. Accounting firms often provide auditing services to businesses.

Auditing

Auditors have the responsibility of checking the quality of the financial information prepared by the accounting system. There are two types of auditors:
1. *external* — who check the financial accounts and report to the shareholders
2. *internal* — who are employed internally to check the quality and effectiveness of the accounting system that produces the information.

Public sector accounting

This is a specialised area of accounting dealing with accounting practices for government instrumentalities covering federal, State and local government.

ACCOUNTING CONCEPTUAL FRAMEWORK

Over the years, the accounting profession evolved without a defined set of guiding principles. Confusion often arose as different firms used varying methods to correct similar problems. This made comparison of financial reports between companies and over time difficult, as information was interpreted in different ways by different people. For this reason, a conceptual framework, in the form of a number of concept statements, is being developed to provide a set of guiding principles for the accounting profession. Statements of accounting concepts are discussed in more detail on page 6.

Accountants themselves have developed traditional ways of doing things. This is reflected in the Accounting Conventions, which are generally accepted accounting principles which have been used for many years. These conventions (or accepted practices) include those described below.

Accounting entity convention

For accounting purposes, the business of a **sole trader** or a **partnership** is regarded as a separate accounting entity; that is, a being in its own right. Only the transactions of the business or the partnership are recorded. The personal financial dealings of the owner/s are completely separate to, and distinct from, those of the business.

Continuity of activity convention

Under the **continuity of activity** convention, the business is regarded as an ongoing entity that will continue to operate in the future.

Historical cost convention

Under the **historical cost** convention, all transactions are recorded as they occur and at the monetary value at that time. Assets are recorded at their value (original cost) at the time of purchase.

Accounting period convention

This concept divides the accounting life of the business into periods of equal length, usually a year, but may be quarterly or even monthly. This makes comparisons with previous results easier, assists in determining profit or loss and allows for matching revenues earned with expenses incurred during the period.

The most common reporting period is the financial year; that is, from 1 July to 30 June. This period coincides with the assessment period set down by the Australian Taxation Office.

Accounting monetary convention

Under the **monetary convention**, all transactions of the business are recorded in money terms. A transaction is the exchange of goods or services for money.

Accounting equation convention

This is based on the concept that, at all times, the total assets of the business are equal to the total liabilities of the business, together with the owner's equity. This is stated as:

$$\text{Assets} = \text{Liabilities} + \text{Owner's Equity}.$$

ACCOUNTING STANDARDS AND CONCEPT STATEMENTS

Accounting involves identifying, measuring and communicating economic information to users to enable them to make the best possible decisions about the allocation of resources now or in the future and to verify past decisions. Because financial reports are an essential element in accounting, it was decided that there was a need for a broad set of principles to underlie the preparation and presentation of these financial statements for external users.

Accounting Standards

The accounting profession (namely the Institute of Chartered Accountants in Australia and the Australian Society of Certified Practising Accountants, together with the Australian Accounting Standards Board and the Australian Accounting Research Foundation) has developed the **Accounting Standards**. These provide specific rules on how particular types of financial transaction should be dealt with in the accounting records. There are two groups of accounting standards.

1. **AASB Standards** are issued by the Australian Accounting Standards Board and apply to corporate entities. These standards have the legal backing of the Corporations Law.
2. **AAS Standards** are issued by the Australian Accounting Research Foundation on behalf of the Institute of Chartered Accountants in Australia and the Australian Society of Certified Practising Accountants. They are not legally binding and are applicable to all non-corporate entities as well as to a large number of public sector entities.

Statements of Accounting Concepts

The Australian Accounting Research Foundation, together with the Australian Accounting Standards Board, is developing an Accounting Conceptual Framework which will provide a set of broad principles for financial accounting. Those Statements of Accounting Concepts (**SACs**) which have been issued to date are:
- SAC 1 Definition of the **Reporting Entity**
- SAC 2 Objective of General Purpose Financial Reporting
- SAC 3 Qualitative Characteristics (Qualities) of Financial Reporting
- SAC 4 Definition and Recognition of the Elements of Financial Statements.

Concepts statements are broad in scope and provide guidance on points that are not covered in the Standards, whereas points covered in the Standards are specific and are backed by legislation.

ACCOUNTING ENTITY VERSUS LEGAL ENTITY

For accounting purposes, the business of a sole trader or a partnership is regarded as a separate accounting entity; that is, a being in its own right. Only the transactions of the business or the partnership are recorded. The personal financial dealings of the owner/s are completely separate to, and distinct from, those of the business.

An accounting entity is not necessarily a **legal entity**. For accounting purposes, a business is always a separate accounting entity, but it must be incorporated (become a **company**) in order to be regarded as a legal entity. As a legal entity it is regarded as being entirely separate from its owners. It can sue and be sued, enter into contracts and own property in its own name.

ACCOUNTING CONCEPTS AND TERMS

Accounting entity — an organisation which is regarded as a separate economic unit for accounting purposes

Accounting equation — an equation based on the concept that at all times the total assets of the business are equal to the total liabilities and the owner's equity in the business. It is stated as:

$$\text{Assets} = \text{Liabilities} + \text{Owner's Equity}.$$

Accounts payable (**trade creditors**) — persons or businesses from whom the business purchases trading goods on credit. These goods are purchased to be sold at a profit at a later date. As the business owes money to these persons or businesses, accounts payable are a liability of the business.

Accounts receivable (**trade debtors**) — persons or businesses to whom the business sells trading goods on credit. As these persons and businesses owe money to the business, accounts receivable are an asset of the business.

Assets — items of value owned or controlled by the business as a result of past transactions and which are expected to be of benefit in the future. SAC 4 defines assets as: '... future economic benefits controlled by the entity as a result of past transactions or other past events'.

Balance date — the last day of the reporting period (for example, 30 June). This is when adjustments are made and the **accounts** balanced. The expense and revenue accounts are closed off and final accounts prepared to determine profit or loss. Final accounts consist of a **trading statement**, a **profit and loss statement** and a **balance sheet**.

Chart of accounts — an index, map or guide to the location of accounts in the **general ledger**. The numerous ledger accounts are arranged in an orderly sequence so that individual accounts can be located readily; for example, a classified listing of all accounts contained in the general ledger would constitute a chart of accounts.

Double entry — a system of recording transactions in terms of the accounting equation, which is based on the concept that total debits are always equal to total credits; that is, for every **debit entry** there is a corresponding **credit entry** and vice versa

Expense — decreases in owner's equity as a result of the cost of providing goods or services to customers. Expenses are the opposite of revenues and represent the amount of assets a business uses up or the amount of costs a business incurs in the process of earning revenue (for example, purchases, rent and salaries).

Expense recognition principle — expenses should be recorded in the accounting period in which the asset is used or liability incurred in the process of earning revenue.

Inventory (stock) — goods held for resale in the ordinary course of business

Journal — a book of original entry used to record transactions as they occur, showing date, nature, amount and names of parties involved

Ledger — a book of secondary entry, which classifies transactions under individual account headings. Entries must not be made in the ledger/s until details of transactions are recorded in the journals.

Liabilities — future economic obligations of an entity as a result of past transactions. They represent the external equities of a business and consist of amounts owed to persons or businesses other than the owner. SAC 4 defines liabilities as: '... future sacrifices of economic benefits that the entity is presently obliged to make to other entities as a result of past transactions or other past events'.

Owner's equity — the residual interest in the assets of the business after the deduction of liabilities, illustrated as:

Owner's Equity = Assets − Liabilities.

It is the internal equity of the business and represents the amount of money that the business owes to the owner. Owner's equity is also known as proprietorship. SAC 4 defines owner's equity as: '... the residual interest in the assets of the entity after deduction of its liabilities'.

For a sole trader, this represents the net investment of the **proprietor** in the business; that is, the amount of capital invested, plus any profits and less any losses or drawings by the proprietor.

Reporting period — a period of time, generally one year, over which the life of a business is divided for accounting purposes

Revenue — increases in owner's equity resulting from the sale of goods or provision of services (both cash and credit transactions) to customers, plus any income received from investments during the reporting period under review

Revenue recognition principle — a principle which recognises that revenue should be recorded in the **accounting period** in which it is earned rather than when the cash or asset is received

Sundry creditors — persons or businesses from whom the business purchases something, other than trading goods on credit (for example, a non-current asset such as a new computer for the business). As these transactions fall into the category of 'non-trade' or 'other' receivables, their accounts should be kept separately from the Accounts Payable (trade creditors) account.

Sundry debtors — persons or businesses to whom the business sells something, other than trading goods on credit (for example, a non-current asset such as a printer which has outlived its usefulness to the business). As these transactions fall into the category of 'non-trade' or 'other' receivables, their accounts should be kept separately from the Accounts Receivable (trade debtors) account.

EXERCISE 1.1

1. What is the accounting term given to the last day of the reporting period?
2. Express the accounting equation in two different ways.
3. What is another term for owner's equity?
4. What are two terms for a person or business from whom the business purchases trading goods on credit?
5. Into which book are details of transactions first recorded?
6. What is the term for the system which records transactions in terms of the accounting equation?
7. What is the term for goods which are purchased and held for resale in order to make a profit?
8. What is the term for a guide to the location of accounts in the general ledger?
9. What is the term for a person or business from whom a business purchases an item of office equipment on credit?
10. What is the term for a person or business to whom a business sells trading goods on credit?

MAIN TYPES OF BUSINESS OWNERSHIP

Sole trader (or sole proprietor)

A sole trader is a person who conducts a business for his or her own benefit and owns and controls the business. The owner receives all the profits and bears all the losses.

A sole trader is *not* a separate legal entity and is said to have unlimited liability. (Liability is an obligation to pay debts or amounts owing.) This means that if the business cannot pay its debts, the owner may be sued and his or her personal property sold to pay these debts. However, for accounting purposes, the business is regarded as a separate entity. This means that only the transactions of the business are recorded.

The personal financial dealings of the proprietor are completely separate from those of the business.

Partnership

A partnership is made up of two or more persons who combine in a business to share the profits and risk the losses. There may be a minimum of two persons in a partnership and a maximum of 20.

Ownership of the business is shared in agreed proportions, according to a partnership agreement which, although not mandatory, may be drawn up when the business is formed. Control of the business is as stipulated in this agreement. Partnerships are not separate legal entities. As in the case of the sole trader, the individual partners are personally liable for the debts of the business and their personal assets may be sold to meet the obligations of the business.

A partnership, like a sole trader, is not a legal entity. Any business property owned must be owned in the names of the owners. It is the owners who are legal entities. They can sue and be sued, enter into contracts and own property in their own names.

Company

When a company is formed, a separate legal entity is created. A company can sue or be sued in its own name. It can buy, own or sell property and it can enter into a legal contract.

Ownership of a company is in the hands of the shareholders whose interests are represented by shares in the capital of the company. The shareholders are not personally liable for the debts of any shares held in the company, but are said to have **limited liability**; that is, a liability limited to the fully paid up value of any shares held in the company.

Control is in the hands of a board of directors elected by the shareholders to run the company properly. Profits are shared by the shareholders in the form of dividends based on the number of shares held. A company must be registered with the Corporate Affairs Commission.

There are two main types of company:
1. **private** (or proprietory) **company**. This form of ownership is suitable for small companies where the owner (or owners) are involved in the day-to-day running of the business. The following restrictions apply.
    - There may be a minimum of two and a maximum of 50 shareholders.
    - The words *Pty Ltd (Proprietary Limited)* must appear in the company name.
    - Shares or ownership may not be sold to the general public — potential investors are approached and invited to purchase shares.
2. **public company**. This form of ownership is chosen by very large companies. Members of the public may buy shares in the company and shares are offered for sale on the Stock Exchange. Restrictions are as follows.
    - The minimum number of shareholders is five; the maximum number is unlimited.
    - The word *Limited (or Ltd)* must appear in the company name.
    - Public companies are subject to strict government control.

Cooperative

A cooperative is a type of limited company where the shareholders are also the customers of the business. Examples of cooperatives are producer cooperatives (for example, citrus growers may form a cooperative to market their fruit) and consumer cooperatives (for example, consumers may form a cooperative to bulk purchase groceries from wholesalers).

Franchise

A franchise allows individuals, partnerships or companies to purchase an outlet for a fee and a percentage of profit. Examples of franchises are McDonald's, and Jim's Mowing. The franchisee purchases the franchise from the franchisor and signs an agreement to run the franchise in the way set down by the franchisor. The franchisor trains the franchisee in how to run the franchise and gives ongoing help where required.

Other types of business, although not formed to make a profit for members, are:
- professional associations
- societies
- charities
- clubs.

Many government and semi-government authorities are also run like a business (for example, Australia Post). These authorities are owned by the federal or State governments which appoint a board (or commission) and a manager to run them. In the current climate of 'user pays', many of these authorities are expected to compete with private providers; for example, Telecom competes with Optus, and TAFE institutions compete with private educational providers.

EXERCISE 1.2

Answer true (T) or false (F) to the following. (Place either 'T' or 'F' in the box provided.)

1. James and Munro, electrical contractors, form a business, agreeing to share costs and profits equally. This is a partnership. ☐
2. TAFE New South Wales is a public company. ☐
3. A private company may have a maximum of 50 shareholders. ☐
4. Public company shareholders have limited liability. ☐
5. In a cooperative, the owners may also be the customers of the business. ☐
6. Pizza Hut is a franchise business. ☐
7. Profits, in the form of dividends, are paid to shareholders of a public company. ☐
8. The words *Pty Ltd* appear in the name of a private company. ☐
9. A partnership may have only two partners. ☐
10. A sole trader receives all the profits and bears all the losses of his or her business. ☐

THE ACCOUNT

The account is the basic unit used in accounting to summarise business transactions. Accounts are classified as follows:
- assets
- liabilities
- owner's equity.

Assets

Assets are economic resources owned or controlled by an entity as a result of past transactions, which are expected to be of benefit in the future. Examples of assets are:
- cash (refers to coin, currency, cheques etc.)
- accounts receivable. When a business sells goods or services on credit, the Accounts Receivable account records these transactions.
- land
- office equipment
- office furniture.

A separate account is kept for each type of asset.

Liabilities

A liability is an economic entity's future obligation as a result of past transactions. Examples of liabilities are:
- accounts payable. When a business purchases goods or services on credit, the Accounts Payable account records these transactions. It is the opposite of the Accounts Receivable account.
- mortgage.

A separate account is kept for each type of liability.

Owner's equity

Owner's equity is the owner's claim on the assets of the business. Owner's equity is represented by two accounts:
1. *capital*. The owner's investment in the business is recorded in the Capital account.
2. **drawings**. When the owner withdraws cash or other assets from the business for personal use, the assets of both the business and owner's equity are decreased. Withdrawals are recorded separately in the Drawings account and represent a decrease in the owner's equity. As the amount of drawings *increases*, so the owner's equity *decreases*.

THE ACCOUNTING EQUATION

The accounting equation is based on the concept that at all times the total assets of the business are equal to the total equities. The accounting equation is stated as:

Assets = Equities

```
           ┌──────────────┬──────────────┐
           │   External   │   Internal   │
           │   Liability  │   Liability  │
           └──────┬───────┴───────┬──────┘
                  │               │
           ┌──────┴───────┐┌──────┴───────┐
           │  Liabilities ││   Owner's    │
           │              ││    Equity    │
           └──────────────┘└──────────────┘
```

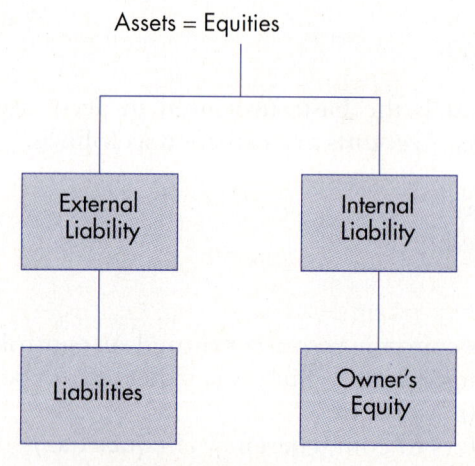

Assets = Liabilities + Owner's Equity

Equities can be divided into two parts. One is the internal liability of the business, which is the amount of owner's equity (owner's investment), and the other is the external liability, representing those liabilities incurred by the business through outsiders (for example, the bank and creditors).

The accounting equation may be expressed as:

$$\text{Assets} = \text{Liabilities} + \text{Owner's Equity}$$

or

$$\text{Owner's equity} = \text{Assets} - \text{Liabilities}$$

or

$$\text{Liabilities} = \text{Assets} - \text{Owner's Equity}.$$

EXERCISE 1.3

Identify the following as assets, liabilities or owner's equity.

	Assets	Liabilities	Owner's equity
(a) Amounts owed to trade creditors			
(b) Capital			
(c) Motor vehicles			
(d) Buildings			
(e) Amounts due from trade debtors			
(f) Mortgage			
(g) Cash at bank			
(h) Equipment owned			
(i) Bank overdraft			
(j) Inventory on hand			

EXERCISE 1.4

In each of the following examples, you are required to calculate the owner's equity.
(a) Land $20 000, Building $30 000, Cash at bank $25 000, Mortgage $16 000
(b) Inventory $5000, Cash at bank $4000, Motor vehicle $3500, Equipment $2000, Mortgage $10 000
(c) Motor vehicle $4000, Land $20 000, Cash at bank $5000
(d) Inventory $600, Office equipment $900, Trade debtors $1200, Trade creditors $1000
(e) Cash at bank $800, Furniture $750, Inventory $250, Bank loan $300, Trade debtors $200, Trade creditors $150

EXERCISE 1.5

Provide the missing information below.

Assets $	Liabilities $	Owner's equity $
7 000	3000	?
6 000	?	3600
9 500	4700	?
?	3000	5000
10 500	?	6000

Transactions and the accounting equation

In accounting terms, a transaction is defined as an event which affects the financial position of a business. It involves the exchange of money for money's worth of goods or services between two parties. Buying and selling goods and receiving or paying money are transactions. There are two main types of transaction:
1. *cash* — where money is received in exchange for goods or services
2. *credit* — where goods or services are supplied or received on agreement that payment will be made at a later date.

The transaction is the basic operating unit of the business. Cash is used to purchase goods, these goods are then sold, and the cash received for them is used to purchase more goods which, in turn, are sold. This cycle of cash → goods → cash is called the **operating cycle**. Below is a simple illustration of the operating cycle for both cash and credit transactions.

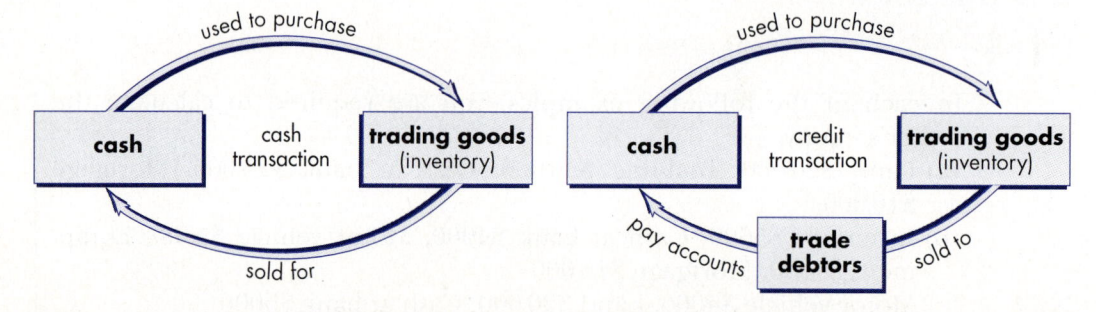

To show how transactions are recorded in terms of the accounting equation, consider the following examples. As you will see, not all businesses commence operation by depositing cash in a business bank account; they may bring a variety of assets and liabilities into the business.

Example 1
New business with cash investment
Vicki Newman decides to open her own business. She deposits $30 000 in a bank account entitled Elite Models. The effect of this transaction on the accounting equation is shown below.

	Assets	=		**Liabilities** +	**Owner's Equity**
Cash at Bank	$30 000	=	Capital		$30 000

Assets ($30 000) = Liabilities + Owner's Equity ($30 000).

This transaction affects two accounts:
1. *Cash at Bank* — an asset account which reflects the amount deposited in the bank account of the business
2. *Capital* — an owner's equity account which reflects the amount that the business owes to the owner.

Example 2
Purchase of existing business with additional asset/s
Roy Stevenson wishes to go into business for himself. He is experienced in the decorating field and purchases an established business, Metro Interiors (a small furnishing store), for $50 000, which includes trading stock valued at $30 000. When he commences trading on 1 August 19XX, his accounting equation is shown as:

	Assets	=		**Liabilities** +	**Owner's Equity**
Cash at Bank	$20 000		Capital		$50 000
Inventory (trading stock)	30 000				
	$50 000	=			$50 000

Assets ($50 000) = Liabilities + Owner's Equity ($50 000).

This transaction affects three accounts:
1. *Cash at Bank* — an asset account which records R. Stevenson's cash investment in the business
2. *Inventory* — an asset account which records the amount of trading stock acquired
3. *Capital* — an owner's equity account which reflects the amount which the business owes to the owner.

Example 3
Ongoing business converting to double-entry system
Michael Tesoriero operates a small retail business, Italia Ceramics. To date, he has recorded his transactions in a cash book, but the business has grown

so rapidly he decides to convert to a double-entry bookkeeping system. On 1 July 19XX, he has the following assets, liabilities and owner's equity:

Assets		=		Liabilities	+	Owner's Equity
Cash at Bank	$10 000		Capital			$21 500
Accounts Receivable	3 000		Accounts Payable	$1 500		
Inventory (trading stock)	6 000		Mortgage	5 000		
Motor Vehicle	9 000					
		=		$6 500	+	$21 500
	$28 000					$28 000

The accounting equation for Italia Ceramics on this date is as follows:

Assets ($28 000) = Liabilities ($6500) + Owner's Equity ($21 500).

Balancing the accounting equation

The amount on the left-hand side of the equation must equal the amount on the right-hand side. This balancing of the equation must be maintained throughout all transactions.

To keep the accounting equation balanced, it is important to realise that an increase or decrease in one account must be offset by a corresponding increase or decrease in another account.

To demonstrate the balancing of the accounting equation, we will consider the transactions of Metro Interiors (proprietor R. Stevenson). Accounts involved in the following transactions are marked with an asterisk. As illustrated on page 15, the opening transaction on 1 August 19XX is:

Transaction 1

	Assets	=		Liabilities	+	Owner's Equity
Cash at Bank*	$20 000		Capital*			$50 000
Inventory (trading stock)*	30 000					
	$50 000	=				$50 000

Transaction 2

On 3 August 19XX, Metro Interiors purchases $7000 of office furniture on credit from Designer Offices. The effect of this transaction on the accounting equation is:

	Assets	=		Liabilities	+	Owner's Equity
Cash	$20 000	=	Capital			$50 000
Inventory	30 000		Sundry Creditor —			
Office Furniture*	7 000		Designer Offices*	$7000		
				$7000	+	$50 000
	$57 000					$57 000

Note: Capital is the internal liability of the business and Sundry Creditor — Designer Offices is the external liability.

Assets ($57 000) = Liabilities ($7000) + Owner's Equity ($50 000).

Metro Interiors has now acquired another asset, office furniture (something it *owns*), but at the same time it has acquired a liability, a sundry creditor (a person or business to whom it *owes* money). The two accounts involved in this transaction are the asset account Office Furniture (which has increased) and the liability account Sundry Creditor — Designer Offices (which has also increased).

Transaction 3
On 5 August 19XX, Metro Interiors purchases a computer for $5000 cash. This transaction affects the accounting equation in the following way:

	Assets	=		Liabilities	+	Owner's Equity
Cash*	$15 000		Capital			$50 000
Inventory	30 000		Sundry Creditor —			
Office Furniture	7 000		Designer Offices	$7000		
Office Equipment*	5 000					
				$7000	+	$50 000
	$57 000	=				$57 000

Assets ($57 000) = Liabilities ($7000) + Owner's Equity ($50 000).

The two accounts involved in this transaction are the asset account Cash (which has decreased) and another asset account Office Equipment (which has increased to reflect the acquisition of the computer).

Transaction 4
On 8 August 19XX, the owner, R. Stevenson, withdrew $500 cash for personal use.

The two accounts affected by this transaction are the asset account Cash and the Drawings account, a negative owner's equity account which records amounts of cash (or stock) withdrawn from the business by the owner.

	Assets	=		Liabilities	+	Owner's Equity
Cash*	$14 500		Capital			$50 000
Inventory	30 000		Sundry Creditor —			
Office Furniture	7 000		Designer Offices	$7000		
Office Equipment	5 000		Drawings*			(500)
				$7000	+	$49 500
	$56 500	=				$56 500

Note: A figure enclosed in parentheses, for example (500), is a negative amount and, when encountered, should be deducted.

Assets ($56 500) = Liabilities ($7000) + Owner's Equity ($49 500).

The withdrawal of $500 cash decreases the asset account Cash and increases the Drawings account. The increase in the Drawings account reduces the amount of owner's equity in the business, as drawings are always recorded as a deduction from owner's equity. Withdrawals by the owner may be in the form of cash, or goods taken from stock for personal use.

These withdrawals cannot be recorded as business expenses as they are to be used for personal expenses. Withdrawals by the owner from a business decrease the owner's equity in the business.

Transaction 5
On 15 August 19XX, Metro Interiors purchases shop fittings on credit from Custom Interiors Ltd for $6000, paying a cash deposit of $1000.

Assets	=		Liabilities	+	Owner's Equity
Cash*	$13 500	Capital			$50 000
Inventory	30 000	Sundry Creditor —			
Office Furniture	7 000	Designer Offices	$ 7 000		
Office Equipment	5 000	Drawings			(500)
Shop Fittings*	6 000	Sundry Creditor —			
		Custom Interiors Ltd*	5 000		
			$12 000	+	$49 500
$61 500	=				$61 500

Assets ($61 500) = Liabilities ($12 000) + Owner's Equity ($49 500).

This transaction involves three accounts — Metro Interiors acquires an asset (Shop Fittings), the asset account Cash has decreased because the business withdrew money ($1000) to pay a cash deposit, and a liability was created in the form of a Sundry Creditor (Custom Interiors Ltd) to which Metro Interiors owes $5000 for shop fittings purchased on credit. (Note that Custom Interiors Ltd is not a trade creditor as shop fittings are not for resale.)

TRANSACTION ANALYSIS CHART

A transaction analysis chart is useful for examining the effects that business transactions have on the accounting equation and for help in answering the following questions.
- Which accounts are affected by the transaction?
- What types of account are affected, for example, asset, liability or owner's equity account?
- Is the account increased or decreased by the transaction?
- What is the amount of increase or decrease in the account?

It also helps you to write a brief summary of the transaction.

Set out below is an analysis chart for transactions discussed for Metro Interiors.

TRANSACTION ANALYSIS CHART
METRO INTERIORS

Trans. no./ Date	Accounts affected	Type of account*	Inc. or dec.	Amount ($)	Summary
19XX Aug. 1	Cash Inventory Capital	A A OE	Inc. Inc. Inc.	20 000 30 000 50 000	Initial investment by R. Stevenson in business $50 000: Cash — $20 000; Stock — $30 000 Business owes owner $50 000
3	Office Furniture Sundry Creditor — Designer Offices	A L	Inc. Inc.	7 000 7 000	Purchase of asset (office furniture) on credit. Liability is acquired in the form of a sundry creditor — Designer Offices.
5	Office Equipment Cash at Bank	A A	Inc. Dec.	5 000 5 000	Purchase of asset (computer) for $5000 cash
8	Cash Drawings	A OE	Dec. Dec.	500 500	Withdrawal by owner of $500 cash for personal use. This reduces the owner's investment in the business by $500.
15	Cash Shop Fittings Sundry Creditor — Custom Interiors	A A L	Dec. Inc. Inc.	1 000 6 000 5 000	$1000 cash used as deposit on asset (shop fittings) — cost $6000. Balance of $5000 is owed to sundry creditor — Custom Interiors Ltd.

* A = Asset, L = Liability, OE = Owner's Equity

OWNER'S EQUITY AND THE CAPITAL ACCOUNT

Owner's equity (or proprietorship, or capital) is the amount that the proprietor originally invested at the commencement of the business. It is the internal equity of the business and is recorded in the general ledger as the Capital account, which, at the end of the reporting period, shows the following details:
- the amount of capital which is owed by the business to the proprietor
- *plus* any additional capital invested in the business by the proprietor
- *less* any drawings the proprietor takes from the business (in the form of inventory or other assets, cash, or cheques drawn on the business for cash or for the payment of private expenses)
- *plus* any profit the business earns — or *less* any loss which the business incurs.

We can now expand the accounting equation to include profit and loss.

$$\text{Assets} = \text{Liabilities} + \text{Owner's Equity} + \text{Profit.}$$

if

$$\text{Profit} = \text{Revenue} - \text{Expenses,}$$

therefore

$$\text{Assets} = \text{Liabilities} + \text{Owner's Equity} + \text{Revenue} - \text{Expenses}$$

where

(a) *profit* is the excess of revenue over expenses for a given period. (If there is an excess of expenses over revenue for a given period, a loss results.)
(b) *revenues* is the increase in owner's equity resulting from selling goods or providing services, plus any income received from other sources for a given period.
(c) *expenses* are decreases in owner's equity arising from the costs of operating the business.

In a loss situation, the equation would be stated as:

$$\text{Assets} = \text{Liabilities} + \text{Owner's Equity} - \text{Loss}$$

where

loss is the excess of expenses over revenue.

If we consider some revenue and expenses for Metro Interiors for the month of August 19XX, we can ascertain if the business made a profit (or a loss) and observe the effect on the expanded accounting equation:

$$\text{Assets} = \text{Liabilities} + \text{Owner's Equity} + \text{Revenue} - \text{Expenses.}$$

Using this expanded accounting equation, we will continue to analyse the following transactions for Metro Interiors.

Transaction 6
On 16 August 19XX, Metro Interiors sells goods on credit, valued at $18 000. The effect of this transaction on the accounting equation is shown at the top of page 21:
The two accounts affected by this transaction are:
1. *Sales* — a revenue account which is *increased* to record the revenue from credit sales of trading goods
2. *Accounts Receivable* — an asset account which is *increased* to reflect the amount owing to the business by trade debtors.

The Sales account is used to record credit sales of trading stock. During the course of the business, inventory is depleted and replenished on a recurring basis as stock is sold and then replaced. Sales of trading stock are recorded in the Sales account as a revenue of the business.

Account	Assets	= Liabilities +	Owner's Equity +	Revenue –	Expenses
Cash	$13 500				
Capital			$50 000		
Inventory	30 000				
Office Furniture	7 000				
Sundry Creditor					
— Designer Offices		$ 7 000			
Office Equipment	5 000				
Drawings			(500)		
Shop Fittings	6 000				
Sundry Creditor					
— Custom Interiors		5 000			
Sales*				$18 000	
Accounts Receivable*	18 000				
	$79 500 =	$12 000 +	$49 500	+ $18 000	

Assets ($79 500) = Liabilities ($12 000) + Owner's Equity ($49 500) + Revenue ($18 000).

The business has also acquired an asset account, Accounts Receivable, in which details of transactions with trade debtors (persons or businesses to whom Metro Interiors sell trading goods on credit) are recorded. This account is increased to reflect the increase in amounts owing by trade debtors.

Transaction 7
On 18 August 19XX, Metro Interiors purchases $10 000 of trading goods (also known as trading stock) on credit. The effect of this transaction on the expanded accounting equation is as follows:

Account	Assets	= Liabilities +	Owner's Equity +	Revenue –	Expenses
Cash	$13 500				
Capital			$50 000		
Inventory	30 000				
Office Furniture	7 000				
Sundry Creditor					
— Designer Offices		$ 7 000			
Office Equipment	5 000				
Drawings			(500)		
Shop Fittings	6 000				
Sundry Creditor					
— Custom Interiors		5 000			
Sales				$18 000	
Accounts Receivable	18 000				
Purchases*					$10 000
Accounts Payable*		10 000			
	$79 500 =	$22 000 +	$49 500	+ $18 000	– $10 000

Assets ($79 500) = Liabilities ($22 000) + Owner's Equity ($49 500) + Revenue ($18 000) – Expenses ($10 000).

The two accounts affected by this transaction are:
1. *Purchases* — an expense account which is *increased* to record the expense of purchasing trading goods on credit
2. *Accounts Payable* — a liability account which is *increased* to reflect the amount owing to trade creditors.

The Purchases account is used to record credit purchases of trading stock. Replacements or additions to trading stock are recorded in the Purchases account as an expense of the business.

The business has also acquired a liability account, Accounts Payable, in which details of transactions with trade creditors (persons or businesses from which Metro Interiors has purchased trading goods on credit) are recorded. The Accounts Payable account has increased to reflect the amount owing to trade creditors.

Transaction 8
Metro Interiors paid **wages** to employees ($1000) on 23 August 19XX. The effect of this transaction on the accounting equation is as follows:

Account	Assets	= Liabilities	+ Owner's Equity	+ Revenue	− Expenses
Cash*	$12 500				
Capital			$50 000		
Inventory	30 000				
Office Furniture	7 000				
Sundry Creditor — Designer Offices		$ 7 000			
Office Equipment	5 000				
Drawings			(500)		
Shop Fittings	6 000				
Sundry Creditor — Custom Interiors		5 000			
Sales				$18 000	
Accounts Receivable	18 000				
Purchases					$10 000
Accounts Payable		10 000			
Wages Expense*					1 000
	$78 500 =	$22 000 +	$49 500	+ $18 000 −	$11 000

Assets ($78 500) = Liabilities ($22 000) + Owner's Equity ($49 500) + Revenue ($18 000) − Expenses ($11 000).

The Wages Expense account has increased to reflect the increase in that account and the Cash account has decreased to reflect the amount drawn to meet the wages expense.

Transaction 9
On 28 August 19XX, Metro Interiors paid an electricity account of $400. The effect of this transaction on the accounting equation of Metro Interiors is shown at the top of the following page.

CHAPTER 1: THE ACCOUNTING ENVIRONMENT | 23

Account	Assets	= Liabilities	+ Owner's Equity	+ Revenue	− Expenses
Cash*	$12 100				
Capital			$50 000		
Inventory	30 000				
Office Furniture	7 000				
Sundry Creditor					
— Designer Offices		$ 7 000			
Office Equipment	5 000				
Drawings			(500)		
Shop Fittings	6 000				
Sundry Creditor					
— Custom Interiors		5 000			
Sales				$18 000	
Accounts Receivable	18 000				
Purchases					$10 000
Accounts Payable		10 000			
Wages Expense					1 000
Electricity*					400
	$78 100 =	$22 000 +	$49 500	+ $18 000 −	$11 400

Assets ($78 100) = Liabilities ($22 000) + Owner's Equity ($49 500) + Revenue ($18 000)
− Expenses ($11 400).

The two accounts affected by this transaction are the Cash account which has *decreased* and the Electricity expense account which has *increased*.

Transaction 10
On 29 August 19XX, R. Stevenson invests a further $10 000 in the business. This has the following effect on the accounting equation:

Account	Assets	= Liabilities	+ Owner's Equity	+ Revenue	− Expenses
Cash*	$22 100				
Capital*			$60 000		
Inventory	30 000				
Office Furniture	7 000				
Sundry Creditor					
— Designer Offices		$ 7 000			
Office Equipment	5 000				
Drawings			(500)		
Shop Fittings	6 000				
Sundry Creditor					
— Custom Interiors		5 000			
Sales				$18 000	
Accounts Receivable	18 000				
Purchases					$10 000
Accounts Payable		10 000			
Wages Expense					1 000
Electricity					400
	$88 100 =	$22 000 +	$59 500	+ $18 000 −	$11 400

Assets ($88 100) = Liabilities ($22 000) + Owner's Equity ($59 500) + Revenue ($18 000)
− Expenses ($11 400).

The investment of $10 000 by R. Stevenson increases the Cash account while reflecting an increase in the owner's equity account, Capital.

We can now complete the Transaction Analysis Chart for Metro Interiors to record those transactions from 16 August 19XX to date (see page 19).

TRANSACTION ANALYSIS CHART
METRO INTERIORS (cont'd)

Trans. no./ Date	Accounts affected	Type of account*	Inc. or dec.	Amount $	Summary
19XX Aug.16	Sales A/cs Receivable	R A	Inc. Inc.	18 000 18 000	Sales of trading goods on credit which result in increase in amount owed by trade debtors/creditors
18	Purchases A/cs Payable	E L	Inc. Inc.	10 000 10 000	Purchase of trading goods of $10 000 on credit resulting in increase in amount owed to trade creditors
23	Wages Cash	E A	Inc. Dec.	1 000 1 000	Increase in expense (Wages) which results in decrease in asset (Cash)
28	Electricity Cash	E A	Inc. Dec.	400 400	Increase in expense (Electricity) which results in decrease in asset (Cash)
29	Cash Capital	A OE	Inc. Inc.	10 000 10 000	Owner invests a further $10 000 in the business.

* A = Asset, L = Liability, OE = Owner's Equity, R = Revenue, E = Expense

PROFIT AND LOSS STATEMENT

The purpose of the profit and loss statement is to measure the performance of the business and to determine whether the business has made a profit (or incurred a loss) *for a period of time.* The profit and loss statement 'matches' the revenue earned during the reporting period against the expenses incurred in earning that revenue during the same period. The difference between the revenue and expenses for the period represents the net profit (or **net loss**). The owner's equity in the business is increased by profit and decreased by loss (that is, he or she is entitled to any profit that is made, or bears any loss).

This profit (or loss) is what links the profit and loss statement to the **owner's equity account** (Capital) in the balance sheet. The amount of capital, which represents the owner's investment, is increased by a profit and decreased by a loss.

To summarise the revenue and expense transactions of Metro Interiors, we will prepare a profit and loss statement for the month ended 31 August 19XX. As the revenue earned by Metro Interiors exceeds the expenses of the business for the month, a profit has been made.

```
            PROFIT AND LOSS STATEMENT FOR METRO INTERIORS
                     for month ended 31 August 19XX
                       (Profit = Revenue − Expenses)

     Revenue:
       Sales                                                      $18 000
     Less Expenses:
       Purchases                                  $10 000
       Wages                                        1 000
       Electricity                                    400          11 400

     Profit                                                       $ 6 600
```

BALANCE SHEET

The balance sheet is a statement of assets, liabilities and owner's equity (also known as proprietorship) of a business *at a particular date*, usually at the last date of a given trading period; for example, as at 30 June 19XX, being the last day in the financial year (1 July 19XX to 30 June 19XX). It is a statement of what the business owns (or is owed) on a particular day. At the beginning of the next trading period, the balance sheet ceases to present a true picture of the business's financial position, owing to changes caused by further transactions occurring from the very first day in the new reporting period.

The balance sheet for Metro Interiors follows.

```
                      BALANCE SHEET OF METRO INTERIORS
                              as at 31 August 19XX
                       (Assets = Liabilities + Owner's Equity)

  Assets                             Liabilities
    Cash                 $22 100       Accounts Payable   $10 000
    Accounts Receivable   18 000       Sundry Creditors    12 000    $22 000
    Inventory             30 000
    Office Furniture       7 000
    Office Equipment       5 000     Owner's Equity
    Shop Fittings          6 000       Capital            $60 000
                                       Plus Profit          6 600
                                                          $66 600
                                       Less Drawings          500     66 100

                        $88 100                                      $88 100
```

It is important to remember that assets, liabilities and owner's equity are balance sheet items, whereas revenue and expenses are profit and loss items. This is especially important when doing computerised bookkeeping as accounts must be classified as either Profit and Loss (P/L) or Balance Sheet (B/S) when setting up the chart of accounts.

PROFIT AND LOSS STATEMENT FOR METRO INTERIORS
for month ended 31 August 19XX
(Profit = Revenue − Expenses)

Revenue	$18 000
Less Expenses	11 400
Profit	**$ 6 600**

BALANCE SHEET OF METRO INTERIORS
as at 31 August 19XX
(Assets = Liabilities + Owner's Equity)

Assets	$88 100	Liabilities		$22 000
		Owner's Equity		
		Capital	$60 000	
		Plus Profit	6 600	
			$66 600	
		Less Drawings	500	66 100
	$88 100			$88 100

From the abbreviated representations of the Profit and Loss Statement and Balance Sheet of Metro Interiors above, you can see that the profit has been transferred from the Profit and Loss Statement to the owner's equity section of the Balance Sheet, where it appears as an addition to Capital.

EXERCISE 1.6

For each of the following, identify the items as assets, liabilities, owner's equity, revenue or expenses. Use the letters A = Assets, L = Liabilities, OE = Owner's Equity, R = Revenue, E = Expenses.

Account	Type	Account	Type	Account	Type
Accounts Payable		Sales		Interest Received	
Cash at Bank		Commission Received		Purchases	
Rent Paid		Wages Paid		Interest Paid on Bank Loan	
Electricity Paid		Sundry Creditor		Sundry Debtor	
Accounts Receivable		Bank Loan		Office Equipment	
Mortgage		Motor Vehicles		Capital	
Drawings		Office Furniture		Motor Vehicle Expenses	

EXERCISE 1.7

For each of the following transactions, indicate how the accounts involved will be affected. The first entry has been done for you.

Transaction	Accounts affected	Increase or decrease
Bought plant and equipment for cash	Plant and equipment Cash	Increase Decrease
Cash sales		
Sold old typewriter for cash		
Bought new computer on credit from Superbytes Ltd, paying cash deposit		
Paid electricity		
Owner invests extra cash in business.		
Paid Superbytes Ltd (sundry creditor) $500		
Received $150 from a trade debtor		
Bought office desk on credit from Credenza Ltd, paying cash deposit		
Owner withdrew cash for personal use.		
Borrowed $10 000 from A. Levitt		
Sold old motor vehicle for cash		
Bought trading goods on credit from West Pty Ltd		
Repaid A. Levitt $5000		

EXERCISE 1.8

For each of the following transactions, indicate how the accounts involved will be affected.

Transaction	Accounts affected	Increase or decrease
Made initial cash investment in business		
Bought motor vehicle on credit from Acme Motors, paying cash deposit		
Purchased trading goods on credit		
Sold office desk for cash		
Paid wages		
Sold trading goods on credit		
Owner withdrew cash for personal use.		

EXERCISE 1.9

Anne Watson commences business on 1 July 19XX. From the information below, and following the example given for Metro Interiors:

1. apply the accounting equation to transactions (i)–(vii) (which appear on pages 29–31), showing which two accounts are involved, and that the accounting equation:

    Assets = Liabilities + Owner's Equity + Revenue − Expenses

    is maintained throughout all transactions

2. complete a transaction analysis chart for Anne's Fashions to show:
    (a) which accounts are affected by each transaction
    (b) the nature of each account affected (for example, an asset, liability or owner's equity account)
    (c) whether each account is increased or decreased by the transaction
    (d) the amount of increase or decrease
    (e) a brief summary of the transaction.
    Use the blank transaction analysis chart for Anne's Fashions which is provided on page 32.

Transactions
(i) Anne Watson commences Anne's Fashions with $60 000 cash and $20 000 inventory.

Example

Account	Assets =	Liabilities +	Owner's Equity +	Revenue –	Expenses
Cash	$60 000				
Inventory	20 000				
Capital (A. Watson)			$80 000		
	$80 000 =	+	$80 000 +	–	

(ii) Fixtures and fittings purchased for shop for $5000 cash

Account	Assets =	Liabilities +	Owner's Equity +	Revenue –	Expenses
	=	+	+	–	

(iii) A cash register purchased for $500 cash

Account	Assets =	Liabilities +	Owner's Equity +	Revenue –	Expenses
	=	+	+	–	

(iv) Credit sales amounting to $12 000

Account	Assets	=	Liabilities + Owner's Equity + Revenue − Expenses
	=		+ + −

(v) Shop premises purchased for $60 000 by obtaining a mortgage for the same amount from the bank

Account	Assets	=	Liabilities + Owner's Equity + Revenue − Expenses
	=		+ + −

(vi) Paid rent of $1000

Account	Assets	=	Liabilities + Owner's Equity + Revenue − Expenses
	___ = ___		___ + ___ + ___ − ___

(vii) Purchased $8000 of trading goods on credit

Account	Assets	=	Liabilities + Owner's Equity + Revenue − Expenses
	___ = ___		___ + ___ + ___ − ___

TRANSACTION ANALYSIS CHART
ANNE'S FASHIONS (Proprietor A. Watson)

Trans. no./ Date	Accounts affected	Type of account*	Inc. or dec.	Amount ($)	Summary

* A = Asset, L = Liability, OE = Owner's Equity, R = Revenue, E = Expense

EXERCISE 1.10

Robert Hartley commences business on 1 May 19XX, trading as Hartley Pharmacy. You are required to complete a transaction analysis chart for Hartley Pharmacy to show:
(a) which accounts are affected by each transaction
(b) the nature of each account affected (for example, an asset account)
(c) whether each account is increased or decreased by the transaction
(d) the amount of increase or decrease
(e) a brief summary of the transaction.

Use a copy of the blank transaction analysis chart provided on page 539. Make sure that you add the name of the business and the proprietor at the top of the chart (see example on page 32).

Transactions
  (i) Robert Hartley commences business trading as Hartley Pharmacy with the following assets and liabilities:
  Cash at bank $30 000, Premises $50 000, Inventory $20 000, Mortgage $40 000.
 (ii) A delivery vehicle is purchased on credit for $20 000 from Titan Trucks Ltd, paying a cash deposit of $5000.
(iii) Trading goods are purchased on credit from suppliers for $10 000.
(iv) Robert Hartley withdraws $350 cash for personal use.
 (v) Hartley Pharmacy sells $800 trading goods on credit.
(vi) Robert Hartley invests a further $10 000 capital in his business by depositing the cash in the bank account of Hartley Pharmacy.
(vii) A computer is purchased for $2500 cash.

EXERCISE 1.11

Complete a transaction analysis chart for the following.
(a) J. Davenport commences business by paying $10 000 into the bank account of Bayside Bakers.
(b) Fixtures and fittings are purchased on credit ($1200) from Bakery Supplies, paying a cash deposit of $200.
(c) Shop equipment is bought (cash register) for $750 cash.
(d) A second-hand van is purchased on credit from City Autos for $2500.
(e) An amount of $200 is paid off the **debt** with Bakery Supplies.

Use a copy of the blank transaction analysis chart provided on page 539. Make sure that you add the name of the business and the proprietor at the top of the chart (see example on page 32).

EXERCISE 1.12

Complete a transaction analysis chart for the following.
(a) Roy Seville pays $15 000 into a bank account entitled Figaro's Barber Shoppe.
(b) Hairdressing equipment ($600) is purchased on credit from Hair Supply Ltd.
(c) A barber's chair is purchased from Salon Supplies on credit for $2000, paying a cash deposit of $800.
(d) Roy Seville withdraws $450 from the business for personal use.
(e) An amount owing of $500 is paid to Salon Supplies.

Use a copy of the blank transaction analysis chart provided on page 539. Make sure that you add the name of the business and the proprietor at the top of the chart (see example on page 32).

RECORDING TRANSACTIONS

To date, we have been keeping a record of each transaction for Metro Interiors by examining the effect each transaction had on the accounting equation and changing the accounts accordingly. However, with perhaps thousands of transactions taking place daily in a business enterprise, it is not practical to follow this procedure. For this reason, details of increases and decreases resulting from transactions are recorded in accounts.

Recording increases and decreases in the accounts

An account is the basic recording unit used in accounting. We have already discussed the types or classification of accounts (for example, asset, liability, owner's equity, revenue and expense). However, most commonly, use of the term *account* refers to the account in which details of increases and decreases are summarised. An account is kept for each asset, liability, owner's equity, revenue and expense item. The accounts are usually kept together in a ledger (named after the large book in which account details were recorded for many years) and are referred to as ledger accounts. Nowadays, ledgers in book form or as a card system still exist, but it is more likely that the ledger forms part of an accounting software package on a computer.

Format of ledger accounts

There are two formats used for ledger accounts:
1. the T-account (traditional style)
2. the 3-column account (statement style).

T-account (traditional style)

This is called a T-account because it resembles the shape of the letter 'T'. It provides a quick way to check the effects of transactions on the accounts involved. The left side of a T-account is called the debit side and the right side is called the credit side.

Format of a T-account

Debit				Credit			
Date	Particulars	Fol.	Amount	Date	Particulars	Fol.	Amount

Balancing a T-account

The T-account must be balanced off at the end of each month. This is done by totalling both sides, deducting the amount on the smallest side from the amount on the largest side and carrying this balance forward to the next month, as shown in the following example.

ACCOUNT OF A DEBTOR

Debit side			Credit side		
Date	Particulars	Amount	Date	Particulars	Amount
June 1 15	Balance Sales	200.00 350.00	June 30	Sales Returns Cash Disc. Allowed Balance (c/d)	50.00 300.00 6.00 194.00
		550.00			550.00
July 1	Balance (b/d)	194.00			

3-column account (statement style)

This style of account is widely used in business and computerised book-keeping and is the style used in this text.

Format of a 3-column account

Date	Particulars	Fol.	Debit	Credit	Balance

The 3-column ledger account contains a debit column, a credit column and a balance column, instead of a debit side and a credit side.

Balancing a 3-column account

This style of account is self-balancing in that the **account balance** is calculated and entered in the balance column after each transaction. The balance must always be designated as a debit (Dr) or credit (Cr) balance. An entry in the debit column decreases a credit balance and an entry in the credit column increases a credit balance. Similarly, an entry in the debit column increases a debit balance and an entry in the credit column decreases a debit balance.

The balance column shows the difference between the debits and credits as a running balance after each entry, for example:

ACCOUNT OF A DEBTOR

Date		Particulars	Debit	Credit	Balance
June	1	Balance	200.00		200.00 Dr
	15	Sales	350.00		550.00 Dr
	30	Sales Returns		50.00	500.00 Dr
		Cash		300.00	200.00 Dr
		Discount Allowed		6.00	194.00 Dr

When using the 3-column format, it is essential to check additions and subtractions carefully and ensure that entries are made in the correct ledger column.

Once each transaction is analysed and it has been determined which accounts are affected and which accounts are increased/decreased, the details of the transactions are recorded using the double-entry system of bookkeeping.

The double-entry system

The double-entry system is based on the concept that there are two sides to every transaction and that *at least* two accounts are affected by every transaction. In fact, it is named for the fact that at least two entries are required to record every transaction. The double-entry system records transactions in terms of the accounting equation:

Assets = Liabilities + Owner's Equity + Revenue − Expenses

which states that at all times, *total debits* are equal to *total credits*; that is, for every debit entry there is a corresponding credit entry and vice versa.

The term *debit* originates from the latin word *debitum* meaning debt. In accounting, it is used to refer to the left side of a T-account (that is, the debit side) or to the debit column of a 3-column account. The term *credit* refers to the other side of a T-bar account (that is, the credit side) or to the credit column of a 3-column account. A useful way of remembering this is that the word *credit* contains an 'r' as does the word *right*.

Increases and decreases in accounts are governed by the type of accounts involved in a transaction. For each type of account, increases are recorded on one side of the account and decreases on the other.

Debit entry

A debit entry is made on the left-hand (debit) side of a T-account or in the debit column of a 3-column account.

T-account

Debit	Credit
xxxx.xx	

3-column account

Debit	Credit	Balance
xxxx.xx		xxxx.xx Dr

Credit entry

A credit entry is made on the right-hand (credit) side of a T-account or in the credit column of a 3-column account.

T-account			3-column account		
Debit	Credit		Debit	Credit	Balance
	xxxx.xx			xxxx.xx	xxxx.xx Cr

ANALYSING TRANSACTIONS

When analysing transactions, as well as determining:
- which two accounts are involved in the transaction
- what types of accounts are involved
- whether there will be an increase or decrease in each of these accounts as a result of the transaction,

you will also need to determine:
- which of these accounts should be debited or credited.

The following rules will help you.

Asset accounts
- An increase in an asset account is recorded on the debit side of an account.
- A decrease in an asset account is recorded on the credit side of an account.

Liability accounts
- An increase in a liability account is recorded on the credit side of an account.
- A decrease in a liability account is recorded on the debit side of an account.

Owner's equity accounts
- An increase in an owner's equity account is recorded on the credit side of an account.
- A decrease in an owner's equity account is recorded on the debit side of an account.

Revenue accounts
- An increase in a revenue account is recorded on the credit side of an account.
- A decrease in a revenue account is recorded on the debit side of an account.

Expense accounts
- An increase in an expense account is recorded on the debit side of an account.
- A decrease in an expense account is recorded on the credit side of an account.

You will need to learn the above rules, but it will be helpful to keep a copy of the rules alongside you while you work until you become familiar with them. The rules of debit and credit may be summarised as in the following table.

Type of account	Nature of account	To record increase	To record decrease
Asset	Debit	Debit	Credit
Liability	Credit	Credit	Debit
Owner's equity	Credit	Credit	Debit
Revenue	Credit	Credit	Debit
Expense	Debit	Debit	Credit

To illustrate these rules simply, each type of account is shown below in both T-account and 3-column account format.

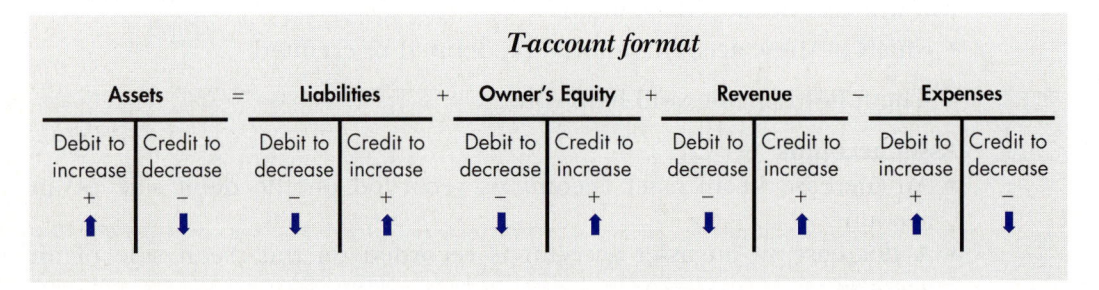

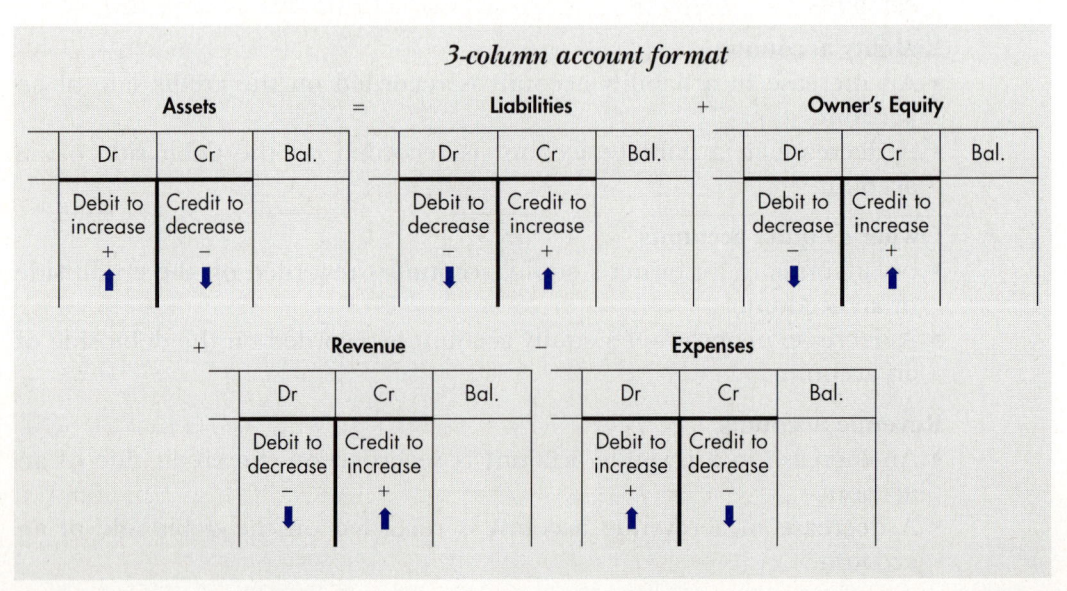

T-account format

Assets = Liabilities + Owner's Equity + Revenue − Expenses

Assets		Liabilities		Owner's Equity		Revenue		Expenses	
Debit to increase + ↑	Credit to decrease − ↓	Debit to decrease − ↓	Credit to increase + ↑	Debit to decrease − ↓	Credit to increase + ↑	Debit to decrease − ↓	Credit to increase + ↑	Debit to increase + ↑	Credit to decrease − ↓

3-column account format

Assets = **Liabilities** + **Owner's Equity**

Dr	Cr	Bal.	Dr	Cr	Bal.	Dr	Cr	Bal.
Debit to increase + ↑	Credit to decrease − ↓		Debit to decrease − ↓	Credit to increase + ↑		Debit to decrease − ↓	Credit to increase + ↑	

+ **Revenue** − **Expenses**

Dr	Cr	Bal.	Dr	Cr	Bal.
Debit to decrease − ↓	Credit to increase + ↑		Debit to increase + ↑	Credit to decrease − ↓	

If you look closely at the 3-column format, you can see that the debit and credit columns serve exactly the same function as the debit and credit sides of the T-account format, the main difference being the additional column to record balance figures.

An increase in an asset or expense account must be offset by a corresponding:
- decrease in another asset or expense account
- increase in a liability, owner's equity or revenue account
- a combination of both.

A decrease in an asset or expense account is offset by a corresponding:
- increase in another asset or expense account
- decrease in a liability, owner's equity or revenue account
- a combination of both.

An increase in a liability, owner's equity or revenue account is offset by a corresponding:
- decrease in another liability, owner's equity or revenue account
- decrease in an asset or expense account
- a combination of both.

When we refer to the 'normal' balance of an account, we refer to the side on which increases occur. If we look at the diagram on page 38, we can see that:
- asset and expense accounts increase on the debit side, so the normal balance of asset and expense accounts is 'debit'. Another way of expressing this is to say that assets and expenses are 'debit balance' accounts.

Similarly we can now say that:
- liabilities, owner's equity and revenue accounts increase on the credit side, so the normal balance of these accounts is 'credit'. Therefore, liabilities, owner's equity and revenues are 'credit balance' accounts.

This is illustrated as follows.

Assets	=	Liabilities	+	Owner's Equity	+	Revenue	–	Expenses
Debit to increase / Credit to decrease		Debit to decrease / Credit to increase		Debit to decrease / Credit to increase		Debit to decrease / Credit to increase		Debit to increase / Credit to decrease
Normal balance		Normal balance		Normal balance		Normal balance		Normal balance

You may find the table on the following page helpful. It sets out the nature of most of the asset, liability, owner's equity, revenue and expense accounts with which you will be working. It is to help you decide which accounts should be debited and which accounts should be credited and is *not* to be confused with a chart of accounts with which you will work in a later chapter.

KNOW YOUR ACCOUNTS — CLASSIFICATION OF ACCOUNTS

These accounts are DEBIT by nature.	These accounts are CREDIT by nature.
Asset accounts *Current assets* Cash at Bank Inventory Accounts Receivable (trade debtors) Sundry Debtors (non-trade receivables) *Investments* Commonwealth Bonds *Non-current assets* Land Buildings Plant and Machinery Motor Vehicles Office Equipment Furniture and Fittings **Expense accounts** Purchases (Purchases Returns and Allowances)* Discount Allowed Advertising Bad Debts Bank Charges Cartage/Freight Inwards Cartage/Freight Outwards Customs Duty Electricity General Expenses Insurance Interest Expense Postage Rent Expense Repairs and Maintenance Telephone Wages and Salaries Expense	**Liability accounts** *Current liabilities* Accounts Payable (trade creditors) Sundry Creditors (non-trade payables) Sales Tax Payable Net Wages Payable Group Tax Payable Superannuation Payable Medical Insurance Payable Group Savings Payable Union Dues Payable *Long-term liabilities* Mortgage **Owner's equity accounts** Capital (Drawings)* **Revenue accounts** Sales (Sales Returns and Allowances)* Discount Received Interest Revenue Rent Revenue
To record an INCREASE in these account balances, make an entry on the DEBIT side/column of the ledger.	To record an INCREASE in these account balances, make an entry on the CREDIT side/column of the ledger.
To record a DECREASE in these account balances, make an entry on the CREDIT side/column of the ledger.	To record a DECREASE in these account balances, make an entry on the DEBIT side/column of the ledger.

Note: Those accounts marked with an asterisk are 'negative' accounts; for example, Purchases Returns and Sales Returns, which are accounts that accumulate details of deductions from their companion accounts, Purchases and Sales respectively. Drawings is also a negative account accumulating deductions from the Capital account. These accounts are treated in the opposite manner to their associated accounts.

We can now use the rules on page 40 to show whether the accounts involved in the transactions of Metro Interiors are debited or credited and the resulting increases and decreases in these accounts. The accounts involved in each transaction are marked with an asterisk. The 3-column format is used so that you can see the effect of each entry on the account balance.

1. R. Stevenson commenced business as Metro Interiors with the following assets and liabilities:
   - cash at bank $20 000, inventory (trading stock) $30 000 and owner's equity (capital) $50 000.
   - Debit the Cash at Bank account (to record increase) $20 000
   - Debit the Inventory account (to record increase) $30 000
   - Credit the Capital account (to record increase) $50 000

Cash at Bank

Dr	Cr	Bal.
*20 000		20 000 Dr

Inventory

Dr	Cr	Bal.
*30 000		30 000 Dr

Capital

Dr	Cr	Bal.
	*50 000	50 000 Cr

2. Office furniture is purchased on credit from Designer Offices, $7000.
   - Debit the Office Furniture account (to increase) $7000
   - Credit the Sundry Creditor — Designer Offices account (to increase) $7000

Office Furniture

Dr	Cr	Bal.
*7000		7000 Dr

Sundry Creditor — Designer Offices

Dr	Cr	Bal.
	*7000	7000 Cr

3. A computer is purchased for cash, $5000.
   - Debit the Office Equipment account (to increase) $5000
   - Credit the Cash at Bank account (to decrease) $5000

Office Equipment

Dr	Cr	Bal.
*5000		5000 Dr

Cash at Bank

Dr	Cr	Bal.
20 000		20 000 Dr
	*5000	15 000 Dr

4. R. Stevenson withdraws $500 cash from the bank account of Metro Interiors for private expenses.
   - Debit the Drawings account (to increase) $500
   - Credit the Cash at Bank account (to decrease) $500

Drawings				Cash at Bank		
Dr	Cr	Bal.		Dr	Cr	Bal.
*500		500 Dr		20 000		20 000 Dr
					5000	15 000 Dr
					*500	14 500 Dr

5. Shop fittings are purchased ($6000) with $1000 cash deposit and $5000 on credit from Custom Interiors Ltd.
   - Debit the Shop Fittings account (to increase) $6000
   - Credit the Cash at Bank account (to decrease) $1000
   - Credit the Sundry Creditor — Custom Interiors Ltd account (to increase) $5000

Shop Fittings				Cash at Bank				Sundry Creditor — Custom Interiors Ltd		
Dr	Cr	Bal.		Dr	Cr	Bal.		Dr	Cr	Bal.
*6000		6000 Dr		20 000		20 000 Dr			*5000	5000 Cr
					5000	15 000 Dr				
					500	14 500 Dr				
					*1000	13 500 Dr				

6. Trading goods are sold on credit, $18 000.
   - Debit the Accounts Receivable account (to increase) $18 000
   - Credit the Sales account (to increase) $18 000

Accounts Receivable				Sales		
Dr	Cr	Bal.		Dr	Cr	Bal.
*18 000		18 000 Dr			*18 000	18 000 Cr

7. Trading goods are purchased on credit, $10 000.
   - Debit the Purchases account (to increase) $10 000
   - Credit the Accounts Payable account (to increase) $10 000

Purchases				Accounts Payable		
Dr	Cr	Bal.		Dr	Cr	Bal.
*10 000		10 000 Dr			*10 000	10 000 Cr

8. Metro Interiors pays wages amounting to $1000.
   - Debit the Wages account (to increase) $1000
   - Credit the Cash at Bank account (to decrease) $1000

Wages				Cash at Bank		
Dr	Cr	Bal.		Dr	Cr	Bal.
*1000		1000 Dr		20 000		20 000 Dr
					5000	15 000 Dr
					500	14 500 Dr
					1000	13 500 Dr
					*1000	12 500 Dr

9. The electricity account is paid, $400.
   - Debit the Electricity account (to increase) $400
   - Credit the Cash at Bank account (to decrease) $400

Electricity				Cash at Bank		
Dr	Cr	Bal.		Dr	Cr	Bal.
*400		400 Dr		20 000		20 000 Dr
					5000	15 000 Dr
					500	14 500 Dr
					1000	13 500 Dr
					1000	12 500 Dr
					*400	12 100 Dr

10. The owner invests an additional $10 000 in the business.
    - Debit the Cash at Bank account (to increase) $10 000
    - Credit the Capital account (to increase) $10 000

Cash at Bank				Capital — R. Stevenson		
Dr	Cr	Bal.		Dr	Cr	Bal.
20 000		20 000 Dr			50 000	50 000 Cr
	5000	15 000 Dr			*10 000	60 000 Cr
	500	14 500 Dr				
	1000	13 500 Dr				
	1000	12 500 Dr				
	400	12 100 Dr				
*10 000		22 100 Dr				

If you study transactions 1–10 on pages 41–43, you will see that in every transaction the debit entry is accompanied by a corresponding credit entry and vice versa, and that at all times the total amount of debits is equal to the total amount of credits. To check this, list all accounts that have a debit balance and all accounts that have a credit balance. If the total of the debit balances is equal to the total of the credit balances, the accounting equation balance has been maintained; for example:

$$\text{Assets} = \text{Liabilities} + \text{Owner's Equity} + \text{Revenue} - \text{Expenses}.$$

This is reflected in the following:

METRO INTERIORS (Proprietor — R. Stevenson)			
Debit balances		**Credit balances**	
Cash at Bank	$ 22 100	Capital	$ 60 000
Inventory	30 000	Sundry Creditor — Designer Offices	7 000
Office Furniture	7 000	Sundry Creditor — Custom Interiors Ltd	5 000
Office Equipment	5 000	Sales	18 000
Drawings	500	Accounts Payable	10 000
Shop Fittings	6 000		
Accounts Receivable	18 000		
Purchases	10 000		
Wages Expense	1 000		
Electricity	400		
	$100 000		$100 000

This is called a trial balance. If you look at the list of debit and credit balances, it is easy to see that total debits are equal to total credits. However, did you notice that all asset and expense accounts are listed on the debit side and all liability, owner's equity and revenue accounts are listed on the credit side? If we apply this to the accounting equation, we can now say that:

$$\text{Assets} + \text{Expenses} = \text{Liabilities} + \text{Owner's Equity} + \text{Revenue}.$$

If you learn to express the accounting equation in this format, you will find it easy to remember that asset and expense accounts are debited and that liabilities, owner's equity and revenue accounts are credited.

In order to analyse transactions, you should be able to:
- decide which accounts are affected by the transaction
- determine which types of account are involved in the transaction (for example, asset, liability, owner's equity, revenue or expense account)
- determine whether the account has been increased or decreased by the transaction
- use all the above information and apply your debit/credit rules to determine whether each account is debited or credited
- write a brief summary of the transaction.

All the above activities can be carried out very simply by completing a transaction analysis chart. As you analyse a transaction, note in the appropriate columns the results of your determination.

Metro Interiors' transaction analysis chart (see pages 19 and 24) has been expanded to include a debit or credit column. After applying the above rules it appears as shown on page 45.

TRANSACTION ANALYSIS CHART
METRO INTERIORS (Proprietor — R. Stevenson)

Trans. no./ Date	Accounts affected	Type of account*	Inc. or dec.	Dr or Cr	Amount ($)	Summary
19XX Aug. 1	Cash at Bank Inventory Capital	A A OE	Inc. Inc. Inc.	Dr Dr Cr	20 000 30 000 50 000	R. Stevenson commenced business with $20 000 cash and $30 000 stock. Business owes $50 000 to owner.
3	Office Furniture Sundry Creditor — Designer Offices	A L	Inc. Inc.	Dr Cr	7 000 7 000	Purchase of asset (office furn.) on credit. Liability acquired in form of Sundry Creditor — Designer Offices.
5	Office Equipment Cash at Bank	A A	Inc. Dec.	Dr Cr	5 000 5 000	Purchase of asset (computer) for $5000 cash
8	Cash at Bank Drawings	A OE	Dec. Dec.	Cr Dr	500 500	Owner withdrew $500 cash for personal use. This reduces owner's investment in business by $500.
15	Cash at Bank Shop Fittings Sundry Creditor — Custom Interiors Ltd	A A L	Dec. Inc. Inc.	Cr Dr Cr	1 000 6 000 5 000	$1000 cash used as deposit on asset (shop fittings) — cost $6000. Balance $5000 owed to Sundry Creditor — Custom Interiors Ltd.
16	Sales Accounts Receivable	R A	Inc. Inc.	Cr Dr	18 000 18 000	Sale of trading goods on credit which results in increase in amount owed by trade debtors
16	Purchases Accounts Payable	E L	Inc. Inc.	Dr Cr	10 000 10 000	Purchase of trading goods ($10 000) on credit resulting in increase in amount owed to trade creditors
23	Wages Cash at Bank	E A	Inc. Dec.	Dr Cr	1 000 1 000	Increase in expense (Wages) which results in decrease in asset (Cash)
28	Electricity Cash at Bank	E A	Inc. Dec.	Dr Cr	400 400	Increase in expense (Electricity) with a corresponding decrease in asset (Cash)
29	Cash at Bank Capital	A OE	Inc. Inc.	Dr Cr	10 000 10 000	Owner invests a further $10 000 in the business.

* A = Asset, L = Liability, OE = Owner's Equity, R = Revenue, E = Expense

EXERCISE 1.13

Indicate the normal balance of the following accounts.

Account type	Normal balance
Asset	
Liability	
Owner's equity	
Revenue	
Expense	

For each of the following exercises (1.14 to 1.18), circle the correct answer.

EXERCISE 1.14

The account debited to record the purchase of a motor vehicle on credit with a cash deposit is:
(a) Cash
(b) Sundry Creditor
(c) Motor Vehicle
(d) Purchases.

EXERCISE 1.15

The purchase of an item of office equipment for cash is recorded by:
(a) debit to Cash and a credit to Office Equipment
(b) debit to Cash and a debit to Office Equipment
(c) debit to Office Equipment and a credit to Cash
(d) credit to Cash and a credit to Office Equipment.

EXERCISE 1.16

The account debited for payment of cash owed to trade creditors is:
(a) Accounts Payable
(b) Accounts Receivable
(c) Cash
(d) Purchases.

EXERCISE 1.17

Cash received from debtors is recorded by:
(a) debit to Cash and a debit to Accounts Receivable
(b) debit to Accounts Receivable and a credit to Cash
(c) credit to Cash and a credit to Accounts Receivable
(d) debit to Cash and a credit to Accounts Receivable.

EXERCISE 1.18

The account credited to record the purchase of a computer for cash is:
(a) Office Equipment
(b) Cash
(c) Accounts Payable
(d) Purchases.

Using copies of the relevant masters, on pages 539 and 540, complete exercises 1.19 and 1.20 as follows.
(a) Analyse each transaction and record details on a transaction analysis chart.
(b) Following the examples given already in the demonstration exercise for Metro Interiors, prepare accounts, in 3-column format, for each asset, liability, owner's equity, revenue and expense, and record increases and decreases resulting from the transactions.
(c) Prepare a list of debit and credit balances to ensure that the accounting equation:

> Assets + Expenses = Liabilities + Owner's Equity + Revenue

has been maintained.

EXERCISE 1.19

19XX
Sept. 1 Amanda Grassi commenced business by depositing $30 000 in a bank account entitled Grassi Wine Cellars.
3 A delivery van is purchased costing $8500 on credit from Fleet Vans, paying a cash deposit of $2500.
6 Bottled wine is purchased for resale on credit from Theo & Co. for $6000.
9 Amanda withdrew $1000 cash from the business to pay some personal expenses.
15 Sales are credited to the Sports Club of $12 000.
20 Wages are paid to a shop assistant of $250.
26 Cash sales are made of $185.
29 An amount owing of $700 is received from the Sports Club

EXERCISE 1.20

19XX
May 1   Tran Minh commenced business trading as TM Computers with the following assets and liabilities: cash $20 000, inventory (computers and parts) $30 000, bank loan $10 000.
    4   Office furniture is purchased on account (that is, on credit) from Office Supplies Ltd ($3500).
    8   Sales are credited amounting to $5300.
    10 An amount of $80 cash is paid for advertising in a local paper.
    15 An amount of $500 is withdrawn for personal use.
    21 A copier is purchased on credit from Copy Cats ($1200), paying a cash deposit of $200.
    25 Computer parts for resale are purchased on credit ($2500).
    29 An amount of $600 is received from trade debtors.
    30 An amount of $2000 is paid to trade creditors.

KEEPING A RECORD OF TRANSACTIONS

The **accounting** (or bookkeeping) **cycle** is broken down into manageable components, as shown in the following diagram.

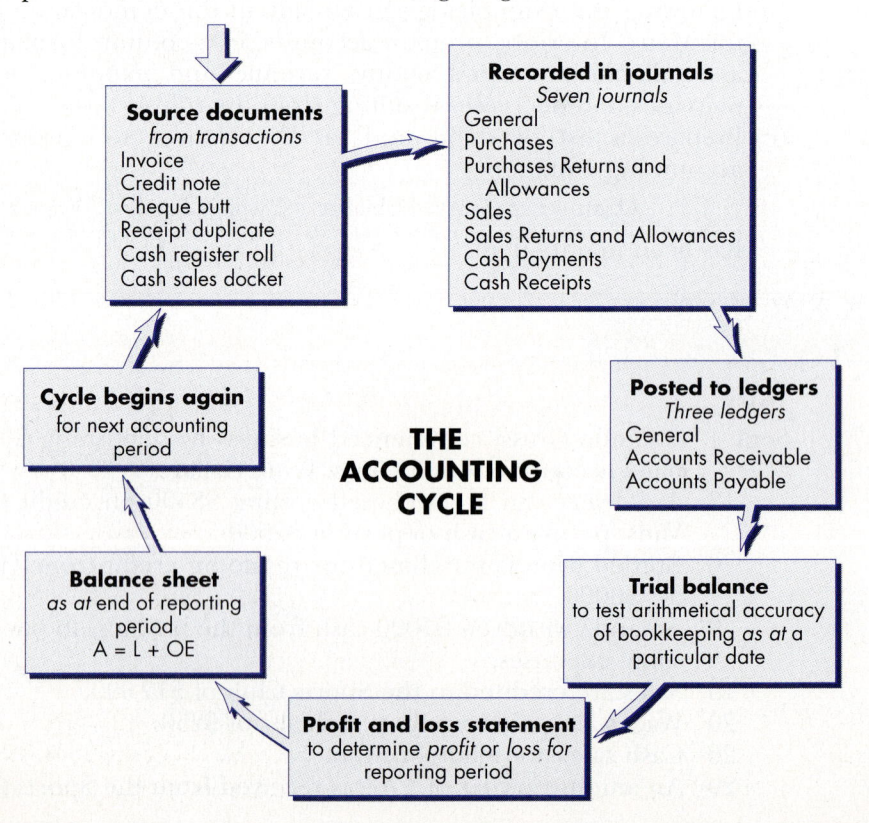

THE ACCOUNTING CYCLE

Source documents
from transactions
Invoice
Credit note
Cheque butt
Receipt duplicate
Cash register roll
Cash sales docket

Recorded in journals
Seven journals
General
Purchases
Purchases Returns and Allowances
Sales
Sales Returns and Allowances
Cash Payments
Cash Receipts

Posted to ledgers
Three ledgers
General
Accounts Receivable
Accounts Payable

Trial balance
to test arithmetical accuracy of bookkeeping *as at* a particular date

Profit and loss statement
to determine *profit* or *loss* for reporting period

Balance sheet
as at end of reporting period
A = L + OE

Cycle begins again
for next accounting period

Financial source documents

Financial source documents provide physical evidence of transactions. As they flow through a business they are checked, sorted and then batched into like groups ready for entering into the journals. Source documents are covered in detail in chapter 2, 'Financial source documents'.

Journals

Journals are books of original entry and, as such, are the first place that details of transactions are recorded from source documents. At the end of each month, these details are posted to the ledger. The journals used in a business consist of:

Trading (or specialised) journals
These include:
- accounts payable journals in which are recorded details of transactions with trade creditors — purchases journal, purchases returns and allowances journal and cash payments journal
- accounts receivable journals in which are recorded details of transactions with trade debtors — sales journal, sales returns and allowances journal and cash receipts journal.

General journal
In this are recorded details of transactions that cannot be recorded in any of the above trading journals.

You will learn more about journals in chapter 3, 'Preparation of journals'.

Ledgers

A ledger is an aggregation of all accounts which make up the accounting records of a business. The ledger may exist as a book-style ledger, a card system or a collection of computer records. A ledger account is maintained for every asset, liability and owner's equity account, including revenue and expense accounts. The latter two accounts are grouped with owner's equity, as revenue increases owner's equity, and expenses decrease owner's equity. The principal ledger used in an accounting system is the general ledger.

General ledger

The general ledger contains all the accounts of a business. These include **control accounts** for the **accounts payable ledger** and the **accounts receivable ledger**, which record the amounts owed by the trade creditors and trade debtors (in total). The individual details for each individual trade creditor and trade debtor are kept in subsidiary ledgers.

Subsidiary ledgers

Subsidiary ledgers are those ledgers into which detailed information for each element of the control accounts in the general ledger is recorded.

Subsidiary ledgers comprise:
- accounts payable ledger (also called **creditors' ledger**) in which details of accounts of individual trade creditors are recorded. These trade creditors are represented, in total, by the Accounts Payable Control account in the general ledger.
- accounts receivable ledger (also called **debtors' ledger**) in which details of accounts of individual trade debtors are recorded. These trade debtors are represented, in total, by the Accounts Receivable Control account in the general ledger.

At the end of the reporting period, a schedule of balances is prepared from the account balances in each of the subsidiary ledgers. The total of these balances must agree with the balance of the relevant control account in the general ledger as shown in the diagram below.

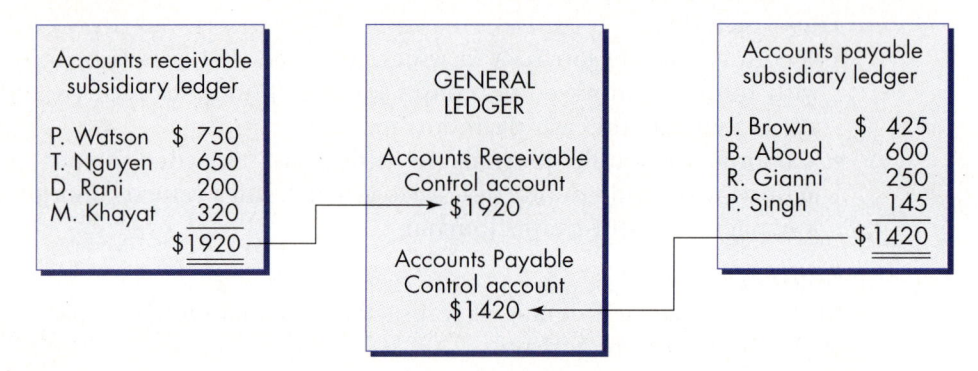

Accounts receivable subsidiary ledger		GENERAL LEDGER	Accounts payable subsidiary ledger	
P. Watson	$ 750	Accounts Receivable Control account $1920	J. Brown	$ 425
T. Nguyen	650		B. Aboud	600
D. Rani	200		R. Gianni	250
M. Khayat	320	Accounts Payable Control account $1420	P. Singh	145
	$1920			$1420

Organising the ledger

To allow prompt retrieval of accounting data from within the ledger, it is necessary to devise an index, or guide (for example, a classified listing of all accounts in the ledger). This is done by using coding to relate items of data belonging to one classification. Coding consists of allocating numbers in a systematic manner to various items of data with common characteristics. In an accounting system, it is used to establish a chart of accounts.

Chart of accounts

This is a listing of all accounts contained in the general ledger. The purpose of a chart of accounts is to organise the ledger accounts in a systematic order so that any account can be found quickly. This is especially important in a large business.

The accounts are usually categorised according to their classification in the accounting equation:

Assets = Liabilities + Owner's Equity.

Accounts are then listed under their particular classification (for example, **current asset**, **current liability**, expense). In a computerised accounting system, the chart of accounts is automatically created as the software package is configured to suit the individual requirements of the business during the setting up phase.

For a manual accounting system, the ledger must be set up with account names and numbers consistent with the chart of accounts. For exercises in this text, students will list only those accounts required to complete a particular exercise. Examples are:

- **block coding**. Each category in the ledger is assigned a block of numbers. For example:

  Assets (1–99):
  1. Cash at Bank
  2. Accounts Receivable

  Liabilities (100–199):
  100 Accounts Payable
  101 Sales Tax

- **numeric coding**. Each category in the ledger is assigned a number and the accounts are numbered consecutively within the category. For example:

  1. Assets:
     1.1 Cash at Bank
     1.2 Accounts Receivable

  2. Liabilities:
     2.1 Accounts Payable
     2.2 Sales Tax

- **alpha-numeric coding**. Each category in the ledger is assigned an alphabetic character. Each specific account within this category is then assigned a number. For example:

  Assets:
  A1 Cash at Bank
  A2 Accounts Receivable

  Liabilities:
  L1 Accounts Payable
  L2 Sales Tax

For exercises in this text the following numerically coded chart of accounts is used:

CHART OF ACCOUNTS		
Asset accounts 1 *Current assets* 　1.1　Cash at Bank 　1.2　Inventory 　1.3　Accounts Receivable 　　　Control 　1.4　Petty Cash 　1.5　Sundry Debtor 2 *Non-current assets* 　2.1　Land 　2.2　Buildings 　2.3　Plant and Machinery 　2.4　Furniture and Fittings 　2.5　Motor Vehicles 　2.6　Office Equipment 　2.7　Office Furniture	3 **Expense accounts** 　3.1　Purchases 　3.2　(Purchases, Returns 　　　and Allowances) 　3.3　Discount Allowed 　3.4　Advertising 　3.5　Bad Debts 　3.6　Bank Charges 　3.7　Electricity 　3.8　General Expenses 　3.9　Insurance 　3.10 Interest Expense 　3.11 Postage 　3.12 Rent Expense 　3.13 Repairs and 　　　Maintenance 　3.14 Stationery 　3.15 Telephone 　3.16 Travel Expenses 　3.17 Wages and Salaries	**Liability accounts** 4 *Current liabilities* 　4.1　Accounts Payable 　　　Control 　4.2　Sales Tax 　4.3　Sundry Creditor 5 *Long-term liabilities* 　5.1　Mortgage 6 **Owner's equity accounts** 　6.1　Capital 　6.2　(Drawings) 7 **Revenue accounts** 　7.1　Sales 　7.2　(Sales Returns and 　　　Allowances) 　7.3　Discount Received 　7.4　Interest Revenue 　7.5　Rent Revenue

Trial balance

At the end of each month, a trial balance is extracted from the general ledger to test the mathematical accuracy of a bookkeeper's work. All accounts with debit balances are totalled and compared with the total of all those accounts with credit balances. If the work is accurate, total debits will always equal total credits. You will learn more about ledgers, including how to post to the ledgers and extract a trial balance in chapter 4, 'Posting to the ledgers'.

Profit and loss statement

At the end of the reporting period, the revenue and expense accounts in the general ledger are closed to the Profit and Loss account, in order to determine the **net profit** (or loss) for the reporting period and prepare the profit and loss statement. Net profit, which increases owner's equity, represents an excess of revenue over expenditure. If expenditure exceeds revenue, a net loss has occurred, which decreases owner's equity. The net profit (or loss) is then transferred to the owner's Capital account.

Balance sheet

This is a listing of all asset, liability and owner's equity account balances *as at* balance date (the date the books are closed and the financial reports prepared). The owner's equity account is decreased by any withdrawals by the owner and by any loss, and increased by any additional contributions of capital by the owner and by any profit. Once the financial position of the business has been ascertained at balance date, the whole accounting cycle commences again for the next reporting period.

CHAPTER 2

Financial source documents

WHEN you have studied this chapter and completed the exercises, you should be competent in the following skills. Tick each skill when you have completed the relevant section.

LEARNING OUTCOMES

1. Identify and prepare appropriate business source documents for purchases, sales, receipts and remittances.

2. Check incoming and outgoing business source documents for accuracy of contents.

3. Note discrepancies in business source documents and take appropriate action or refer to appropriate authority for rectification.

4. Sort business source documents into batches of like transactions and distribute to appropriate person/section for processing within specified times.

▼

TYPES OF BUSINESS DOCUMENT

Whenever a financial transaction takes place in a business organisation, a document is prepared to record details of the transaction. These details then become the source of an entry in the accounting records. Business documents (or financial source documents) form the basis for most entries made to the accounting system. Set out below is a summary of business documents typically used in the accounting section of a business. These are known as financial source documents. Not all of these originate an entry in the bookkeeping system; however, they all have a specific purpose in the financial activities of the business in that they provide tangible proof of transactions, whether they be between departments (internal) or with external parties.

Business document	Purpose	Financial source document
Purchase requisition	Internal document requesting purchase of goods	
Purchase order	Request to supplier for supply of goods on credit	
Invoice*	Charge to customer for goods supplied on credit	Yes
Delivery docket	Accompanies delivery of goods supplied on credit	
Credit note*	Allows customer a reduction in price charged for goods supplied on credit	Yes
Statement of account	Monthly account sent to customer of summary transactions for month	
Remittance advice	Prepared and forwarded with cheque showing details of payment	
Bank deposit slip	Details of daily banking to accompany bank deposit	

CHAPTER 2: FINANCIAL SOURCE DOCUMENTS | 55

Business document	Purpose	Financial source document
Bank deposit book	Bank deposit forms in book format for listing large numbers of cheque details for bank deposit	
Cheque form/butt*	An order to bank to pay nominated person	Yes, cheque butt
Receipt*	Written acknowledgement of cash received	Yes
Cash register roll* (internal cash register record)	Record of daily cash sales from cash register and includes cash/cheques and credit card sales	Yes
Cash register receipt	Tear-off receipt from cash register	
Cash sales docket*	Written receipt for cash sale (sometimes issued in addition to cash register receipt)	Yes, if no cash register receipt issued
Credit card sales voucher	Records credit card (for example, Bankcard, MasterCard, Visa) purchase by customer	
Credit card credit voucher	Records credit card allowance to customer for returns or overcharge	
Credit card merchant summary	Summarises and is attached to daily credit card sales and returns and banked with daily deposit	

* Documents that originate an entry in the books of account

    The way these documents flow within a business provides a series of checks and balances to safeguard the assets of the business. They are an important part of the internal control system of the business. (The internal control system is discussed later in this chapter.)

    The diagrams at the top of page 56 represent the flow of source documents for the selling and purchasing cycles within a business. Each source document will be explained in turn on the following pages.

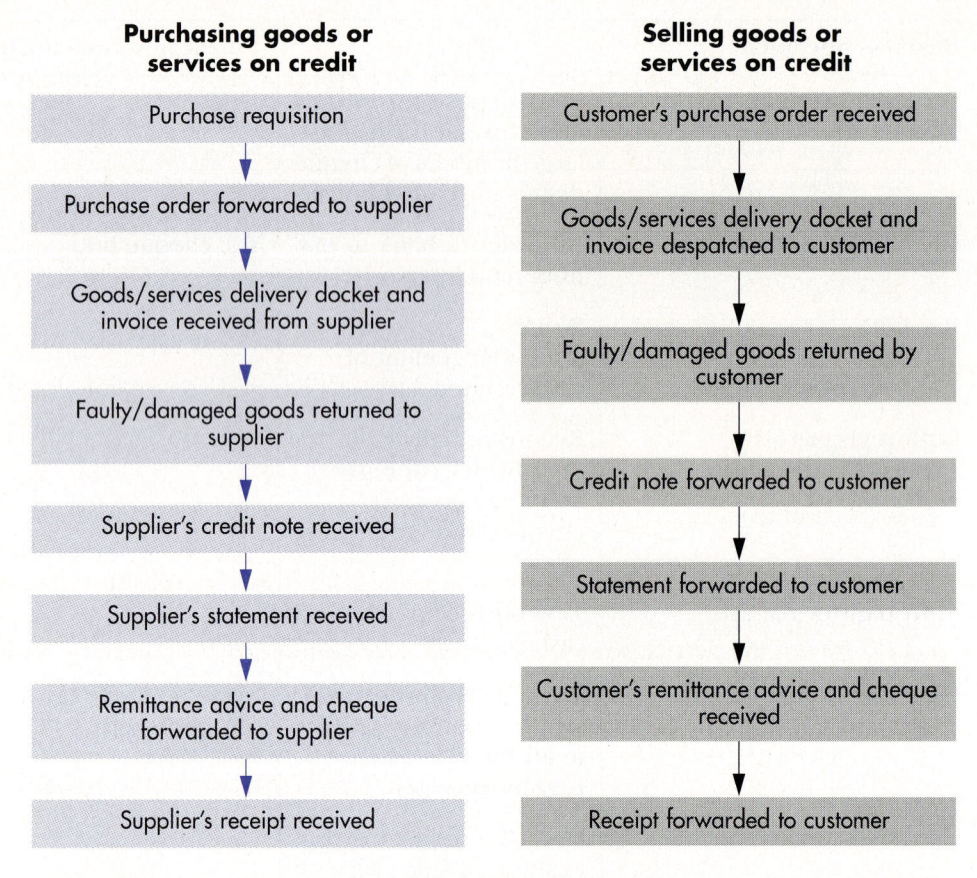

Purchasing goods or services on credit

- Purchase requisition
- Purchase order forwarded to supplier
- Goods/services delivery docket and invoice received from supplier
- Faulty/damaged goods returned to supplier
- Supplier's credit note received
- Supplier's statement received
- Remittance advice and cheque forwarded to supplier
- Supplier's receipt received

Selling goods or services on credit

- Customer's purchase order received
- Goods/services delivery docket and invoice despatched to customer
- Faulty/damaged goods returned by customer
- Credit note forwarded to customer
- Statement forwarded to customer
- Customer's remittance advice and cheque received
- Receipt forwarded to customer

As most of the exercises in this chapter are based on the selling and purchasing activities of J. Mason, clothing manufacturer, an extract from his organisational chart is shown below.

Extract from the organisational chart of J. Mason

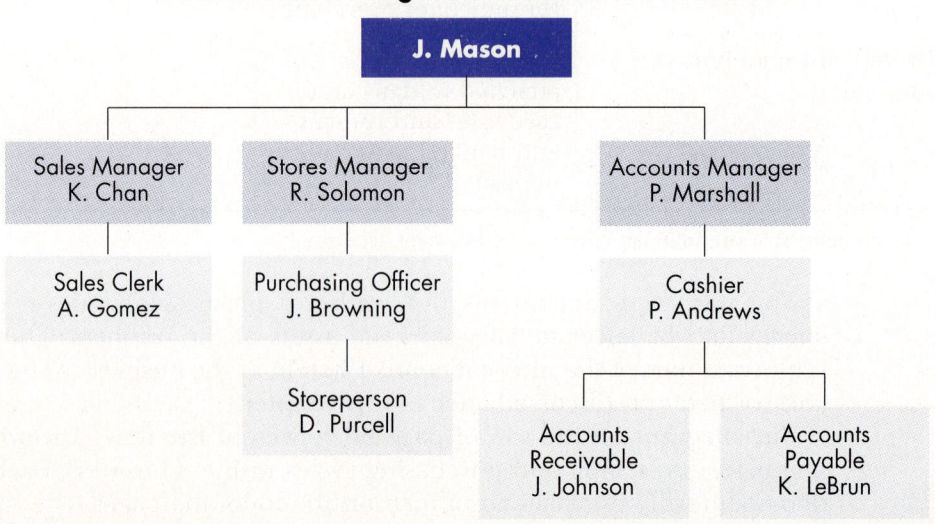

J. Mason

- Sales Manager — K. Chan
  - Sales Clerk — A. Gomez
- Stores Manager — R. Solomon
  - Purchasing Officer — J. Browning
    - Storeperson — D. Purcell
- Accounts Manager — P. Marshall
  - Cashier — P. Andrews
    - Accounts Receivable — J. Johnson
    - Accounts Payable — K. LeBrun

Purchase requisition

The **purchase requisition** is an internal document passed from one department to another requesting the supply of goods. The purchase of goods from outside suppliers is usually controlled by the purchasing department in a large firm, or, in a small business, the purchasing officer.

If the goods required are in store, a stores requisition (instead of a purchase requisition) would be completed, approved by the officer in charge of the department requiring the goods and sent to the officer in charge of the stores department for processing. However, if the goods requested are out of stock or are required for a special job, a purchase requisition is completed and forwarded to the purchasing department. A purchase requisition provides a record of the purchases that have been approved.

Some firms require the person requesting the goods to do the groundwork; in other words, to check with suppliers, obtain prices, delivery dates and so on, and send all material to the purchasing department where the decision is made whether to place an order and with whom.

Placing an order is referred to as 'raising' a purchase order (see page 541). If a purchase order is raised, the number of the purchase order sent to the supplier is quoted on the purchase requisition. This is the first step in a trail of documentation that will accumulate for this purchase.

Documentation pertaining to transactions forms part of an 'audit trail' — a system by which any number of transactions may be traced back to their source.

A purchase requisition shows the following:
- date and number of purchase requisition
- department/person requesting goods
- number, type and description of goods requested
- list price (not always current) and approximate cost of goods
- name of firm which will supply goods
- signature of person requesting goods
- signature of person authorising purchase
- number of purchase order raised.

Somewhere on a purchase requisition the words *Not a purchase order* or *Requisition only* should be included. Some firms have an imprint (such as a watermark) printed on the requisition forms so they cannot be confused with purchase orders.

Example

Jonas Agnetti, Cutting Department Manager at J. Mason's clothing manufacturing company, sent the purchase requisition shown below to J. Browning, Purchasing Officer. It was prepared in duplicate, with distribution as follows:
- original to stores department
- duplicate retained in cutting department.

<table>
<tr><td colspan="5" align="center">**J. Mason**
401 Denning Highway
NORTH PERTH WA 6006</td></tr>
<tr><td colspan="5">No.: 342
Date: 29 December 19XX</td></tr>
<tr><td colspan="3">To: J. Browning
     Purchasing Officer</td><td colspan="2">**Purchase Requisition**</td></tr>
<tr><td colspan="3">From: J. Agnetti
      Cutting Department Manager</td><td colspan="2">This is not a purchase order.</td></tr>
<tr><th>QUANTITY</th><th>UNIT</th><th>DESCRIPTION</th><th>LIST PRICE</th><th>ESTIMATED COST</th></tr>
<tr><td>8</td><td>only</td><td>'Bonform' dressmaker dummies</td><td>$80.00</td><td>$640.00</td></tr>
<tr><td>6</td><td>prs</td><td>Industrial cutting shears</td><td>35.00</td><td>210.00</td></tr>
<tr><td colspan="3">Suggested supplier:
P. Eastman
29 Newman Road
CLAREMONT WA 6010
Purchase Order Yes ✓ No ☐ No. 283</td><td colspan="2">Requested by: *J. Agnetti*
Date: 29 December 19XX
Authorised by: *J. Browning*
Date: 2 January 19XX</td></tr>
</table>

Purchase order

The **purchase order** is a formal request for the supply of goods on credit, generated by the purchasing firm (customer) and sent to the supplier of the goods or services. It documents the agreement between the customer (buyer) and the supplier (seller). It is an accountable document and is sequentially numbered. It sets out:
- date and order number
- name and address of firm ordering goods
- contact person
- name and address of firm supplying goods
- delivery instructions
- date goods required
- quantity, details and price of goods ordered (the total cost of the order is not generally included on the purchase order)
- amount of sales tax payable, or sales tax exemption number if applicable (these are explained on pages 60–61)
- signature of authorised person on behalf of the purchaser.

In the purchase requisition shown above, J. Browning, as the officer in charge of the purchasing department, has approved the purchase

and authorised the raising of Purchase Order No. 283, shown below. The purchase order is usually prepared in quadruplicate, with distribution as follows:
- original to supplier
- duplicate to receiving dock
- triplicate to accounts department
- quadruplicate retained by purchasing department.

J. Mason
401 Denning Highway
NORTH PERTH WA 6006

No.: 283

Date: 2 January 19XX

To: P. Eastman
29 Newman Road
CLAREMONT WA 6010

Purchase Order

Please supply the goods listed below, quoting the above order number.

QUANTITY	DESCRIPTION	APPROX. UNIT PRICE	ESTIMATED TOTAL
8 only	'Bonform' dressmaker dummies	$80.00	$640.00
6 prs	Industrial cutting shears	35.00	210.00

Deliver to: Warehouse

Delivery required by: 10 January 19XX

Authorised by: *J. Browning*

EXERCISE 2.1 Purchase orders

Make three copies of the blank purchase order master provided on page 541 and add the J. Mason header as shown in the example above. Prepare the purchase orders for the following transactions.

1. Purchase Order No. 2501, on 5 December 19XX, to P. Eastman, 29 Newman Road, Claremont, WA 6010, for:
   20 × 20 cm zippers @ $4.50 each
   500 × 2.5 cm rose buttons @ $0.20 each
   350 × 2.0 cm pearl buttons @ $0.18 each.
   Goods are required as soon as possible and are to be delivered to the warehouse.

2. Purchase Order No. 2502, on 5 December 19XX, to H. Lime, 48 Argyle Road, Midland, WA 6056, for:
200 m floral cotton @ $4.50 per metre
150 m printed linen @ $6.60 per metre.
   Goods are required as soon as possible and are to be delivered to the warehouse.
3. Purchase Order No. 2503, on 6 December 19XX, to N. Lilly, 53 Conroy Street, Fremantle, WA 6160, for:
48 × shoulder pad sets @ $1.00 each
40 × spools of white thread @ $1.50 per spool.
   Goods are required by 20 December 19XX and are to be delivered to the factory.

Invoice

An **invoice** is issued when goods are purchased on credit. It is made out by the supplier and the original copy is sent to the purchaser of the goods or services. The invoice may accompany the goods or may be mailed at a later date.

An invoice is prepared for each delivery of goods and shows the amount of money that the buyer owes to the seller for the goods. An invoice is an accountable document and is numbered sequentially but it is not signed. It shows the following details:
- name and address of supplier/seller
- date and invoice number
- name and address of customer/buyer
- customer order number
- delivery instructions
- quantity, details and price of goods
- trade discount (if any)
- amount of sales tax payable (if applicable)
- total amount of invoice
- terms of trading.

The invoice is prepared in duplicate, with distribution as follows:
- original to customer
- duplicate retained by supplier for entry in the accounting records.

Trade discount

Trade discount is allowed by a manufacturer to a wholesaler, or by a wholesaler to a retailer. It is shown on the invoice as a deduction from the selling price. If trade discount is allowed, it is always *subtracted* from the total value of the invoice *before* sales tax is calculated and added. Trade discount is deducted at the time the goods are sold.

Sales tax

Sales tax is charged by the Federal Government on the wholesale price of certain classes of goods. All wholesalers and some manufacturers who sell directly to retailers are registered with the Australian Taxation Office and issued with a sales tax registration number. Sales tax is added to the invoice price of goods sold. The seller does not keep this money, but acts as an unpaid collector and remits the tax collected to the government on a regular basis, usually monthly.

For sales tax purposes, goods are classified as follows.
- *Taxable goods.* These are goods sold to a retailer on which tax is chargeable at the rate specified for that particular class of goods.
- *Goods on which sales tax is not payable.* When a wholesaler sells to a retailer, the retailer pays sales tax (if chargeable) on the goods bought. However, when a wholesaler purchases these goods from the manufacturer, the sales tax registration number is quoted on the purchase order. This alerts the manufacturer not to charge sales tax on this sale, as manufacturers collect sales tax only when they sell directly to a retailer. It is left to the wholesaler to collect the tax when selling the goods to the retailer. This registration number is often called a 'sales tax exemption number'. Some charitable, religious and educational organisations, providing they meet certain guidelines and supply a statement to this effect, are not charged sales tax on goods purchased by them.
- *Exempt goods.* These are goods on which sales tax is not payable at any time.

It is important to remember that a business is required to record sales tax only on its *selling* operations. When goods are purchased, sales tax, if payable, is the responsibility of the business from which the goods were purchased (that is, the person selling the goods).

Cash discount

Cash discount does not appear on the invoice, but is allowed to trade debtors (customers) to encourage prompt payment of amounts owing. When payment is made, and if a discount is allowed, it is recorded in the accounting records as Discount Allowed. When a cash discount is received from trade creditors (suppliers), it is recorded in the accounting records as Discount Received.

Where this discount is allowed, it is specified under the 'Terms of Trading' which appear at the bottom of the invoice as a percentage. For example, '$2\frac{1}{2}\%$ 7 days or net 30 days' indicates that if an invoice is paid within seven days, $2\frac{1}{2}$ per cent may be deducted from the amount owing before payment is remitted. Otherwise, the full amount should be paid in 30 days.

Some firms also have a limit on the time allowed for claims for returns and allowances. This is stated along with the terms of trading on the bottom of the invoice. The term 'E & O E' at the bottom of the invoice on page 62 stands for 'errors and omissions excepted'. This means that, although an invoice may contain calculation errors, the correct amount should be paid.

In the example of an invoice given on page 62, J. Mason sells merchandise on credit to Maud's Boutique (Purchase Order No. 121).

J. Mason
401 Denning Highway
NORTH PERTH WA 6006

Invoice No.: 371

Date: 3 January 19XX

Cust. Order No.: 121

Maud's Boutique
84 Trent Road
RYDE NSW 2112

Invoice

QUANTITY	DESCRIPTION	UNIT PRICE	TOTAL
24	Ladies' dresses	$21.50	$516.00
12	Ladies' silk T-shirts	29.25	351.00
			867.00
	Less Trade Discount @ 10%		86.70
			780.30
	Plus Sales Tax @ 15%		117.05
			$897.35

Terms: $2\frac{1}{2}$% 7 days or net 30 days   No claims accepted after 7 days

E & O E

EXERCISE 2.2 *Invoices*

J. Mason sells the following goods on credit. You are required to prepare the invoices for these goods. J. Mason gives a trade discount of 10%, and sales tax of 15% is to be charged on all goods. (Copy the blank invoice master provided on page 542 and add the J. Mason header, as shown on the example of an invoice above.)

1. On 16 December 19XX, on Invoice No. 508 to L. Wells, 28 Waverley Road, Canning Vale WA 6155 (Customer Order No. 6025), for:
   12 × ladies' dresses @ $55.00 each
   24 × skirts @ $27.50 each
   36 × prs slacks @ $23.00 pr.

2. On 18 December 19XX, on Invoice No. 509 to T. Abbott, 162 Ryan Road, Fremantle WA 6160 (Customer Order No. 1179), for:
   24 × slack suits @ $75.00 each
   12 × ladies' dresses @ $40.00 each.

3. On 19 December 19XX, on Invoice No. 510 to M. Adams, 410 Venetia Street, East Perth WA 6004 (Customer Order No. 4351), for:
   50 × blouses @ $25.00 each
   25 × prs slacks @ $18.00 pr.

Delivery docket

The **delivery docket** provides proof that the goods have been delivered. It is forwarded with the goods and is signed by the customer as evidence that the goods arrived in good order and condition. The customer retains a copy for the records.

It is important that the customer checks the goods as soon as possible after they are received as some firms have a limit on the time allowed for returns. This is usually stated on the invoice as part of the trading terms. Quite often, the delivery docket uses a similar format to that of an invoice with the pricing details blanked out. The delivery docket shows:
- date
- name of supplier
- name of customer
- name of carrier (if external carrier used)
- brief description of goods.

The delivery docket is another form of internal control, enabling goods to be checked against the delivery docket and the delivery docket to be checked against the original purchase order.

The delivery docket is usually prepared in triplicate, with distribution as follows:
- original signed by customer and returned to supplier
- duplicate given to customer
- triplicate retained by carrier (if external).

In the example of a delivery docket below, J. Mason has forwarded goods to Maud's Boutique, the original docket has been signed by M. Coutsis (proprietor) and returned to J. Mason.

Date: 3 January 19XX

J. Mason
401 Denning Highway
NORTH PERTH WA 6006

No.: 1274

Customer Order No. 121

To:

Maud's Boutique
84 Trent Road
RYDE NSW 2112

Delivery Docket

QUANTITY	DESCRIPTION	PRICE
24	Ladies' dresses	
12	Ladies' silk T-shirts	

The above-mentioned goods have been received in good order and condition.

Received by: *M. Coutsis*

Credit note

A **credit note** is issued by a supplier when goods which have been invoiced to the customer (buyer) are returned by the customer to the supplier (seller). Reasons for return of goods include:
- short delivery
- damaged, incorrect or faulty goods supplied
- incorrect information on invoice
- goods not as described on invoice.

A credit note is made out in duplicate by the supplier (seller). The original is forwarded to the customer (purchaser) and the duplicate is retained for record purposes.

In the example shown below, Maud's Boutique has returned eight ladies' dresses with incorrectly stitched collars and the credit note has been issued accordingly.

J. Mason
401 Denning Highway
NORTH PERTH WA 6006

Credit Note No.: 524
Date: 10 January 19XX
Invoice No.: 371

Maud's Boutique
84 Trent Road
RYDE NSW 2112

Credit Note

QUANTITY	DESCRIPTION	UNIT PRICE	TOTAL
8	Ladies' dresses	$21.50	$172.00
	Less Trade Discount @ 10%		17.20
			154.80
	Plus Sales Tax 15%		23.22
			$178.02

Reason for return: Incorrectly stitched collars

Terms: $2\frac{1}{2}$% 7 days, otherwise net 30 days   No claims accepted after 7 days

---

Both the invoice and the credit note are completed by the supplier (seller). The invoice shows the amount owing and the credit note reduces that amount as appropriate. A credit note is usually printed in red to distinguish it from an invoice and shows the following details:
- name and address of supplier/seller
- date and credit note number
- name and address of customer/purchaser

- number of invoice to which it refers
- quantity, details and price of goods
- amount of trade discount (if allowed on invoice)
- amount of sales tax
- credit note total
- details of allowance.

If trade discount and sales tax apply, the same rates used on the invoice are used in the credit note. The credit note is prepared in duplicate, with distribution as follows:
- original to customer
- duplicate retained by the supplier for entry in the accounting records.

EXERCISE 2.3 *Credit notes*

The following goods were returned to J. Mason. Use a copy of the blank credit note master provided on page 543 and add the J. Mason header. Prepare the necessary credit notes.

1. On 20 December 19XX, Credit Note No. 536 was issued for 2 ladies' dresses @ $55 each, which were returned by L. Wells because they were faulty (Invoice No. 508) (see page 62 for address details).
2. On 21 December 19XX, Credit Note No. 537 was issued for 4 slack suits @ $75 each, which were returned by T. Abbott because they were faulty (Invoice No. 509) (see page 62 for address details).
3. On 22 December 19XX, Credit Note No. 538 was issued for 2 pairs of ladies' slacks @ $18 each and 3 ladies' blouses @ $25 each, which were returned by M. Adams because they were not as ordered (Invoice No. 510) (see page 62 for address details).

Cheque

A **cheque** provides a convenient method of drawing funds from a bank account. A cheque is an order to the bank to pay, on demand, the amount of money written on the cheque to the person named on the cheque.

The authority to draw a cheque is given on an approval for payment slip or cheque requisition form, after verifying that the goods or services itemised on the invoice were properly ordered and received. Most businesses require one of these forms to be attached to the account, duly signed by the authorising officer, before a cheque is drawn. Others require only that the person authorising payment of invoices should, after checking that all is correct, place an 'Approved for payment' stamp on the invoice to be paid and initial it in the appropriate places.

Before a cheque is drawn, documentation should be sighted to show that invoices and statements have been checked and the amount to be paid is correct. A cheque can then be drawn up for the amount due.

There are three parties to a cheque. These are:
1. *the **drawer*** — the person who draws and signs the cheque and whose account is to be charged (In some companies, one person may write out or prepare the cheque and another person may sign it on behalf of the business.)
2. *the **drawee*** — the bank and branch on which the cheque is drawn (the drawer's bank)
3. *the **payee*** — the person or firm named on the face of the cheque.

All money paid out of the business is by cheque drawn on the business bank account (except for small items paid for out of petty cash). Cash is *never* taken from the cash register to make any payments.

A cheque consists of two parts — the cheque form itself and the **cheque butt**. Details of the payment are entered on the cheque butt which remains in the cheque book for recording in the cash payments journal. The completed cheque form itself is then detached and posted to the creditor in settlement of an outstanding account. The cheque shows the following:
- date
- drawee (the bank on which the cheque is drawn)
- payee (the person to whom the money is to be paid)
- amount of the cheque (in words and figures)
- signature of the person authorised to sign the cheque on behalf of the drawer
- some form of 'crossing' for security.

'Crossed' cheques

A cheque is 'crossed' to prevent unauthorised persons from cashing it. The most common forms of 'crossing' are:
- two parallel lines drawn across the face of a cheque to signify that the cheque must be paid into a bank account. It cannot be paid out in cash.
- the addition of the words *not negotiable* between these lines. This is a warning that anyone receiving the cheque has a claim to the cheque only as good as that of the person receiving it. It provides protection for both drawer and payee in that, if the cheque is stolen or lost, it can be traced to the person (or firm) into whose bank account it is paid. The rightful owner can then demand payment from the person who banked the cheque. Anyone who accepts a 'not negotiable' cheque does so at his or her own risk.
- the words *account payee only* included in the crossing. These are an instruction that the cheque must be paid into the bank of the payee only.

The name of the bank account on which the cheque is drawn is printed at the bottom of the cheque, together with a coded entry consisting of three parts.
1. *Cheque number.* This is the same as the number on the cheque butt.
2. *BSB number.* This is in two parts: the first part identifies the bank and the State, the second part identifies the branch.
3. *Account number.* This is a unique number allocated to the account when it was established.

The drawer of the cheque must be careful to observe the following.
- All alterations on a cheque must be initialled by the drawer.
- Fraudulent use of a cheque may be prevented by:
  (a) writing the amount in words as closely as possible to the dollar sign
  (b) using a dash instead of a decimal point when writing figures
  (c) taking care not to leave spaces that might permit the insertion of additional words or figures.
- Words and figures must agree.
- Check that the date is correct. Post-dated cheques are illegal and a cheque that is more than 12 months old is a 'stale' cheque.
- Cheques must be signed by a person or persons authorised to sign.
- For security, cheques should be crossed and marked 'Not negotiable'.

Example

J. Mason receives the **purchases invoice** shown below from P. Eastman for goods ordered on Purchase Order No. 283. Verification has been received that the goods have arrived in good order and condition and all documentation is with the accounts department.

P. EASTMAN
Suppliers to the Clothing Industry
29 Newman Road
CLAREMONT WA 6010

Invoice No.: 1135
Date: 5 January 19XX
Cust. Order No.: 283

J. Mason
401 Denning Highway
NORTH PERTH WA 6006

Invoice

QUANTITY	DESCRIPTION	UNIT PRICE	TOTAL
8 only	Dressmaker dummies	$82.00	$656.00
6 prs	Industrial dressmaker shears	32.00	192.00
			848.00
	Less 10% Trade Discount		84.80
			763.20
	Plus 15% Sales Tax		114.48
			$877.68

Terms: $2\frac{1}{2}$% 7 days or net 30 days   No claims accepted after 7 days
E & O E

The accounts clerk now completes a cheque requisition form (or approval for payment slip) to enable a cheque to be drawn in payment of this invoice to take advantage of the cash discount for prompt settlement. An example of a cheque requisition form is shown on page 68. An approval for payment slip serves the same purpose.

J. Mason
Cheque Requisition

Date: 10 January 19XX

Cheque payable to: P. Eastman

Address: 29 Newman Road
CLAREMONT **State:** WA **P'code:** 6010

Date	Particulars	Invoice No.	Credit No.	Receipt No.	Debit	Credit	Total
10.1.XX	Invoice	1135			877.68		877.68

Authorised by:

Cheque No.	0000132	Amount owing $	877 | 68
Cheque date	10 January 19XX	Less discount	21 | 94
Cheque amount	$855.74		
Discount	$21.94	Amount payable $	855 | 74

After the cheque requisition is authorised, a cheque is drawn in payment of this invoice to take advantage of the trading terms of P. Eastman's cash discount of $2\frac{1}{2}$% if paid within seven days. This cheque is depicted below.

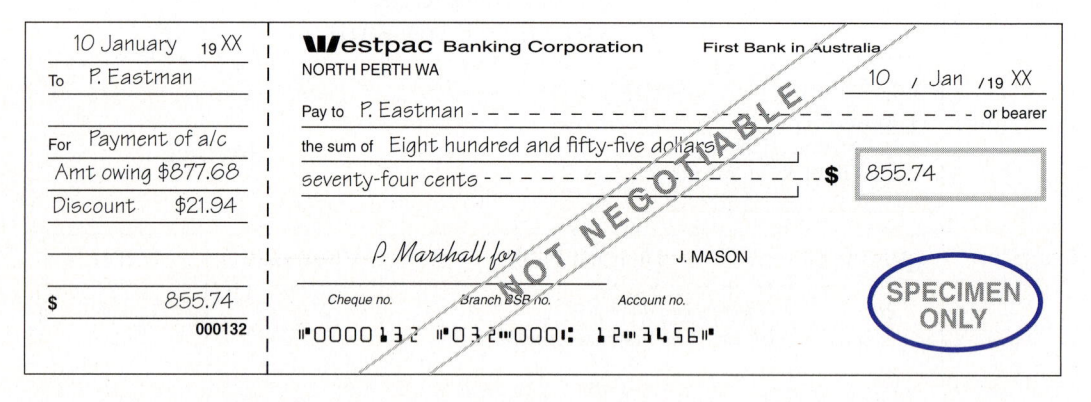

Cheque stub:
10 January 19XX
To P. Eastman
For Payment of a/c
Amt owing $877.68
Discount $21.94
$ 855.74
000132

Cheque:
Westpac Banking Corporation — First Bank in Australia
NORTH PERTH WA
10 / Jan /19 XX
Pay to P. Eastman — or bearer
the sum of Eight hundred and fifty-five dollars seventy-four cents — $ 855.74
P. Marshall for J. MASON
Cheque no. 000132 Branch BSB no. 032-000 Account no. 12-3456
NOT NEGOTIABLE
SPECIMEN ONLY

Remittance advice

A **remittance** (or payment) **advice** is prepared for the benefit of the payee (the person or firm to whom the cheque is made payable) and is included with the cheque when the account is paid. It assists the creditor (supplier) to identify the sender of the cheque and to credit it to the correct account. All details of the payment, including details of invoices, credit notes or deductions claimed, should be listed on the advice.

A remittance advice is commonly in the form of a tear-off slip attached to the monthly statement of account. This portion is detached and returned with the payment. The duplicate copy of the remittance advice is retained for record purposes.

The following remittance advice would be attached to J. Mason's cheque before mailing.

J. Mason
401 Denning Highway
NORTH PERTH WA 6006

Remittance Advice

To: P. Eastman
29 Newman Road
CLAREMONT WA 6010

Date: 10 January 19XX

Date	Particulars	Ref.	Debit $	Credit $	Balance $
19XX Jan. 10	Invoice	1135	877.68		877.68

Details of payment

Balance owing	$877	68
less Discount	21	94
Cheque amount	$855	74

Petty cash

It is normal business practice for all payments to be made by cheque. This is because cheques provide written records of amounts paid out in both the company's and the bank's records, whereas cash is easy to misappropriate.

However, cash is needed to pay for small day-to-day expenses of a business, such as tea and coffee, magazines and newspapers, flowers, parking fees, postage and bus and train fares.

For this purpose, businesses operate a **petty cash system**. To make a claim, the member of staff who spent the money must complete a **petty cash voucher**. A receipt for the amount spent should be attached to the petty cash voucher. The voucher is signed by the person claiming the payment. In some instances, the claim must also be signed by the claimant's supervisor authorising the payment. All payments made from the petty cash fund must be supported by a petty cash voucher, an example of which is shown below.

Petty Cash Voucher

Date: 6-2-XX

DEBIT: Admin. dept.

Particulars: Flowers for reception desk

$ 6-00

Received: C. Grabham

The operation and maintenance of the petty cash fund is covered in detail in chapter 6, 'Cash control'.

EXERCISE 2.4 — Remittance advices and cheques

As the accounts payable clerk for J. Mason, use copies of the blank masters on pages 544 and 545 to complete remittance advices (add the J. Mason header) and prepare cheques for signature for the following accounts which have been passed for payment.

1. On 12 December 19XX, paid Invoice No. 236 (dated 10 December 19XX) for $256.00 for trading goods received from P. Eastman, 29 Newman Road, Claremont, WA 6010. The discount allowed by this firm for prompt payment is $6.40.
2. On 14 December 19XX, paid Invoice No. 754 (dated 12 December 19XX) for $235.60 for computer software purchased from M. Chater, 72 Rundle Mall, Adelaide SA 5000.
3. On 14 December 19XX, paid Invoice No. 324 (dated 9 December 19XX) for $580.00 for trading goods received from L. Pastor, 241 Queen's Road, Mt Gambier, SA 5290. Discount allowed by this firm for prompt payment is $14.50.

Receipt

Cash received by a business is usually in the form of notes and coins, cheques or credit card vouchers. Money that is paid directly into the firm's bank account by direct deposit or electronic transfer is also regarded as cash received.

When a business receives cash, a **receipt** is issued as proof that the goods have been paid for. This usually takes one of two forms.

1. In the case of a cash sale, the **cash register receipt** or the **cash sale docket** serves as a receipt. As this is a cash transaction, this form of receipt does not need to show the name of the person from whom the money is received. The total cash sales for the day are recorded by the cash register on the **cash register roll**. (Cash register receipts and rolls are discussed in more detail on page 74.)
2. When cash is received in any other way, for example, through the mail (by cheque) or paid directly into the firm's bank account (direct deposit or electronic transfer), a receipt must be made out showing:
    - receipt number
    - date
    - name of firm issuing the receipt (supplier/seller)
    - name of person from whom the money was received (customer/purchaser)
    - amount received, in words and figures
    - reason for payment, such as payment of account or rent, wages etc.
    - whether payment is by cash or cheque
    - whether discount is allowed and the amount of discount
    - the total of the account (amount received plus the discount allowed)
    - signature of the receiver (person authorised to sign on behalf of business).

The receipt is made out in duplicate with distribution as follows:
- original forwarded to customer
- duplicate retained for entry in the accounting records.

In the example shown below, a receipt was made out on 6 December 19XX for a cheque received from M. Adams (of Maud's Boutique) for $1413.75 in payment of the November account (total $1450.00). J. Mason forwards the receipt to Maud's Boutique which has taken advantage of the cash discount of $36.25 for early settlement.

```
J. Mason                                    No. 284
                                            Receipt

                    Date    6 December         19XX

RECEIVED from    M. Adams

the sum of    Fourteen hundred and thirteen    dollars

and    seventy-five                            cents

being for    Payment of November account    of

                            Cash/cheque    $1413    75
                            Discount          36    25
                            $               1450    00

Signed    P. Andrews
```

EXERCISE 2.5 Receipts

On 6 December 19XX, J. Mason received the following payments. You are required to prepare a receipt for each of these amounts. Use copies of the blank receipt master provided on page 546.

1. A cheque is received from L. Wells for $487.50 in payment of the November account ($500.00). Discount allowed for prompt payment of $12.50 has been deducted (Receipt No. 285).
2. A cheque is received from L. Bryant for $740 in payment for a second-hand computer (Receipt No. 286).
3. A cheque is received from T. Abbott for $766.48 in payment of the November account ($786.00). Discount allowed for prompt payment of $19.52 has been deducted (Receipt No. 287).

Statement of account

The **statement of account** is prepared by the supplier and forwarded to the customer at the end of the month. It summarises the trading transactions for the month, showing relevant invoice and credit note numbers, and is virtually a copy of the debtor's ledger account in the books of the supplier. It lists:
- the balance outstanding at the beginning of the month (showing amounts overdue 30, 60 or 90 days as well as the current amount outstanding). This breakdown of the total amount outstanding is called **'ageing'** the balance.
- invoices and credit notes in date order
- payments received for the month
- discounts allowed for the month
- balance owing at the end of the month.

Large firms use a cyclical billing system to help spread the workload throughout the month. The debtors' ledger is divided into alphabetical sections, for example, A–G, H–M and so on, and statements for each section are sent out on a different day of the month. For example, statements for A–G might go out on the 10th, and those for H–M on the 20th.

In the example shown below, J. Mason forwards the statement for the month of December 19XX to Maud's Boutique summarising transactions for that month.

J. Mason
401 Denning Highway
NORTH PERTH WA 6006

Statement of Account

for the month of

December 19 XX

To:
Maud's Boutique
84 Trent Road
RYDE NSW 2112

Date	Particulars	Ref.	Debit	Credit	Balance
19XX					
Dec. 1	Opening balance				724.80
5	Invoice	286	572.50		1297.30
6	Receipt	182		706.68	590.62
	Discount			18.12	572.50
14	Invoice	298	362.80		935.30
22	Credit note	341		122.50	812.80

Current	30 days	60 days	90 days	Please pay final amount in this column
$812.80				

EXERCISE 2.6

Statements of account

Using a copy of the blank statement master provided on page 547, prepare a statement for the month of December 19XX for each of the following. (Add the J. Mason header to the top of each statement.)

1. To L. Wells, 28 Waverley Road, Canning Vale WA 6155:

Dec.	1	Opening balance	$ 500.00
	5	Inv. 477	$ 303.00
	15	Rec. 285	$ 487.50
		Discount	$ 12.50
	16	Inv. 508	$2223.18
	20	C/note 536	$ 113.85

2. To T. Abbott, 162 Ryan Road, Fremantle WA 6160:

Dec.	1	Opening balance	$ 786.00
	10	Inv. 489	$ 602.50
	15	Rec. 286	$ 766.48
		Discount	$ 19.52
	16	Inv. 509	$2359.80
	21	C/note 537	$ 315.50
	22	Inv. 520	$1115.00

3. To M. Adams, 410 Venetia Street, East Perth WA 6004:

Dec.	1	Opening balance	$1450.00
	2	Inv. 460	$ 503.50
	6	Rec. 294	$1413.75
		Discount	$ 36.25
	10	Inv. 490	$1274.00
	16	Inv. 510	$1759.50
	22	C/note 538	$ 114.89

Records of cash sales

When cash is received in exchange for goods or services, most businesses, for security purposes, use a cash register. This has the advantage of recording details of all transactions internally on the cash register roll, as well as generating a receipt for each individual sale.

Cash register receipt

This is a tear-off receipt produced by the cash register for one sale (see the example opposite). It records:
- the issuing firm's name
- date
- amount of cash sale
- sales tax (if any)
- total value of sale
- cash tendered
- change given.

```
        J. Mason
        15/01/XX

Shears              $70.00
Sales tax            14.00
TOTAL               $84.00

Amount tendered    $100.00
Change               16.00
        THANK YOU
```

Cash sale docket

Sometimes a customer may require a more detailed form of receipt for business purposes. The example below shows a typical cash sale docket which may be issued along with the cash register receipt, to which it should be attached. It is made out in duplicate for record purposes.

Cash Sale Docket

No. 372   Date   15 January 19XX
Received from   P. Algenoni

Description	Price	Total	
1 only pr. Electric Cutting Shears	$70.00	$70	00
Plus Sales Tax @ 20%		14	00
Total		$84	00

J. Mason
Per *A. Gomez* $84.00

Cash register roll

The daily cash sales total is recorded internally by the cash register on the cash register roll. At the end of the day's trading (or at regular intervals throughout the day, depending on the cash-secure policy of the business), the cash register is balanced and a print-out obtained. An example of a typical cash register roll print-out is shown opposite.

```
          J. Mason
     Cash Register No. 3
      15 January 19XX

Total Sales        $3794.64
Total Sales Tax      948.66
DAILY TOTAL       $4743.30
```

Credit card sales voucher

Many transactions are carried out using credit cards. The credit card supplier (for example, Bankcard, Visa, American Express or Diners Club) derives income from commission charged on sales made using its credit card.

When goods are purchased with a credit card, the merchant (the seller of the goods) records details of the sale on a **credit card sales voucher** (see the example below). The voucher is recorded in triplicate and distributed as follows:
- original to the credit card supplier
- duplicate to the purchaser (card holder)
- triplicate retained by the merchant.

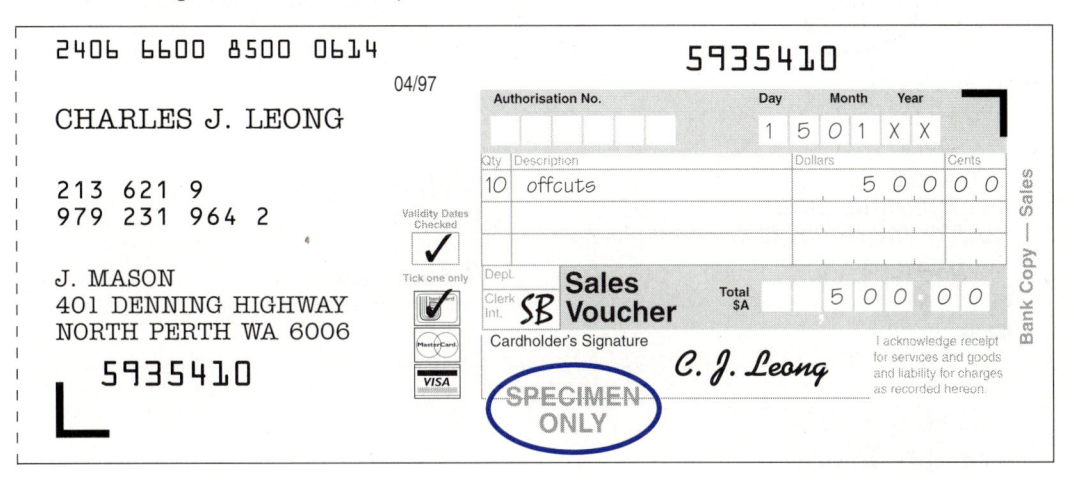

```
2406 6600 8500 0614                                    5935410
                        04/97
                               Authorisation No.    Day   Month   Year
CHARLES J. LEONG                                    15    01     XX

                               Qty  Description              Dollars      Cents
213 621 9                      10   offcuts                  500          00
979 231 964 2
                   Validity Dates
                   Checked
                   ✓
                   Tick one only  Dept.
J. MASON                          Clerk  Sales         Total
401 DENNING HIGHWAY               Int.   SB Voucher    $A    500    00
NORTH PERTH WA 6006
                                  Cardholder's Signature       I acknowledge receipt
   5935410                                   C. J. Leong       for services and goods
                                                               and liability for charges
                                        SPECIMEN ONLY          as recorded hereon.
```

Credit card credit voucher

When goods that have been purchased with a credit card are returned to the seller (for example, if the goods are faulty), the customer presents the goods and the credit card and a **credit card credit voucher** is made out. This deducts the price of the returned goods from the amount that the customer owes to the credit card supplier. An example is shown below.

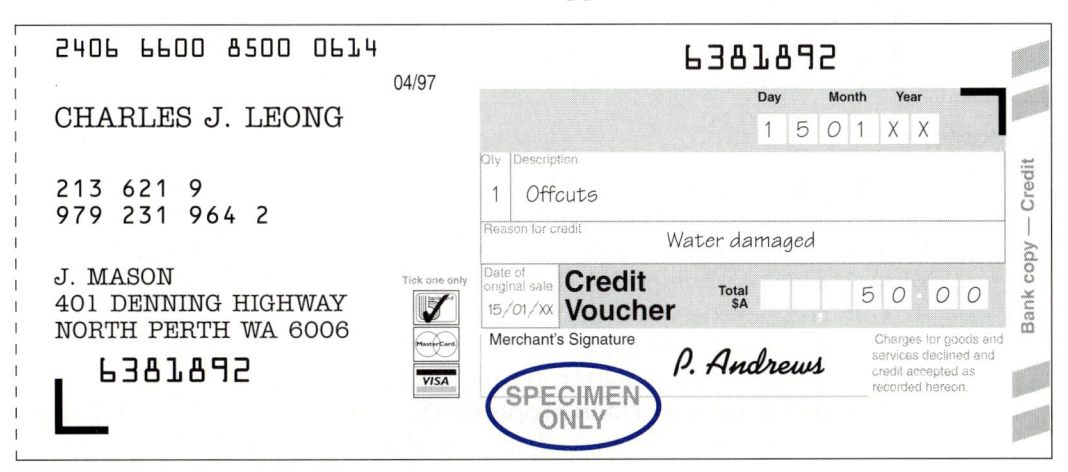

```
2406 6600 8500 0614                                    6381892
                        04/97
                                                    Day   Month   Year
CHARLES J. LEONG                                    15    01     XX

                               Qty  Description
213 621 9                      1    Offcuts
979 231 964 2
                               Reason for credit    Water damaged

                   Tick one only  Date of
J. MASON                          original sale  Credit    Total
401 DENNING HIGHWAY               15/01/XX       Voucher   $A    50    00
NORTH PERTH WA 6006
                                  Merchant's Signature         Charges for goods and
   6381892                                   P. Andrews        services declined and
                                                               credit accepted as
                                        SPECIMEN ONLY          recorded hereon.
```

Credit card merchant summary

The trader records all the credit card sales made for one day on a **credit card merchant summary** slip (see the example below). The total amount of all these sales is entered on the bank deposit slip, along with all other cash receipts for that day. When this is banked, the total amount of the deposit, including the credit card sales, is credited to the account of the merchant.

The commission is charged monthly by the card supplier in the form of a direct debit to the merchant's account.

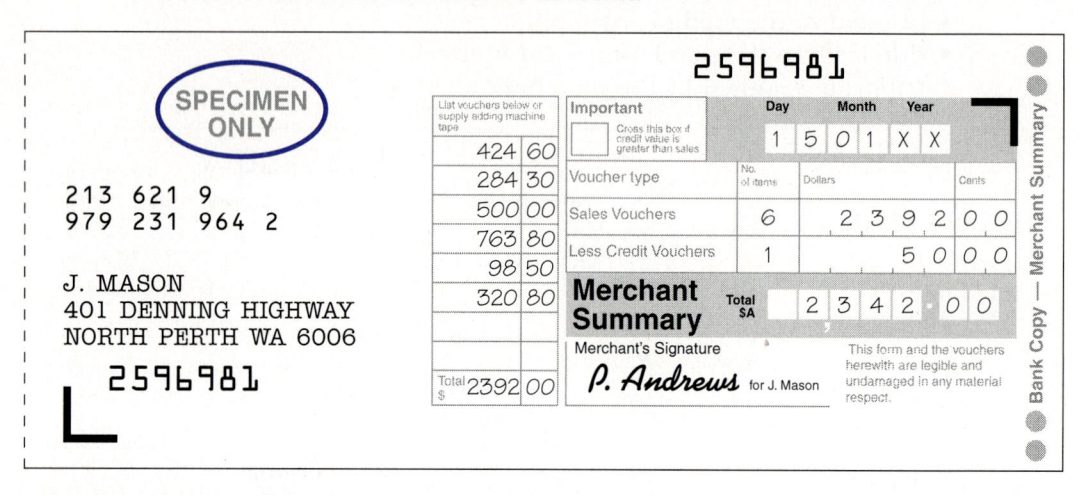

EXERCISE 2.7 *Revision*

What kind of transactions are supported by each of the following documents?
1. Cash sales docket
2. Purchases invoice
3. Credit note from supplier
4. Invoice sent to customer
5. Cheque butt
6. Credit note sent to customer
7. Duplicate receipt
8. Cash sales docket received from supplier

EXERCISE 2.8 *Westport Hardware Supplies*

What documents are used to record each of the following transactions of Westport Hardware Supplies (Proprietor, M. West)?
1. Goods ordered on credit from Handi Tools
2. Telephone account paid
3. Cash received from debtor, B. Aboud, to settle account
4. Goods delivered by Handi Tools to M. West
5. Goods sold on credit to A. Picone, builder

6. Handi Tools send account for goods to M. West
7. Goods purchased for cash from Crescent Timber
8. Faulty goods returned to Handi Tools and allowance received
9. Cash sales made via cash register
10. Cash withdrawn from business by M. West for personal use

EXERCISE 2.9 Central Auto Mart

Using copies of the relevant blank masters provided at the back of the book, complete appropriate documents to record details of transactions between Metal Industries, Ajax Tyres, Downey Engineering, G. B. Wheels and Central Auto Mart. Donald Singh, proprietor of Central Auto Mart (26 Longshore Road, Avonlea 4300), operates an account at the Avonlea branch of the Westpac Banking Corporation.

Date	Transaction	Doc. No.
19XX Apr. 1	Central Auto Mart ordered 10 gearboxes @ $145.00 each from Metal Industries, 27 Carveth Street, Avonlea 4300. Goods to be delivered to Factory Workshop No. 1 as soon as possible. Authorised by Bob Landers.	265
4	Central Auto Mart paid March account from Ajax Tyres (264 City Highway, Avonlea 4300) for $620.00 and received 3% cash discount for prompt payment.	728
7	Central Auto Mart sold (on credit) to Downey Engineering, 255 Thomas Street, Avonlea 4300 (Customer Order No. 126): • 4 sets Headlight Covers @ $23.50 ea. • 3 sets Lambswool Seat Covers @ $160.00 ea. • 6 sets Floor Mats (front) @ $38.00 ea. Trade discount 10% Sales tax applicable 15%	193
10	Metal Industries delivered gearboxes as per order. Donald Singh took delivery of and signed for these gearboxes.	63
13	G. B. Wheels (Prop. G. Archer, 82 High Street, Avonlea 4300) forwarded amount of $409.50 in payment of March account from Central Auto Mart. Early **settlement discount** of $10.50 had been deducted. G. B. Wheels also banks with the Westpac bank at Avonlea.	293
20	Metal Industries sent account for gearboxes, confirming price @ $145.00 ea. and allowing 10% trade discount and sales tax chargeable at 20%.	651
23	Central Auto Mart allowed claim from Downey Engineering for two sets of faulty headlight covers.	333

EXERCISE 2.10 — J. Mason

Using copies of the relevant blank masters provided at the back of the book, prepare the documents required to record the following transactions of J. Mason. Trade discount of 10% is allowed. Sales tax is chargeable at 15% and cash discount is $2\frac{1}{2}\%$ for seven days.

Note: You are required to prepare only those documents that originate with J. Mason.

Date	Transaction	Doc. No.
19XX Mar. 1	J. Mason ordered the following from P. Eastman, 29 Newman Road, Claremont, WA 6010: • 50 × 200 mm zippers @ $2.80 each • 150 m chain trim @ $1.65 m • 60 × 5 cm belt buckles @ $1.20. To be delivered to the factory before 6 March 19XX.	308
3	Sold the following goods on credit to Trendy Togs (Purchase order No. 362) of 128 Rutland Avenue, Carlisle 6101: • 25 silk T-shirts @ $29.25 each • 6 prs denim jeans @ $65.00 each • 4 denim shirts @ $45.00 each.	371
4	J. Mason settles February account of Fantasy Fabrics of 150 Bennet Street, Perth 6000, for $680.00, taking advantage of the $2\frac{1}{2}\%$ cash discount.	733
5	Cheque received from Trendy Togs in payment of February account — $460.00 less $2\frac{1}{2}\%$.	308
10	The following goods are sold on credit to La Mode Fashions, 92 Sherwood Road, West Perth 6005 (Customer Order No. 134): • 10 ladies' polyester dresses @ $40.00 • 5 ladies' blouses @ $25.00 • 6 pairs ladies' rayon slacks @ $23.00.	372
20	Paid *Courier News*, 180 Adelaide Terrace, Perth 6000, amount of $480.00 for advertising.	254
25	Made an allowance to Trendy Togs for returns — two silk T-shirts (flaw in material).	612
28	An allowance is made to La Mode Fashions for two pairs of ladies' rayon slacks (faulty zippers).	613
31	Statement forwarded to Trendy Togs. (Opening balance on 1 March 19XX is $460.00.)	

Bank deposit slip

All monies received by the business should be banked intact daily. This includes all cash and cheques together with credit card sales slips and the merchant summary. No money should be taken from the daily cash takings for any purpose whatsoever.

A bank deposit slip is used to record details of the daily deposit. If the deposit slip is not preprinted with the name of the account and account details, these should be written on the slip. The amount of cash, cheques and credit card summary items should be totalled separately, entered into the appropriate spaces on the deposit slip and added for the deposit total. Where there is no provision for the credit card total, include this amount with the cash total. The details of each cheque banked are also recorded on the deposit slip. Where space is provided for credit card entries, this should be used to record credit card details. Alternatively, credit card details may be itemised on the reverse side of the deposit slip, following the details of cheques (see example on page 80).

A bank deposit slip consists of two parts: the deposit form which is given to the bank with the money, and the tear-off stub which is receipted by the teller and returned to the depositor. A bank deposit slip records:
- account number
- account name
- date of deposit
- branch where account is held
- cheque details
- total value of cash, cheques and credit card receipts
- signature of depositor
- initials of bank teller, on both the form and the tear-off stub.

Example

According to company policy and procedures, all banking for J. Mason is done daily. The day's cash receipts, including all cheques received by mail and the cash takings from the cash register (including cash/cheques/credit card sales), are prepared for banking and a bank deposit slip is completed to accompany the deposit. The reverse of the slip is at the top of page 80. When large numbers of cheques are banked, a deposit slip such as that shown on page 452 would be used.

Westpac Banking Corporation ARBN 007 467 141		
Date	15 / 01 /19 XX	
Deposited for credit of	J. Mason	
Cash	$	7137 · 65
Cheques	$	1578 · 15
Total	$	8715 · 80
Teller		

Westpac Banking Corporation — DEPOSIT
Branch name: NORTH PERTH
For CREDIT of: J. Mason
Paid in by (Signature): P. Andrews
No. chq's: 3
⑊032⑊0001: 12⑊3456⑊
SPECIMEN ONLY

Date	15 / 01 /19XX
Cash	7137 · 65
Cheques See Reverse	1578 · 15
TOTAL $	8715 · 80

Bank Use Only Third party cheque explanation				Bank use only	
Details of cheques *(proceeds will not be available until cleared)*				100	
Drawer *(i.e. Account name on cheque)*	Bank	Branch	Amount	50	Details of Cheques
Maud's Boutique	ANZ	Nth Ryde	792.45	20	
Centre Fashions	Westpac	Alice Springs	383.50	10	
Tropical Trends	Cwlth	Katherine	402.20	5	
Bankcard	$ 770.80			Coin	
MasterCard	424.60			Cash Total	
Visa	1146.60				
TOTAL	$2342.00				
Note: This deposit will be transferred under the Bank's internal procedures. The Bank will not be held responsible for delays in transmission.			Total $ 1578.15		

SPECIMEN ONLY

EXERCISE 2.11 Bank deposit slips

You are required to prepare bank deposit slips for each of the following dates. (Use copies of the blank bank deposit slip (both sides) on page 549 or page 565.)

1. On 18 December 19XX, the following amounts are banked by J. Mason:
   - cheque for $258.00 from L. Morgan drawn on Perth branch of ANZ Bank
   - cheque for $177.20 from K. Matthews drawn on Geelong branch of National Bank
   - cheque for $400.00 from L. Woods drawn on the Claremont branch of Westpac Bank
   - cash amounting to $56.00 ($50.00 note and $6.00 in coin)
   - credit card sales vouchers totalling $180.60 (Bankcard $50.00, MasterCard $70.40, Visa $60.20).

2. On 20 December 19XX, the following amounts are banked by J. Mason:
   - cheque for $440.00 from H. Austin drawn on South Perth branch of Westpac Bank
   - cheque for $1800.00 from Compuco drawn on Albany branch of ANZ Bank
   - cheque for $77.00 from R. Yates drawn on Subiaco branch of Commonwealth Bank
   - cash amounting to $148.50 ($140.00 in notes and $8.50 in coin)
   - credit card sales vouchers totalling $128.40 (Bankcard $46.20, MasterCard $42.10, Visa $40.10).

3. On 24 December 19XX, the following amounts are banked by J. Mason:
   - cheque for $125.00 from T. Nguyen drawn on National Bank, Subiaco, WA
   - cheque for $520.70 from P. Georgiou drawn on Westpac Bank, South Vermont, Vic.
   - cheque for $728.40 from M. Alexander drawn on Commonwealth Bank, Ferndale, WA
   - cash amounting to $254.20 ($250.00 in notes, $4.20 in coin)
   - credit card sales vouchers totalling $521.90 (Bankcard $128.40, MasterCard $183.20, Visa $210.30).

VALIDITY OF SOURCE DOCUMENTS

Source documents are relevant to two main areas of accounting:
- accounts receivable — which are all dealings with debtors, those people to whom the business sells goods or services on credit, and who owe money to the business
- accounts payable — which are all dealings with creditors, those persons or firms from whom the business purchases goods or services on credit, and to whom the business owes money.

Regardless of whether financial source documents are incoming or outgoing, *all* documents should be verified. This involves identifying and correcting errors and/or omissions in any of the documentation. Source documents are an important part of the accounting system of a business (in that all transactions must be supported by some documentation) and the accuracy of the information contained in them is vital. Errors in incoming or outgoing documents have the potential to cost the business money and all efforts should be made to identify mistakes.

All incoming and outgoing source documents should be checked. Depending on whether you work in the accounts receivable or accounts payable section, you should check for the following.

- *Address.* Check that all outgoing invoices to customers (debtors) are correctly addressed and that all incoming invoices belong to the business and represent a valid charge for goods supplied.
- *Cross-reference.* As documents are generated they are cross-referenced to another document. For example, an invoice refers to a purchase order, and a credit note refers to an invoice. Cross-referencing of pre-numbered accountable documents creates an audit trail for checking both internally and externally. It is an important control system for the security of source documents and for the prevention of fraud.
- *Accuracy.* All documents should be checked for accuracy. If errors are located they should be corrected according to the organisation's policies and procedures. This may involve making the necessary correction, or circling the error and referring it to a supervisor who may authorise the correction. In some cases the error may be referred to the originator who would issue a corrected copy. It may also be your responsibility to collect and attach all documents relating to the transaction as part of the verification process.

The following rules apply for correcting errors on accountable documents.
1. Rule a line neatly through the incorrect figure/s.
2. Write the correct figure/s above in black or blue pen.
3. Initial any alterations for reference.
4. The use of erasers or liquid paper is not permitted. Do not overwrite numbers or use pencil or coloured pen.
5. All financial source documents should be checked for arithmetical accuracy. This includes extensions, percentages and totals.

EXERCISE 2.12 Checking financial source documents

In your position as Accounts Receivable Clerk for J. Mason, you are contacted on 5 January by Centre Fashions, 26 Todd Mall, Alice Springs, NT 0870, which requests an allowance for an overcharge for ladies' blouses on your Invoice No. 542. The file copy of this invoice appears below.

J. Mason
401 Denning Highway
NORTH PERTH WA 6006

Invoice No.: 542
Date: 2 January 19XX
Cust. Order No.: 67

Centre Fashions
26 Todd Mall
ALICE SPRINGS NT 0870

Invoice

QUANTITY	DESCRIPTION	UNIT PRICE	TOTAL
12 pr	Ladies' walk shorts	$29.95	$359.40
8 only	Ladies' blouses	32.95	263.60
			623.00
	Less 10% Discount		62.30
			560.70
	Plus 15% Sales Tax		84.11
			$644.81

Terms: $2\frac{1}{2}$% 7 days or net 30 days   No claims accepted after 7 days
E & O E

When checking this invoice, you see that the ladies' blouses should have been charged at $28.95.
(a) Explain how you would correct the invoice.
(b) Complete a credit note (use a copy of the blank master on page 543) to adjust the overcharge.

Note the errors on the invoice in accordance with company policies and procedures and refer it to the Accounts Manager.

Some organisations require that a claim form be completed for returns or claims. Some companies forward a copy to the person or firm making the claim; others fill in the details as supplied by the debtor by mail, telephone or fax. The claim form is attached to the relevant documentation for reference and provides a detailed record of the adjustment.

EXERCISE 2.13 *Checking invoices*

In your position as Accounts Receivable Clerk for J. Mason, you are required to check the following two invoices before they are mailed. You should check for the following:
- correct extensions (quantity × unit price)
- correct additions
- calculation of discount and sales tax.

Remember that trade discount is calculated and deducted *before* sales tax is calculated and added. Errors should be ruled through neatly and the correct amount inserted in pen above the entry. Initial the corrections or have your supervisor verify them.

J. Mason
401 Denning Highway
NORTH PERTH WA 6006

Invoice No.: 548
Date: 6 January 19XX
Cust. Order No.: 362

P. Contos
286 Burwood Road
SPRINGVALE VIC 3171

Invoice

QUANTITY	DESCRIPTION	UNIT PRICE	TOTAL
10 only	Ladies' silk shirts	$59.00	$531.00
5 pairs	Ladies' slacks	49.00	245.00
			776.00
	Less 10% Discount		77.60
			689.40
	Plus 15% Sales Tax		104.76
			$803.16

Terms: $2\frac{1}{2}$% 7 days or net 30 days   No claims accepted after 7 days
E & O E

J. Mason
401 Denning Highway
NORTH PERTH WA 6006

Invoice No.: 549

Date: 8 January 19XX

Cust. Order No.: 241

P. Nguyen
Snappy Fashions
122 Main Street
CLAREMONT WA 6010

Invoice

QUANTITY	DESCRIPTION	UNIT PRICE	TOTAL
15 only	Ladies' silk shirts	$59.00	$ 885.00
6 pairs	Ladies' slacks	49.00	294.00
10 only	Ladies' skirts	27.50	275.00
			1545.00
	Plus 15% Sales Tax		231.75
			1776.76
	Less 10% Trade Discount		177.68
			$1599.08

Terms: $2\frac{1}{2}$ % 7 days or net 30 days   No claims accepted after 7 days

E & O E

INTERNAL CONTROLS AND SECURITY

The measures that a firm employs to ensure security are known as **internal controls**. Internal controls encompass the organisation plan and all related measures the firm adopts to:
- safeguard the assets
- ensure accurate and reliable accounting records
- promote operational efficiency
- encourage adherence to the firm's organisational policies and procedures.

Internal controls consist of two parts: administrative controls and accounting controls.

Administrative controls

Administrative controls are those procedures used to ensure that the business operates efficiently and that organisational policies and procedures are followed. This includes the **audit** function. Auditors have the responsibility of checking the quality of the financial information prepared by the accounting system.

There are two types of auditors:
1. *external* — generally accountants from a separate firm who come into an organisation to check its financial records and report to shareholders
2. *internal* — people employed internally to check the quality and effectiveness of the accounting system that produces the information and then report to management.

Accounting controls

Accounting controls are those procedures that are implemented to ensure the accuracy and reliability of the accounting records and to protect the company's assets from loss or theft. They also provide checks against error and fraud.

For a system of internal control to be effective, it should have the following characteristics.
- *Competent and reliable personnel.* These should be people who are trained to do their job well and whose work is supervised. Job rotation will improve reliability as staff are less likely to commit fraud if another **employee** may uncover some wrongdoing.
- *Assignment of responsibility.* Personnel should be assigned a clearly defined set of duties and should bear responsibility for carrying them out.
- *Proper authorisation.* The policies and procedures should be firmly adhered to. There should be no deviation from these policies without proper authorisation. For example, you may be authorised to accept cheques of under $50 from customers providing they have identification, but for a cheque for $55 you must obtain the proper authorisation.
- *Separation of duties.* Responsibility for transactions should be divided between two or more people or departments. This separation of duties limits the opportunities for fraud and promotes accuracy of accounting records. This aspect of internal control may be further divided as follows.
  - Separate the accounting function of a business from the operating function of the business.
  - Separate accounting from custody of assets. The people involved in the accounting functions should not have access to or handle cash, nor should the cashier and cashier's staff have access to accounting records. If one person was responsible for both, the cash could be misappropriated and the books of account could be falsified.
  - Separate the authorisation of transactions from the custody of assets. People who authorise transactions should not handle cash. For example, the person who authorises payment of a supplier's invoice should not sign the cheque to pay the account. Such a person could authorise payment to himself or herself and then sign the cheque. By separating these duties, only legitimate payments are made.

At all times, this separation of duties should extend to all parts of the organisation so that those people who have access to record-keeping do not handle assets, such as cash or inventory.

Security of financial source documents

Pre-numbering of financial source documents provides security against fraudulent misuse. Each number must be accounted for and none may be destroyed. Should you make an error, do not destroy the document. Refer to your supervisor who will cancel the document and retain the original with the duplicate — in this way, every number is accounted for.

Signatures on source documents should only be those of personnel authorised to sign on behalf of the business. Access to unused pre-numbered documents should be restricted to authorised personnel.

Copies of financial source documents should be:
- maintained in an efficient filing system according to the information handling policies and procedures of the business
- delivered to the records handling (filing) department as soon as possible after generation
- recorded in a file register
- able to be accessed speedily and easily.

Statutory requirements state that these documents should be accessible for a period of seven years, during which time the Australian Taxation Office may call upon the documents for reference.

ACCOUNTABILITY OF SOURCE DOCUMENTS

To preserve the accountability of source documents, every pre-numbered document must be accounted for. There should be no gaps in the numbering sequence. Should a document be damaged, be incorrect or be unuseable for any reason, the word *cancelled*, enclosed in parallel lines, should be written across the original copy of the document, which is retained with the duplicate copies.

BATCHING OF SOURCE DOCUMENTS

As soon as possible the source documents which are generated to record transactions should be sorted into categories for processing. This is called **batching**. Documents of the same type are collected together or 'batched' at the end of a set period, which may be weekly or monthly depending on the volume of transactions, ready to be processed into the accounting system, either manually or electronically.

To allow for prompt entry or retrieval of accounting data from within the accounting system, most businesses use a system of classification and coding. Each account within the system is given a specific code which identifies the category to which it belongs. This code may be alphabetic, numeric or alpha-numeric (a combination of alphabetic and numeric). This coding forms the basis of the chart of accounts which is a listing of all accounts contained in the general ledger.

Each document within a **batch** is coded according to the chart of accounts before processing. This entails recording the account code on each document. Some firms use a rubber stamp imprint which relates the document to its batch control slip (see the example below).

Date	Batch No.	Account Code

A batch control slip is used to record information about a single batch of source documents. It lists the following:
- batch number
- batch type (as per chart of accounts)
- dates covered by documents
- number of documents
- total value of batch
- signature of preparer
- signature of checker.

An example of a typical batch control slip is shown below.

J. Mason Batch Control Slip	
Batch No.	123
Type	Sales Invoices
Date	From 7/01/XX To 11/01/XX
No. of documents	8
Batch total value	$4282.50
Signed	R. Jackson
Checked	J. Le Brun

When completed, the batch control slip is placed on top of the documents which it summarises. The information contained in the documents within the batch is transferred to the appropriate journal either manually or electronically. The journal totals are compared with the batch totals, allowing errors to be corrected at this point.

To batch the documents correctly for entry into the accounting system, the following steps should be followed:
- identify the document
- verify the information contained in it
- sort documents for batching and processing.

When sorted, source documents are coded according to the chart of accounts before batching and processing. An extract from a typical chart of accounts is shown below.

Chart of Accounts of J. Mason			
Revenue		Expense	
Code	Account	Code	Account
110	Sales	410	Purchases
115	Sales Returns	415	Purchases Returns
120	Discount Received	420	Discount Allowed
130	Interest Receivable	430	Advertising
		440	Electricity
		450	Interest Expense
		460	Office Supplies
		470	Rent
		480	Repairs and Maintenance
		490	Wages

In this chart of accounts, a cheque butt for an electricity account would be coded 440, while **sales invoices** would be coded 110.

The documents are then sorted into 'like' groups or 'batched' for entry into the firm's journals (the books of original entry; in other words, those books into which the source documents are first recorded). There are seven journals, as listed below.

Journal	Records
Purchases journal	Purchases of trading goods on credit
Purchases returns and allowances journal	Credit received from supplier for returns and allowances
Sales journal	Sales of trading goods on credit
Sales returns and allowances journal	Credit given to customers for returns and allowances
Cash receipts journal	All receipts of cash/cheques
Cash payments journal	All payments of cash (by cheque)
General journal	All other transactions not included in above journals

The way in which the batched information is processed will depend on the policies and procedures of the business, but the main areas of responsibility are:
- accounts receivable
- accounts payable.

Accounts receivable

This department is responsible for all trade debtors' activity. Trade debtors are the people or businesses who owe money to the company as a result of the sale of goods or services on credit.

The accounts receivable department receives all source documentation relating to money owed by trade debtors to the firm. This includes duplicate copies of:
- invoices sent to trade debtors
- credit notes sent to trade debtors
- statements of account sent to trade debtors
- remittance advices received from trade debtors (original)
- receipts sent to trade debtors.

The accounts receivable department processes the source documents and makes journal entries as listed below.

Source document	Journal
Invoice: Used to record credit sales. Duplicate copy retained after forwarding original with goods to customer.	Sales journal
Credit Note: Used to record credit sales returns. Duplicate copy retained after sending original to debtor (customer) to adjust for damaged goods, overcharges, refunds on containers etc. Usually printed in red.	Sales returns and allowances journal
Receipt: Used to record money (cash/cheques) received. Duplicate copy retained in receipt book after original has been forwarded to acknowledge receipt of payment by debtor.	Cash receipts journal
Cash register roll: Records cash received via cash register. Records day's cash trading.	Cash receipts journal

Accounts payable

This department is responsible for all trade creditors' activity. Trade creditors are those persons or firms to whom the business owes money as a result of the purchase of goods or services from outside firms on credit.

The accounts payable department receives all source documentation relating to money owed by the firm to trade creditors. This includes original copies of:
- purchase orders sent to trade creditors (duplicate copies)
- invoices received from trade creditors

- credit notes received from trade creditors
- delivery dockets received from trade creditors
- statements of account received from trade creditors
- cheque butts from cheques remitted to trade creditors
- remittance advices sent to trade creditors (duplicate copies)
- receipts received from trade creditors.

The accounts payable department processes the source documents and makes journal entries as listed below.

Source document	Journal
Invoice: This is used to record credit purchases. The original copy is received from the supplier.	Purchases journal
Credit Note: This is used to record credit purchases returns and allowances. The original copy is received from the supplier, usually printed in red.	Purchases returns and allowances journal
Cheque butt: This is used to record cash (cheque) payments. All payments made from the business are by cheque.	Cash payments journal

In both departments, the batched information would be processed, either manually or electronically, into the accounting records of the business. A computerised accounting system relies totally on the relation of account numbers to account names as the chart of accounts is the foundation for the ledger file which links all data entered into the system to the correct account number.

EXERCISE 2.14 *Batching documents*

You are required to batch the following documents correctly for entry into the accounting system, as follows.

1. Identify the documents.
2. Verify the information contained in them.
3. Mark each document with 'batch' stamp. (You may need to draw this.)
4. Sort documents for processing.
5. Using a copy of the blank master provided on page 541, complete a batch control slip (Batch No. 138) using the account code from the chart of accounts on page 88.

J. Mason
401 Denning Highway
NORTH PERTH WA 6006

Invoice No.: 532

Date: 14 January 19XX

Cust. Order No.: 321

Top End Fashions
41 Smith Street Mall
DARWIN NT 0801

Date	Batch No.	Account Code

Invoice

QUANTITY	DESCRIPTION	UNIT PRICE	TOTAL
25	Ladies' blouses	$25.00	$ 625.00
12	Ladies' suits	75.00	900.50
			1525.00
	Less 10% Trade Discount		152.50
			1372.50
	Plus 15% Sales Tax		205.88
			$1578.38

Terms: $2\frac{1}{2}$% 7 days or net 30 days   No claims accepted after 7 days

E & O E

J. Mason
401 Denning Highway
NORTH PERTH WA 6006

Invoice No.: 533

Date: 15 January 19XX

Cust. Order No.: 273

Centre Fashions
26 Todd Mall
ALICE SPRINGS NT 0870

Date	Batch No.	Account Code

Invoice

QUANTITY	DESCRIPTION	UNIT PRICE	TOTAL
10 each	Ladies' dresses	$55.00	$ 550.00
25 each	Ladies' skirts	27.50	687.50
10 pairs	Ladies' slacks	23.00	230.00
			1467.50
	Less 10% Trade Discount		146.75
			1320.75
	Plus 15% Sales Tax		198.11
			$1518.86

Terms: $2\frac{1}{2}$% 7 days or net 30 days   No claims accepted after 7 days

E & O E

J. Mason
401 Denning Highway
NORTH PERTH WA 6006

Invoice No.: *534*

Date: *15 January 19XX*

Cust. Order No.: *864*

Invoice

Tropical Trends
180 Katherine Terrace
KATHERINE NT 0850

Date	Batch No.	Account Code

QUANTITY	DESCRIPTION	UNIT PRICE	TOTAL
10 prs	Ladies' walk shorts	$22.50	$ 225.00
15 each	Ladies' silk T-shirts	38.00	570.00
15 each	Ladies' dresses	55.00	825.00
			1620.00
	Less 10% Trade Discount		162.00
			1458.00
	Plus 15% Sales Tax		218.70
			$1676.70

Terms: $2\frac{1}{2}$ % 7 days or net 30 days   No claims accepted after 7 days

E & O E

EXERCISE 2.15 Batching documents

You are required to batch the following documents correctly for entry into the accounting system as follows.
1. Identify the documents.
2. Verify the information contained in them.
3. Mark each document with 'batch' stamp. (You may need to draw this.)
4. Sort documents for processing.
5. Note the date, batch number and account code on each document using the account code from the chart of accounts on page 88.
6. Using a copy of the blank master provided on page 541, complete a batch control slip (Batch No. 139).

Cheque No. 320
Date: *18 January 19XX*

To: CITY REAL ESTATE
For: *Rent*

This cheque: $675.00

Cheque No. 321
Date: *18 January 19XX*

To: WESTERN
       ADVERTISER
For: *Advertising*

This cheque: $86.00

Cheque No. 322
Date: *19 January 19XX*

To: CASH
For: *Wages*

This cheque: $850.00

Cheque No. 323 Date: *19 January 19XX* To: *FAR WEST ELECTRICS* For: *Electricity* This cheque: $200.00	Cheque No. 324 Date: *20 January 19XX* To: *PAPER PRODUCTS* For: *Office Supplies* This cheque: $68.00	Cheque No. 325 Date: *20 January 19XX* To: *F. GELETTO* For: *Repairs and Maintenance* This cheque: $142.00

ELECTRONIC REPORTING SYSTEMS

Computer technology has been of great benefit to the accounting profession. The time has passed when only the largest organisations could afford computerised accounting systems. Today even a small business can afford to keep computerised records, and all accounting staff must be familiar with computer-operated systems.

A computerised accounting system has many advantages over a manual system. The main advantages are outlined below.

Speed

The computer can perform tasks almost instantaneously which, if done manually, would prove extremely time-consuming.

Output

Because of its processing speed, a computer can handle a much larger volume of transactions easily.

Posting

Posting is performed automatically in a computerised system. Manual posting is slow and prone to error. Computerised posting is fast and protects against errors such as:
- double posting
- posting to the wrong account
- posting a debit as a credit and vice versa
- posting the wrong amount.

Error protection

Errors are reduced as a computerised system has error protection features. For example, when entering transactions, the computer gives an error message when entries do not balance. Computers can also perform complex calculations more accurately. However, the accuracy of a computerised system is only ever as accurate as the data entered.

Reports

These are generated automatically in a computerised system. Information which is processed laboriously in a manual system, such as for journals, ledgers, and financial and special reports, is created automatically. The speed with which this information is provided to management to assist with economic planning and decision-making is vital. As with all information, the longer it takes to access, the less useful it becomes.

Printing source documents

The computer can automatically generate many documents used in a business, such as invoices and monthly statements. Errors in mathematical calculations are eliminated.

Automatic adjustments

To perform the accounting function, a specially designed software program must be installed on the computer. This is a set of instructions to tell the computer what to do. Although the accounting procedures remain basically the same whether carried out on a computer or performed manually, there are many savings in time and labour with the use of computers. Set out below is a comparison of the accounting cycle for both manual and computerised systems.

Accounting cycle

Manual system	Computerised system
Transactions are analysed and entered into appropriate journals in date order.	Transactions are analysed and entered into the computer. Journals are prepared automatically. Printouts may be obtained if desired.
Journals are posted to ledger accounts.	Journals are posted to ledger automatically.
The accounts are totalled at the end of the period and the unadjusted trial balance is prepared.	Accounts are totalled at end of period and the unadjusted trial balance is automatically prepared.
Adjusting entries are journalised and posted. Adjusted accounts are totalled.	End-of-period adjusting entries are prepared and entered into the computer. Adjusting and closing entries are automatically prepared and posted by the computer.
Closing entries are journalised and posted. Accounts are totalled and balanced. Post-closing trial balance is prepared.	Post-closing trial balance is automatically prepared.
Financial reports are prepared.	Financial reports are automatically generated.
Reversal entries are journalised and posted for accrual adjustments.	Year-closing procedures automatically adjust for new accounting period.

The table on page 94 represents a simple comparison of a manual and a computerised accounting system. To enter data into a computer, an accounting software program must be loaded and accessed. Data entry is usually via an appropriate menu of selected accounting software.

In a manual accounting system, the procedures from the preparation of the unadjusted trial balance to the preparation of financial reports are carried out on a worksheet before any entries are made to the accounting records. This helps to minimise errors and is useful for preparing interim reports which may be required during the reporting period. All the financial information is gathered together on the worksheet and this helps in the preparation of the financial reports at the end of the reporting period. Once the worksheet is 'balanced', it is a simple procedure to finalise the accounting records and produce the financial reports.

Computers, however, have been able to free accountants from most of the 'number-crunching' activities involved in accounting and allow valuable time for analysis and interpretation of data. Accounting information forms the basis of financial reports and aids management in making decisions and allocating resources, as well as providing useful information for external users of the firm's financial reports, such as shareholders.

CHAPTER 3

Preparation of journals

WHEN you have studied this chapter and completed the exercises, you should be competent in the following skills. Tick each skill when you have completed the relevant section.

LEARNING OUTCOMES

1. Prepare general journal opening entry.
2. Prepare accounts payable journal entries.
   - Correctly enter details of purchase invoices into a columnar purchases journal.
   - Correctly enter details of credit notes into a columnar purchases returns and allowances journal.
   - Correctly enter details of payment vouchers/cheques into a columnar cash payments journal.
3. Prepare accounts receivable journal entries.
   - Correctly enter details of credit sales invoices into a columnar sales journal.
   - Correctly enter details of sales credit notes into a columnar sales returns and allowances journal.
   - Correctly enter details of receipts and cash sales into a columnar cash receipts journal.
4. Prepare general journal miscellaneous entries.
   - Purchase of non-current asset on credit
   - Sale of non-current asset on credit
   - Inventory withdrawals by owner
   - Interest expense (paid to creditors)
   - Interest revenue (received from debtors)
   - Bad debts written off
   - Transfers between accounts (contra)
   - Correction of posting errors

WHAT ARE JOURNALS?

A journal is a book of original entry used to record details of transactions from source documents. The source documents are sorted and batched into like groups. Details of transactions from each of these groups are summarised and recorded in chronological order, showing the names of the parties involved, together with the date and nature of the transaction and the amount involved.

There are seven journals in all (six of which are trading journals). These are used to record details, from source documents, of transactions arising from the purchase and sale of trading stock on credit. Into the trading journals are entered the details of transactions with trade creditors and trade debtors, known in accounting terms as accounts payable and accounts receivable respectively. These trading journals are summarised in the table below.

Journal	Purpose
Accounts payable	
Purchases journal	Records all credit purchases from creditors
Purchases returns and allowances journal	Records details of returns and allowances received from creditors
Cash payments journal	Records all cash (cheque) payments. All payments made from the business are by cheque.
Accounts receivable	
Sales journal	Records all credit sales to trade debtors
Sales returns and allowances journal	Records all returns and allowances made to debtors
Cash receipts journal	Records all money (cash/cheques) received

There are, however, transactions which are not supported by source documents and which, because of their nature, cannot be recorded in either the trading journals or the cash journals. These entries are entered in the general journal.

The text that follows discusses how a business sets up its books — its general journal, its accounts payable journals and its accounts receivable journals.

General journal

The general journal is used to record all transactions which cannot be entered in either the trading journals or the cash journals. Examples of entries recorded in the general journal are:
- the opening entry, which lists assets, liabilities and capital of the business when it is first opened
- purchase and sale of **non-current assets** on credit
- recording interest expense (interest charged by creditors for overdue accounts)
- recording interest revenue (interest charged to debtors for overdue accounts)
- **bad debts** that have been 'written off'
- correction of errors
- inventory drawings (by proprietor for personal use)
- transfers between accounts (a **contra entry**), made when a business conducts both credit purchases and credit sales with the same firm.

General journal entries are not supported by source documents, but each transaction is accompanied by an explanation (hereafter called a narration) of the details of the transaction. General journal entries require written authorisation from the Financial Controller (or other approved person) of a business. This may be in the form of a memorandum. It may also be a special journal voucher used for this purpose, and to which reference may be made in the narration.

The general journal differs from other journals in the following ways.
- All entries must be accompanied by a narration; that is, a short explanation written below the entry to explain the nature of the transaction. Where possible, reference to source documents should form part of the narration. This narration is necessary because this is a general purpose journal with no common nature of recorded transactions.
- In every general journal entry, the account to be debited is entered first and is written close to the date line and the account to be credited is entered on the following line and is indented approximately one centimetre.

The opening entry records details of assets and liabilities introduced to the business by the owner. It is made *once only* in the life of a business and records:

(a) values of cash and assets (equipment, inventory etc.) when a new business is commenced

(b) values of cash, assets, debtors and creditors, when a proprietor with an existing business decides to convert to a double-entry bookkeeping system

(c) values of cash, assets, debtors and creditors, when a proprietor acquires an existing business and wishes to open a new set of books.

General journals can be set out in different ways.
- The basic format is set out on journal paper with a debit and a credit column at the right-hand side of the page (see below).

Date	Particulars	Folio	Debit	Credit

- The columnar (tabular) format is set out on specially ruled paper and, when working with subsidiary ledgers, it provides a simple method for posting totals for trade creditors and trade debtors to the Accounts Payable and Accounts Receivable Control accounts in the general ledger by providing a 'debit' *and* a 'credit' column for *both* trade debtors (accounts receivable) and trade creditors (accounts payable). This is the format used in this chapter (see below).

DEBIT / CREDIT

Accounts receivable	Accounts payable	General	Date	Particulars	Fol.	Accounts receivable	Accounts payable	General

The opening entry for a business may be as simple as recording the amount of capital the owner has invested in a new business.

Example

J. Mason invests $30 000 to commence a new business. This is illustrated as follows.

	Assets	=	Liabilities	+	Owner's Equity
Cash at Bank	$30 000	= Capital			$30 000

If we analyse this transaction, we can see that two accounts are affected — there is an increase in the asset account, Cash at Bank, and an increase in the owner's equity account, Capital. Therefore, we must:

Debit — Cash at Bank account $30 000
Credit — Capital account $30 000

However, in addition to cash, an owner may introduce other assets and liabilities, or the owner of an existing business may wish to convert to a double-entry system of bookkeeping.

Example

J. Mason commences business on 1 January 19XX with the following assets, liabilities and capital:

Cash at bank		$ 5 000.00
Land		20 000.00
Buildings		40 000.00
Plant and machinery		12 000.00
Office equipment		10 000.00
Office furniture		1 000.00
Inventory		1 500.00
Accounts Receivable:		1 118.00
M. Adams	$250.00	
J. Abbott	500.00	
R. Glacken	115.00	
H. Raja	253.00	
Accounts Payable:		1 210.00
H. Lime	300.00	
P. Eastman	200.00	
M. Garcia	510.00	
B. Allar	200.00	
Mortgage		10 000.00
Capital		79 408.00

If you have not been given the amount of capital (the amount of money that the business owes to the owner/s), this must be calculated before the opening entry can be finalised. The value of capital is calculated by deducting the total of external liabilities of the business from the total assets. Remember, the capital (or owner's equity, or proprietorship) is the amount that the business owes to the proprietor/s (owner/s) and is the internal liability of the business. Hence, the accounting equation is expressed thus:

Capital = Assets − Liabilities

$79 408 = $90 618 − $11 210.

This opening entry is illustrated as follows.

Assets	=		Liabilities	+	Owner's Equity
Cash at Bank	$ 5 000	Accounts Payable	$ 1 210		
Land	20 000	Mortgage	10 000		
Buildings	40 000	Capital			$79 408
Plant and Machinery	12 000				
Office Equipment	10 000				
Office Furniture	1 000				
Inventory	1 500				
Accounts Receivable	1 118		$11 210	+	$79 408
	$90 618	=			$90 618

Assets ($90 618) = Liabilities ($11 210) + Capital ($79 408)
Total debits ($90 618) = Total credits ($90 618).

How to record the opening entry

1. List all assets first (things owned by the business), listing names of trade debtors (persons who owe money to the business) immediately below. Sundry debtors are listed separately from Accounts Receivable (trade debtors). The business has received these assets from the owner. Asset accounts have debit balances.
2. Liabilities (what the business owes) are listed next, and indented approximately one centimetre to the right. The names of the trade creditors (persons to whom the business owes money) are listed first then followed by any other external liabilities. Sundry creditors are listed separately from Accounts Payable (trade creditors). Liability accounts have credit balances.
3. Record the amount of capital on the next line. If not supplied, calculate by subtracting the total external liabilities from the total assets. The business owes this amount to the owner. The owner is a creditor. The owner's Capital account has a credit balance.
4. Write a narration (a brief description of the transaction) on the next line and total the columns. Total debits must equal total credits. This proves the arithmetical accuracy of your recording.

Example 1 — basic format

Below is the opening entry for J. Mason set out in the basic (or traditional) format.

GENERAL JOURNAL OF J. MASON

Fol. GJI

Date	Particulars	Fol.	Debit	Credit
19XX Jan 1	Land		20 000.00	
	Buildings		40 000.00	
	Plant and Machinery		12 000.00	
	Office Equipment		10 000.00	
	Office Furniture		1 000.00	
	Cash at Bank		5 000.00	
	Inventory		1 500.00	
	Accounts Receivable		1 118.00	
	M. Adams 250.00			
	J. Abbott 500.00			
	R. Glacken 115.00			
	H. Raja 253.00			
	Accounts Payable			1 210.00
	H. Lime 300.00			
	P. Eastman 200.00			
	M. Garcia 510.00			
	B. Allar 200.00			
	Mortgage			10 000.00
	Capital			79 408.00
	Assets, liabilities and capital at this date		90 618.00	90 618.00

Example 2 — columnar (or tabular) format

As you will be working with subsidiary ledgers, this is the format you will use in this text for all exercises which involve transactions with Accounts Receivable (trade debtors) and Accounts Payable (trade creditors). Below is the opening entry for J. Mason. Study the format carefully, then complete the exercises which follow.

GENERAL JOURNAL OF J. MASON

DEBIT | | | | | | | | CREDIT | | Fol. GJI

Accounts receivable	Accounts payable	General	Date	Particulars	Fol.	Accounts receivable	Accounts payable	General
			19XX Jan. 1	Land				
		20 000.00		Buildings				
		40 000.00		Plant and Machinery				
		12 000.00		Office Equipment				
		10 000.00		Office Furniture				
		1 000.00		Cash at Bank				
		5 000.00		Inventory				
		1 500.00		M. Adams				
250.00				J. Abbott				
500.00				R. Glacken				
115.00				H. Raja				
253.00				H. Lime			300.00	
				P. Eastman			200.00	
				M. Garcia			510.00	
				B. Allar			200.00	
				Mortgage				10 000.00
				Capital				79 408.00
				Being assets, liabilities and capital as at this date.				
1 118.00		89 500.00					1 210.00	89 408.00

If we examine the above entry, it can be seen that:

Capital (or owner's equity) = Assets − (external) Liabilities
$79 408 = $90 618 − $11 210
Total debits ($90 618) = Total credits ($90 618).

EXERCISE
3.1 K. Dominic & Sons

K. Dominic commenced business on 1 May 19XX, trading as K. Dominic & Sons, with the following assets and liabilities:

Cash at bank $18 000; Land $250 000; Buildings $80 000; Motor vehicles $35 000; Office equipment $2550; Office furniture $1890; Inventory $9890; *Accounts Receivable:* J. Wade $240, M. Byrnes $580, G. Mundo $420; *Accounts Payable:* W. Maine $680; Conway & Sons $420; B. Samuels $78; Mortgage $150 000.

1. Calculate the amount of capital (OE = A − L).
2. Following the format on page 102, record the opening entry for K. Dominic & Sons in the general journal. Use a copy of the blank general journal master provided on page 550.)

   Check: Have you applied the accounting equation correctly to ensure that your 'Capital' figure is correct? Is the total of your debit entries equal to the total of your credit entries?

EXERCISE 3.2 B. James & Co.

B. James commenced business on 1 April 19XX, trading as B. James & Co., with the following assets and liabilities:

Cash at bank $12 440; Plant and machinery $18 900; Motor vehicles $15 500; Office equipment $4890; Office furniture $2680; Inventory $5660; *Accounts Receivable:* A. Collins $172; Corella Private Hospital $289; E. & J. White $320; G. McGregor $402; *Accounts Payable:* King & Co. $426; Greenway & Co. $215; F Nguyen $75.

1. Calculate the amount of capital (OE = A − L).
2. Following the format on page 102, record the opening entry for B. James & Co. in the general journal. (Use a copy of the blank general journal master provided on page 550.)

EXERCISE 3.3 Trend Fashions

L. Morrison commenced business on 1 February 19XX, trading as Trend Fashions, with the following assets and liabilities:

Cash at bank $11 765; Land $240 000; Buildings $60 000; Motor vehicles $24 500; Office equipment $6110; Office furniture $2400; Inventory $5295; *Accounts Receivable:* The Dress Shop $320; Jane's Fashion Store $265; H. Taylor & Co. $532; Petrovich & Co. $302; *Accounts Payable:* W. A. Montey $440; G. Hanna $385; W. Laporte $229; J. S. Baxter $88; Mortgage $120 000.

1. Calculate the amount of capital (OE = A − L).
2. Following the format on page 102, record the opening entry for Trend Fashions in the general journal. (Use a copy of the blank general journal master provided on page 550.)

ACCOUNTS PAYABLE JOURNALS

As a means of increasing sales and ultimately net profit, businesses regularly extend credit to persons or firms who purchase their goods or services. As well as extending credit, most business entities expect to receive credit from their own suppliers for goods or services.

The term *accounts payable* refers to those persons or firms from whom the business purchases trading goods on credit. As the business owes money to these suppliers, accounts payable are a liability of the business.

The accounts payable department of a business is responsible for all transactions involving trade creditors; that is, those persons or firms to whom the business owes money as a result of the purchase of trading goods (or services) on credit.

Accounts payable refers only to those goods which are purchased for resale at a profit at a later date; that is, the trading stock (or inventory). Details of transactions with trade creditors are recorded as accounts payable.

A business may also purchase non-current assets on credit. Non-current assets refer to assets which the business owns or controls and which are not intended for resale until their usefulness to the business has been exhausted. Examples of these are plant and machinery, motor vehicles, office equipment and furniture and fittings.

When a non-current asset is purchased on credit, the business acquires a sundry (or non-trade) creditor.

- Details of transactions with sundry creditors are recorded separately in the general journal only and posted to the general ledger, where a separate account is maintained for each sundry creditor.
- Details of transactions with accounts payable (trade creditors) are recorded in the general journal and the accounts payable journals; that is, purchases, purchases returns and allowances and cash payments. Individual details of these journals are posted to the accounts payable ledger which is represented 'in total' in the general ledger by the Accounts Payable Control account.

Set out below is a representation of the document flow for transactions with trade creditors.

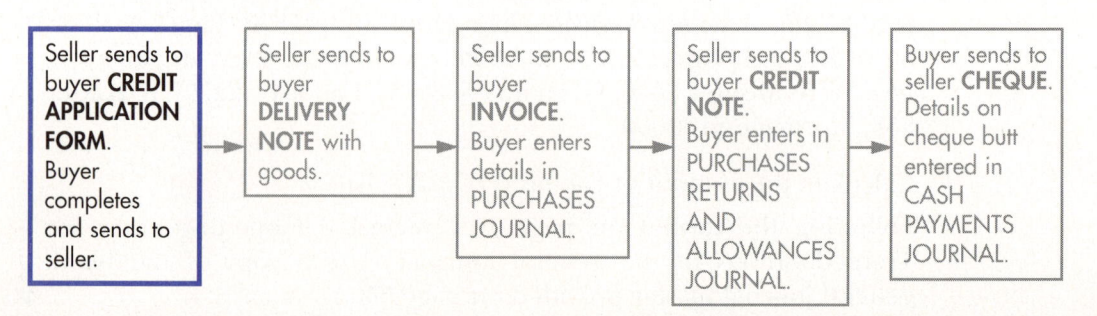

| Seller sends to buyer **CREDIT APPLICATION FORM**. Buyer completes and sends to seller. | Seller sends to buyer **DELIVERY NOTE** with goods. | Seller sends to buyer **INVOICE**. Buyer enters details in PURCHASES JOURNAL. | Seller sends to buyer **CREDIT NOTE**. Buyer enters in PURCHASES RETURNS AND ALLOWANCES JOURNAL. | Buyer sends to seller **CHEQUE**. Details on cheque butt entered in CASH PAYMENTS JOURNAL. |

Credit application

Suppliers do not wish to extend credit to businesses who may not pay their accounts, so before any goods can be purchased, prospective credit customers are requested to furnish details of their credit history to confirm their ability to repay debts. When requested by the seller, the buyer completes a credit application form providing details of persons or firms who will act as credit referees.

Guidelines, similar to the following, may form part of a firm's policies and procedures for using credit from suppliers.
1. Prompt payment of suppliers' accounts is important as credit terms with suppliers are a valuable asset.
2. Take advantage of discount received for prompt payment to ensure that savings are made.

Example

In response to J. Mason's request for credit terms up to $5000, H. Lime forwarded the following credit application form for completion:

CREDIT APPLICATION FORM

H. LIME
48 Argyle Road
MIDLAND WA 6056
Tel: (08) 9663 9471
Fax: (08) 9663 9472

NAME: J. MASON

ADDRESS: 401 Denning Highway, NORTH PERTH

STATE: WA   POSTCODE: 6006

MONTHLY CREDIT REQUIRED: $5000

Credit referees:

Company Name J. Denning & Co.	Company Name P. Eastman & Co.	Company Name N. Lilly
Contact *John Denning*	Contact *Paul Eastman*	Contact *Alan Ullolo*
Telephone No. (08) 9468 4555 Fax No. (08) 9468 4505	Telephone No. (08) 9244 8996 Fax No. (08) 9244 8999	Telephone No. (08) 9331 3468 Fax No. (08) 9331 3472

DECLARATION:

We the undersigned accept responsibility for any debts incurred by this firm jointly or severally:

Signed: .... Signed: ....

Position: .... Position: ....

EXERCISE 3.4 K. Dominic & Sons

Complete credit application forms (using copies of the blank credit application master provided on page 551) for:

K. Dominic & Sons, 24 West Street, Petersham, NSW, 2049
Telephone: (02) 9754 3200, Fax: (02) 9754 3220

who wishes to apply for credit from the following suppliers:

- W. Maine & Co. — $5000 credit per month
  181 Railway Street
  Carlton NSW 2218
  Tel: (02) 9652 8890
  Fax: (02) 9652 8894

- Conway & Sons — $2000 credit per month
  23 Morrison Parade
  Burwood NSW 2134
  Tel: (02) 9651 2378
  Fax: (02) 9651 2380

- D. J. Callaghan — $2000 credit per month
  201 Lancaster Street
  Auburn NSW 2144
  Tel: (02) 9642 1178
  Fax: (02) 9642 1190

Credit referees for K. Dominic & Sons are:
- Kenton Trading Co., Contact: B. J. Kenton, Telephone (02) 9448 7001, Fax: (02) 448 7003
- J. Gilchrist Pty Ltd, Contact: James Geddes, Telephone (02) 9451 6782, Fax: (02) 451 6788
- N. Cameron & Sons, Contact: Ian Jarvie, Telephone (02) 9651 9023, Fax: (02) 651 9044.

Entering details from source documents into journals

Each day the source documents are sorted into batches and entered into their respective journals:

- *Batch 1* — Invoices are entered into the purchases journal.
- *Batch 2* — Credit notes are entered into the purchases returns and allowances journal.
- *Batch 3* — Cheque butts are entered into the cash payments journal.

All journals are totalled at the end of the month.

Purchases journal

The purchases journal is used to record all purchases of trading goods (inventory) on credit; that is, those goods purchased on credit from the firm's trade creditors (*accounts payable*). Transactions are recorded in chronological order.

Format

PURCHASES JOURNAL OF   Fol. PJX

Date	Inv. No.	Particulars (Creditors' account to be credited)	Fol.	Amount	Monthly total

Source document

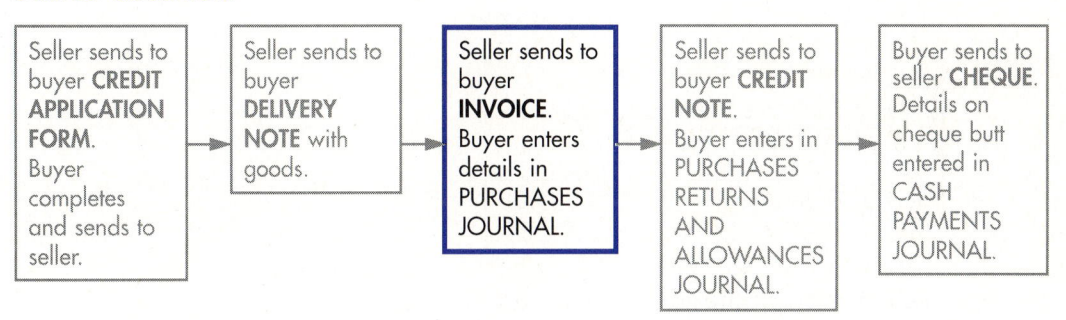

| Seller sends to buyer **CREDIT APPLICATION FORM**. Buyer completes and sends to seller. | → | Seller sends to buyer **DELIVERY NOTE** with goods. | → | **Seller sends to buyer INVOICE. Buyer enters details in PURCHASES JOURNAL.** | → | Seller sends to buyer **CREDIT NOTE**. Buyer enters in PURCHASES RETURNS AND ALLOWANCES JOURNAL. | → | Buyer sends to seller **CHEQUE**. Details on cheque butt entered in CASH PAYMENTS JOURNAL. |

The source document from which the information for the purchases journal is obtained is the original of the purchase invoice received from the supplier.

Example

J. Mason received the following original invoices from his suppliers (trade creditors).

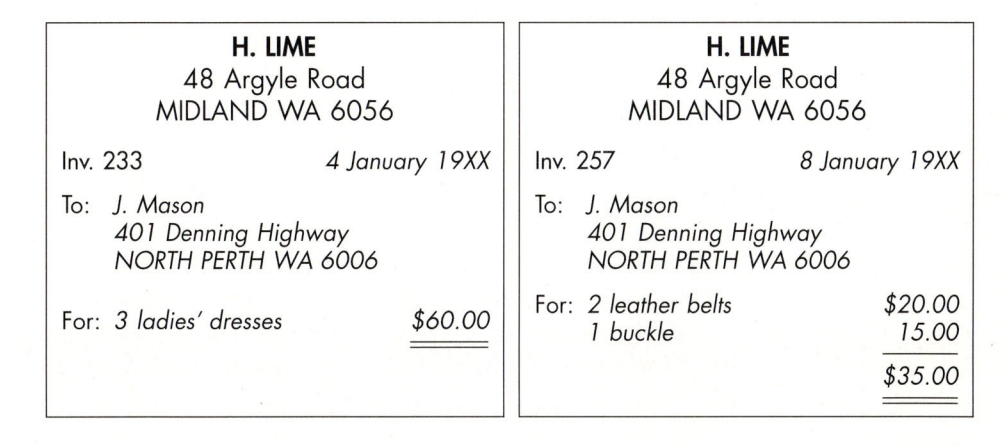

```
           H. LIME
        48 Argyle Road
       MIDLAND WA 6056

Inv. 233              4 January 19XX

To:   J. Mason
      401 Denning Highway
      NORTH PERTH WA 6006

For:  3 ladies' dresses        $60.00
                               ======
```

```
           H. LIME
        48 Argyle Road
       MIDLAND WA 6056

Inv. 257              8 January 19XX

To:   J. Mason
      401 Denning Highway
      NORTH PERTH WA 6006

For:  2 leather belts          $20.00
      1 buckle                  15.00
                               $35.00
                               ======
```

```
┌─────────────────────────────────┐  ┌─────────────────────────────────┐
│          P. EASTMAN             │  │          P. EASTMAN             │
│        29 Newman Road           │  │        29 Newman Road           │
│       CLAREMONT WA 6010         │  │       CLAREMONT WA 6010         │
│                                 │  │                                 │
│  Inv. 612      12 January 19XX  │  │  Inv. 622      15 January 19XX  │
│                                 │  │                                 │
│  To:  J. Mason                  │  │  To:  J. Mason                  │
│       401 Denning Highway       │  │       401 Denning Highway       │
│       NORTH PERTH WA 6006       │  │       NORTH PERTH WA 6006       │
│                                 │  │                                 │
│  For: 6 prs slacks      $68.00  │  │  For: 2 denim skirts    $28.00  │
└─────────────────────────────────┘  └─────────────────────────────────┘

┌─────────────────────────────────┐
│           N. LILLY              │
│        53 Conroy Street         │
│       FREMANTLE WA 6160         │
│                                 │
│  Inv. 479      24 January 19XX  │
│                                 │
│  To:  J. Mason                  │
│       401 Denning Highway       │
│       NORTH PERTH WA 6006       │
│                                 │
│  For: 3 silk blouses    $45.00  │
└─────────────────────────────────┘
```

Entering transactions in the purchases journal

Information from the invoices on page 107 and above is entered in the purchases journal as shown below:

PURCHASES JOURNAL OF J. MASON   Fol. PJX

Date	Inv. No.	Particulars (Creditor's account to be credited)	Fol.	Amount	Monthly total
19XX					
Jan. 3	233	H. Lime		60.00	
8	257	H. Lime		35.00	
12	612	P. Eastman		68.00	
15	622	P. Eastman		28.00	
24	479	N. Lilly		45.00	
31					236.00

It should be noted that exercises for K. Dominic & Sons, B. James & Co. and Trend Fashions continue through entry in all journals, posting to all ledgers and trial balance. Students should keep their completed exercises for these three companies as they will be used throughout this book.

EXERCISE 3.5 K. Dominic & Sons

You are employed as bookkeeper for K. Dominic & Sons. The following invoices have been received for trading goods purchased during the month of May 19XX. You are required to enter the transactions in the purchases journal. (Use a copy of the blank purchases journal master provided on page 552.)

W. MAINE & CO.
181 Railway Street
CARLTON NSW 2218

Inv. 237   5 May 19XX

To: K. Dominic & Sons
      24 West Street
      PETERSHAM NSW 2049

25 men's woollen jumpers $500.00

CONWAY & SONS
23 Morrison Parade
BURWOOD NSW 2134

Inv. 125   8 May 19XX

To: K. Dominic & Sons
      24 West Street
      PETERSHAM NSW 2049

10 prs boys' jeans $140.00

D. J. CALLAGHAN
201 Lancaster Street
AUBURN NSW 2144

Inv. 98   15 May 19XX

To: K. Dominic & Sons
      24 West Street
      PETERSHAM NSW 2049

50 men's shirts $400.00
4 men's shirts   500.00
                                $900.00

W. MAINE & CO.
181 Railway Street
CARLTON NSW 2218

Inv. 251   20 May 19XX

To: K. Dominic & Sons
      24 West Street
      PETERSHAM NSW 2049

24 prs men's socks $ 48.00
20 prs boys' jeans   280.00
                                $328.00

CONWAY & SONS
23 Morrison Parade
BURWOOD NSW 2134

Inv. 147   20 May 19XX

To: K. Dominic & Sons
      24 West Street
      PETERSHAM NSW 2049

25 men's shirts $250.00

EXERCISE 3.6 B. James & Co.

You are the bookkeeper for B. James & Co. The following invoices have been received for trading goods purchased during April 19XX. Enter the transactions in the purchases journal. (Use a copy of the blank purchases journal master on page 552.)

KING & CO.
48 Westleigh Street
THORNLEIGH NSW 2120

Inv. 1127   4 April 19XX

To: B. James & Co.
     48 William Street
     PARRAMATTA NSW 2150

For: Trading goods $457.00

L. THOMPSON & SONS
29 Greenway Street
WAVERLEY NSW 2024

Inv. 885   10 April 19XX

To: B. James & Co.
     48 William Street
     PARRAMATTA NSW 2150

For: Trading goods $98.67

KING & CO.
48 Westleigh Street
THORNLEIGH NSW 2120

Inv. 1145   15 April 19XX

To: B. James & Co.
     48 William Street
     PARRAMATTA NSW 2150

For: Trading goods $368.00

GREENWAY & CO.
28 Treadway Street
RYDALMERE NSW 2116

Inv. 98   24 April 19XX

To: B. James & Co.
     48 William Street
     PARRAMATTA NSW 2150

For: Trading goods $1254.80

L. THOMPSON & SONS
29 Greenway Street
WAVERLEY NSW 2024

Inv. 946   28 April 19XX

To: B. James & Co.
     48 William Street
     PARRAMATTA NSW 2150

For: Trading goods $467.00

GREENWAY & CO.
28 Treadway Street
RYDALMERE NSW 2116

Inv. 125   29 April 19XX

To: B. James & Co.
     48 William Street
     PARRAMATTA NSW 2150

For: Trading goods $125.25

WILLIAMS & SONS
48 Gray Road
RYDE NSW 2112

Inv. 157   30 April 19XX

To: B. James & Co.
     48 William Street
     PARRAMATTA NSW 2150

For: Trading goods $560.00

EXERCISE 3.7 Trend Fashions

You are employed as bookkeeper for Trend Fashions. The following invoices have been received for trading goods purchased during the month of February 19XX. You are required to enter the transactions in the purchases journal. (Use a copy of the blank purchases journal master provided on page 552.)

W. A. MONTEY
28 Melody Road
RYDE NSW 2112

Inv. 201   2 February 19XX

To: Trend Fashions
     28 Bayswater Road
     BONDI NSW 2026

For: Trading goods $405.60

J. S. BAXTER
48 Weston Street
SUTHERLAND NSW 2232

Inv. 304   6 February 19XX

To: Trend Fashions
     28 Bayswater Road
     BONDI NSW 2026

For: Trading goods $236.94

G. HANNA
465 Kent Street
SYDNEY NSW 2000

Inv. 235   9 February 19XX

To: Trend Fashions
     28 Bayswater Road
     BONDI NSW 2026

For: Trading goods $983.56

W. A. MONTEY
28 Melody Road
RYDE NSW 2112

Inv. 667   10 February 19XX

To: Trend Fashions
     28 Bayswater Road
     BONDI NSW 2026

For: Trading goods $56.78

J. S. BAXTER
48 Weston Street
SUTHERLAND NSW 2232

Inv. 345   15 February 19XX

To: Trend Fashions
     28 Bayswater Road
     BONDI NSW 2026

For: Trading goods $436.90

L. BEETSON
91 Wilson Street
PADDINGTON NSW 2021

Inv. 91   20 February 19XX

To: Trend Fashions
     28 Bayswater Road
     BONDI NSW 2026

For: Trading goods $125.50

W. A. MONTEY
28 Melody Road
RYDE NSW 2112

Inv. 745   28 February 19XX

To: Trend Fashions
     28 Bayswater Road
     BONDI NSW 2026

For: Trading goods $1270.50

Purchases returns and allowances journal

The purchases returns and allowances journal is used to record details of:
- all returns of trading (inventory) goods to creditors (accounts payable)
- allowances received for faulty or damaged goods
- overcharges on purchase invoices.

Format

PURCHASES RETURNS AND ALLOWANCES JOURNAL OF   Fol. PRX

Date	CN No.	Particulars (Creditor's account to be debited)	Fol.	Amount	Monthly total

Source document

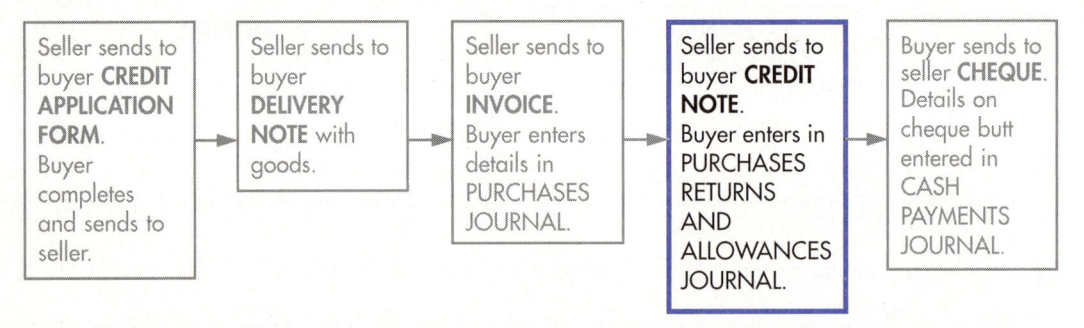

Seller sends to buyer **CREDIT APPLICATION FORM**. Buyer completes and sends to seller. → Seller sends to buyer **DELIVERY NOTE** with goods. → Seller sends to buyer **INVOICE**. Buyer enters details in PURCHASES JOURNAL. → Seller sends to buyer **CREDIT NOTE**. Buyer enters in PURCHASES RETURNS AND ALLOWANCES JOURNAL. → Buyer sends to seller **CHEQUE**. Details on cheque butt entered in CASH PAYMENTS JOURNAL.

The source document from which the information for the purchases returns and allowances journal is obtained is the credit note received from the supplier.

Example

J. Mason received the following original credit notes from his suppliers.

```
        H. LIME
     48 Argyle Road
    MIDLAND WA 6056

CN No. 111           12 January 19XX
(Ref. Inv. 233)

To:  J. Mason
     401 Denning Highway
     NORTH PERTH WA 6006

By return — faulty goods        $15.00
```

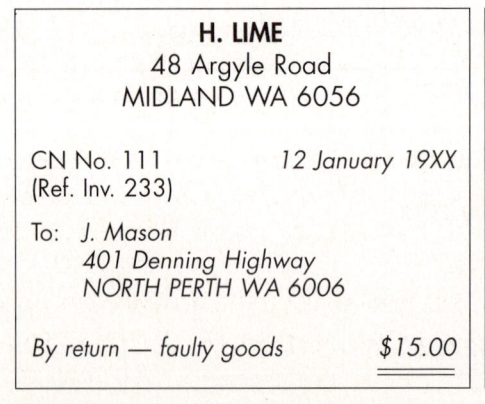

```
        P. EASTMAN
     29 Newman Road
    CLAREMONT WA 6010

CN No. 321           18 January 19XX
(Ref. Inv. 612)

To:  J. Mason
     401 Denning Highway
     NORTH PERTH WA 6006

By return — faulty goods        $10.00
```

```
              N. LILLY
          53 Conroy Street
         FREMANTLE WA 6160

29 January 19XX           CN No. 456

To:   J. Mason
      401 Denning Highway
      NORTH PERTH WA 6006

By overcharge (Inv. 479)      $20.00
```

Entering transactions in the purchases returns and allowances journal

Information from the credit notes on page 112 and above is entered in the purchases returns and allowances journal as shown below:

PURCHASES RETURNS AND ALLOWANCES JOURNAL OF J. MASON   Fol. PJX

Date	CN No.	Particulars (Creditor's account to be debited)	Fol.	Amount	Monthly total
19XX					
Jan. 12	111	H. Lime		15.00	
18	321	P. Eastman		10.00	
29	456	N. Lilly		20.00	
					45.00

EXERCISE 3.8   K. Dominic & Sons

You are employed as bookkeeper for K. Dominic & Sons. The following credit notes have been received from suppliers for trading goods returned during the month of May 19XX. You are required to enter the transactions into the purchases returns and allowances journal. (Use a copy of the blank purchases returns and allowances journal master provided on page 552.)

```
         W. MAINE & CO.
         181 Railway Street
         CARLTON NSW 2218

CN No. 111              20 May 19XX

To:   K. Dominic & Sons
      24 West Street
      PETERSHAM NSW 2049

By return — faulty goods (Ref. Inv. 237)
10 men's woollen jumpers      $200.00
```

```
         D. J. CALLAGHAN
        201 Lancaster Street
        AUBURN NSW 2144

CN No. 54               25 May 19XX

To:   K. Dominic & Sons
      24 West Street
      PETERSHAM NSW 2049

By return — faulty goods (Ref. Inv. 98)
2 men's suits                 $250.00
```

EXERCISE 3.9 — B. James & Co.

You are employed as bookkeeper for B. James & Co. The following credit notes have been received from suppliers for trading goods returned during the month of April 19XX. You are required to enter the transactions into the purchases returns and allowances journal. (Use a copy of the blank purchases returns and allowances journal master provided on page 552.)

KING & CO.
48 Westleigh Street
THORNLEIGH NSW 2120

CN No. 37   20 April 19XX

Ref. Inv. 1127

To: B. James & Co.
     48 William Street
     PARRAMATTA NSW 2150

By return — faulty goods $57.00

GREENWAY & CO.
28 Treadway Street
RYDALMERE NSW 2116

CN No. 12   24 April 19XX

To: B. James & Co.
     48 William Street
     PARRAMATTA NSW 2150

By return — faulty goods $105.00

(Ref. Inv. No. 98)

EXERCISE 3.10 — Trend Fashions

You are employed as bookkeeper for Trend Fashions. The following credit notes have been received from suppliers for trading goods returned during the month of February 19XX. You are required to enter the transactions into the purchases returns and allowances journal. (Use a copy of the blank purchases returns and allowances journal master provided on page 552.)

CN No. 98   16 February 19XX

G. HANNA
465 Kent Street
SYDNEY NSW 2000

To: Trend Fashions
     28 Bayswater Road
     BONDI NSW 2026

(Ref. Inv. 235)

By return — faulty goods $51.00

CN No. 14   21 February 19XX

J. S. BAXTER
43 Weston Street
SUTHERLAND NSW 2232

To: Trend Fashions
     28 Bayswater Road
     BONDI NSW 2026

(Ref. Inv. 304)

By return — damaged goods $26.94

Putting it together

3A Ace Hardware Store

You are employed as bookkeeper for Ace Hardware Store. The following invoices and credit notes have been received during the month of October 19XX. You are required to enter the details of the transactions in the purchases and purchases returns and allowances journals. (Use a copy of the blank masters provided on page 552.)

Invoices received

Inv. 989	5 October 19XX
W. TINDALE & CO.	
12 Oakdale Road	
BLACKTOWN NSW 2148	
To: Ace Hardware Store	
27 Fox Road	
DURAL NSW 2148	
For: 2 L white undercoat	$ 36.00
6 L white plastic gloss	120.00
	$156.00

Inv. 224	8 October 19XX
G. ATKINS PTY LTD	
35 Symons Road	
BROOKVALE NSW 2100	
To: Ace Hardware Store	
27 Fox Road	
DURAL NSW 2148	
For: 2 doz. kitchen canisters	$504.00
12 mixing bowls	60.00
	$564.00

Inv. 98	21 October 19XX
B. DANIEL & SON	
28 Peters Road	
LIDCOMBE NSW 2141	
To: Ace Hardware Store	
27 Fox Road	
DURAL NSW 2148	
For: 12 large crystal vases	$240.00

Inv. 1005	28 October 19XX
W. TINDALE & CO.	
12 Oakdale Road	
BLACKTOWN NSW 2148	
To: Ace Hardware Store	
27 Fox Road	
DURAL NSW 2148	
For: 10 L blue gloss	$200.00
20 L green undercoat	360.00
	$560.00

Credit notes received

CN 23	28 October 19XX
W. TINDALE & CO.	
12 Oakdale Road	
BLACKTOWN NSW 2148	
To: Ace Hardware Store	
27 Fox Road	
DURAL NSW 2148	
By return — damaged goods (Ref. Inv. 989)	
2 L white undercoat	$36.00

CN 44	29 October 19XX
G. ATKINS PTY LTD	
35 Symons Road	
BROOKVALE NSW 2100	
To: Ace Hardware Store	
27 Fox Road	
DURAL NSW 2148	
By return — oversupply Inv. 224	
2 kitchen canisters	$42.00

3B The Video & Record Store

You are employed as bookkeeper for The Video & Record Store. The following invoices and credit notes have been received during the month of April 19XX. You are required to enter the details of the transactions in the purchases and purchases returns and allowances journals. (Use a copy of the blank masters provided on page 552.)

Invoices received

DEL VIDEO CO.
29 Watson Road
SUNDALE QLD 4215

Inv. 724   4 April 19XX

To: The Video & Record Store
       4 Verona Road
       BALLINA NSW 2478

For: 6 VHS videos $215.70
        3 Stereo videos   315.70
                               $531.40

CLASSIC RECORDS PTY LTD
401 City Road
PRESTON VIC 3072

Inv. 1224   8 April 19XX

To: The Video & Record Store
       4 Verona Road
       BALLINA NSW 2478

For: 12 cassette sets $126.00
        10 CDs   250.00
                             $376.00

D. J. RECORD CO.
25 Morton Road
BRISBANE QLD 4000

Inv. 456   12 April 19XX

To: The Video & Record Store
       4 Verona Road
       BALLINA NSW 2478

3 double CD sets $ 90.00
6 boxed CDs   300.00
                           $390.00

VINTAGE VIDEOS
523 City Road
NEWTOWN NSW 2042

Inv. 1127   20 April 19XX

To: The Video & Record Store
       4 Verona Road
       BALLINA NSW 2478

For: 10 VHS videos $350.95

CLASSIC RECORDS PTY LTD
401 City Road
PRESTON VIC 3072

Inv. 1290   27 April 19XX

To: The Video & Record Store
       4 Verona Road
       BALLINA NSW 2478

10 video disks $252.00
3 CD sets   150.00
                           $402.00

DEL VIDEO CO.
29 Watson Road
SUNDALE QLD 4215

Inv. 770   28 April 19XX

To: The Video & Record Store
       4 Verona Road
       BALLINA NSW 2478

For: 10 VHS videos $359.50
        8 VHS videos   143.80
                              $503.30

Credit notes received

```
         DEL VIDEO CO.
         29 Watson Road
         SUNDALE QLD 4215

CN No. 26                27 April 19XX
To:  The Video & Record Store
     4 Verona Road
     BALLINA NSW 2478
By overcharge
— Invoice 724                 $100.00
```

```
         D. J. RECORD CO.
         25 Morton Road
         BRISBANE QLD 4000

CN No. 127               27 April 19XX
To:  The Video & Record Store
     4 Verona Road
     BALLINA NSW 2478
By return — damaged goods
(Ref. Inv. 456)
     1 double CD              $30.00
```

```
         VINTAGE VIDEOS
         53 City Road
         NEWTOWN NSW 2042

CN 49                    29 April 19XX
To:  The Video & Record Store
     4 Verona Road
     BALLINA NSW 2478
By return — faulty goods
(Ref. Inv. 1127)
     1 VHS video              $35.95
```

Cash payments journal

The cash payments journal is used to record:
(a) all cash payments (cheques) for:
- cash purchases of trading goods (inventory)
- expenses — such as wages, rent, advertising
- amounts paid to creditors
- cash drawings — money drawn by proprietor for personal use
- cash purchases of non-current (fixed) assets, for example, motor vehicles, office equipment
- petty cash — imprest amount and reimbursement of expenses

(b) bank charges as per bank statement
(c) discount received — this is received from creditors for prompt payment of their account according to their trading terms.

Format

The format shown below is the format used in this text.

CASH PAYMENTS JOURNAL OF   Fol. CPX

Date	Chq. No.	Particulars (Account to be debited)	Fol.	Discount received	Trade creditors	General	Bank

However, where a firm has a large volume of regular payments, extra columns are provided for this purpose. This makes posting easier as only the totals of the columns are posted to the relevant accounts. For example:

CASH PAYMENTS JOURNAL OF   Fol. CPX

Date	Chq. No.	Particulars (Account to be debited)	Fol.	Discount received	Trade creditors	Purchases	Wages	General	Bank

Source documents

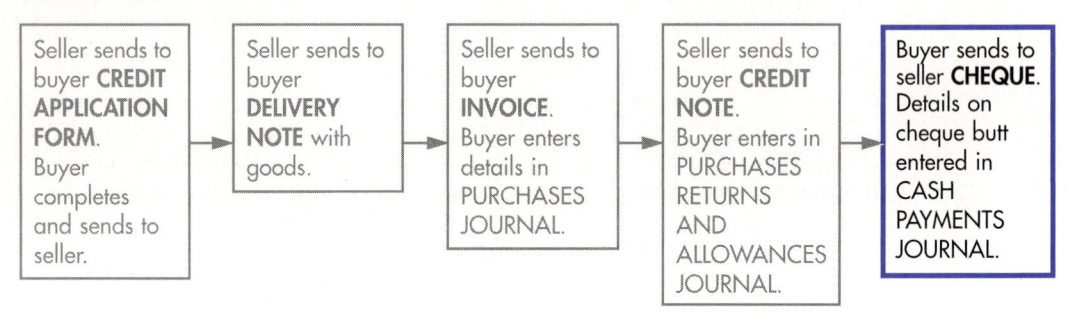

| Seller sends to buyer **CREDIT APPLICATION FORM**. Buyer completes and sends to seller. | → | Seller sends to buyer **DELIVERY NOTE** with goods. | → | Seller sends to buyer **INVOICE**. Buyer enters details in PURCHASES JOURNAL. | → | Seller sends to buyer **CREDIT NOTE**. Buyer enters in PURCHASES RETURNS AND ALLOWANCES JOURNAL. | → | Buyer sends to seller **CHEQUE**. Details on cheque butt entered in CASH PAYMENTS JOURNAL. |

The source documents from which the information for the cash payments journal is obtained are:
(a) cheque butts
(b) bank statement (not used in this chapter).

Example
The following are cheque butts for cheques made out by J. Mason.

```
Cheque No. 264
Date: 13 January 19XX

To:   H. LIME
For:  Payment of Account

This cheque:   $332.50
Discount:        17.50
```

```
Cheque No. 265
Date: 24 January 19XX

To:   P. EASTMAN
For:  Payment of Account

This cheque:   $142.50
Discount:         7.50
```

```
Cheque No. 266
Date: 26 January 19XX

To:   CASH
For:  Wages

This cheque:   $150.00
```

```
Cheque No. 267
Date: 28 January 19XX

To:   THE ESTATE AGENT
For:  Rent

This cheque:    $40.00
```

```
Cheque No. 268
Date: 30 January 19XX

To:   N. LILLY
For:  Payment of Account

This cheque:    $25.00
```

Entering transactions in the cash payments journal

Information from the cheque butts is entered in the cash payments journal as shown below:

CASH PAYMENTS JOURNAL OF J. MASON   Fol. CP1

Date	Chq. No.	Particulars (Account to be debited)	Fol.	Discount received	Trade creditors	General	Bank*
19XX							
Jan. 13	264	H. Lime		17.50	332.50		332.50
25	265	P. Eastman		7.50	142.50		142.50
26	266	Wages				150.00	150.00
28	267	Rent				40.00	40.00
	268	N. Lilly			25.00		25.00
				25.00	500.00	190.00	690.00

* *Note*: The total amount of each cheque is entered in the 'Bank' column.

When payment is being made to **personal accounts** (creditors), the cheque butt will show either 'Payment of Account'; that is, payment is being made for total amount owing, or 'Payment on Account' — that is; part payment of amount owing. The name of the creditor is shown after 'To'. Enter the name of the creditor in the 'Account to be debited' column, the amount paid in the 'Trade creditors' column and the discount in the 'Discount received' column. This is necessary as these amounts will affect the balance owing for goods or services purchased on credit.

When payment is being made for non-personal accounts (for example, Rent or Office Equipment) enter the name of the expense account (for example, Wages) or the asset account (for example, Motor Vehicles) in the 'Accounts to be debited' column. The name of the expense or asset is shown on the cheque butt after 'For'. Do *not* enter the name of the person to whom the cheque is made out. Amounts entered in the 'Bank' column are actual amounts paid out. The amount of discount received is *not* added to this figure.

As these accounts are being paid directly (that is, by cheque or cash), recording the name of the person to whom the cheque is made out is not necessary. The amount is entered in the appropriate account column (for example, wages may have a separate column) or the 'General' column.

When entering an amount for petty cash imprest (that is, the opening of the petty cash float), enter 'Petty cash' in the 'Accounts to be debited' column. When entering amounts for petty cash reimbursement, enter the names of the accounts on which the money was spent (for example, Stationery, Postage) in the 'General' column and the total amount of the cheque in the 'Bank' column.

EXERCISE 3.11   K. Dominic & Sons

You are employed as bookkeeper for K. Dominic & Sons. From the following cheque butts for cheques made out in May 19XX, you are required to enter the transactions in the cash payments journal. (Use a copy of the blank cash payments journal master provided on page 553.)

Cheque No. 114 Date: *14 May 19XX* To: *RAMSEY & CO.* For: *Rent* This cheque: $500.00	Cheque No. 115 Date: *15 May 19XX* To: *H. DEANE & CO.* For: *Advertising* This cheque: $55.00	Cheque No. 116 Date: *15 May 19XX* To: *CONWAY & SONS* For: *Payment of Account* This cheque: $399.00 Discount: 21.00
Cheque No. 117 Date: *20 May 19XX* To: *CASH* For: *Petty Cash Imprest* This cheque: $150.00	Cheque No. 118 Date: *20 May 19XX* To: *W. MAINE & CO.* For: *Payment of Account* This cheque: $646.00 Discount: 34.00	Cheque No. 119 Date: *28 May 19XX* To: *W. KING* For: *Repairs and Maintenance* This cheque: $83.00

EXERCISE 3.12   B. James & Co.

You are employed as bookkeeper for B. James & Co. From the following cheque butts for cheques made out in April 19XX, you are required to enter the transactions in the cash payments journal. (Use a copy of the blank cash payments journal master provided on page 553.)

Cheque No. 148 Date: *12 April 19XX* To: *M. MORGAN* For: *Stationery* This cheque: $68.00	Cheque No. 149 Date: *14 April 19XX* To: *KING & CO.* For: *Payment of Account* This cheque: $561.60 Discount: 14.40	Cheque No. 150 Date: *24 April 19XX* To: *SYDNEY ELECTRICITY* For: *Electricity* This cheque: $180.00
Cheque No. 151 Date: *24 April 19XX* To: *GREENWAY & CO.* For: *Payment of Account* This cheque: $63.38 Discount: 1.62	Cheque No. 152 Date: *28 April 19XX* To: *CASH* For: *Purchases* This cheque: $100.00	Cheque No. 153 Date: *28 April 19XX* To: *SOMMERS MOTORS* For: *Motor Vehicle* This cheque: $17 000.00

EXERCISE 3.13 Trend Fashions

You are employed as bookkeeper for Trend Fashions. From the following cheque butts for cheques made out in February 19XX, you are required to enter the transactions in the cash payments journal. (Use a copy of the blank cash payments journal master provided on page 553.)

Cheque No. 334 Date: *15 February 19XX* To: JAMES CARTER & CO. For: *Repairs and Maintenance* This cheque: $150.00	Cheque No. 335 Date: *20 February 19XX* To: CASH For: *Wages* This cheque: $1076.00	Cheque No. 336 Date: *20 February 19XX* To: W. A. MONTEY For: *Payment of Account* This cheque: $312.00 Discount: 8.00
Cheque No. 337 Date: *25 February 19XX* To: D. DEANE For: *Advertising* This cheque: $120.00	Cheque No. 338 Date: *25 February 19XX* To: G. HANNA For: *Payment of Account* This cheque: $492.35 Discount: 12.65	Cheque No. 339 Date: *28 February 19XX* To: CASH For: *Petty Cash Reimbursement* Stationery $15.00 Travel expenses 80.00 This cheque: $95.00

Putting it together

3C A. Thomas & Co.

You are employed as bookkeeper for A. Thomas & Co. From the following invoices and credit notes received from your suppliers, and from the cheque butts for cheques made out during the month of November 19XX, you are required to enter the details in the purchases, purchases returns and allowances and cash payments journals, respectively. (Use copies of the relevant blank masters provided on pages 552–553.)

Invoices received

K. JAMES 28 Collins Street MELBOURNE VIC 3000 Inv. 1245　　　　8 November 19XX To:　A. Thomas & Co. 　　495 Richard Street 　　GRANVILLE NSW 2142 For: Trading goods　　　　$405.50	**N. HUNTER & SONS** 45 Prospect Street TAMWORTH NSW 2340 Inv. 902　　　　10 November 19XX To:　A. Thomas & Co. 　　495 Richard Street 　　GRANVILLE NSW 2142 For: Trading goods　　　　$89.75
G. WILKINSON PTY LTD 61 Clyde Street AUBURN NSW 2144 Inv. 4579　　　　15 November 19XX To:　A. Thomas & Co. 　　495 Richard Street 　　GRANVILLE NSW 2142 For: Trading goods　　　　$506.70	**K. JAMES** 28 Collins Street MELBOURNE VIC 3000 Inv. 1300　　　　20 November 19XX To:　A. Thomas & Co. 　　495 Richard Street 　　GRANVILLE NSW 2142 For: Trading goods　　　　$237.80
G. WILKINSON PTY LTD 61 Clyde Street AUBURN NSW 2144 Inv. 4701　　　　28 November 19XX To:　A. Thomas & Co. 　　495 Richard Street 　　GRANVILLE NSW 2142 For: Trading goods　　　　$560.00	**N. HUNTER & SONS** 45 Prospect Street TAMWORTH NSW 2340 Inv. 958　　　　28 November 19XX To:　A. Thomas & Co. 　　495 Richard Street 　　GRANVILLE NSW 2142 For: Trading goods　　　　$1274.85
R. & M. MENZIES 48 Johnson Street ALBURY NSW 2640 Inv. 325　　　　30 November 19XX To:　A. Thomas & Co. 　　495 Richard Street 　　GRANVILLE NSW 2142 For: Trading goods　　　　$1560.00	

Credit notes received

N. HUNTER & SONS 45 Prospect Street TAMWORTH NSW 2340	**K. JAMES** 28 Collins Street MELBOURNE VIC 3000
CN No. 460 15 November 19XX	CN No. 361 16 November 19XX

To: A. Thomas & Co.
  495 Richard Street
  GRANVILLE NSW 2142
	To: A. Thomas & Co.
	  495 Richard Street
	  GRANVILLE NSW 2142

By return — faulty goods (Ref. Inv. 902) $9.75	By overcharge Inv. 1245 $20.00

Cheque butts

Cheque No. 080 Date: 5 November 19XX To: CASH For: Wages This cheque: $2300.00	Cheque No. 081 Date: 10 November 19XX To: THE COUNTY COUNCIL For: Electricity This cheque: $390.00	Cheque No. 082 Date: 10 November 19XX To: ACME ADVERTISERS For: Advertising This cheque: $140.50
Cheque No. 083 Date: 12 November 19XX To: A. THOMAS For: Drawings This cheque: $200.00	Cheque No. 084 Date: 12 November 19XX To: CASH For: Purchases This cheque: $48.00	Cheque No. 085 Date: 20 November 19XX To: N. HUNTER & SONS For: Payment of Account This cheque: $78.00 Discount: 2.00
Cheque No. 086 Date: 20 November 19XX To: CASH For: Wages This cheque: $2300.00	Cheque No. 087 Date: 24 November 19XX To: K. JAMES For: Payment of Account This cheque: $375.50 Discount: 10.00	Cheque No. 088 Date: 24 November 19XX To: G. WILKINSON PTY LTD For: Payment of Account This cheque: $500.00

Cheque No. 089
Date: 30 November 19XX
 	
To: WALSH & CO.
For: Office Furniture
   (Desk and chair)
 	
This cheque: $570.00
	Cheque No. 090
	Date: 30 November 19XX
	
	To: CASH
	For: Petty Cash
	   Reimbursement
	   Postage $27.00
	   Stationery 40.00
	   Repairs 15.00
	
	This cheque: $82.00
		Cheque No. 091
		Date: 30 November 19XX
		
		To: CASH
		For: Purchases
		
		This cheque: $160.00

3D Bryant's Newsagency

You are employed as bookkeeper for Bryant's Newsagency. From the following invoices and credit notes received from your suppliers, and from the cheque butts for cheques made out during the month of July 19XX, you are required to enter the details in the purchases, purchases returns and allowances and cash payments journals respectively. (Use copies of the relevant blank masters provided on pages 552–553.)

Invoices received

GAZETTE PRESS
402 Elizabeth Street
SYDNEY NSW 2000

Inv. 983   2 July 19XX

To: Bryant's Newsagency
      362 Pacific Highway
      PYMBLE NSW 2073

For: *Trading goods* $1598.00

STATIONERY SUPPLIERS
88 Wilde Street
ARTARMON NSW 2064

Inv. 406   4 July 19XX

To: Bryant's Newsagency
      362 Pacific Highway
      PYMBLE NSW 2073

For: *Trading goods* $148.00

PRINT PUBLISHERS
98 Church Street
BRISBANE QLD 4000

Inv. 901   10 July 19XX

To: Bryant's Newsagency
      362 Pacific Highway
      PYMBLE NSW 2073

For: *Trading goods* $1480.00

NATIONAL JOURNALS
67 Menzies Street
BELCONNEN ACT 2617

Inv. 48   10 July 19XX

To: Bryant's Newsagency
      362 Pacific Highway
      PYMBLE NSW 2073

For: *Trading goods* $2367.85

STATIONERY SUPPLIERS
88 Wilde Street
ARTARMON NSW 2064

Inv. 453   15 July 19XX

To: Bryant's Newsagency
      362 Pacific Highway
      PYMBLE NSW 2073

For: *Trading goods* $423.80

GAZETTE PRESS
402 Elizabeth Street
SYDNEY NSW 2000

Inv. 1123   18 July 19XX

To: Bryant's Newsagency
      362 Pacific Highway
      PYMBLE NSW 2073

For: *Trading goods* $2000.00

NATIONAL JOURNALS
67 Menzies Street
BELCONNEN ACT 2617

Inv. 77　　　　　　　　30 July 19XX

To:　Bryant's Newsagency
　　　362 Pacific Highway
　　　PYMBLE NSW 2073

For: Trading goods　　　$483.70

Credit notes received

PRINT PUBLISHERS
98 Church Street
BRISBANE QLD 4000

CN No. 99　　　　　　20 July 19XX

To:　Bryant's Newsagency
　　　362 Pacific Highway
　　　PYMBLE NSW 2073

By return — faulty goods

(Inv. 901)　　　　　　　$100.00

STATIONERY SUPPLIERS
88 Wilde Street
ARTARMON NSW 2064

CN No. 45　　　　　　20 July 19XX

To:　Bryant's Newsagency
　　　362 Pacific Highway
　　　PYMBLE NSW 2073

By overcharge

Inv. 406　　　　　　　　$23.00

GAZETTE PRESS
402 Elizabeth Street
SYDNEY NSW 2000

CN No. 234　　　　　　30 July 19XX

To:　Bryant's Newsagency
　　　362 Pacific Highway
　　　PYMBLE NSW 2073

By return — damaged goods

(Ref. Inv. 1123)　　　　$98.00

Cheque butts

Cheque No. 70
Date: 4 July 19XX

To:　CASH
For: Wages

This cheque:　　$2400.00

Cheque No. 71
Date: 5 July 19XX

To:　CASH
For: Petty Cash Imprest

This cheque:　　$100.00

Cheque No. 72
Date: 10 July 19XX

To:　CASH
For: Purchases

This cheque:　　$136.00

Cheque No. 73 Date: 11 July 19XX To: SYDNEY ELECTRICITY For: Electricity This cheque: $650.00	Cheque No. 74 Date: 11 July 19XX To: GAZETTE PRESS For: Payment of Account This cheque: $1568.00 Discount: 30.00	Cheque No. 75 Date: 18 July 19XX To: CASH For: Wages This cheque: $2760.00
Cheque No. 76 Date: 19 July 19XX To: ADAMS AGENCY For: Advertising This cheque: $150.00	Cheque No. 77 Date: 20 July 19XX To: STATIONERY SUPPLIERS For: Payment on Account This cheque: $125.00	Cheque No. 78 Date: 30 July 19XX To: PRINT PUBLISHERS For: Payment of Account This cheque: $1340.00 Discount: 40.00
Cheque No. 79 Date: 30 July 19XX To: CASH For: Repairs This cheque: $210.00	Cheque No. 80 Date: 31 July 19XX To: CASH For: Purchases This cheque: $700.00	Cheque No. 81 Date: 31 July 19XX To: CASH For: Petty Cash Reimbursement Postage $35.00 Stationery 20.00 Travel 35.00 This cheque: $90.00

ACCOUNTS RECEIVABLE JOURNALS

As a means of increasing sales and ultimately net profit, businesses regularly extend credit to persons or firms who purchase their goods or services. The term 'accounts receivable' refers to those persons or firms to whom the business sells trading goods on credit. As these firms owe money to the business, accounts receivable (or trade debtors, as they are known) are an asset of the business.

The accounts receivable department of a business is responsible for all transactions involving trade debtors; that is, those persons or firms from whom the business receives money as a result of the sale of trading goods (or services) on credit.

Accounts receivable refers only to those transactions which involve the sale of trading goods which have been purchased for resale at a profit at a later date; that is, the trading stock (or inventory) of the business. Inventory is a current asset which will be used up during the current trading period. Details of transactions with trade debtors are recorded as accounts receivable.

A business may also sell non-current assets on credit. Non-current assets refer to assets which the business owns or controls and which are not intended for resale until their usefulness to the business has been exhausted. Examples are plant and machinery, motor vehicles, office equipment and furniture and fittings.

When a non-current asset is sold on credit, the business acquires a sundry (or non-trade) debtor. Details of transactions with sundry debtors are recorded separately from trade debtors, as can be seen from the following examples.

- Details of transactions with accounts receivable (trade debtors) are recorded in the general journal and the accounts receivable journals (that is, sales, sales returns and allowances and cash receipts). Individual details of these journals are posted to the accounts receivable ledger and represented 'in total' only in the general ledger by the Accounts Receivable Control account.
- Details of transactions with sundry debtors are recorded only in the general journal and are posted to the general ledger, where a separate account is maintained for each sundry debtor.

Entering details of source documents

Each day the source documents are sorted into batches and entered into their respective journals:

- *Batch 1 —* Invoices are entered into the sales journal.
- *Batch 2 —* Credit notes are entered into the sales returns and allowances journal.
- *Batch 3 —* Receipts, cash sales invoices/dockets/cash register roll details are entered into the cash receipts journal.

All journals are totalled at the end of the month.

Sales journal

The sales journal records details of all credit sales of trading goods (inventory) to the firm's customers. In accounting terms, those persons or firms to whom a business sells trading goods on credit are referred to as *trade debtors*; they are also known as accounts receivable.

Format

SALES JOURNAL OF   Fol. SJX

Date	Inv. No.	Particulars (Debtor's account to be debited)	Fol.	Sales	Sales tax	Debtors' total

Source document

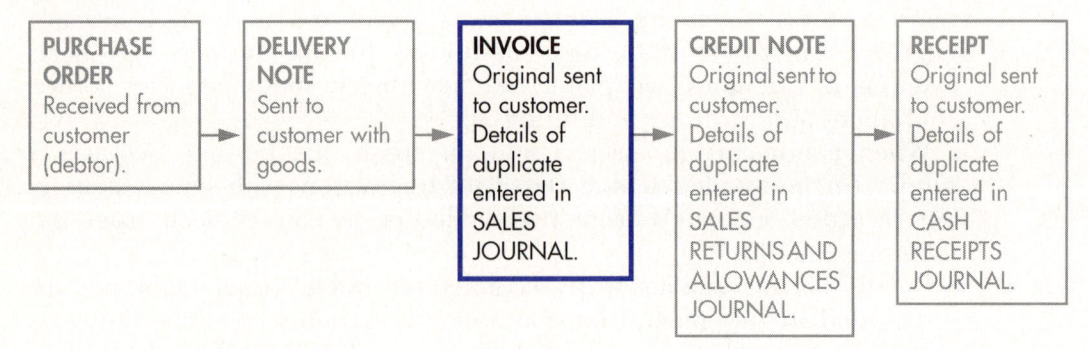

PURCHASE ORDER	DELIVERY NOTE	**INVOICE**	CREDIT NOTE	RECEIPT
Received from customer (debtor).	Sent to customer with goods.	**Original sent to customer. Details of duplicate entered in SALES JOURNAL.**	Original sent to customer. Details of duplicate entered in SALES RETURNS AND ALLOWANCES JOURNAL.	Original sent to customer. Details of duplicate entered in CASH RECEIPTS JOURNAL.

The source document from which the information for the sales journal is obtained is the duplicate copy of the sales invoice forwarded to the customer.

Example

The following are duplicates of sales invoices sent by J. Mason to his customers.

Inv. 371   1 January 19XX

To: M. Adams
      84 Trent Road
      RYDE NSW 2112

4 ladies' dresses @ $21.50 ea.	$86.00
Less 5% Trade Discount	4.30
	81.70
Plus 15% Sales Tax	12.25
	$93.95

Inv. 372   10 January 19XX

To: J. Abbott
      67 Crane Street
      BLACKTOWN NSW 2148

8 women's cardigans @ $22 each	$176.00
Less 5% Trade Discount	8.80
	167.20
Plus 15% Sales Tax	25.08
	$192.28

Inv. 373   21 January 19XX

To: L. Wells
      149 Fletcher Road
      CHATSWOOD NSW 2067

3 ladies' dresses @ $46 ea.	$138.00
Less 5% Trade Discount	6.90
	131.10
Plus 15% Sales Tax	19.66
	$150.76

Inv. 374   29 January 19XX

To: E. Garton
      91 Murdoch Road
      NEWPORT NSW 2106

3 prs slacks @ $20 pr	$60.00
Less 5% Trade Discount	3.00
	57.00
Plus 15% Sales Tax	8.55
	$65.55

Entering the transactions in the sales journal

The format of the sales journal differs from the format of the purchases journal. When a wholesaler sells to a retailer (or a manufacturer sells directly to a retailer), sales tax is payable on certain classes of goods, owing to the fact that, as a seller of trading goods, the business must by law, charge sales tax on various categories of goods. The amount of sales tax is fixed by State governments and the federal government.

Sales tax, when applicable, is an amount collected by the seller of the trading goods. The amount of sales tax is recorded when goods are sold, and the seller must remit this amount to the Australian Taxation Department by a specified date during the following month. Therefore, it is necessary for this amount to be recorded in the sales journal.

The sales invoice also shows trade discount. Trade discount is a discount allowed by a manufacturer to a wholesaler or a wholesaler to a retailer. It is a discount given when large quantities of goods are purchased or to a buyer in the same trade. *Trade discount is* not *recorded in the books of account.*

Trade discount should not be confused with the discount given for prompt payment; that is, discount received which is recorded in the cash payments journal, or discount allowed which is recorded in the cash receipts journal.

Note: Trade discount is calculated on the actual selling price of the goods before sales tax is added.

Information from the sales invoices is entered in the sales journal as shown below:

SALES JOURNAL OF J. MASON   Fol. SJX

Date	Inv. No.	Particulars (Debtor's account to be debited)	Fol.	Sales	Sales tax	Debtors' total
19XX						
Jan. 1	371	M. Adams		81.70	12.25	93.95
10	372	J. Abbott		167.20	25.08	192.28
21	373	L. Wells		131.10	19.66	150.76
29	374	E. Garton		57.00	8.55	65.55
				437.00	65.54	502.54

Note: In many computer accounting packages, the transactions are entered into the sales journal at the time the invoices are produced.

EXERCISE 3.14 K. Dominic & Sons

You are employed as bookkeeper for K. Dominic & Sons. The duplicates of the invoices sent to customers for trading goods supplied during the month of May 19XX are shown on page 130. You are required to enter the transactions in the sales journal. (Use a copy of the blank sales journal master provided on page 554.)

```
Inv. 463                    3 May 19XX        Inv. 464                    10 May 19XX

To:  J. Wade                                   To:  M. Byrnes
     77 Gold Street                                 14 McFee Road
     DRUMMOYNE NSW 2047                             LANE COVE NSW 2066

10 prs boys' jeans @ $18 ea.   $180.00         2 doz girls' blouses
Less 10% Trade Discount          18.00           @ $11.60 ea.              $278.40
                                ───────        Less 10% Trade Discount      27.84
                                162.00                                    ───────
Plus 15% Sales Tax               24.30                                     250.56
                                ───────        Plus 15% Sales Tax           37.59
                               $186.30                                    ───────
                                ═══════                                   $288.15
                                                                          ═══════

Inv. 465                   18 May 19XX         Inv. 466                    20 May 19XX

To:  R. Cotter & Sons                          To:  J. Wade
     12 Flynn Avenue                                77 Gold Street
     ASHFIELD NSW 2131                              DRUMMOYNE NSW 2047

12 girls' dresses @ $36 ea.   $360.00          24 prs boys' socks @ $1.50 pr  $36.00
Less 10% Trade Discount         36.00          Less 10% Trade Discount         3.60
                              ───────                                        ───────
                              324.00                                          32.40
Plus 15% Sales Tax             48.10           Plus 15% Sales Tax              4.86
                              ───────                                        ───────
                             $372.10                                         $37.26
                              ═══════                                        ═══════
```

EXERCISE 3.15 B. James & Co.

You are employed as bookkeeper for B. James & Co. Following are the duplicates of the invoices sent to customers for trading goods supplied during the month of April 19XX. You are required to enter the transactions in the sales journal. (Use a copy of the blank sales journal master provided on page 554.)

```
Inv. 22                    3 April 19XX        Inv. 23                    10 April 19XX

To:  A. Collins                                To:  Corella Private Hospital
     80 Watson Avenue                               225 North Road
     RYDE NSW 2112                                  CARLINGFORD NSW 2118

48 ctns soap powder                            5 doz tins fruit @ $13 per doz.  $65.00
  @ $17.50 per ctn            $840.00                                           ═══════
Less 5% Trade Discount          42.00          Sales Tax Exempt
                              ───────
                              798.00
Plus 12.5% Sales Tax           19.95
                              ───────
                             $817.95
                              ═══════
```

CHAPTER 3: PREPARATION OF JOURNALS | 131

Inv. 24	15 April 19XX
To: E. & J. White	
18 Thompson Road	
EASTWOOD NSW 2122	
6 doz tins jam @ $15.75 doz.	$ 94.50
2 doz tins orange juice	
@ $23 per doz.	46.00
	140.50
Less 5% Trade Discount	7.02
	133.48
Plus 12.5% Sales Tax	16.68
	$150.16

Inv. 25	15 April 19XX
To: K. Carter & Co.	
88 Cambridge Street	
EPPING NSW 2121	
2 doz bottles sauce	
@ $16 per doz.	$32.00
1 carton SR flour	35.00
	67.00
Less 5% Trade Discount	3.35
	63.65
Plus 12.5% Sales Tax	7.96
	$71.61

Inv. 26	20 April 19XX
To: E. & J. White	
18 Thompson Road	
EASTWOOD NSW 2122	
5 ctns detergent @ $24 ctn	$120.00
1 doz tins coffee	
@ $48 per doz.	48.00
	168.00
Less 10% Trade Discount	16.80
	151.20
Plus 12.5% Sales Tax	18.87
	$170.07

Inv. 27	28 April 19XX
To: A. Collins	
80 Watson Avenue	
RYDE NSW 2112	
3 doz tins ham	
@ $66 per doz.	$198.00
6 doz pkts biscuits	
@ $9.36 per doz.	56.16
	254.16
Less 5% Trade Discount	12.71
	241.45
Plus 12.5% Sales Tax	30.18
	$271.63

EXERCISE 3.16 *Trend Fashions*

You are employed as bookkeeper for Trend Fashions. Below and on page 132 are the duplicates of the invoices sent to customers for trading goods supplied during the month of February 19XX. You are required to enter the transactions in the sales journal. (Use a copy of the blank sales journal master provided on page 554.)

Inv. 508	10 February 19XX
To: Jane's Fashion Store	
28 Byron Road	
LISMORE NSW 2480	
10 dresses @ $40 each	$400.00
Less 10% Trade Discount	40.00
	360.00
Plus 15% Sales Tax	54.00
	$414.00

Inv. 509	12 February 19XX
To: The Dress Shop	
35 Wylie Street	
MONA VALE NSW 2103	
25 prs slacks @ $14 pr	$375.00
Less 10% Trade Discount	37.50
	337.50
Plus 15% Sales Tax	50.63
	$388.13

```
Inv. 510                 15 February 19XX        Inv. 511                 20 February 19XX
To:  Dianne's Boutique                           To:  H. Taylor & Co.
     63 Candy Street                                  181 George Street
     GOSFORD NSW 2250                                 PARRAMATTA NSW 2150
6 blouses @ $17.50 ea.      $105.00              10 prs slacks @ $10 pr    $100.00
12 belts @ $5 ea.             60.00              20 skirts @ $15 ea.        300.00
                             165.00                                         400.00
Less 10% Trade Discount       16.50              Less 10% Trade Discount     40.00
                             148.50                                         360.00
Plus 15% Sales Tax            22.80              Plus 15% Sales Tax          54.00
                            $171.30                                        $414.00


Inv. 512                 25 February 19XX        Inv. 513                 25 February 19XX
To:  The Dress Shop                              To:  Jane's Fashion Store
     35 Wylie Street                                  28 Byron Road
     MONA VALE NSW 2103                               LISMORE NSW 2480
20 dresses @ $25 ea.        $500.00              5 blazers @ $70 ea.       $350.00
Less 10% Trade Discount       50.00              Less 10% Trade Discount     35.00
                             450.00                                         315.00
Plus 15% Sales Tax            67.50              Plus 15% Sales Tax          47.25
                            $517.50                                        $362.25
```

Sales returns and allowances journal

The sales returns and allowances journal records details of:
- all returns of trading (inventory) goods by debtors
- allowances made for faulty or damaged goods
- overcharges on sales invoices.

Format

SALES RETURNS AND ALLOWANCES JOURNAL OF   Fol. SRX

Date	CN No.	Particulars (Debtor's account to be credited)	Fol.	Sales returns	Sales tax	Debtors' total

Source document

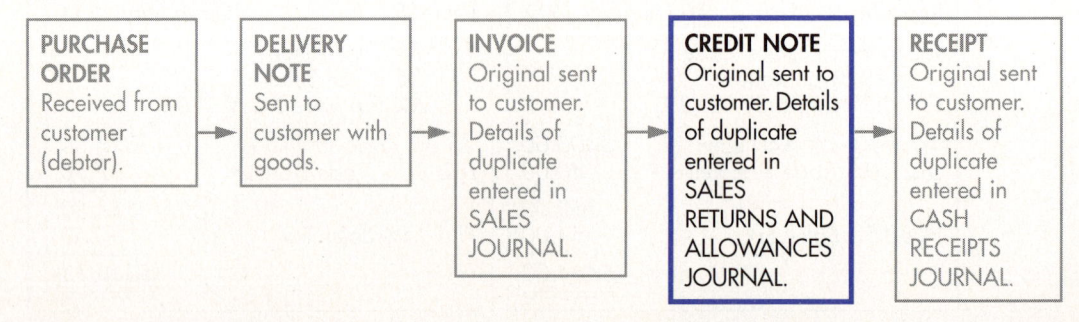

PURCHASE ORDER Received from customer (debtor). → **DELIVERY NOTE** Sent to customer with goods. → **INVOICE** Original sent to customer. Details of duplicate entered in SALES JOURNAL. → **CREDIT NOTE** Original sent to customer. Details of duplicate entered in SALES RETURNS AND ALLOWANCES JOURNAL. → **RECEIPT** Original sent to customer. Details of duplicate entered in CASH RECEIPTS JOURNAL.

The source documents from which the information for the sales returns and allowances journal is obtained are the duplicates of credit notes sent to customers.

Example

Below are duplicates of credit notes sent to customers by J. Mason.

CN No. 86	28 January 19XX
To: J. Abbott	
67 Crane Street	
BLACKTOWN NSW 2148	
By return — faulty goods (Inv. 372)	
1 woman's cardigan	$22.00
Less 5% Trade Discount	1.10
	20.90
Plus 15% Sales Tax	3.13
	$24.03

CN No. 87	28 January 19XX
To: M. Adams	
84 Trent Road	
RYDE NSW 2112	
By return — oversupply (Inv. 371)	
1 lady's dress	$21.50
Less 5% Trade Discount	1.07
	20.43
Plus 15% Sales Tax	3.06
	$23.49

CN No. 88	30 January 19XX
To: E. Garton	
91 Murdoch Road	
NEWPORT NSW 2105	
By return — faulty goods (Inv. 374)	
2 prs slacks @ $20 pr	$40.00
Less 5% Trade Discount	2.00
	38.00
Plus: 15% Sales Tax	5.70
	$43.70

Remember: The same rates for trade discount and sales tax apply to the credit note as they did to the invoice.

Entering transactions in the sales returns and allowances journal

Information from the duplicate credit notes is entered in the sales returns and allowances journal as below:

SALES RETURNS AND ALLOWANCES JOURNAL OF J. MASON   Fol. SRX

Date	CN No.	Particulars (Debtor's account to be credited)	Fol.	Sales returns	Sales tax	Debtors' total
19XX						
Jan. 28	86	J. Abbott		20.90	3.13	24.03
	87	M. Adams		20.43	3.06	23.49
30	88	E. Garton		38.00	5.70	43.70
				79.33	11.89	91.22

EXERCISE 3.17 — K. Dominic & Sons

You are employed as bookkeeper for K. Dominic & Sons. The following are duplicates of credit notes sent to customers for trading goods returned during the month of May 19XX. You are required to enter the transactions in the sales returns and allowances journal. (Use a copy of the sales returns and allowances master provided on page 555.)

CN No. 42	18 May 19XX
To: J. Wade	
77 Gold Street	
DRUMMOYNE NSW 2047	
By return — damaged goods (Inv. 463)	
2 prs boys' jeans @ $18 pr	$36.00
Less 10% Trade Discount	3.60
	32.40
Plus 15% Sales Tax	4.86
	$37.26

CN No. 43	21 May 19XX
To: R. Cotter & Sons	
12 Flynn Avenue	
ASHFIELD NSW 2131	
By return — faulty goods (Inv. 465)	
2 girls' dresses @ $36 ea.	$72.00
Less 10% Trade Discount	7.20
	64.80
Plus 15% Sales Tax	9.72
	$74.52

EXERCISE 3.18 — B. James & Co.

You are employed as bookkeeper for B. James & Co. The following are duplicates of credit notes sent to customers for trading goods returned during the month of April 19XX. You are required to enter the transactions in the sales returns and allowances journal. (Use a copy of the sales returns and allowances master provided on page 555.)

CN No. 85	13 April 19XX
To: A. Collins	
80 Watson Street	
RYDE NSW 2112	
By return — faulty goods (Ref. Inv. 22)	
12 ctns soap powder @ $17.50 per ctn	$210.00
Less 5% Trade Discount	10.50
	199.50
Plus 12.5% Sales Tax	24.94
	$224.44

CN No. 86	21 April 19XX
To: K. Carter & Co.	
77 Cambridge Street	
EPPING NSW 2121	
By return — damaged goods (Ref. Inv. 25)	
1 carton SR flour	$35.00
Less 5% Trade Discount	1.75
	33.25
Plus 12.5% Sales Tax	4.16
	$37.41

EXERCISE 3.19   Trend Fashions

You are employed as bookkeeper for Trend Fashions. The following are duplicates of credit notes sent to customers for trading goods returned during the month of February 19XX. You are required to enter the transactions in the sales returns and allowances journal. (Use a copy of the sales returns and allowances master provided on page 555.)

CN No. 12	20 February 19XX
To: The Dress Shop 35 Wylie Street MONA VALE NSW 2103	
By return — (oversupply) — Ref. Inv. 509	
5 prs slacks @ $14 ea.	$70.00
Less 10% Trade Discount	7.00
	63.00
Plus 15% Sales Tax	9.45
	$72.45

CN No. 13	27 February 19XX
To: Dianne's Boutique 63 Candy Street GOSFORD NSW 2250	
By return (faulty goods) — Ref. Inv. 2250	
6 belts @ $5 ea.	$30.00
Less 10% Trade Discount	3.00
	27.00
Plus 15% Sales Tax	4.05
	$31.05

Putting it together

3E   Austral Wool Co.

You are employed as bookkeeper by Austral Wool Co. From the duplicates of invoices and credit notes sent to customers during the month of July 19XX, you are required to enter the details of the transactions in the sales and sales returns and allowances journals. (Use copies of the relevant masters provided on pages 554 and 555.)

Duplicates of invoices

Inv. 104	2 July 19XX
To: D. A. Dixon 59 Cox Road TAREE NSW 2430	
50 pkts 8 ply wool	$625.00
50 pkts 12 ply wool	750.00
	1375.00
Less 10% Trade Discount	137.50
	1237.50
Plus 12.5% Sales Tax	154.69
	$1392.19

Inv. 105	5 July 19XX
To: The Hills School 220 Old Northern Road GLENORIE NSW 2157	
60 pkts 4 ply wool	$550.00
Sales Tax exempt	

Inv. 106	9 July 19XX

To: J. M. Cummings
    81 Castlereagh Street
    DUBBO NSW 2830

6 lambswool underlays	$230.00
Less 10% Trade Discount	23.00
	207.00
Plus 15% Sales Tax	31.05
	$238.05

Inv. 107	12 July 19XX

To: The Craft Shop
    104 Mains Road
    TWEED HEADS NSW 2485

20 pkts 12 ply wool	$180.00
10 pkts 4 ply wool	75.00
	255.00
Less 10% Trade Discount	25.50
	229.50
Plus 12.5% Sales Tax	28.69
	$258.19

Inv. 108	18 July 19XX

To: J. M. Cummings
    81 Castlereagh Street
    DUBBO NSW 2830

20 wheel covers	$150.00
10 prs seat covers	440.00
	590.00
Less 10% Trade Discount	59.00
	531.00
Plus 15% Sales Tax	79.65
	$610.65

Inv. 109	25 July 19XX

To: D. A. Dixon
    59 Cox Road
    TAREE NSW 2485

20 pkts baby wool	$315.00
Less 10% Trade Discount	31.50
	283.50
Plus 12.5% Sales Tax	35.44
	$318.94

Duplicates of credit notes

CN No. 45	15 July 19XX

To: D. A. Dixon
    59 Cox Road
    TAREE NSW 2485

By return — (Inv. 104)

10 pkts 12 ply wool	$150.00
Less 10% Trade Discount	15.00
	135.00
Plus 25% Sales Tax	16.88
	$151.88

CN No. 46	27 July 19XX

To: The Craft Shop
    104 Mains Road
    TWEED HEADS NSW 2485

By return — (Inv. 107)

5 pkts 12 ply wool	$75.00
Less 10% Trade Discount	7.50
	67.50
Plus 25% Sales Tax	8.44
	$75.94

CN No. 47	30 July 19XX

To: The Hills School
    220 Old Northern Road
    GLENORIE NSW 2157

Overcharge on Inv. 105	$100.00

CHAPTER 3: PREPARATION OF JOURNALS | 137

3F *The Leather Goods Co.*

You are employed as bookkeeper by The Leather Goods Co. Following are the duplicates of invoices and credit notes sent to customers during the month of April 19XX. You are required to enter the details of the transactions in the sales and sales returns and allowances journals. (Use copies of the relevant masters provided on pages 554 and 555.)

Duplicates of invoices

Inv. 94	2 April 19XX
To: Avenue Handbags	
23 Park Street	
HURSTVILLE NSW 2220	
12 ladies' handbags	$240.00
Less 15% Trade Discount	36.00
	204.00
Plus 12.5% Sales Tax	25.50
	$229.50

Inv. 95	5 April 19XX
To: M. A. Sampson & Co.	
90 Chambers Road	
WAGGA WAGGA NSW 2650	
24 key cases	$260.00
Less 15% Trade Discount	39.00
	221.00
Plus 12.5% Sales Tax	27.63
	$248.63

Inv. 96	9 April 19XX
To: Jane's Fashion Store	
58 Queen Street	
WEST RYDE NSW 2114	
12 leather wallets	$240.00
10 ladies' wallets	96.00
	336.00
Less 15% Trade Discount	50.40
	285.60
Plus 12.5% Sales Tax	35.70
	$321.30

Inv. 97	12 April 19XX
To: Trend Setters	
Shop 23, Westfield Centre	
ORANGE NSW 2800	
6 leather belts	$56.00
24 key cases (initialled)	84.00
	140.00
Less 15% Trade Discount	21.00
	119.00
Plus 12.5% Sales Tax	14.88
	$133.88

Inv. 98	20 April 19XX
To: M. A. Sampson & Co.	
90 Chambers Road	
WAGGA WAGGA NSW 2650	
6 briefcases	$540.00
6 'Executive' cases	680.00
	1220.00
Less 15% Trade Discount	183.00
	1037.00
Plus 12.5% Sales Tax	129.63
	$1166.63

Inv. 99	23 April 19XX
To: Avenue Handbags	
23 Park Street	
HURSTVILLE NSW 2220	
10 ladies' handbags	$320.00
8 leather wallets	160.00
	480.00
Less 15% Trade Discount	72.00
	408.00
Plus 12.5% Sales Tax	51.00
	$459.00

Duplicates of credit notes

CN No. 26		15 April 19XX
To:	Jane's Fashion Store	
	58 Queen Street	
	WEST RYDE NSW 2114	
By return (Inv. 96)		
3 leather wallets		$60.00
Less 15% Trade Discount		9.00
		51.00
Plus 12.5% Sales Tax		6.38
		$57.38

CN No. 27		28 April 19XX
To:	M. A. Sampson & Co.	
	90 Chambers Road	
	WAGGA WAGGA NSW 2650	
By return (Inv. 98)		
3 briefcases		$270.00
Less 15% Trade Discount		40.50
		229.50
Plus 12.5% Sales Tax		28.63
		$258.13

Cash receipts journal

The cash receipts journal records details of:
(a) all money (cash/cheques) received by the business, which may consist of:
- amounts received from debtors for sale of trading goods on credit
- cash sales of trading goods
- additional capital (cash contributions) by proprietor/s of the business
- amounts received from the sale of assets (for example, motor vehicles, office equipment)
- amounts received from revenue items (for example, rent revenue from a rental property, interest revenue from investments)

(b) discount allowed — a discount allowed to debtors for prompt payment of accounts
(c) reversal entry for dishonoured cheque.

Format

CASH RECEIPTS JOURNAL OF J. MASON   Fol. CR1

Date	Rec. No.	Particulars (Account to be credited)	Fol.	Discount allowed	Trade debtors	Sales	Sales tax	General	Bank

Source documents

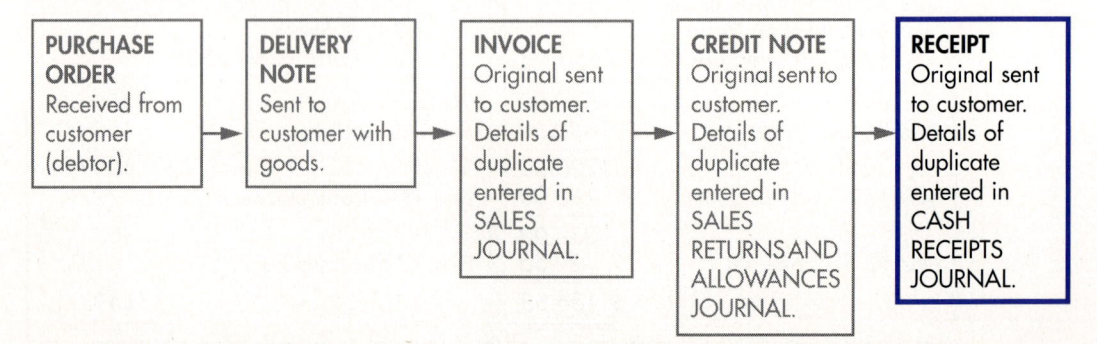

PURCHASE ORDER	DELIVERY NOTE	INVOICE	CREDIT NOTE	RECEIPT
Received from customer (debtor).	Sent to customer with goods.	Original sent to customer. Details of duplicate entered in SALES JOURNAL.	Original sent to customer. Details of duplicate entered in SALES RETURNS AND ALLOWANCES JOURNAL.	Original sent to customer. Details of duplicate entered in CASH RECEIPTS JOURNAL.

The source documents from which the information for the cash receipts journal is obtained are:
(a) duplicate copies of receipts
(b) cash sales invoices/dockets/cash register rolls
(c) bank statement
(d) credit card merchant summaries, for example Bankcard, Visa, MasterCard.

Example
Duplicate of receipts made out by J. Mason

Rec. No. 23 Date: *29/1/19XX* Rec'd from *M. ADAMS* the sum of *Two hundred & nine dollars* For: *Payment of Account* Cash/Chq. $209.00 Discount 11.00 Amt Owing $220.00	Rec. No. 24 Date: *30/1/19XX* Rec'd from *J. ABBOTT* the sum of *Four hundred & ninety-eight dollars twenty cents* For: *Payment of Account* Cash/Chq. $498.20 Discount 31.80 Amt Owing $530.00	Rec. No. 25 Date: *31/1/19XX* Rec'd from *L. WELLS* the sum of *One hundred dollars* For: *Payment on Account* Cash/Chq. $100.00
Rec. No. 26 Date: *31/1/19XX* Rec'd from *J. MASON* the sum of *One thousand dollars* For: *Capital (additional money paid in by owner)* Cash/Chq. $1000.00	Rec. No. 27 Date: *31/1/19XX* Rec'd from *REALTY CO.* the sum of *Four hundred dollars* For: *Rent Revenue* Cash/Chq. $400.00	Rec. No. 28 Date: *31/1/19XX* Rec'd from *OFFICE SUPPLIERS* the sum of *Twenty-five dollars* For: *Office Equipment (sale of calculator)* Cash/Chq. $25.00

Cash sales dockets

No. 81
Date: *5/1/19XX*
 	
Sales $127.50
Sales Tax   22.50
               $150.00
	No. 82
	Date: *10/1/19XX*
	
	Sales $180.00
	Sales Tax 20.00
	               $200.00
		No. 83
		Date: *29/1/19XX*
		
		Total Sales $23.50

Entering transactions in the cash receipts journal

Information from the receipts and cash sales invoices/dockets/cash register rolls is entered into the cash receipts journal as follows:

CASH RECEIPTS JOURNAL OF J. MASON   Fol. CRX

Date	Rec. No.	Particulars (Account to be credited)	Fol.	Discount allowed	Trade debtors	Sales	Sales tax	General	Bank*
19XX Jan. 5	CS	Sales				127.50	22.50		150.00
10	CS	Sales				180.00	20.00		200.00
29	23	M. Adams		11.00	209.00				
	CS	Sales				23.50			232.50
30	24	J. Abbott		31.80	498.20				498.20
31	25	L. Wells			100.00				
	26	Capital						1000.00	
	27	Rent Revenue						400.00	
	28	Office Equipment						25.00	1525.00
				42.80	807.20	331.00	42.50	1425.00	2605.70

Note: The total amount banked each day is entered in the 'Bank' column with a line ruled under all amounts that make up the total banked. This provides a record of daily banking and is useful for comparing the firm's cash records with those of the bank as the bank statement shows only total amount of deposits.

EXERCISE 3.20   K. Dominic & Sons

You are employed as bookkeeper for K. Dominic & Sons. You are required to enter the cash receipts journal from the following duplicates of receipts and cash sales dockets for money received during the month of May 19XX. (Use a copy of the cash receipts journal master provided on page 556.)

Note: When money has been received from debtors (personal accounts), the receipt will show 'Payment of Account'; that is, payment is being made for total amount owing, or 'Payment on Account' (that is, part payment). The name of the debtor is shown after 'From:'. Enter the name of the debtor in the 'Trade debtors' column and the discount in the 'Discount allowed' column. This is necessary as these amounts together make the total amount owed by the trade debtor.

When payment is being made for non-personal accounts, enter the *name* of the account (for example, Capital, Rent Received, Office Equipment) in the 'General' column. Do *not* enter the name of the person or firm to whom the receipt is made out. As these monies have been received directly (by cheque or cash), the name of the person to whom the receipt is made out is not necessary.

When entering amounts from cash sales invoices/dockets/cash register rolls, enter the name of the account as sales and the amount in the 'Sales' column. Sales tax is recorded in the 'Sales tax' column.

Duplicates of receipts

Rec. No. 201 Date: *2/5/19XX* Rec'd from *J. WADE* the sum of *Four hundred & ninety dollars fifty cents* For: *Payment of Account* Cash/Chq. $409.50 Discount 10.50 Amt Owing $420.00	Rec. No. 202 Date: *10/5/19XX* Rec'd from *L. PEARSON & CO.* the sum of *Five hundred dollars* For: *Rent Revenue* Cash/Chq. $500.00	Rec. No. 203 Date: *10/5/19XX* Rec'd from *K. DOMINIC* the sum of *Ten thousand dollars* For: *Additional Capital* Cash/Chq. $10 000.00
Rec. No. 204 Date: *28/5/19XX* Rec'd from *R. COTTER & SONS* the sum of *Two hundred & eighty-nine dollars fourteen cents* For: *Payment of Account* Cash/Chq. $289.14 Discount 8.44 Amt Owing $297.58	Rec. No. 205 Date: *28/5/19XX* Rec'd from *WOOD CAR SALES* the sum of *Five thousand dollars* For: *Motor Vehicle (sold for cash)* Cash/Chq. $5000.00	Rec. No. 206 Date: *29/5/19XX* Rec'd from *M. BYRNES* the sum of *One hundred dollars* For: *Payment on Account* Cash/Chq. $100.00

Cash sales dockets

No. 44
Date: *9/5/19XX*
 	
Sales $467.50
Sales Tax   82.50
                 $550.00
	No. 45
	Date: *22/5/19XX*
	
	Sales $200.60
	Sales Tax 35.40
	                 $236.00
		No. 46
		Date: *28/5/19XX*
		
		Sales $417.40
		Sales Tax 62.60
		                 $480.00

EXERCISE 3.21 — B. James & Co.

You are employed as bookkeeper for B. James & Co. You are required to enter the cash receipts journal from the following duplicates of receipts made out and cash sales dockets for money received during the month of April 19XX. (Use a copy of the cash receipts journal master provided on page 556.)

Duplicates of receipts

Rec. No. 301
Date: 10/4/19XX

Rec'd from D. BASSETT
the sum of Eighty dollars

For: Office Equipment
(Cash sale of printer)

Cash/Chq.	$80.00

Rec. No. 302
Date: 20/4/19XX

Rec'd from A. COLLINS
the sum of Seventy dollars twenty cents

For: Payment of Account

Cash/Chq.	$70.20
Discount	1.80
Amt Owing	$72.00

Rec. No. 303
Date: 20/4/19XX

Rec'd from B. JAMES
the sum of Twelve thousand dollars

For: Capital (Additional money paid in by owner)

Cash/Chq.	$12 000.00

Rec. No. 304
Date: 20/4/19XX

Rec'd from CORELLA PRIVATE HOSPITAL
the sum of Three hundred & seventy-nine dollars twenty-eight cents

For: Payment of Account

Cash/Chq.	$379.28
Discount	9.72
Amt Owing	$389.00

Rec. No. 305
Date: 25/4/19XX

Rec'd from D. SIMMS
the sum of Five hundred dollars

For: Office Equipment
(Cash sale of computer)

Cash/Chq.	$500.00

Rec. No. 306
Date: 29/4/19XX

Rec'd from E. & J. WHITE
the sum of Three hundred & ten dollars forty cents

For: Payment of Account

Cash/Chq.	$310.40
Discount	9.60
Amt Owing	$320.00

Cash sales dockets

No. 44
Date: 12/4/19XX

Sales	$172.70
Sales Tax	30.50
	$203.20

No. 45
Date: 15/4/19XX

Sales	$348.50
Sales Tax	61.50
	$410.00

No. 46
Date: 25/4/19XX

Sales	$516.40
Sales Tax	92.10
	$608.50

EXERCISE 3.22 Trend Fashions

You are employed as bookkeeper for Trend Fashions. You are required to enter the cash receipts journal from the following duplicates of receipts made out and cash sales dockets for money received during the month of February 19XX. (Use a copy of the cash receipts journal on page 556.)

Duplicates of receipts

Rec. No. 75 Date: *15/2/19XX* Rec'd from *R. MORGAN* the sum of *One hundred dollars* For: *Office Furniture (Desk sold for cash)* Cash/Chq. $100.00	Rec. No. 76 Date: *20/2/19XX* Rec'd from *KIM FASHIONS* the sum of *Six hundred dollars* For: *Rent Revenue* Cash/Chq. $600.00	Rec. No. 77 Date: *21/2/19XX* Rec'd from *THE DRESS SHOP* the sum of *Two hundred & ninety-six dollars* For: *Payment of Account* Cash/Chq. $296.00 Discount 24.00 Amt Owing $320.00
Rec. No. 78 Date: *23/2/19XX* Rec'd from *JANE'S FASHION STORE* the sum of *Two hundred & forty-six dollars forty-five cents* For: *Payment of Account* Cash/Chq. $246.45 Discount 18.55 Amt Owing $265.00	Rec. No. 79 Date: *27/2/19XX* Rec'd from *H TAYLOR & CO.* the sum of *Four hundred & ninety-seven dollars seventy-six cents* For: *Payment of Account* Cash/Chq. $497.76 Discount 34.24 $532.00	Rec. No. 80 Date: *27/2/19XX* Rec'd from *DALE & JAMES* the sum of *Eighty-eight dollars* For: *Office Equipment (Cash register sold for cash)* Cash/Chq. $88.00

Cash sales dockets

No. 210 Date: *15/2/19XX* Sales $168.30 Sales Tax 29.70 $198.00	No. 211 Date: *18/2/19XX* Sales $476.00 Sales Tax 84.00 $560.00	No. 212 Date: *27/2/19XX* Sales $471.20 Sales Tax 83.20 $554.40

Putting it together

3G Moore Camera Traders

You are employed as bookkeeper for Moore Camera Traders. From the duplicates of invoices and credit notes and receipts sent to customers and cash sales dockets for the month of March 19XX, you are required to enter the transactions in the sales, sales returns and allowances and cash receipts journals respectively. (Use copies of the relevant masters provided on pages 554–556.)

Duplicates of invoices

Inv. 926	4 March 19XX
To: D. Hunt & Sons	
47 Kingston Road	
CRONULLA NSW 2230	
2 x reflex cameras	$480.00
Less 10% Trade Discount	48.00
	432.00
Plus 25% Sales Tax	108.00
	$540.00

Inv. 927	6 March 19XX
To: M. Holland	
213 Holmes Street	
CAMPBELLTOWN NSW 2560	
2 x auto focus cameras	$1224.00
Less 10% Trade Discount	122.40
	1101.60
Plus 25% Sales Tax	275.40
	$1377.00

Inv. 928	12 March 19XX
To: H. Rayner	
52 Spelson Road	
KIAMA NSW 2535	
1 x video unit	$2169.00
Less 10% Trade Discount	216.90
	1952.10
Plus 25% Sales Tax	488.03
	$2440.13

Inv. 929	24 March 19XX
To: M. Holland	
213 Holmes Street	
CAMPBELLTOWN NSW 2560	
20 rolls x 35 mm film	$210.00
Less 10% Trade Discount	21.00
	189.00
Plus 25% Sales Tax	47.25
	$236.25

Inv. 930	24 March 19XX
To: St David's School	
17 Fraser Street	
HABERFIELD NSW 2045	
1 x video camera	$2470.00
Less Special Discount	120.00
	$2350.00
Sales Tax Exempt	

Inv. 931	28 March 19XX
To: D. Hunt & Sons	
47 Kingston Road	
CRONULLA NSW 2230	
1 x zoom lens	$289.00
Less 10% Trade Discount	28.90
	260.10
Plus 25% Sales Tax	65.03
	$325.13

Duplicates of credit notes

CN No. 156	24 March 19XX

To: M. Holland
     213 Holmes Street
     CAMPBELLTOWN NSW 2560

By return — faulty goods (Inv. 927)

1 × auto focus camera	$612.00
Less 10% Trade Discount	61.20
	550.80
Plus 25% Sales Tax	137.70
	$688.50

CN No. 157	24 March 19XX

To: St David's School
     17 Fraser Road
     HABERFIELD NSW 2045

Overcharge Inv. 930 $200.00

Duplicates of receipts

Rec. No. 121
Date: *12/3/19XX*

Rec'd from *D. MOORE*
the sum of *One thousand five hundred dollars*

For: *Capital (Additional money paid in by owner)*

Cash/Chq. $1500.00

Rec. No. 122
Date: *15/3/19XX*

Rec'd from *EVANS & ROSS*
the sum of *Four hundred & eighty dollars*

For: *Rent Revenue*

Cash/Chq. $480.00

Rec. No. 123
Date: *22/3/19XX*

Rec'd from *M. HOLLAND*
the sum of *Six hundred & fifty-four dollars eight cents*

For: *Payment of Account*

Cash/Chq.	$654.08
Discount	34.42
Amt Owing	$688.50

Rec. No. 124
Date: *25/3/19XX*

Rec'd from *ST DAVID'S SCHOOL*
the sum of *One thousand dollars*

For: *Payment on Account*

Cash/Chq. $1000.00

Rec. No. 125
Date: *30/3/19XX*

Rec'd from *D. HUNT & SONS*
the sum of *Five hundred & thirteen dollars*

For: *Payment of Account*

Cash/Chq.	$513.00
Discount	27.00
Amt Owing	$540.00

Rec. No. 126
Date: *31/3/19XX*

Rec'd from *ST DAVID'S SCHOOL*
the sum of *One thousand & fifty-one dollars sixty-four cents*

For: *Payment of Account*

Cash/Chq.	$1051.64
Discount	98.36
Amt Owing	$1150.00

Cash sales dockets

No. 24		No. 25		No. 26	
Date: 12/3/19XX		Date: 18/3/19XX		Date: 22/3/19XX	
Sales	$83.70	Sales	$98.60	Sales	$41.20
Sales Tax	14.80	Sales Tax	17.40	Sales Tax	7.30
	$98.50		$116.00		$48.50

No. 27		No. 28		No. 29	
Date: 25/3/19XX		Date: 30/3/19XX		Date: 31/3/19XX	
Sales	$350.20	Sales	$87.32	Sales	$60.76
Sales Tax	61.80	Sales Tax	15.40	Sales Tax	10.72
	$412.00		$102.72		$71.48

3H K. Preston Pty Ltd

You are employed as bookkeeper for K. Preston Pty Ltd. From the duplicates of invoices and credit notes and receipts sent to customers and cash sales dockets for the month of August 19XX, you are required to enter the transactions in the sales, sales returns and allowances and cash receipts journals respectively. (Use copies of the relevant masters provided on pages 554–556.)

Duplicates of invoices

Inv. 561	3 August 19XX
To: Chester Private Hospital	
45 Saxon Road	
BELMONT WA 6104	
For: Trading goods	$295.00
Less Special Discount	25.00
	$270.00
Sales Tax Exempt	

Inv. 562	5 August 19XX
To: N. Coleman & Co.	
127 Jacaranda Avenue	
MOSMAN PARK WA 6012	
For: Trading goods	$461.50
Less 15% Trade Discount	69.23
	392.27
Plus 20% Sales Tax	78.45
	$470.72

Inv. 563	15 August 19XX
To: A. Sayer Pty Ltd 15 Ninth Avenue ESPERANCE WA 6450	
For: Trading goods	$181.60
Less 15% Trade Discount	27.24
	154.36
Plus 20% Sales Tax	30.87
	$185.23

Inv. 564	15 August 19XX
To: N. Coleman & Co. 127 Jacaranda Avenue MOSMAN PARK WA 6012	
For: Trading goods	$432.75
Less 15% Trade Discount	64.91
	367.84
Plus 12.5% Sales Tax	45.98
	$413.82

Inv. 565	20 August 19XX
To: Wright & Day 23 Oxford Road ALBANY WA 6012	
For: Trading goods	$124.70
Less 10% Trade Discount	12.47
	112.23
Plus 20% Sales Tax	22.45
	$134.68

Inv. 566	22 August 19XX
To: D. Hartman 91 Westleigh Street BUNBURY WA 6012	
For: Trading goods	$ 98.62
Less 15% Trade Discount	14.79
	83.83
Plus 20% Sales Tax	16.77
	$100.60

Inv. 567	24 August 19XX
To: St Paul's Private School 45 Saxon Road BELMONT WA 6012	
For: Trading goods	$369.00
Less Special Discount	40.00
	$329.00
Sales Tax Exempt	

Inv. 568	30 August 19XX
To: A. Sayer Pty Ltd 15 Ninth Avenue ESPERANCE WA 6012	
For: Trading goods	$300.19
Less 10% Trade Discount	30.02
	270.17
Plus 17.5% Sales Tax	47.28
	$317.45

Duplicates of credit notes

CN No. 152	28 August 19XX
To: N. Coleman & Co. 91 Westleigh Street BUNBURY WA 6230	
By return — faulty goods (Inv. 562)	
Trading goods	$115.38
Less 15% Trade Discount	17.31
	98.07
Plus 20% Sales Tax	19.61
	$117.68

CN No. 153	28 August 19XX
To: Wright & Day 23 Oxford Road ALBANY WA 6530	
By return — oversupply (Inv. 565)	
Trading goods	$49.31
Less 10% Trade Discount	4.93
	44.38
Plus 20% Sales Tax	8.88
	$53.26

```
CN No. 154              30 August 19XX

To:  Chester Private Hospital
     45 Saxon Road
     BELMONT WA 6104

Overcharge Inv. 561         $10.00
```

Duplicates of receipts

Rec. No. 72 Date: *5/8/19XX* Rec'd from *GEORGE'S MOTORS* the sum of *Two thousand dollars* For: *Motor Vehicle (car sold for cash)* Cash/Chq. $2000.00	Rec. No. 73 Date: *10/8/19XX* Rec'd from *K. PRESTON* the sum of *One thousand two hundred dollars* For: *Capital (additional money paid in by owner)* Cash/Chq. $1200.00	Rec. No. 74 Date: *15/8/19XX* Rec'd from *N. COLEMAN & CO.* the sum of *Three hundred & twenty dollars* For: *Payment of Account* Cash/Chq. $320.00 Discount 33.00 Amt Owing $353.00
Rec. No. 75 Date: *26/8/19XX* Rec'd from *D. HARTMAN* the sum of *Sixty-four dollars* For: *Payment of Account* Cash/Chq. $64.00 Discount 3.06 Amt Owing $67.06	Rec. No. 76 Date: *30/8/19XX* Rec'd from *WRIGHT & DAY* the sum of *Eighty-three dollars eighty-six cents* For: *Payment of Account* Cash/Chq. $78.98 Discount 2.44 Amt Owing $81.42	Rec. No. 77 Date: *31/8/19XX* Rec'd from *A. SAYER PTY LTD* the sum of *Two hundred dollars* For: *Payment on Account* Cash/Chq. $200.00

Cash sales dockets

No. 12
Date: *5/8/19XX*
 	
Cash Sales $112.50
Sales Tax   14.08
 	
               $126.58
	No. 13
	Date: *15/8/19XX*
	
	Cash Sales $49.70
	Sales Tax 9.94
	
	               $59.64
		No. 14
		Date: *26/8/19XX*
		
		Cash Sales $238.59
		
		Sales Tax Exempt

GENERAL JOURNAL MISCELLANEOUS ENTRIES

Following are entries which, because of their nature, cannot be entered into the trading journals. They are entered into the general journal and, although these transactions occur infrequently in the life of the business, it is important to know the correct procedures for recording them. Some of these entries involve *cash* in the transaction and, with the exception of the opening entry, all cash which comes into or goes out of the business must be recorded in either the cash receipts or the cash payments journal. In these transactions, therefore, it is necessary to make an entry in the general journal *and* in the relevant cash journal, according to the type of transaction. The following examples are based on the transactions of J. Mason whose transactions are recorded in the demonstration exercises, and form part of his ongoing business activity.

Purchase and sale of non-current assets on credit

Non-current assets are those assets that the business owns or controls and which are not intended for resale until their usefulness to the business has been exhausted. Examples of these are plant and machinery, motor vehicles, office equipment and furniture and fittings.

When a non-current asset is purchased or sold on credit, the business acquires a sundry (non-trade) creditor and a sundry (non-trade) debtor. Details of transactions with sundry debtors and sundry creditors are recorded separately from those with trade debtors and trade creditors.

When making general journal entries it is necessary to analyse each transaction to determine:

(a) which accounts are affected by the transaction
(b) what type of accounts (for example, Asset, Liability, Owner's Equity, Revenue or Expense)
(c) whether there is an increase or decrease in the accounts affected as a result of the transaction
(d) which account/s should be debited and which account/s should be credited to record increases or decreases.

Purchase of a non-current asset on credit

Example
On 5 January 19XX, J. Mason purchased a computer on credit for $12 000 from Propert's Computers.

Accounts affected:
- Office Equipment — asset account — increase
- Sundry Creditor — Propert's Computers — liability account — increase.

Apply the debit/credit rule:

| *Debit* — to increase asset account. | *Debit* — to decrease liability account. |
| *Credit* — to decrease asset account. | *Credit* — to increase liability account. |

General journal entry:

> *Debit* — Office Equipment account
> *Credit* — Sundry Creditor — Prophet's Computers account.

The asset account, Office Equipment, is debited to increase the value of this account to reflect the purchase of the computer. At the same time, the business has acquired a sundry creditor, a liability of the business. The Sundry Creditor's account is credited to record the amount owing by J. Mason. The general journal entry is as follows:

EXTRACT OF GENERAL JOURNAL OF J. MASON

DEBIT | | | | | | CREDIT | | Fol. GJ1

Accounts receivable	Accounts payable	General	Date	Particulars	Fol.	Accounts receivable	Accounts payable	General
		12 000.00	19XX Jan. 5	Office Equipment Sundry Creditor — Propert's Computers Purchase of computer on credit.				12 000.00*

Note: The credit entry for a sundry creditor is entered in the 'General' column. The 'accounts payable' column is used to record details of transactions with trade creditors *only*, so that the totals of these columns may be posted to the Accounts Payable Control account in the general ledger.

Sale of a non-current asset on credit

Example

On 7 January 19XX, J. Mason sold a dot matrix printer, on credit, to H. Larson for $150.

Accounts affected:
- Sundry Debtor — H. Larson — asset account — increase
- Office Equipment — asset account — decrease.

Apply the debit/credit rule:

> *Debit* — to increase asset account.
> *Credit* — to decrease asset account.

General journal entry:

> *Debit* — Sundry Debtor — H. Larson account
> *Credit* — Office Equipment account.

This entry increases the amount owed to the business by a sundry debtor (an asset) and correspondingly decreases the balance in the appropriate 'asset' account to reflect the sale of the asset.

Remember:

> Debit to *increase* an asset account. | Debit to *decrease* a liability account.
> Credit to *decrease* an asset account. | Credit to *increase* a liability account.

The general journal entry is as follows:

EXTRACT OF GENERAL JOURNAL OF J. MASON

DEBIT — CREDIT — Fol. GJ1

Accounts receivable	Accounts payable	General	Date	Particulars	Fol.	Accounts receivable	Accounts payable	General
		150.00*	19XX Jan. 7	H. Larson — Sundry Debtor Office Equipment Sale of printer on credit.				150.00

Note: The debit entry for a sundry debtor is entered in the 'General' column. The accounts receivable column is used to record details of transactions with trade debtors *only*, so that the totals of these columns may be posted to the Accounts Receivable Control account in the general ledger.

Inventory (stock) drawings by owner

The term *inventory* (or stock) *drawings* is used when the owner of a business takes goods from the business for personal use.

Withdrawals of inventory by the owner are recorded in the Drawings account. This is a *negative* owner's equity account because it ultimately decreases the owner's equity Capital account. It is kept separately from the Capital account, and is shown on the balance sheet at the end of the reporting period as a deduction from the Capital account. The debit/credit rule for the owner's equity (Capital) account is:

> *Debit* — to decrease Owner's Equity account.
> *Credit* — to increase Owner's Equity account.

However, the debit/credit rule for the Drawings account is the reverse of that for the Capital account.

> *Debit* — to increase Drawings account.
> *Credit* — to decrease Drawings account.

Inventory drawings are taken from the trading goods which have been purchased for the purpose of resale in order to make a profit. Goods purchased in order to make a profit are referred to as 'purchases'. Therefore, when inventory withdrawals by the owner occur, the value of 'purchases' is decreased.

When inventory drawings occur, the two accounts affected are:
- Drawings — a negative owner's equity account — increase
- Purchases — an expense account — decrease

Example

On 23 January 19XX, J. Mason took from the business for personal use, trading goods valued at $50.

Apply the debit/credit rule:

| Debit — to increase negative owner's equity account. | Debit — to increase expense account. |
| Credit — to decrease negative owner's equity account. | Credit — to decrease expense account. |

Note that as the Drawings account is a negative owner's equity account, it is treated in the opposite manner to a normal owner's equity account; that is, debit to decrease and credit to increase.

General journal entry:

Debit — Drawings account
Credit — Purchases account.

The Drawings account is increased by the value of the inventory withdrawn by the owner and the Purchases account is decreased by the same amount. The general journal entry is as follows:

EXTRACT OF GENERAL JOURNAL OF J. MASON

DEBIT / CREDIT — Fol. GJ1

Accounts receivable	Accounts payable	General	Date	Particulars	Fol.	Accounts receivable	Accounts payable	General
		50.00	19XX Jan. 23	Drawings Purchases Owner took goods for personal use.				50.00

Interest expense charged by creditors on overdue accounts

If a business, for various reasons, neglects to pay an account by the due date and allows it to remain outstanding for a number of months, it may find itself in the position of having to pay **interest** to a creditor.

Example

J. Mason owes the sum of $200 to B. Allar and it is six months overdue. J. Mason's trading terms with this trade creditor allow him to be charged interest on the overdue account at the rate of 5% per annum. The accounts affected are:

- Interest Expense — expense account
- B. Allar (trade creditor) — liability account.

Apply the debit/credit rule:

| Debit — to increase expense account. | Debit — to decrease liability account. |
| Credit — to decrease expense account. | Credit — to increase liability account. |

General journal entry:
> *Debit* — Interest Expense account
> *Credit* — B. Allar account.

Interest expense is debited with the amount of interest payable, being 5% (calculated as $200 \times 5\% = \$10 \div 2 = \$5$), to increase the amount of interest expense by that amount. Expense accounts are maintained in the general ledger. B. Allar's account is credited to increase the amount owing to this creditor by the amount of interest expense payable. The general journal entry is as follows:

EXTRACT OF GENERAL JOURNAL OF J. MASON   Fol. GJX

DEBIT						CREDIT		
Accounts receivable	Accounts payable	General	Date	Particulars	Fol.	Accounts receivable	Accounts payable	General
		5.00	19XX Jan. 31	Interest Expense B. Allar Interest payable on creditor's overdue acount.			5.00*	

Interest revenue (interest charged on overdue debtors' accounts)

When a debtor, for various reasons, neglects to pay an account by the due date and allows it to remain outstanding for a number of months, the debtor may be charged interest on the outstanding amount.

*The 'Accounts Payable' column is used to record details of transactions with trade creditors so that the total of this column may be posted to the credit side of the Accounts Payable Control account in the general ledger.

Example
J. Glacken's account has been outstanding for 4 months. On 31 January 19XX, J. Mason charges J. Glacken interest at the rate of 4% per annum on the outstanding amount of $115. The accounts affected are:
- J. Glacken (trade debtor) — asset account
- Interest Revenue — revenue account.

Apply the debit/credit rule:

Debit — to *increase* an expense account. *Credit* — to *decrease* an expense account.	*Debit* — to *decrease* a revenue account. *Credit* — to *increase* a revenue account.

General journal entry:
> *Debit* — J. Glacken account
> *Credit* — Interest Revenue account.

J. Glacken's account is debited with the amount of interest charged, being $1.53 (calculated as $115.00 × 4% = $4.60 ÷ 3 = $1.53), to increase the amount owed by this debtor. Interest Revenue, a revenue account, is credited to increase this revenue account by the amount charged to the debtor. Revenue accounts are maintained in the general ledger.

EXTRACT OF GENERAL JOURNAL OF J. MASON

DEBIT						CREDIT		Fol. GJ1
Accounts receivable	Accounts payable	General	Date	Particulars	Fol.	Accounts receivable	Accounts payable	General
1.53*			19XX Jan. 31	J. Glacken Interest Revenue Interest charged on debtor's overdue account.				1.53

*The 'Accounts Receivable' column is used to record details of transactions with trade debtors so that the total of this column may be posted to the debit side of the Accounts Receivable Control account in the general ledger.

Bad debts written off

During the life of any business it becomes apparent that some debtors are unable, for various reasons, to settle their accounts. When it becomes obvious that an amount of money owing to the business by the debtor is irrecoverable, it is written off as a bad debt.

Example

It has become obvious that J. Glacken, a debtor of J. Mason, will never be able to pay his account of $116.53. On 31 March 19XX, J. Mason decides to write the amount off as a bad debt.

The two accounts affected are:
- Bad Debts — expense account
- J. Glacken (trade debtor) — asset account.

Apply the debit/credit rule:

Debit — to *increase* an expense account.	*Debit* — to *decrease* an asset account.
Credit — to *decrease* an expense account.	*Credit* — to *increase* an asset account.

General journal entry:
  Debit — Bad Debts account
  Credit — J. Glacken account.

The Bad Debts account is an expense account and is debited to record the increase in bad debts expense. Expense accounts are maintained in the general ledger. J. Glacken's account is credited with the amount written off, to remove details of the outstanding amount from the accounting records. The general journal entry is as follows:

EXTRACT OF GENERAL JOURNAL OF J. MASON

DEBIT   CREDIT   Fol. GJ1

Accounts receivable	Accounts payable	General	Date	Particulars	Fol.	Accounts receivable	Accounts payable	General
		116.53	19XX Mar. 31	Bad Debts J. Glacken Amount written off as irrecoverable.		116.53*		

The following examples of bad debts partly written off and bad debts recovered are for your information only and are not included as transactions to be worked in this text.

Bad debts partly written off

When a debtor has been declared bankrupt, the business has a claim on the assets of the debtor. However, there may be other creditors, also, with a claim on those assets, so each creditor may recoup only a percentage of the amount owing; for example, he or she may receive only 40 cents from every dollar owed. In this case the amount of debt to be written off is decreased by the amount recouped.

*The 'Accounts Receivable' column is used to record details of transactions with trade debtors so that the total of this column may be posted to the credit side of the Accounts Receivable Control account in the general ledger.

Example

Let us suppose that J. Mason recoups 40 cents in the dollar for J. Glacken's debt of $116.53. J. Mason recovers $46.61 ($116.53 × 0.40c), which is recorded as a receipt of cash in the cash receipts journal. This reduces the amount irrecoverable in J. Glacken's account to $69.92 and this amount is then written off in the manner described above.

Bad debts recovered

Occasionally, a debtor whose account has been written off as irrecoverable manages to overcome the financial difficulties and is able to reimburse creditors for their losses. This enables the debtor to regain his or her credit standing among business peers.

Example

We will assume that J. Mason receives a cheque for $116.53 on 18 June 19XX from J. Glacken, whose account for the same amount was previously written off as irrecoverable. J. Glacken's account is reopened and his account debited with this amount. An account, Bad Debts Recovered, is credited with the same amount. This reduces the amount of loss to J. Mason, incurred when J. Glacken's account was written off as a bad debt. The Bad Debts Recovered account offsets the Bad Debts account, thus having the effect of reducing the Bad Debts expense for J. Mason. The amount is then recorded in the cash receipts journal to record the receipt of J. Glacken's cheque for $116.53 in settlement of his account, which is reopened when he is restored as a debtor in good standing.

Transfers between accounts (contra entries)

When a business conducts credit sales and credit purchases with the *same person or firm*, accounts are generally settled by 'setting off' one amount against the other. This avoids both parties involved having to exchange cheques for amounts outstanding and allows accounts to be settled promptly. This type of transaction is known as a contra transaction and is recorded by an entry in the general journal.

Example

For demonstration purposes, let us assume that L. Burrough is both a trade creditor *and* a trade debtor of J. Mason. Consider the following transactions.

19XX
Mar. 2 J. Mason sells goods to L. Burrough (trade debtor) for $200
     8 J. Mason purchases goods from L. Burrough (trade creditor) for $250

When the two amounts are set off against each other, at the end of the month, J. Mason owes L. Burrough (trade creditor) an amount of $50. (*Caution*: Do *not* use this amount when recording the transaction.) On 31 March 19XX, L. Burrough's account is settled by contra.

Apply the debit/credit rule:

| Debit — to increase asset account. | Debit — to decrease liability account. |
| Credit — to decrease asset account. | Credit — to increase asset account. |

1. Select the *lesser* amount involved in the two transactions, that is $200.
   Debit — L. Burrough (trade creditor) — $200 (to decrease liability account)
   Credit — L. Burrough (trade debtor) — $200 (to decrease asset account).
2. This leaves a balance of $50 owing by J. Mason who would be required to forward a cheque to L. Burrough to settle the account. When the account of L. Burrough (trade creditor) is debited, the amount owing by J. Mason is reduced to $50. When the account of L. Burrough (trade debtor) is credited, the account balance is reduced to zero.

The general journal entry is as follows:

EXTRACT OF GENERAL JOURNAL OF J. MASON

DEBIT | | | | | | | CREDIT | | Fol. GJ1

Accounts receivable	Accounts payable	General	Date	Particulars	Fol.	Accounts receivable	Accounts payable	General
	200.00*		19XX Mar. 31	L. Burrough (creditor) L. Burrough (debtor) Account settled by contra.		200.00**		

*The 'Accounts Payable' column is used to record details of transactions with trade creditors so that the total of this column may be posted to the debit side of the Accounts Payable Control account in the general ledger.

**The 'Accounts Receivable' column is used to record details of transactions with trade debtors so that the total of this column may be posted to the credit side of the Accounts Receivable Control account in the general ledger.

Correction of errors

It is a generally accepted rule of bookkeeping that errors should be corrected by an entry in the general journal. This helps to minimise the risk of fraudulent manipulation of figures in the accounting records. Errors which are detected after the monthly balance procedures, are corrected by means of general journal entries.

If the error is such that only *one* side of a double-entry account is incorrect because of a simple clerical error, it is *not* possible to use a general journal entry. In this case you are permitted to rule out the incorrect figure and neatly insert the correct figure above the incorrect one. *Erasers and correcting fluid must not be used.* This type of error is usually detected when the trial balance is being prepared and the totals of the debit and credit columns do not agree.

The trial balance is a listing of all account balances at a particular time. Under the double-entry system of bookkeeping total debits are, at all times, equal to total credits.

It is important to remember that adjustments made to accounts of trade creditors and trade debtors in the accounts payable and accounts receivable ledgers, must also be reflected in the Accounts Payable and Accounts Receivable Control accounts in the general ledger.

Listed below are examples of errors which may be detected at trial balance:
- amounts posted to wrong accounts
- errors in addition
- figures transposed when recording journals or posting to ledgers (for example, $520 instead of $502), resulting in a wrong amount being recorded
- clerical errors, including errors made in extensions or totals on invoices, recording transactions in journals, or in posting details from journals to ledgers. All of these errors result in incorrect figures being posted to ledger accounts. These errors often remain undetected until customers check their monthly statements, which are based on information extracted from their ledger accounts.

Transposition of figures

Example 1: (Accounts payable)

At the end of the month, J. Mason's financial controller discovers that an amount of $150 for accounts payable creditor, M. Garcia, was incorrectly entered in the general journal opening entry as $510. This means that M. Garcia's amount is overstated by $360 ($510 less $150) resulting in capital being understated by the same amount.

Accounts affected:
- M. Garcia (trade creditor) — liability account
- Capital — owner's equity account.

Apply the debit/credit rule:

Debit — to decrease liability account.	Debit — to decrease owner's equity account.
Credit — to increase liability account.	Credit — to increase owner's equity account.

General journal entry:
  Debit — M. Garcia — with amount of overstatement ($360)
  Credit — Capital — with amount of understatement ($360).

The Accounts Payable (trade creditor's) account, M. Garcia, is debited to reduce the amount owing and the owner's equity account, Capital, is credited to increase the amount of capital. The general journal entry is as follows:

EXTRACT OF GENERAL JOURNAL OF J. MASON   Fol. GJ1

DEBIT						CREDIT		
Accounts receivable	Accounts payable	General	Date	Particulars	Fol.	Accounts receivable	Accounts payable	General
	360.00*		19XX Jan. 24	M. Garcia Capital Correction of error				360.00

*The 'Accounts Payable' column is used to record details of transactions with trade creditors so that the total of this column may be posted to the debit side of the Accounts Payable Control account in the general ledger.

Remember:

Debit — to decrease an owner's equity account.	Credit — to increase an owner's equity account.

Example 2: (Accounts receivable)

After the monthly balancing procedures, it was found that the amount owed to the business by H. Raja (a trade debtor) was recorded in the general journal opening entry of J. Mason as $253 instead of $235. The amount owing by H. Raja has been overstated by $18 ($253 less $235). Capital has also been overstated by the same amount. Accounts affected:
- Capital — owner's equity account
- H. Raja (trade debtor) — asset account.

Apply the debit/credit rule:

Debit — to increase asset account. *Credit* — to decrease asset account.	*Debit* — to decrease owner's equity account. *Credit* — to increase owner's equity account.

General journal entry:
Debit — Capital — with amount of overstatement ($18)
Credit — H. Raja — with amount of overstatement ($18).

The Capital account is debited to reduce the amount of owner's equity and the Trade Debtor's account is credited to reduce the amount owing. The general journal entry is as follows:

EXTRACT OF GENERAL JOURNAL OF J. MASON

DEBIT / CREDIT / Fol. GJ1

Accounts receivable	Accounts payable	General	Date	Particulars	Fol.	Accounts receivable	Accounts payable	General
		18.00	19XX Jan. 10	Capital H. Raja Correction of error.		18.00*		

Following is a simple illustration of the effect on the Capital account, when debtors' and creditor's balances are stated incorrectly. Let us assume that assets for J. Mason total $500 and that creditors' accounts totalling $255 are overstated by $55. The accounting equation is:

*The 'Accounts Receivable' column is used to record details of transactions with trade debtors so that the total of this column may be posted to the credit side of the Accounts Receivable Control account in the general ledger.

   Assets − Liabilities = Owner's Equity
   $500   − $255   = $245.

When the liabilities are reduced by the $55 overstatement, the owner's equity account, Capital, is *increased*. The accounting equation is:

   Assets − Liabilities = Owner's Equity
   $500   − $200   = $300.

However, if we assume that J. Mason's liabilities total $200 and assets, consisting of debtors' accounts totalling $500 are overstated by $50, the accounting equation is:

   Assets − Liabilities = Owner's Equity
   $500   − $200   = $300.

When assets are reduced by the $50 overstatement, the accounting equation is:

   Assets − Liabilities = Owner's Equity
   $450   − $200   = $250.

This results in a *decrease* in the Capital account.

Posting amount to incorrect creditor's account in accounts payable ledger

Example

On 4 January, it was discovered that an amount of $50 owing to H. Lime had been incorrectly credited to P. Eastman's account in the accounts payable ledger. The accounts affected are those of individual creditors in the accounts payable (trade creditors') subsidiary ledger.

Accounts affected are:
- H. Lime (Trade Creditor) — liability account
- P. Eastman (Trade Creditor) — liability account.

Apply the debit/credit rule:

> *Debit* — to decrease liability account.
> *Credit* — to increase liability account.

General journal entry:
Debit — P. Eastman's account (to decrease)
Credit — H. Lime's account (to increase).

The amount of $50 incorrectly credited to P. Eastman is cancelled and H. Lime's account is correctly increased by $50.

When these transactions are posted to the general ledger, the total value of the Accounts Payable Control account remains unaltered as the increase of $50 in H. Lime's account is offset by the cancelling of the amount of $50 from P. Eastman's account. The general journal entry is as follows:

EXTRACT OF GENERAL JOURNAL OF J. MASON

DEBIT | | | | | | CREDIT | | Fol. GJ1

Accounts receivable	Accounts payable	General	Date	Particulars	Fol.	Accounts receivable	Accounts payable	General
	50.00*		19XX Jan. 4	P. Eastman H. Lime Correction of error.			50.00**	

*The 'Accounts Payable' column is used to record details of debit transactions with trade creditors so that the total of this column may be posted to the debit side of the Accounts Payable Control account in the general ledger.

**The 'Accounts Payable' column is used to record details of credit transactions with trade creditors so that the total of this column may be posted to the credit side of the Accounts Payable Control account in the general ledger.

Posting amount to incorrect debtor's account in accounts receivable ledger

Example

On 10 January, J. Mason found that an amount of $30 owed by J. Abbott had been debited, incorrectly, to M. Adams' account in the accounts receivable ledger.

The accounts affected are:
- J. Abbott (trade debtor) — asset account
- M. Adam (trade debtor) — asset account

Apply the debit/credit rule:

> *Debit* — to increase asset account.
> *Credit* — to decrease asset account.

General journal entry:

Debit — J. Abbott's account (to increase)
Credit — M. Adam's account (to decrease).

The amount of $30 incorrectly debited to M. Adams' account is cancelled, and J. Abbott's account is correctly increased by $30.

When these transactions are posted to the general ledger, the total value of the Accounts Receivable Control account remains unaltered as the increase of $30 in J. Abbott's account is offset by cancellation of the amount of $30 from M. Adams' account. The general journal entry is as follows:

EXTRACT OF GENERAL JOURNAL OF J. MASON

Fol. GJX

Accounts receivable (DEBIT)	Accounts payable	General	Date	Particulars	Fol.	Accounts receivable (CREDIT)	Accounts payable	General
30.00*			19XX Jan. 10	J. Abbott M. Adams Correction of error.		30.00**		

*The 'Accounts Receivable' column is used to record details of debit transactions with trade debtors so that the total of this column may be posted to the debit side of the Accounts Receivable Control account in the general ledger.

**The 'Accounts Receivable' column is used to record details of credit transactions with trade debtors so that the total of this column may be posted to the credit side of the Accounts Receivable Control account in the general ledger.

General journal miscellaneous entries

The following is a summary of steps to be followed for
1. Purchase of non-current asset on credit
    Debit — Asset account
    Credit — Sundry Creditor's account

2. Sale of non-current asset on credit
   Debit — Sundry Debtor's account
   Credit — Asset account
3. Inventory drawings by owner (proprietor)
   Debit — Drawings account
   Credit — Purchases account
4. Interest expense charged by creditors on overdue accounts
   Debit — Interest Expense account
   Credit — Trade Creditor's account
5. Interest revenue charged to debtors on overdue accounts
   Debit — Trade Debtor's account
   Credit — Interest Revenue account
6. (a) Bad debts written off
   Debit — Bad Debts account
   Credit — Trade Debtor's account
   (b) Bad debts partly written off
   Debit — Bad Debts account (with amount to be written off)
   Credit — Trade Debtor's account (with amount to be written off)
   Note: Cash received in the above transactions is recorded in the cash receipts journal in the usual manner.
   (c) Bad debts recovered
   Debit — Trade Debtor's account (reopened when cheque received)
   Credit — Bad Debts Recovered account
   Note: Cash received in the above transactions is recorded in the cash receipts journal in the usual manner.
7. Transfer between accounts (contra entries). Select the lesser amount involved in the transaction.
   Debit — Trade Creditor's account
   Credit — Trade Debtor's account
8. Correction of errors. Decide which account/s are involved and which account/s should be increased/decreased.
   - when creditors' accounts are involved
     Debit — creditor's account to reduce balance
     Credit — creditor's account to increase balance
   - when debtors' accounts are involved
     Debit — debtor's account to increase balance
     Credit — debtor's account to increase balance
   - when asset accounts are involved
     Debit — asset account to increase balance
     Credit — asset account to decrease balance
   - when liability accounts are involved
     Debit — liability account to decrease balance
     Credit — liability account to increase balance
   - when owner's equity accounts are involved
     Debit — owner's equity account to decrease balance
     Credit — owner's equity account to increase balance

Putting it together

Shown below are the completed miscellaneous general journal entries for J. Mason for the month of January 19XX.

GENERAL JOURNAL OF J. MASON

Fol. GJ1

\<DEBIT\> Accounts receivable	Accounts payable	General	Date	Particulars	Fol.	\<CREDIT\> Accounts receivable	Accounts payable	General
	50.00		Jan. 4	P. Eastman 　　H. Lime Correction of error.			50.00	
		12 000.00	5	Office Equipment 　　Sundry Creditor — 　　　　Propert's Computers Purchase of computer on credit.				12 000.00
		150.00	7	H. Larson — 　　Sundry Debtor 　　　　Office Equipment Sale of printer on credit.				150.00
30.00			10	J. Abbott 　　M. Adams Correction of error.		30.00		
		18.00		Capital 　　H. Raja Correction of error.		18.00		
		50.00	23	Drawings 　　Purchases Owner took goods for personal use.				50.00
	360.00			M. Garcia 　　Capital Correction of error.				360.00
		5.00	31	Interest Expense 　　B. Allar Interest payable on creditor's overdue account.			5.00	
1.53				J. Glacken 　　Interest Revenue Interest charged on debtor's overdue account.				1.53
		116.53		Bad Debts 　　J. Glacken Bad debt written off.		116.53		
31.53	410.00	12 339.53				164.53	55.00	12 561.53

Total debits ($12 781.06) = Total credits ($12 781.06)

3I K. Dominic & Sons

You are required to enter the following transactions into the general journal of K. Dominic & Sons. (Use a copy of the blank general journal master provided on page 550.)

1. On 5 May 19XX, K. Dominic & Sons purchased a photocopier on credit from Imagemakers Ltd for $10 000
2. On 7 May, an amount of $180 owed by J. Wade, incorrectly debited to M. Byrnes, was corrected.
3. On 16 May 19XX, sold office desk on credit to Ace Secretarial Service for $500.
4. Received advice on 19 May 19XX that G. Mundo was bankrupt. Amount owing of $420 is written off.
5. On 20 May, owner took goods valued at $300 for personal use.
6. On 25 May 19XX, paid interest expense @ 10% per annum to B. Samuel on account of $78 overdue for three months.

3J B. James & Co.

You are required to enter the following transactions into the general journal of B. James & Co. (Use a copy of the blank general journal master provided on page 550.)

1. On 6 April 19XX, F. Nguyen's account of $75 in opening entry was incorrectly recorded and should have been $57.
2. On 8 April, B. James attended to the following posting errors.
   — An amount of $100 owed by Corella Private Hospital and wrongly debited to A. Collins' account was corrected.
   — An amount of $150 owing to King & Co. and wrongly credited to Greenway and Co. was corrected.
3. Laser printer was purchased on credit, on 11 April 19XX, from Technics Ltd, $2000.
4. On 30 April, charged G. McGregor's account, interest on amount of $402 overdue for six months @ 10% per annum.

3K Trend Fashions

You are required to record the following transactions into the general journal of Trend Fashions. (Use a copy of the blank general journal master provided on page 550.)

1. On 7 February, the financial controller for Trend Fashions authorised correction of posting error for amount of $120 which should have been credited to G. Hanna, but was incorrectly credited to W. A. Montey's account.

2. Motor vehicle purchased on credit ($21 000) from Schaeffer Motors on 16 February 19XX.

3. On 18 February 19XX, sold old motor vehicle to R. Mustafa on credit for $9500.

4. Laser printer purchased on credit for $1100 from Compusupply Co., on 22 February 19XX.

5. Sold inkjet printer on credit to H. Rostov for $300 on 22 February 19XX.

6. On 27 February, goods valued at $520 taken by owner for personal use.

CHAPTER 4

Posting to the ledgers

WHEN you have studied the four sections of this chapter and completed the exercises, you should be competent in the following skills. Tick each skill when you have completed the relevant section.

LEARNING OUTCOMES

Section 1 (pages 168–205)
1. Explain the purpose of the general ledger.
2. Post to the general ledger from the following journals, maintaining the accounting equation:
   - general journal
   - accounts payable journals: purchases journal; purchases returns and allowances journal; cash payments journal
   - accounts receivable journals: sales journal; sales returns and allowances journal; cash receipts journal.
3. Extract an accurate trial balance of the general ledger.

Section 2 (pages 205–237)
1. Explain the purpose of the accounts payable ledger.
2. Post to the accounts payable ledger from the following journals, maintaining the accounting equation:
   - general journal
   - purchases journal
   - purchases returns and allowances journal
   - cash payments journal.
3. Prepare a list of creditors' balances and reconcile with the Accounts Payable Control account in the general ledger.
4. Reconcile invoices for payment to creditors:
   - Process, correct and authorise invoices for payment.
   - Identify any discrepancies between invoices and delivery notes and report to nominated person/section for resolution.

- Identify errors in invoice charges and report to nominated person/section for correction.
- Rectify discrepancies and errors as directed.
- Resolve and/or refer credit enquiries to nominated person/section for resolution.

Section 3 (pages 237–285)
1. Explain the purpose of the accounts receivable ledger.
2. Post to the accounts receivable ledger from the following journals, maintaining the accounting equation:
   - general journal
   - sales journal
   - sales returns and allowances journal
   - cash receipts journal.
3. Prepare a list of debtors' balances and reconcile with the Accounts Receivable Control account in the general ledger.
4. Prepare statements for debtors.

Section 4 (pages 286–337)
1. Compare cash records with bank statements.
2. Adjust cash journals for dishonoured cheques, bank fees and direct bank debits; total cash journals and post to general ledger.
3. Prepare a bank reconciliation statement incorporating unpresented cheques and deposits not yet credited.

SECTION 1: THE GENERAL LEDGER

A ledger consists of a collection of accounts. It is used in conjunction with the double-entry system of bookkeeping. Ledgers may be in the form of a book, a card system or part of a computerised accounting package.

The principal ledger used in a business is called the general ledger. All accounts of the business are represented in this ledger. The purpose of the general ledger is:

(a) to classify transactions under account names
(b) to ascertain the balance of each account.

At the end of the month, the accounts are balanced and a trial balance is prepared.

The account format used in this text is the 3-column (statement style) ledger account, as follows.

Date	Particulars	Fol.	Debit	Credit	Balance

Subsidiary ledgers

As a business expands, the amount of credit transactions handled on a daily basis increases. It becomes cumbersome to keep a record of all accounts in the general ledger. Imagine the size of the general ledger for a large organisation if it contained every account, including the balances of individual trade debtors' and trade creditors' accounts.

To overcome this problem, the ledger posting procedure is divided into three sections:
1. principal ledger — the general ledger
2. accounts payable ledger (or trade creditors' ledger)
3. accounts receivable ledger (or trade debtors' ledger).

The subsidiary ledgers are usually divided into a number of sections. For example, they may be divided into names commencing with A–C, D–G, H–M, and so on. This provides the following benefits:
- Work flows continuously.
- Staff are responsible for maintaining small sections, so that a number of people can work on these ledgers at the same time.
- Each section can be balanced independently.
- Money flows into and out of the business on a continuous basis.
- Accounting errors can be easily located.
- Information contained in the general ledger is kept confidential.

Details of all accounts belonging to individual trade creditors are posted to the accounts payable ledger and details of all accounts belonging to individual trade debtors are posted to the accounts receivable ledger.

It is important to remember that the general ledger is still the main ledger into which *all* information relating to the financial dealings of the business

is recorded. Even though itemised details of individual trade creditors' and trade debtors' transactions are recorded in the subsidiary ledgers, the general ledger contains all these details *in total*, in the following two accounts:
1. Accounts Payable Control account, in which *totals* of all transactions with trade creditors are recorded
2. Accounts Receivable Control account, in which *totals* of all transactions with trade debtors are recorded.

You must always post to the control accounts in the general ledger *before* posting to the individual accounts in the subsidiary ledgers.

Posting to the general ledger

At the end of each month:
- the amounts in the journals are posted to the general ledger
- a trial balance is extracted from the balances in the general ledger.

To post from the journals to the ledgers, carry out the following.
1. From the journals, ascertain the names of the accounts to be posted.
2. Set up ledger accounts as per the format shown, following the order designated in the chart of accounts.
3. Decide whether the account is to be debited or credited.
4. Record the following information in the ledger account:
    (a) date
    (b) particulars — the name of the other account/s involved in the transaction (there are always at least two accounts involved in any transaction)
    (c) **folio number** — enter the journal page number in the 'Folio' column as a cross-reference
    (d) amount — entered in either the 'Debit' or 'Credit' column
    (e) account balance — determined by either adding or subtracting from the previous balance according to the account type.
5. Insert the ledger folio reference number in the 'Folio' column of the journal.

Journals are posted to the ledgers in the following order.
1. General journal
2. Accounts payable journals
    (a) Purchases journal
    (b) Purchases returns and allowances journal
    (c) Cash payments journal
3. Accounts receivable journals
    (a) Sales journal
    (b) Sales returns and allowances journal
    (c) Cash receipts journal

The general journal is posted before the trading journals so that opening balances for asset, liability and owner's equity accounts are recorded in the appropriate accounts in the general ledger.

Posting from the general journal

The first entry posted from the general journal is the opening entry. Steps for posting from both the basic format and the columnar format are listed below.

Basic format

In the general ledger, carry out the following.
1. *Debit* amounts listed against individual accounts in the 'Debit' column, for example Land, Buildings, etc. (see ① below).
2. *Credit* amounts listed against individual accounts in the 'Credit' column, for example Mortgage and Capital (see ② below).
3. *Debit* the Accounts Receivable Control account with the amount in the 'Debit' column (see ③ below).
4. *Credit* the Accounts Payable Control account with the amount in the 'Credit' column (see ④ below).

GENERAL JOURNAL OF J. MASON   Fol. GJ1

Date	Particulars		Folio	Debit	Credit
19XX Jan. 1	Land		2.1	20 000.00	
	Buildings		2.2	40 000.00	
	Plant and Machinery		2.3	12 000.00	
	Office Equipment ①		2.6	10 000.00	
	Office Furniture		2.7	1 000.00	
	Cash at Bank		1.1	5 000.00	
	Inventory		1.2	1 500.00	
	Accounts Receivable ③		1.3	1 118.00	
	M. Adams	250.00			
	J. Abbott	500.00			
	R. Glacken	115.00			
	H. Raja	253.00			
	Accounts Payable ④		4.1		1 210.00
	H. Lime	300.00			
	P. Eastman	200.00			
	M. Garcia	510.00			
	B. Allar	200.00			
	Mortgage ②		5.1		10 000.00
	Capital		6.1		79 408.00
	Assets, liabilities and capital at this date			90 618.00	90 618.00

Columnar (tabular) format

This form of general journal is used in conjunction with subsidiary ledgers and makes posting to the control accounts in the general ledger easier. Instead of posting individual transactions with trade debtors and trade creditors, only the 'totals' of the relevant 'control' columns from the general journal are posted to the control accounts. Postings to trade debtors' and trade creditors' personal accounts — in the accounts receivable and accounts payable ledgers respectively — are carried out in the normal manner. You will learn more about this in the following sections of this chapter.

The posting procedures for the general journal in a columnar format are as follows. In the general ledger:

1. *Debit* individual accounts (Land, Buildings etc.) with amounts in the 'General' column on the debit side (see ① below).
2. *Credit* individual accounts (Mortgage and Capital) with amounts in the 'General' column on the credit side (see ② below).
3. *Debit* the Accounts Receivable Control account with the 'total' of the 'Accounts receivable' column on the debit side (see ③ below).
4. *Debit* the Accounts Payable Control account with the 'total' of the 'Accounts payable' column on the debit side (see ④ below).
5. *Credit* the Accounts Receivable Control account with the 'total' of the 'Accounts receivable' column on the credit side (see ⑤ below).
6. *Credit* the Accounts Payable Control account with the 'total' of the 'Accounts payable' column on the credit side (see ⑥ below).

Amounts for sundry debtors and sundry creditors are posted to their accounts in the general ledger. Thus, their accounts are maintained separately from those of the trade debtors and trade creditors which are maintained in the accounts receivable and accounts payable subsidiary journals.

GENERAL JOURNAL OF J. MASON

DEBIT / CREDIT — Fol. GJ1

Accounts receivable	Accounts payable	General	Date	Particulars	Fol.	Accounts receivable	Accounts payable	General
			19XX					
		20 000.00	Jan. 1	Land	2.1			
		40 000.00		Buildings	2.2			
		12 000.00		Plant and Machinery	2.3			
		10 000.00	①	Office Equipment	2.4			
		1 000.00		Office Furniture	2.7			
		5 000.00		Cash at Bank	1.1			
		1 500.00		Inventory	1.2			
250.00				M. Adams				
500.00				J. Abbott				
115.00				R. Glacken				
253.00				H. Raja				
				H. Lime			300.00	
				P. Eastman			200.00	
				M. Garcia			510.00	
				B. Allar			200.00	②
			②	Mortgage	5.1			10 000.00
				Capital	6.1			79 408.00
③ 1 118.00	④ TOTAL	89 500.00		Being assets, liabilities and capital as at this date.		⑤ TOTAL	⑥ 1 210.00	89 408.00
(1.3)							(4.1)	

Folio references

When posting from the general journal, folio references are inserted alongside each entry in the general journal to indicate to which account in the general ledger the amounts have been posted. Folio references for amounts posted to the Accounts Receivable and Accounts Payable Control accounts are inserted below the Accounts receivable and Accounts payable columns (where appropriate) as shown in the example on page 171. Folio references will be inserted for trade debtors and trade creditors when their details are posted to the accounts receivable and accounts payable ledgers respectively.

Preparing to post

Before commencing to post to the ledgers from the journals, it is recommended that you prepare a chart of accounts and set up 'skeleton' ledgers for each exercise from the chart of accounts. In business, ledgers are usually arranged in loose-leaf form, allowing easy insertion of additional pages when required. For class work, leave at least six writing lines between accounts, allowing additional lines for control accounts in the general ledger and, if using T-style accounts, for those accounts which need to be 'balanced' each month.

Set out below is a chart of accounts prepared for J. Mason.

CHART OF ACCOUNTS OF J. MASON		

1. Current Assets
  1.1 Cash at Bank
  1.2 Inventory
  1.3 Accounts Receivable
      Control
  1.4 Sundry Debtor — H. Larson
 	
2. Non-current Assets
  2.1 Land
  2.2 Buildings
  2.3 Plant and Machinery
  2.4 Motor Vehicles
  2.5 Furniture and Fittings
  2.6 Office Equipment
  2.7 Office Furniture
	3. Expenses
	  3.1 Purchases
	  3.2 (Purchases Returns and
	      Allowances)
	  3.3 Discount Allowed
	  3.4 Bad Debts
	  3.5 Interest Expense
	  3.6 Wages and Salaries
	
	4. Current Liabilities
	  4.1 Accounts Payable
	      Control
	  4.2 Sales Tax
	  4.6 Sundry Creditor —
	      Propert's Computers
		5. Long-term Liabilities
		  5.1 Mortgage
		
		6. Owner's Equity
		  6.1 Capital
		  6.2 (Drawings)
		
		7. Revenue
		  7.1 Sales
		  7.2 (Sales Returns and
		      Allowances)
		  7.3 Discount Received
		  7.4 Interest Revenue

The following show how J. Mason's general ledger will look when the general journal opening entry is posted.

GENERAL LEDGER OF J. MASON

Cash at Bank   1.1

Date	Particulars	Fol.	Debit	Credit	Balance
19XX Jan. 1	Capital	GJ1	5 000.00		5 000.00 Dr

Inventory   1.2

Date	Particulars	Fol.	Debit	Credit	Balance
19XX Jan. 1	Capital	GJ1	1 500.00		1 500.00 Dr

Accounts Receivable Control   1.3

Date	Particulars	Fol.	Debit	Credit	Balance
19XX Jan. 1	Capital	GJ1	1 118.00		1 118.00 Dr

Land   2.1

Date	Particulars	Fol.	Debit	Credit	Balance
19XX Jan. 1	Capital	GJ1	20 000.00		20 000.00 Dr

Buildings   2.2

Date	Particulars	Fol.	Debit	Credit	Balance
19XX Jan. 1	Capital	GJ1	40 000.00		40 000.00 Dr

Plant and Machinery   2.3

Date	Particulars	Fol.	Debit	Credit	Balance
19XX Jan. 1	Capital	GJ1	12 000.00		12 000.00 Dr

Office Equipment   2.6

Date	Particulars	Fol.	Debit	Credit	Balance
19XX Jan. 1	Capital	GJ1	10 000.00		10 000.00 Dr

Office Furniture   2.7

Date	Particulars	Fol.	Debit	Credit	Balance
19XX Jan. 1	Capital	GJ1	1 000.00		1 000.00 Dr

Accounts Payable Control 4.1

Date	Particulars	Fol.	Debit	Credit	Balance
19XX Jan. 1	Capital	GJ1		1 210.00	1 210.00 Cr

Mortgage 5.1

Date	Particulars	Fol.	Debit	Credit	Balance
19XX Jan. 1	Capital	GJ1		15 000.00	15 000.00 Cr

Capital 6.1

Date	Particulars	Fol.	Debit	Credit	Balance
19XX Jan. 1	Sundries	GJ1		79 408.00	79 408.00 Cr

Cross-references

Each transaction is **cross-referenced** when it is recorded in the ledger. Each entry made in the ledger has an equal debit or credit. For a debit entry, the cross-reference is the name of the account credited, and for a credit entry, the cross-reference is the name of the account debited. For example, the individual debit accounts in the opening entry are cross-referenced 'Capital', but the cross-reference for the Capital account is 'Sundries' to encompass all the debit accounts involved in the transaction.

Cross-referencing has two important functions:
- it provides a means of checking the accounts if errors are suspected
- it serves as a reminder of the double-entry effect of each transaction.

Accounting equation verified

Assets		=	Liabilities + Owner's Equity	
Cash at Bank	$ 5 000.00	Accounts Payable Control	$ 1 210.00
Inventory	1 500.00	Mortgage	10 000.00
Accounts Receivable Control	1 118.00	Capital	79 408.00
Land	20 000.00		
Buildings	40 000.00		
Plant and Machinery	12 000.00		
Office Equipment	10 000.00		
Office Furniture	1 000.00		
Total debits	$90 618.00	= **Total credits**	$90 618.00

CHAPTER 4: POSTING TO THE LEDGERS | 175

At the end of the month, the following miscellaneous general journal entries are posted to J. Mason's general ledger. The general ledger will be illustrated after each step, with entries for each new step highlighted in italic type.

GENERAL JOURNAL OF J. MASON Fol. GJ1

| \-\-\- DEBIT \-\-\- |||| | | \-\-\- CREDIT \-\-\- |||
Accounts receivable	Accounts payable	General	Date	Particulars	Fol.	Accounts receivable	Accounts payable	General
	50.00		Jan. 4	P. Eastman H. Lime Correction of error.			50.00	

		12 000.00	5	Office Equipment
				    Sundry Creditor —
				    Propert's Computers
				Purchase of computer on credit.
					2.6
					
					4.7
								12 000.00

		150.00	7	H. Larson —
				    Sundry Debtor
				    Office Equipment
				Sale of printer on credit.
					1.5
					2.6
								150.00

30.00			10	J. Abbott M. Adams Correction of error.		30.00		
		18.00	10	Capital H. Raja Correction of error.	6.1	18.00		
		50.00	23	Drawings Purchases Owner took goods for personal use.	6.2 3.1			50.00
	360.00		31	M. Garcia Capital Correction of error.	6.1			360.00
		5.00	31	Interest Expense B. Allar Interest payable on creditor's overdue account.	3.10		5.00	
1.53			31	J. Glacken Interest Revenue Interest charged on debtor's overdue account.	7.4			1.53
		116.53	31	Bad Debts J. Glacken Bad debt written off.	3.5	116.53		
31.53	410.00	12 339.53				164.53	55.00	12 561.53
(1.3)	(4.1)					(1.3)	(4.1)	

Total debits, $12 781.06 = Total credits, $12 781.06

At the end of the month, the remainder of the general journal entries are posted. This is done transaction by transaction, posting each account involved to the debit or credit column of each account according to the transaction being processed. When completed, J. Mason's ledger will appear as follows. (Italic type has been used here to draw attention to entries for each new step.)

GENERAL LEDGER OF J. MASON

Cash at Bank 1.1

Date	Particulars	Fol.	Debit	Credit	Balance
19XX Jan. 1	Capital	GJ1	5 000.00		5 000.00 Dr

Inventory 1.2

Date	Particulars	Fol.	Debit	Credit	Balance
19XX Jan. 1	Capital	GJ1	1 500.00		1 500.00 Dr

Accounts Receivable Control 1.3

Date	Particulars	Fol.	Debit	Credit	Balance
19XX Jan. 1	Capital	GJ1	1 118.00		1 118.00 Dr
31	Sundries	GJ1	31.53		1 149.53 Dr
	Sundries	GJ1		164.53	985.00 Dr

Sundry Debtor — H. Larson 1.5

Date	Particulars	Fol.	Debit	Credit	Balance
19XX Jan. 7	Office equipment	GJ1	150.00		150.00 Dr

Land 2.1

Date	Particulars	Fol.	Debit	Credit	Balance
19XX Jan. 1	Capital	GJ1	20 000.00		20 000.00 Dr

Buildings 2.2

Date	Particulars	Fol.	Debit	Credit	Balance
19XX Jan. 1	Capital	GJ1	40 000.00		40 000.00 Dr

Plant and Machinery 2.3

Date	Particulars	Fol.	Debit	Credit	Balance
19XX Jan. 1	Capital	GJ1	12 000.00		12 000.00 Dr

Office Equipment 2.6

Date	Particulars	Fol.	Debit	Credit	Balance

19XX
Jan. 1
5
 	
7
	Capital
	Sundry creditor —
	  Propert's Computers
	Sundry debtor —
	  H. Larson
		GJ1
		
		GJ1
		
		GJ1
			10 000.00
			
			12 000.00
				
				150.00
					10 000.00 Dr
					
					22 000.00 Dr
					
					21 850.00 Dr

Office Furniture 2.7

Date	Particulars	Fol.	Debit	Credit	Balance
19XX Jan. 1	Capital	GJ1	1 000.00		1 000.00 Dr

Purchases 3.1

Date	Particulars	Fol.	Debit	Credit	Balance
19XX Jan. 23	Drawings	GJ1		50.00	50.00 Cr

Bad Debts 3.5

Date	Particulars	Fol.	Debit	Credit	Balance
19XX Jan. 31	J. Glacken	GJ1	116.53		116.53 Dr

Interest Expense 3.10

Date	Particulars	Fol.	Debit	Credit	Balance
19XX Jan. 31	B. Allar	GJ1	5.00		5.00 Dr

Accounts Payable Control 4.1

Date	Particulars	Fol.	Debit	Credit	Balance
19XX Jan. 1 31	Capital Sundries Sundries	GJ1 GJ1 GJ1	 410.00	1 210.00 55.00	1 210.00 Cr 800.00 Cr 855.00 Cr

Sundry Creditor — Propert's Computers 4.7

Date	Particulars	Fol.	Debit	Credit	Balance
19XX Jan. 5	Office equipment	GJ1		12 000.00	12 000.00 Cr

Mortgage 5.1

Date	Particulars	Fol.	Debit	Credit	Balance
19XX Jan. 1	Capital	GJ1		10 000.00	10 000.00 Cr

Capital 6.1

Date	Particulars	Fol.	Debit	Credit	Balance
19XX Jan. 1 10 31	Sundries H. Raja (correction) M. Garcia (correction)	GJ1 GJ1 GJ1	 18.00 	79 408.00 360.00	79 408.00 Cr 79 390.00 Cr 79 750.00 Cr

Drawings 6.2

Date	Particulars	Fol.	Debit	Credit	Balance
19XX Jan. 23	Purchases	GJ1	50.00		50.00 Dr

Interest Revenue 7.4

Date	Particulars	Fol.	Debit	Credit	Balance
19XX Jan. 31	J. Glacken	GJ1		1.53	1.53 Cr

EXERCISE 4.1 K. Dominic & Sons

K. Dominic & Sons' general journal is reproduced on page 179. You are required to carry out the following.
1. Prepare the chart of accounts for K. Dominic & Sons using the chart of accounts on page 172 as a guide.
2. Post details from the general journal to the general ledger. Use as many copies as you need of the blank ledger master provided on page 540. Don't forget to include the name of the ledger at the top of the first page (see example on page 172).

GENERAL JOURNAL OF K. DOMINIC & SONS

Fol. GJ1

DEBIT						CREDIT		
Accounts receivable	Accounts payable	General	Date	Particulars	Fol.	Accounts receivable	Accounts payable	General
			19XX					
		250 000.00	May 1	Land				
		80 000.00		Buildings				
		35 000.00		Motor Vehicles				
		2 550.00		Office Equipment				
		1 890.00		Office Furniture				
		18 000.00		Cash at Bank				
		9 890.00		Inventory				
240.00				J. Wade				
580.00				M. Byrnes				
420.00				G. Mundo				
				W. Maine			680.00	
				Conway & Sons			420.00	
				B. Samuels			78.00	
				Mortgage				150 000.00
				Capital				247 392.00
				Assets, liabilities and capital as at this date.				
1240.00		397 330.00					1178.00	397 392.00
		10 000.00	5	Office Equipment				
				Sundry Creditor—				
				Imagemakers				10 000.00
				Photocopier purchased on credit.				
180.00			7	J. Wade				
				M. Byrnes		180.00		
				Correction of posting error.				
			16	Sundry Debtor — Ace				
		500.00		Secretarial Service				
				Office Furniture				500.00
				Office desk sold on credit.				
		420.00	19	Bad Debts				
				G. Mundo		420.00		
				Bad debt written off.				
		300.00	20	Drawings				
				Purchases				300.00
				Owner took goods for personal use.				
		1.95	25	Interest Expense				
				B. Samuel			1.95	
				Interest paid on overdue account.				
180.00		11 221.95				600.00	1.95	10 800.00

EXERCISE 4.2 *B. James & Co.*

The general journal for B. James & Co. is reproduced on page 180.
1. Prepare the chart of accounts for B. James & Co. using the chart of accounts on page 172 as a guide.
2. Post details from the general journal to the general ledger. Use as many copies as you need of the blank ledger master provided on page 540. Don't forget to include the name of the ledger at the top of the first page (see example on page 172).

GENERAL JOURNAL OF B. JAMES & CO.

Fol. GJ1

Accounts receivable (Dr)	Accounts payable (Dr)	General (Dr)	Date	Particulars	Fol.	Accounts receivable (Cr)	Accounts payable (Cr)	General (Cr)
		18 900.00	19XX Apr. 1	Plant and Machinery				
		15 500.00		Motor Vehicles				
		4 890.00		Office Equipment				
		2 680.00		Office Furniture				
		12 440.00		Cash at Bank				
		5 660.00		Inventory				
172.00				A. Collins				
289.00				Corella Private Hosp.				
320.00				E. & J. White				
402.00				G. McGregor				
				King & Co.			426.00	
				Greenway & Co.			215.00	
				F. Nguyen			75.00	
				Capital				60 537.00
				Assets, liabilities and capital at this date.				
1183.00		60 070.00					716.00	60 537.00
	18.00		6	F. Nguyen				
				Capital				18.00
				Correction of error.				
100.00			8	Corella Private Hosp.				
				A. Collins		100.00		
				Correction of error.				
	150.00		8	Greenway & Co.				
				King & Co.			150.00	
				Correction of error.				
		2 000.00	11	Office Equipment				
				Sundry Creditor — Technics Ltd				2 000.00
				Laser printer purchased on credit.				
20.10			30	G. McGregor				
				Interest Revenue				20.10
				Interest charged on debtor's overdue account (6 months).				
120.10	168.00	2 000.00				100.00	150.00	2 038.10

EXERCISE 4.3 *Trend Fashions*

The general journal for Trend Fashions is reproduced on page 181.
1. Prepare the chart of accounts for Trend Fashions using the chart of accounts on page 172 as a guide.
2. Post details from the general journal to the general ledger. Use as many copies as you need of the blank ledger master provided on page 540. Don't forget to include the name of the ledger at the top of the first page (see example on page 172).

GENERAL JOURNAL OF TREND FASHIONS

Fol. GJ1

Accounts receivable (Dr)	Accounts payable (Dr)	General (Dr)	Date	Particulars	Fol.	Accounts receivable (Cr)	Accounts payable (Cr)	General (Cr)
		240 000.00	19XX Feb. 1	Land				
		60 000.00		Buildings				
		24 500.00		Motor Vehicles				
		6 110.00		Office Equipment				
		2 400.00		Office Furniture				
		11 765.00		Cash at Bank				
		5 295.00		Inventory				
320.00				The Dress Shop				
265.00				Jane's Fashion Store				
532.00				H. Taylor & Co.				
302.00				Petrovich & Co.				
				W. A. Montey			440.00	
				G. Hanna			385.00	
				W. Laporte			229.00	
				J. S. Baxter			88.00	
				Mortgage				120 000.00
				Capital				230 347.00
				Assets, liabilities and capital as at this date.				
1419.00		350 070.00					1142.00	350 347.00
	120.00		7	W. A. Montey				
				G. Hanna			120.00	
				Correction of error.				
		21 000.00	16	Motor Vehicles				
				Sundry Creditor — Schaeffer Motors				21 000.00
				Motor vehicle purchased on credit.				
		9 500.00	18	Sundry Debtor — R. Mustafa				
				Motor Vehicles				9 500.00
				Motor vehicle sold on credit.				
		1 100.00	22	Office Equipment				
				Sundry Creditor — Compusupply Co.				1 100.00
				Laser printer purchased on credit.				
		300.00	22	Sundry Debtor — H. Rostov				
				Office Equipment				300.00
				Inkjet printer sold on credit.				
		520.00	27	Drawings				
				Purchases				520.00
				Owner took goods for personal use.				
	120.00	32 420.00					120.00	32 420.00

Posting from the accounts payable journals to the general ledger

From the purchases journal

The posting procedure for posting details from the purchases journal to the general ledger is illustrated below.
- Debit the Purchases account with the *total* amount of purchases for the month (see ① below).
- Credit the Accounts Payable Control account with the *total* amount of purchases for the month (see ② below).

PURCHASES JOURNAL OF J. MASON Fol. PJ1

Date	Inv. no.	Particulars (Creditor's account to be credited)	Fol.	Amount	Monthly total
19XX					
Jan. 3	233	H. Lime		60.00	
8	257	H. Lime		35.00	
12	612	P. Eastman		68.00	
15	622	P. Eastman		28.00	
24	479	N. Lilly		45.00	
31		① Dr Purchases	3.1		
		② Cr Accounts Payable Control	4.1		236.00

① *Debit* Purchases account.
② *Credit* Accounts Payable Control account.
  Total debits, $236.00 = Total credits, $236.00

As each journal is posted, the changes to each account are shown in italics so you can see how posting from each journal builds in the ledger accounts to provide a history of transactions.

GENERAL LEDGER OF J. MASON

Purchases 3.1

Date	Particulars	Fol.	Debit	Credit	Balance
19XX					
Jan. 23	Drawings	GJ1		50.00	50.00 Cr
31	Accounts payable ①	PJ1	236.00		186.00 Dr

Accounts Payable Control 4.1

Date	Particulars	Fol.	Debit	Credit	Balance
19XX					
Jan. 1	Capital	GJ1		1210.00	1210.00 Cr
31	Sundries	GJ2		55.00	1265.00 Cr
	Sundries	GJ2	410.00		855.00 Cr
	Purchases ②	PJ1		236.00	1091.00 Cr

Folio numbers of ledger accounts are inserted in the journal as the items are posted. The folio numbers of the two general ledger accounts, Accounts Payable Control and Purchases, are placed alongside the total in the journal.

From the purchases returns and allowances journal

The posting procedure for posting details from the purchases returns and allowances journal to the general ledger is shown below.
- Credit the Purchases Returns and Allowances account with the *total* amount of purchases returns for the month (see ① below).
- Debit the Accounts Payable Control account with the *total* amount of purchases returns for the month (see ② below).

PURCHASES RETURNS AND ALLOWANCES JOURNAL OF J. MASON Fol. PR1

Date	CN no.	Particulars (Creditor's account to be debited)	Fol.	Amount	Monthly total
19XX					
Jan. 12	111	H. Lime		15.00	
18	321	P. Eastman		10.00	
29	456	N. Lilly		20.00	
31		① Dr Accounts Payable Control	4.1		
		② Cr Purchases Returns	3.2		45.00

① *Debit* Accounts Payable Control account.
② *Credit* Purchases Returns account.

Total debits, $45.00 = Total credits, $45.00

GENERAL LEDGER OF J. MASON

Purchases Returns and Allowances 3.2

Date	Particulars	Fol.	Debit	Credit	Balance
19XX					
Jan. 31	Accounts payable ②	PR1		45.00	45.00 Cr

Accounts Payable Control 4.1

Date	Particulars	Fol.	Debit	Credit	Balance
19XX					
Jan. 1	Capital	GJ1		1210.00	1210.00 Cr
31	Sundries	GJ2		55.00	1265.00 Cr
	Sundries	GJ2	410.00		855.00 Cr
	Purchases	PJ1		236.00	1091.00 Cr
	Purchases returns ①	PR1	45.00		1046.00 Cr

From the cash payments journal

The folio references for the two general ledger accounts, Accounts Payable Control and Purchases Returns and Allowances, are inserted alongside the 'total' amount.

From the cash payments journal

The posting procedure for posting details from the cash payments journal to the general ledger is shown below.

- Credit the Cash at Bank account with the *total* of the 'Bank' column (see ① below).
- Debit the Accounts Payable Control account with the *total* of the 'Accounts payable/Trade creditors' column (see ② below).
- Debit the Accounts Payable Control account with the *total* of the 'Discount received' column (see ③ below).
- Credit the Discount Received account with the *total* of the 'Discount received' column (see ④ below).
- Debit individual expense accounts (Wages, Rent, etc.) with the amounts in the 'General' column (see ⑤ below). Do not post trade creditors' individual amounts to the general ledger — they will be posted to the accounts payable ledger in the next section of your course.

Insert folio references in brackets below the columns.

CASH PAYMENTS JOURNAL OF J. MASON   Fol. CP1

Date	Chq. no.	Particulars (Account to be debited)	Fol.	Discount received	Trade creditors	General	Bank
19XX							
Jan. 13	264	H. Lime		17.50	332.50		332.50
25	265	P. Eastman		7.50	142.50		142.50
26	266	Wages ⑤	3.17			150.00	150.00
28	267	Rent	3.14			40.00	40.00
	268	N. Lilly			25.00		25.00
31				25.00	500.00	190.00	690.00
				(4.1/7.3)	(4.1)		(1.1)
				③ ④	②		①

① *Credit* Cash at Bank account with the *total* of the 'Bank' column.
② *Debit* Accounts Payable Control account with the *total* of the 'Trade creditors' column.
③ *Debit* Accounts Payable Control account with the *total* of the 'Discount received' column.
④ *Credit* Discount Received account with the *total* of the 'Discount received' column.
⑤ *Debit* individual expense accounts (Wages, Rent, etc.) with the amounts in the 'General' column.

Total debits, $715.00 ($500.00 + $25.00 + $190.00) = Total credits, $715.00 ($690.00 + $25.00)

GENERAL LEDGER OF J. MASON

Cash at Bank 1.1

Date	Particulars	Fol.	Debit	Credit	Balance
19XX					
Jan. 1	Capital	GJ1	5000.00		5000.00 Dr
31	Cash payments ①	CP1		690.00	4310.00 Dr

Accounts Payable Control 4.1

Date	Particulars	Fol.	Debit	Credit	Balance
19XX					
Jan. 1	Capital	GJ1		1210.00	1210.00 Cr
31	Sundries	GJ2		55.00	1265.00 Cr
	Sundries	GJ2	410.00		855.00 Cr
	Purchases	PJ1		236.00	1091.00 Cr
	Purchases returns	PR1	45.00		1046.00 Cr
	Cash payments ②	CP1	500.00		546.00 Cr
	Discount received ③	CP1	25.00		521.00 Cr

Rent 3.14

Date	Particulars	Fol.	Debit	Credit	Balance
19XX					
Jan. 28	Cash payments ⑤	CP1	40.00		40.00 Dr

Wages 3.17

Date	Particulars	Fol.	Debit	Credit	Balance
19XX					
Jan. 26	Cash payments ⑤	CP1	150.00		150.00 Dr

Discount Received 7.3

Date	Particulars	Fol.	Debit	Credit	Balance
19XX					
Jan. 31	Accounts payable ④	CP1		25.00	25.00 Cr

EXERCISE 4.4 K. Dominic & Sons

Using the ledger accounts prepared in exercise 4.1 (page 178), continue to post the amounts from the following purchases, purchases returns and allowances and cash payments journals to the general ledger of K. Dominic & Sons. Use as many copies as you need of the blank ledger master provided on page 540. Don't forget to include the name of the ledger at the top of the first page (see example on page 172).

PURCHASES JOURNAL OF K. DOMINIC & SONS — Fol. PJ1

Date	Inv. no.	Particulars (Creditor's account to be credited)	Fol.	Amount	Monthly total
19XX					
May 5	237	W. Maine & Co.		500.00	
8	125	Conway & Sons		140.00	
15	98	D. J. Callaghan		900.00	
20	251	W. Maine & Co.		328.00	
	147	Conway & Sons		250.00	
31					2118.00

PURCHASES RETURNS AND ALLOWANCES JOURNAL OF K. DOMINIC & SONS — Fol. PR1

Date	CN no.	Particulars (Creditor's account to be debited)	Fol.	Amount	Monthly total
19XX					
May 20	111	W. Maine & Co.		200.00	
25	54	D. J. Callaghan		250.00	
31					450.00

CASH PAYMENTS JOURNAL OF K. DOMINIC & SONS — Fol. CP1

Date	Chq. no.	Particulars (Account to be debited)	Fol.	Discount received	Trade creditors	General	Bank
19XX							
May 14	114	Rent				500.00	500.00
15	115	Advertising				55.00	55.00
	116	Conway & Sons		21.00	399.00		399.00
17	117	Petty Cash				150.00	150.00
20	118	W. Maine & Co.		34.00	646.00		646.00
28	119	Repairs and Maintenance				83.00	83.00
31				55.00	1045.00	788.00	1833.00

EXERCISE 4.5   B. James & Co.

Using the ledger accounts prepared in exercise 4.2 (page 179), continue to post the amounts from the following purchases, purchases returns and allowances and cash payments journals to the general ledger of B. James & Co. Use as many copies as you need of the blank ledger master provided on page 540. Don't forget to include the name of the ledger at the top of the first page (see example on page 172).

PURCHASES JOURNAL OF B. JAMES & CO. Fol. PJ1

Date	Inv. no.	Particulars (Creditor's account to be credited)	Fol.	Amount	Monthly total
19XX					
Apr. 4	1127	King & Co.		457.00	
10	885	L. Thompson & Sons		98.67	
15	1145	King & Co.		368.00	
24	98	Greenway & Co.		1254.80	
28	946	L. Thompson & Sons		467.00	
29	125	Greenway & Co.		125.25	
30	157	Williams & Sons		560.00	
					3330.72

PURCHASES RETURNS AND ALLOWANCES JOURNAL OF B. JAMES & CO. Fol. PR1

Date	CN no.	Particulars (Creditor's account to be debited)	Fol.	Amount	Monthly total
19XX					
Apr. 20	37	King & Co.		57.00	
24	12	Greenway & Co.		105.00	
30					162.00

CASH PAYMENTS JOURNAL OF B. JAMES & CO. Fol. CP1

Date	Chq. no.	Particulars (Account to be debited)	Fol.	Discount received	Trade creditors	General	Bank
19XX							
Apr. 12	148	Stationery				68.00	68.00
14	149	King & Co.		14.40	561.60		561.60
24	150	Electricity				180.00	180.00
151	Greenway & Co.		1.62	63.38		63.38	
28	152	Purchases				100.00	100.00
153	Motor Vehicles				17 000.00	17 000.00	
30				16.02	624.98	17 348.00	17 972.98

EXERCISE 4.6 Trend Fashions

Using the ledger accounts prepared in exercise 4.3 (page 180), continue to post the amounts from the following purchases, purchases returns and allowances and cash payments journals to the general ledger of Trend Fashions. Use as many copies as you need of the blank ledger master provided on page 540. Don't forget to include the name of the ledger at the top of the first page (see example on page 172).

PURCHASES JOURNAL OF TREND FASHIONS — Fol. PJ1

Date	Inv. no.	Particulars (Creditor's account to be credited)	Fol.	Amount	Monthly total
19XX					
Feb. 2	201	W. A. Montey		405.60	
6	304	J. S. Baxter		236.94	
9	235	G. Hanna		983.56	
10	667	W. A. Montey		56.78	
15	345	J. S. Baxter		436.90	
20	91	L. Beetson		125.50	
28	745	W. A. Montey		1270.50	
					3515.78

PURCHASES RETURNS AND ALLOWANCES JOURNAL OF TREND FASHIONS — Fol. PR1

Date	CN no.	Particulars (Creditor's account to be debited)	Fol.	Amount	Monthly total
19XX					
Feb. 16	98	G. Hanna		51.00	
21	14	J. S. Baxter		26.94	
28					77.94

CASH PAYMENTS JOURNAL OF TREND FASHIONS — Fol. CP1

Date	Chq. no.	Particulars (Account to be debited)	Fol.	Discount received	Trade creditors	General	Bank
19XX							
Feb. 15	334	Repairs and Maintenance				150.00	150.00
20	335	Wages				1076.00	1076.00
	336	W. A. Montey		8.00	312.00		312.00
25	337	Advertising				120.00	120.00
	338	G. Hanna		12.65	492.35		492.35
28	339	Petty Cash Reimbursement					
		Stationery				15.00	
		Travel Expenses				80.00	95.00
28				20.65	804.35	1441.00	2245.35

Posting from the accounts receivable journals

From the sales journal

The posting procedure for posting details from the sales journal to the general ledger is illustrated below.

- Debit the Accounts Receivable Control account with the *total* amount of the 'Debtors' total' column (see ① below). This column records the total amount owing by customers for goods received.
- Credit the Sales Tax Payable account with the *total* amount of sales tax for the month (see ② below).
- Credit the Sales account with the *total* amount of sales for the month (see ③ below).

Insert folio references in brackets below the columns.

SALES JOURNAL OF J. MASON   Fol. SJ1

Date	Inv. no.	Particulars (Debtor's account to be debited)	Fol.	Sales	Sales tax	Debtors' total
19XX						
Jan. 1	371	M. Adams		81.70	12.25	93.95
10	372	J. Abbott		167.20	25.08	192.28
21	373	L. Wells		131.10	19.66	150.76
29	374	E. Garton		57.00	8.55	65.55
31				437.00	65.54	502.54
				(7.1) ③	(4.3) ②	(1.3) ①

① *Debit* Accounts Receivable Control account.
② *Credit* Sales Tax Payable account.
③ *Credit* Sales account.

Total debits, $502.54 = Total credits, $502.54 ($437.00 + $65.54)

GENERAL LEDGER OF J. MASON

Accounts Receivable Control   1.3

Date	Particulars	Fol.	Debit	Credit	Balance
19XX					
Jan. 1	Capital	GJ1	1118.00		1118.00 Dr
31	Sundries	GJ1	31.53		1149.53 Dr
	Sundries	GJ1		164.53	985.00 Dr
	Sales ①	SJ1	502.54		1487.54 Dr

Sales Tax Payable   4.3

Date	Particulars	Fol.	Debit	Credit	Balance
19XX					
Jan. 31	Accounts receivable ②	SJ1		65.54	65.54 Cr

Sales 7.1

Date	Particulars	Fol.	Debit	Credit	Balance
19XX Jan. 31	Accounts receivable ③	SJ1		437.00	437.00 Cr

It should be noted that folio numbers of ledger accounts should be inserted in the journals as the items are posted.

Posting from the sales returns and allowances journal

The posting procedure for posting details from the sales returns and allowances journal to the general ledger is illustrated below.
- Credit the Accounts Receivable Control account with the *total* amount of the 'Debtors' total' column (see ① below). This column records the total amount of returns and allowances by/due customers for the month.
- Debit the Sales Tax Payable account with the *total* amount of sales tax for the month (see ② below).
- Debit the Sales Returns account with the *total* amount of sales returns for the month (see ③ below).

Insert folio references below the 'total' figures in each column.

SALES RETURNS AND ALLOWANCES JOURNAL OF J. MASON   Fol. SR1

Date	CN no.	Particulars (Debtor's account to be credited)	Fol.	Sales returns	Sales tax	Debtors' total
19XX Jan. 28 30 31	86 87 88	J. Abbott M. Adams E. Garton		20.90 20.43 38.00	3.13 3.06 5.70	24.03 23.49 43.70
				79.33	11.89	91.22
				(7.2) ③	(4.3) ②	(1.3) ①

① *Credit* Accounts Receivable Control account.
② *Debit* Sales Tax Payable account.
③ *Debit* Sales Returns account.

Total debits, $91.22 ($79.33 + $11.89) = Total credits, $91.22

GENERAL LEDGER OF J. MASON
Accounts Receivable Control 1.3

Date	Particulars	Fol.	Debit	Credit	Balance
19XX Jan. 1 31	Capital Sundries Sundries Sales Sales returns ①	GJ1 GJ1 GJ1 SJ1 SR1	1118.00 31.53 502.54 	 164.53 91.22	1118.00 Dr 1149.53 Dr 985.00 Dr 1487.54 Dr 1396.32 Dr

Sales Tax Payable 4.3

Date	Particulars	Fol.	Debit	Credit	Balance
19XX Jan. 31	Accounts receivable Accounts receivable ②	SJ1 SR1	11.89	65.54	65.54 Cr 53.65 Cr

Sales Returns 7.2

Date	Particulars	Fol.	Debit	Credit	Balance
19XX Jan. 31	Accounts receivable ③	SR1	79.33		79.33 Dr

Posting from the cash receipts journal

The posting procedure for posting details from the cash receipts journal to the general ledger is shown below.

- Debit the Cash at Bank account with the *total* of the 'Bank' column to record increase in asset account, Cash (see ① on page 192).
- Credit the Accounts Receivable Control account with the *total* of the 'Accounts receivable/Trade debtors' column to decrease amounts owing by trade creditors (see ② on page 192).
- Credit the Accounts Receivable Control account with the *total* of the 'Discount allowed' column to record the amount of discount allowed to trade debtors for prompt payment (see ③ on page 192). (Amount received + discount allowed = amount originally owed.)
- Credit the Sales account with the *total* of the 'Sales' column to record increase in revenue account, Sales (see ④ on page 192).
- Credit the Sales Tax Payable account with the *total* of the 'Sales tax' column to record increase in liability account, Sales Tax (see ⑤ on page 192).
- Debit the Discount Allowed account with the *total* of the 'Discount allowed' column to record increase in expense account, Discount Allowed (see ⑥ on page 192).
- Credit individual **nominal accounts** (pertaining to revenue and expense accounts, for example Rent Revenue), asset and capital accounts with amounts in the 'General' column (see ⑦ on page 192). Do not post trade debtors' individual amounts to the general ledger — they will be posted to the accounts receivable ledger later in your course.

Insert folio references in the 'Folio' column alongside each entry, or below column as appropriate.

CASH RECEIPTS JOURNAL OF J. MASON   Fol. CR1

Date	Rec. no.	Particulars (Account to be credited)	Fol.	Discount allowed	Trade debtors	Sales	Sales tax	General	Bank
19XX									
Jan. 5	CS	Sales	7.1			127.50	22.50		150.00
10	CS	Sales	7.1			180.00	20.00		200.00
29	23	M. Adams		11.00	209.00				
	CS	Sales	7.1			23.50			232.50
30	24	J. Abbott		31.80	498.20				498.20
31	25	L. Wells			100.00				
	26	Capital	6.1					1000.00	
	27	Rent Revenue ⑦	7.5					400.00	
	28	Office Equipment	2.6					25.00	
									1525.00
				42.80	807.20	331.00	42.50	1425.00	2605.70
				(1.3/3.3)	(1.3)	(7.1)	(4.3)		(1.1)
				③ ⑥	②	④	⑤		①

① *Debit* Cash at Bank account.
② *Credit* Accounts Receivable Control account.
③ *Credit* Accounts Receivable Control account.
④ *Credit* Sales account.
⑤ *Credit* Sales Tax Payable account.
⑥ *Debit* Discount Allowed account.
⑦ *Credit* individual nominal, asset and capital accounts.

Total debits, $2648.50 ($2605.70 + $42.80) = Total credits, $2648.50
($42.80 + $807.20 + $331.00 + $42.50 + $1425.00)

GENERAL LEDGER OF J. MASON
Cash at Bank   1.1

Date	Particulars	Fol.	Debit	Credit	Balance
19XX					
Jan. 1	Capital	GJ1	5 000.00		5 000.00 Dr
31	Cash payments	CP1		685.00	4 315.00 Dr
	Cash receipts ①	CR1	2 605.70		6 920.70 Dr

Accounts Receivable Control   1.3

Date	Particulars	Fol.	Debit	Credit	Balance
19XX					
Jan. 1	Capital	GJ1	1 118.00		1 118.00 Dr
31	Sundries	GJ1	31.53		1 149.53 Dr
	Sundries	GJ1		164.53	985.00 Dr
	Sales	SJ1	502.54		1 487.54 Dr
	Sales returns	SR1		91.22	1 396.32 Dr
	Cash receipts ②	CR1		807.20	589.12 Dr
	Discount allowed ③	CR1		42.80	546.32 Dr

Office Equipment 2.6

Date	Particulars	Fol.	Debit	Credit	Balance
19XX					
Jan. 1	Capital	GJ1	10 000.00		10 000.00 Dr
5	Sundry creditor — Propert's Computers	GJ1	12 000.00		22 000.00 Dr
7	Sundry debtor — H. Larson	GJ1		150.00	21 850.00 Dr
31	Cash receipts ⑦	CR1		25.00	21 825.00 Dr

Discount Allowed 3.3

Date	Particulars	Fol.	Debit	Credit	Balance
19XX					
Jan. 31	Accounts receivable ⑥	CR1	42.80		42.80 Dr

Sales Tax Payable 4.3

Date	Particulars	Fol.	Debit	Credit	Balance
19XX					
Jan. 31	Accounts receivable	SJ1		65.54	65.54 Cr
	Accounts receivable	SR1	11.89		53.65 Cr
	Cash receipts ⑤	CR1		42.50	96.15 Cr

Capital 6.1

Date	Particulars	Fol.	Debit	Credit	Balance
19XX					
Jan. 1	Sundries	GJ1		79 408.00	79 408.00 Cr
10	H. Raja (correction)	GJ1	18.00		79 390.00 Cr
31	M. Garcia (correction)	GJ1		360.00	79 750.00 Cr
26	Cash receipts ⑦	CR1		1 000.00	80 750.00 Cr

Sales 7.1

Date	Particulars	Fol.	Debit	Credit	Balance
19XX					
Jan. 31	Accounts receivable	SJ1		437.00	437.00 Cr
	Cash receipts ④	CR1		331.00	768.00 Cr

Rent Revenue 7.5

Date	Particulars	Fol.	Debit	Credit	Balance
19XX					
Jan. 28	Cash receipts ⑦	CR1		400.00	400.00 Cr

EXERCISE 4.7   K. Dominic & Sons

Using the ledger prepared through exercises 4.1 and 4.4, post the amounts from the following sales, sales returns and allowances and cash receipts journals to the general ledger of K. Dominic & Sons. Use as many copies as you need of the blank ledger master provided on page 540. Don't forget to include the name of the ledger at the top of the first page (see example on page 172).

SALES JOURNAL OF K. DOMINIC & SONS — Fol. SJ1

Date	Inv. no.	Particulars (Debtor's account to be debited)	Fol.	Sales	Sales tax	Debtors' total
19XX May 3	463	J. Wade		162.00	24.30	186.30
10	464	M. Byrnes		250.56	37.59	288.15
18	465	R. Cotter & Sons		324.00	48.10	372.10
20	466	J. Wade		32.40	4.86	37.26
31				768.96	114.85	883.81

SALES RETURNS AND ALLOWANCES JOURNAL OF K. DOMINIC & SONS — Fol. SR1

Date	CN no.	Particulars (Debtor's account to be credited)	Fol.	Sales returns	Sales tax	Debtors' total
19XX May 18	42	J. Wade		32.40	4.86	37.26
21	43	R. Cotter & Sons		64.80	9.72	74.52
31				97.20	14.58	111.78

CASH RECEIPTS JOURNAL OF K. DOMINIC & SONS — Fol. CR1

Date	Rec. no.	Particulars (Account to be credited)	Fol.	Discount allowed	Trade debtors	Sales	Sales tax	General	Bank
19XX May 2	201	J. Wade		10.50	409.50				409.50
9	CS	Sales				467.50	82.50		550.00
10	202	Rent Revenue						500.00	
	203	Capital						10 000.00	10 500.00
22	CS	Sales				200.60	35.40		236.00
28	203	R. Cotter & Sons		8.44	289.14				
	204	Motor Vehicles						5 000.00	
	CS	Sales				417.40	62.60		5 769.14
29	205	M. Byrnes			100.00				100.00
31				18.94	798.64	1 085.50	180.50	15 500.00	17 564.64

EXERCISE 4.8 B. James & Co.

Using the ledger prepared through exercises 4.2 and 4.5, post the amounts from the following sales, sales returns and allowances and cash receipts journals to the general ledger for B. James & Co. Use as many copies as you need of the blank ledger master provided on page 540. Don't forget to include the name of the ledger at the top of the first page (see example on page 172).

SALES JOURNAL OF B. JAMES & CO. Fol. SJ1

Date	Inv. no.	Particulars (Debtor's account to be debited)	Fol.	Sales	Sales tax	Debtors' total
19XX						
Apr. 3	22	A. Collins		798.00	19.95	817.95
10	23	Corella Private Hospital		65.00		65.00
15	24	E. & J. White		133.48	16.68	150.16
	25	K. Carter & Co.		63.65	7.96	71.61
20	26	E. & J. White		151.20	18.87	170.07
28	27	A. Collins		241.45	30.18	271.63
30				1452.78	93.64	1546.42

SALES RETURNS AND ALLOWANCES JOURNAL OF B. JAMES & CO. Fol. SR1

Date	CN no.	Particulars (Debtor's account to be credited)	Fol.	Sales returns	Sales tax	Debtors' total
19XX						
Apr. 13	85	A. Collins		199.50	24.94	224.44
21	86	K. Carter & Co.		33.25	4.16	37.41
30				232.75	29.10	261.85

CASH RECEIPTS JOURNAL OF B. JAMES & CO. Fol. CR1

Date	Rec. no.	Particulars (Account to be credited)	Fol.	Discount allowed	Trade debtors	Sales	Sales tax	General	Bank
19XX									
Apr. 3	301	Office Equipment						80.00	80.00
12	CS	Sales				172.70	30.50		203.20
15	CS	Sales				348.50	61.50		410.00
20	302	A. Collins		1.80	70.20				
	303	Capital						12 000.00	
	304	Corella Private Hospital		9.72	379.28				12 449.48
25	305	Office Equipment						500.00	1 108.50
	CS	Sales				516.40	92.10		
29	306	E. & J. White		9.60	310.40				310.40
30				21.12	759.88	1037.60	184.10	12 580.00	14 561.58

EXERCISE 4.9 — Trend Fashions

Using the ledger accounts prepared through exercises 4.3 and 4.6, post the amounts from the following sales, sales returns and allowances and cash receipts journals to the general ledger for Trend Fashions. Use as many copies as you need of the blank ledger master provided on page 540. Don't forget to include the name of the ledger at the top of the first page (see example on page 172).

SALES JOURNAL OF TREND FASHIONS — Fol. SJ1

Date	Inv. no.	Particulars (Debtor's account to be debited)	Fol.	Sales	Sales tax	Debtors' total
19XX						
Feb. 10	508	Jane's Fashion Store		360.00	54.00	414.00
12	509	The Dress Shop		337.50	50.63	388.13
15	510	Dianne's Boutique		148.50	22.80	171.30
20	511	H. Taylor & Co.		360.00	54.00	414.00
25	512	The Dress Shop		450.00	67.50	517.50
	513	Jane's Fashion Store		315.00	47.25	362.25
28				1971.00	296.18	2267.18

SALES RETURNS AND ALLOWANCES JOURNAL OF TREND FASHIONS — Fol. SR1

Date	CN no.	Particulars (Debtor's account to be credited)	Fol.	Sales returns	Sales tax	Debtors' total
19XX						
Feb. 20	12	The Dress Shop		63.00	9.45	72.45
27	13	Dianne's Boutique		27.00	4.05	31.05
28				90.00	13.50	103.50

CASH RECEIPTS JOURNAL OF TREND FASHIONS — Fol. CR1

Date	Rec. no.	Particulars (Account to be credited)	Fol.	Discount allowed	Trade debtors	Sales	Sales tax	General	Bank
19XX									
Feb. 15	75	Office Furniture						100.00	
	CS	Sales				168.30	29.70		298.00
18	CS	Sales				476.00	84.00		560.00
20	76	Rent Revenue						600.00	
	77	The Dress Shop		24.00	296.00				896.00
23	78	Jane's Fashion Store		18.55	246.45				246.45
27	79	H. Taylor & Co.		34.24	497.76				
	80	Office Equipment						88.00	
	CS	Sales				471.20	83.20		1140.16
28				76.79	1040.21	1115.50	196.90	788.00	3140.61

The completed general ledger

When posting from all journals has been completed, J. Mason's general ledger appears as follows.

GENERAL LEDGER OF J. MASON

Cash at Bank — 1.1

Date	Particulars	Fol.	Debit	Credit	Balance
19XX					
Jan. 1	Capital	GJ1	5 000.00		5 000.00 Dr
31	Cash payments	CP1		690.00	4 310.00 Dr
	Cash receipts	CR1	2 605.70		6 915.70 Dr

Inventory — 1.2

Date	Particulars	Fol.	Debit	Credit	Balance
19XX					
Jan. 1	Capital	GJ1	1 500.00		1 500.00 Dr

Accounts Receivable Control — 1.3

Date	Particulars	Fol.	Debit	Credit	Balance
19XX					
Jan. 1	Capital	GJ1	1 118.00		1 118.00 Dr
31	Sundries	GJ1	31.53		1 149.53 Dr
	Sundries	GJ1		164.53	985.00 Dr
	Sales	SJ1	502.54		1 487.54 Dr
	Sales returns	SR1		91.22	1 396.32 Dr
	Cash receipts	CR1		807.20	589.12 Dr
	Discount allowed	CR1		42.80	546.32 Dr

Sundry Debtor — H. Larson — 1.5

Date	Particulars	Fol.	Debit	Credit	Balance
19XX					
Jan. 7	Office equipment	GJ1	150.00		150.00 Dr

Land — 2.1

Date	Particulars	Fol.	Debit	Credit	Balance
19XX					
Jan. 1	Capital	GJ1	20 000.00		20 000.00 Dr

Buildings — 2.2

Date	Particulars	Fol.	Debit	Credit	Balance
19XX					
Jan. 1	Capital	GJ1	40 000.00		40 000.00 Dr

Plant and Machinery 2.3

Date	Particulars	Fol.	Debit	Credit	Balance
19XX Jan. 1	Capital	GJ1	12 000.00		12 000.00 Dr

Office Equipment 2.6

Date	Particulars	Fol.	Debit	Credit	Balance

19XX
Jan. 1
5
 	
7
 	
31
	Capital
	Sundry creditor —
	  Propert's Computers
	Sundry debtor —
	  H. Larson
	Cash receipts
		GJ1
		
		GJ1
		
		GJ1
		CR1
			10 000.00
			
			12 000.00
				
				150.00
				25.00
					10 000.00 Dr
					
					22 000.00 Dr
					
					21 850.00 Dr
					21 825.00 Dr

Office Furniture 2.7

Date	Particulars	Fol.	Debit	Credit	Balance
19XX Jan. 1	Capital	GJ1	1 000.00		1 000.00 Dr

Purchases 3.1

Date	Particulars	Fol.	Debit	Credit	Balance
19XX Jan. 23 31	Drawings Accounts payable	GJ1 PJ1	 236.00	50.00	50.00 Cr 186.00 Dr

Purchases Returns and Allowances 3.2

Date	Particulars	Fol.	Debit	Credit	Balance
19XX Jan. 31	Accounts payable	PR1		45.00	45.00 Cr

Discount Allowed 1.3

Date	Particulars	Fol.	Debit	Credit	Balance
19XX Jan. 31	Accounts receivable	CR1	42.80		42.80 Dr

Bad Debts 3.5

Date	Particulars	Fol.	Debit	Credit	Balance
19XX Jan. 31	J. Glacken	GJ1	116.53		116.53 Dr

Interest Expense 3.10

Date	Particulars	Fol.	Debit	Credit	Balance
19XX Jan. 31	B. Allar	GJ1	5.00		5.00 Dr

Rent Expense 3.14

Date	Particulars	Fol.	Debit	Credit	Balance
19XX Jan. 28	Cash payments	CP1	40.00		40.00 Dr

Wages Expense 3.17

Date	Particulars	Fol.	Debit	Credit	Balance
19XX Jan. 26	Cash payments	CP1	150.00		150.00 Dr

Accounts Payable Control 4.1

Date	Particulars	Fol.	Debit	Credit	Balance
19XX Jan. 1	Capital	GJ1		1 210.00	1 210.00 Cr
31	Sundries	GJ2		55.00	1 265.00 Cr
	Sundries	GJ2	410.00		855.00 Cr
	Purchases	PJ1		236.00	1 091.00 Cr
	Purchases returns	PR1	45.00		1 046.00 Cr
	Cash payments	CP1	500.00		546.00 Cr
	Discount received	CP1	25.00		521.00 Cr

Sales Tax Payable 4.3

Date	Particulars	Fol.	Debit	Credit	Balance
19XX Jan. 31	Accounts receivable	SJ1		65.54	65.54 Cr
	Accounts receivable	SR1	11.89		53.65 Cr
	Cash receipts	CR1		42.50	96.15 Cr

Sundry Creditor — Propert's Computers 4.7

Date	Particulars	Fol.	Debit	Credit	Balance
19XX Jan. 5	Office equipment	GJ1		12 000.00	12 000.00 Cr

Mortgage 5.1

Date	Particulars	Fol.	Debit	Credit	Balance
19XX Jan. 1	Capital	GJ1		10 000.00	10 000.00 Cr

Capital 6.1

Date	Particulars	Fol.	Debit	Credit	Balance
19XX Jan. 1 10 31 26	Sundries H. Raja (correction) M. Garcia (correction) Cash receipts	GJ1 GJ1 GJ1 CR1	18.00	79 408.00 360.00 1 000.00	79 408.00 Cr 79 390.00 Cr 79 750.00 Cr 80 750.00 Cr

Drawings 6.2

Date	Particulars	Fol.	Debit	Credit	Balance
19XX Jan. 23	Purchases	GJ1	50.00		50.00 Dr

Sales 7.1

Date	Particulars	Fol.	Debit	Credit	Balance
19XX Jan. 31	Accounts receivable Cash receipts	SJ1 CR1		437.00 331.00	437.00 Cr 768.00 Cr

Sales Returns 7.2

Date	Particulars	Fol.	Debit	Credit	Balance
19XX Jan. 31	Accounts receivable	SR1	79.33		79.33 Dr

Discount Received 7.3

Date	Particulars	Fol.	Debit	Credit	Balance
19XX Jan. 31	Accounts payable	CP1		25.00	25.00 Cr

Interest Revenue 7.4

Date	Particulars	Fol.	Debit	Credit	Balance
19XX Jan. 31	J. Glacken	GJ1		1.53	1.53 Cr

Rent Revenue 7.5

Date	Particulars	Fol.	Debit	Credit	Balance
19XX Jan. 28	Cash receipts	CR1		400.00	400.00 Cr

Extracting a trial balance

A **trial balance** is a list of general ledger account balances *as at* a particular date. It is a procedure which is undertaken, usually at the end of each month, to test the mathematical accuracy of the bookkeeping.

The format for a trial balance is as follows.

TRIAL BALANCE OF XXXXXXXXX
as at XX XXXXXXX 19XX

Account no.	Account name	Debit	Credit

The trial balance tests the accuracy of the bookkeeping after posting to the ledgers and balancing ledger accounts. It will not, of course, identify **compensating errors** or errors made when making the original entries in the journals.

Remember: The total of debit entries *must equal* the total of credit entries, stated in the accounting equation as follows:

Assets + Expenses = Liabilities + Owner's Equity + Revenue.

If your trial balance is incorrect, carry out the following.
1. Check the trial balance:
   (a) additions
   (b) entries on wrong side
   (c) omissions
   (d) accuracy of entries from ledger — **transposition errors** (digits in wrong order), wrong amount etc.
   (e) halve the difference between totals and look for that amount entered on the wrong side of the trial balance.

2. Check ledger accounts:
   (a) opening balances
   (b) additions
   (c) posting from journals, such as transactions entered on the wrong side of an account
   (d) transposed figures.

Example

All posting procedures having been completed, a trial balance (see below) is to be extracted from J. Mason's general ledger.

All account balances are listed and classified as either a debit balance or a credit balance. The completed trial balance for J. Mason as at 31 January 19XX is shown below.

TRIAL BALANCE OF J. MASON
as at 31 January 19XX

Account no.	Account name	Debit	Credit
1.1	Cash at Bank	6 915.70	
1.2	Inventory	1 500.00	
1.3	Accounts Receivable Control	546.32	
1.5	Sundry Debtor — H. Larson	150.00	
2.1	Land	20 000.00	
2.2	Buildings	40 000.00	
2.3	Plant and Machinery	12 000.00	
2.6	Office Equipment	21 825.00	
2.7	Office Furniture	1 000.00	
3.1	Purchases	186.00	
3.2	Purchases Returns and Allowances		45.00
3.3	Discount Allowed	42.80	
3.5	Bad Debts	116.53	
3.10	Interest Expense	5.00	
3.14	Rent Expense	40.00	
3.17	Wages Expense	150.00	
4.1	Accounts Payable Control		521.00
4.3	Sales Tax Payable		96.15
4.7	Sundry Creditor — Propert's Computers		12 000.00
5.1	Mortgage		10 000.00
6.1	Capital		80 750.00
6.2	Drawings	50.00	
7.1	Sales		768.00
7.2	Sales Returns and Allowances	79.33	
7.3	Discount Received		25.00
7.4	Interest Revenue		1.53
7.5	Rent Revenue		400.00
		104 606.68	104 606.68

EXERCISE 4.10 K. Dominic & Sons

Using the ledger accounts prepared through exercises 4.1, 4.4 and 4.7, prepare a trial balance for K. Dominic & Sons as at 31 May 19XX. Use a copy of the trial balance master provided on page 557.

EXERCISE 4.11 B. James & Co.

Using the ledger accounts prepared through exercises 4.2, 4.5 and 4.8, prepare a trial balance for B. James & Co. as at 30 April 19XX. Use a copy of the trial balance master provided on page 557.

EXERCISE 4.12 Trend Fashions

Using the ledger accounts prepared through exercises 4.3, 4.6 and 4.9, prepare a trial balance for Trend Fashions as at 28 February 19XX. Use a copy of the trial balance master provided on page 557.

EXERCISE 4.13 H. Ayad & Co.

From the following general ledger account balances, prepare a trial balance for H. Ayad & Co. as at 30 April 19XX. Use a copy of the trial balance master provided on page 557.

Cash at Bank	5 590.00
Accounts Receivable Control	2 489.00
Sundry Debtor — J. Rankin	580.00
Accounts Payable Control	1 998.75
Sundry Creditor — Westwood Motors	12 500.00
Sundry Creditor — The Desk Set	500.00
Motor Vehicles	22 950.00
Office Equipment	3 675.00
Office Furniture	1 295.60
Discount Allowed	203.00
Discount Received	198.00
Land	398 000.00
Buildings	200 000.00
Mortgage	250 000.00
Inventory	7 430.00
Purchases	5 640.00
Purchases Returns and Allowances	410.00
Sales	8 945.00
Sales Returns and Allowances	543.00
Wages Expense	8 430.00
Advertising	555.00
Electricity	480.00
Stationery	224.00
Sales Tax Payable	803.00
Petty Cash	250.00
Capital	382 979.85

In this and the following exercises, you will need to determine whether these accounts have a debit balance or a credit balance. To do this, determine what type of account it is (for example, whether an asset, liability, owner's equity, expense or revenue account) and apply the rules of debit and credit:

Cash at Bank = Asset account   Normal balance of asset account = Debit.

(*Hint*: Until you become more familiar with 'normal' account balances, consult the chart on page 40.)

EXERCISE 4.14 N. Tomesetti & Sons

From the following general ledger account balances, prepare the trial balance for N. Tomasetti & Sons as at 30 September 19XX. Use a copy of the trial balance master provided on page 557.

Cash at Bank	18 942.00
Motor Vehicles	30 225.00
Accounts Receivable Control	12 265.50
Sundry Debtor — C. Ranatunga	850.00
Accounts Payable Control	9 443.00
Sundry Creditor — Northside Motors	15 000.00
Sundry Creditor — Copy Cats Ltd	1 200.00
Discount Received	540.00
Land	350 000.00
Mortgage	150 000.00
Rent Revenue	2 500.00
Buildings	150 000.00
Wages Expense	7 000.00
Sales Tax Payable	1 115.60
Petty Cash	300.00
Advertising	750.00
Stationery	405.00
Office Equipment	4 950.00
Office Furniture	2 309.00
Discount Allowed	743.00
Plant and Equipment	20 540.00
Purchases	8 660.00
Sales	10 778.00
Purchases Returns	204.00
Sales Returns	310.00
Inventory	18 745.60
Drawings	400.00
Repairs and Maintenance	780.00
Capital	437 394.50

Reconciling with subsidiary ledgers

When posting to the general ledger is finalised for the month, a trial balance is prepared to check the accuracy of the bookkeeping. After posting to the accounts payable and accounts receivable subsidiary ledgers is finalised, a schedule of creditors' balances and a schedule of debtors' balances are prepared. These consist of a listing of the account balances in the accounts payable and accounts receivable ledgers. These account balances are then totalled to ascertain for the month:
- the amount owing to trade creditors, and
- the amount owed by trade debtors.

The balance of the Accounts Payable Control account in the general ledger should agree with the total of the schedule of creditors' balances in the accounts payable ledger. Also, the balance of the Accounts Receivable Control account in the general ledger should agree with the total of the schedule of debtors' balances in the accounts receivable ledger.

Reconciling the control accounts in the general ledger with the schedules of debtors' and creditors' balances will be covered in detail in the sections 'Posting to the accounts payable ledger' (below) and 'Posting to the accounts receivable ledger' (page 237).

SECTION 2: THE ACCOUNTS PAYABLE LEDGER

The accounts payable ledger contains details of transactions for individual trade creditors. From this information the business can determine how much it owes each individual trade creditor and the past history of its transactions with each trade creditor; in other words, the amounts owing, credits received and payments made.

Posting to the accounts payable ledger

Trade creditors' accounts are only posted 'in total' to the general ledger and are represented in that ledger by the Accounts Payable Control account. Dealings with trade creditors are processed by the accounts payable department which is responsible for recording the accounts payable journals and posting details of individual transactions with trade creditors to the accounts payable ledger.

At the end of each month:
- post individual trade creditors' amounts to the accounts payable ledger
- insert the ledger folio reference number in the 'Folio' column of the journal.

Journals are posted to ledgers in the following order:
1. general journal
2. purchases journal
3. purchases returns and allowances journal
4. cash payments journal.

From the general journal

Basic format

The posting of the opening entry from the general journal (basic format) to the accounts payable ledger is carried out by crediting the individual trade creditors' accounts with individual amounts (see ① below). Folio numbers of accounts payable ledger accounts are inserted in the journals as the items are posted and are placed in the 'Folio' column alongside the amount posted.

GENERAL JOURNAL OF J. MASON　　　　　　　　　　　　　Fol. GJ1

Date	Particulars		Folio	Debit	Credit
19XX Jan. 1	Land Buildings Plant and Machinery Office Equipment Office Furniture Cash at Bank Inventory Accounts Receivable 　M. Adams 　J. Abbott 　R. Glacken 　H. Raja Accounts Payable 　H. Lime 　P. Eastman　① 　M. Garcia 　B. Allar Mortgage Capital	 250.00 500.00 115.00 253.00 300.00 200.00 510.00 200.00	 AP1 AP2 AP3 AP4	20 000.00 40 000.00 12 000.00 10 000.00 1 000.00 5 000.00 1 500.00 1 118.00	 1 210.00 10 000.00 79 408.00
	Assets, liabilities and capital at this date			90 618.00	90 618.00

In the accounts payable ledger:
① Individual trade creditors' amounts are posted to the 'Credit' column of relevant accounts in the accounts payable ledger.

Columnar format

The following illustrates the posting of the opening entry in the general journal (columnar format) to the accounts payable ledger:

1. *Credit* individual creditors' accounts with amounts in the 'Accounts payable' column from the *credit* side of the general journal.
2. *Debit* individual creditors' accounts with amounts in the 'Accounts payable' column from the *debit* side of the general journal.

Folio numbers of Accounts Payable Ledger accounts are inserted in the journals as the items are posted and are placed in the 'Folio' column alongside the account name.

GENERAL JOURNAL OF J. MASON

Fol. GJ1

| DEBIT ||| | | | CREDIT |||
Accounts receivable	Accounts payable	General	Date	Particulars	Fol.	Accounts receivable	Accounts payable	General
		20 000.00 40 000.00 12 000.00 10 000.00 1 000.00 5 000.00 1 500.00	19XX Jan. 1	Land Buildings Plant and Machinery Office Equipment Office Furniture Cash at Bank Inventory				

250.00
500.00
115.00
253.00
	②
	THIS
	COLUMN
			①②	M. Adams
				J. Abbott
				R. Glacken
				H. Raja
				  H. Lime
				  P. Eastman
				  M. Garcia
				  B. Allar
				Mortgage
				Capital
				Being assets,
				liabilities and capital
				as at this date.
					AP1
					AP2
					AP3
					AP4
							①
							THIS
							COLUMN
							300.00
							200.00
							510.00
							200.00
								10 000.00
								79 408.00

1118.00		89 500.00					1210.00	89 408.00

In the accounts payable ledger:
① *Credit* individual creditors' accounts with amounts in the 'Accounts payable' column from the *credit* side of the general journal.
② *Debit* individual creditors' accounts with amounts in the 'Accounts payable' column from the *debit* side of the general journal.
Insert folio references alongside account name.

When details of trade creditors' transactions are posted from the general journal opening entry, J. Mason's accounts payable ledger will appear as follows.

ACCOUNTS PAYABLE LEDGER OF J. MASON

H. Lime   AP1

Date	Particulars	Fol.	Debit	Credit	Balance
19XX Jan. 1	Capital	GJ1		300.00	300.00 Cr

P. Eastman   AP2

Date	Particulars	Fol.	Debit	Credit	Balance
19XX Jan. 1	Capital	GJ1		200.00	200.00 Cr

M. Garcia   AP3

Date	Particulars	Fol.	Debit	Credit	Balance
19XX Jan. 1	Capital	GJ1		510.00	510.00 Cr

B. Allar   AP4

Date	Particulars	Fol.	Debit	Credit	Balance
19XX Jan. 1	Capital	GJ1		200.00	200.00 Cr

Following the posting procedures outlined above, the remainder of the general journal entries for January are posted to the accounts payable ledger.

GENERAL JOURNAL OF J. MASON (continued)

DEBIT   CREDIT   Fol. GJ1

Accounts receivable	Accounts payable	General	Date	Particulars	Fol.	Accounts receivable	Accounts payable	General
	50.00		Jan. 4	P. Eastman H. Lime Correction of error.	AP2 AP1		50.00	

		12 000.00	5	Office Equipment
				  Sundry Creditor —
				    Propert's
				    Computers
				Purchase of
				computer on credit.
								12 000.00

		150.00	7	H. Larson —
				  Sundry Debtor
				    Office Equipment
				Sale of printer on
				credit.
								150.00

30.00			10	J. Abbott M. Adams Correction of error.		30.00		
		18.00	10	Capital H. Raja Correction of error.			18.00	
		50.00	23	Drawings Purchases Owner took goods for personal use.				50.00
	360.00		31	M. Garcia Capital Correction of error.	AP3			360.00
		5.00	31	Interest Expense B. Allar Interest payable on creditor's overdue account.	AP4		5.00	
1.53			31	J. Glacken Interest Revenue Interest charged on debtor's overdue account.				1.53
		116.53	31	Bad Debts J. Glacken Bad debt written off.		116.53		
31.53	410.00	12 339.53				164.53	55.00	12 561.53

When trade creditors' transactions for January are posted from the remainder of the general journal entries, J. Mason's accounts payable ledger will appear as follows. Note how the various transactions affect the amounts owed to trade creditors.

ACCOUNTS PAYABLE LEDGER OF J. MASON

H. Lime — AP1

Date	Particulars	Fol.	Debit	Credit	Balance
19XX					
Jan. 1	Capital	GJ1		300.00	300.00 Cr
4	P. Eastman (correction) ①	GJ1		50.00	350.00 Cr

P. Eastman — AP2

Date	Particulars	Fol.	Debit	Credit	Balance
19XX					
Jan. 1	Capital	GJ1		200.00	200.00 Cr
4	H. Lime (correction) ②	GJ1	50.00		150.00 Cr

M. Garcia — AP3

Date	Particulars	Fol.	Debit	Credit	Balance
19XX					
Jan. 1	Capital	GJ1		510.00	510.00 Cr
31	Capital (correction) ②	GJ1	360.00		150.00 Cr

B. Allar — AP4

Date	Particulars	Fol.	Debit	Credit	Balance
19XX					
Jan. 1	Capital	GJ1		200.00	200.00 Cr
31	Interest expense ①	GJ1		5.00	205.00 Cr

From the purchases journal

The individual amounts for the trade creditors are posted to the accounts payable ledger by crediting the trade creditors' accounts with the individual amounts (see ① on page 210).

Insert folio references in the 'Folio' column alongside each entry.

PURCHASES JOURNAL OF J. MASON
Fol. PJX

Date	Inv. no.	Particulars (Creditor's account to be credited)	Fol.	Amount	Monthly total
19XX					
Jan. 3	233	H. Lime	AP1	60.00	
8	257	H. Lime	AP2	35.00	
12	612	P. Eastman ①	AP2	68.00	
15	622	P. Eastman	AP2	28.00	
24	479	N. Lilly	AP5	45.00	
31					236.00

① *Credit* individual trade creditors' accounts.

After the purchases journal has been posted, J. Mason's accounts payable ledger appears as follows.

ACCOUNTS PAYABLE LEDGER OF J. MASON

H. Lime AP1

Date	Particulars	Fol.	Debit	Credit	Balance
19XX					
Jan. 1	Capital	GJ1		300.00	300.00 Cr
4	P. Eastman (correction)	GJ1		50.00	350.00 Cr
3	Purchases ①	PJ1		60.00	410.00 Cr
8	Purchases ①	PJ1		35.00	445.00 Cr

P. Eastman AP2

Date	Particulars	Fol.	Debit	Credit	Balance
19XX					
Jan. 1	Capital	GJ1		200.00	200.00 Cr
4	H. Lime (correction)	GJ1	50.00		150.00 Cr
12	Purchases ①	PJ1		68.00	218.00 Cr
15	Purchases ①	PJ1		28.00	246.00 Cr

M. Garcia AP3

Date	Particulars	Fol.	Debit	Credit	Balance
19XX					
Jan. 1	Capital	GJ1		510.00	510.00 Cr
31	Capital (correction)	GJ1	360.00		150.00 Cr

B. Allar — AP4

Date	Particulars	Fol.	Debit	Credit	Balance
19XX					
Jan. 1	Capital	GJ1		200.00	200.00 Cr
31	Interest expense	GJ1		5.00	205.00 Cr

N. Lilly — AP5

Date	Particulars	Fol.	Debit	Credit	Balance
19XX					
Jan. 24	Purchases ①	PJ1		45.00	45.00 Cr

From the purchases returns and allowances journal

The individual amounts for the trade creditors are posted to the accounts payable ledger by debiting the trade creditors' accounts with individual amounts (see ① below).

Insert folio references in the 'Folio' column alongside each entry.

PURCHASES RETURNS AND ALLOWANCES JOURNAL OF J. MASON Fol. PR1

Date	Inv. no.	Particulars (Creditor's account to be debited)	Fol.	Amount	Monthly total
19XX					
Jan. 12	111	H. Lime	AP1	15.00	
18	321	P. Eastman ①	AP2	10.00	
29	456	N. Lilly	AP5	20.00	
31					$45.00

① *Debit* individual trade creditors' accounts.

After the purchases returns and allowances journal has been posted, J. Mason's accounts payable ledger appears as follows.

ACCOUNTS PAYABLE LEDGER OF J. MASON

H. Lime — AP1

Date	Particulars	Fol.	Debit	Credit	Balance
19XX					
Jan. 1	Capital	GJ1		300.00	300.00 Cr
4	P. Eastman (correction)	GJ1		50.00	350.00 Cr
3	Purchases	PJ1		60.00	410.00 Cr
8	Purchases	PJ1		35.00	445.00 Cr
12	Purchases returns ①	PR1	15.00		430.00 Cr

P. Eastman   AP2

Date	Particulars	Fol.	Debit	Credit	Balance
19XX					
Jan. 1	Capital	GJ1		200.00	200.00 Cr
4	H. Lime (correction)	GJ1	50.00		150.00 Cr
12	Purchases	PJ1		68.00	218.00 Cr
15	Purchases	PJ1		28.00	246.00 Cr
18	Purchases returns ①	PR1	10.00		236.00 Cr

M. Garcia   AP3

Date	Particulars	Fol.	Debit	Credit	Balance
19XX					
Jan. 1	Capital	GJ1		510.00	510.00 Cr
31	Capital (correction)	GJ1	360.00		150.00 Cr

B. Allar   AP4

Date	Particulars	Fol.	Debit	Credit	Balance
19XX					
Jan. 1	Capital	GJ1		200.00	200.00 Cr
31	Interest expense	GJ1		5.00	205.00 Cr

N. Lilly   AP5

Date	Particulars	Fol.	Debit	Credit	Balance
19XX					
Jan. 24	Purchases	PJ1		45.00	45.00 Cr
29	Purchases returns ①	PR1	20.00		25.00 Cr

From the cash payments journal

The individual amounts for the trade creditors are posted to the accounts payable ledger by debiting the individual trade creditors' accounts with:

1. the amount recorded in the 'Trade creditors' column (see ① on page 213)
2. the amount recorded in the 'Discount received' column (see ② on page 213).

Insert folio references in the 'Folio' column alongside each entry.

CASH PAYMENTS JOURNAL OF J. MASON Fol. CP1

Date	Chq. no.	Particulars (Account to be debited)	Fol.	Discount received	Trade creditors	General	Bank
19XX				②	①		
Jan. 13	264	H. Lime	AP1	17.50	332.50		332.50
25	265	P. Eastman	AP2	7.50	142.50		142.50
26	266	Wages Expense				150.00	150.00
28	267	Rent				40.00	40.00
	268	N. Lilly	AP5		25.00		25.00
31				25.00	500.00	190.00	690.00

Debit the individual trade creditors' accounts with:
① amount recorded in 'Trade creditors' column.
② amount recorded in 'Discount received' column.

Folio references for individual accounts are entered in the 'Folio' column of the cash payments journal as each item is posted to the ledger.

After the cash payments journal has been posted, J. Mason's accounts payable ledger appears as follows.

ACCOUNTS PAYABLE LEDGER OF J. MASON

H. Lime AP1

Date	Particulars	Fol.	Debit	Credit	Balance
19XX					
Jan. 1	Capital	GJ1		300.00	300.00 Cr
4	P. Eastman (correction)	GJ1		50.00	350.00 Cr
3	Purchases	PJ1		60.00	410.00 Cr
8	Purchases	PJ1		35.00	445.00 Cr
12	Purchases returns	PR1	15.00		430.00 Cr
13	Cash payments ①	CP1	332.50		97.50 Cr
	Discount received ②	CP1	17.50		80.00 Cr

P. Eastman AP2

Date	Particulars	Fol.	Debit	Credit	Balance
19XX					
Jan. 1	Capital	GJ1		200.00	200.00 Cr
4	H. Lime (correction)	GJ1	50.00		150.00 Cr
12	Purchases	PJ1		68.00	218.00 Cr
15	Purchases	PJ1		28.00	246.00 Cr
18	Purchases returns	PR1	10.00		236.00 Cr
24	Cash payments ①	CP1	142.50		93.50 Cr
	Discount received ②	CP1	7.50		86.00 Cr

M. Garcia — AP3

Date	Particulars	Fol.	Debit	Credit	Balance
19XX					
Jan. 1	Capital	GJ1		510.00	510.00 Cr
31	Capital (correction)	GJ1	360.00		150.00 Cr

B. Allar — AP4

Date	Particulars	Fol.	Debit	Credit	Balance
19XX					
Jan. 1	Capital	GJ1		200.00	200.00 Cr
31	Interest expense	GJ1		5.00	205.00 Cr

N. Lilly — AP5

Date	Particulars	Fol.	Debit	Credit	Balance
19XX					
Jan. 24	Purchases	PJ1		45.00	45.00 Cr
29	Purchases returns	PR1	20.00		25.00 Cr
30	Cash payments ①	CP1	25.00		0.00

The completed accounts payable ledger

At the end of the month when all details of transactions with individual trade creditors have been posted to the accounts payable ledger of J. Mason, a schedule of creditors' balances is prepared.

Schedule of creditors' balances

A schedule of creditors' balances is a listing of all outstanding balances in the accounts payable ledger. It is prepared to show the total amount owing to *trade* creditors at the end of the month. The balances of the trade creditors' accounts are listed and totalled.

For example, the schedule of creditors' balances taken from the accounts payable ledger of J. Mason shows the following.

J. MASON
Schedule of Creditors' Balances
as at 31 January 19XX

AP1	H. Lime	$ 80.00
AP2	P. Eastman	86.00
AP3	M. Garcia	150.00
AP4	B. Allar	205.00
		$521.00

Reconciling the schedule of creditors' balances

The steps taken to reconcile the schedule of creditors' balances with the Accounts Payable Control account in the general ledger are as follows:
1. From the accounts payable ledger, prepare a list of outstanding balances to show the total amount owing to trade creditors at the end of the month.
2. In the general ledger, access the Accounts Payable Control account.
3. Compare the total of the schedule of creditors' balances with the balance of the Accounts Payable Control account. Totals should agree.

For comparison purposes, the schedule of creditors' balances and the Accounts Payable Control account from J. Mason's general ledger are shown below. If you examine them, you can see that the final balance in the Accounts Payable Control account in the general ledger agrees with the total of the schedule of creditors' balances compiled from the account balances in the accounts payable ledger.

Accounts Payable Control 4.1

Date	Particulars	Fol.	Debit	Credit	Balance
19XX					
Jan. 1	Capital	GJ1		1210.00	1210.00 Cr
31	Sundries	GJ2		55.00	1265.00 Cr
	Sundries	GJ2	410.00		855.00 Cr
	Purchases	PJ1		236.00	1091.00 Cr
	Purchases returns	PR1	45.00		1046.00 Cr
	Cash payments	CP1	500.00		546.00 Cr
	Discount received	CP1	25.00		521.00 Cr

J. MASON
Schedule of Creditors' Balances
as at 31 January 19XX

AP1	H. Lime	$ 80.00
AP2	P. Eastman	86.00
AP3	M. Garcia	150.00
AP4	B. Allar	205.00
		$521.00

EXERCISE 4.15 K. Dominic & Sons

From the general journal and accounts payable journals of K. Dominic & Sons, reproduced on pages 216–217, you are required to carry out the following.
1. Post all relevant amounts to the accounts payable ledger for K. Dominic & Sons. Use as many copies as you need of the blank ledger master provided on page 558. Don't forget to include the name of the ledger at the top of the first page (see example on page 207).
2. Prepare a schedule of creditors' balances as at 31 May 19XX.
3. Reconcile the schedule of creditors' balances with the Accounts Payable Control account in the general ledger which you prepared for exercise 4.7 (page 194) in the general ledger section.

GENERAL JOURNAL OF K. DOMINIC & SONS

Fol. GJ1

Accounts receivable (Dr)	Accounts payable (Dr)	General (Dr)	Date	Particulars	Fol.	Accounts receivable (Cr)	Accounts payable (Cr)	General (Cr)
		250 000.00	19XX May 1	Land				
		80 000.00		Buildings				
		35 000.00		Motor Vehicles				
		2 550.00		Office Equipment				
		1 890.00		Office Furniture				
		18 000.00		Cash at Bank				
		9 890.00		Inventory				
240.00				J. Wade				
580.00				M. Byrnes				
420.00				G. Mundo				
				W. Maine			680.00	
				Conway & Sons			420.00	
				B. Samuels			78.00	
				Mortgage				150 000.00
				Capital				247 392.00
				Assets, liabilities and capital as at this date.				
1240.00		397 330.00					1178.00	397 392.00
		10 000.00	5	Office Equipment				
				Sundry creditor — Imagemakers				10 000.00
				Purchased photocopier on credit.				
	180.00		7	J. Wade				
				M. Byrnes		180.00		
				Correction of posting error.				
			16	Sundry Debtor — Ace Secretarial Service				
		500.00		Office Furniture				500.00
				Office desk sold on credit.				
		420.00	19	Bad Debts				
				G. Mundo		420.00		
				Bad debt written off.				
		300.00	20	Drawings				
				Purchases				300.00
				Owner took goods for personal use.				
		1.95	25	Interest Expense				
				B. Samuel			1.95	
				Interest paid on overdue account.				
	180.00	11 221.95				600.00	1.95	10 800.00

PURCHASES JOURNAL OF K. DOMINIC & SONS
Fol. PJ1

Date	Inv. no.	Particulars (Creditor's account to be credited)	Fol.	Amount	Monthly total
19XX					
May 5	237	W. Maine & Co.		500.00	
8	125	Conway & Sons		140.00	
15	98	D. J. Callaghan		900.00	
20	251	W. Maine & Co.		328.00	
	147	Conway & Sons		250.00	
31					2118.00

PURCHASES RETURNS AND ALLOWANCES JOURNAL OF K. DOMINIC & SONS
Fol. PR1

Date	CN no.	Particulars (Creditor's account to be debited)	Fol.	Amount	Monthly total
19XX					
May 20	111	W. Maine & Co.		200	
25	54	D. J. Callaghan		250	
31					450.00

CASH PAYMENTS JOURNAL OF K. DOMINIC & SONS
Fol. CP1

Date	Chq. no.	Particulars (Account to be debited)	Fol.	Discount received	Trade creditors	General	Bank
19XX							
May 14	114	Rent				500.00	500.00
15	115	Advertising				55.00	55.00
	116	Conway & Sons		21.00	399.00		399.00
17	117	Petty Cash				150.00	150.00
20	118	W. Maine & Co.		34.00	646.00		646.00
28	119	Repairs and Maintenance				83.00	83.00
31				55.00	1045.00	788.00	1833.00

EXERCISE 4.16 B. James & Co.

From the general journal and the accounts payable journals of B. James & Co., reproduced on pages 218–219, you are required to carry out the following.

1. Post all relevant amounts to the accounts payable ledger for B. James & Co. Use as many copies as you need of the blank ledger master provided on page 558. Don't forget to include the name of the ledger at the top of the first page (see example on page 207).

2. Prepare a schedule of creditors' balances as at 30 April 19XX.
3. Reconcile the schedule of creditors' balances with the Accounts Payable Control account from the general ledger of B. James & Co., which you prepared in exercise 4.8 (page 195) in the general ledger section.

GENERAL JOURNAL OF B. JAMES & CO.

Fol. GJ1

Accounts receivable	Accounts payable	General	Date	Particulars	Fol.	Accounts receivable	Accounts payable	General
			19XX					
		18 900.00	Apr. 1	Plant and Machinery				
		15 500.00		Motor Vehicles				
		4 890.00		Office Equipment				
		2 680.00		Office Furniture				
		12 440.00		Cash at Bank				
		5 660.00		Inventory				
172.00				A. Collins				
				Corella Private				
289.00				Hospital				
320.00				E. & J. White				
402.00				G. McGregor				
				King & Co.			426.00	
				Greenway & Co.			215.00	
				F. Nguyen			75.00	
				Capital				60 537.00
				Assets, liabilities and				
1 183.00		60 070.00		capital at this date.			716.00	60 537.00
	18.00		6	F. Nguyen				
				Capital				18.00
				Correction of error.				
			8	Corella Private				
100.00				Hospital				
				A. Collins		100.00		
				Correction of error.				
	150.00		8	Greenway & Co.				
				King & Co.			150.00	
				Correction of error.				
		2 000.00	11	Office Equipment				
				Sundry creditor —				
				Technics Ltd				2 000.00
				Laser printer				
				purchased on credit.				
20.10			30	G. McGregor				
				Interest Revenue				20.10
				Interest charged on				
				debtor's overdue				
				account (6 months).				
120.10	168.00	2 000.00				100.00	150.00	2 038.10

PURCHASES JOURNAL OF B. JAMES & CO.
Fol. PJ1

Date	Inv. no.	Particulars (Creditor's account to be credited)	Fol.	Amount	Monthly total
19XX					
Apr. 4	1127	King & Co.		457.00	
10	885	L. Thompson & Sons		98.67	
15	1145	King & Co.		368.00	
24	98	Greenway & Co.		1254.80	
28	946	L. Thompson & Sons		467.00	
29	125	Greenway & Co.		125.25	
30	157	Williams & Sons		560.00	
					3330.72

PURCHASES RETURNS AND ALLOWANCES JOURNAL OF B. JAMES & CO.
Fol. PR1

Date	CN no.	Particulars (Creditor's account to be debited)	Fol.	Amount	Monthly total
19XX					
Apr. 20	37	King & Co.		57.00	
24	12	Greenway & Co.		105.00	
30					162.00

CASH PAYMENTS JOURNAL OF B. JAMES & CO.
Fol. CP1

Date	Chq. no.	Particulars (Account to be debited)	Fol.	Discount received	Trade creditors	General	Bank
19XX							
Apr. 12	148	Stationery				68.00	68.00
14	149	King & Co.		14.40	561.60		561.60
24	150	Electricity				180.00	180.00
	151	Greenway & Co.		1.62	63.38		63.38
28	152	Purchases				100.00	100.00
	153	Motor Vehicles				17 000.00	17 000.00
30				16.02	624.98	17 348.00	17 972.98

EXERCISE
4.17   *Trend Fashions*

From the general journal and the accounts payable journals of Trend Fashions, reproduced on pages 220–221, you are required to carry out the following.

1. Post all relevant amounts to the accounts payable ledger for Trend Fashions. Use as many copies as you need of the blank ledger master provided on page 558. Don't forget to include the name of the ledger at the top of the first page (see example on page 207).
2. Prepare a schedule of creditors' balances as at 28 February 19XX.

3. Reconcile the schedule of creditors' balances with the Accounts Payable Control account in the general ledger, which you prepared for exercise 4.9 (page 196) in the general ledger section.

GENERAL JOURNAL OF TREND FASHIONS   Fol. GJ1

\\ DEBIT \\						\\ CREDIT \\		
Accounts receivable	Accounts payable	General	Date	Particulars	Fol.	Accounts receivable	Accounts payable	General
			19XX					
		240 000.00	Feb. 1	Land				
		60 000.00		Buildings				
		24 500.00		Motor Vehicles				
		6 110.00		Office Equipment				
		2 400.00		Office Furniture				
		11 765.00		Cash at Bank				
		5 295.00		Inventory				
320.00				The Dress Shop				
265.00				Jane's Fashion Store				
532.00				H. Taylor & Co.				
302.00				Petrovich & Co.				
				W. A. Montey			440.00	
				G. Hanna			385.00	
				W. Laporte			229.00	
				J. S. Baxter			88.00	
				Mortgage				120 000.00
				Capital				230 347.00
				Assets, liabilities and capital as at this date.				
1419.00		350 070.00					1142.00	350 347.00
	120.00		7	W. A. Montey				
				G. Hanna			120.00	
				Correction of error.				
		21 000.00	16	Motor Vehicles				
				Sundry Creditor — Schaeffer Motors				21 000.00
				Motor vehicle purchased on credit.				
			18	Sundry Debtor —				
		9 500.00		R. Mustafa				
				Motor Vehicles				9 500.00
				Motor vehicle sold on credit.				
		1 100.00	22	Office Equipment				
				Sundry Creditor — Compusupply Co.				1 100.00
				Laser printer purchased on credit.				
			22	Sundry Debtor —				
		300.00		H. Rostov				
				Office Equipment				300.00
				Inkjet printer sold on credit.				
		520.00	27	Drawings				
				Purchases				520.00
				Owner took goods for personal use.				
	120.00	32 420.00					120.00	32 420.00

PURCHASES JOURNAL OF TREND FASHIONS   Fol. PJ1

Date	Inv. no.	Particulars (Creditor's account to be credited)	Fol.	Amount	Monthly total
19XX					
Feb. 2	201	W. A. Montey		405.60	
6	304	J. S. Baxter		236.94	
9	235	G. Hanna		983.56	
10	667	W. A. Montey		56.78	
15	345	J. S. Baxter		436.90	
20	91	L. Beetson		125.50	
28	745	W. A. Montey		1270.50	
					3515.78

PURCHASES RETURNS AND ALLOWANCES JOURNAL OF TREND FASHIONS
Fol. PR1

Date	CN no.	Particulars (Creditor's account to be debited)	Fol.	Amount	Monthly total
19XX					
Feb. 16	98	G. Hanna		51.00	
21	14	J. S. Baxter		26.94	
28					77.94

CASH PAYMENTS JOURNAL OF TREND FASHIONS   Fol. CP1

Date	Chq. no.	Particulars (Account to be debited)	Fol.	Discount received	Trade creditors	General	Bank
19XX							
Feb. 15	334	Repairs and Maintenance				150.00	150.00
20	335	Wages				1076.00	1076.00
	336	W. A. Montey		8.00	312.00		312.00
25	337	Advertising				120.00	120.00
	338	G. Hanna		12.65	492.35		492.35
28	339	Petty Cash Reimbursement					
		Stationery				15.00	
		Travel Expenses				80.00	95.00
				20.65	804.35	1441.00	2245.35

EXERCISE 4.18

The Handicraft Shop

The Handicraft Shop commenced trading on 1 July 19XX with the following assets, liabilities and capital:

Motor Vehicles		$23 000.00
Furniture and Fittings		9 000.00
Office Equipment		4 500.00
Office Furniture		2 100.00
Cash at Bank		7 890.00
Accounts Receivable (Trade Debtors)		1 377.00
J. Schultz	$455.00	
L. Morovitz	320.00	
K. Lang	602.00	
Accounts Payable (Trade Creditors)		2 864.00
Tapestry Supplies	870.00	
Woollen Mills	340.00	
A. B. Wells & Co.	890.00	
Craft Importers Ltd	764.00	
Capital		45 003.00

The following source documents were received during the month of July.

Invoices received

TAPESTRY SUPPLIES
147 Clarence Street
SYDNEY NSW 2000

Inv. 704   2 July 19XX

To: The Handicraft Shop
      Westfield Shopping Centre
      PARRAMATTA NSW 2150

For: Trading goods $48.00

RILEY WHOLESALE CO.
10 Westerway Street
CAMPSIE NSW 2194

Inv. 8940   7 July 19XX

To: The Handicraft Shop
      Westfield Shopping Centre
      PARRAMATTA NSW 2150

For: Trading goods $125.50

WOOLLEN MILLS
18 Murray Street
WANGARATTA VIC 3677

Inv. 987   15 July 19XX

To: The Handicraft Shop
      Westfield Shopping Centre
      PARRAMATTA NSW 2150

For: Trading goods $548.00

CRAFT IMPORTERS LTD
89 Bridge Street
EPPING NSW 2121

Inv. 66   15 July 19XX

To: The Handicraft Shop
      Westfield Shopping Centre
      PARRAMATTA NSW 2150

For: Trading goods $780.50

```
┌─────────────────────────────────────┐  ┌─────────────────────────────────────┐
│         RILEY WHOLESALE CO.         │  │          A. B. WELLS & CO.          │
│          10 Westerway Street        │  │            94 Forest Way            │
│           CAMPSIE NSW 2194          │  │         SHEPPARTON VIC 3630         │
│                                     │  │                                     │
│  Inv. 9010              20 July 19XX│  │  Inv. 462               20 July 19XX│
│                                     │  │                                     │
│  To:   The Handicraft Shop          │  │  To:   The Handicraft Shop          │
│        Westfield Shopping Centre    │  │        Westfield Shopping Centre    │
│        PARRAMATTA NSW 2150          │  │        PARRAMATTA NSW 2150          │
│                                     │  │                                     │
│  For: Trading goods        $465.00  │  │  For: Trading goods       $1205.60  │
└─────────────────────────────────────┘  └─────────────────────────────────────┘

┌─────────────────────────────────────┐  ┌─────────────────────────────────────┐
│         CRAFT IMPORTERS LTD         │  │            WOOLLEN MILLS            │
│            89 Bridge Street         │  │           18 Murray Street          │
│           EPPING NSW 2121           │  │         WANGARATTA VIC 3677         │
│                                     │  │                                     │
│  Inv. 80                20 July 19XX│  │  Inv. 1049              30 July 19XX│
│                                     │  │                                     │
│  To:   The Handicraft Shop          │  │  To:   The Handicraft Shop          │
│        Westfield Shopping Centre    │  │        Westfield Shopping Centre    │
│        PARRAMATTA NSW 2150          │  │        PARRAMATTA NSW 2150          │
│                                     │  │                                     │
│  For: Trading goods        $450.00  │  │  For: Trading goods       $1780.50  │
└─────────────────────────────────────┘  └─────────────────────────────────────┘
```

Credit notes received

```
┌─────────────────────────────────────┐  ┌─────────────────────────────────────┐
│         CRAFT IMPORTERS LTD         │  │          A. B. WELLS & CO.          │
│            89 Bridge Street         │  │            94 Forest Way            │
│           EPPING NSW 2121           │  │         SHEPPARTON VIC 3630         │
│                                     │  │                                     │
│  CN No. 904             28 July 19XX│  │  CN No. 562             29 July 19XX│
│                                     │  │                                     │
│  To:   The Handicraft Shop          │  │  To:   The Handicraft Shop          │
│        Westfield Shopping Centre    │  │        Westfield Shopping Centre    │
│        PARRAMATTA NSW 2150          │  │        PARRAMATTA NSW 2150          │
│                                     │  │                                     │
│  By return damaged goods   $105.50  │  │  Overcharge Inv. 462       $100.00  │
│  (Ref. Inv. 66)                     │  │                                     │
└─────────────────────────────────────┘  └─────────────────────────────────────┘
```

Cheque butts

```
┌──────────────────────────┐  ┌──────────────────────────┐  ┌──────────────────────────┐
│ Cheque No. 106           │  │ Cheque No. 107           │  │ Cheque No. 108           │
│ Date: 7 July 19XX        │  │ Date: 7 July 19XX        │  │ Date: 10 July 19XX       │
│                          │  │                          │  │                          │
│ To:   CASH               │  │ To:   CASH               │  │ To:   WESTFIELD CENTRE   │
│ For:  Petty Cash Imprest │  │ For:  Wages              │  │ For:  Rent               │
│                          │  │                          │  │                          │
│ This cheque:    $100.00  │  │ This cheque:   $3760.00  │  │ This cheque:    $800.00  │
└──────────────────────────┘  └──────────────────────────┘  └──────────────────────────┘
```

Cheque No. 109 Date: *15 July 19XX* To: *A. B. WELLS & CO.* For: *Payment of Account* This cheque: $867.75 *Discount:* 22.25	Cheque No. 110 Date: *15 July 19XX* To: *CRAFT IMPORTERS LTD* For: *Payment of Account* This cheque: $682.50 *Discount:* 17.50	Cheque No. 111 Date: *21 July 19XX* To: *CASH* For: *Wages* This cheque: $3760.00
Cheque No. 112 Date: *25 July 19XX* To: *CASH* For: *Purchases* This cheque: $205.50	Cheque No. 113 Date: *25 July 19XX* To: *TAPESTRY SUPPLIES* For: *Payment of Account* This cheque: $822.90 *Discount:* 21.10	Cheque No. 114 Date: *30 July 19XX* To: *CRAFT ADVERTISER* For: *Advertising* This cheque: $140.00

- On 8 July, it was found that an amount of $64 owing to Tapestry Supplies was incorrectly credited to Craft Importers Ltd.
- On 16 July, a fax machine was purchased on credit from Amadeus Supplies for $1560.
- On 20 July, Woollen Mills charged The Handicraft Shop interest of 5% on their account of $340 which was outstanding for 3 months.
- On 21 July, a motor vehicle was purchased on credit from Woolfe Motors for $18 500.
- On 22 July, the amount in the opening entry for Tapestry Supplies was found to have been incorrectly recorded as $870. It should have been $780.
- On 25 July, the proprietor took trading goods to the value of $68 for personal use.

You are required to carry out the following.

1. Prepare journals from the source documents and the information supplied. Use copies of the relevant journal masters provided at the back of this book.
2. Post journal entries, relating to trade creditors only, to the accounts payable ledger. Use as many copies as you need of the blank ledger master provided on page 558. Don't forget to include the name of the ledger at the top of the first page (see example on page 207).
3. Prepare a schedule of creditors' balances for The Handicraft Shop as at 31 July 19XX.

EXERCISE 4.19   The Book Store

The Book Store commenced trading on 1 May 19XX with the following assets, liabilities and owner's equity.

Premises		$250 000.00
Motor Vehicles		20 000.00
Furniture and Fittings		8 000.00
Office Equipment		3 400.00
Cash at Bank		9 770.00
Inventory		8 790.00
Accounts Receivable (Trade Debtors)		1 229.00
K. Lewin	$602.00	
R. Riaz	56.00	
D. Dominico	220.00	
F. McIntyre	351.00	
Accounts Payable (Trade Creditors)		2 243.00
Master Publishing Co.	550.00	
N. Austin & Co.	224.00	
Deakin Publishers	369.00	
Lyons Press	800.00	
Kimberley Cards	300.00	
Mortgage		80 000.00
Capital		218 946.00

The following source documents were received during the month of May.

Invoices received

Inv. 93	3 May 19XX
MASTER PUBLISHING CO.	
83 Bridge Street	
SYDNEY NSW 2000	
To: The Book Store	
23 Hunter Street	
NEWCASTLE NSW 2300	
For: Trading goods	$168.00

Inv. 401	5 May 19XX
LYONS PRESS	
240 Great North Road	
DRUMMOYNE NSW 2047	
To: The Book Store	
23 Hunter Street	
NEWCASTLE NSW 2300	
For: Trading goods	$950.00

Inv. 115	10 May 19XX
N. AUSTIN & CO.	
104 King William Street	
ADELAIDE SA 5000	
To: The Book Store	
23 Hunter Street	
NEWCASTLE NSW 2300	
For: Trading goods	$849.50

Inv. 117	10 May 19XX
M. BRODIE & SONS	
45 Atkins Street	
GEELONG VIC 3330	
To: The Book Store	
23 Hunter Street	
NEWCASTLE NSW 2300	
For: Trading goods	$1428.75

Inv. 509		15 May 19XX
	DEAKIN PUBLISHERS	
	14 Curtin Square	
	FORREST ACT 2603	
To:	The Book Store	
	23 Hunter Street	
	NEWCASTLE NSW 2300	
For:	Trading goods	$758.90

Inv. 130		20 May 19XX
	N. AUSTIN & CO.	
	104 King William Street	
	ADELAIDE SA 5000	
To:	The Book Store	
	23 Hunter Street	
	NEWCASTLE NSW 2300	
For:	Trading goods	$235.00

Inv. 158		28 May 19XX
	M. BRODIE & SONS	
	45 Atkins Street	
	GEELONG VIC 3330	
To:	The Book Store	
	23 Hunter Street	
	NEWCASTLE NSW 2300	
For:	Trading goods	$1273.80

Inv. 134		28 May 19XX
	MASTER PUBLISHING CO.	
	83 Bridge Street	
	SYDNEY NSW 2000	
To:	The Book Store	
	23 Hunter Street	
	NEWCASTLE NSW 2300	
For:	Trading goods	$590.00

Credit notes received

CN No. 46		15 May 19XX
	N. AUSTIN & CO.	
	104 King William Street	
	ADELAIDE SA 5000	
To:	The Book Store	
	23 Hunter Street	
	NEWCASTLE NSW 2300	
By return — faulty goods		
(Ref. Inv. 115)		$49.50

CN No. 015		18 May 19XX
	MASTER PUBLISHING CO.	
	83 Bridge Street	
	SYDNEY NSW 2000	
To:	The Book Store	
	23 Hunter Street	
	NEWCASTLE NSW 2300	
By return — damaged goods		
(Ref. Inv. 93)		$18.00

CN No. 162		28 May 19XX
	M. BRODIE & SONS	
	45 Atkins Street	
	GEELONG VIC 3330	
To:	The Book Store	
	23 Hunter Street	
	NEWCASTLE NSW 2300	
By overcharge Inv. 117		$100.00

Cheque butts

Cheque No. 065 Date: *5 May 19XX* To: *CASH* For: *Wages* This cheque: *$1500.00*	Cheque No. 066 Date: *7 May 19XX* To: *ADAMS ADVERTISING* For: *Advertising* This cheque: *$78.90*	Cheque No. 067 Date: *7 May 19XX* To: *N. AUSTIN & CO.* For: *Payment of Account* This cheque: *$215.00* Discount: *9.00*
Cheque No. 068 Date: *12 May 19XX* To: *HUNTER ELECTRICITY* For: *Electricity* This cheque: *$380.00*	Cheque No. 069 Date: *15 May 19XX* To: *MASTER PUBLISHING* For: *Payment of Account* This cheque: *$390.00* Discount: *10.00*	Cheque No. 070 Date: *15 May 19XX* To: *DEAKIN PUBLISHERS* For: *Payment on Account* This cheque: *$200.00*
Cheque No. 071 Date: *20 May 19XX* To: *CASH* For: *Wages* This cheque: *$1550.00*	Cheque No. 072 Date: *20 May 19XX* To: *LYONS PRESS* For: *Payment of Account* This cheque: *$768.00* Discount: *32.00*	Cheque No. 073 Date: *28 May 19XX* To: *A. H. PLUMBING* For: *Repairs* This cheque: *$75.00*

- On 2 May, an amount of $150 owing to Deakin Publishers incorrectly credited to Master Publishing Co. was corrected.
- On 5 May, a computer was purchased on credit from Achille Computers for $8950.
- On 10 May, Kimberley Cards charged The Book Store 2.5 per cent p.a. interest on their account of $300, which was overdue for 4 months.
- On 18 May, Deakin Publishers' opening general journal entry should have been recorded as $396, not $369.
- On 25 May, an office desk was purchased on credit from H. Ahmed & Co. for $500.
- On 28 May, the proprietor took goods ($95) for own use.

You are required to carry out the following.
1. Prepare journals from the source documents and the information supplied. Use copies of the relevant journal masters at the back of this book.
2. Post journal entries, relating to trade creditors only, to the accounts payable ledger. Use as many copies as you need of the blank ledger masters provided on page 558. Don't forget to include the name of the ledger at the top of the first page (see example on page 207).
3. Prepare a schedule of creditors' balances for The Book Store as at 31 May 19XX.

Reconciling invoices for payment to creditors

When goods are received they are usually accompanied by a delivery note which states the quantity and description of the goods. The invoice is sent by mail later. (In some cases the goods are accompanied by the invoice and a delivery note is not used.)

When the goods arrive they should be checked to verify that the correct type and quantity of goods have been received and have arrived in good condition. The delivery note should be checked with the purchase order that was sent to the supplier.

When the invoice is received this should be checked against the delivery note. The price of the goods stated on the invoice should also be checked against the purchase order and delivery note. The calculations on the invoice should also be checked.

If there is any discrepancy, the accounts payable clerk should report this to the appropriate person or section to be resolved or rectified. The supplier will be contacted either by using a debit note or by telephone or fax.

EXERCISE 4.20 D. Swan

On 1 August 19XX, D. Swan commenced business as D. Swan Pty Ltd with the following assets, liabilities and capital.

Land		$300 000.00
Buildings		150 000.00
Motor Vehicles		27 500.00
Office Equipment		10 100.00
Office Furniture		7 540.00
Inventory		6 591.00
Cash at Bank		8 420.00
Accounts Receivable		2 745.00
R. Merrill	$1 205.00	
P. Kee	110.00	
M. Bush	1 330.00	
W. Frost Pty Ltd	100.00	
Accounts Payable		1 314.00
R. Douglas	140.00	
W. Frost Pty Ltd	68.00	
A. Parker Pty Ltd	560.00	
N. Williams	300.00	
A. Gomez	246.00	
Mortgage		180 000.00
Capital		331 582.00

The following delivery notes, invoices and credit notes were received and cheques were sent during the month of August 19XX.

Delivery notes received

Delivery Note No. 203
1 August 19XX

R. DOUGLAS
18 Lombard Street
SUTHERLAND NSW 2232

To: D. Swan Pty Ltd
64 Clifford Road
PENSHURST NSW 2222

6 boxes HD computer disks

Delivery Note No. 111
8 August 19XX

W. FROST & CO.
39 Wren Street
TURELLA NSW 2205

To: D. Swan Pty Ltd
64 Clifford Road
PENSHURST NSW 2222

6 boxes continuous fax paper
12 boxes A4 printer paper

Delivery Note No. 12
8 August 19XX

A. PARKER PTY LTD
88 Stafford Road
CAMMERAY NSW 2062

To: D. Swan Pty Ltd
64 Clifford Road
PENSHURST NSW 2222

24 boxes paperclips
2 photocopier toner sets

Delivery Note No. 53
8 August 19XX

SEFTON PRODUCTS
142 Telford Street
HOMEBUSH NSW 2077

To: D. Swan Pty Ltd
64 Clifford Road
PENSHURST NSW 2222

5 laser printer cartridges
10 boxes A4 printer paper

Delivery Note No. 111
20 August 19XX

W. FROST & CO.
39 Wren Street
TURELLA NSW 2205

To: D. Swan Pty Ltd
64 Clifford Road
PENSHURST NSW 2222

1 bubble jet printer
12 boxes printer paper

Delivery Note No. 57
22 August 19XX

A. PARKER PTY LTD
88 Stafford Road
CAMMERAY NSW 2062

To: D. Swan Pty Ltd
64 Clifford Road
PENSHURST NSW 2222

25 boxes A4 photocopier paper

Invoices received

Inv. 480   4 August 19XX

R. DOUGLAS
18 Lombard Street
SUTHERLAND NSW 2232

To: D. Swan Pty Ltd
     64 Clifford Road
     PENSHURST NSW 2222

12 boxes HD computer disks
  @ $9.00 per box $108.00

Inv. 1436   10 August 19XX

W. FROST & CO.
39 Wren Street
TURELLA NSW 2205

To: D. Swan Pty Ltd
     64 Clifford Road
     PENSHURST NSW 2222

6 boxes continuous fax paper
  @ $5.50 per box $ 33.00
12 boxes A4 printer paper
  @ $6.10 per box   73.20
                                  $106.20

Inv. 678   11 August 19XX

A. PARKER PTY LTD
88 Stafford Road
CAMMERAY NSW 2062

To: D. Swan Pty Ltd
     64 Clifford Road
     PENSHURST NSW 2222

24 boxes paperclips
  @ $0.50 per box $ 12.00
2 photocopier toner sets
  @ $45 per set   90.00
                                  $102.00

Inv. 968   11 August 19XX

SEFTON PRODUCTS
142 Telford Street
HOMEBUSH NSW 2077

To: D. Swan Pty Ltd
     64 Clifford Road
     PENSHURST NSW 2222

5 laser printer cartridges
  @ $22.50 each $112.50
10 boxes A4 printer paper
  @ $6.00 per box   60.00
                                  $172.50

Inv. 1521   24 August 19XX

W. FROST & CO.
39 Wren Street
TURELLA NSW 2205

To: D. Swan Pty Ltd
     64 Clifford Road
     PENSHURST NSW 2222

1 bubble jet printer, J182
  @ $580 $580.00
12 boxes printer paper
  @ $6 per box   72.00
                                  $652.00

Inv. 725   26 August 19XX

A. PARKER PTY LTD
88 Stafford Road
CAMMERAY NSW 2062

To: D. Swan Pty Ltd
     64 Clifford Road
     PENSHURST NSW 2222

50 boxes A4 photocopier paper
  @ $3.60 per box $180.00

Credit notes received

```
CN No. 39                 25 August 19XX
            R. DOUGLAS
          18 Lombard Street
        SUTHERLAND NSW 2232

To:   D. Swan Pty Ltd
      64 Clifford Road
      PENSHURST NSW 2222

Ref. Inv. 480
6 boxes HD computer disks
  @ $9 per box overdelivered    $54.00
```

```
CN No. 304                27 August 19XX
         A. PARKER PTY LTD
          88 Stafford Road
         CAMMERAY NSW 2062

To:   D. Swan Pty Ltd
      64 Clifford Road
      PENSHURST NSW 2222

Overcharge Inv. 678            $10.00
```

```
CN No. 95                 28 August 19XX
         A. PARKER PTY LTD
          88 Stafford Road
         CAMMERAY NSW 2062

To:   D. Swan Pty Ltd
      64 Clifford Road
      PENSHURST NSW 2222

By return — damaged goods
(Ref. Inv. 725)
20 boxes A4 photocopier paper
  @ $3.60 per box              $72.00
```

Cheque butts

```
Cheque No. 203
Date: 4 August 19XX

To:   CASH
For:  Wages

This cheque:    $1460.00
```

```
Cheque No. 204
Date: 4 August 19XX

To:   CASH
For:  Petty Cash Imprest

This cheque:    $200.00
```

```
Cheque No. 205
Date: 5 August 19XX

To:   R. DOUGLAS
For:  Payment of Account

This cheque:    $397.70
Discount:         12.30
```

```
Cheque No. 206
Date: 10 August 19XX

To:   R. J. SOMERS
For:  Advertising

This cheque:    $140.00
```

```
Cheque No. 207
Date: 15 August 19XX

To:   Sydney Electricity
For:  Electricity

This cheque:    $298.00
```

```
Cheque No. 208
Date: 20 August 19XX

To:   CASH
For:  Purchases

This cheque:    $45.00
```

Cheque No. 209 Date: *20 August 19XX* To: *A. GOMEZ* For: *Payment of Account* This cheque: $239.85 *Discount:* 6.15	Cheque No. 210 Date: *24 August 19XX* To: *W. FROST & CO.* For: *Payment of Account* This cheque: $23.40 *Discount:* 0.60	Cheque No. 211 Date: *28 August 19XX* To: *CASH* For: *Wages* This cheque: $3400.00
Cheque No. 212 Date: *28 August 19XX* To: *N. ELGAR* For: *Stationery* This cheque: $198.00	Cheque No. 213 Date: *29 August 19XX* To: *A. PARKER PTY LTD* For: *Payment of Account* This cheque: $491.40 *Discount:* 12.60	

- On 8 August, an amount of $56 owing to W. Frost & Co. was incorrectly credited to the account of A. Parker Pty Ltd.
- On 10 August, a photocopier was purchased on credit from Spartacus Suppliers for $2500.
- On 12 August, N. Williams charged D. Swan Pty Ltd 3 per cent p.a. interest on their account of $300 which was overdue for 3 months.
- On 18 August, an executive desk was purchased on credit from M. Munz & Co. for $500.
- D. Swan conducts both credit purchases and credit sales with W. Frost & Co. On 24 August W. Frost & Co.'s account is settled by contra.
- On 28 August, R. Douglas's opening general journal entry should have been recorded as $410, not $140.
- On 29 August, the proprietor took goods valued at $240 for personal use.

You are required to carry out the following. Use copies of the relevant masters provided at the back of this book.
1. Prepare the general journal opening entry.
2. Check the invoices received for accuracy and against delivery notes and report any discrepancies to your superior. Enter the invoices into the purchases journal.
3. Check the credit notes received and report any discrepancies to your superior. Enter the credit notes into the purchases returns and allowances journal.
4. Enter details of cheques into the cash payments journal.
5. Enter the general journal miscellaneous transactions.
6. Post the relevant details from all journals to the accounts payable ledger.
7. Prepare a schedule of creditors' balances for D. Swan as at 31 August 19XX.

EXERCISE 4.21

Jane's Gift Store

Jane Carmody commenced business on 2 November 19XX trading as Jane's Gift Store with the following assets, liabilities and capital.

Furniture and Fittings		$ 5 000.00
Office Equipment		3 060.00
Office Furniture		2 100.00
Inventory (Stock)		9 980.00
Cash at Bank		7 111.00
Accounts Receivable		3 480.00
R. Dabney	$670.00	
C. Forrester	720.00	
R. Fairfax	830.00	
E. Taylor	560.00	
G. Jensen	400.00	
Jewellery Manufacturers	300.00	
Accounts Payable		1 935.00
Gordon Wholesale Co.	308.00	
D. & B. Coleman	162.00	
Dural Homecrafts	450.00	
Jewellery Manufacturers	595.00	
Handcraft Suppliers	420.00	
Loan		4 000.00
Capital		24 796.00

The following delivery notes, invoices and credit notes were received and cheques were sent during the month of November 19XX.

Delivery notes received

Delivery Note 101   2 November 19XX

JEWELLERY MANUFACTURERS
181 Jordan Road
CHATSWOOD NSW 2067

To: Jane's Gift Store
     56 Wylie Street
     LISMORE NSW 2480

6 opal brooches
6 gold pendants & chains

Delivery Note 502   5 November 19XX

GORDON WHOLESALE CO.
19 Massey Street
WOLLONGONG NSW 2500

To: Jane's Gift Store
     56 Wylie Street
     LISMORE NSW 2480

8 porcelain figurines

Delivery Note 42   6 November 19XX

WHITE STATIONERY SUPPLIES
58 Grosvenor Street
LAMBTON NSW 2299

To: Jane's Gift Store
     56 Wylie Street
     LISMORE NSW 2480

200 sheets gift wrapping paper
100 gift boxes

Delivery Note 133   12 November 19XX

JEWELLERY MANUFACTURERS
181 Jordan Road
CHATSWOOD NSW 2067

To: Jane's Gift Store
     56 Wylie Street
     LISMORE NSW 2480

6 ladies' gold watches
6 men's gold watches

```
Delivery Note 87    16 November 19XX
         D. & B. COLEMAN
           80 Bryan Street
         KOGARAH NSW 2217

To:  Jane's Gift Store
     56 Wylie Street
     LISMORE NSW 2480

3 'Rose' tea sets
```

```
Delivery Note 567    16 November 19XX
       GORDON WHOLESALE CO.
           19 Massey Street
       WOLLONGONG NSW 2500

To:  Jane's Gift Store
     56 Wylie Street
     LISMORE NSW 2480

10 prs pewter candlesticks
10 prs pewter salt & pepper shakers
```

```
Delivery Note 75    18 November 19XX
         DURAL HOMECRAFTS
         195 Old Northern Road
           DURAL NSW 2158

To:  Jane's Gift Store
     56 Wylie Street
     LISMORE NSW 2480

24 tablecloths
```

```
Delivery Note 502    18 November 19XX
       GORDON WHOLESALE CO.
           19 Massey Street
       WOLLONGONG NSW 2500

To:  Jane's Gift Store
     56 Wylie Street
     LISMORE NSW 2480

6 ovenware dishes
12 crystal figures
```

Invoices received

```
Inv. 243              6 November 19XX
     JEWELLERY MANUFACTURERS
            181 Jordan Road
         CHATSWOOD NSW 2067

To:  Jane's Gift Store
     56 Wylie Street
     LISMORE NSW 2480

6 opal brooches @ $100 each  $600.00
6 gold pendants & chains
    @ $90 each                540.00
                            $1240.00
```

```
Inv. 446              7 November 19XX
       GORDON WHOLESALE CO.
           19 Massey Street
       WOLLONGONG NSW 2500

To:  Jane's Gift Store
     56 Wylie Street
     LISMORE NSW 2480


8 porcelain figurines
    @ $40.60 each             $324.80
```

```
Inv. 148             10 November 19XX
     WHITE STATIONERY SUPPLIES
           58 Grosvenor Street
          LAMBTON NSW 2299

To:  Jane's Gift Store
     56 Wylie Street
     LISMORE NSW 2480

200 sheets gift wrapping paper
    @ 50c per sheet         $100.00
100 gift boxes
    @ $2 each                200.00
                            $300.00
```

```
Inv. 261             15 November 19XX
     JEWELLERY MANUFACTURERS
            181 Jordan Road
         CHATSWOOD NSW 2067

To:  Jane's Gift Store
     56 Wylie Street
     LISMORE NSW 2480

12 ladies' gold watches
    @ $75 each              $ 900.00
6 men's gold watches
    @ $65 each                390.00
                            $1290.00
```

```
Inv. 549                    20 November 19XX

              D. & B. COLEMAN
                 80 Bryan Street
                KOGARAH NSW 2217

   To:   Jane's Gift Store
         56 Wylie Street
         LISMORE NSW 2480

   3 'Rose' tea sets
       @ $75 each                      $225.00
                                       =======
```

```
Inv. 500                    20 November 19XX

              GORDON WHOLESALE CO.
                 19 Massey Street
               WOLLONGONG NSW 2500

   To:   Jane's Gift Store
         56 Wylie Street
         LISMORE NSW 2480

   10 prs pewter candlesticks
       @ $67 pr                        $670.00
   10 prs pewter salt & pepper
       shakers @ $26.60 pr              266.00
                                       $936.00
                                       =======
```

```
Inv. 83                     25 November 19XX

              DURAL HOMECRAFTS
              195 Old Northern Road
                 DURAL NSW 2158

   To:   Jane's Gift Store
         56 Wylie Street
         LISMORE NSW 2480

   24 tablecloths @ $26 each           $624.00
                                       =======
```

```
Inv. 527                    27 November 19XX

              GORDON WHOLESALE CO.
                 19 Massey Street
               WOLLONGONG NSW 2500

   To:   Jane's Gift Store
         56 Wylie Street
         LISMORE NSW 2480

   6 ovenware dishes
       @ $15.00 ea                    $ 90.00
   12 crystal figures
       @ $25.50 ea                     306.00
                                       $396.00
                                       =======
```

Credit notes received

```
CN No. 84                   18 November 19XX

            JEWELLERY MANUFACTURERS
                 181 Jordan Road
               CHATSWOOD NSW 2067

   To:   Jane's Gift Store
         56 Wylie Street
         LISMORE NSW 2480

   Overcharge Invoice 243              $100.00
                                       =======
```

```
CN No. 176                  19 November 19XX

              GORDON WHOLESALE CO.
                 19 Massey Street
               WOLLONGONG NSW 2500

   To:   Jane's Gift Store
         56 Wylie Street
         LISMORE NSW 2480

   By return — damaged goods (Inv. 446)
   2 porcelain figurines
       @ $40.60 each                    $81.20
                                        ======
```

```
CN No. 403          29 November 19XX
     JEWELLERY MANUFACTURERS
          181 Jordan Road
        CHATSWOOD NSW 2067

To:  Jane's Gift Store
     56 Wylie Street
     LISMORE NSW 2480

Ref. Inv. 261 — overcharge
(for 6 watches not delivered)
6 ladies' gold watches
    @ $75 each              $450.00
```

Cheque butts

Cheque No. 054 Date: 7 November 19XX To: CONSOLIDATED PAPERS For: Advertising This cheque: $76.00	Cheque No. 055 Date: 7 November 19XX To: TINDALE AGENCY For: Rent This cheque: $400.00	Cheque No. 056 Date: 17 November 19XX To: NRCC For: Electricity This cheque: $240.00
Cheque No. 057 Date: 17 November 19XX To: D. & B. COLEMAN For: Payment of Account This cheque: $252.20 Discount: 7.80	Cheque No. 058 Date: 17 November 19XX To: DURAL HOMECRAFTS For: Payment of Account This cheque: $341.44 Discount: 10.56	Cheque No. 059 Date: 17 November 19XX To: GORDON WHOLESALE For: Payment of Account This cheque: $370.50 Discount: 9.50
Cheque No. 060 Date: 28 November 19XX To: CASH For: Purchases This cheque: $130.00	Cheque No. 061 Date: 28 November 19XX To: JEWELLERY MFRS For: Payment of Account This cheque: $280.25 Discount: 14.75	Cheque No. 062 Date: 28 November 19XX To: WHITE STATIONERY For: Payment of Account This cheque: $291.00 Discount: 9.00

- On 6 November, an amount of $98 owing to D. & B. Coleman and incorrectly credited to Dural Homecrafts was corrected.
- On 11 November, a glass display cabinet was purchased on credit for $750 from Shop Fitters.
- On 15 November, Gordon Wholesale & Co.'s opening general journal entry should have been recorded as $380 not $308.
- On 20 November, a computer was purchased from Techno Supplies on credit for $3500.

- On 22 November, Handcraft Suppliers charged Jane's Gift Store interest at 5 per cent p.a. on its account of $420 which was overdue for 6 months.
- On 26 November, Jane Carmody (proprietor) took goods to the value of $385 for personal use.
- On 27 November, account with Jewellery Manufacturers is settled by contra.

You are required to carry out the following. Use copies of the relevant masters provided at the back of this book.
1. Prepare the general journal opening entry.
2. Check the invoices received for accuracy and against delivery notes and report any discrepancies to your superior. Enter the invoices into the purchases journal.
3. Check the credit notes received and report any discrepancies to your superior. Enter the credit notes into the purchases returns and allowances journal.
4. Enter the cheque details into the cash payments journal.
5. Enter the miscellaneous general journal transactions.
6. Post all relevant amounts to the accounts payable ledger.
7. Prepare a schedule of creditors' balances for Jane's Gift Store as at 30 November 19XX.

SECTION 3: THE ACCOUNTS RECEIVABLE LEDGER

The accounts receivable ledger contains details of transactions for individual trade debtors. From this information the business can determine how much each individual trade debtor owes and the past history of its transactions with the trade debtor, such as amounts due, credits given and monies received. The accounts receivable ledger is also used to prepare the statements of account at the end of each month.

Trade debtors' accounts are only posted 'in total' to the general ledger and are represented in that ledger by the Accounts Receivable Control account. Dealings with trade debtors are processed by the accounts receivable department, which is responsible for recording the accounts receivable journals and posting details of individual transactions with trade debtors to the accounts receivable ledger.

Posting to the accounts receivable ledger

At the end of each month:
- post individual trade debtors' amounts to the accounts receivable ledger
- insert the ledger folio reference number in the 'Folio' column of the journal.

Journals are posted to the accounts receivable ledger in the following order:
1. general journal
2. sales journal
3. sales returns and allowances journal
4. cash receipts journal.

From the general journal

Basic format

The opening entry from the general journal (basic format) is posted to the accounts receivable ledger by debiting individual trade debtors' accounts with the individual amounts (see ① below).

Folio numbers of accounts receivable ledger accounts are inserted in the journals as the items are posted and are placed in the 'Folio' column alongside the amount posted.

GENERAL JOURNAL OF J. MASON   Fol. GJ1

Date	Particulars		Folio	Debit	Credit
19XX Jan. 1	Land			20 000.00	
	Buildings			40 000.00	
	Plant and Machinery			12 000.00	
	Office Equipment			10 000.00	
	Office Furniture			1 000.00	
	Cash at Bank			5 000.00	
	Inventory			1 500.00	
	Accounts Receivable			1 118.00	
	M. Adams	250.000	AR1		
	J. Abbott	500.00	AR2		
	R. Glacken	115.00	AR3		
	H. Raja	253.00	AR4		
	Accounts Payable				1 210.00
	H. Lime	300.00			
	P. Eastman	200.00			
	M. Garcia	510.00			
	B. Allar	200.00			
	Mortgage				10 000.00
	Capital				79 408.00
	Assets, liabilities and capital at this date			90 618.00	90 618.00

In the accounts receivable ledger:
① Individual trade debtors' amounts are posted to the 'Debit' column of relevant accounts in the accounts receivable ledger.

Columnar format

The following illustrates the posting of the opening entry in the general journal (columnar format) to the accounts receivable ledger:
1. *Debit* individual debtors' accounts with the amounts in the 'Accounts receivable' column from the *debit* side of the general journal.
2. *Credit* individual debtors' accounts with amounts in the 'Accounts receivable' column from the *credit* side of the general journal.

Folio numbers of the accounts receivable ledger accounts are inserted in the journals as the items are posted and are placed in the 'Folio' column alongside the account name.

CHAPTER 4: POSTING TO THE LEDGERS | 239

GENERAL JOURNAL OF J. MASON   Fol. GJ1

Accounts receivable (DEBIT)	Accounts payable (DEBIT)	General (DEBIT)	Date	Particulars	Fol.	Accounts receivable (CREDIT)	Accounts payable (CREDIT)	General (CREDIT)
		20 000.00 40 000.00 12 000.00	19XX Jan. 1	Land Buildings Plant and Machinery Office Equipment Office Furniture Cash at Bank Inventory				
250.00 500.00 115.00 253.00 ① THIS COLUMN		10 000.00 1 000.00 5 000.00 1 500.00		M. Adams J. Abbott ⎫ R. Glacken ⎬ ①② H. Raja ⎭ H. Lime P. Eastman M. Garcia B. Allar Mortgage Capital Being assets, liabilities and capital as at this date.	AR1 AR2 AR3 AR4 ①	② THIS COLUMN 300.00 200.00 510.00 200.00		10 000.00 79 408.00
1 118.00		89 500.00					1 210.00	89 408.00

In the accounts receivable ledger:
① *Debit* individual debtors' accounts with the amounts in the 'Accounts receivable' column from the *debit* side of the general journal.
② *Credit* individual debtors' accounts with the amounts in the 'Accounts receivable' column from the *credit* side of the general journal.
Insert folio references alongside account name.

When details of trade debtors' transactions are posted from the general journal opening entry, J. Mason's accounts receivable ledger will appear as follows.

ACCOUNTS RECEIVABLE LEDGER OF J. MASON

M. Adams   AR1

Date	Particulars	Fol.	Debit	Credit	Balance
19XX Jan. 1	Capital ①	GJ1	250.00		250.00 Dr

J. Abbott   AR2

Date	Particulars	Fol.	Debit	Credit	Balance
19XX Jan. 1	Capital ①	GJ1	500.00		500.00 Dr

R. Glacken   AR3

Date	Particulars	Fol.	Debit	Credit	Balance
19XX Jan. 1	Capital ①	GJ1	115.00		115.00 Dr

H. Raja   AR4

Date	Particulars	Fol.	Debit	Credit	Balance
19XX Jan. 1	Capital ①	GJ1	253.00		253.00 Dr

Following the posting procedures outlined above, the remainder of the general journal entries for January are posted to the accounts payable ledger.

GENERAL JOURNAL OF J. MASON (continued)

DEBIT   CREDIT   Fol. GJ1

Accounts receivable	Accounts payable	General	Date	Particulars	Fol.	Accounts receivable	Accounts payable	General
	50.00		Jan. 4	P. Eastman H. Lime Correction of error.			50.00	

		12 000.00	5	Office Equipment
				  Sundry Creditor
				    — Propert's
				    Computers
				Purchase of
				computer on credit.
								12 000.00

		150.00	7	H. Larson —
				  Sundry Debtor
				    Office Equipment
				Sale of printer on
				credit.
								150.00

30.00			10	J. Abbott M. Adams Correction of error.	AR2 AR1	30.00		
		18.00	10	Capital H. Raja Correction of error.	AR4	18.00		
		50.00	23	Drawings Purchases Owner took goods for personal use.				50.00
	360.00		31	M. Garcia Capital Correction of error.				360.00
		5.00	31	Interest Expense B. Allar Interest payable on creditor's overdue account.			5.00	
1.53			31	J. Glacken Interest Revenue Interest charged on debtor's overdue account.	AR3			1.53
		116.53	31	Bad Debts J. Glacken Bad debt written off.	AR3	116.53		
31.53	410.00	12 339.53				164.53	55.00	12 561.53

When trade debtors' transactions for January are posted from the remainder of the general journal entries, J. Mason's accounts receivable ledger will appear as follows. Note how the various transactions affect the amounts owed to the business by trade debtors (indicated by italic type).

ACCOUNTS RECEIVABLE LEDGER OF J. MASON

M. Adams — AR1

Date	Particulars	Fol.	Debit	Credit	Balance
19XX Jan. 1	Capital	GJ1	250.00		250.00 Dr
10	J. Abbott (correction) ②	GJ2		30.00	220.00 Dr

J. Abbott — AR2

Date	Particulars	Fol.	Debit	Credit	Balance
19XX Jan. 1	Capital	GJ1	500.00		500.00 Dr
10	M. Adams (correction) ①	GJ2	30.00		530.00 Dr

R. Glacken — AR3

Date	Particulars	Fol.	Debit	Credit	Balance
19XX Jan. 1	Capital	GJ1	115.00		115.00 Dr
31	Interest revenue ①	GJ2	1.53		116.53 Dr
31	Bad debts ②	GJ2		116.53	0.00

H. Raja — AR4

Date	Particulars	Fol.	Debit	Credit	Balance
19XX Jan. 1	Capital	GJ1	253.00		253.00 Dr
10	Capital (correction) ②	GJ2		18.00	235.00 Dr

From the sales journal

The individual amounts for the trade debtors are posted to the accounts receivable ledger in the following manner, by debiting individual trade debtors' accounts with the individual amounts in the 'Debtors' total' column (see ① on page 242).

Insert folio references in the 'Folio' column alongside each entry.

SALES JOURNAL OF J. MASON
Fol. SJ1

Date	Inv. no.	Particulars (Debtor's account to be debited)	Fol.	Sales	Sales tax	Debtors' total
19XX						①
Jan. 1	371	M. Adams	AR1	81.70	12.25	93.95
10	372	J. Abbott	AR2	167.20	25.08	192.28
21	373	L. Wells ①	AR5	131.10	19.66	150.76
29	374	E. Garton	AR6	57.00	8.55	65.55
31				437.00	65.54	502.54
				(7.1)	(4.3)	(1.3)

① *Debit* individual trade debtors' accounts with the individual amounts in the 'Debtors' total' column.

Folio references for individual accounts are entered in the 'Folio' column of the sales journal as each item is posted to the accounts receivable ledger. Invoice numbers from the sales journal are recorded in the ledger to provide an audit trail (a documented record for each transaction). Invoice numbers are placed in brackets after the transaction is recorded, for example, Sales (Inv. 231).

After the sales journal has been posted, J. Mason's accounts receivable ledger appears as follows.

ACCOUNTS RECEIVABLE LEDGER OF J. MASON

M. Adams
AR1

Date	Particulars	Fol.	Debit	Credit	Balance
19XX					
Jan. 1	Capital	GJ1	250.00		250.00 Dr
10	J. Abbott (correction)	GJ2		30.00	220.00 Dr
1	Sales (Inv. 371) ①	SJ1	93.95		313.95 Dr

J. Abbott
AR2

Date	Particulars	Fol.	Debit	Credit	Balance
19XX					
Jan. 1	Capital	GJ1	500.00		500.00 Dr
10	M. Adams (correction)	GJ2	30.00		530.00 Dr
12	Sales (Inv. 372) ①	SJ1	192.28		722.28 Dr

R. Glacken — AR3

Date	Particulars	Fol.	Debit	Credit	Balance
19XX					
Jan. 1	Capital	GJ1	115.00		115.00 Dr
31	Interest revenue	GJ2	1.53		116.53 Dr
31	Bad debts	GJ2		116.53	0.00

H. Raja — AR4

Date	Particulars	Fol.	Debit	Credit	Balance
19XX					
Jan. 1	Capital	GJ1	253.00		253.00 Dr
10	Capital (correction)	GJ2		18.00	235.00 Dr

L. Wells — AR5

Date	Particulars	Fol.	Debit	Credit	Balance
19XX					
Jan. 21	Sales (Inv. 373) ①	SJ1	150.76		150.76 Dr

E. Garton — AR6

Date	Particulars	Fol.	Debit	Credit	Balance
19XX					
Jan. 29	Sales (Inv. 374) ①	SJ1	65.55		65.55 Dr

From the sales returns and allowances journal

The individual amounts for the trade debtors are posted to the accounts receivable ledger by crediting individual debtors' accounts with the individual amounts from the 'Debtors' total' column (see ① below).

Insert folio references in the 'Folio' column alongside each entry.

SALES RETURNS AND ALLOWANCES JOURNAL OF J. MASON Fol. SR1

Date	CN no.	Particulars (Debtor's account to be credited)	Fol.	Sales	Sales tax	Debtors' total
19XX						①
Jan. 28	86	J. Abbott	AR2	20.90	3.13	24.03
	87	M. Adams ①	AR1	20.43	3.06	23.49
30	88	E. Garton	AR6	38.00	5.70	43.70
31				79.33	11.89	91.22

① *Credit* individual trade debtors' accounts with the individual amounts in the 'Debtors' total' column.

Folio references for individual accounts are entered in the 'Folio' column of the sales returns and allowances journal as each item is posted to the accounts receivable ledger. Credit note numbers from the sales journal are recorded in the ledger to provide an audit trail. Credit note numbers are placed in brackets after the transaction is recorded, for example, Sales returns (CN 456).

After the sales returns and allowances journal has been posted, J. Mason's accounts receivable ledger will appear as shown below.

ACCOUNTS RECEIVABLE LEDGER OF J. MASON

M. Adams — AR1

Date	Particulars	Fol.	Debit	Credit	Balance
19XX					
Jan. 1	Capital	GJ1	250.00		250.00 Dr
10	J. Abbott (correction)	GJ2		30.00	220.00 Dr
1	Sales (Inv. 371)	SJ1	93.95		313.95 Dr
28	Sales returns (CN 87) ①	SR1		23.49	290.46 Dr

J. Abbott — AR2

Date	Particulars	Fol.	Debit	Credit	Balance
19XX					
Jan. 1	Capital	GJ1	500.00		500.00 Dr
10	M. Adams (correction)	GJ2	30.00		530.00 Dr
	Sales (Inv. 372)	SJ1	192.28		722.28 Dr
28	Sales returns (CN 86) ①	SR1		24.03	698.25 Dr

R. Glacken — AR3

Date	Particulars	Fol.	Debit	Credit	Balance
19XX					
Jan. 1	Capital	GJ1	115.00		115.00 Dr
31	Interest revenue	GJ2	1.53		116.53 Dr
31	Bad debts	GJ2		116.53	0.00

H. Raja — AR4

Date	Particulars	Fol.	Debit	Credit	Balance
19XX					
Jan. 1	Capital	GJ1	253.00		253.00 Dr
10	Capital (correction)	GJ2		18.00	235.00 Dr

L. Wells
AR5

Date	Particulars	Fol.	Debit	Credit	Balance
19XX Jan. 21	Sales (Inv. 373)	SJ1	150.76		150.76 Dr

E. Garton
AR6

Date	Particulars	Fol.	Debit	Credit	Balance
19XX Jan. 29	Sales (Inv. 374)	SJ1	65.55		65.55 Dr
30	Sales returns (CN 88) ①	SR1		43.70	21.85 Dr

From the cash receipts journal

The individual amounts for the trade debtors are posted to the accounts receivable ledger by crediting the individual trade debtors' personal accounts with:

(a) the amount recorded in the 'Trade debtors' column (see ① below), and

(b) the amount recorded in the 'Discount allowed' column (see ② below).

Insert the folio reference alongside each entry.

CASH RECEIPTS JOURNAL OF J. MASON   Fol. CR1

Date	Rec. no.	Particulars (Account to be credited)	Fol.	Discount allowed	Trade debtors	Sales	Sales tax	General	Bank
				②	①				
19XX Jan. 5	CS	Sales				127.50	22.50		150.00
10	CS	Sales				180.00	20.00		200.00
29	23 CS	M. Adams ①, ② Sales	AR1	11.00	209.00	23.50			232.50
30	24	J. Abbott ①, ②	AR2	31.80	498.20				498.20
31	25 26 27 28	L. Wells ①, ② Capital Rent Revenue Office Equipment	AR4		100.00			1000.00 400.00 25.00	1525.00
				42.80	807.20	331.00	42.50	1425.00	2605.70

Credit individual trade debtors' personal accounts with:
① amount recorded in the 'Trade debtors' column, and
② amount recorded in the 'Discount allowed' column.

Folio references for individual accounts are entered in the 'Folio' column of the cash receipts journal as each item is posted to the ledger.

After the cash receipts journal has been posted, J. Mason's accounts receivable ledger appears as follows.

ACCOUNTS RECEIVABLE LEDGER OF J. MASON

M. Adams — AR1

Date	Particulars	Fol.	Debit	Credit	Balance
19XX					
Jan. 1	Capital	GJ1	250.00		250.00 Dr
10	J. Abbott (correction)	GJ2		30.00	220.00 Dr
1	Sales (Inv. 371)	SJ1	93.95		313.95 Dr
28	Sales returns (CN 87)	SR1		23.49	290.46 Dr
29	Cash receipts ①	CR1		209.00	81.46 Dr
	Discount allowed ②	CR1		11.00	70.46 Dr

J. Abbott — AR2

Date	Particulars	Fol.	Debit	Credit	Balance
19XX					
Jan. 1	Capital	GJ1	500.00		500.00 Dr
10	M. Adams (correction)	GJ2	30.00		530.00 Dr
	Sales (Inv. 372)	SJ1	192.28		722.28 Dr
28	Sales returns (CN 86)	SR1		24.03	698.25 Dr
30	Cash receipts ①	CR1		498.20	200.05 Dr
	Discount allowed ②	CR1		31.80	168.25 Dr

R. Glacken — AR3

Date	Particulars	Fol.	Debit	Credit	Balance
19XX					
Jan. 1	Capital	GJ1	115.00		115.00 Dr
31	Interest revenue	GJ2	1.53		116.53 Dr
31	Bad debts	GJ2		116.53	0.00

H. Raja — AR4

Date	Particulars	Fol.	Debit	Credit	Balance
19XX					
Jan. 1	Capital	GJ1	253.00		253.00 Dr
10	Capital (correction)	GJ2		18.00	235.00 Dr

L. Wells   AR5

Date	Particulars	Fol.	Debit	Credit	Balance
19XX					
Jan. 21	Sales (Inv. 373)	SJ1	150.76		150.76 Dr
31	Cash receipts ①	CR1		100.00	50.76 Dr

E. Garton   AR6

Date	Particulars	Fol.	Debit	Credit	Balance
19XX					
Jan. 29	Sales (Inv. 374)	SJ1	65.55		65.55 Dr
30	Sales returns (CN 88)	SR1		43.70	21.85 Dr

Schedule of debtors' balances

A schedule of debtors' balances is a listing of all outstanding balances in the accounts receivable ledger. It is prepared to show the total amount owed by trade debtors at the end of the month. The balances of the trade debtors' accounts are listed and totalled.

Example

Taken from the accounts receivable journal of J. Mason, the schedule of debtors' balances for J. Mason shows:

J. MASON
Schedule of Debtors' Balances
as at 31 January 19XX

AR1	M. Adams	$ 70.46
AR2	J. Abbott	168.25
AR4	H. Raja	235.00
AR5	L. Wells	50.76
AR6	E. Garton	21.85
		$546.32

Reconciling the schedule of debtors' balances

The steps taken to reconcile the schedule of debtors' balances with the Accounts Receivable Control account in the general ledger are as follows:
1. From the accounts receivable ledger, prepare a list of outstanding balances to show the total amount owing to the business by trade debtors at the end of the month.
2. In the general ledger, access the Accounts Receivable Control account.
3. Compare the total of the schedule of debtors' balances with the balance of the Accounts Receivable Control account. Totals should agree.

For comparison purposes, the schedule of debtors' balances and the Accounts Receivable Control account from J. Mason's general ledger are shown below. If you examine them, you can see that the final balance in the Accounts Receivable Control account in the general ledger agrees with the total of the schedule of debtors' balances compiled from the account balances in the accounts receivable ledger.

J. MASON
Schedule of Debtors' Balances
as at 31 January 19XX

AR1	M. Adams	$ 40.46
AR2	J. Abbott	198.25
AR4	H. Raja	235.00
AR5	L. Wells	50.76
AR6	E. Garton	21.85
		$546.32

Accounts Receivable Control 1.3

Date	Particulars	Fol.	Debit	Credit	Balance
19XX					
Jan. 1	Capital	GJ1	1118.00		1118.00 Dr
31	Sundries	GJ1	31.53		1149.53 Dr
	Sundries	GJ1		164.53	985.00 Dr
	Sales	SJ1	502.54		1487.54 Dr
	Sales returns	SR1		91.22	1396.32 Dr
	Cash receipts	CR1		807.20	589.12 Dr
	Discount allowed	CR1		42.80	546.32 Dr

EXERCISE 4.22   K. Dominic & Sons

From the general journal and the accounts receivable journals of K. Dominic & Sons, reproduced on pages 249–250, you are required to carry out the following.

1. Post all relevant amounts to the accounts receivable ledger of K. Dominic & Sons. Use as many copies as you need of the blank ledger master provided on page 559. Don't forget to include the name of the ledger at the top of the first page (see example on page 239).
2. Prepare a schedule of debtors' balances as at 31 May 19XX.
3. Reconcile the schedule of debtors' balances with the Accounts Receivable Control account from the general ledger, which you prepared for exercise 4.7 (page 194) in the general ledger section.

GENERAL JOURNAL OF K. DOMINIC & SONS

Fol. GJ1

Debit Accounts receivable	Debit Accounts payable	Debit General ledger	Date	Particulars	Fol.	Credit Accounts receivable	Credit Accounts payable	Credit General
			19XX					
		250 000.00	May 1	Land				
		80 000.00		Buildings				
		35 000.00		Motor Vehicles				
		2 550.00		Office Equipment				
		1 890.00		Office Furniture				
		18 000.00		Cash at Bank				
		9 890.00		Inventory				
240.00				J. Wade				
580.00				M. Byrnes				
420.00				G. Mundo				
				W. Maine			680.00	
				Conway & Sons			420.00	
				B. Samuels			78.00	
				Mortgage				150 000.00
				Capital				247 392.00
				Assets, liabilities and capital as at this date.				
1240.00		397 330.00					1178.00	397 392.00
		10 000.00	5	Office Equipment				
				Sundry Creditor — Imagemakers				10 000.00
				Photocopier purchased on credit.				
180.00			7	J. Wade				
				M. Byrnes		180.00		
				Correction of posting error.				
			16	Sundry Debtor — Ace Secretarial Service				
		500.00		Office Furniture				500.00
				Office desk sold on credit.				
		420.00	19	Bad Debts				
				G. Mundo		420.00		
				Bad debt written off.				
		300.00	20	Drawings				
				Purchases				300.00
				Owner took goods for personal use.				
		1.95	25	Interest Expense				
				B. Samuel			1.95	
				Interest paid on overdue account.				
180.00		11 221.95				600.00	1.95	10 800.00

SALES JOURNAL OF K. DOMINIC & SONS Fol. SJ1

Date	Inv. no.	Particulars (Debtor's account to be debited)	Fol.	Sales	Sales tax	Debtors' total
19XX May 3	463	J. Wade		162.00	24.30	186.30
10	464	M. Byrnes		250.56	37.59	288.15
18	465	R. Cotter & Sons		324.00	48.10	372.10
20	466	J. Wade		32.40	4.86	37.26
31				768.96	114.85	883.81

SALES RETURNS AND ALLOWANCES JOURNAL OF K. DOMINIC & SONS Fol. SR1

Date	CN no.	Particulars (Debtor's account to be credited)	Fol.	Sales returns	Sales tax	Debtors' total
19XX May 18	42	J. Wade		32.40	4.86	37.26
21	43	R. Cotter & Sons		64.80	9.72	74.52
31				97.20	14.58	111.78

CASH RECEIPTS JOURNAL OF K. DOMINIC & SONS Fol. CR1

Date	Rec. no.	Particulars (Account to be credited)	Fol.	Discount allowed	Trade debtors	Sales	Sales tax	General	Bank
19XX May 2	201	J. Wade		10.50	409.50				409.50
9	CS	Sales				467.50	82.50		550.00
10	202	Rent Revenue						500.00	
	203	Capital						10 000.00	10 500.00
22	CS	Sales				200.60	35.40		236.00
28	204	R. Cotter & Sons		8.44	289.14				
	205	Motor Vehicles						5 000.00	
	CS	Sales				417.40	62.60		5 769.14
29	206	M. Byrnes			100.00				100.00
31				18.94	798.64	1085.50	180.50	15 500.00	17 564.64

EXERCISE 4.23 B. James & Co.

From the general journal and accounts receivable journals of B. James & Co., reproduced on pages 251–252, you are required to carry out the following.
1. Post all relevant amounts to the accounts receivable ledger of B. James & Co. Use as many copies as you need of the blank ledger master provided on page 559. Don't forget to include the name of the ledger at the top of the first page (see example on page 239).

2. Prepare a schedule of debtors' balances as at 30 April 19XX.
3. Reconcile the schedule of debtors' balances with the Accounts Receivable Control account from the general ledger, which you prepared for exercise 4.8 (page 195) in the general ledger section.

GENERAL JOURNAL OF B. JAMES & CO.

DEBIT — CREDIT — Fol. GJ1

Accounts receivable	Accounts payable	General	Date	Particulars	Fol.	Accounts receivable	Accounts payable	General
			19XX					
		18 900.00	Apr. 1	Plant and Machinery				
		15 500.00		Motor Vehicles				
		4 890.00		Office Equipment				
		2 680.00		Office Furniture				
		12 440.00		Cash at Bank				
		5 660.00		Inventory				
172.00				A. Collins				
				Corella Private				
289.00				Hospital				
320.00				E. & J. White				
402.00				G. McGregor				
				King & Co.			426.00	
				Greenway & Co.			215.00	
				F. Nguyen			75.00	
				Capital				60 537.00
				Assets, liabilities and				
1183.00		60 070.00		capital at this date.			716.00	60 537.00
	18.00		6	F. Nguyen				
				Capital				18.00
				Correction of posting error.				
			8	Corella Private				
100.00				Hospital				
				A. Collins			100.00	
				Correction of posting error.				
	150.00		8	Greenway & Co.				
				King & Co.			150.00	
				Correction of posting error.				
		2 000.00	11	Office Equipment				
				Sundry Creditor —				
				Technics Ltd				2 000.00
				Laser printer purchased on credit.				
20.10			30	G. McGregor				
				Interest Revenue				20.10
				Interest charged on debtor's overdue account (6 months).				
120.10	168.00	2 000.00				100.00	150.00	2 038.10

SALES JOURNAL OF B. JAMES & CO. — Fol. SJ1

Date	Inv. no.	Particulars (Debtor's account to be debited)	Fol.	Sales	Sales tax	Debtors' total
19XX						
Apr. 3	22	A. Collins		798.00	19.95	817.95
10	23	Corella Private Hospital		65.00		65.00
15	24	E. & J. White		133.48	16.68	150.16
	25	K. Carter & Co.		63.65	7.96	71.61
20	26	E. & J. White		151.20	18.87	170.07
28	27	A. Collins		241.45	30.18	271.63
30				1452.78	93.64	1546.42

SALES RETURNS AND ALLOWANCES JOURNAL OF B. JAMES & CO. — Fol. SR1

Date	CN no.	Particulars (Debtor's account to be credited)	Fol.	Sales returns	Sales tax	Debtors' total
19XX						
Apr. 13	85	A. Collins		199.50	24.94	224.44
21	86	K. Carter & Co.		33.25	4.16	37.41
30				232.75	29.10	261.85

CASH RECEIPTS JOURNAL OF B. JAMES & CO. — Fol. CR1

Date	Rec. no.	Particulars (Account to be credited)	Fol.	Discount allowed	Trade debtors	Sales	Sales tax	General	Bank
19XX									
Apr. 10	301	Office Equipment						80.00	80.00
12	CS	Sales				172.70	30.50		203.20
15	CS	Sales				348.50	61.50		410.00
20	302	A. Collins		1.80	70.20				
	303	Capital						12 000.00	
	304	Corella Pte. Hosp.		9.72	379.28				12 449.48
25	305	Office Equipment						500.00	
	CS	Sales				516.40	92.10		1 108.50
29	306	E. & J. White		9.60	310.40				310.40
30				21.12	759.88	1037.60	184.10	12 580.00	14 561.58

EXERCISE 4.24 *Trend Fashions*

From the general journal and accounts receivable journals of Trend Fashions, reproduced on pages 253–254, you are required to carry out the following.
1. Post all relevant amounts to the accounts receivable ledger of Trend Fashions. Use as many copies as you need of the blank ledger master on page 559. Don't forget to include the name of the ledger at the top of the first page (see example on page 239).

CHAPTER 4: POSTING TO THE LEDGERS | 253

2. Prepare a schedule of debtors' balances as at 28 February 19XX.
3. Reconcile the schedule of debtors' balances with the Accounts Receivable Control account from the general ledger, which you prepared for exercise 4.9 (page 196) in the general ledger section.

GENERAL JOURNAL OF TREND FASHIONS
Fol. GJ1

Accounts receivable (DR)	Accounts payable (DR)	General (DR)	Date	Particulars	Fol.	Accounts receivable (CR)	Accounts payable (CR)	General (CR)
		240 000.00	19XX Feb. 1	Land				
		60 000.00		Buildings				
		24 500.00		Motor Vehicles				
		6 110.00		Office Equipment				
		2 400.00		Office Furniture				
		11 765.00		Cash at Bank				
		5 295.00		Inventory				
320.00				The Dress Shop				
265.00				Jane's Fashion Store				
532.00				H. Taylor & Co.				
302.00				Petrovich & Co.				
				W. A. Montey			440.00	
				G. Hanna			385.00	
				W. Laporte			229.00	
				J. S. Baxter			88.00	
				Mortgage				120 000.00
				Capital				230 347.00
				Assets, liabilities and capital as at this date.				
1419.00		350 070.00					1142.00	350 347.00
	120.00		7	W. A. Montey				
				G. Hanna			120.00	
				Correction of posting error.				
		21 000.00	16	Motor Vehicles				
				Sundry Creditor — Schaeffer Motors				21 000.00
				Motor vehicle purchased on credit.				
		9 500.00	18	Sundry Debtor — R. Mustafa				
				Motor Vehicles				9 500.00
				Motor vehicle sold on credit.				
		1 100.00	22	Office Equipment				
				Sundry Creditor — Compusupply Co.				1 100.00
				Laser printer purchased on credit.				
		300.00	22	Sundry Debtor — H. Rostov				
				Office Equipment				300.00
				Inkjet printer sold on credit.				
		520.00	27	Drawings				
				Purchases				520.00
				Goods taken by owner for personal use.				
	120.00	32 420.00					120.00	32 420.00

SALES JOURNAL OF TREND FASHIONS Fol. SJ1

Date	Inv. no.	Particulars (Debtor's account to be debited)	Fol.	Sales	Sales tax	Debtors' total
19XX						
Feb. 10	508	Jane's Fashion Store		360.00	54.00	414.00
12	509	The Dress Shop		337.50	50.63	388.13
15	510	Dianne's Boutique		148.50	22.80	171.30
20	511	H. Taylor & Co.		360.00	54.00	414.00
25	512	The Dress Shop		450.00	67.50	517.50
	513	Jane's Fashion Store		315.00	47.25	362.25
28				1971.00	296.18	2267.18

SALES RETURNS AND ALLOWANCES JOURNAL OF TREND FASHIONS Fol. SR1

Date	CN no.	Particulars (Debtor's account to be credited)	Fol.	Sales returns	Sales tax	Debtors' total
19XX						
Feb. 20	12	The Dress Shop		63.00	9.45	72.45
27	13	Dianne's Boutique		27.00	4.05	31.05
28				90.00	13.50	103.50

CASH RECEIPTS JOURNAL OF TREND FASHIONS Fol. CR1

Date	Rec. no.	Particulars (Account to be credited)	Fol.	Discount allowed	Trade debtors	Sales	Sales tax	General	Bank
19XX									
Feb. 15	75	Office Furniture						100.00	
	CS	Sales				168.30	29.70		298.00
18	CS	Sales				476.00	84.00		560.00
20	76	Rent Revenue						600.00	
	77	The Dress Shop		24.00	296.00				896.00
23	78	Jane's Fashion Store		18.55	246.45				246.45
27	79	H. Taylor & Co.		34.24	497.76				
	80	Office Equipment						88.00	
	CS	Sales				471.20	83.20		1140.16
28				76.79	1040.21	1115.50	196.90	788.00	3140.61

EXERCISE 4.25 David Clarke Pty Ltd

David Clarke commenced business on 1 February 19XX with the following assets, liabilities and capital.

Land		$250 000.00
Buildings		120 000.00
Motor Vehicles		42 000.00
Office Equipment		10 500.00
Office Furniture		8 760.00
Inventory		9 540.00
Cash at Bank		6 660.00
Accounts Receivable		3 536.84
Tosca Trading Co.	$ 254.20	
Da Silva Bros	603.64	
J. Stephens Pty Ltd	66.00	
The Cooking School	636.00	
S. Pampas & Sons	1457.00	
A. Ernst & Co.	520.00	
Accounts Payable		1 531.00
T. Wagner	890.00	
L. Sumeigi	431.00	
M. Sumovich	210.00	
Mortgage		100 000.00
Capital		349 465.84

The following invoices, credit notes and receipts were sent to customers and cash sales dockets were made out during the month of February 19XX.

Duplicates of invoices

```
Inv. 242                    2 February 19XX

To:   Da Silva Bros
      140 Donald Street
      BALLARAT VIC 3350

For: 3 silver carving sets          $144.00
Less 20% Trade Discount               28.80
                                     ------
                                     115.20
Plus 15% Sales Tax                    17.28
                                     ------
                                    $132.48
                                     ======
```

```
Inv. 243                    5 February 19XX

To:   J. Stephens Pty Ltd
      28 Carter Street
      BENDIGO VIC 3550

For: 1 'Westleigh' dinner set       $750.00
     2 stoneware dinner sets         160.00
                                     ------
                                     910.00
Less 20% Trade Discount              182.00
                                     ------
                                     728.00
Plus 15% Sales Tax                   109.20
                                     ------
                                    $837.20
                                     ======
```

Inv. 244	14 February 19XX

To: S. Pampas & Sons
442 Canterbury Road
CANTERBURY NSW 2193

For: 6 S/S roasters	$300.00
Less 20% Trade Discount	60.00
	240.00
Plus 15% Sales Tax	36.00
	$276.00

Inv. 245	20 February 19XX

To: Tosca Trading Co.
93 Exeter Street
BRISBANE QLD 4000

For: 18 sherry glasses	$ 48.00
18 champagne flutes	216.00
	264.00
Less 20% Trade Discount	52.80
	211.20
Plus 15% Sales Tax	31.68
	$242.88

Inv. 246	24 February 19XX

To: The Cooking School
80 Florence Street
TOOWOOMBA QLD 4350

For: 1 S/S carving set	$50.00
2 coffee pots	40.00
	90.00
Less Special Discount	18.00
	$72.00

Inv. 247	26 February 19XX

To: S. Pampas & Sons
442 Canterbury Road
CANTERBURY NSW 2193

For: 6 stoneware dinner sets	$480.00
Less 20% Trade Discount	96.00
	384.00
Plus 15% Sales Tax	57.60
	$441.60

Duplicates of credit notes

CN No. 72	20 February 19XX

To: J. Stephens Pty Ltd
28 Carter Street
BENDIGO VIC 3550

By return — damaged goods
(Ref. Inv. 234)

3 crystal vases	$45.00
Less 20% Trade Discount	9.00
	36.00
Plus 15% Sales Tax	5.40
	$41.40

CN No. 73	26 February 19XX

To: Tosca Trading Co.
93 Exeter Street
BRISBANE QLD 4000

By return — damaged goods
(Ref. Inv. 245)

18 sherry glasses	$48.00
Less 20% Trade Discount	9.60
	38.40
Plus 15% Sales Tax	5.76
	$44.16

CN No. 74	28 February 19XX

To: The Cooking School
80 Florence Street
TOOWOOMBA QLD 4350

Overcharge Inv. 239	$10.00

Duplicates of receipts

Rec. No. 104	Rec. No. 105	Rec. No. 106
Date: *10/2/19XX*	Date: *15/2/19XX*	Date: *20/2/19XX*
Rec'd from *J. STEPHENS P/L* the sum of *Sixty-four dollars thirty-five cents*	Rec'd from *D. CLARKE* the sum of *One thousand dollars*	Rec'd from *S. PAMPAS & SONS* the sum of *One thousand dollars*
For: *Payment of Account*	For: *Capital (Additional money paid in by owner)*	For: *Payment on Account*
Cash/Chq. $64.35 Discount 1.65 Amt. Owing $66.00	Cash/Chq. $1000.00	Cash/Chq. $1000.00

Rec. No. 107	Rec. No. 108	Rec. No. 109
Date: *20/2/19XX*	Date: *27/2/19XX*	Date: *28/2/19XX*
Rec'd from *DA SILVA BROS* the sum of *Five hundred and seventy-three dollars forty-four cents*	Rec'd from *THE COOKING SCHOOL* the sum of *Three hundred and forty-six dollars*	Rec'd from *KAY BUSINESS MACHINES* the sum of *Four hundred and fifty dollars*
For: *Payment of Account*	For: *Payment of Account*	For: *Office Equipment (Printer sold for cash)*
Cash/Chq. $573.44 Discount 30.20 Amt. Owing $603.64	Cash/Chq. $346.00 Discount 20.00 Amt Owing $366.00	Cash/Chq. $450.00

Cash sales dockets

No. 005	No. 006	No. 007
Date: *3/2/19XX*	Date: *10/2/19XX*	Date: *15/2/19XX*
Cash Sales $76.00 Sales Tax 19.00 $95.00	Cash Sales $128.00 Sales Tax 32.00 $160.00	Cash Sales $256.00 Sales Tax 64.00 $320.00

No. 008	No. 009
Date: *16/2/19XX*	Date: *23/2/19XX*
Cash Sales $752.00 Sales Tax 188.00 $940.00	Cash Sales $158.40 Sales Tax 39.60 $198.00

- On 8 February, a dot matrix printer was sold on credit to J. Trang for $250.00.
- On 12 February, it was found that The Cooking School's opening general journal entry was incorrectly recorded as $636.00 instead of $366.00.
- Also on 12 February, D. Clarke Pty Ltd charged Tosca Trading interest of 3 per cent p.a. on its account of $254.20 which was overdue for 3 months.
- On 15 February, a motor vehicle was sold on credit to B. Pearson for $10 600.00.
- On 20 February, A. Ernst's account for $520.00 was considered irrecoverable and should be written off as a bad debt.

You are required to carry out the following. Use copies of the relevant masters provided at the back of this book.

1. Prepare the opening entry.
2. Enter the invoices into the sales journal.
3. Enter the credit notes into the sales returns and allowances journal.
4. Enter the receipts and cash sales dockets into the cash receipts journal.
5. Enter the general journal miscellaneous entries.
6. Post all amounts relating to trade debtors to the accounts receivable ledger.
7. Prepare a schedule of debtors' balances as at 28 February 19XX.

Preparing statements for debtors

A statement of account is usually sent to the debtor (purchaser) by the creditor (seller) at the end of the month. It lists:
- the balance outstanding at the beginning of the month (showing amounts overdue for 30, 60 or 90 days as well as the current amount outstanding — this is called 'ageing' accounts)
- invoices
- credit notes
- payments received
- discount allowed

  } in date order

- balance owing at the end of the month.

In many businesses, the statement of account is a copy of the debtor's account in the accounts receivable ledger and the statement is prepared from the ledger account.

Large firms use a cyclical billing system in which the debtors' ledger is divided into alphabetical sections, for example, A–G, H–M, and so on.

Statements for each section are sent out on a different day of the month, for example A–G on 10th, H–M on 20th. This is to spread the workload throughout the month.

An example of a statement of account is shown below.

STATEMENT OF ACCOUNT

J. Mason
401 Denning Highway
NORTH PERTH WA 6006

TO:
E. Garton
91 Murdoch Road
NEWPORT NSW 2106

FOR THE MONTH OF
December 19 XX

Date	Particulars	Debit	Credit	Balance
Dec. 1	Balance			560.00
5	Inv. 248	201.50		761.50
10	Inv. 269	748.00		1509.50
16	CN 018		48.00	1461.50
20	Rec. No. 448		560.00	901.50

Current	30 days	60 days	90 days	Please pay final amount in this column
901.50				

EXERCISE 4.26 — David Clarke Pty Ltd

Prepare a statement of account for each of the following debtors using their ledger accounts for the month of February 19XX. (Use copies of the blank statement of account master provided on page 547 and add the header: D. Clarke Pty Ltd, 201 Phillip Street, Bendigo, Vic. 3550.)

1. Tosca Trading Co.
2. Da Silva Bros
3. J. Stephens Pty Ltd
4. The Cooking School
5. S. Pampas & Sons

EXERCISE 4.27 Gem Supply Co.

B. Ormonde commenced business on 1 June 19XX trading as Gem Supply Co. with the following assets, liabilities and capital.

Premises		$300 000.00
Motor Vehicles		24 780.00
Furniture and Fittings		12 100.00
Office Equipment		10 200.00
Stock		6 970.00
Cash at Bank		5 576.00
Accounts Receivable		4 814.66
A. & S. Wallace	$1 102.50	
The Jewel Store	491.00	
K. Hunt Pty Ltd	820.00	
Freeman Jewellers	763.00	
Cheshire Hospital	60.00	
A. Dixon & Co.	508.16	
Maxime & Co.	850.00	
L. Voss	220.00	
Accounts Payable		1 540.00
Connegrave & Co.	231.00	
P. Fogel Pty Ltd	765.00	
R. Shute	544.00	
Mortgage		85 000.00
Capital		277 900.66

The following invoices, credit notes and receipts were sent to customers and cash sales dockets were made out during the month of June 19XX.

Duplicates of invoices

Inv. 231		5 June 19XX
To: Maxime & Co.		
Shop 28, Regency Arcade		
NEWCASTLE NSW 2300		
For: 3 sapphire rings		$ 525.00
2 emerald rings		400.00
		925.00
Less 10% Trade Discount		92.50
		832.50
Plus 33⅓% Sales Tax		277.22
		$1109.72

Inv. 232		8 June 19XX
To: The Jewel Store		
201 McIntyre Street		
CASINO NSW 2470		
For: 2 × 498 cm gold chains		$100.00
3 ladies' gold watches		280.00
		380.00
Less 10% Trade Discount		38.00
		342.00
Plus 25% Sales Tax		85.50
		$427.50

Inv. 233	12 June 19XX
To: K. Hunt Pty Ltd 56 Wilson Road GEELONG VIC 3220	
For: 10 quartz alarm clocks	$550.00
Less 10% Trade Discount	55.00
	495.00
Plus 15% Sales Tax	74.25
	$569.25

Inv. 234	15 June 19XX
To: A. & S. Wallace 45 Alfred Street CAMPSIE NSW 2194	
For: 6 men's digital watches	$480.00
4 white gold bracelets	320.00
	800.00
Less 10% Trade Discount	80.00
	720.00
Plus 25% Sales Tax	180.00
	$900.00

Inv. 235	20 June 19XX
To: Maxime & Co. Shop 28, Regency Arcade NEWCASTLE NSW 2300	
For: 6 × 55 cm gold chains	$450.00
3 'Leaf' gold brooches	150.00
	600.00
Less 5% Trade Discount	30.00
	570.00
Plus 25% Sales Tax	142.50
	$712.50

Inv. 236	20 June 19XX
To: Freeman Jewellers 181 Conway Road TOWNSVILLE QLD 4810	
For: 6 ladies' gold watches	$560.00
Less 10% Trade Discount	56.00
	504.00
Plus 25% Sales Tax	126.00
	$630.00

Inv. 237	25 June 19XX
To: The Jewel Store 201 McIntyre Street CASINO NSW 2470	
For: 8 travel clocks	$160.00
Less 10% Trade Discount	16.00
	144.00
Plus 15% Sales Tax	21.60
	$165.60

Inv. 238	29 June 19XX
To: K. Hunt Pty Ltd 56 Wilson Road GEELONG VIC 3220	
For: 6 'Leaf' gold brooches	$300.00
Less 10% Trade Discount	30.00
	270.00
Plus 25% Sales Tax	67.50
	$337.50

Duplicates of credit notes

CN No. 69	25 June 19XX
To: A. & S. Wallace 45 Alfred Street CAMPSIE NSW 2194	
By return — faulty goods (Ref. Inv. 234)	
2 men's digital watches	$160.00
Less 10% Trade Discount	16.00
	144.00
Plus 25% Sales Tax	36.00
	$180.00

CN No. 70	25 June 19XX
To: Cheshire Private Hospital 83 Taylor Street BONDI NSW 2026	
By return — oversupply (Inv. 229)	
1 nurse's watch	$25.00
Less Special Discount	5.00
	$20.00

Duplicates of receipts

Rec. No. 132	Rec. No. 133	Rec. No. 134
Date: 10/6/19XX	Date: 20/6/19XX	Date: 24/6/19XX
Rec'd from B. ORMONDE the sum of *Five thousand dollars*	Rec'd from A. & S. WALLACE the sum of *One thousand and seventy-five dollars*	Rec'd from A. DIXON & CO. the sum of *Four hundred and ninety-five dollars forty-six cents*
For: *CAPITAL (Additional money paid in by owner)*	For: *Payment of Account*	For: *Payment of Account*
Cash/Chq. $5000.00	Cash/Chq. $1075.00 Discount 27.50 Amt Owing $1102.50	Cash/Chq. $495.46 Discount 12.70 Amt Owing $508.16

Rec. No. 135	Rec. No. 136	Rec. No. 137
Date: 26/6/19XX	Date: 30/6/19XX	Date: 30/6/19XX
Rec'd from CHESHIRE HOSPITAL the sum of *Forty dollars*	Rec'd from MAXIME & CO. the sum of *Five hundred dollars*	Rec'd from D. MOSS the sum of *Six hundred dollars*
For: *Payment of Account*	For: *Payment on Account*	For: *Rent Revenue*
Cash/Chq. $40.00	Cash/Chq. $500.00	Cash/Chq. $600.00

Cash sales dockets

No. 11	No. 12	No. 13
Date: 10/6/19XX	Date: 15/6/19XX	Date: 20/6/19XX
Cash Sales $550.00 Sales Tax 110.00 $660.00	Cash Sales $600.00 Sales Tax 150.00 $750.00	Cash Sales $220.00 Sales Tax Exempt

No. 14	No. 15	No. 16
Date: 26/6/19XX	Date: 27/6/19XX	Date: 30/6/19XX
Cash Sales $670.00 Sales Tax 165.00 $835.00	Cash Sales $102.00 Sales Tax Exempt	Cash Sales $98.75 Sales Tax 22.00 $120.75

- On 7 June, a display cabinet was sold on credit to G. Johns for $250.
- On 12 June, Gem Supply Co. charged The Jewel Store interest of 5 per cent p.a. on its account of $491 which was overdue for 4 months.
- Also on 12 June, L. Voss's account was considered irrecoverable and written off as a bad debt.
- On 20 June, a computer was sold on credit to V. Bryon for $500.
- On 28 June, Freeman Jewellers' opening general journal entry should have been $736 not $763.

You are required to carry out the following. Use copies of the relevant masters provided at the back of this book.

1. Prepare the general journal opening entry.
2. Enter the invoices into the sales journal.
3. Enter the credit notes into the sales returns and allowances journal.
4. Enter the receipts and cash sales dockets into the cash receipts journal.
5. Enter the general journal entries.
6. Post details of all amounts relating to trade debtors to the accounts receivable ledger.
7. Prepare a schedule of debtors' balances as at 30 June 19XX.
8. Prepare statements of account for the following. (Use a copy of the blank statement of account master provided on page 547 and add the header: Gem Supply Co., 62 Murray Street, Newcastle, NSW 2300.)
    (a) A. & S. Wallace
    (b) K. Hunt Pty Ltd
    (c) The Jewel Store
    (d) Maxime & Co.

EXERCISE 4.28 Bo-Peep Clothing Co.

R. Fox commenced trading on 1 September 19XX as Bo-Peep Clothing Co. with the following assets, liabilities and capital.

Land		$300 000.00
Buildings		120 000.00
Motor Vehicles		55 000.00
Office Equipment		12 900.00
Office Furniture		6 770.00
Stock		8 423.00
Cash at Bank		8 943.00
Accounts Receivable		2 590.24
S. Walters & Co.	$480.00	
Humpty Dumpty Kindergarten	100.00	
M. Bright & Co.	207.00	
K. Armour	340.00	
B. Lamb Pty Ltd	700.00	
Kiddi-Clothes	273.24	
K. Lee	380.00	
W. Yurich	110.00	
Accounts Payable		2 292.00
Clothing Manufacturers	890.00	
P. Kee & Sons	756.00	
R. Cartwright	646.00	
Mortgage		115 000.00
Capital		397 334.24

The following invoices, credit notes and receipts were sent to customers and cash sales dockets were made out during the month of September 19XX.

Duplicates of invoices

Inv. 40	3 September 19XX
To:	S. Walters & Co.
	93 Rose Street
	KOGARAH NSW 2217

For:	12 baby's dresses	$240.00
	10 baby's cardigans	100.00
		340.00
Less 10% Trade Discount		34.00
		306.00
Plus 15% Sales Tax		45.90
		$351.90

Inv. 41	8 September 19XX
To:	Kiddi-Clothes Pty Ltd
	123 Coronation Road
	KINGSTON ACT 2604

For:	24 boy's jogger suits	$432.00
Less 10% Trade Discount		43.20
		388.80
Plus 15% Sales Tax		58.32
		$447.12

Inv. 42	15 September 19XX
To:	M. Bright & Co.
	14 Lynch Street
	KINGAROY QLD 4610

For:	6 girl's denim skirts	$ 42.00
	12 prs boy's jeans	144.00
		186.00
Less 10% Trade Discount		18.60
		167.40
Plus 15% Sales Tax		25.11
		$192.51

Inv. 43	18 September 19XX
To:	B. Lamb Pty Ltd
	37 Riverview Street
	TAREE NSW 2430

For:	24 baby's feeders	$48.00
	12 baby's singlets	18.00
		66.00
Less 10% Trade Discount		6.60
		59.40
Plus 15% Sales Tax		8.91
		$68.31

Inv. 44	22 September 19XX
To:	Kiddi-Clothes Pty Ltd
	123 Coronation Road
	KINGSTON ACT 2604

For:	10 girl's dresses	$300.00
Less 10% Trade Discount		30.00
		270.00
Plus 15% Sales Tax		40.50
		$310.50

Inv. 45	29 September 19XX
To:	M. Bright & Co.
	14 Lynch Street
	KINGAROY QLD 4610

For:	18 prs boy's shorts	$153.00
	18 girl's floral blouses	72.00
		225.00
Less 10% Trade Discount		22.50
		202.50
Plus 15% Sales Tax		30.38
		$232.88

```
Inv. 46              29 September 19XX

To:  Humpty Dumpty Kindergarten
     88 Atkins Street
     LORNE VIC 3232

For: 20 child's coveralls        150.00
Less 20% Trade Discount           30.00
                                 $120.00

Sales Tax Exempt
```

Duplicates of credit notes

```
CN No. 025         10 September 19XX

To:  S. Walters & Co.
     93 Rose Street
     KOGARAH NSW 2217

By return — damaged goods
(Ref. Inv. 40)
6 baby's dresses               $120.00
Less 10% Trade Discount          12.00
                                108.00
Plus 15% Sales Tax               16.20
                               $124.20
```

```
CN No. 026         24 September 19XX

To:  Kiddi-Clothes Pty Ltd
     123 Coronation Road
     KINGSTON ACT 2604

By return — faulty goods
(Ref. Inv. 41)
2 boy's jogger suits            $36.00
Less 10% Trade Discount           3.60
                                 32.40
Plus 15% Sales Tax                4.86
                                $37.26
```

```
CN No. 027         28 September 19XX

To:  Humpty Dumpty Kindergarten
     88 Atkins Street
     LORNE VIC 3232

Overcharge Inv. 37              $10.00
```

Duplicates of receipts

```
Rec. No. 82
Date: 10/9/19XX

Rec'd from M. BRIGHT &
CO.
the sum of Two hundred
and one dollars eighty-
three cents

For: Payment of Account

Cash/Chq.      $201.83
Discount          5.17
Amt Owing      $207.00
```

```
Rec. No. 83
Date: 10/9/19XX

Rec'd from R. FOX
the sum of One thousand
dollars

For: Capital
     (Additional money
     paid by owner)

Cash/Chq.     $1000.00
```

```
Rec. No. 84
Date: 25/9/19XX

Rec'd from HUMPTY
DUMPTY
KINDERGARTEN
the sum of Eighty-seven
dollars seventy-five cents

For: Payment of Account

Cash/Chq.       $87.75
Discount          2.25
Amt Owing       $90.00
```

Rec. No. 85	Rec. No. 86	Rec. No. 87
Date: *25/9/19XX*	Date: *28/9/19XX*	Date: *28/9/19XX*
Rec'd from *B. LAMB PTY LTD*	Rec'd from *KIDDI-CLOTHES*	Rec'd from *OFFICE TRADERS*
the sum of *Four hundred dollars*	the sum of *Two hundred and sixty-six dollars forty-one cents*	the sum of *Five hundred and fifty dollars*
For: *Payment on Account*	For: *Payment of Account*	For: *Office Equipment (Cash sale of typewriter)*
Cash/Chq. $400.00	Cash/Chq. $266.41 Discount 6.83 Amt Owing $273.24	Cash/Chq. $550.00

Cash sales dockets

No. 136	No. 137	No. 138
Date: *3/9/19XX*	Date: *10/9/19XX*	Date: *16/9/19XX*
Cash Sales $155.50 Sales Tax 20.00 $175.50	Cash Sales $305.00 Sales Tax 58.40 $363.40	Cash Sales $240.00 Sales Tax Exempt

No. 139	No. 140	No. 141
Date: *21/9/19XX*	Date: *28/9/19XX*	Date: *30/9/19XX*
Cash Sales $560.00 Sales Tax 105.10 $665.10	Cash Sales $230.00 Sales Tax 92.40 $322.40	Cash Sales $198.00 Sales Tax Exempt

- On 3 September, a motor vehicle was sold on credit to A. Haddad for $12 500.
- On 10 September, Bo-Peep Clothing charged K. Lee interest at 4 per cent p.a. on his account of $380 which was outstanding for 6 months.
- On 12 September, it was found that K. Armour's opening general journal entry should have been recorded as $430 not $340.
- On 20 September, a fax machine was sold on credit for $230 to D. Procter.
- On 22 September, W. Yurich's account, considered irrecoverable, was written off as a bad debt.

You are required to carry out the following. Use copies of relevant masters provided at the back of this book.

1. Prepare the general journal opening entry.
2. Enter the invoices into the sales journal.

3. Enter the credit notes into the sales returns and allowances journal.
4. Enter the receipts and cash sales dockets into the cash receipts journal.
5. Enter the general journal entries.
6. Post all amounts relating to trade debtors to the accounts receivable ledger.
7. Prepare a schedule of debtors' balances as at 30 September 19XX.
8. Prepare statements of account for the following. (Use a copy of the blank statement of account master provided on page 547 and add the header: Bo-Peep Clothing Co., 88 Cambridge Street, Bankstown, NSW 2200.)
   (a) S. Walters & Co.
   (b) Humpty Dumpty Kindergarten
   (c) M. Bright & Co.
   (d) B. Lamb Pty Ltd

Putting it together

The guides that follow summarise the posting rules that have been covered in the preceding text. You may find these a useful reference when attempting the following exercises.

GUIDE FOR POSTING GENERAL JOURNAL TO LEDGERS

POSTING SOURCE	DESTINATION LEDGER	ACTION
General journal — Basic format 1. TOTAL of trade debtors' amounts in 'DEBIT' column	**General ledger**	DR Accounts Receivable Control account
2. TOTAL of trade creditors' amounts in 'CREDIT' column		CR Accounts Payable Control account
3. INDIVIDUAL amounts in 'DEBIT' column (excluding trade debtors)		DR individual accounts
4. INDIVIDUAL amounts in 'CREDIT' column (excluding trade creditors)		CR individual accounts
5. INDIVIDUAL trade debtors' amounts	**Accounts receivable ledger**	DR individual trade debtors' accounts
6. INDIVIDUAL trade creditors' amounts	**Accounts payable ledger**	CR individual trade creditors' accounts

(*continued*)

Guide for posting General Journal to ledgers (*continued*)

POSTING SOURCE	DESTINATION LEDGER	ACTION
General journal — Columnar (tabular) format 1. DEBIT SIDE total of 'ACCOUNTS RECEIVABLE' column	**General ledger**	DR Accounts Receivable Control account
2. DEBIT SIDE total of 'ACCOUNTS PAYABLE' column		DR Accounts Payable Control account
3. CREDIT SIDE total of 'ACCOUNTS RECEIVABLE' column		CR Accounts Receivable Control account
4. CREDIT SIDE total of 'ACCOUNTS PAYABLE' column		CR Accounts Payable Control account
5. DEBIT SIDE individual amounts in 'GENERAL' column		DR individual accounts
6. CREDIT SIDE individual amounts in 'GENERAL' column		CR individual accounts
7. DEBIT SIDE individual amounts in 'ACCOUNTS RECEIVABLE' column	**Accounts receivable ledger**	DR individual trade debtors' accounts
8. DEBIT SIDE individual amounts in 'ACCOUNTS PAYABLE' column	**Accounts payable ledger**	DR individual trade creditors' accounts
9. CREDIT SIDE individual amounts in 'ACCOUNTS RECEIVABLE' column	**Accounts receivable ledger**	CR individual trade debtors' accounts
10. CREDIT SIDE individual amounts in 'ACCOUNTS PAYABLE' column	**Accounts payable ledger**	CR individual trade creditors' accounts

GUIDE FOR POSTING TRADING JOURNALS TO LEDGERS

POSTING SOURCE	DESTINATION LEDGER	ACTION
Purchases journal 1. Total 'AMOUNT' column	**General ledger**	(a) DR Purchases account (b) CR Accounts Payable Control account
2. INDIVIDUAL entries	**Accounts payable ledger**	CR individual trade creditors' accounts
Purchases returns journal 1. Total 'AMOUNT' column	**General ledger**	(a) CR Purchases Returns account (b) DR Accounts Payable Control account
2. Individual entries	**Accounts payable ledger**	DR individual trade creditors' accounts

POSTING SOURCE	DESTINATION LEDGER	ACTION
Cash payments journal		
1. Total 'BANK' column	General ledger	CR Cash at Bank account (what goes out)
2. Total 'TRADE CREDITORS' column		DR Accounts Payable Control account
3. Total 'DISCOUNT RECEIVED' column		(a) DR Accounts Payable Control account (b) CR Discount Received account
4. INDIVIDUAL nominal entries in 'GENERAL' column		DR Individual nominal accounts (Wages, Rent, etc.)
5. INDIVIDUAL personal entries in 'General' column	Accounts payable ledger	DR individual creditors' accounts with: (a) amount in 'Accounts Payable' column (b) amount in 'Discount Received' column
Sales journal		
1. Total 'SALES' column	General ledger	CR Sales account
2. Total 'SALES TAX' column		CR Sales Tax account
3. Total 'TOTAL' column		DR Accounts Receivable Control account
4. INDIVIDUAL entries	Accounts receivable ledger	DR individual trade debtors' accounts with amount in 'TOTAL' column
Sales returns journal		
1. Total 'SALES RETURNS' column	General ledger	DR Sales Returns account
2. Total 'SALES TAX' column		DR Sales Tax account
3. Total 'TOTAL' column		CR Accounts Receivable Control account
4. INDIVIDUAL entries	Accounts receivable ledger	DR individual trade debtors' accounts with amount in 'TOTAL' column
Cash receipts journal		
1. Total 'BANK' column	General ledger	DR Cash at Bank account (what comes in)
2. Total 'SALES' column		CR Sales account
3. Total 'SALES TAX' column		CR Sales Tax account
4. Total 'TRADE DEBTORS' column		CR Accounts Receivable account
5. Total 'DISCOUNT ALLOWED' column		(a) CR Accounts Receivable account (b) DR Discount Allowed account
6. INDIVIDUAL nominal entries in 'GENERAL' column		CR individual nominal, asset or capital accounts
7. INDIVIDUAL personal entries	Accounts receivable ledger	CR individual debtors' accounts with: (a) amount in 'Accounts Receivable' column (b) amount in 'Discount Allowed' column

4A M. Kendall & Co.

The following journals for M. Kendall & Co. are shown below and on pages 271–273: the general journal, purchases journal, purchases returns and allowances journal, cash payments journal, sales journal, sales returns and allowances journal and cash receipts journal.

You are required to carry out the following. Use copies of the relevant masters provided at the back of this book.

1. Prepare a chart of accounts.
2. Post amounts from all journals to the general ledger.
3. Prepare a trial balance as at 31 May 19XX.
4. Post all journals to subsidiary ledgers.
5. Prepare schedules of debtors' and creditors' balances.
6. Reconcile the Accounts Payable and Accounts Receivable Control accounts in the general ledger with the schedules of creditors' and debtors' balances.

GENERAL JOURNAL OF M. KENDALL & CO.

Fol. GJ1

DEBIT							CREDIT		
Accounts receivable	Accounts payable	General	Date	Particulars	Fol.	Accounts receivable	Accounts payable	General
			19XX						
		5 693.50	May 1	Cash at Bank				
		300 000.00		Land				
		180 000.00		Buildings				
		9 480.00		Motor Vehicles				
		2 340.00		Office Equipment				
793.00				R. Barry				
383.50				T. Logan				
289.00				F. R. Shelley				
231.50				S. Underwood				
650.00				M. Pikler				
290.00				R. Eaton				
				A. Thornton			346.00	
				F. M. Rushton			729.50	
				T. K. Trading Co.			112.48	
				Gilbert Supplies			519.40	
				K. Pears			540.00	
				Mortgage				6 000.00
				Capital				491 903.12
				Assets, liabilities and capital at this date.				
2637.00		497 513.50					2247.38	497 903.12

GENERAL JOURNAL OF M. KENDALL & CO. (continued)

Fol. GJ1

Accounts receivable (Dr)	Accounts payable (Dr)	General (Dr)	Date	Particulars	Fol.	Accounts receivable (Cr)	Accounts payable (Cr)	General (Cr)
		120.00	May 8	Drawings Purchases Proprietor took goods for own use.				120.00

		1 000.00	14	Sundry Debtor —
				  W. Zammit
				    Office Equipment
				Computer sold on credit.
								1 000.00

6.50			15	M. Pikler Interest Revenue Interest charged on overdue a/c.				6.50

		21 000.00	20	Motor Vehicles
				  Sundry Creditor —
				    Deane Motors
				Motor vehicle purchased on credit.
								21 000.00

		290.00	20	Bad Debts R. Eaton Account written off as irrecoverable.		290.00		

		9 480.00	23	Sundry Debtor —
				  S. Flynne
				    Motor Vehicles
				Motor vehicle sold on credit.
								9 480.00

		3.37	23	Interest Expense K. Pears Interest paid to creditor on overdue a/c.			3.37	

		4 560.00	28	Office Equipment
				  Sundry Creditor —
				    Computec
				Computer and printer purchased on credit.
								4 560.00

300.00			31	T. Logan R. Barry Correction of error.		300.00		
306.50		36 453.37				590.00	3.37	36 166.50

PURCHASES JOURNAL OF M. KENDALL & CO.   Fol. PJ1

Date	Inv. no.	Particulars (Creditor's account to be credited)	Fol.	Amount	Monthly total
19XX					
May 3	92	T. K. Trading		64.70	
7	144	A. Thornton		198.35	
12	333	F. M. Rushton		423.00	
20	115	T. K. Trading		190.10	
24	546	C. Martin		262.70	
28	360	F. M. Rushton		48.90	
	179	A. Thornton		458.00	
31	591	C. Martin		563.70	
					2209.45

PURCHASES RETURNS AND ALLOWANCES JOURNAL OF M. KENDALL & CO.   Fol. PR1

Date	CN no.	Particulars (Creditor's account to be debited)	Fol.	Amount	Monthly total
19XX					
May 24	31	T. K. Trading		23.10	
27	44	F. M. Rushton		47.60	
30	112	C. Martin		65.60	
31					136.30

CASH PAYMENTS JOURNAL OF M. KENDALL & CO.   Fol. CP1

Date	Chq. no.	Particulars (Account to be debited)	Fol.	Discount received	Trade creditors	Wages	General	Bank
19XX								
May 2	630	Petty Cash					200.00	200.00
4	631	Wages				2460.00		2460.00
	632	F. M. Rushton		40.25	689.25			689.25
10	633	Electricity					198.00	198.00
	634	Advertising					155.00	155.00
15	635	Petty Cash Reimbursement						
		Stationery					55.00	
		Postage					42.70	
		Repairs					12.00	109.70
18	636	Wages				2880.00		2880.00
	637	Purchases					148.00	148.00
	638	Gilbert Supplies		38.50	480.90			480.90
24	639	Purchases					230.00	230.00
	640	A. Thornton		26.00	320.00			320.00
26	641	Drawings					100.00	100.00
28	642	T. K. Trading			100.00			100.00
31				104.75	1590.15	5340.00	1140.70	8070.85

SALES JOURNAL OF M. KENDALL & CO. Fol. SJ1

Date	Inv. no.	Particulars (Debtor's account to be debited)	Fol.	Sales	Sales tax	Debtors' total
19XX						
May 4	680	T. Logan		261.00	68.50	329.50
10	681	R. Barry		104.50	25.50	130.00
	682	S. Underwood		98.00		98.00
15	683	T. Logan		426.50	121.00	547.50
20	684	W. Ross		116.00	23.00	139.00
	685	F. R. Shelley		48.20	4.60	52.80
28	686	R. Barry		316.00	101.20	417.20
30	687	W. Ross		107.10	24.20	131.30
31				1477.30	368.00	1845.30

SALES RETURNS AND ALLOWANCES JOURNAL OF M. KENDALL & CO. Fol. SR1

Date	CN no.	Particulars (Debtor's account to be credited)	Fol.	Sales returns	Sales tax	Debtors' total
19XX						
May 25	572	T. Logan		120.00	34.50	154.50
28	573	S. Underwood		12.00		12.00
30	574	R. Barry		52.25	12.70	64.95
31				184.25	47.20	231.45

CASH RECEIPTS JOURNAL OF M. KENDALL & CO. Fol. CR1

Date	Rec. no.	Particulars (Account to be credited)	Fol.	Discount allowed	Trade debtors	Sales	Sales tax	General	Bank
19XX									
May 3	CS	Sales				120.50	32.45		152.95
10	221	F. R. Shelley		24.00	265.00				
	222	Capital						3500.00	
	CS	Sales				225.00	42.90		4032.90
18	223	Office Equipment						65.00	65.00
20	224	T. Logan			500.00				
	225	S. Underwood		11.50	220.00				
	CS	Sales				1263.50			1983.50
24	CS	Sales				183.20	46.15		229.35
26	226	R. Barry		33.00	460.00				460.00
30	CS	Sales				1148.20	37.10		1185.30
31				68.50	1445.00	2940.40	158.60	3565.00	8109.00

4B General Traders Ltd

The following journals for General Traders Ltd are shown below and on pages 275–277: the general journal, purchases journal, purchases returns and allowances journal, cash payments journal, sales journal, sales returns and allowances journal and cash receipts journal.

You are required to carry out the following. Use copies of the relevant masters provided at the back of this book.

1. Prepare a chart of accounts.
2. Post amounts from all journals to the general ledger.
3. Prepare a trial balance as at 31 March 19XX.
4. Post all journals to subsidiary ledgers.
5. Prepare schedules of debtors' and creditors' balances.
6. Reconcile the Accounts Payable and Accounts Receivable Control accounts in the general ledger with the schedules of creditors' and debtors' balances.

GENERAL JOURNAL OF GENERAL TRADERS LIMITED

Fol. GJ1

Accounts receivable (DR)	Accounts payable (DR)	General (DR)	Date	Particulars	Fol.	Accounts receivable (CR)	Accounts payable (CR)	General (CR)
		8 540.00	19XX Mar. 1	Cash at Bank				
		3 773.00		Inventory				
		200.00		Petty Cash				
		220 000.00		Land				
		112 000.00		Buildings				
		25 500.00		Motor Vehicles				
		7 780.00		Office Equipment				
		5 598.00		Office Furniture				
275.36				W. Marsh & Co.				
205.00				T. Bilby				
213.21				Jones & King				
144.64				Simpson & James				
120.00				B. Sumegi				
199.24				J. Cable Pty Ltd				
				Morgan Import Co.			342.80	
				Whitby Kitchen Products			650.80	
				M. Pringle			180.00	
				Ajax Plastics P/L			259.10	
				Cole Paint Supply Co.			1745.75	
				Capital				381 370.00
				Assets, liabilities and capital at this date.				
1157.45		383 391.00					3178.45	381 370.00

GENERAL JOURNAL OF GENERAL TRADERS LIMITED (continued)

Fol. GJ1

DEBIT						CREDIT		
Accounts receivable	Accounts payable	General	Date	Particulars	Fol.	Accounts receivable	Accounts payable	General
		90.00	Mar. 7	Drawings Purchases Proprietor took goods for own use.				90.00

		22 500.00	14	Motor Vehicles
				   Sundry Creditor —
				     M. R. Motors
				Motor vehicle purchased on credit.
								22 500.00

2.05			18	T. Bilby Interest Revenue Interest charged on overdue a/c.				2.05

		3 100.00	29	Office Equipment
				   Sundry Creditor —
				     Boyd's Computerland
				Computer purchased on credit.
								3 100.00

		250.00	29	Sundry Debtor —
				   F. Richards
				     Office Equipment
				Printer sold on credit.
								250.00

		8 900.00	29	Sundry Debtor —
				   J. Booth
				     Motor Vehicles
				Motor vehicle sold on credit.
								8 900.00

		2.25	31	Interest Expense M. Pringle Interest charged by creditor on overdue a/c.			2.25	
		120.00	31	Bad Debts B. Sumegi Account written off as irrecoverable.		120.00		
	215.00		31	Cole Paint Supply Co. Morgan Import Co. Correction of posting error.			215.00	
2.05	215.00	34 962.25				120.00	217.25	34 842.05

PURCHASES JOURNAL OF GENERAL TRADERS LIMITED   Fol. PJ1

Date	Inv. no.	Particulars (Creditor's account to be credited)	Fol.	Amount	Monthly total
19XX					
Mar. 2	742	Cole Paint Supply Co.		1035.00	
3	1127	Morgan Import Co. Pty Ltd		118.80	
10	762	Ajax Plastics Pty Ltd		92.50	
15	196	Whitby Kitchen Products		399.60	
23	874	Cole Paint Supply Co.		1543.50	
30	1201	Morgan Import Co. Pty Ltd		1340.70	
31					4530.10

PURCHASES RETURNS AND ALLOWANCES JOURNAL OF GENERAL TRADERS LIMITED
Fol. PR1

Date	CN no.	Particulars (Creditor's account to be debited)	Fol.	Amount	Monthly total
19XX					
Mar. 1	92	Ajax Plastics Pty Ltd		10.00	
12	881	Cole Paint Supply Co.		300.00	
28	111	Morgan Import Co. Pty Ltd		24.00	
31					334.00

CASH PAYMENTS JOURNAL OF GENERAL TRADERS LIMITED   Fol. CP1

Date	Chq. no.	Particulars (Account to be debited)	Fol.	Discount received	Trade creditors	Wages	General	Bank
19XX								
Mar. 2	520	Purchases					98.00	98.00
4	521	Wages				1075.00		1075.00
11	522	Wages				1090.00		1090.00
	523	Petty Cash Reimbursement						
		Postage					27.00	
		Stationery					12.00	
		Advertising					36.00	75.00
18	524	Wages				1090.00		1090.00
		Purchases					36.00	36.00
23	525	Advertising					75.00	75.00
26	526	Wages				1090.00		1090.00
	527	Whitby Kitchen Products			500.00			500.00
	528	Ajax Plastics P/L		19.10	240.00			240.00
30	529	Office Furniture					550.00	550.00
	530	Cole Paint Supply Co.			1000.00			1000.00
31				19.10	1740.00	4345.00	834.00	6919.00

SALES JOURNAL OF GENERAL TRADERS LIMITED   Fol. SJ1

Date	Inv. no.	Particulars (Debtor's account to be debited)	Fol.	Sales	Sales tax	Debtors' total
19XX						
Mar. 2	228	Jones & King		263.70	39.56	303.26
5	229	W. Marsh & Co.		217.35	32.60	249.95
10	230	J. Cable Pty Ltd		84.60	12.69	97.29
	231	Jones & King		245.25	36.79	282.04
15	232	Simpson & James		33.38	5.01	38.39
28	234	W. Marsh & Co.		511.65	76.75	588.40
31				1355.93	203.40	1559.33

SALES RETURNS AND ALLOWANCES JOURNAL OF GENERAL TRADERS LIMITED   Fol. SR1

Date	CN no.	Particulars (Debtor's account to be credited)	Fol.	Sales returns	Sales tax	Debtors' total
19XX						
Mar. 8	203	Jones & King		54.00	8.10	62.10
20	204	Simpson & James		11.02	1.65	12.67
31				65.02	9.75	74.77

CASH RECEIPTS JOURNAL OF GENERAL TRADERS LIMITED   Fol. CR1

Date	Rec. no.	Particulars (Account to be credited)	Fol.	Discount allowed	Trade debtors	Sales	Sales tax	General	Bank
19XX									
Mar. 3	CS	Sales				200.00			200.00
10	404	Capital						5000.00	
	CS	Sales				430.00	47.00		5477.00
12	CS	Sales				380.00			380.00
15	405	Jones & King		13.00	200.21				
	CS	Sales				58.00	6.80		265.01
20	406	Office Furniture						75.00	75.00
28	407	J. Cable Pty Ltd		19.24	180.00				180.00
30	408	Simpson & James			100.00				
	CS	Sales				150.00			250.00
31	409	W. Marsh & Co.		68.40	1045.31				1045.31
				100.64	1525.52	1218.00	53.80	5075.00	7872.32

4C The Toy Warehouse

Below and on pages 279–281 are the general journal, purchases journal, purchases returns and allowances journal, cash payments journal, sales journal, sales returns and allowances journal and cash receipts journal for The Toy Warehouse.

You are required to carry out the following. Use copies of the relevant masters provided at the back of this book.

1. Prepare a chart of accounts.
2. Post amounts from all journals to the general ledger.
3. Prepare a trial balance as at 31 August 19XX.
4. Post all journals to subsidiary ledgers.
5. Prepare schedules of debtors' and creditors' balances.
6. Reconcile the Accounts Payable and Accounts Receivable Control accounts in the general ledger with the schedules of creditors' and debtors' balances.

GENERAL JOURNAL OF THE TOY WAREHOUSE

Fol. GJ1

Accounts receivable (DR)	Accounts payable (DR)	General (DR)	Date	Particulars	Fol.	Accounts receivable (CR)	Accounts payable (CR)	General (CR)
			19XX					
		8 754.00	Aug. 1	Cash at Bank				
		8 328.00		Inventory				
		300.00		Petty Cash				
		150 000.00		Land				
		120 000.00		Buildings				
		11 480.00		Motor Vehicles				
		3 690.00		Office Equipment				
		2 285.00		Office Furniture				
990.00				B. Jenkins				
330.00				L. Gustafson				
750.00				G. Snow & Sons				
79.00				B. O'Leary				
1 296.50				Gordon Bros				
897.60				J. Laurie Pty Ltd				
				Hornsby Doll Co.			1 530.00	
				Kinder Toys P/L			1 257.50	
				G. Mallory			500.00	
				Paulson Imports			686.00	
				Toymakers P/L			377.00	
				Mortgage				50 000.00
				Capital				254 829.60
				Assets, liabilities and capital at this date.				
4343.10		304 837.00					4350.50	304 829.60

GENERAL JOURNAL OF THE TOY WAREHOUSE (continued)

Fol. GJ1

DEBIT						CREDIT		
Accounts receivable	Accounts payable	General	Date	Particulars	Fol.	Accounts receivable	Accounts payable	General
		120.00	Aug. 5	Drawings Purchases Proprietor took goods for own use.				120.00

		3 310.00	18	Office Equipment
				   Sundry Creditor —
				      G. Hamilton & Co.
				Photocopier purchased on credit.
								3 310.00

		12 500.00	24	Sundry Debtor —
				   T. Unwin
				      Motor Vehicles
				Motor vehicle sold on credit.
								12 500.00

		18 900.00	24	Motor Vehicles
				   Sundry Creditor —
				      Vanderfield
				      Car Sales
				Van purchased on credit.
								18 900.00

		79.00	24	Bad Debts B. O'Leary Account written off as irrecoverable.		79.00		

		1 300.00	28	Office Furniture
				   Sundry Creditor—
				      Prestige Office
				      Furniture
				Desk and chairs purchased on credit.
								1 300.00

3.30			31	L. Gustafson Interest Revenue Interest charged to debtor on overdue a/c.				3.30
		2.47	31	Interest Expense G. Mallory Interest charged by creditor on overdue a/c.			2.47	
3.30		36 211.47				79.00	2.47	36 133.30

PURCHASES JOURNAL OF THE TOY WAREHOUSE   Fol. PJ1

Date	Inv. no.	Particulars (Creditor's account to be credited)	Fol.	Amount	Monthly total
19XX					
Aug. 3	2268	Paulson Imports		807.50	
8	203	Kinder Toys Pty Ltd		648.00	
10	302	Hornsby Doll Co.		1134.75	
18	234	Kinder Toys Pty Ltd		975.00	
23	353	Hornsby Doll Co.		1303.00	
	504	Toymakers Pty Ltd		200.00	
27	2291	Paulson Imports		684.00	
30	642	Toymakers Pty Ltd		355.00	
31					6107.25

PURCHASES RETURNS AND ALLOWANCES JOURNAL OF THE TOY WAREHOUSE
Fol. PR1

Date	CN no.	Particulars (Creditor's account to be debited)	Fol.	Amount	Monthly total
19XX					
Aug. 3	89	Hornsby Doll Co.		150.00	
10	1160	Paulson Imports		192.00	
31					342.00

CASH PAYMENTS JOURNAL OF THE TOY WAREHOUSE   Fol. CP1

Date	Chq. no.	Particulars (Account to be debited)	Fol.	Discount received	Trade creditors	General	Bank
19XX							
Aug. 4	320	Purchases				150.00	150.00
	321	Electricity				195.00	195.00
10	322	Wages				2450.00	2450.00
12	323	Hornsby Doll Co.			1200.00		1200.00
14	324	Petty Cash Reimbursement					
		Stationery				15.00	
		Postage				35.00	
		Travel Expenses				30.00	80.00
16	325	Advertising				295.00	295.00
24	326	Wages				2450.00	2450.00
	327	Paulson Imports		43.00	643.00		643.00
	328	Kinder Toys			1000.00		1000.00
30	329	Toymakers Pty Ltd		27.00	350.00		350.00
31	330	Drawings				850.00	850.00
	BS	Bank Charges				45.00	45.00
				70.00	3193.00	6515.00	9708.00

SALES JOURNAL OF THE TOY WAREHOUSE Fol. SJ1

Date	Inv. no.	Particulars (Debtor's account to be debited)	Fol.	Sales	Sales tax	Debtors' total
19XX						
Aug. 2	1456	J. Laurie Pty Ltd		456.87	91.37	548.24
4	1457	Gordon Bros		549.95	109.99	659.94
10	1458	G. Snow & Sons		786.25	157.25	943.50
18	1459	Mary Muffet Toys		142.37	28.47	170.84
25	1460	Gordon Bros		561.00	112.20	673.20
28	1461	B. Jenkins		604.35	120.87	725.22
30	1462	G. Snow & Sons		816.00	163.20	979.20
31	1463	The Children's Hospital		176.00		176.00
				4092.79	783.35	4876.14

SALES RETURNS AND ALLOWANCES JOURNAL OF THE TOY WAREHOUSE Fol. SR1

Date	CN no.	Particulars (Debtor's account to be credited)	Fol.	Sales returns	Sales tax	Debtors' total
19XX						
Aug. 25	44	B. Jenkins		99.45	19.89	119.34
26	45	Gordon Bros		165.32	33.06	198.38
31	46	G. Snow & Sons		144.50	28.90	173.40
				409.27	81.85	491.12

CASH RECEIPTS JOURNAL OF THE TOY WAREHOUSE Fol. CR1

Date	Rec. no.	Particulars (Account to be credited)	Fol.	Discount allowed	Trade debtors	Sales	Sales tax	General	Bank
19XX									
Aug. 5	CS	Sales				550.00	47.50		597.50
10	91	Gordon Bros			750.00				
	CS	Sales				98.00			848.00
12	CS	Sales				167.00	25.00		192.00
18	CS	Sales				485.00			485.00
20	92	G. Snow & Sons		45.00	705.00				705.00
25	93	Capital						1000.00	1000.00
27	94	B. Jenkins		50.00	940.00				
	95	J. Laurie Pty Ltd			500.00				
	CS	Sales				325.00			1765.00
30	96	Mary Muffet Toys			170.84				170.84
31				95.00	3065.84	1625.00	72.50	1000.00	5763.34

4D Jackson's Wholesale Stationers

Below and on pages 283–285 are the general journal, purchases journal, purchases returns and allowances journal, cash payments journal, sales journal, sales returns and allowances journal and cash receipts journal for Jackson's Wholesale Stationers.

You are required to carry out the following. Use copies of the relevant masters provided at the back of this book.

1. Prepare a chart of accounts.
2. Post amounts from all journals to the general ledger.
3. Prepare a trial balance as at 30 September 19XX.
4. Post all journals to subsidiary ledgers.
5. Prepare schedules of debtors' and creditors' balances.
6. Reconcile the Accounts Payable and Accounts Receivable Control accounts in the general ledger with the schedules of creditors' and debtors' balances.

GENERAL JOURNAL OF JACKSON'S WHOLESALE STATIONERS

DEBIT / CREDIT — Fol. GJ1

Accounts receivable	Accounts payable	General	Date	Particulars	Fol.	Accounts receivable	Accounts payable	General
			19XX					
		5 610.00	Sept. 1	Cash at Bank				
		9 874.00		Inventory				
		300.00		Petty Cash				
		80 000.00		Land				
		90 000.00		Buildings				
		28 540.00		Motor Vehicles				
		5 990.00		Office Equipment				
		3 110.00		Office Furniture				
464.33				M. W. Anderson & Co.				
690.18				James Black & Sons				
210.00				Klein & Vanstone				
527.16				Simpson Stationers				
1309.40				Les Stephens Pty Ltd				
400.00				Mardu & Singh				
				Austral Stamp Co.			589.50	
				Greenway Co. P/L			495.00	
				William Gray P/L			1041.25	
				R. McIntyre & Co.			742.00	
				Stationery Suppliers P/L			780.00	
				Carmody & Co.			335.00	
				Capital				223 042.32
				Assets, liabilities and capital at this date.				
3601.07		223 424.00					3982.75	223 042.32

GENERAL JOURNAL OF JACKSON'S WHOLESALE STATIONERS (continued)

Fol. GJ1

Accounts receivable	Accounts payable	General	Date	Particulars	Fol.	Accounts receivable	Accounts payable	General
		160.00	Sept. 7	Drawings Purchases Proprietor took goods for own use.				160.00
		23 000.00	10	Motor Vehicles Sundry Creditor — Preston Car Sales Car purchased on credit.				23 000.00
		12 500.00	10	Sundry Debtor — B. English Motor Vehicles Car sold on credit.				12 500.00
		210.00	24	Bad Debts Klein & Vanstone Account written off as irrecoverable.		210.00		
		580.00	28	Office Furniture Sundry Creditor — Hughes & Jackson Desk purchased on credit.				580.00
3.00			28	Mardu & Singh Interest Revenue Interest charged on debtor's overdue a/c.				3.00
		300.00	30	Sundry Debtor — T. Wilson Office Equipment Printer sold on credit.				300.00
		10.41	30	Interest Expense William Gray P/L Interest charged by creditor on overdue a/c.			10.41	
3.00		36 760.41				210.00	10.41	36 543.00

PURCHASES JOURNAL OF JACKSON'S WHOLESALE STATIONERS Fol. PJ1

Date	Inv. no.	Particulars (Creditor's account to be credited)	Fol.	Amount	Monthly total
19XX					
Sept. 3	203	R. McIntyre & Co.		545.00	
5	921	Austral Stamp Co.		201.25	
	336	Greenway Co. Pty Ltd		244.00	
11	290	Stationery Suppliers Pty Ltd		550.00	
	246	R. McIntyre & Co.		2632.40	
15	980	Austral Stamp Co.		205.00	
30					4377.65

PURCHASES RETURNS AND ALLOWANCES JOURNAL OF JACKSON'S WHOLESALE STATIONERS

Fol. PR1

Date	CN no.	Particulars (Creditor's account to be debited)	Fol.	Amount	Monthly total
19XX					
Sept. 12	51	R. McIntyre & Co.		100.00	
24	89	Austral Stamp Co.		162.50	
30					262.50

CASH PAYMENTS JOURNAL OF JACKSON'S WHOLESALE STATIONERS Fol. CP1

Date	Chq. no.	Particulars (Account to be debited)	Fol.	Discount received	Trade creditors	Wages	General	Bank
19XX								
Sept. 3	649	Advertising					95.00	95.00
5	650	Wages				2550.00		2550.00
6	651	Carmody & Co.		30.00	305.00			305.00
	652	Austral Stamp Co.		35.50	554.00			554.00
	653	Petty Cash Reimbursement						
		Stationery					23.50	
		Postage					56.00	79.50
12	654	Wages				2560.00		2560.00
	655	Purchases					150.00	150.00
18	656	Office Equipment					576.00	576.00
19	657	Wages				2750.00		2750.00
20	658	Drawings					150.00	150.00
	659	R. McIntyre & Co.			500.00			500.00
	660	Stationery Suppliers		24.00	756.00			756.00
	661	Electricity					273.00	273.00
	BS	Bank Charges					27.00	27.00
30				89.50	2115.00	7860.00	1350.50	11325.50

SALES JOURNAL OF JACKSON'S WHOLESALE STATIONERS Fol. SJ1

Date	Inv. no.	Particulars (Debtor's account to be debited)	Fol.	Sales	Sales tax	Debtors' total
19XX						
Sept. 5	89	Simpson Stationers		237.20	35.58	272.78
8	90	M. W. Anderson & Co.		240.00	36.00	276.00
	91	James Black & Sons		561.20	84.18	645.38
12	92	M. W. Anderson & Co.		196.00	29.40	225.40
18	93	Simpson Stationers		681.60	102.24	783.84
20	94	Les Stephens Pty Ltd		792.00	118.80	910.80
30	95	James Black & Sons		471.20	70.68	541.88
				3179.20	476.88	3656.08

SALES RETURNS AND ALLOWANCES JOURNAL OF JACKSON'S WHOLESALE STATIONERS Fol. SR1

Date	CN no.	Particulars (Debtor's account to be credited)	Fol.	Sales returns	Sales tax	Debtors' total
19XX						
Sept. 10	22	Simpson Stationers		31.20	6.00	37.20
20	23	Les Stephens Pty Ltd		120.00	23.00	143.00
30	24	M. W. Anderson & Co.		40.00	6.00	46.00
				191.20	35.00	226.20

CASH RECEIPTS JOURNAL OF JACKSON'S WHOLESALE STATIONERS Fol. CR1

Date	Rec. no.	Particulars (Account to be credited)	Fol.	Discount allowed	Trade debtors	Sales	Sales tax	General	Bank
19XX									
Sept. 2	CS	Sales				567.00	100.00		
	93	Capital						5000.00	5667.00
5	CS	Sales				90.50			90.50
9	94	M. W. Anderson		32.03	432.30				
	95	Simpson Stationers		27.16	500.00				
	CS	Sales				468.00	51.50		1451.80
15	CS	Sales				263.50	45.50		309.00
23	96	Les Stephens P/L			1000.00				
	97	James Black & Sons			450.00				1450.00
27	CS	Sales				480.00	35.00		515.00
30	98	Office Equipment						3500.00	3500.00
				59.19	2382.30	1869.00	232.00	8500.00	12983.30

SECTION 4: BANK RECONCILIATION PROCEDURES

This section is for students doing Module NOS 240 'Accounting to trial balance'.

Reconciling the cash records

When a business receives and pays out money, records are kept by both the business (internal records) and the bank (external records). There are therefore two distinct points of view in respect to financial records. The point of view of the business is represented by the Cash at Bank account in the general ledger. When a business has money in its bank account, the bank is a debtor of the business. Debtors are an asset, and assets always have a debit balance in the bookkeeping records of the business. When a business owes money to the bank (for example, a bank overdraft) the business has a liability. Liabilities always have a credit balance in the bookkeeping records of the business.

The bank's point of view is represented by the bank statement. When a business has money in its bank account, the bank, in reality, owes that money to the business. Therefore, the bank has a liability. Liabilities always have a credit balance in the bank's ledger. When the business owes money to the bank (for example, a bank overdraft), the business is the bank's debtor. Debtors are an asset, and assets always have a debit balance in the bank's ledger.

Therefore, a debit balance in the Cash at Bank account in the general ledger of the business corresponds to a credit balance in the bank statement. Similarly, a credit balance in the Cash at Bank account in the general ledger of the business corresponds to a debit balance in the bank statement.

This relationship is illustrated in the following table.

Situation	Cash at Bank account	Bank statement
Business has money in its bank account.	Debit balance	Credit balance (CR)
Business has overdrawn its bank account or operates an overdraft as a result of an agreement with the bank.	Credit balance	Debit balance (DR)

Because there are these two different perspectives, it is therefore necessary for the business to ensure that its own records (the Cash at Bank account in the general ledger) agree (or reconcile) with those kept by the bank (the bank statement, which is a copy of the individual account of the business in the bank's ledger). By way of example, a bank statement for A. French & Sons for the month of February 19XX is shown on page 287.

Statement of Account

Westpac Banking Corporation
MYRTLEVILLE NSW

SPECIMEN ONLY

This statement: **FEBRUARY**

A. French & Sons
256 Airport Road
MYRTLEVILLE NSW 2834

Account No. **86423**
Sheet No. **220**

Name of account: **A. FRENCH & SONS**

Date	Particulars	Debit	Credit	Balance
19XX				
1 FEB.	BROUGHT FORWARD			5320.00 CR
2 FEB.	C/C		315.00	5635.00 CR
3 FEB.	C/C		292.00	5927.00 CR
	00079	480.00		5447.00 CR
4 FEB.	00080	360.00		5087.00 CR
8 FEB.	C/C		500.00	5587.00 CR
10 FEB.	00082	600.00		4987.00 CR
11 FEB.	00083	150.00		4837.00 CR
12 FEB.	00084	182.00		4655.00 CR
14 FEB.	00085	300.00		4355.00 CR
	C/C		1042.00	5397.00 CR
17 FEB.	00087	85.00		5312.00 CR
20 FEB.	FEE	9.80		5302.20 CR
	CHQ BK	6.00		5296.20 CR
	C/C		506.00	5802.20 CR
24 FEB.	DD — B. Witherspoon		360.00	6162.20 CR
	STATE GOVT TAX ON WITHDRAWALS	3.60		6158.60 CR
	STATE GOVT TAX ON DEPOSITS	4.80		6153.80 CR
28 FEB.	RTD — J. Corelli	292.00		5861.80 CR

Last statement to: **31 JAN.**
This statement to: **28 FEB.**
Total debits: **2473.20**
Total credits: **3015.00**

CR credit
OD overdrawn

Proceeds of cheques etc. accepted for collection will not be available until cleared.
All entries for the last few business days are subject to verification and authorisation.
Any items not paid or withdrawn will be adjusted by reversal entry on a later statement.
Please see reverse for additional information.

To reconcile the cash records, a business prepares a bank reconciliation statement. How this is done is described in some detail from page 291 onwards.

Overdraft

The term 'overdraft' means, literally, 'overdrawn account'. When a business realises that funds are low, and that issuing further cheques may result in its account being overdrawn, the bank should be notified. The bank manager may be willing to accommodate the situation provided that cash is deposited within the next day or so. For example, the wages cheque may be due to be paid on Friday, but funds will not be deposited until Monday.

A business may, however, make an arrangement with its bank to overdraw its current account. This is what is known as an 'overdraft'. It means that the business can still draw cheques although there are no funds in the account. A limit is placed on the amount by which the account may be overdrawn and the business pays interest on the daily balance by which the account is overdrawn. Many firms borrow money from the bank to finance their operations by this method.

In an overdraft situation, the amount outstanding to the bank is increased when cheques are paid, and decreased when deposits are made.

Dishonoured cheques

Before we go on to look at bank reconciliation statements in detail, we must first consider dishonoured cheques, which have a bearing on the reconciliation of financial records.

When a bank refuses to make payment on a cheque, the cheque becomes a dishonoured cheque. A cheque becomes dishonoured if:
- the account has been closed
- the account does not have sufficient funds in it to cover the transaction
- a 'stop payment' notice has been issued to the bank by the customer
- the bank has received notice of the customer's death, placement in protective custody, or bankruptcy
- the cheque is 'stale', in other words, dated over twelve months previously
- the cheque is 'post-dated', in other words, dated in the future.

When a cheque is dishonoured, it is returned to the drawer (the person or firm who owns the account on which the cheque is drawn) by the drawer's bank with the notation 'RTD' (return to drawer). This information also appears on the bank statement (see the bank statement on page 287).

Recording a dishonoured cheque in the accounting records

When a cheque is received from a debtor, a receipt is sent to the debtor, the cheque is deposited and the debtor's account is credited with the amount of the cheque plus the amount of discount allowed for prompt payment (if any). However, if the cheque is dishonoured — if there are insufficient funds to meet the cheque — the bank returns the cheque to the drawer. This means that although the business has recorded the transaction, no money has been received.

When a business discovers that a cheque from one of its debtors has been dishonoured, it must be recorded in the books of account in the following manner.

Method 1: Reversal entry in cash receipts journal (used in this text)
To record details of a dishonoured cheque, a reversal entry is made in the cash receipts journal. The cash receipt and the discount allowed are entered as a reversal entry in the cash receipts book. Negative amounts are indicated by placing brackets around the figures or writing them in red ink.

Example
On 12 February 19XX, A. French & Sons was informed that a cheque received from J. Corelli for $292.00 was dishonoured. Discount of $8.00 had been allowed for prompt payment. Details of the dishonoured cheque (shown in italics) are entered in the cash receipts journal of A. French as follows.

CASH RECEIPTS JOURNAL OF A. FRENCH & SONS   Fol. CR1

Date	Rec. no.	Particulars (Account to be credited)	Fol.	Discount allowed	Trade debtors	Sales	Sales tax	General	Bank
19XX Feb. 1		Balance	b/f						5320.00
2	CRR	Sales				270.00	45.00		315.00
3	042	J. Corelli		8.00	292.00				292.00
8	043 CRR	F. Bronte Sales			150.00	297.50	52.50		500.00
12	D/C	*J. Corelli dishonoured chq.*		*(8.00)*	*(292.00)*				*(292.00)*
14	044 CRR	M. Dickens Sales		7.00	260.00	680.00	102.00		1042.00
20	CRR	Sales				440.00	66.00		506.00
25	CRR	Sales				820.00	123.00		943.00

This is the method used in this text, as it is the easiest and most convenient method, allowing both the cash and the discount to be reversed with *one* entry in *one* journal. Posting details of the dishonour from this entry is simplified as all details are contained in the one journal (cash receipts). It also provides a simple method of tracing the transaction back to the original receipt number.

Method 2: Cash payments journal
The details of the dishonoured cheque are entered into the cash payments journal. When posted, the debtor's account is debited and the amount owing is increased to the correct amount.

CASH PAYMENTS JOURNAL OF A. FRENCH & SONS   Fol. CP1

Date	Chq. no.	Particulars (Account to be debited)	Fol.	Discount received	Trade creditors	General	Bank
19XX							
Feb. 3	079	Electricity				480.00	480.00
4	080	Advertising				360.00	360.00
5	081	T. Nguyen		20.00	780.00		780.00
10	082	Wages				600.00	600.00
11	083	Petty Cash Imprest				150.00	150.00
12	084	Purchases				182.00	182.00
	D/C	Debtor: J. Corelli (dishonoured chq.)				292.00*	292.00
14	085	Drawings				300.00	300.00
16	086	A. Lucchese		16.00	624.00		624.00
17	087	Petty Cash Reimbursement					
		Postage				36.00	
		Stationery				15.00	
		Travel				25.00	
		Sundries				9.00	85.00
28				36.00	1404.00	2449.00	3853.00

* This entry concerns a debtor and cannot be recorded in the 'Accounts payable' column, but is recorded in the 'General' column of the cash payments journal. Similarly, the amount of discount allowed cannot be reversed through the cash payments journal as there is only a column for 'Discount received'. Consequently, when using this method an additional entry must also be made in the general journal to record reversal of discount allowed.

The Accounts Receivable Control account in the general ledger and the debtor's individual account in the accounts receivable (trade debtors') ledger are debited to increase the amount owed by the debtor.

If discount has been allowed to the debtor for prompt payment, it is written back into the Accounts Receivable Control account and the individual trade debtors' account in the accounts receivable ledger. This is done with the following general journal entry:

- *debit* — Accounts Receivable (J. Corelli)
- *credit* — Discount Allowed.

The disadvantage of this method is that it utilises the cash payments journal — normally used to record details of transactions with trade creditors — to record details of a transaction with a trade debtor. Also, if discount has been allowed to the debtor for prompt payment, an additional entry must be made in the general journal to reverse the discount. This would involve the use of three journals:

1. *cash receipts journal* — to record the original receipt from J. Corelli
2. *cash payments journal* — to record the dishonour of the cheque
3. *general journal* — to record the discount allowed written back.

Bank statement

The dishonoured cheque will also be shown on A. French's bank statement at the end of the month (see the bank statement on page 287). Dishonoured cheques are recorded as RTD (return to drawer) in the bank statement.

Preparing a bank reconciliation statement

The bank reconciliation statement provides a link between the records of the business and those of the bank. Those items which appear on the bank statement, but not in the business records, are recorded in the appropriate cash journals.

However, as alterations or additions may not be made to the bank statement (which is a true and accurate record of the firm's bank account), those details which appear in the business records but not on the bank statement are included in the bank reconciliation statement which is used to reconcile the two records.

As we have already mentioned, it is important to recognise that there will be differences between a bank's records and the records of a business. The Cash at Bank account in the general ledger of the business and the bank statement may disagree for the reasons listed below.

1. The business may have drawn cheques that had not been presented to the bank at the time the bank statement was issued. These are called unpresented cheques.
2. The business may have deposited cash, cheques and/or credit card receipts (noted as C/C on the bank statement) after the bank statement was issued. These are called outstanding deposits.
3. The bank may have deposits (credits) or withdrawals (debits) of which the business is not aware, for example:
   (a) bank charges (FEE, CHQ BK)
   (b) financial institutions duty (FID)[1]
   (c) government debits tax (BADT)[2]
   (d) direct deposits (DD)
   (e) periodical payments (PP)
   (f) interest on bonds
   (g) interest on a bank overdraft/mortgage
   (h) dishonoured cheques (RTD)
   (i) electronic transfers (TFR).

---

1. Financial institutions duty is a State government duty on all dutiable credits, which includes deposits, automatic credits, transfers between accounts and interest credits. It is accrued daily and debited when the account is credited with interest earnings. This may appear on the bank statement as 'State Govt Tax on Deposits'.
2. Government debits tax is a State government duty charged on each withdrawal from an account which has a cheque book facility. The tax is accrued daily and debited on the last day of each month. This may appear on the bank statement as 'State Govt Tax on Withdrawals'.

A bank reconciliation statement is prepared to account for these differences. The steps involved in preparing this statement are listed in the table below.

STEP	ACTION
1	Check to see whether the opening balance in the bank statement (the balance at the top of the statement) and the balance brought down (b/d) at the beginning of the month in the Cash at Bank account agree. If so, tick both figures. If they do not agree, refer to the previous month's bank reconciliation statement.
2	Compare the entries in the 'Credit' column of the bank statement with those in the 'Bank' column of the cash receipts journal. Tick all entries that agree — both in the bank statement and the cash receipts journal.
3	Record any unticked entries in the 'Credit' column of the bank statement in the cash receipts journal. Once you have done this, tick the entry in both the bank statement and the cash receipts journal.
4	Compare the entries in the 'Debit' column of the bank statement (ticking both the cheque number and the amount) with those in the 'Bank' column of the cash payments journal. Tick all entries that agree — both in the bank statement and the cash payments journal.
5	Record any unticked entries in the 'Debit' column of the bank statement in the cash payments journal. Once you have done this, tick the entry in both the bank statement and the cash payments journal. Note: All entries in the bank statement should now be ticked.[3]
6	Total all columns in the cash receipts and cash payments journals and show the balance brought down (b/d) at the reconciliation date. Any items in the cash receipts and cash payments journals that are not ticked are included in the bank reconciliation statement.[4]
7	Post the totals of the 'Bank' column of both the cash receipts and cash payments journals to the Cash at Bank account in the general ledger.
8	Balance the Cash at Bank account in the general ledger.

3. The exceptions here are previously reconciled cheques and outstanding deposits which are listed on the previous month's bank reconciliation statement. This topic is covered in detail later in this chapter.
4. The exceptions here are dishonoured cheques which are recorded as a negative entry in the cash receipts journal.

There are a number of points to watch carefully when you are preparing a bank reconciliation statement. These are listed below.
(a) Always begin with the final balance in the bank statement.
(b) If the final balance in the bank statement is a credit balance (that is, the business has money in the bank), you *add* outstanding deposits and *deduct* unpresented cheques.
(c) If the final balance in the bank statement is a debit balance (that is, the business owes money[5] to the bank), you *add* unpresented cheques and *deduct* outstanding deposits.
(d) The final figure in the bank reconciliation statement *must* agree with the balance b/d in the Cash at Bank account in the general ledger.

When the bank statement shows a credit balance

When the bank statement shows a credit balance, that is, when the business has money in the bank, the bank reconciliation statement should be set out in the following manner.

BANK RECONCILIATION STATEMENT OF J. MASON
as at 30 March 19XX

Credit balance as per bank statement				$1463.00
Add: Outstanding deposits (i.e. any unticked entry in cash receipts journal)				310.00
				1773.00
Less: Unpresented cheques (i.e. any unticked entry in cash payments journal and previous bank reconciliation statement)		094	270.00	
		098	102.00	372.00
Debit balance as per Cash at Bank account in general ledger				$1401.00

Example

On pages 294–295 are the bank statement (extract), cash receipts journal, cash payments journal and Cash at Bank account of A. French & Sons. Items which appear in both the bank statement *and* the cash receipts and/or cash payments journals have been ticked. Those items which appear on the bank statement but *not* in the cash receipts and/or cash payments journals have been entered into the appropriate cash receipts or cash payments journal in italics. (Refer to page 292 for instructions on how this is done.)

---

5. This indicates that the account is overdrawn, and generally means that the business has an overdraft arrangement with the bank.

Statement of Account
Westpac Banking Corporation
MYRTLEVILLE NSW

SPECIMEN ONLY

This statement: **FEBRUARY**

A. French & Sons
256 Airport Road
MYRTLEVILLE NSW 2834

Account No. **86423**

Sheet No. **220**

Name of account: **A. FRENCH & SONS**

Date	Particulars	Debit	Credit	Balance
19XX				
1 FEB.	BROUGHT FORWARD			5320.00 CR
2 FEB.	C/C		✓ 315.00	5635.00 CR
3 FEB.	C/C		✓ 292.00	5927.00 CR
	00079 ✓	✓ 480.00		5447.00 CR
4 FEB.	00080 ✓	✓ 360.00		5087.00 CR
8 FEB.	C/C		✓ 500.00	5587.00 CR
10 FEB.	00082 ✓	✓ 600.00		4987.00 CR
11 FEB.	00083 ✓	✓ 150.00		4837.00 CR
12 FEB.	00084 ✓	✓ 182.00		4655.00 CR
14 FEB.	00085 ✓	✓ 300.00		4355.00 CR
	C/C		✓ 1042.00	5397.00 CR
17 FEB.	00087 ✓	✓ 85.00		5312.00 CR
20 FEB.	FEE	✓ 9.80		5302.20 CR
	CHQ BK	✓ 6.00		5296.20 CR
	C/C		✓ 506.00	5802.20 CR
24 FEB.	DD — B. Witherspoon		✓ 360.00	6162.20 CR
	STATE GOVT TAX ON WITHDRAWALS	✓ 3.60		6158.60 CR
	STATE GOVT TAX ON DEPOSITS	✓ 4.80		6153.80 CR
28 FEB.	RTD — J. Corelli	✓ 292.00		5861.80 CR

CASH RECEIPTS JOURNAL OF A. FRENCH & SONS
Fol. CR1

Date	Rec. no.	Particulars (Account to be credited)	Fol.	Discount allowed	Trade debtors	Sales	Sales tax	General	Bank	
19XX										
Feb. 2	CRR	Sales				270.00	45.00		✓	315.00
3	042	J. Corelli		8.00	292.00				✓	292.00
8	043	F. Bronte			150.00					
	CRR	Sales				297.50	52.50		✓	500.00
12	D/C	J. Corelli — dishonoured cheque		(8.00)	(292.00)				✓	(292.00)
14	044	M. Dickens		7.00	260.00					
	CRR	Sales				680.00	102.00		✓	1042.00
20	CRR	Sales				440.00	66.00		✓	506.00
25	CRR	Sales				820.00	123.00			943.00
24	B220	B. Witherspoon			360.00				✓	360.00
28				7.00	770.00	2507.50	388.50			3666.00

CASH PAYMENTS JOURNAL OF A. FRENCH & SONS

Fol. CP1

Date	Chq. no.	Particulars (Account to be debited)	Fol.	Discount received	Sundry creditors	Purchases	Wages	General	Bank
19XX									
Feb. 3	079 ✓	Electricity						480.00	480.00 ✓
4	080 ✓	Advertising						360.00	360.00 ✓
5	081	T. Nguyen		20.00	780.00				780.00
10	082 ✓	Wages					600.00		600.00 ✓
11	083 ✓	Petty Cash Imprest						150.00	150.00 ✓
12	084 ✓	Purchases				182.00			182.00 ✓
14	085 ✓	Drawings						300.00	300.00 ✓
16	086	A. Lucchese		16.00	624.00				624.00
17	087 ✓	Petty Cash Reimbursement							
		Postage						36.00	
		Stationery						15.00	
		Travel						25.00	
28	B220	Sundries						9.00	85.00 ✓
		Fee						9.80	9.80 ✓
		Cheque Book						6.00	6.00 ✓
		State Govt tax on withdrawals						3.60	3.60 ✓
		State Govt tax on deposits						4.80	4.80 ✓
28				36.00	1404.00	182.00	600.00	1399.20	3585.20

GENERAL LEDGER OF A. FRENCH

Cash at Bank 1.1

Date	Particulars	Fol.	Debit	Credit	Balance
19XX					
Feb. 1	Balance	b/d			5320.00 Dr
28	Sundries	CR1	3666.00		8986.00 Dr
	Sundries	CP1		3585.20	5400.80 Dr

When the cash receipts and cash payments journals have been totalled and posted to the Cash at Bank account in the general ledger for the month, the bank reconciliation statement can be prepared as follows.

BANK RECONCILIATION STATEMENT OF A. FRENCH & SONS
as at 28 February 19XX

Credit balance as per bank statement				$5861.80
Add: Outstanding deposits				943.00
				6804.80
Less: Unpresented cheques		081	780.00	
		086	624.00	1404.00
Debit balance as per Cash at Bank account in general ledger				$5400.80

Checking for errors

Let us now recap what we have done in the example on pages 293–295.
1. We compared the bank statement extract of A. French & Sons with its cash receipts and cash payments journals. In a real-life situation, we would also look at the previous month's bank reconciliation statement.
2. We ticked those items common to both the bank statement and the cash receipts and cash payments journals.
3. We added those unticked items on the bank statement to either the cash receipts or cash payments journals as appropriate.
4. We added and balanced the cash journals and posted details to the general ledger and the appropriate subsidiary ledger.
5. We then prepared the bank reconciliation statement which took account of any outstanding deposits and unpresented cheques.

But what if you do not balance? First, you should check to see that you have not made one of the following most common errors in the preparation of the bank reconciliation statement:
(a) adding figures incorrectly — usually in cash journals
(b) recording an incorrect balance carried down from the previous period in the Cash at Bank account in the general ledger
(c) omitting to tick off an item in the cash journals (for example, a cheque that has been presented)
(d) overlooking an unpresented cheque
(e) failing to consult the previous month's bank reconciliation statement
(f) ticking a cheque that has not been presented
(g) transposing figures when recording (for example, recording bank charges of $5.40 listed on the bank statement as $4.50 in the cash payments journal).

If this does not uncover the discrepancy, you may find it simpler to redo the whole procedure. Use a different coloured pen for the new ticks or cross-tick the originals.

EXERCISE 4.29   *D. Bennett*

On pages 297–298 are the bank statement (extract), cash receipts journal, cash payments journal and Cash at Bank account for D. Bennett. You are required to carry out the following.
1. Compare the cash receipts and cash payments journals with the bank statement for May 19XX.
2. Adjust the cash journals by adding items that are in the bank statement but not in the cash journals.
3. Post details to the Cash at Bank account in the general ledger.
4. Prepare a bank reconciliation statement as at 31 May 19XX. This must agree with the balance in the Cash at Bank account in the general ledger. Use copies of the relevant masters provided at the back of this book.

Statement of Account

Westpac Banking Corporation
DENHAM GROVE NSW

SPECIMEN ONLY

This statement: **MAY**

Mr D. Bennett
56 Highland Street
DENHAM GROVE NSW

Account No. **723–615**
Sheet No. **21**

Name of account: **D. BENNETT**

Date	Particulars	Debit	Credit	Balance
19XX				
1 MAY	BROUGHT FORWARD			18 000.00 CR
2 MAY	C/C		223.20	18 223.20 CR
10 MAY	C/C		550.00	18 773.20 CR
11 MAY	C/C		10 736.00	29 509.20 CR
16 MAY		62114 500.00		29 009.20 CR
		62115 55.00		28 954.20 CR
21 MAY		62118 646.00		28 308.20 CR
22 MAY		62117 150.00		28 158.20 CR
28 MAY	C/C		5 769.14	33 927.34 CR
	DD — P. West		326.40	34 253.74 CR
	FEE	7.40		34 246.34 CR
	CHQ BK	8.00		34 238.34 CR
29 MAY	STATE GOVT TAX ON WITHDRAWALS	2.30		34 236.04 CR
	STATE GOVT TAX ON DEPOSITS	4.20		34 231.84 CR
30 MAY	RTD — R. Lee	223.20		34 008.64 CR

CASH RECEIPTS JOURNAL OF D. BENNETT   Fol. CR1

Date	Rec. no.	Particulars (Account to be credited)	Fol.	Discount allowed	Trade debtors	Sales	Sales tax	General	Bank
19XX May 2	201	R. Lee		16.80	223.20				223.20
10	CRR	Sales				481.25	68.75		550.00
11	202	Rent Revenue						500.00	
	203	Capital						10 000.00	
	CRR	Sales				206.50	29.50		10 736.00
28	203	G. Christos		8.44	289.14				
	204	Motor Vehicles						5 000.00	
	CRR	Sales				420.00	60.00		5 769.14
29	205	M. Fox			100.00				100.00

CASH PAYMENTS JOURNAL OF D. BENNETT
Fol. CP1

Date	Chq. no.	Particulars (Account to be debited)	Fol.	Discount received	Trade creditors	General	Bank
19XX							
May 14	114	Rent				500.00	500.00
15	115	Advertising				55.00	55.00
	116	Coffey & Sons		21.00	399.00		399.00
17	117	Petty Cash (Imprest)				150.00	150.00
20	118	Johnson Bros		34.00	646.00		646.00
28	119	Repairs and Maintenance				83.00	83.00

GENERAL LEDGER OF D. BENNETT
Cash at Bank 1.1

Date	Particulars	Fol.	Debit	Credit	Balance
19XX					
May 1	Balance	b/d			18 000.00 Dr

EXERCISE 4.30 Savannah Electrics

On pages 299–300 are the bank statement (extract), cash receipts journal, cash payments journal and Cash at Bank account of Savannah Electrics (proprietor, Keith Savannah). You are required to carry out the following.

1. Compare the cash receipts and cash payments journals with the bank statement for November 19XX.
2. Adjust the cash journals by adding items that are in the bank statement but not in the cash journals.
3. Post details to the Cash at Bank account in the general ledger.
4. Prepare a bank reconciliation statement as at 30 November 19XX. This must agree with the balance in the Cash at Bank account in the general ledger.

Use copies of the relevant masters provided at the back of this book.

Statement of Account

Westpac Banking Corporation
SPRINGFIELD NSW

SPECIMEN ONLY

This statement: **NOVEMBER**

Mr K. Savannah
Savannah Electrics
420 Tennyson Road
SPRINGFIELD NSW 2317

Account No. **527-111**
Sheet No. **48**

Name of account: **SAVANNAH ELECTRICS**

Date	Particulars		Debit	Credit	Balance
19XX					
1 NOV.	BROUGHT FORWARD				4640.00 CR
2 NOV.	C/C			138.00	4778.00 CR
4 NOV.		31866	342.00		4436.00 CR
5 NOV.	C/C			481.50	4917.50 CR
8 NOV.		31867	232.05		4685.45 CR
9 NOV.	C/C			459.15	5144.60 CR
10 NOV.	DD — A. Stamnos			383.20	5527.80 CR
11 NOV.		31868	168.60		5359.20 CR
		31869	480.90		4878.30 CR
15 NOV.	C/C			184.60	5062.90 CR
17 NOV.		31871	260.00		4802.90 CR
19 NOV.		31872	175.50		4627.40 CR
21 NOV.	C/C			689.65	5317.05 CR
29 NOV.		31873	520.60		4796.45 CR
	RTD — P. Taylor		184.60		4611.85 CR
30 NOV.	FEE		6.80		4605.05 CR
	CHQ BK		12.50		4592.55 CR
	STATE GOVT TAX ON WITHDRAWALS		6.50		4586.05 CR
	STATE GOVT TAX ON DEPOSITS		5.80		4580.25 CR

CASH RECEIPTS JOURNAL OF SAVANNAH ELECTRICS

Fol. CR1

Date	Rec. no.	Particulars (Account to be credited)	Fol.	Discount allowed	Trade debtors	Sales	Sales tax	General	Bank
19XX									
Nov. 1	CRR	Sales				120.00	18.00		138.00
4	CRR	Sales				64.00	8.00		
	461	Elite Engineering		10.50	409.50				481.50
8	CRR	Sales				406.00	53.15		459.15
14	462	P. Taylor		4.62	184.60				184.60
20	CRR	Sales				185.00	4.65		
	463	Rent Revenue						500.00	689.65
28	CRR	Sales				220.00	33.00		
	464	K. Bowman			205.00				458.00

CASH PAYMENTS JOURNAL OF SAVANNAH ELECTRICS Fol. CP1

Date	Chq. no.	Particulars (Account to be debited)	Fol.	Discount received	Trade creditors	Purchases	General	Bank
19XX								
Nov. 3	866	Purchases				342.00		342.00
7	867	T. Hobbs		5.95	232.05			232.05
10	868	Purchases				168.60		168.60
14	869	Wages					480.90	480.90
16	870	Advertising					84.00	84.00
	871	Electricity					260.00	260.00
18	872	M. Kong		4.50	175.50			175.50
28	873	Wages					520.60	520.60
29	874	Purchases				204.00		204.00

GENERAL LEDGER OF SAVANNAH ELECTRICS

Cash at Bank 1.1

Date	Particulars	Fol.	Debit	Credit	Balance
19XX					
Nov. 1	Balance	b/d			4640.00 Dr

EXERCISE 4.31 Marinos & Co.

On pages 301–302 are the bank statement (extract), cash receipts journal, cash payments journal and Cash at Bank account of Marinos & Co. You are required to carry out the following.

1. Compare the cash receipts and cash payments journals with the bank statement for February 19XX.
2. Adjust the cash journals by adding items that are in the bank statement but not in the cash journals.
3. Post details to the Cash at Bank account in the general ledger.
4. Prepare a bank reconciliation statement as at 28 February 19XX. This must agree with the balance in the Cash at Bank account in the general ledger.

Use copies of the relevant masters provided at the back of this book.

Statement of Account

Westpac Banking Corporation
CLIFTON WATERS   NSW

SPECIMEN ONLY

This statement: **FEBRUARY**

Marinos & Co.
184 Bayview Parade
CLIFTON WATERS NSW 2456

Account No. **238–411**
Sheet No. **31**

Name of account: **MARINOS & CO**

Date	Particulars		Debit	Credit	Balance
19XX					
1 FEB.	BROUGHT FORWARD				6241.80 CR
4 FEB.	C/C			368.00	6609.80 CR
		21418	282.90		6326.90 CR
6 FEB.		21419	351.00		5975.90 CR
8 FEB.		21421	280.00		5695.90 CR
9 FEB.	C/C			687.00	6382.90 CR
10 FEB.		21422	510.00		5872.90 CR
		21426	155.50		5717.40 CR
		21424	243.75		5473.65 CR
		21425	48.26		5425.39 CR
	DD — B. Shipman			286.20	5711.59 CR
13 FEB.	C/C			28.60	5740.19 CR
15 FEB.	C/C			589.15	6329.34 CR
16 FEB.	RTD — G. Jackson		376.00		5953.34 CR
18 FEB.	CHQ BK		12.50		5940.84 CR
20 FEB.	FEE		10.00		5930.84 CR
	STATE GOVT TAX ON WITHDRAWALS		5.60		5925.24 CR
	STATE GOVT TAX ON DEPOSITS		4.80		5920.44 CR
24 FEB.		21427	542.60		5377.84 CR
26 FEB.	C/C			260.00	5637.84 CR

CASH RECEIPTS JOURNAL OF MARINOS & CO.   Fol. CR1

Date	Rec. no.	Particulars (Account to be credited)	Fol.	Discount allowed	Trade debtors	Sales	Sales tax	General	Bank
19XX									
Feb. 2	CRR	Sales				320.00	48.00		368.00
8	CRR	Sales				222.00	30.15		
	167	A. Vella		11.15	434.85				687.00
12	168	Commission Revenue						28.60	28.60
14	169	G. Jackson			376.00				
	CRR	Sales				189.50	23.65		589.15
25	170	Rent Revenue						260.00	260.00
27	171	A. Vella		5.50	214.50				214.50

CASH PAYMENTS JOURNAL OF MARINOS & CO. Fol. CP1

Date	Chq. no.	Particulars (Account to be debited)	Fol.	Discount received	Trade creditors	Purchases	General	Bank
19XX								
Feb. 2	418	Purchases				282.90		282.90
5	419	A. Chang		9.00	351.00			351.00
7	420	Purchases				145.60		145.60
	421	Rent Expense					280.00	280.00
9	422	Wages					510.00	510.00
	423	Purchases				163.80		163.80
	424	S. Brown		6.25	243.75			243.75
	425	Purchases				48.26		48.26
	426	Advertising					155.50	155.50
23	427	Wages					542.60	542.60
	428	M. Popolous		4.90	191.10			191.10

GENERAL LEDGER OF MARINOS & CO.
Cash at Bank 1.1

Date	Particulars	Fol.	Debit	Credit	Balance
19XX					
Feb. 1	Balance	b/d			6241.80 Dr

Checking unpresented cheques and/or outstanding deposits from previous month

Unpresented cheques and outstanding deposits in the previous month's bank reconciliation statement are those entries which appeared in the cash receipts and cash payments journals in the previous month but did not appear on the bank statement for that month.

When the balance at the beginning of the month in the Cash at Bank account in the general ledger and the *first* balance in the bank statement do not agree, it is necessary to go to the previous month's bank reconciliation statement and tick items which appear both on it and on the bank statement. Any unticked items in the previous month's bank reconciliation statement will go into the current month's bank reconciliation statement and will continue to be carried forward until the bank has 'caught up' on these transactions.

EXERCISE 4.32 *Busy Bee Craft Supplies*

On pages 303–304 are the bank statement (extract), cash receipts journal, cash payments journal and Cash at Bank account of Busy Bee Craft Supplies (proprietor, Lauren Schmidt) for July 19XX, together with the bank reconciliation statement as at 30 June 19XX. You are required to carry out the following.
1. Compare the cash receipts journal, cash payments journal and previous month's bank reconciliation statement with the bank statement for July.
2. Adjust the cash journals by adding items that are in the bank statement but not in the cash journals.

3. Post details to the Cash at Bank account in the general ledger.
4. Prepare a bank reconciliation statement as at 31 July 19XX. This must agree with the balance in the Cash at Bank account in the general ledger.

Use copies of the relevant masters provided at the back of this book.

BANK RECONCILIATION STATEMENT OF BUSY BEE CRAFT SUPPLIES
as at 30 June 19XX

Credit balance as per bank statement				$3762.80
Add: Outstanding deposits				420.60
				4183.40
Less: Unpresented cheques	33183	72.80		
	33184	195.60		268.40
Debit balance as per Cash at Bank account in general ledger				$3915.00

Statement of Account

Westpac Banking Corporation
BELLMAINE VIC 3832

SPECIMEN ONLY

This statement: JULY

Ms L. Schmidt
Busy Bee Craft Supplies
240 Heritage Drive
BELLMAINE VIC 3832

Account No. 142–641
Sheet No. 83

Name of account: BUSY BEE CRAFT SUPPLIES

Date	Particulars	Debit		Credit	Balance
19XX					
1 JULY	BROUGHT FORWARD				3762.80 CR
2 JULY	C/C			420.60	4183.40 CR
		33183	72.80		4110.60 CR
		33184	195.60		3915.00 CR
4 JULY	C/C			175.50	4090.50 CR
5 JULY		33186	80.00		4010.50 CR
7 JULY	C/C			332.00	4342.50 CR
8 JULY		33187	120.00		4222.50 CR
9 JULY	C/C			414.50	4637.00 CR
10 JULY	RTD — J. Carling		175.50		4461.50 CR
	FEE		18.20		4443.30 CR
11 JULY	C/C			180.00	4623.30 CR
15 JULY	CHQ BK		12.50		4610.80 CR
	C/C			325.25	4936.05 CR
17 JULY		33190	150.00		4786.05 CR
		33188	175.50		4610.55 CR
18 JULY	DD — V. Elwood		82.00		4692.55 CR
19 JULY		33191	85.80		4606.75 CR
21 JULY	C/C			220.00	4826.75 CR
		33192	230.00		4596.75 CR
	STATE GOVT TAX ON WITHDRAWALS		7.80		4588.95 CR
	STATE GOVT TAX ON DEPOSITS		5.90		4583.05 CR
25 JULY		33193	135.00		4448.05 CR

CASH RECEIPTS JOURNAL OF BUSY BEE CRAFT SUPPLIES Fol. CR1

Date	Rec. no.	Particulars (Account to be credited)	Fol.	Discount allowed	Trade debtors	Sales	Sales tax	General	Bank
19XX July 3	262	J. Carling		4.50	175.50				175.50
6	CRR	Sales				282.60	49.40		332.00
8	263	P. Retzos		5.50	214.50				
	CRR	Sales				175.00	25.00		414.50
10	CRR	Sales				157.50	22.50		180.00
14	264	M. Chenery		4.75	185.25				
	CRR	Sales				122.50	17.50		325.25
20	CRR	Sales				187.00	33.00		220.00
26	265	J. Carling		5.75	224.25				224.25

CASH PAYMENTS JOURNAL OF BUSY BEE CRAFT SUPPLIES Fol. CP1

Date	Chq. no.	Particulars (Account to be debited)	Fol.	Discount received	Trade creditors	Purchases	General	Bank
19XX July 4	186	Purchases				80.00		80.00
7	187	Wages					120.00	120.00
11	188	D. Katz		4.50	175.50			175.50
13	189	Advertising					46.70	46.70
16	190	Petty Cash (Imprest)					150.00	150.00
18	191	A. Chang		2.20	85.80			85.80
20	192	Rent Expense					230.00	230.00
24	193	Wages					135.00	135.00
30	194	Purchases				98.80		98.80

GENERAL LEDGER OF BUSY BEE CRAFT SUPPLIES
Cash at Bank 1.1

Date	Particulars	Fol.	Debit	Credit	Balance
19XX July 1	Balance	b/d			3915.00 Dr

EXERCISE
4.33 *Sovereign Enterprises*

On pages 305–306 are the bank statement (extract), cash receipts journal, cash payments journal and Cash at Bank account in the general ledger of Sovereign Enterprises for May 19XX, together with the bank reconciliation statement as at 30 April 19XX. You are required to carry out the following.
1. Compare the cash receipts journal, cash payments journal and previous month's bank reconciliation statement with the bank statement for May.
2. Adjust the cash journals by adding items that are in the bank statement but not in the cash journals.

3. Post details to the Cash at Bank account in the general ledger.
4. Prepare a bank reconciliation statement as at 31 May 19XX. This must agree with the balance in the Cash at Bank account in the general ledger.

Use copies of the relevant masters provided at the back of this book.

BANK RECONCILIATION STATEMENT OF SOVEREIGN ENTERPRISES
as at 30 April 19XX

Credit balance as per bank statement				$7692.84
Add:	Outstanding deposits			363.90
				8056.74
Less:	Unpresented cheques	38716	82.60	
		38719	358.40	441.00
Debit balance as per Cash at Bank account in general ledger				$7615.74

Statement of Account

Westpac Banking Corporation
MANNERTON QLD

SPECIMEN ONLY

This statement: MAY

Sovereign Enterprises
763 Boulder Highway
MANNERTON QLD 4821

Account No. 934–721
Sheet No. 36

Name of account: SOVEREIGN ENTERPRISES

Date	Particulars		Debit	Credit	Balance
19XX					
1 MAY	BROUGHT FORWARD				7692.84 CR
2 MAY	C/C			363.90	8056.74 CR
3 MAY		38716	82.60		7974.14 CR
4 MAY	C/C			504.40	8478.54 CR
5 MAY		38721	376.82		8101.72 CR
		38719	358.40		7743.32 CR
		38722	341.25		7402.07 CR
6 MAY	C/C			481.71	7883.78 CR
9 MAY		38723	280.50		7603.28 CR
11 MAY	C/C			666.32	8269.60 CR
12 MAY	FEE		12.40		8257.20 CR
15 MAY		38725	440.00		7817.20 CR
16 MAY	DD — B. Timms			386.80	8204.00 CR
18 MAY	CHQ BK		26.00		8178.00 CR
19 MAY	INTEREST ON C'TH BONDS			56.80	8234.80 CR
20 MAY	RTD — A. Lawrence		504.40		7730.40 CR
21 MAY	C/C			513.78	8244.18 CR
22 MAY		38726	264.80		7979.38 CR
23 MAY	STATE GOVT TAX ON WITHDRAWALS		8.60		7970.78 CR
	STATE GOVT TAX ON DEPOSITS		7.80		7962.98 CR
29 MAY		38729	495.40		7467.58 CR
		38728	214.50		7253.08 CR
	C/C			233.00	7486.08 CR

CASH RECEIPTS JOURNAL OF SOVEREIGN ENTERPRISES — Fol. CR1

Date	Rec. no.	Particulars (Account to be credited)	Fol.	Discount allowed	Trade debtors	Sales	Sales tax	General	Bank
19XX May 3	656	A. Lawrence		15.60	504.40				504.40
5	CRR	Sales				425.00	56.71		481.71
10	657	D. Lam		9.18	296.82				
	CRR	Sales				321.30	48.20		666.32
20	CRR	Sales				168.70	21.10		
	658	J. Kostera		10.02	323.98				513.78
28	CRR	Sales				202.60	30.40		233.00
30	CRR	Sales				156.30	19.54		175.84

CASH PAYMENTS JOURNAL OF SOVEREIGN ENTERPRISES — Fol. CP1

Date	Chq. no.	Particulars (Account to be debited)	Fol.	Discount received	Trade creditors	Purchases	General	Bank
19XX May 4	721	Purchases				376.82		376.82
	722	M. Thompson		8.75	341.25			341.25
8	723	Elite Engineering		7.20	280.50			280.50
	724	Purchases				93.75		93.75
14	725	Wages					440.00	440.00
21	726	Advertising					264.80	264.80
	727	Purchases				185.75		185.75
25	728	F. Gregg		5.50	214.50			214.50
28	729	Wages					495.40	495.40

GENERAL LEDGER OF SOVEREIGN ENTERPRISES
Cash at Bank 1.1

Date	Particulars	Fol.	Debit	Credit	Balance
19XX May 1	Balance	b/d			7615.74 Dr

EXERCISE 4.34 *K. Cheung & Sons*

On pages 307–308 are the bank statement (extract), cash receipts journal, cash payments journal and Cash at Bank account in the general ledger of K. Cheung & Sons for August 19XX, together with the bank reconciliation statement as at 31 July 19XX. You are required to carry out the following.
1. Compare the cash receipts journal, cash payments journal and previous month's bank reconciliation statement with the bank statement for August 19XX.
2. Adjust the cash journals by adding items that are in the bank statement but not in the cash journals.
3. Post details to the Cash at Bank account in the general ledger.

4. Prepare a bank reconciliation statement as at 31 August 19XX. This must agree with the balance in the Cash at Bank account in the general ledger.

Use copies of the relevant masters provided at the back of this book.

BANK RECONCILIATION STATEMENT OF K. CHEUNG & SONS
as at 31 July 19XX

Credit balance as per bank statement				$8296.76
Add:	Outstanding deposits			428.96
				8725.72
Less:	Unpresented cheques	42757	184.70	
		42760	363.40	548.10
Debit balance as per Cash at Bank account in general ledger				$8177.62

Statement of Account

Westpac Banking Corporation
BAYVILLE NSW

SPECIMEN ONLY

This statement: AUGUST

K. Cheung & Sons
27 Bayside Drive
BAYVILLE NSW 2124

Account No. 764-351
Sheet No. 18

Name of account: K. CHEUNG & SONS

Date	Particulars		Debit	Credit	Balance
19XX					
1 AUG.	BROUGHT FORWARD				8296.76 CR
2 AUG.	C/C			428.96	8725.72 CR
		42760	363.40		8362.32 CR
3 AUG.	C/C			142.40	8504.72 CR
5 AUG.		42762	273.00		8231.72 CR
7 AUG.		42757	184.70		8047.02 CR
	C/C			379.05	8426.07 CR
8 AUG.	INTEREST ON MORTGAGE		221.10		8204.97 CR
9 AUG.		42763	284.20		7920.77 CR
11 AUG.	C/C			465.60	8386.37 CR
12 AUG.		42764	516.80		7869.57 CR
	DD — P. Artemis		234.80		8104.37 CR
15 AUG.	C/C			170.88	8275.25 CR
16 AUG.		42766	186.90		8088.35 CR
		42767	212.00		7876.35 CR
17 AUG.	FEE		12.60		7863.75 CR
18 AUG.	RTD — M. Tregonna		180.00		7683.75 CR
20 AUG.	CHQ BK		25.00		7658.75 CR
22 AUG.	C/C			395.34	8054.09 CR
24 AUG.	STATE GOVT TAX ON WITHDRAWALS		7.20		8046.89 CR
	STATE GOVT TAX ON DEPOSITS		6.40		8040.49 CR
		42768	349.44		7691.05 CR
25 AUG.	INTEREST ON C'TH BONDS			152.40	7843.45 CR
31 AUG.		42770	79.80		7763.65 CR

CASH RECEIPTS JOURNAL OF K. CHEUNG & SONS   Fol. CR1

Date	Rec. no.	Particulars (Account to be credited)	Fol.	Discount allowed	Trade debtors	Sales	Sales tax	General	Bank
19XX									
Aug. 2	CRR	Sales				126.58	15.82		142.40
6	161	K. Johnson		8.00	312.00				
	CRR	Sales				59.60	7.45		379.05
10	CRR	Sales				238.00	47.60		
	162	N. Tregonna			180.00				465.60
14	CRR	Sales				148.60	22.28		170.88
21	163	A. Benson		4.00	156.00				
	CRR	Sales				212.75	26.59		395.34
28	164	J. Wade		6.80	268.32				
	165	Rent Revenue						484.00	752.32

CASH PAYMENTS JOURNAL OF K. CHEUNG & SONS   Fol. CP1

Date	Chq. no.	Particulars (Account to be debited)	Fol.	Discount received	Trade creditors	Purchases	General	Bank
19XX								
Aug. 2	762	P. Lee		7.00	273.00			273.00
8	763	Purchases				284.20		284.20
11	764	Wages					516.80	516.80
	765	Repairs and Maintenance					82.30	82.30
15	766	Purchases				186.90		186.90
	767	Rent Expense					212.00	212.00
23	768	R. Kearney		8.96	349.44			349.44
	769	Purchases				187.50		187.50
30	770	Petty Cash Reimbursement						
		Travel					28.00	
		Postage					33.00	
		General Expenses					18.80	79.80

GENERAL LEDGER OF K. CHEUNG & SONS
Cash at Bank   1.1

Date	Particulars	Fol.	Debit	Credit	Balance
19XX Aug. 1	Balance	b/d			8177.62 Dr

When the business owes money to the bank

When the final balance on the bank statement is a *debit* balance (DR), this means that the business owes money to the bank. When this situation occurs, the bank reconciliation statement is set out as follows.

BANK RECONCILIATION STATEMENT OF J. MASON
as at 31 March 19XX

Debit balance as per bank statement				$1463.00
Add: Unpresented cheques	094	270.00		
	098	102.00		372.00
				1835.00
Less: Outstanding deposits				310.00
Credit balance as per Cash at Bank account in general ledger				$1525.00

In the above example, the business begins the period owing money to the bank (bank overdraft). The unpresented cheques are added, which increases the amount the business owes to the bank. The outstanding deposits are then deducted and the amount owing to the bank is decreased.

A credit balance in the Cash at Bank account in the general ledger is shown as follows.

GENERAL LEDGER OF J. MASON

Cash at Bank 1.1

Date	Particulars	Fol.	Debit	Credit	Balance
19XX Apr. 1	Balance	b/d			1525.00 Cr

EXERCISE 4.35 *Ace Motor Spares*

On pages 310–311 are the bank statement (extract), cash receipts journal, cash payments journal and Cash at Bank account in the general ledger of Ace Motor Spares (proprietor, G. Ferremo) for October 19XX, together with the bank reconciliation statement as at 30 September 19XX.

1. Compare the cash receipts journal, cash payments journal and the previous month's bank reconciliation statement with the bank statement for October.
2. Adjust the cash journals by adding items that are in the bank statement but not in the cash journals.
3. Post details to the Cash at Bank account in the general ledger.
4. Prepare a bank reconciliation statement as at 31 October 19XX. This must agree with the balance in the Cash at Bank account in the general ledger.

Use copies of the relevant masters provided at the back of this book.

BANK RECONCILIATION STATEMENT OF ACE MOTOR SPARES
as at 30 September 19XX

Debit balance as per bank statement				$4283.00
Add: Unpresented cheques	415	72.80		
	418	186.40		259.20
				4542.20
Less: Outstanding deposits				204.80
Credit balance as per Cash at Bank account in general ledger				$4337.40

Statement of Account

Westpac Banking Corporation
RUTHVEN WA

SPECIMEN ONLY

This statement: **OCTOBER**

Mr G. Ferremo
Ace Motor Spares
81 Kingsley Road
RUTHVEN WA 6346

Account No.: **814–912**
Sheet No.: **46**

Name of account: **ACE MOTOR SPARES**

Date	Particulars		Debit	Credit	Balance
19XX					
1 OCT.	BROUGHT FORWARD				4283.00 DR
2 OCT.	C/C			204.80	4078.20 DR
		82418	186.40		4264.60 DR
3 OCT.	C/C			411.75	3852.85 DR
4 OCT.		82421	180.00		4032.85 DR
6 OCT.		82422	234.00		4266.85 DR
		82415	72.80		4339.65 DR
7 OCT.	C/C			135.00	4204.65 DR
9 OCT.		82424	280.00		4484.65 DR
11 OCT.		82425	420.00		4904.65 DR
12 OCT.	INTEREST ON OVERDRAFT		163.00		5067.65 DR
	C/C			707.50	4360.15 DR
14 OCT.	FEE		48.00		4408.15 DR
15 OCT.	DD — K. Monroe		156.40		4251.75 DR*
		82423	126.00		4377.75 DR
17 OCT.	C/C			726.75	3651.00 DR
19 OCT.	INTEREST ON C'TH BONDS			48.50	3602.50 DR
20 OCT.	CHQ BK		25.00		3627.50 DR
21 OCT.		82427	75.00		3702.50 DR
23 OCT.	C/C			99.80	3602.70 DR
24 OCT.	STATE GOVT TAX ON WITHDRAWALS		8.20		3610.90 DR
	STATE GOVT TAX ON DEPOSITS		7.40		3618.30 DR
26 OCT.		82428	186.80		3805.10 DR

*Note: 15 OCT DD — K. Monroe shows 156.40 in Credit column, balance 4251.75 DR

CASH RECEIPTS JOURNAL OF ACE MOTOR SPARES   CR1

Date	Rec. no.	Particulars (Account to be credited)	Fol.	Discount allowed	Trade debtors	Sales	Sales tax	General	Bank
19XX Oct. 2	CRR 514	Sales Custom Cars		4.50	175.50	210.00	26.25		411.75
6	CRR	Sales				120.00	15.00		135.00
11	515 CRR	Metro Auto Sales Sales			280.00	380.00	47.50		707.50
16	CRR 516	Sales Speedy Car Repairs		12.00	468.00	230.00	28.75		726.75
22	CRR	Sales				88.70	11.10		99.80
29	517 518	Custom Cars Rent Revenue		4.65	181.35			380.00	561.35

CASH PAYMENTS JOURNAL OF ACE MOTOR SPARES   Fol. CP1

Date	Chq. no.	Particulars (Account to be debited)	Fol.	Discount received	Trade creditors	Purchases	General	Bank
19XX Oct. 3	421	Purchases				180.00		180.00
5	422	M. Caruana		6.00	234.00			234.00
	423	Purchases				126.00		126.00
8	424	Electricity					280.00	280.00
10	425	Rent Expense					420.00	420.00
14	426	Repairs and Maintenance					84.60	84.60
20	427	K. Wong			75.00			75.00
24	428	Purchases				186.80		186.80
28	429	L. Wilson		8.00	312.00			312.00

GENERAL LEDGER OF ACE MOTOR SPARES
Cash at Bank   1.1

Date	Particulars	Fol.	Debit	Credit	Balance
19XX Oct. 1	Balance	b/d			4337.40 Cr

EXERCISE 4.36   W. Guthrie

The bank statement extract, cash receipts journal, cash payments journal and Cash at Bank account in the general ledger of W. Guthrie for March 19XX, together with the bank reconciliation statement as at 28 February 19XX are shown on pages 312–313. You are required to carry out the following.
1. Compare the cash receipts journal, cash payments journal and the previous month's bank reconciliation statement with the bank statement for March.
2. Adjust the cash journals by adding items that are in the bank statement but not in the cash journals.
3. Post details to the Cash at Bank account in the general ledger.

4. Prepare a bank reconciliation statement as at 31 March 19XX. This must agree with the balance in the Cash at Bank account in the general ledger.

   Use copies of the relevant masters provided at the back of this book.

BANK RECONCILIATION STATEMENT OF W. GUTHRIE
as at 28 February 19XX

Debit balance as per bank statement				$2668.40
Add: Unpresented cheques	213	426.80		
	215	394.75		821.55
				3489.95
Less: Outstanding deposits				562.80
Credit balance as per Cash at Bank account in general ledger				$2927.15

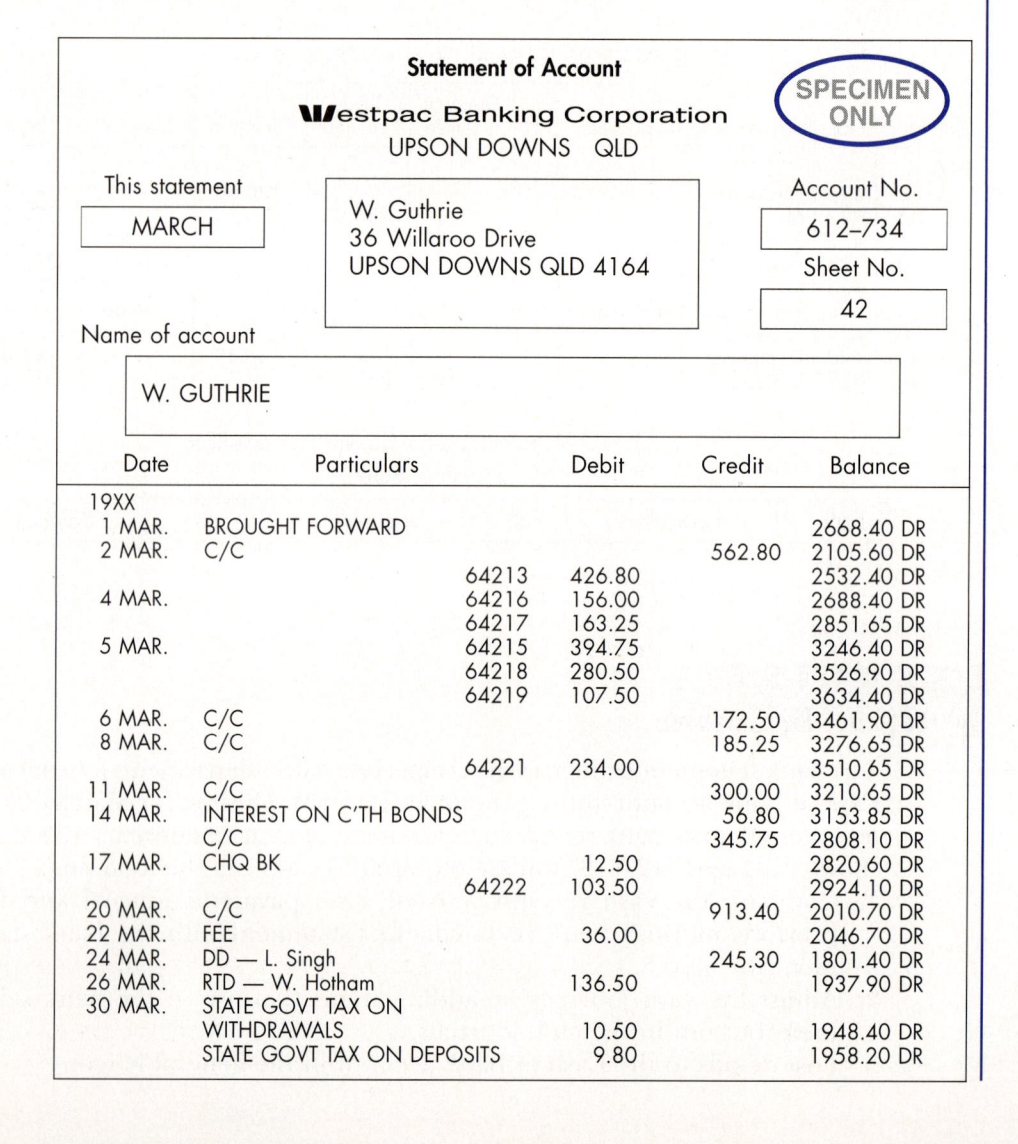

Statement of Account

Westpac Banking Corporation
UPSON DOWNS   QLD

SPECIMEN ONLY

This statement: MARCH

W. Guthrie
36 Willaroo Drive
UPSON DOWNS QLD 4164

Account No. 612–734
Sheet No. 42

Name of account: W. GUTHRIE

Date	Particulars		Debit	Credit	Balance
19XX					
1 MAR.	BROUGHT FORWARD				2668.40 DR
2 MAR.	C/C			562.80	2105.60 DR
		64213	426.80		2532.40 DR
4 MAR.		64216	156.00		2688.40 DR
		64217	163.25		2851.65 DR
5 MAR.		64215	394.75		3246.40 DR
		64218	280.50		3526.90 DR
		64219	107.50		3634.40 DR
6 MAR.	C/C			172.50	3461.90 DR
8 MAR.	C/C			185.25	3276.65 DR
		64221	234.00		3510.65 DR
11 MAR.	C/C			300.00	3210.65 DR
14 MAR.	INTEREST ON C'TH BONDS			56.80	3153.85 DR
	C/C			345.75	2808.10 DR
17 MAR.	CHQ BK		12.50		2820.60 DR
		64222	103.50		2924.10 DR
20 MAR.	C/C			913.40	2010.70 DR
22 MAR.	FEE		36.00		2046.70 DR
24 MAR.	DD — L. Singh			245.30	1801.40 DR
26 MAR.	RTD — W. Hotham		136.50		1937.90 DR
30 MAR.	STATE GOVT TAX ON WITHDRAWALS		10.50		1948.40 DR
	STATE GOVT TAX ON DEPOSITS		9.80		1958.20 DR

CASH RECEIPTS JOURNAL OF W. GUTHRIE   Fol. CR1

Date	Rec. no.	Particulars (Account to be credited)	Fol.	Discount allowed	Trade debtors	Sales	Sales tax	General	Bank
19XX Mar. 3	CRR	Sales				150.00	22.50		172.50
4	168	K. Robinson		4.50	185.25				185.25
6	CRR	Sales				255.00	45.00		300.00
13	CRR 169	Sales W. Hotham		3.50	136.50	186.00	23.25		345.75
17	CRR 170	Sales Rent Revenue				416.00	62.40	435.00	913.40
26	CRR 171	Sales K. Robinson			198.20	395.25	69.75		663.20

CASH PAYMENTS JOURNAL OF W. GUTHRIE   Fol. CP1

Date	Chq. no.	Particulars (Account to be debited)	Fol.	Discount received	Trade creditors	Purchases	General	Bank
19XX Mar. 3	216	R. de Campo		4.00	156.00			156.00
	217	Purchases				163.25		163.25
4	218	Rent Expense					280.50	280.50
	219	Advertising					107.50	107.50
	220	Purchases				86.80		86.80
7	221	K. Minh		6.00	234.00			234.00
16	222	Petty Cash Reimbursement General expenses Postage Travel					25.00 42.00 36.50	103.50
20	223	Purchases				72.60		72.60

GENERAL LEDGER OF W. GUTHRIE
Cash at Bank   1.1

Date	Particulars	Fol.	Debit	Credit	Balance
19XX Mar. 1	Balance	b/d			2927.15 Cr

EXERCISE 4.37   Westside Productions

On pages 314–315 are the bank statement (extract), cash receipts journal, cash payments journal and Cash at Bank account in the general ledger of Westside Productions (proprietor, James North) for September 19XX, together with the bank reconciliation statement as at 31 August 19XX. You are required to carry out the following.

1. Compare the cash receipts journal, cash payments journal and the previous month's bank reconciliation statement with the bank statement for September.
2. Adjust the cash journals by adding items that are in the bank statement but not in the cash journals.

3. Post details to the Cash at Bank account in the general ledger.
4. Prepare a bank reconciliation statement as at 30 September 19XX. This must agree with the balance in the Cash at Bank account in the general ledger.

Use copies of the relevant masters provided at the back of this book.

BANK RECONCILIATION STATEMENT OF WESTSIDE PRODUCTIONS
as at 31 August 19XX

Debit balance as per bank statement				$4898.90
Add: Unpresented cheques	309	186.70		
	311	92.90		279.60
				5178.50
Less: Outstanding deposits				311.96
Credit balance as per Cash at Bank account in general ledger				$4866.54

Statement of Account
Westpac Banking Corporation
IVANHOE   SA

SPECIMEN ONLY

This statement: SEPTEMBER

Mr J. North
Westside Productions
76 Berril Road
IVANHOE SA 5432

Account No. 172–818
Sheet No. 92

Name of account: WESTSIDE PRODUCTIONS

Date	Particulars		Debit	Credit	Balance
19XX					
1 SEPT.	BROUGHT FORWARD				4898.90 DR
2 SEPT.	C/C			311.96	4586.94 DR
		24309	186.70		4773.64 DR
3 SEPT.		24314	268.12		5041.76 DR
4 SEPT.	C/C			412.20	4629.56 DR
		24311	92.90		4722.46 DR
5 SEPT.		24313	128.40		4850.86 DR
6 SEPT.		24315	286.80		5137.66 DR
7 SEPT.	C/C			186.00	4951.66 DR
10 SEPT.	C/C			257.60	4694.06 DR
11 SEPT.		24317	238.45		4932.51 DR
		24318	360.00		5292.51 DR
12 SEPT.	FEE		23.80		5316.31 DR
14 SEPT.	C/C			481.70	4834.61 DR
15 SEPT.	CHQ BK		12.50		4847.11 DR
16 SEPT.	TFR — J. Weiss			276.90	4570.21 DR
17 SEPT.		24320	96.80		4667.01 DR
21 SEPT.	C/C			315.00	4352.01 DR
22 SEPT.	INTEREST ON OVERDRAFT		28.80		4380.81 DR
23 SEPT.	RTD — Hi-Lite Signs		186.00		4566.81 DR
26 SEPT.		24321	274.60		4841.41 DR
	STATE GOVT TAX ON WITHDRAWALS		11.20		4852.61 DR
	STATE GOVT TAX ON DEPOSITS		9.80		4862.41 DR

CHAPTER 4: POSTING TO THE LEDGER | 315

CASH RECEIPTS JOURNAL OF WESTSIDE PRODUCTIONS   Fol. CR1

Date	Rec. no.	Particulars (Account to be credited)	Fol.	Discount allowed	Trade debtors	Sales	Sales tax	General	Bank
19XX Sept. 3	626 CRR	Ace Posters Sales		6.50	253.50	138.00	20.70		412.20
6	627	Hi-Lite Signs			186.00				186.00
9	CRR	Sales				224.00	33.60		257.60
13	CRR 628	Sales Rent Revenue				197.00	24.70	260.00	481.70
20	CRR	Sales				280.00	35.00		315.00
27	629	Ace Posters		9.25	360.75				360.75

CASH PAYMENTS JOURNAL OF WESTSIDE PRODUCTIONS   Fol. CP1

Date	Chq. no.	Particulars (Account to be debited)	Fol.	Discount received	Trade creditors	Purchases	General	Bank
19XX Sept. 2	313	Purchases				128.40		128.40
	314	Rainbow Paints		6.88	268.12			268.12
5	315	Wages					286.80	286.80
	316	Purchases				156.75		156.75
10	317	Purchases				238.45		238.45
	318	Rent Expense					360.00	360.00
16	319	Insurance					148.00	148.00
	320	Advertising					96.80	96.80
25	321	Wages					274.60	274.60
	322	Universal Paper Co.		8.00	312.00			312.00

GENERAL LEDGER OF WESTSIDE PRODUCTIONS

Cash at Bank   1.1

Date	Particulars	Fol.	Debit	Credit	Balance
19XX Sept. 1	Balance	b/d			4866.54 Cr

Credit balance in both bank statement and Cash at Bank account

The situation can arise in which the bank statement shows a *credit* balance — indicating that the business has money in its bank account — but, when the outstanding deposits are added and the unpresented cheques deducted, the business actually *owes* money to the bank, in other words the account is temporarily overdrawn. Interest is charged on the overdrawn amount and shown on the next bank statement.

BANK RECONCILIATION STATEMENT OF J. MASON
as at 31 August 19XX

Credit balance as per bank statement				$4375.00
Add: Outstanding deposits				100.00
				4475.00
Less: Unpresented cheques	430	1195.00		
	436	500.00		
	441	5000.00	6695.00	
Credit balance as per Cash at Bank account in general ledger				$2220.00

EXERCISE 4.38 — Custom Interiors

Below and on pages 317–318 are the bank statement (extract), cash receipts journal, cash payments journal and Cash at Bank account in the general ledger of Custom Interiors (proprietor, R. Ghidini) for June 19XX, together with the bank reconciliation statement as at 31 May 19XX. You are required to carry out the following.

1. Compare the cash receipts journal, cash payments journal and the previous month's bank reconciliation statement with the bank statement for June.
2. Adjust the cash journals by adding items that are in the bank statement but not in the cash journals.
3. Post details to the Cash at Bank account in the general ledger.
4. Prepare a bank reconciliation statement as at 30 June 19XX. This must agree with the balance in the Cash at Bank account in the general ledger.

Use copies of the relevant masters provided at the back of this book.

BANK RECONCILIATION STATEMENT OF CUSTOM INTERIORS
as at 31 May 19XX

Credit balance as per bank statement				$ 609.00
Add: Outstanding deposits				445.00
				1054.00
Less: Unpresented cheques	589	157.00		
	591	76.50	233.50	
Debit balance as per Cash at Bank account in general ledger				$ 820.50

Statement of Account

Westpac Banking Corporation
HYDE PARK   NSW

SPECIMEN ONLY

This statement: **JUNE**

Mr R. Ghidini
Custom Interiors
82 Maple Avenue
HYDE PARK NSW 2061

Account No.: **246–183**
Sheet No.: **32**

Name of account: **CUSTOM INTERIORS**

Date	Particulars		Debit	Credit	Balance
19XX					
1 JUNE	BROUGHT FORWARD				609.00 CR
2 JUNE	C/C			445.00	1054.00 CR
		43591	76.50		977.50 CR
3 JUNE	C/C			383.25	1360.75 CR
4 JUNE		43592	180.00		1180.75 CR
		43593	234.00		946.75 CR
6 JUNE		43595	280.00		666.75 CR
7 JUNE	C/C			364.50	1031.25 CR
10 JUNE		43596	328.00		703.25 CR
12 JUNE	FEE		18.40		684.85 CR
	C/C			77.40	762.25 CR
		43589	157.00		605.25 CR
13 JUNE		43597	200.00		405.25 CR
16 JUNE	C/C			88.20	493.45 CR
18 JUNE	RTD — P. Zammit		150.00		343.45 CR
19 JUNE		43598	280.00		63.45 CR
20 JUNE	CHQ BK		12.50		50.95 CR
22 JUNE	C/C			291.30	342.25 CR
26 JUNE	STATE GOVT TAX ON WITHDRAWALS		7.20		335.05 CR
	STATE GOVT TAX ON DEPOSITS		6.80		328.25 CR
28 JUNE		43600	182.40		145.85 CR

CASH RECEIPTS JOURNAL OF CUSTOM INTERIORS   Fol. CR1

Date	Rec. no.	Particulars (Account to be credited)	Fol.	Discount allowed	Trade debtors	Sales	Sales tax	General	Bank
19XX									
June 2	717	W. Bradley		4.75	185.25				
	CRR	Sales				176.00	22.00		383.25
6	CRR	Sales				142.00	17.75		
	718	L. Roberts		5.25	204.75				364.50
11	CRR	Sales				68.80	8.60		77.40
15	CRR	Sales				78.40	9.80		88.20
21	719	P. Zammit			150.00				
	CRR	Sales				125.60	15.70		291.30
26	720	Commission Revenue						236.00	236.00

CASH PAYMENTS JOURNAL OF CUSTOM INTERIORS   Fol. CP1

Date	Chq. no.	Particulars (Account to be debited)	Fol.	Discount received	Trade creditors	Purchases	General	Bank
19XX								
June 3	592	Advertising					180.00	180.00
	593	R. Singh		6.00	234.00			234.00
5	594	Rent Expense					263.00	263.00
	595	Wages					280.00	280.00
9	596	Purchases				328.00		328.00
12	597	N. Aldini			200.00			200.00
18	598	Wages					280.00	280.00
20	599	Purchases				256.80		256.80
27	600	Repairs and Maintenance					182.40	182.40

GENERAL LEDGER OF CUSTOM INTERIORS

Cash at Bank   1.1

Date	Particulars	Fol.	Debit	Credit	Balance
19XX June 1	Balance	b/d			820.50 Dr

EXERCISE 4.39 — F. Groenig

On pages 319–320 are the bank statement (extract), cash receipts journal, cash payments journal and Cash at Bank account in the general ledger of F. Groenig for December 19XX, together with the bank reconciliation statement as at 30 November 19XX. You are required to carry out the following.

1. Compare the cash receipts journal, cash payments journal and the previous month's bank reconciliation statement with the bank statement for December.
2. Adjust the cash journals by adding items that are in the bank statement but not in the cash journals.
3. Post details to the Cash at Bank account in the general ledger.
4. Prepare a bank reconciliation statement as at 31 December 19XX. This must agree with the balance in the Cash at Bank account in the general ledger.

Use copies of the relevant masters provided at the back of this book.

BANK RECONCILIATION STATEMENT OF F. GROENIG
as at 30 November 19XX

Credit balance as per bank statement				$363.90
Add: Outstanding deposits				484.80
				848.70
Less: Unpresented cheques	718	294.80		
	721	86.30		381.10
Debit balance as per Cash at Bank account in general ledger				$467.60

Statement of Account

Westpac Banking Corporation
LAMBERT VALE   VIC

SPECIMEN ONLY

This statement
DECEMBER

Mr F. Groenig
198 Camperdown Road
LAMBERT VALE VIC 3121

Account No.
336–141

Sheet No.
28

Name of account

F. GROENIG

Date	Particulars		Debit	Credit	Balance
19XX					
1 DEC.	BROUGHT FORWARD				363.90 CR
2 DEC.	C/C			484.80	848.70 CR
		52718	294.80		553.90 CR
		52724	386.00		167.90 CR
3 DEC.	C/C			178.04	345.94 CR
6 DEC.	C/C			437.75	783.69 CR
7 DEC.		52725	312.00		471.69 CR
8 DEC.	FEE		18.20		453.49 CR
10 DEC.	INTEREST ON MORTGAGE		32.80		420.69 CR
11 DEC.	C/C			325.95	746.64 CR
12 DEC.	CHQ BK		12.50		734.14 CR
16 DEC.	TFR — J. Needham			210.00	944.14 CR
		52727	206.90		737.24 CR
	STATE GOVT TAX ON WITHDRAWALS		9.60		727.64 CR
	STATE GOVT TAX ON DEPOSITS		8.40		719.24 CR
18 DEC.		52723	235.00		484.24 CR
19 DEC.	C/C			281.40	765.64 CR
20 DEC.	RTD — R. Silva		150.00		615.64 CR
21 DEC.		52728	347.10		268.54 CR
23 DEC.	INTEREST ON C'TH BONDS			162.80	431.34 CR
29 DEC.		52730	409.50		21.84 CR

CASH RECEIPTS JOURNAL OF F. GROENIG
Fol. CR1

Date	Rec. no.	Particulars (Account to be credited)	Fol.	Discount allowed	Trade debtors	Sales	Sales tax	General	Bank
19XX Dec. 2	067	B. McBride		4.56	178.04				178.04
5	CRR	Sales				190.00	23.75		
	068	Rent Revenue						224.00	437.75
10	069	R. Silva			150.00				
	CRR	Sales				156.40	19.55		325.95
18	070	L. Rush		4.10	159.90				
	CRR	Sales				108.00	13.50		281.40
26	071	B. McBride		5.20	197.80				197.80

CASH PAYMENTS JOURNAL OF F. GROENIG
Fol. CP1

Date	Chq. no.	Particulars (Account to be debited)	Fol.	Discount received	Trade creditors	Purchases	General	Bank
19XX Dec. 1	723	Repairs and Maintenance					235.00	235.00
3	724	Wages					386.00	386.00
6	725	V. Hyam		8.00	312.00			312.00
11	726	Advertising					268.80	268.80
16	727	Petty Cash Reimbursement						
		General expenses					78.60	
		Postage					59.00	
		Travel					69.30	206.90
20	728	R. Prentice		8.90	347.10			347.10
26	729	Purchases				382.60		382.60
28	730	M. Torresan		10.50	409.50			409.50

GENERAL LEDGER OF F. GROENIG
Cash at Bank 1.1

Date	Particulars	Fol.	Debit	Credit	Balance
19XX Dec. 1	Balance	b/d			467.60 Dr

When both the bank statement and Cash at Bank account in the general ledger show a debit balance

According to the bank statement, a business owes money to the bank (debit balance). However, when the unpresented cheques are added and the outstanding deposits deducted, the business has money in the bank (debit balance in the Cash at Bank account in the general ledger).

When the bank statement shows a debit balance, the bank reconciliation statement is set out as shown below.

BANK RECONCILIATION STATEMENT OF J. MASON
as at 31 March 19XX

Debit balance as per bank statement				$2365.00
Add: Unpresented cheques	501	120.00		
	512	60.00		180.00
				2545.00
Less: Outstanding deposits				3600.00
Debit balance as per Cash at Bank account in general ledger				$1055.00

EXERCISE 4.40 Timemaster Clocks

Below and on pages 322–323 are the bank statement (extract), cash receipts journal, cash payments journal and Cash at Bank account in the general ledger of Timemaster Clocks (proprietor, P. Tranh) for April 19XX, together with the bank reconciliation statement as at 31 March 19XX. You are required to carry out the following.

1. Compare the cash receipts journal, cash payments journal and previous month's bank reconciliation statement with the bank statement for April.
2. Adjust the cash journals with additional items from the bank statement.
3. Post details to the Cash at Bank account in the general ledger.
4. Prepare a bank reconciliation statement as at 30 April 19XX. This must agree with the balance in the Cash at Bank account in the general ledger.

Use copies of the relevant masters provided at the back of this book.

BANK RECONCILIATION STATEMENT OF TIMEMASTER CLOCKS
as at 31 March 19XX

Debit balance as per bank statement				$2300.00
Add: Unpresented cheques	198	130.00		
	200	50.00		180.00
				2480.00
Less: Outstanding deposits				576.00
Credit balance as per Cash at Bank account in general ledger				$1904.00

Statement of Account
Westpac Banking Corporation
TARWANNA NSW

SPECIMEN ONLY

This statement: **APRIL**

Mr P. Tranh
Timemaster Clocks
73 Anzac Drive
TARWANNA NSW 2076

Account No. **521–440**
Sheet No. **74**

Name of account: **TIMEMASTER CLOCKS**

Date	Particulars		Debit	Credit	Balance
19XX					
1 APR.	BROUGHT FORWARD				2300.00 DR
2 APR.	C/C			576.00	1724.00 DR
3 APR.	C/C			762.40	961.69 DR
		26198	130.00		1091.60 DR
4 APR.		26201	226.80		1318.40 DR
6 APR.	C/C			1295.00	23.40 DR
7 APR.		26204	238.85		262.25 DR
8 APR.		26202	210.40		472.65 DR
10 APR.	INTEREST ON OVERDRAFT		289.60		762.25 DR
		26200	50.00		812.25 DR
11 APR.		26205	153.75		966.00 DR
		26206	183.88		1149.88 DR
13 APR.	C/C			639.45	510.43 DR
15 APR.	FEE		38.00		548.43 DR
16 APR.	RTD — T. Limos		188.00		736.43 DR
17 APR.		26207	215.60		952.03 DR
18 APR.	CHQ BK		12.50		964.53 DR
20 APR.	INTEREST ON C'TH BONDS			328.00	636.53 DR
	C/C			416.00	220.53 DR
24 APR.		26208	283.74		504.27 DR
	STATE GOVT TAX ON WITHDRAWALS		13.80		518.07 DR
	STATE GOVT TAX ON DEPOSITS		9.20		527.27 DR
25 APR.	TFR — K. Hows			262.50	264.77 DR

CASH RECEIPTS JOURNAL OF TIMEMASTER CLOCKS
Fol. CR1

Date	Rec. no.	Particulars (Account to be credited)	Fol.	Discount allowed	Trade debtors	Sales	Sales tax	General	Bank
19XX									
Apr. 2	CRR 921	Sales R. Bennett		9.60	374.40	339.50	48.50		762.40
5	CRR 922	Sales Office Equipment				293.12	41.88	960.00	1295.00
12	CRR 923	Sales K. Ng & Co.		7.55	294.45	300.00	45.00		639.45
19	CRR 924	Sales T. Limos			188.00	193.80	34.20		416.00
28	925 926 927 CRR	Commission Revenue Capital R. Bennett Sales		3.90	152.10	235.80	35.38	286.00 2000.00	2709.28

CHAPTER 4: POSTING TO THE LEDGER | 323

CASH PAYMENTS JOURNAL OF TIMEMASTER CLOCKS   Fol. CP1

Date	Chq. no.	Particulars (Account to be debited)	Fol.	Discount received	Trade creditors	Purchases	General	Bank
19XX								
Apr. 3	201	Purchases				226.80		226.80
	202	Wages					210.40	210.40
6	203	Advertising					174.80	174.80
	204	J. Ransom & Co.		6.15	238.85			238.85
10	205	Electricity					153.75	153.75
	206	A. Georgiou		4.72	183.88			183.88
16	207	Wages					215.60	215.60
23	208	A. Gomez		7.26	283.74			283.74
28	209	Purchases				138.30		138.30

GENERAL LEDGER OF TIMEMASTER CLOCKS

Cash at Bank   1.1

Date	Particulars	Fol.	Debit	Credit	Balance
19XX					
Apr. 1	Balance	b/d			1904.00 Cr

EXERCISE
4.41 Ayoub & Co.

On pages 324–325 are the bank statement (extract), cash receipts journal, cash payments journal and Cash at Bank account in the general ledger of Ayoub & Co. for November 19XX, together with the bank reconciliation statement as at 31 October 19XX. You are required to carry out the following.

1. Compare the cash receipts journal, cash payments journal and the previous month's bank reconciliation statement with the bank statement for November.
2. Adjust the cash journals by adding items that are in the bank statement but not in the cash journals.
3. Post details to the Cash at Bank account in the general ledger.
4. Prepare a bank reconciliation statement as at 30 November 19XX. This must agree with the balance in the Cash at Bank account in the general ledger.

Use copies of the relevant masters provided at the back of this book.

BANK RECONCILIATION STATEMENT OF AYOUB & CO.
as at 31 October 19XX

Debit balance as per bank statement				$1682.40
Add: Unpresented cheques	432	302.86		
	434	27.96		330.82
				2013.22
Less: Outstanding deposits				728.40
Credit balance as per Cash at Bank account in general ledger				$1284.82

Statement of Account
Westpac Banking Corporation
BANKSFORD NSW

SPECIMEN ONLY

This statement: **NOVEMBER**

Mr M. Ayoub
Ayoub & Co.
27 Lansdown Terrace
BANKSFORD NSW 2324

Account No. **163–738**
Sheet No. **52**

Name of account: AYOUB & CO.

Date	Particulars		Debit	Credit	Balance
19XX					
1 NOV.	BROUGHT FORWARD				1682.40 DR
2 NOV.	C/C			728.40	954.00 DR
		56432	302.86		1256.86 DR
3 NOV.	C/C			325.45	931.41 DR
4 NOV.		56434	27.96		959.37 DR
		56436	185.25		1144.62 DR
5 NOV.	C/C			533.28	611.34 DR
6 NOV.		56437	146.90		758.24 DR
		56438	231.00		989.24 DR
8 NOV.	C/C			244.38	744.86 DR
11 NOV.		56440	84.80		829.66 DR
14 NOV.	C/C			303.25	526.41 DR
16 NOV.	CHQ BK		25.00		551.41 DR
18 NOV.		56442	236.00		787.41 DR
		56441	126.70		914.11 DR
	FEE		18.60		932.71 DR
	TFR — L. Cheng			177.80	754.91 DR
21 NOV.	C/C			585.50	169.41 DR
22 NOV.	STATE GOVT TAX ON WITHDRAWALS		9.60		179.01 DR
	STATE GOVT TAX ON DEPOSITS		7.80		186.81 DR
25 NOV.		56443	152.10		338.91 DR
26 NOV.	INTEREST ON MORTGAGE		180.00		518.91 DR

CASH RECEIPTS JOURNAL OF AYOUB & CO.

Fol. CR1

Date	Rec. no.	Particulars (Account to be credited)	Fol.	Discount allowed	Trade debtors	Sales	Sales tax	General	Bank
19XX Nov. 2	CRR	Sales				283.00	42.45		325.45
4	CRR 182	Sales K. Dinh		8.00	312.00	196.70	24.58		533.28
7	CRR	Sales				212.50	31.88		244.38
13	CRR	Sales				263.70	39.55		303.25
20	183 CRR	A. Geary Sales		6.45	251.55	296.80	37.15		585.50
26	CRR 184	Sales Capital				304.60	38.10	3000.00	3342.70

CASH PAYMENTS JOURNAL OF AYOUB & CO.

Fol. CP1

Date	Chq. no.	Particulars (Account to be debited)	Fol.	Discount received	Trade creditors	Purchases	General	Bank
19XX Nov. 3	436	W. Economos		4.75	185.25			185.25
5	437	Purchases				146.90		146.90
	438	Rent Expense					231.00	231.00
10	439	Repairs and Maintenance					38.00	38.00
	440	Advertising					84.80	84.80
17	441	Electricity					126.70	126.70
	442	Purchases				236.00		236.00
24	443	C. Townsend		3.90	152.10			152.10
27	444	Purchases				128.50		128.50

GENERAL LEDGER OF AYOUB & CO.

Cash at Bank

1.1

Date	Particulars	Fol.	Debit	Credit	Balance
19XX Nov. 1	Balance	b/d			1284.82 Cr

Reconciling over two consecutive periods

The following exercises cover two consecutive periods of time. They highlight the importance of constantly checking the current month's bank statement against the previous month's bank reconciliation statement as well as against the current month's records.

EXERCISE 4.42 B. Stratton & Sons

Below and on pages 327–329 are the bank statements (extracts) and cash journals for March and April 19XX for B. Stratton & Sons, together with the Cash at Bank account in the general ledger at 1 March 19XX and the bank reconciliation statement as at 28 February 19XX. You are required to carry out the following.

1. Compare records for March 19XX.
2. Adjust the cash journals with additional items from the March bank statement.
3. Total the cash journals for March and post relevant details to the Cash at Bank account in the general ledger.
4. Prepare a bank reconciliation statement as at 31 March 19XX — this must agree with the balance in the Cash at Bank account in the general ledger at this date.
5. Compare records for April 19XX.
6. Adjust the cash journals with additional items from the April bank statement.
7. Total the cash journals for April and post relevant details to the Cash at Bank account in the general ledger.
8. Prepare a bank reconciliation statement as at 30 April 19XX. This must agree with the balance in the Cash at Bank account in the general ledger at this date.

Use copies of the relevant masters provided at the back of this book.

BANK RECONCILIATION STATEMENT OF B. STRATTON & SONS
as at 28 February 19XX

Credit balance as per bank statement				$7552.60
Add: Outstanding deposits				684.90
				8237.50
Less: Unpresented cheques	280	283.00		
	281	98.24		381.24
Debit balance as per Cash at Bank account in general ledger				$7856.26

GENERAL LEDGER OF B. STRATTON & SONS

Cash at Bank 1.1

Date	Particulars	Fol.	Debit	Credit	Balance
19XX Mar. 1	Balance	b/d			7856.26 Dr

Statement of Account

Westpac Banking Corporation
WESTVILLE WA

SPECIMEN ONLY

This statement: **MARCH**

B. Stratton & Sons
176 Central Road
WESTVILLE WA 6160

Account No. **581-364**
Sheet No. **18**

Name of account: **B. STRATTON & SONS**

Date	Particulars		Debit	Credit	Balance
19XX					
1 MAR.	BROUGHT FORWARD				7552.60 CR
2 MAR.	C/C			684.90	8237.50 CR
		33280	283.00		7954.50 CR
4 MAR.	C/C			270.00	8224.50 CR
		33283	331.50		7893.00 CR
11 MAR.	C/C			329.25	8222.25 CR
		33285	72.00		8150.25 CR
		33284	160.00		7990.25 CR
16 MAR.		33286	84.00		7906.25 CR
17 MAR.	C/C			175.50	8081.75 CR
19 MAR.	DD — P. Manuel			86.00	8167.75 CR
		33287	115.05		8052.70 CR
22 MAR.	C/C			458.00	8510.70 CR
23 MAR.	CHQ BK		25.00		8485.70 CR
25 MAR.		33289	399.75		8085.95 CR
26 MAR.		33281	98.24		7987.71 CR
27 MAR.	STATE GOVT TAX ON WITHDRAWALS		10.20		7977.51 CR
	STATE GOVT TAX ON DEPOSITS		5.70		7971.81 CR

CASH RECEIPTS JOURNAL OF B. STRATTON & SONS

Fol. CR1

Date	Rec. no.	Particulars (Account to be credited)	Fol.	Discount allowed	Trade debtors	Sales	Sales tax	General	Bank
19XX									
Mar. 3	CRR	Sales				240.00	30.00		270.00
10	141	K. Chan		3.25	126.75				
	CRR	Sales				180.00	22.50		329.25
16	142	R. Manetta		4.50	175.50				175.50
21	143	P. Bowes			98.00				
	CRR	Sales				320.00	40.00		458.00
30	144	J. Allen		5.65	219.35				219.35

CASH PAYMENTS JOURNAL OF B. STRATTON & SONS Fol. CP1

Date	Chq. no.	Particulars (Account to be debited)	Fol.	Discount received	Trade creditors	Purchases	General	Bank
19XX								
Mar. 3	283	M. Jason		8.50	331.50			331.50
10	284	Electricity					160.00	160.00
	285	Purchases				72.00		72.00
15	286	Advertising					84.00	84.00
18	287	L. Fabiani		2.95	115.05			115.05
20	288	Purchases				126.00		126.00
24	289	L. Chan		10.25	399.75			399.75
28	290	Rent Expense					320.00	320.00

Statement of Account
Westpac Banking Corporation
WESTVILLE WA

SPECIMEN ONLY

This statement: **APRIL**

B. Stratton & Sons
176 Central Road
WESTVILLE WA 6160

Account No. **581-364**
Sheet No. **19**

Name of account: **B. STRATTON & SONS**

Date	Particulars		Debit	Credit	Balance
19XX					
1 APR.	BROUGHT FORWARD				7971.81 CR
2 APR.	C/C			219.35	8191.16 CR
		33288	126.00		8065.16 CR
3 APR.		33291	264.60		7800.56 CR
5 APR.	C/C			604.35	8404.91 CR
		33290	320.00		8084.91 CR
7 APR.		33293	237.90		7847.01 CR
11 APR.		33295	175.50		7671.51 CR
		33294	255.00		7416.51 CR
13 APR.	C/C			426.00	7842.51 CR
16 APR.	FEE		16.80		7825.71 CR
17 APR.	DD — K. Ormond			156.80	7982.51 CR
18 APR.		33296	200.00		7782.51 CR
19 APR.	PP — G. Parkes		246.00		7536.51 CR
	C/C			223.00	7759.51 CR
20 APR.	CHQ BK		25.00		7734.51 CR
25 APR.		33298	182.40		7552.11 CR
		33297	273.00		7279.11 CR
	STATE GOVT TAX ON WITHDRAWALS		11.70		7267.41 CR
	STATE GOVT TAX ON DEPOSITS		5.60		7261.81 CR
26 APR.	RTD — P. Bowes		124.00		7137.81 CR

CASH RECEIPTS JOURNAL OF B. STRATTON & SONS Fol. CR1

Date	Rec. no.	Particulars (Account to be credited)	Fol.	Discount allowed	Trade debtors	Sales	Sales tax	General	Bank
19XX Apr. 4	145 CRR	K. Chan Sales		6.90	269.10	298.00	37.25		604.35
12	146 CRR	R. Manetta Sales		6.25	243.75	162.00	20.25		426.00
18	CRR 147	Sales P. Bowes			124.00	88.00	11.00		223.00
24	CRR 148	Sales R. Brown		7.95	310.05	138.50	17.35		465.90

CASH PAYMENTS JOURNAL OF B. STRATTON & SONS Fol. CP1

Date	Chq. no.	Particulars (Account to be debited)	Fol.	Discount received	Trade creditors	Purchases	General	Bank
19XX Apr. 2	291	Purchases				264.60		264.60
6	292	Insurance					380.80	380.80
	293	L. Chan		6.10	237.90			237.90
10	294	Rent Expense					255.00	255.00
	295	M. Jason		4.50	175.50			175.50
17	296	Petty Cash (Imprest)					200.00	200.00
	297	L. Fabiani		7.00	273.00			273.00
24	298	Advertising					182.40	182.40
29	299	Purchases				156.70		156.70

EXERCISE 4.43 *Lakeside Engineering*

On pages 330–333 are the bank statements (extracts) and cash journals for August and September 19XX for Lakeside Engineering, together with the Cash at Bank account in the general ledger at 1 August 19XX and the bank reconciliation statement as at 31 July 19XX. You are required to carry out the following. Use copies of the relevant masters provided at the back of this book.

1. Compare records for August 19XX.
2. Adjust the cash journals with additional items from the August bank statement.
3. Total the cash journals for August and post relevant details to the Cash at Bank account in the general ledger.
4. Prepare a bank reconciliation statement as at 31 August 19XX — this must agree with the balance in the Cash at Bank account in the general ledger at this date.
5. Compare records for September 19XX.
6. Adjust the cash journals with additional items from the September bank statement.
7. Total the cash journals for September and post relevant details to the Cash at Bank account in the general ledger.
8. Prepare a bank reconciliation statement as at 30 September 19XX. This must agree with the balance in the Cash at Bank account in the general ledger at this date.

BANK RECONCILIATION STATEMENT OF LAKESIDE ENGINEERING
as at 31 July 19XX

Debit balance as per bank statement				$4583.96
Add: Unpresented cheques	821	462.80		
	824	203.15		665.95
				5249.91
Less: Outstanding deposit				1286.37
Credit balance as per Cash at Bank account in general ledger				$3963.54

GENERAL LEDGER OF LAKESIDE ENGINEERING

Cash at Bank　　　　　　　　　　1.1

Date	Particulars	Fol.	Debit	Credit	Balance
19XX Aug. 1	Balance	b/d			3963.54 Cr

Statement of Account

Westpac Banking Corporation
MUNMORAH NSW

SPECIMEN ONLY

This statement: **AUGUST**

Lakeside Engineering
301 Bay Drive
MUNMORAH NSW 2881

Account No.: **313-116**
Sheet No.: **43**

Name of account: **LAKESIDE ENGINEERING**

Date	Particulars		Debit	Credit	Balance
19XX					
1 AUG.	BROUGHT FORWARD				4583.96 DR
2 AUG.	C/C			1286.37	3297.59 DR
		11824	203.15		3500.74 DR
3 AUG.	C/C			651.15	2849.59 DR
		11821	462.80		3312.39 DR
4 AUG.		11825	230.00		3542.39 DR
		11826	370.50		3912.89 DR
9 AUG.	C/C			508.38	3404.51 DR
11 AUG.		11828	50.00		3454.51 DR
13 AUG.	DD — T. Randall			206.70	3247.81 DR
15 AUG.	CHQ BK		12.50		3260.31 DR
19 AUG.	STATE GOVT TAX ON WITHDRAWALS		8.60		3268.91 DR
	STATE GOVT TAX ON DEPOSITS		5.90		3274.81 DR
20 AUG.	C/C			479.10	2795.71 DR
21 AUG.		11830	225.00		3020.71 DR
24 AUG.	RTD — P. Contos		249.60		3270.31 DR
26 AUG.	PP — Insurance		204.60		3474.91 DR

CASH RECEIPTS JOURNAL OF LAKESIDE ENGINEERING Fol. CR1

Date	Rec. no.	Particulars (Account to be credited)	Fol.	Discount allowed	Trade debtors	Sales	Sales tax	General	Bank
19XX									
Aug. 2	CRR	Sales				272.00	34.00		
	612	K. Houang		8.85	345.15				651.15
8	613	R. Chabra		7.67	299.13				
	CRR	Sales				186.00	23.25		508.38
19	614	P. Contos		6.40	249.60				
	CRR	Sales				204.00	25.50		479.10
28	CRR	Sales				342.00	42.75		
	615	Rent Revenue						296.00	680.75

CASH PAYMENTS JOURNAL OF LAKESIDE ENGINEERING Fol. CP1

Date	Chq. no.	Particulars (Account to be debited)	Fol.	Discount received	Trade creditors	Purchases	General	Bank
19XX								
Aug. 3	825	Rent					230.00	230.00
	826	Metal Industries Ltd		9.50	370.50			370.50
10	827	Purchases				186.00		186.00
	828	Petty Cash Reimbursement						
		Postage					28.00	
		Travel					22.00	50.00
20	829	Forge Supply Co.		6.25	243.75			243.75
	830	Purchases				225.00		225.00

Statement of Account
Westpac Banking Corporation
MUNMORAH NSW

SPECIMEN ONLY

This statement: **SEPTEMBER**

Lakeside Engineering
301 Bay Drive
MUNMORAH NSW 2881

Account No. **313–116**
Sheet No. **44**

Name of account: **LAKESIDE ENGINEERING**

Date	Particulars		Debit	Credit	Balance
19XX					
1 SEPT.	BROUGHT FORWARD				3474.91 DR
	C/C			680.75	2794.16 DR
2 SEPT.		11829	243.75		3037.91 DR
	C/C			679.20	2358.71 DR
3 SEPT.		11831	273.00		2631.71 DR
8 SEPT.		11827	186.00		2817.71 DR
10 SEPT.	C/C			476.85	2340.86 DR
13 SEPT.	FEE		10.60		2351.46 DR
		11833	230.00		2581.46 DR
16 SEPT.	DD — D. Caman			203.86	2377.60 DR
17 SEPT.		11834	249.60		2627.20 DR
18 SEPT.	STATE GOVT TAX ON WITHDRAWALS		7.40		2634.60 DR
	STATE GOVT TAX ON DEPOSITS		4.90		2639.50 DR
20 SEPT.	C/C			451.93	2187.57 DR
21 SEPT.		11835	208.50		2396.07 DR
22 SEPT.	INTEREST ON MORTGAGE		264.80		2660.87 DR
24 SEPT.		11836	196.40		2857.27 DR

CASH RECEIPTS JOURNAL OF LAKESIDE ENGINEERING Fol. CR1

Date	Rec. no.	Particulars (Account to be credited)	Fol.	Discount allowed	Trade debtors	Sales	Sales tax	General	Bank
19XX Sept. 1	616 CRR	K. Huang Sales		7.55	294.45	342.00	42.75		679.20
9	CRR 617	Sales M. Ford		6.40	249.60	202.00	25.25		476.85
20	CRR 618	Sales Rent Revenue				138.60	17.33	296.00	451.93
26	619 CRR	R. Chabra Sales		6.70	261.30	148.80	18.60		428.70

CASH PAYMENTS JOURNAL OF LAKESIDE ENGINEERING Fol. CP1

Date	Chq. no.	Particulars (Account to be debited)	Fol.	Discount received	Trade creditors	Purchases	General	Bank
19XX Sept. 2	831	Forge Supply Co.		7.00	273.00			273.00
8	832	Purchases				158.90		158.90
12	833	Rent					230.00	230.00
16	834	Metal Industries Ltd		6.40	249.60			249.60
20	835	Purchases				208.50		208.50
23	836	Electricity					196.40	196.40
27	837	C. Pagonis		3.34	130.26			130.26

EXERCISE 4.44 Merino Products

On pages 334–337 are the bank statements (extracts) and cash journals for October and November 19XX for Merino Products, together with the Cash at Bank account in the general ledger at 1 October 19XX and the bank reconciliation statement as at 30 September 19XX. You are required to carry out the following. Use copies of the relevant masters provided at the back of this book.

1. Compare the records for October 19XX.
2. Adjust the cash journals with additional items from the October bank statement.
3. Total the cash journals for October and post relevant details to the Cash at Bank account in the general ledger.
4. Prepare a bank reconciliation statement as at 31 October 19XX — this must agree with the balance in the Cash at Bank account in the general ledger at this date.
5. Compare the records for November 19XX.
6. Adjust the cash journals with additional items from the November bank statement.
7. Total the cash journals for November and post relevant details to the Cash at Bank account in the general ledger.
8. Prepare a bank reconciliation statement as at 30 November 19XX. This must agree with the balance in the Cash at Bank account in the general ledger at this date.

BANK RECONCILIATION STATEMENT OF MERINO PRODUCTS
as at 30 September 19XX

Credit balance as per bank statement				$3678.45
Add:	Outstanding deposits			288.60
				3967.05
Less:	Unpresented cheques	210	187.90	
		212	276.45	464.35
Debit balance as per Cash at Bank account in general ledger				$3502.70

GENERAL LEDGER OF MERINO PRODUCTS

Cash at Bank 1.1

Date	Particulars	Fol.	Debit	Credit	Balance
19XX Oct. 1	Balance	b/d			3502.70 Dr

Statement of Account
Westpac Banking Corporation
JUMBUCK VIC

SPECIMEN ONLY

This statement: **OCTOBER**

Merino Products
176 Woolley Road
JUMBUCK VIC 3881

Account No. **222-363**
Sheet No. **28**

Name of account: **MERINO PRODUCTS**

Date	Particulars		Debit	Credit	Balance
19XX					
1 OCT.	BROUGHT FORWARD				3678.45 CR
		42210	187.90		3490.55 CR
	C/C			288.60	3779.15 CR
2 OCT.		42213	128.95		3650.20 CR
3 OCT.	C/C			830.25	4480.45 CR
4 OCT.		42214	204.50		4275.95 CR
8 OCT.		42215	281.00		3994.95 CR
12 OCT.	FEE		18.20		3976.75 CR
	C/C			400.35	4377.10 CR
13 OCT.	DD — G. Youssef			246.75	4623.85 CR
15 OCT.		42216	189.50		4434.35 CR
16 OCT.	CHQ BK		12.50		4421.85 CR
19 OCT.		42212	276.45		4145.40 CR
21 OCT.	C/C			484.08	4629.48 CR
23 OCT.		42217	248.00		4381.48 CR
	STATE GOVT TAX ON WITHDRAWALS		9.90		4371.58 CR
	STATE GOVT TAX ON DEPOSITS		8.70		4362.88 CR
25 OCT.	INTEREST ON C'TH BONDS			168.40	4531.28 CR
26 OCT.	RTD — Victor & Hale		132.60		4398.68 CR
28 OCT.	INTEREST ON MORTGAGE		235.00		4163.68 CR
29 OCT.		42220	87.05		4076.63 CR

CASH RECEIPTS JOURNAL OF MERINO PRODUCTS
Fol. CR1

Date	Rec. no.	Particulars (Account to be credited)	Fol.	Discount allowed	Trade debtors	Sales	Sales tax	General	Bank
19XX									
Oct. 2	CRR 333	Sales K. de Silva		11.25	438.75	348.00	43.50		830.25
11	CRR 334	Sales Victor & Hale		3.40	132.60	238.00	29.75		400.35
19	CRR 335	Sales Rent Revenue				149.40	18.68	316.00	484.08
28	CRR 336	Sales P. Mossman		7.15	278.85	183.80	22.98		485.63

CASH PAYMENTS JOURNAL OF MERINO PRODUCTS
Fol. CP1

Date	Chq. no.	Particulars (Account to be debited)	Fol.	Discount received	Trade creditors	Purchases	General	Bank
19XX								
Oct. 1	213	Purchases				128.95		128.95
3	214	Advertising					204.50	204.50
7	215	K. Poulos		7.20	281.00			281.00
12	216	Electricity					189.50	189.50
18	217	Rent Expense					248.00	248.00
23	218	Purchases				216.85		216.85
26	219	R. Graham		7.95	310.05			310.05
27	220	Petty Cash Reimbursement						
		Postage					29.75	
		Travel					24.80	
		General Expenses					32.50	87.05

Statement of Account
Westpac Banking Corporation
JUMBUCK   VIC

SPECIMEN ONLY

This statement: NOVEMBER

Merino Products
176 Woolley Road
JUMBUCK VIC 3881

Account No. 222-363
Sheet No. 29

Name of account: MERINO PRODUCTS

Date	Particulars	Debit	Credit	Balance
19XX				
1 NOV.	BROUGHT FORWARD			4076.63 CR
2 NOV.	C/C		485.63	4562.26 CR
	42218	216.85		4345.41 CR
	42221	292.45		4052.96 CR
3 NOV.	C/C		465.99	4518.95 CR
4 NOV.	42222	212.55		4306.40 CR
	42223	302.30		4004.10 CR
8 NOV.	42224	248.00		3756.10 CR
10 NOV.	C/C		297.96	4054.06 CR
13 NOV.	PP — Insurance	385.00		3669.06 CR
14 NOV.	42219	310.05		3359.01 CR
16 NOV.	C/C		681.63	4040.64 CR
	42225	356.00		3684.64 CR
18 NOV.	TFR — C. Zarkos		206.60	3891.24 CR
	42226	316.88		3574.36 CR
20 NOV.	42227	189.75		3384.61 CR
23 NOV.	FEE	18.40		3366.21 CR
	TFR — P. Adams		138.25	3504.46 CR
	C/C		509.78	4014.24 CR
25 NOV.	STATE GOVT TAX ON WITHDRAWALS	6.80		4007.44 CR
	STATE GOVT TAX ON DEPOSITS	5.60		4001.84 CR
28 NOV.	42229	356.00		3645.84 CR

CASH RECEIPTS JOURNAL OF MERINO PRODUCTS Fol. CR1

Date	Rec. no.	Particulars (Account to be credited)	Fol.	Discount allowed	Trade debtors	Sales	Sales tax	General	Bank
19XX Nov. 2	337	A. Fabos		6.56	255.84				
	CRR	Sales				186.80	23.35		465.99
9	CRR	Sales				143.30	17.91		
	338	Interest Revenue						136.75	297.96
15	339	P. Mossman		10.05	391.95				
	CRR	Sales				257.50	32.18		681.63
23	310	Rent Revenue						316.00	
	CRR	Sales				172.25	21.53		509.78
27	311	K. de Silva		4.58	178.72				178.72

CASH PAYMENTS JOURNAL OF MERINO PRODUCTS Fol. CP1

Date	Chq. no.	Particulars (Account to be debited)	Fol.	Discount received	Trade creditors	Purchases	General	Bank
19XX Nov. 1	221	Purchases				292.45		292.45
3	222	Samuel & Sons		5.45	212.55			212.55
	223	Purchases				302.30		302.30
7	224	Rent Expense					248.00	248.00
13	225	Wages					356.00	356.00
	226	K. Poulos		8.12	316.88			316.88
19	227	Purchases				189.75		189.75
	228	Repairs and Maintenance					163.60	163.60
27	229	Wages					356.00	356.00
	230	K. Hong		4.95	193.05			193.05

CHAPTER 5
Cash records

WHEN you have studied this chapter and completed the exercises, you should be competent in the following skills. Tick each skill when you have completed the relevant section.

LEARNING OUTCOMES

1. Receive and document payments/takings.
   - Receive and count cash correctly and give correct change when necessary.
   - Receive cheques and credit card payments and verify same according to organisational procedures.
   - Complete receipts accurately and issue according to organisational policies and procedures.

2. Sort source documents and accurately record relevant information into cash book.
   - Sort and batch source documents and accurately record relevant transactions in cash book.
   - Balance cash book and carry balance down to commence new period.
   - Identify and rectify discrepancies by checking accuracy of recording, correcting errors and referring to appropriate authority in accordance with organisational policies and procedures.

3. Reconcile cash records and prepare a bank reconciliation statement.
   - Adjust cash book for dishonoured cheques, bank charges and direct bank debits; total and balance cash book.
   - Identify and rectify discrepancies by comparing cash book with bank statement, identifying errors and taking appropriate action or referring to appropriate authority for rectification.

▼

RECEIVING AND DOCUMENTING PAYMENTS/TAKINGS

In business, the term 'cash' is used to include cash and/or cheques. It is received as a result of:
- cash sales
- credit card sales
- cheques for payment of goods supplied or services rendered.

Cash sales

When a cash sale is made, the customer pays cash in exchange for goods or services. The money is placed in the cash register, change is given and a cash register receipt or a hand-written cash sales docket is supplied.

Receiving cash and giving change

When goods or services are paid for by cash, the customer pays a sum of money. The amount owed is deducted from the amount paid and the change is given to the customer.

Example
You are attending to a cash sale, where the amount payable is $32.45 and the customer tenders a $50 note. You proceed in the following manner.
1. Count and call out loud the amount received from the customer (that is, a $50 note).
2. Place the $50 note on the ledge of the cash register in full view. This avoids any possible dispute about the amount of money the customer handed over. (Notes of $10 or more are kept outside the cash register drawer until change is given to verify that the change is correct in relation to the amount tendered.)
3. Key in the amount of the sale (for example, $32.45).
4. Key in the amount tendered (that is, $50.00).
5. The register shows the amount of change to be given (that is, $17.55).
6. Count the change out loud into your hand. Place the $50 note in the register and close the drawer.
7. Hand the receipt to the customer and count the change out loud into the customer's hand.

The above is a very simple example of a cash register transaction. Modern electronic cash registers are actually point-of-sale computers that perform many other accounting functions for a business.

If you work in a business where the cash register does not automatically compute the change, you will have to calculate it manually. The amount of change to be given is calculated as follows:

Amount tendered − Amount of sale = Change given.

This is demonstrated as:

Amount tendered	$50.00
Less Amount of sale	32.45
Change given	$17.55

As it would be cumbersome to have to perform a manual subtraction every time you wanted to give change, the following simple method helps you to give change quickly and accurately. It is basically a self-balancing method.

1. Ring up the amount of the sale on the register (that is, $32.45).
2. Place the $50 note on the ledger above the drawer.
3. Count out the change into your hand in the following way.
   - (a) Say amount of sale $32.45
   - (b) Pick up 5 cents and say $32.50
   - (c) Pick up 50 cents and say $33.00
   - (d) Pick up a $2 coin and say $35.00
   - (e) Pick up a $5 note and say $40.00
   - (f) Pick up a $10 note and say $50.00
4. Hand the receipt to the customer and count out the change in the following way.
   - (a) Give 5 cents and say $32.50
   - (b) Give 50 cents and say $33.00
   - (c) Give a $2 coin and say $35.00
   - (d) Give a $5 note and say $40.00
   - (e) Give a $10 note and say $50.00

When giving change, always give as few notes and coins as possible; for example, do not give five 20 cent coins when you can give a $1 coin.

EXERCISE 5.1 *Giving change*

Complete the following table by calculating the change to be given and the denominations used to make up the change for each of the sale transactions.

Amount of sale ($)	Amount tendered ($)	Change given ($)	Denominations
26.50	40.00	13.50	Notes 1 × $10 Coins 1 × $2 1 × $1 1 × 50c
52.80	70.00		
4.75	20.00		
10.35	15.00		
11.25	20.00		
24.60	40.60		

Cash summary slip

A cash summary slip, similar to that shown below, is used to record amounts of cash and coin received. It is completed in the following way.
1. List the number of notes in each denomination in the 'Number' column.
2. Calculate the value of each denomination and enter in the 'Amount' column.
3. Calculate totals for 'Total notes', 'Total coin' and 'Total cash'.

CASH SUMMARY SLIP		
Cash register no.:	**Date:**	
Denomination	Number	Amount
Notes: $100		
$50		
$20		
$10		
$5		
TOTAL NOTES		
Coin: $2.00		
$1.00		
$0.50		
$0.20		
$0.10		
$0.05		
TOTAL COIN		
TOTAL CASH		

Cash register summary slip

After completing the cash summary slip, the amount of cash received is recorded on a cash register summary slip, along with other details. (An example of a cash register summary slip is shown at right.) When completed, it is signed by both supervisor and cashier.

Both the cash summary and cash register summary slips are of assistance when banking the day's takings.

CASH REGISTER SUMMARY SLIP	
Date	
Register no.	
Cash	
Cheques	
Credit card — Bankcard	
— MasterCard	
— Visa	
TOTAL	
Checked: Cashier	
Supervisor	

EXERCISE 5.2 — *Counting the daily takings*

As cashier for J. Mason, you are requested to count the daily takings from cash registers numbers 5 and 7 and complete a cash summary slip and a cash register summary slip for each. (Use copies of the blank masters provided on page 560.) Total takings are as listed in the following table.

Register 5		Register 7			
Notes	Coin	Notes	Coin	Cheques ($)	Credit card vouchers ($)
$100 × 46	$2.00 × 83	$100 × 42	$2.00 × 74	324.80	215.85 (B)
$50 × 38	$1.00 × 72	$50 × 56	$1.00 × 86	126.40	82.40
$20 × 36	$0.50 × 53	$20 × 43	$0.50 × 49	282.60	54.60 (M/C)
$10 × 48	$0.20 × 64	$10 × 62	$0.20 × 75		186.20 (V)
$5 × 62	$0.10 × 47	$5 × 98	$0.10 × 68		
	$0.05 × 38		$0.05 × 72		

Note: B = Bankcard; M/C = MasterCard; V = Visa

Credit card sales

Customers may elect to finalise cash sales by using a credit card. These cards are issued by banks (for example, Bankcard, MasterCard and Visa) or by providers such as American Express or Diners Club International. For those cards provided by banks, the following procedure should be observed.

1. Check the expiry date on the card (to see if the card is still valid).
2. Check the credit limit on the card.
3. Check the bulletin list of numbers of cards that have been stolen or fraudulently used. If you have any concerns, refer to your supervisor.
4. If the value of the sale is above the 'floor' limit (i.e. the limit above which the transaction should be checked), contact the card supplier for the authorisation. A code is usually given to be entered on the sales slip. Without this code, the card supplier will not pay the sale.
5. Use the card to imprint customer details on the credit card sales voucher and check that these details are clear.
6. Fill in other details required on the sales voucher.
7. Ask the customer to sign the sales voucher.
8. Validate the signature on the sales voucher by checking it against the signature on the credit card.
9. If they match, ring up the sale on the cash register.
10. Return the credit card to the customer, together with the customer's copy of the sales voucher.

Where firms use a computerised point-of-sale cash register, the card is inserted into a special slot in the register along with a blank credit card form. The register then 'reads' the card and produces a fully detailed form for the customer's signature. In other cases, the details of the sale are recorded on a register slip containing all the customer's account details. The customer signs this slip and receives a duplicate copy, along with the return of his or her credit card.

Procedures for other credit card providers vary according to the type of card in use. Shown below is a sample of a completed credit card sales voucher.

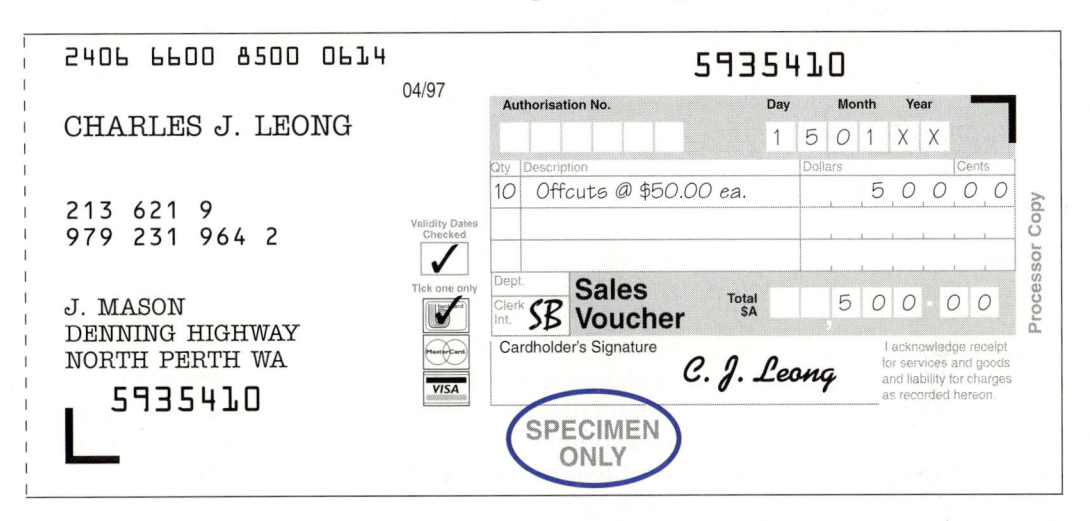

```
2406 6600 8500 0614          5935410
                04/97
                         Authorisation No.        Day   Month   Year
CHARLES J. LEONG                                   15    01     XX

                         Qty  Description           Dollars    Cents
                         10   Offcuts @ $50.00 ea.   500       00
213 621 9
979 231 964 2            Validity Dates
                         Checked ✓
                         Tick one only
                         Dept.        Sales       Total
J. MASON                 Clerk  SB   Voucher      $A      500.00
DENNING HIGHWAY          Int.
NORTH PERTH WA           Cardholder's Signature      I acknowledge receipt
                                                     for services and goods
    5935410                         C. J. Leong      and liability for charges
                                                     as recorded hereon.
                              SPECIMEN
                                ONLY
```

If goods purchased by credit card are returned, a credit card credit voucher needs to be completed, as shown below.

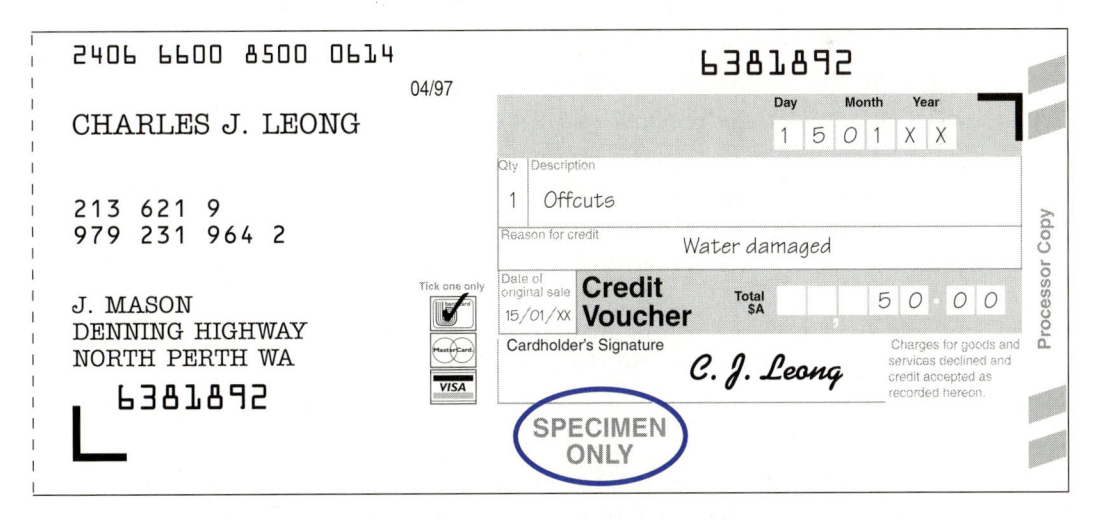

```
2406 6600 8500 0614          6381892
                04/97
                                                  Day   Month   Year
CHARLES J. LEONG                                   15    01     XX

                         Qty  Description
                         1    Offcuts
213 621 9
979 231 964 2            Reason for credit
                                     Water damaged
                         Date of      Credit
J. MASON                 original sale              Total
DENNING HIGHWAY          15/01/XX    Voucher        $A      50.00
NORTH PERTH WA           Cardholder's Signature      Charges for goods and
                                                     services declined and
    6381892                         C. J. Leong      credit accepted as
                                                     recorded hereon.
                              SPECIMEN
                                ONLY
```

These credit card sales (and credit) vouchers are then listed on a Credit Card Merchant Summary. The processor's copy of the Merchant Summary, together with the processor's copies of the individual sales (and credit) vouchers, is placed in the envelope provided and deposited at the bank with the daily takings, where they are treated as a cash deposit. Shown below is a sample of a completed Credit Card Merchant Summary.

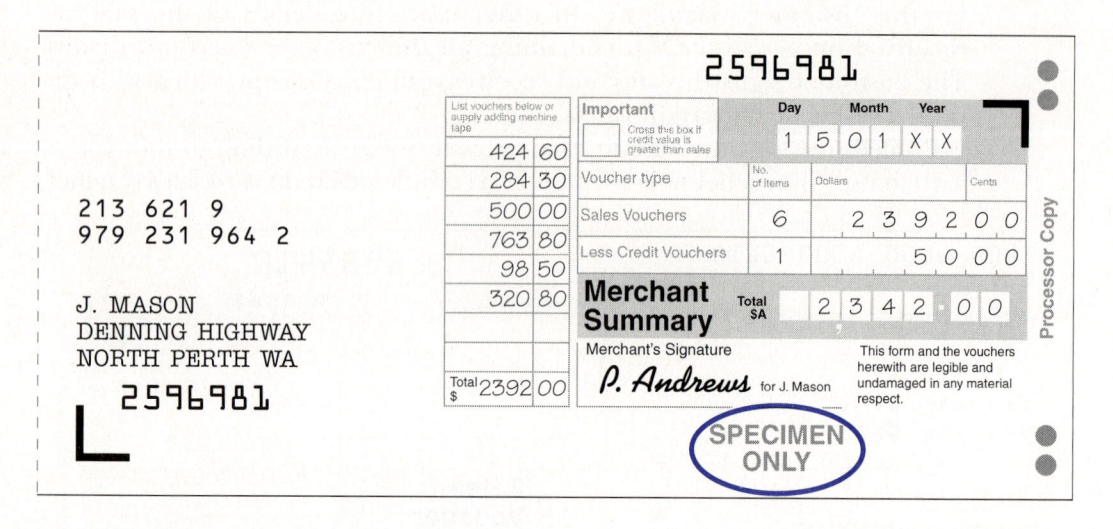

```
                                              2596981
                List vouchers below    Important         Day    Month   Year
                or supply adding
                machine tape           Cross this box if  1 5   0 1    X X
                                       credit value is
                                       greater than sales
                         424 60
                         284 30        Voucher type   No. of   Dollars    Cents
   213 621 9             500 00                       Items
   979 231 964 2         763 80        Sales Vouchers   6      2 3 9 2   0 0
                          98 50        Less Credit
                         320 80        Vouchers        1            5 0 0 0
   J. MASON                            Merchant       Total
   DENNING HIGHWAY                     Summary        $A     2 3 4 2  0 0
   NORTH PERTH WA
                                       Merchant's Signature   This form and the vouchers
   2596981                                                    herewith are legible and
                          Total 2392 00  P. Andrews  for J. Mason  undamaged in any material
                          $                                   respect.

                                           SPECIMEN
                                             ONLY
```

EFTPOS sales

Many businesses, such as retail stores, supermarkets and service stations, provide this service to customers. EFTPOS is an acronym for Electronic Funds Transfer at Point of Sale. This is a facility that enables funds to be electronically transferred from the customer's bank account to the bank account of the business.

Procedures for handling EFTPOS sales are as follows.

1. The customer's credit card is inserted in the Pinpad.
2. The customer enters account PIN details. Look away from the customer while PIN details are being entered.
3. The amount of the transaction is entered.
4. The customer checks the amount and presses 'OK'.

The funds are then electronically transferred. The amount in the customer's bank account is decreased by the amount of the sale while the amount in the bank account of the business is increased by the amount of the sale.

The cash register prints an external receipt for the customer and also records details internally on the cash register roll.

Payment by cheque

Some customers wish to pay for goods and services by cheque. Firms usually have strict policies regarding the acceptance of cheques for cash sales. Some will not accept cheques for cash sales unless prior arrangements have been made. Others will accept them only if proof of identification is offered (for example, a driver's licence).

Where cheques are accepted, your firm's policies and procedures for accepting cheques should be strictly adhered to. You should do the following.
1. Request identification in the form of a driver's licence.
2. Ensure the date on the cheque is correct.
3. Ask that the cheque be made out in the firm's name, preferably 'crossed' for security purposes. A 'cash' or open cheque should never be accepted. This is like cash and can be stolen.
4. Write the name and address of the drawer (that is, the person who owns the bank account on which the cheque is drawn), together with the number of the drawer's driver's licence on the back of the cheque.
5. Compare the signature on the cheque with the signature on the driver's licence. Ensure that they match. If you have any concerns, refer to your supervisor.
6. Ring up the sale on the cash register, and place the cheque in the cash register drawer.
7. Hand the cash register receipt to the customer with the goods. A cash sales docket may also be completed if the customer requires a more detailed receipt.

For a cheque to be valid, it should contain the following information:
- date
- cheque number. This should be preprinted on the face of the cheque.
- name of the drawer (that is, the person who owns the bank account on which the cheque is drawn)
- name of the drawee (that is, the bank or other institution on which the cheque is drawn)
- name of the payee (that is, the person or firm receiving the money)
- amount of the cheque, in both words and figures. (These should agree.)
- signature of person authorised to sign the cheque
- The cheque should be 'crossed' with two parallel lines and the words *not negotiable* written or stamped across the face of the cheque. This ensures that the cheque will be paid into a bank account and gives protection against someone banking the cheque if it is stolen.

Issuing receipts

A receipt should be issued for all money received. For cash sales, this may be in the form of a cash register receipt or a hand-written cash sales docket. A cash sales docket is often issued in addition to a cash register receipt if the customer needs proof of purchase for accounting or tax purposes.

Examples of typical receipts are shown below:

ABC Hardware	RECEIPT No. 22	No. 231 CASH SALE DOCKET
Register No. 3 27/2/XX Paint $486 10 @ $48.60 ea. Sales Tax 42 Total Sales $528 THANK YOU	Date: 28 February 19XX From: John Wright & Sons Amount of: Two hundred and fifty-three dollars For: Payment of account Cash/cheque $253.00 Discount 9.00 $262.00 Signed *J. Smith*	Date: 31 May 19XX To: White Plains Printing | Number	Description	Amount
10	4-ring binders @ $6.20 ea.	$62.00
		$62.00 | Signed: *S. Britten*

A receipt should show:
- date
- payer's name (that is, the name of the person or firm paying the money)
- amount of the transaction in words and figures
- authorised signature on behalf of the payee (that is, the name of the person or firm receiving the money).

VERIFYING THE DAY'S TAKINGS

Cash registers record all cash transactions on a roll or tape inside the register. At the end of the day, cash sales are determined by 'balancing' the amount on the cash register against the day's takings. This is done as follows.

1. The cash register is closed off and 'totalled'. The amount recorded on the cash register roll for the day should equal:

   Cash (notes and coin) + Cheques + Credit vouchers – Amount of daily **change float**.

2. If the amounts disagree, the takings should be re-counted and the supervisor notified. Most firms have particular procedures to be followed in the event of 'deficiencies' and 'surpluses'.

Security of cash

Cash is the most liquid asset of any business. It is easily transferred between people and therefore can be easily misappropriated.

For this reason, businesses implement policies and procedures to control the handling and recording of cash. These may include a requirement that:
- all payments and receipts be properly documented and recorded as they are made or issued

- all payments be properly authorised
- cash held on premises be kept securely
- cash receipts be deposited *intact* in the firm's bank account daily, with no payments made from the daily cash takings
- all payments be made by cheque (exceptions being payments that are made from an established petty cash system)
- electronic/mechanical aids, such as a cash register, be used to verify cash received for the day. (The total of the daily cash receipts is printed on the internal cash register roll. This total should agree with the total amount of cash, cheques and credit card sales vouchers in the register.)
- reconciliation procedures be implemented which provide an effective system of internal control over cash. Examples of such accounting procedures are:
    (a) bank reconciliation procedures
    (b) reconciliation of daily takings (for example, comparing the daily cash summary with the cash register record)
    (c) reconciliation of petty cash (that is, comparing the petty cash vouchers with receipts and cash on hand).

Reconciliation is one of the most important internal controls of a business.

Additional procedures which provide an effective means of internal control are:

- ensuring that duties and responsibilities that involve the handling of cash are separated from those that involve the recording of cash
- rotating job functions. Employees are less likely to commit fraud if they think that a deficiency will be discovered by replacement staff.
- encouraging employees to take holidays when due. Again, the opportunity to commit fraud is diminished as relieving staff may discover any dishonest activities.

Large retail businesses like Woolworths or Coles Myer have special staff who 'read' the cash registers at intervals throughout the day. They total the registers, do a cash count and then remove most of the cash for banking. The cashier is left with a small change float. This practice has the following benefits.

1. Accuracy of transactions at each register is monitored daily.
2. Cashiers change frequently throughout the day so accountability is maintained across shifts.
3. Registers have less cash on hand so are less likely to be targeted by robbers.
4. Excess cash is banked quickly. Some firms use this cash to take advantage of overnight money market rates.

Ethics and accountability

The organisational policies and procedures of a firm define the conduct required of all people employed by that firm. All staff, not just those who handle cash, should be made aware of the firm's policy of honesty and integrity at all times. Staff should be quite clear about the need for accountability and for procedures that are transparent and open to scrutiny. They should be encouraged to see these provisions positively.

Attitudes, beliefs and experiences govern an individual's personal code of ethics. Firms will often use ethical dilemmas as educational tools in helping employees both to recognise corruption or unethical behaviour and to examine their own responses.

The following scenario outlines a possible ethical dilemma an employee might face.

> *You are in charge of petty cash within your office. A colleague, who is also a friend of yours, has accidentally left her wallet at home. She needs $60 to visit the dentist after work, as she is in pain with a toothache. She has lent you money in the past. Unfortunately, you have only $10 in your wallet. You know that she is honest and reliable. Do you lend her cash from the petty cash float?*

Ethical dilemmas, such as the one above, may be discussed with your teacher. From your own experience, you may be able to recount similar situations where you were uncertain about what to do.

As part of the internal control structure of the business, compliance with organisational policies and procedures should be promoted to employees at all times.

MAINTAINING A CASH BOOK

Most firms maintain a cash receipts journal, a cash payments journal and a Cash at Bank account in the general ledger. However, to maintain tighter control over cash, some firms elect to keep a cash book (which combines all of the above elements into one record). A cash book also provides a simple but effective way of tracing money flow for a sole trader who is commencing a new business.

The layout of a cash book is as follows.
- Receipts are recorded on left-hand pages and payments are recorded on right-hand pages.
- The amount of cash brought forward (b/f) from the last period is listed at the commencement of records for a period.
- The amount of cash carried forward (c/f) to the next period is listed at the end of records for a period.

At the end of the period, the balancing procedure is carried out as follows:

Balance b/f	XXXX.XX
Add Receipts	XXXX.XX
	XXXX.XX
Less Payments	XXX.XX
Balance c/f	XXXX.XX

As there is no Cash at Bank account in the general ledger, the cash book must be consulted for the balance of the bank account for trial balance purposes.

Format of a cash book

The format of the cash book varies according to the needs of each business. Some books have a 'Bank balance' column so that the balance of the firm's bank account is known at all times. This is called a self-balancing cash book, as there is no need to perform calculations to establish the balance in the bank account.

The following two examples illustrate what the cash receipts and cash payments pages (hereafter called 'books') of a cash book might look like.

CASH RECEIPTS BOOK OF J. MASON

Date	Rec. no.	Particulars	Fol.	Discount allowed	Trade debtors	Sales	Sales tax	General	Bank*

* This column records the total amount *banked* each day. This amount must agree with the amount shown on the bank deposit slip.

CASH PAYMENTS BOOK OF J. MASON

Date	Chq. no.	Particulars	Fol.	Discount received	Trade creditors	Purchases	Wages	General	Bank*

* This column records the total amount of each cheque.

The following example shows (in a simplified way) typical facing pages of a cash book. Note that cash receipts are recorded on the left-hand side of the cash book, and cash payments on the right.

CASH BOOK OF J. MASON

Cash receipts				Cash payments			
Date	Particulars		Bank	Date	Particulars		Bank
Feb. 1	Balance	b/d	5320.00				
2–28	Various receipts		3306.00	Feb. 2–28	Various payments		3561.00
				28	Balance	c/d	5065.00
			8626.00				8626.00
Mar. 1	Balance	b/d	5065.00				

Even though the basic format of the cash book may change, the information contained remains unaltered. An alternative format is shown below.

CASH BOOK OF J. MASON

Cash receipts			Cash payments		
Date	Particulars	Total	Total	Particulars	Date
Feb. 1	Balance b/d	5320.00			
2–28	Various receipts	3306.00	3561.00	Various payments	Feb. 2–28
		8626.00	3561.00		
28	Balance c/d		5065.00		
		8626.00	8626.00		
Mar. 1	Balance b/d	5065.00			

In subsequent pages of this text (for example page 354), due to space constraints, the cash receipts book is shown before (not beside) the cash payments book.

Recording receipts and payments in a cash book

The cash book should be written up daily from source documents, including:
- cash receipts — cash register roll (internal cash register record of day's takings) and duplicates of receipts sent to debtors
- cash payments — cheque butts

A firm's cash transactions are entered in:
- the cash receipts book when money is received by the business
- the cash payments book when money is paid out by the business.

Procedures for cash receipts

The following procedures should be followed to process cash receipts and to enter relevant information in the cash book.
1. The cashier makes out a receipt in duplicate showing the amount received from the debtor as well as any cash discount which has been allowed. The original is forwarded to the debtor and the duplicate retained in the receipt book.
   (a) Cheques received from debtors are included with the daily banking.
   (b) Information on the duplicate receipts is entered in the cash receipts book.
2. After the daily takings are counted, verified and banked, details from the cash register roll are recorded in the cash receipts book as sales.
   (a) Details are recorded daily from the cash register roll.
   (b) Details are recorded from a duplicate cash sales docket only if no cash register receipt is issued at the same time.
3. The total amount of duplicate receipts plus the amount shown on the cash register roll (or duplicate cash sales dockets) must equal the amount of money banked for the day (as shown on the bank deposit slip).
4. Details of amounts paid by debtors must be separated from details of receipts from other sources (for example, for cash sales of goods or services or for the sale of assets).

Details entered in the cash receipts book are:
- date
- receipt number or cash register roll number
- name of debtor or name of ledger account to which the amount received is posted (for example debtor's name, sales, rent received, capital etc.)
- amount of discount allowed, entered in the 'Discount allowed' column. (See the following note.)
- amounts of transactions with trade debtors, entered in the 'Debtors' column
- amounts of cash sales, entered in the 'Sales' column
- amount of sales tax, entered in the 'Sales tax' column
- amounts for receipts from sources other than above, entered in the 'General' column
- total amount of cash received for the day, entered in the 'Bank' column.

Note: The **discount allowed** represents that part of a debtor's account which has not been received, so it is not recorded in either the 'Debtors' or 'Bank' column but in a separate column called 'Discount allowed'. From this column, it is posted to the 'Credit' column of the debtor's account to record the amount which has been allowed for prompt payment. (See the following example.)

DEBTOR'S ACCOUNT

Date	Particulars	Fol.	Debit	Credit	Balance
19XX					
July 1	Balance (assumed)	b/d			268.00 Dr
10	Cash	CR1		261.30	6.70 Dr
	Discount allowed	CR1		6.70	0.00

In accordance with double-entry rules, it is also posted to the debit column in the Discount Allowed account to record the increase in the amount of discount allowed by the business. (See the following example.)

DISCOUNT ALLOWED ACCOUNT

Date	Particulars	Fol.	Debit	Credit	Balance
19XX					
July 1	Balance (assumed)	b/d			42.50 Dr
31	Accounts receivable	CR1	6.70		49.20 Dr

Procedures for cash payments

When payment is made to creditors (firms to whom the business owes money), a cheque is drawn for each creditor. The cheque is sent (along with a remittance advice) to the creditor and the cheque butt becomes the source document for writing up the cash payments book.

The following information is shown on the cheque butt:
- date
- cheque number
- name of firm (or person) to whom the cheque is made payable
- details of what the payment is for (for example, payment of account, electricity or rent)
- amount of discount received, if any.

Details entered in the cash payments book are:
- date
- cheque number
- name of creditor or name of ledger account to which payment is charged (for example creditor's name, rent, electricity or rates)
- amount of discount received, entered in the 'Discount received' column. (See the following note.)
- amounts of transactions with trade creditors, entered in the 'Creditors' column
- amounts for purchases, wages and drawings, entered in the 'General' column
- total amount of each cash payment, entered in the 'Bank' column.

Note: The **discount received** represents that part of a creditor's account which has not been paid, so it is not recorded in either the 'Creditors' or 'Bank' column. From the 'Discount received' column, it is posted to the 'Debit' column of the creditor's account to record the amount which has been deducted for prompt payment. (See the following example.)

CREDITOR'S ACCOUNT

Date	Particulars	Fol.	Debit	Credit	Balance
19XX					
July 1	Balance (assumed)	b/d			192.00 Cr
17	Cash	CP1	187.20		4.80 Cr
	Discount received	CP1	4.80		0.00

In accordance with double-entry rules, it is also posted to the credit of the Discount Received account to record the increase in the amount of discount received by the business. (See the following example.)

DISCOUNT RECEIVED ACCOUNT

Date	Particulars	Fol.	Debit	Credit	Balance
19XX					
July 1	Balance (assumed)	b/d			56.00 Cr
17	Accounts payable	CP1		4.80	60.80 Cr

Example
You work for A. French & Sons and are responsible for keeping the cash book up to date. Sort and batch the following source documents and write up the receipts and payments sections of the cash book. (See pages 86–90 in chapter 2.) The amount of cash in the bank account on 1 February 19XX is $5320.00.

Duplicates of receipts

Rec. No. 42
Date: *3 February 19XX*
Rec'd from *J. CORELLI* the sum of *Two hundred and ninety-two dollars*
For: *Payment of January Account*
Cash/Chq. $292.00
Discount   8.00
Amt Owing $300.00

Rec. No. 43
Date: *8 February 19XX*
Rec'd from *F. BRONTE* the sum of *One hundred and fifty dollars*
For: *Payment on Account*
Cash/Chq. $150.00

Rec. No. 44
Date: *14 February 19XX*
Rec'd from *M. DICKENS* the sum of *Two hundred and sixty dollars*
For: *Payment of January Account*
Cash/Chq. $260.00
Discount   7.00
Amt Owing $267.00

Cheque butts

Cheque No. 79
Date: *3 February 19XX*
To: SYDNEY ELECTRICITY
For: *Electricity*
This cheque: $480.00

Cheque No. 80
Date: *4 February 19XX*
To: MADISON ADVERTISING
For: *Advertising*
This cheque: $360.00

Cheque No. 81
Date: *5 February 19XX*
To: T. NGUYEN
For: *Payment of Account*
This cheque: $780.00
Discount: 20.00

Cheque No. 82
Date: *10 February 19XX*
To: CASH
For: *Wages*
This cheque: $600.00

Cheque No. 83
Date: *11 February 19XX*
To: CASH
For: *Petty Cash Imprest*
This cheque: $150.00

Cheque No. 84
Date: *12 February 19XX*
To: CASH
For: *Purchases*
This cheque: $182.00

Cheque No. 85
Date: *14 February 19XX*
To: CASH
For: *Drawings*
This cheque: $300.00

Cheque No. 86
Date: *16 February 19XX*
To: A. LUCCHESE
For: *Payment of Account*
This cheque: $624.00
Discount: 16.00

Cheque No. 87
Date: *17 February 19XX*
To: CASH
For: *Petty Cash Reimbursement*
Postage $36.00
Stationery   15.00
Travel   25.00
Sundries   9.00
This cheque: $85.00

Cash register records

Cash Register Record 2/2/19XX		
Sales		$270.00
Sales Tax		45.00
Total Sales		$315.00

Cash Register Record 8/2/19XX		
Sales		$297.50
Sales Tax		52.50
Total Sales		$350.00

Cash Register Record 14/2/19XX		
Sales		$680.00
Sales Tax		102.00
Total Sales		$782.00

| Cash Register Record | | | Cash Register Record | |
20/2/19XX			25/2/19XX	
Sales	$440.00		Sales	$820.00
Sales Tax	66.00		Sales Tax	123.00
Total Sales	$506.00		Total Sales	$943.00

CASH RECEIPTS BOOK OF A. FRENCH & SONS

Date	Rec. no.	Particulars	Fol.	Discount allowed	Trade debtors	Sales	Sales tax	General	Bank
19XX									
Feb. 1		Balance	b/f						5320.00
2	CRR	Sales				270.00	45.00		315.00
3	042	J. Corelli		8.00	292.00				292.00
8	043	F. Bronte			150.00				
	CRR	Sales				297.50	52.50		500.00
14	044	M. Dickens		7.00	260.00				
	CRR	Sales				680.00	102.00		1042.00
20	CRR	Sales				440.00	66.00		506.00
25	CRR	Sales				820.00	123.00		943.00

CASH PAYMENTS BOOK OF A. FRENCH & SONS

Date	Chq. no.	Particulars	Fol.	Discount received	Trade creditors	Purchases	Wages	General	Bank
19XX									
Feb. 3	079	Electricity						480.00	480.00
4	080	Advertising						360.00	360.00
5	081	T. Nguyen		20.00	780.00				780.00
10	082	Wages					600.00		600.00
11	083	Petty Cash Imprest						150.00	150.00
12	084	Purchases				182.00			182.00
14	085	Drawings						300.00	300.00
16	086	A. Lucchese		16.00	624.00				624.00
17	087	Petty Cash Reimbursement							
		Postage						36.00	
		Stationery						15.00	
		Travel						25.00	
		Sundries						9.00	85.00

Recording dishonoured cheques

Under normal business arrangements, when a business receives a cheque from a debtor, it sends the debtor a receipt, the cheque is deposited in the bank account of the business and the debtor's account is credited with the amount of the cheque, plus the amount of discount allowed for prompt payment (if any).

However, a bank may then refuse to make payment on the cheque (that is, the cheque becomes a **dishonoured cheque**). A cheque becomes dishonoured if:
- the account has been closed
- the account does not have sufficient funds in it to cover the transaction
- a 'stop payment' notice has been issued to the bank by the customer
- the bank has received notice of the customer's death, placement in protective custody, or bankruptcy
- the cheque is 'stale' (that is, dated over twelve months previously)
- the cheque is 'post-dated' (that is, dated in the future).

If a cheque becomes dishonoured, the bank returns the cheque to the drawer (the person or firm who owns the account on which the cheque is drawn). The notation 'RTD' (return to drawer) is marked on the cheque and recorded on the **bank statement**. This means that although the business has recorded the transaction, no money has been received.

When it discovers that a cheque from one of its debtors has been dishonoured, the business must enter the amount of the cash receipt (and any discount) as a reversal entry in its cash receipts book. (Negative amounts are indicated by placing brackets around the figures.) This allows both the cash amount (and the amount of any discount) to be reversed, and provides a method of tracing the transaction back to the original receipt number.

Example

On 12 February 19XX, A. French & Sons was informed that a cheque received from J. Corelli for $292.00 was dishonoured. A discount of $8.00 had been allowed for prompt payment.

The following entry (shown in italics) records the dishonoured cheques in the Cash Receipts Book of A. French & Sons.

CASH RECEIPTS BOOK OF A. FRENCH & SONS

Date	Rec. no.	Particulars	Fol.	Discount allowed	Trade debtors	Sales	Sales tax	General	Bank
19XX Feb. 1		Balance	b/f						5320.00
2	CRR	Sales				270.00	45.00		315.00
3	042	J. Corelli		8.00	292.00				292.00
8	043 CRR	F. Bronte Sales			150.00	297.50	52.50		500.00
12	D/C	*J. Corelli — dishonoured cheque*		*(8.00)*	*(292.00)*				*(292.00)*
14	044 CRR	M. Dickens Sales		7.00	260.00	680.00	102.00		1042.00
20	CRR	Sales				440.00	66.00		506.00
25	CRR	Sales				820.00	123.00		943.00

The dishonoured cheque will also be shown on A. French & Sons' bank statement at the end of the month. Bank statements are discussed in detail in the next section.

Balancing the cash book

At the end of the period (usually monthly), the cash book is balanced and the balance carried down to commence the next period. To balance the cash book, the following steps should be taken.

1. Total both sides of the cash book (receipts and payments).
2. Subtract the lesser total from the greater total. The difference is called the balance.
3. Enter the balance (in the 'Bank' column) as the next entry (do not leave blank lines) on the side of the cash book having the lesser total as follows:

$$\text{Balance c/d} \quad \$XXX.XX.$$

(*Note*: The annotation 'c/d', which means 'carried down', is written in the folio column.)

4. Total both sides of the cash book and enter totals on the first line available on both sides. (The total must be on the *same line* on *both* sides.)
5. Enter the balance on the first available line on the side of the cash book having the greater total as follows:

$$\text{Balance b/d} \quad \$XXX.XX.$$

(*Note*: The annotation 'b/d', which means 'brought down', is written in the folio column.)

Example

The simplified version of A. French & Sons' cash book below shows the key amounts identified as part of the balancing procedure. Examples to illustrate this information in more detail follow thereafter.

CASH BOOK OF A. FRENCH & SONS

	Cash receipts				Cash payments	
Date	Particulars		Bank	Date	Particulars	Bank
Feb. 1	Balance	b/d	5320.00			
2–28	Various receipts		3306.00	Feb. 2–28	Various payments	3561.00
				28	Balance c/d	5065.00
			8626.00			8626.00
Mar. 1	Balance	b/d	5065.00			

CASH RECEIPTS BOOK OF A. FRENCH & SONS

Date	Rec. no.	Particulars	Fol.	Discount allowed	Trade debtors	Sales	Sales tax	General	Bank
19XX Feb. 1		Balance	b/f						5320.00
2	CRR	Sales				270.00	45.00		315.00
3	042	J. Corelli		8.00	292.00				292.00
8	043	F. Bronte			150.00				
	CRR	Sales				297.50	52.50		500.00
12	D/C	J. Corelli — dishonoured cheque		(8.00)	(292.00)				(292.00)
14	044	M. Dickens		7.00	260.00				
	CRR	Sales				680.00	102.00		1042.00
20	CRR	Sales				440.00	66.00		506.00
25	CRR	Sales				820.00	123.00		943.00
				7.00	410.00	2507.50	388.50		8626.00
Mar. 1		Balance	b/d						5065.00

(*Note*: the annotations 'b/f' and 'c/f' which mean 'brought forward' and 'carried forward' are written in the folio column. They are used when moving to the next page.)

CASH PAYMENTS BOOK OF A. FRENCH & SONS

Date	Chq. no.	Particulars	Fol.	Discount received	Trade creditors	General	Bank
19XX Feb. 3	079	Electricity				480.00	480.00
4	080	Advertising				360.00	360.00
5	081	T. Nguyen		20.00	780.00		780.00
10	082	Wages				600.00	600.00
11	083	Petty Cash Imprest				150.00	150.00
12	084	Purchases				182.00	182.00
14	085	Drawings				300.00	300.00
16	086	A. Lucchese		16.00	624.00		624.00
17	087	Petty Cash Reimbursement					
		Postage				36.00	
		Stationery				15.00	
		Travel				25.00	
		Sundries				9.00	85.00
				36.00	1404.00	2157.00	3561.00
28		Balance	c/d				5065.00
							8626.00

Checking the accuracy of the cash book

To verify that you have carried out all procedures accurately, the following actions should be taken.
1. When information from all source documents has been entered, verify your work by ticking off documents (i.e. tick the document itself) and cash book entries. This is the time to enter any information you may have omitted, or to delete any entry that you may have recorded twice.
2. In the cash receipts book, check that you have entered the total amount banked for each day. A line is ruled across the columns (excluding the 'Discount' column) to indicate which amounts are included in that day's banking.
3. In the cash payments book, check that you have entered the amount of each cheque drawn in the 'Bank' column as well as in dissection columns.
4. Rule off and total all columns.
5. Verify the mathematical accuracy of your work by adding totals across the columns (do not include the 'Discount' columns). The total of these columns should agree with the total of the 'Bank' column (before 'Balance b/f' is included).

Different types of cash books

Firms may use different types of cash books. Three of these are described below.

Columnar cash book

Whereas some firms include a column in their cash book for revenue or expenditure that occurs on a regular basis (for example purchases, wages or rent), many firms operate a columnar (or multi-column) cash book which may have up to 32 columns.

All revenue and expenditure is recorded in this cash book. Each item is recorded in a 'Bank' column and also posted to its particular revenue or expenditure column in much the same way as we have discussed so far, but on a much larger scale.

Some businesses, especially small businesses, record all business transactions in a columnar cash book and at the end of the reporting period hand it to the accountant for balancing, reconciliation and preparation of financial reports.

The advantages for a business, especially a small business, in keeping a columnar cash book are that:
- records are kept in one place
- it may be maintained by one person (for example, the owner)
- sensitive information is more secure owing to the limited access.

Some disadvantages in keeping a columnar cash book may be that:
- posting to columns is tedious and time-consuming
- posting across a large number of columns is prone to error
- only one person can work on the cash book at any one time. This may be a problem where large volumes of source documents need to be processed.

Commercial cash book

There are a number of commercial cash book systems on the market. They are known as 'one-write' systems because they use a series of carbon-impregnated forms which require details to be entered once only, on the top form. The forms are positioned on a special copy holder in such a way that when the top form is completed, details are recorded simultaneously, and in the correct position, on every other form in the holder.

An example of a one-write system is the Cash Receipts System marketed by Kalamazoo (Aust.) Pty Ltd. Completion of the receipt, using this system, automatically records information on both the bank deposit slip and on a page of the cash receipts book. When the cash receipts page is filled up, it is placed into the cash receipts book, which is set up on a loose-leaf basis.

One of the main advantages of a one-write system is the elimination of transposition errors which can occur when information is being copied from one place to another. The obvious disadvantage of the system is that only one person can work on the cash book at any one time.

Electronic (computerised) cash book

The procedures followed when processing information by computer are the same as those used in a manual system. (See the following table.)

Manual system	**Computerised system**
Account balances are recorded in the ledger at the beginning of the period.	Same
Transactions are entered into journals.	Transactions are entered into computer. Journals are automatically prepared.
Journals are posted to ledger accounts.	Journals are posted to ledger automatically.
Account balances at the end of the period are calculated manually.	Account balances are calculated by computer.
Trial balance is manually calculated and worksheet is prepared.	Trial balance is automatically prepared. End-of-period adjusting entries are entered into the computer.
The worksheet is used to: • prepare financial statements • journalise and post adjusting entries • journalise and post closing entries.	The computer automatically prepares financial statements and posts adjusting and closing entries.

Most computerised accounting systems consist of a number of linked 'specific-purpose' accounting modules, one of which is a cash book module. Most cash book accounting modules have features and facilities similar to the following.

- Transaction lists are generated and printed automatically.
- The bank deposit slip is generated and printed automatically.
- Cheques and remittance advices may be printed automatically.
- The bank reconciliation statement is generated and printed automatically.
- Regular payments, such as lease and rent payments, are automatically reported.
- The module is integrated with other modules, such as accounts receivable, accounts payable, and the general ledger, so that data are exchanged between modules.
- The module caters for large volumes of income and expenditure.
- The business knows the exact amount of total income and total expenditure at any time.

The prime advantages of a computerised cash book system are as follows.
- Large volumes of transactions can be processed speedily.
- Effort and possible errors incurred by re-keying the same data are eliminated as processing is automatic.
- A high level of security is afforded, with multi-level password protection for sensitive data. (For example, staff can enter the data bank, but are denied access to confidential material.)

Many small businesses use a spreadsheet to control cash. It is set up as a multi-column (columnar) cash book, but information is posted to the correct columns automatically. The advantages of using a spreadsheet to keep control of revenue and expenditure include:
- elimination of tedious and error-prone manual posting to columns
- increased speed and accuracy of work
- automatic calculation of total income and total expenditure for the period
- ability to meet the specific needs of a particular business through customised spreadsheet design.

To complete the following exercises, use copies of the blank cash book masters provided on pages 561–562.

EXERCISE 5.3 L. Brasch & Co.

The receipts, cash register records and cheque butts for L. Brasch & Co. for March 19XX are shown on page 361. The cash book of L. Brasch & Co. shows a debit balance of $8260.00 on 1 March 19XX. You are required to carry out the following.
1. Verify the documents. (If there are inconsistencies between the amounts in figures and the amounts in words, assume that the amounts in figures are correct.)
2. Enter details of the documents into the receipts and payments pages of the cash book.
3. Check that the documents have been entered correctly by ticking off both the documents and the cash book entries.

4. Verify the accuracy of your cash book by totalling all columns, cross-adding total columns and balancing with the 'Bank' column.
5. Balance the cash book and show balance b/d at 1 April 19XX.

Duplicates of receipts

Rec. No. 172
Date: 6 March 19XX

Rec'd from M. ARGY
the sum of One hundred and ninety-five dollars

For: Payment of February Account

Cash/Chq.	$195.00
Discount	5.00
Amt Owing	$200.00

Rec. No. 173
Date: 26 March 19XX

Rec'd from W. CHIE
the sum of Two hundred and forty-two dollars twenty-five cents

For: Payment of February Account

Cash/Chq.	$224.25
Discount	5.75
Amt Owing	$230.00

Cash register records

Cash Register Record
6/3/19XX

Sales	$319.37
Sales Tax	45.63
Total Sales	$365.00

Cash Register Record
18/3/19XX

Sales	$250.25
Sales Tax	35.75
Total Sales	$286.00

Cash Register Record
30/3/19XX

Sales	$264.62
Sales Tax	37.88
Total Sales	$302.50

Cheque butts

Cheque No. 20671
Date: 1 March 19XX

To: CASH
For: Purchases

This cheque: $175.00

Cheque No. 20672
Date: 4 March 19XX

To: P. ELLAM
For: Payment of April Account

This cheque: $409.50
Discount: 10.50

Cheque No. 20673
Date: 9 March 19XX

To: CITY REAL ESTATE
For: Rent

This cheque: $380.00

Cheque No. 20674
Date: 20 March 19XX

To: HARBOURSIDE GAZETTE
For: Advertising

This cheque: $150.00

Cheque No. 20675
Date: 27 March 19XX

To: L. DAVIS
For: Payment of April Account

This cheque: $146.25
Discount: 3.75

Cheque No. 20676
Date: 31 March 19XX

To: CASH
For: Wages

This cheque: $500.00

EXERCISE 5.4 G. Easton & Sons

The receipts, cash register records and cheque butts for G. Easton & Sons for September 19XX are shown below and on page 363. The cash book of G. Easton & Sons shows a debit balance of $6736.50 on 1 September 19XX. You are required to carry out the following.

1. Verify the documents. (If there are any inconsistencies between the amounts in figures and the amounts in words, assume that the amounts in figures are correct.)
2. Enter details of the documents into the receipts and payments pages of the cash book.
3. Check that the documents have been entered correctly by ticking off both documents and cash book entries.
4. Verify the accuracy of your cash book by totalling all columns, cross-adding total columns and balancing with the 'Bank' column.
5. Balance the cash book and show balance b/d at 1 October 19XX.

Duplicates of receipts

Rec. No. 333	
Date: 7 September 19XX	
Rec'd from T. de SOUZA the sum of Four hundred and sixty-eight dollars	
For: Payment of August Account	
Cash/Chq.	$468.00
Discount	12.00
Amt Owing	$480.00

Rec. No. 334	
Date: 14 September 19XX	
Rec'd from B. BOWERMAN the sum of Three hundred and twelve dollars	
For: Payment of August Account	
Cash/Chq.	$312.00
Discount	8.00
Amt Owing	$320.00

Rec. No. 335	
Date: 29 September 19XX	
Rec'd from M. O'BRIEN the sum of Two hundred and eighty dollars	
For: Sale of Office Equipment (old calculator)	
Cash/Chq.	$286.00

Cash register records

Cash Register Record 23/9/19XX	
Sales	$369.25
Sales Tax	52.75
Total Sales	$422.00

Cash Register Record 29/9/19XX	
Sales	$512.40
Sales Tax	73.20
Total Sales	$585.60

Cheque butts

Cheque No. 45283	
Date: 5 September 19XX	
To: CASH	
For: Purchases	
This cheque:	$185.00

Cheque No. 45284	
Date: 12 September 19XX	
To: N. USHER	
For: Payment of August Account	
This cheque:	$214.50
Discount:	5.50

Cheque No. 45285	
Date: 19 September 19XX	
To: CASH	
For: Wages	
This cheque:	$360.00

Cheque No. 45286	Cheque No. 45287	Cheque No. 45288
Date: *26 September 19XX*	Date: *29 September 19XX*	Date: *30 September 19XX*
To: K. GALLETA	To: CASH	To: CASH
For: *Payment of August Account*	For: *Rent*	For: *Wages*
This cheque: $370.50	This cheque: $265.00	This cheque: $360.00
Discount: 9.50		

EXERCISE 5.5   *J. Marczan*

The receipts, cash register records and cheque butts for J. Marczan for May 19XX are shown below and on page 364. The cash book of J. Marczan shows a debit balance of $4721.30 on 1 May 19XX. You are required to carry out the following.

1. Verify the documents. (If there are any inconsistencies between the amounts in figures and the amounts in words, assume the amounts in figures are correct.)
2. Enter details of the documents into the receipts and payments pages of the cash book.
3. Check that the documents have been entered correctly by ticking off both documents and cash book entries.
4. Verify the accuracy of your cash book by totalling all columns, cross-adding total columns and balancing with the 'Bank' column.
5. Balance the cash book and show balance b/d at 1 June 19XX.

Duplicates of receipts

Rec. No. 459	Rec. No. 460
Date: *13 May 19XX*	Date: *30 May 19XX*
Rec'd from R. CHEW the sum of *Four hundred and nine dollars*	Rec'd from N. WEEKS the sum of *Three hundred and sixty-six dollars sixty cents*
For: *Payment of April Account*	For: *Payment of April Account*
Cash/Chq. $409.50	Cash/Chq. $366.60
Discount 10.50	Discount 9.40
Amt Owing $420.00	Amt Owing $376.00

Cash register records

Cash Register Record 6/5/19XX		Cash Register Record 20/5/19XX		Cash Register Record 25/5/19XX	
Sales	$285.95	Sales	$352.36	Sales	$340.65
Sales Tax	40.85	Sales Tax	50.34	Sales Tax	48.65
Total Sales	$326.80	Total Sales	$402.70	Total Sales	$389.30

Cheque butts

Cheque No. 92811 Date: 4 May 19XX	Cheque No. 92812 Date: 11 May 19XX	Cheque No. 92813 Date: 17 May 19XX
To: CASH For: Wages	To: S. FORD For: Payment of April Account	To: CASH For: Wages
This cheque: $350.00	This cheque: $354.90 Discount: 9.10	This cheque: $350.00

Cheque No. 92814 Date: 24 May 19XX	Cheque No. 92815 Date: 28 May 19XX	Cheque No. 92816 Date: 31 May 19XX
To: CASH For: Rent	To: CASH For: Purchases	To: S. CONNELL For: Payment of April Account
This cheque: $230.00	This cheque: $496.80	This cheque: $397.80 Discount: 10.20

EXERCISE 5.6 *Porter Art Supplies*

The receipts, cash register records and cheque butts for Porter Art Supplies for August 19XX are shown on page 365. The cash book of Porter Art Supplies shows a debit balance of $3821.60 on 1 August 19XX. You are required to carry out the following.

1. Verify the documents. (If there are any inconsistencies between the amounts in figures and the amounts in words, assume that the amounts in figures are correct.)
2. Enter the documents into the receipts and payments pages of the cash book.
3. Check that the documents have been entered correctly by ticking off both documents and cash book entries.
4. Verify the accuracy of your cash book by totalling all columns, cross-adding total columns and balancing with the 'Bank' column.
5. Balance the cash book and show balance b/d at 1 September 19XX.

Duplicates of receipts

Rec. No. 306	Rec. No. 307	Rec. No. 308
Date: *5 August 19XX*	Date: *12 August 19XX*	Date: *23 August 19XX*
Rec'd from *A. BOLT* the sum of *One hundred and seventy-five dollars fifty cents*	Rec'd from *P. HAND* the sum of *One hundred and thirty-six dollars twenty cents*	Rec'd from *C. ROBERTS* the sum of *Two hundred and four dollars seventy-five cents*
For: *Payment of July Account*	For: *Payment of July Account*	For: *Payment of July Account*
Cash/Chq. $175.50 *Discount* 4.50 *Amt Owing* $180.00	Cash/Chq. $132.60 *Discount* 3.40 *Amt Owing* $136.00	Cash/Chq. $204.75 *Discount* 5.25 *Amt Owing* $210.00

Cash register records

Cash Register Record 7/8/19XX	Cash Register Record 17/8/19XX	Cash Register Record 29/8/19XX
Sales $ 98.85 Sales Tax 14.15 Total Sales $113.00	Sales $151.82 Sales Tax 21.68 Total Sales $173.50	Sales $184.10 Sales Tax 26.30 Total Sales $210.40

Cheque butts

Cheque No. 51596	Cheque No. 51597	Cheque No. 51598
Date: *6 August 19XX*	Date: *9 August 19XX*	Date: *11 August 19XX*
To: *CASH* For: *Purchases*	To: *CASH* For: *Wages*	To: *R. WHITE* For: *Payment of July Account*
This cheque: $382.20	This cheque: $250.00	This cheque: $276.90 Discount: 7.10

Cheque No. 51599	Cheque No. 51600
Date: *23 August 19XX*	Date: *26 August 19XX*
To: *CASH* For: *Wages*	To: *W. NOLAN* For: *Payment of July Account*
This cheque: $250.00	This cheque: $356.86 Discount: 9.15

EXERCISE 5.7 Nationwide Suppliers

The receipts, cash register records and cheque butts for Nationwide Suppliers for November 19XX are shown below and on page 367. The cash book of Nationwide Suppliers shows a debit balance of $4159.30 on 1 November 19XX. You are required to carry out the following.

1. Verify the documents. (If there are any inconsistencies between the amounts in figures and the amounts in words, assume that the amounts in figures are correct.)
2. Enter the documents into the receipts and payments pages of the cash book.
3. Check that the documents have been entered correctly by ticking off both documents and cash book entries.
4. Verify the accuracy of your cash book by totalling all columns, cross-adding total columns and balancing with the 'Bank' column.
5. Balance the cash book and show balance b/d at 1 December 19XX.

Duplicates of receipts

Rec. No. 218	Rec. No. 219	Rec. No. 220
Date: 6 November 19XX	Date: 15 November 19XX	Date: 30 November 19XX
Rec'd from L. HALLAM the sum of One hundred and twenty-one dollars eighty cents	Rec'd from D. REINER the sum of Two hundred and thirty-three dollars	Rec'd from K. ALLENBY the sum of One hundred and eighty-three dollars
For: Payment of October Account	For: Payment on Account	For: Sale of Electronic Typewriter
Cash/Chq. $121.85 Discount 3.15 Amt Owing $125.00	Cash/Chq. $233.00	Cash/Chq. $183.00

Cash register records

Cash Register Record 3/11/19XX	Cash Register Record 6/11/19XX	Cash Register Record 30/11/19XX
Sales $143.76 Sales Tax 20.54 Total Sales $164.30	Sales $184.72 Sales Tax 26.38 Total Sales $211.10	Sales $171.95 Sales Tax 24.55 Total Sales $196.50

Cheque butts

Cheque No. 37336 Date: 7 November 19XX To: CASH For: Purchases This cheque: $183.40	Cheque No. 37337 Date: 8 November 19XX To: CASH For: Wages This cheque: $286.00	Cheque No. 37338 Date: 12 November 19XX To: F. BARNES For: Payment of October Account This cheque: $325.45 Discount: 8.35
Cheque No. 37339 Date: 24 November 19XX To: CASH For: Wages This cheque: $286.00	Cheque No. 37340 Date: 29 November 19XX To: K. WIPITO For: Payment of Account This cheque: $249.60 Discount: 6.40	

RECONCILING THE CASH RECORDS

When a business receives and pays out money, records are kept by both the business (internal records) and the bank (external records). There are therefore two distinct points of view in respect to financial records.

The point of view of the business is represented by the cash book balance. When a business has money in its bank account, the bank is a debtor of the business. Debtors are an asset, and assets always have a debit balance in the bookkeeping records of the business. When a business owes money to the bank (for example, a bank overdraft), the business has a liability. Liabilities always have a credit balance in the bookkeeping records of the business.

The bank's point of view is represented by the bank statement. When a business has money in its bank account, the bank, in reality, owes that money to the business. Therefore, the bank has a liability. Liabilities always have a credit balance in the bank's ledger. When the business owes money to the bank (for example, a bank overdraft), the business is the bank's debtor. Debtors are an asset, and assets normally have a debit balance in the bank's ledger.

Therefore, a debit balance in the cash book of the business corresponds to a credit balance in the bank statement. Similarly, a credit balance in the cash book of the business corresponds to a debit balance in the bank statement.

This relationship is illustrated in the following table.

Situation	Cash book	Bank statement
Business has money in its bank account.	Debit balance	Credit balance (CR)
Business has overdrawn its bank account or operates an overdraft as a result of an agreement with the bank.	Credit balance	Debit balance (DR)

Because there are these two different perspectives, it is necessary for the business to ensure that its own records (the cash book) agrees (or reconciles) with those kept by the bank (the bank statement, which is a copy of the individual account of the business in the bank's ledger). By way of example, a bank statement for A. French & Sons for the month of February 19XX is shown below.

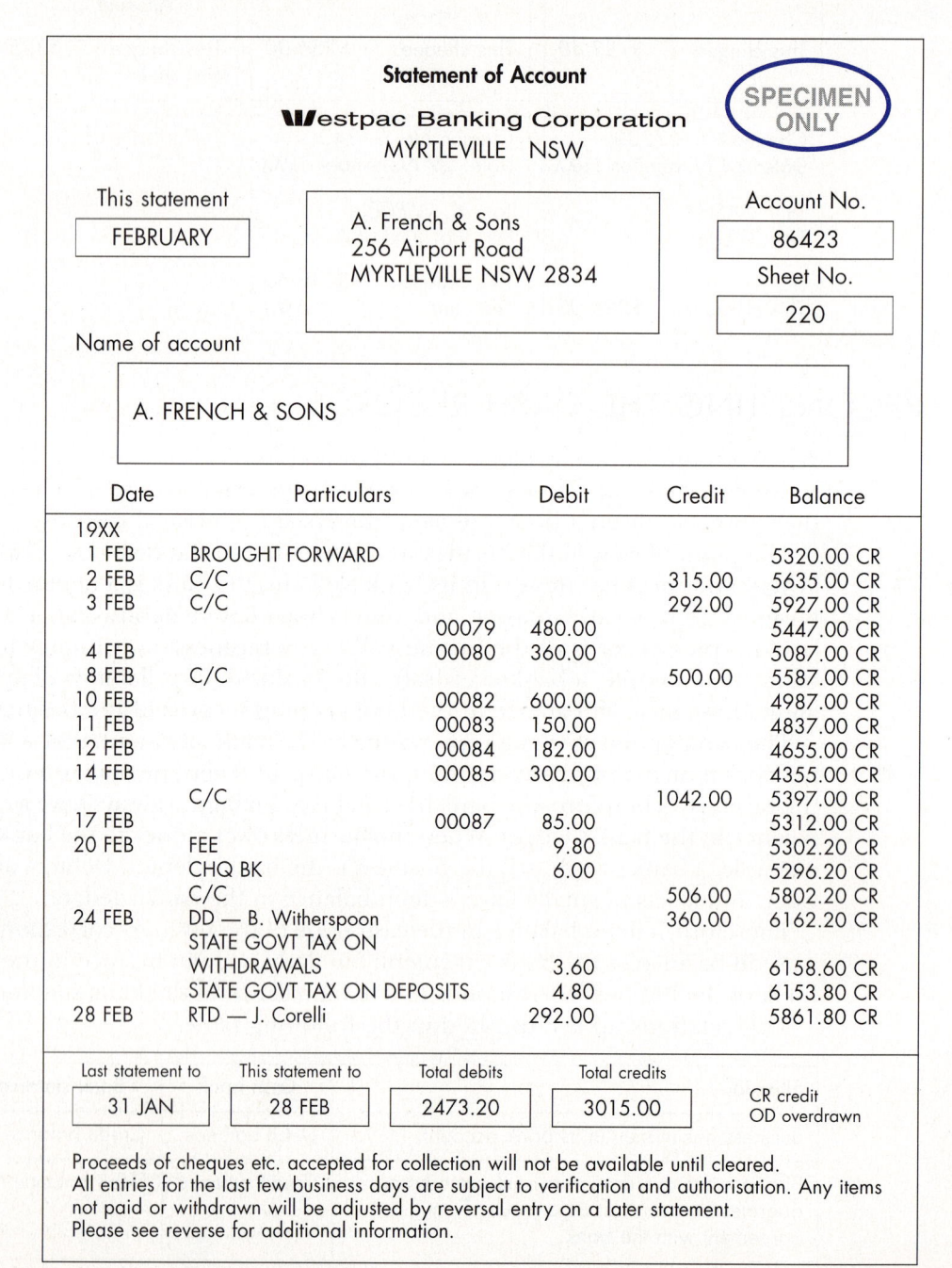

Statement of Account

Westpac Banking Corporation
MYRTLEVILLE NSW

SPECIMEN ONLY

This statement: FEBRUARY

A. French & Sons
256 Airport Road
MYRTLEVILLE NSW 2834

Account No. 86423
Sheet No. 220

Name of account: A. FRENCH & SONS

Date	Particulars		Debit	Credit	Balance
19XX					
1 FEB	BROUGHT FORWARD				5320.00 CR
2 FEB	C/C			315.00	5635.00 CR
3 FEB	C/C			292.00	5927.00 CR
		00079	480.00		5447.00 CR
4 FEB		00080	360.00		5087.00 CR
8 FEB	C/C			500.00	5587.00 CR
10 FEB		00082	600.00		4987.00 CR
11 FEB		00083	150.00		4837.00 CR
12 FEB		00084	182.00		4655.00 CR
14 FEB		00085	300.00		4355.00 CR
	C/C			1042.00	5397.00 CR
17 FEB		00087	85.00		5312.00 CR
20 FEB	FEE		9.80		5302.20 CR
	CHQ BK		6.00		5296.20 CR
	C/C			506.00	5802.20 CR
24 FEB	DD — B. Witherspoon			360.00	6162.20 CR
	STATE GOVT TAX ON WITHDRAWALS		3.60		6158.60 CR
	STATE GOVT TAX ON DEPOSITS		4.80		6153.80 CR
28 FEB	RTD — J. Corelli		292.00		5861.80 CR

Last statement to	This statement to	Total debits	Total credits	
31 JAN	28 FEB	2473.20	3015.00	CR credit OD overdrawn

Proceeds of cheques etc. accepted for collection will not be available until cleared.
All entries for the last few business days are subject to verification and authorisation. Any items not paid or withdrawn will be adjusted by reversal entry on a later statement.
Please see reverse for additional information.

To reconcile the cash records, a business prepares a **bank reconciliation statement**. How this is done is described in some detail below. But, first, we need to know what an overdraft is.

Overdraft

The term 'overdraft' means, literally, 'overdrawn account'. When a business realises that funds are low, and that issuing further cheques may result in its account being overdrawn, the bank should be notified. The bank manager may be willing to accommodate the situation, provided that cash is deposited within the next day or so. For example, the wages cheque may be due to be paid on Friday, but funds will not be deposited until Monday.

A business may, however, make an arrangement with its bank to overdraw its current account. This is known as an 'overdraft'. It means that the business can still draw cheques although there are no funds in the account. A limit is placed on the amount by which the account may be overdrawn and the business pays interest on the daily balance by which the account is overdrawn. Many firms borrow money from the bank to finance their operations by this method.

In an overdraft situation, the amount outstanding to the bank is increased when cheques are paid, and decreased when deposits are made.

PREPARING A BANK RECONCILIATION STATEMENT

As we have already mentioned, it is important to recognise that there will be differences between a bank's records and the records of a business. The cash book of the business and the bank statement may disagree for the reasons listed below.

1. The business may have drawn cheques that had not been presented to the bank at the time the bank statement was issued. These are called unpresented cheques.
2. The business may have deposited cash, cheques and/or credit card receipts (noted as C/C on the bank statement) after the bank statement was issued. These are called outstanding deposits.
3. The bank may have deposits (credits) or withdrawals (debits) of which the business is not aware, for example:
    (a) bank charges (FEE, CHQ BK)
    (b) financial institutions duty (FID). Financial institutions duty is a State government duty on all dutiable credits, which includes deposits, automatic credits, transfers between accounts and interest credits. It is accrued daily and debited when the account is credited with interest earnings. This may appear on the bank statement as 'State Govt Tax on Deposits'.

(c) government debits tax (BAD) or (BADT). Government debits tax is a State government duty charged on each withdrawal from an account which has a cheque book facility. The tax is accrued daily and debited on the last day of each month. This may appear on the bank statement as 'State Govt Tax on Withdrawals'.
(d) direct deposits (DD)
(e) periodical payments (PP)
(f) interest on bonds
(g) interest on a bank overdraft/mortgage
(h) dishonoured cheques (RTD)
(i) electronic transfers (TFR).

A bank reconciliation statement is prepared to account for these differences. The bank reconciliation statement provides a link between the records of the business and those of the bank. Those items that appear on the bank statement, but not in the business records, are recorded in the appropriate cash journals.

However, as alterations or additions may not be made to the bank statement (which is a true and accurate record of the firm's bank account), those details which appear in the business records but not on the bank statement are included in the bank reconciliation statement which is used to reconcile the two records. The steps involved in preparing this statement are listed below.

STEP	ACTION
1	Check to see whether the opening balance in the bank statement (the balance at the top of the statement) and the balance brought down (b/d) at the beginning of the month in the cash book agree. If so, tick both figures. If they do not agree, refer to the previous month's bank reconciliation statement.
2	Compare the entries in the 'Credit' column of the bank statement with those in the 'Bank' column of the cash receipts book. Tick all entries that agree — both in the bank statement and the cash book.
3	Record any unticked entries in the 'Credit' column of the bank statement and in the cash receipts book. (The exceptions here are previously reconciled cheques and outstanding deposits which are listed on the previous month's bank reconciliation statement. This topic is covered in detail, later in this chapter.) Once you have done this, tick the entry in both the bank statement and the cash receipts book.
4	Compare the entries in the 'Debit' column of the bank statement (checking both the cheque number and the amount) with those in the 'Bank' column of the cash payments book. Tick all entries that agree — both in the bank statement and the cash book.

STEP	ACTION
5	Record any unticked entries in the 'Debit' column of the bank statement and in the cash payments book. (The exceptions here are dishonoured cheques which are recorded as a negative entry in the cash receipts book.) Once you have done this, tick the entry in both the bank statement and the cash book. Note: All entries in the bank statement should now be ticked.
6	Total all columns in both the cash receipts book and cash payments book and show the balance brought down (b/d) at the reconciliation date. Any items in the cash book that are not ticked are included in the bank reconciliation statement.

There are a number of points to watch carefully when you are preparing a bank reconciliation statement.

(a) Always begin with the final balance in the bank statement.
(b) If the final balance in the bank statement is a credit balance (that is, the business has money in the bank), you *add* outstanding deposits and *deduct* unpresented cheques.
(c) If the final balance in the bank statement is a debit balance (that is, the business owes money to the bank), you *add* unpresented cheques and *deduct* outstanding deposits.
(d) The final figure in the bank reconciliation statement must agree with the balance b/d in the cash book.

When the bank statement shows a credit balance

When the bank statement shows a credit balance, that is, when the business has money in the bank, the bank reconciliation statement should be set out in the following manner.

BANK RECONCILIATION STATEMENT OF J. MASON
as at 30 March 19XX

Credit balance as per bank statement				$1463.00
Add: Outstanding deposits (i.e. any unticked entry in cash receipts book)				310.00
				1773.00
Less: Unpresented cheques (i.e. any unticked entry in cash payments book and previous bank reconciliation statement)		094	270.00	
		098	102.00	372.00
Debit balance as per cash book				$1401.00

Example

Items which appear in both the bank statement *and* cash book extracts for A. French & Sons (shown below) have been ticked. Those items which appear on the bank statement but not in the cash book have been entered into the appropriate section of the cash book in italics, and have also been ticked.

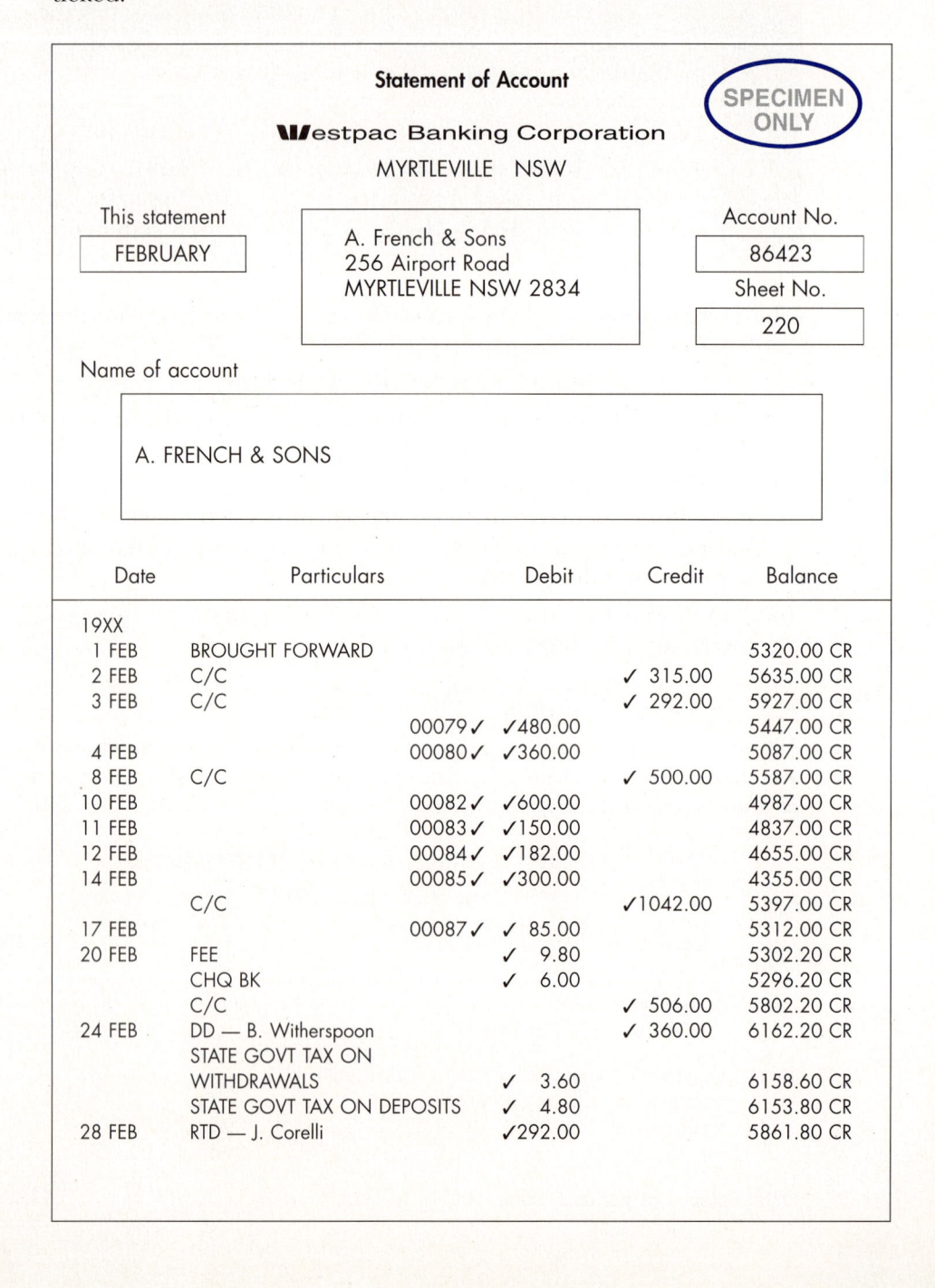

Statement of Account

Westpac Banking Corporation

MYRTLEVILLE   NSW

SPECIMEN ONLY

This statement: FEBRUARY

A. French & Sons
256 Airport Road
MYRTLEVILLE NSW 2834

Account No. 86423
Sheet No. 220

Name of account: A. FRENCH & SONS

Date	Particulars	Debit		Credit	Balance
19XX					
1 FEB	BROUGHT FORWARD				5320.00 CR
2 FEB	C/C			✓ 315.00	5635.00 CR
3 FEB	C/C			✓ 292.00	5927.00 CR
		00079 ✓	✓480.00		5447.00 CR
4 FEB		00080 ✓	✓360.00		5087.00 CR
8 FEB	C/C			✓ 500.00	5587.00 CR
10 FEB		00082 ✓	✓600.00		4987.00 CR
11 FEB		00083 ✓	✓150.00		4837.00 CR
12 FEB		00084 ✓	✓182.00		4655.00 CR
14 FEB		00085 ✓	✓300.00		4355.00 CR
	C/C			✓1042.00	5397.00 CR
17 FEB		00087 ✓	✓ 85.00		5312.00 CR
20 FEB	FEE		✓ 9.80		5302.20 CR
	CHQ BK		✓ 6.00		5296.20 CR
	C/C			✓ 506.00	5802.20 CR
24 FEB	DD — B. Witherspoon			✓ 360.00	6162.20 CR
	STATE GOVT TAX ON WITHDRAWALS		✓ 3.60		6158.60 CR
	STATE GOVT TAX ON DEPOSITS		✓ 4.80		6153.80 CR
28 FEB	RTD — J. Corelli		✓292.00		5861.80 CR

CASH RECEIPTS BOOK OF A. FRENCH & SONS

Date	Rec. no.	Particulars	Fol.	Discount allowed	Trade debtors	Sales	Sales tax	General	Bank	
19XX Feb. 1		Balance	b/f						5320.00	✓
2	CRR	Sales				270.00	45.00		315.00	✓
3	042	J. Corelli		8.00	292.00				292.00	✓
	043	F. Bronte			150.00					
8	CRR	Sales				297.50	52.50		500.00	✓
12	D/C	J. Corelli — dishonoured cheque		(8.00)	(292.00)				(292.00)	✓
	044	M. Dickens		7.00	260.00					
14	CRR	Sales				680.00	102.00		1042.00	✓
20	CRR	Sales				440.00	66.00		506.00	✓
25	CRR	Sales				820.00	123.00		943.00	
24	B220	B. Witherspoon			360.00				360.00	
				7.00	770.00	2507.50	388.50		8986.00	
Mar. 1		Balance	b/d						5400.80	

CASH PAYMENTS BOOK OF A. FRENCH & SONS

Date	Chq. no.	Particulars	Fol.	Discount received	Trade creditors	Purchases	Wages	General	Bank	
19XX Feb. 3	079	Electricity						480.00	480.00	✓
4	080	Advertising						360.00	360.00	✓
5	081	T. Nguyen		20.00	780.00				780.00	
10	082	Wages					600.00		600.00	✓
11	083	Petty Cash Imprest						150.00	150.00	✓
12	084	Purchases				182.00			182.00	✓
14	085	Drawings						300.00	300.00	✓
16	086	A. Lucchese		16.00	624.00				624.00	
17	087	Petty Cash Reimbursement								
		Postage						36.00		
		Stationery						15.00		
		Travel						25.00		
		Sundries						9.00	85.00	✓
28	B220	Fee						9.80	9.80	
		Cheque Book						6.00	6.00	
		State Govt tax on withdrawals						3.60	3.60	
		State Govt tax on deposits						4.80	4.80	
				36.00	1404.00	182.00	600.00	1399.20	3585.20	
28		Balance	c/d						5400.80	
									8986.00	

Those items that remain unticked in the cash book (both receipts and payments) make up the bank reconciliation statement. The bank reconciliation statement that follows is prepared once the cash book has been balanced for the month (as we have done on the previous pages).

BANK RECONCILIATION STATEMENT OF A. FRENCH & SONS
as at 28 February 19XX

Credit balance as per bank statement				$5861.80
Add: Outstanding deposits				943.00
				6804.80
Less: Unpresented cheques	081	780.00		
	086	624.00	1404.00	
Debit balance as per cash book				$5400.80

Checking for errors

1. Let us now recap what we have done in the above example. We compared the bank statement of A. French & Sons with its cash book. (In a real-life situation, we would also look at the previous month's bank reconciliation statement.)
2. We ticked those items common to both the bank statement and the cash book.
3. We recorded the unticked items on the bank statement in the cash book (shown in italics).
4. We added and balanced the cash book.
5. We then prepared the bank reconciliation statement, which took account of any outstanding deposits and unpresented cheques.

But what if you do all these things and you do not balance? First, you should check to see that you have not made one (or more) of the most common errors in preparing the bank reconciliation statement. These are:
- adding figures incorrectly — usually in the cash book
- recording an incorrect balance carried forward from the previous period in the cash book
- omitting to tick off an item in the cash book (for example, a cheque that has been presented)
- overlooking an unpresented cheque
- failing to consult the previous month's bank reconciliation statement
- ticking a cheque that has not been presented
- transposing figures when recording (for example, recording bank charges which appear as $5.40 on the bank statement but are recorded as $4.50 in the cash book).

If this does not uncover the discrepancy, you may find it simpler to redo the whole procedure. Use a different coloured pen for the new ticks or cross-tick the originals.

For the exercises that follow, use copies of the blank cash book masters provided on pages 561–562. Use your own stationery to prepare the bank reconciliation statements.

EXERCISE 5.8 A. Bradley

The cash book extracts and bank statement for A. Bradley for November 19XX are shown below and on page 376. You are required to carry out the following.
1. Compare the cash book with the bank statement for November.
2. Adjust the cash book by adding items that are in the bank statement but not in the cash book.
3. Balance the cash book at the end of November.
4. Prepare a bank reconciliation statement as at 30 November 19XX. This must agree with the cash book balance.

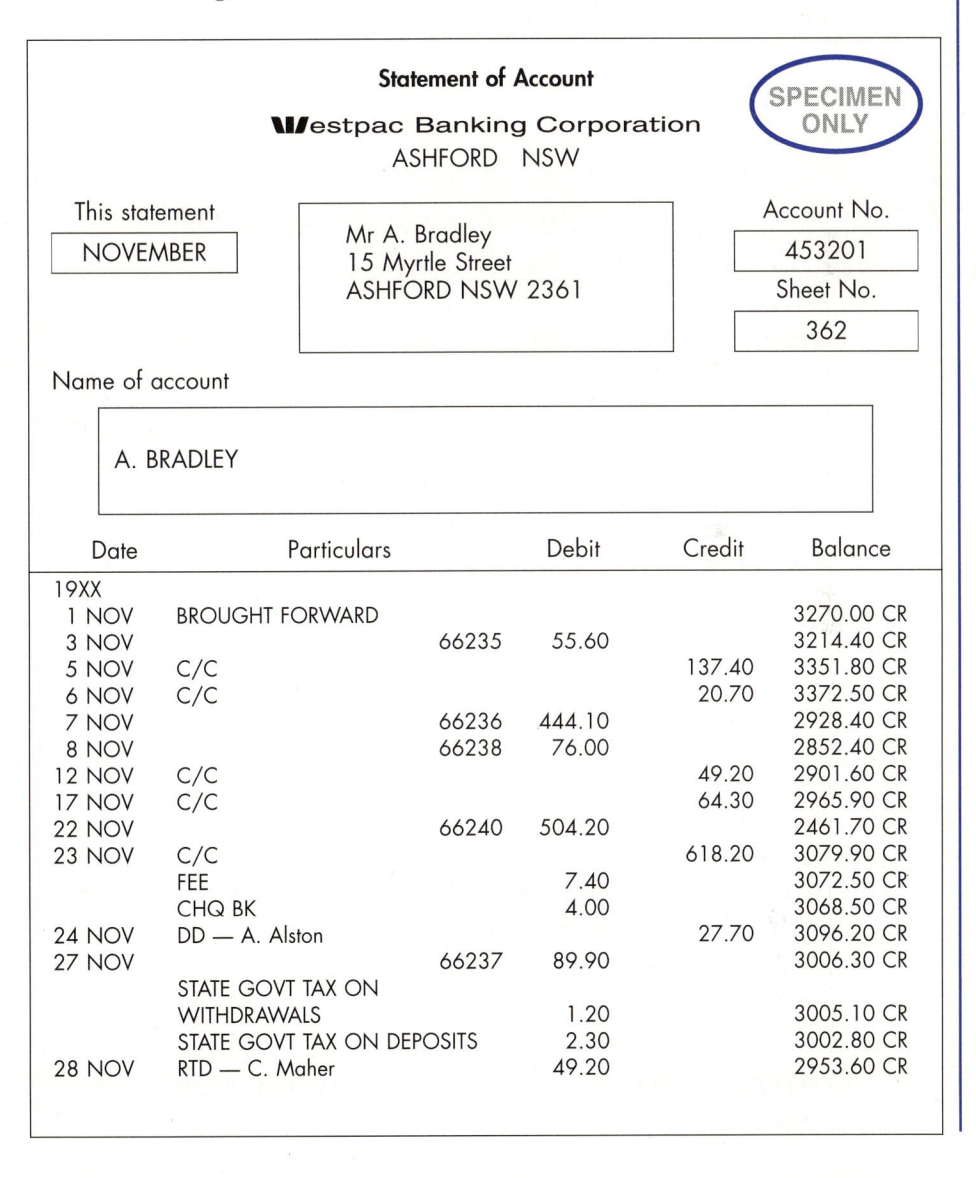

Statement of Account

Westpac Banking Corporation
ASHFORD NSW

SPECIMEN ONLY

This statement: NOVEMBER

Mr A. Bradley
15 Myrtle Street
ASHFORD NSW 2361

Account No. 453201
Sheet No. 362

Name of account: A. BRADLEY

Date	Particulars		Debit	Credit	Balance
19XX					
1 NOV	BROUGHT FORWARD				3270.00 CR
3 NOV		66235	55.60		3214.40 CR
5 NOV	C/C			137.40	3351.80 CR
6 NOV	C/C			20.70	3372.50 CR
7 NOV		66236	444.10		2928.40 CR
8 NOV		66238	76.00		2852.40 CR
12 NOV	C/C			49.20	2901.60 CR
17 NOV	C/C			64.30	2965.90 CR
22 NOV		66240	504.20		2461.70 CR
23 NOV	C/C			618.20	3079.90 CR
	FEE		7.40		3072.50 CR
	CHQ BK		4.00		3068.50 CR
24 NOV	DD — A. Alston			27.70	3096.20 CR
27 NOV		66237	89.90		3006.30 CR
	STATE GOVT TAX ON WITHDRAWALS		1.20		3005.10 CR
	STATE GOVT TAX ON DEPOSITS		2.30		3002.80 CR
28 NOV	RTD — C. Maher		49.20		2953.60 CR

CASH RECEIPTS BOOK OF A. BRADLEY

Date	Rec. no.	Particulars	Fol.	Discount allowed	Trade debtors	Sales	Sales tax	General	Bank
19XX Nov. 1		Balance	b/f						3270.00
4	81	B. Rickard		5.00	37.40				
	CRR	Sales				87.50	12.50		137.40
5	CRR	Sales				17.70	3.00		20.70
11	82	C. Maher			49.20				49.20
16	CRR	Sales				56.26	8.04		64.30
22	83	J. Warren			118.20				
	84	Capital						500.00	618.20
28	CRR	Sales				25.64	3.66		29.30

CASH PAYMENTS BOOK OF A. BRADLEY

Date	Chq. no.	Particulars	Fol.	Discount received	Trade creditors	General	Bank
19XX Nov. 2	235	Purchases				55.60	55.60
3	236	Wages				444.10	444.10
	237	Advertising				89.90	89.90
6	238	Petty Cash Reimbursement					
		Postage				56.00	
		Stationery				20.00	76.00
12	239	J. Fraser		10.00	321.40		321.40
22	240	Wages				504.20	504.20
25	241	J. McKay			164.70		164.70

EXERCISE 5.9 *R. Thomas*

The cash book extracts and bank statement for R. Thomas for July 19XX are on pages 377–378. You are required to carry out the following.
1. Compare the cash book with the bank statement for July.
2. Adjust the cash book by adding items that are in the bank statement but not in the cash book.
3. Balance the cash book at the end of July.
4. Prepare a bank reconciliation statement as at 31 July 19XX. This must agree with the cash book balance.

Statement of Account

Westpac Banking Corporation
FAIRBURN NSW

SPECIMEN ONLY

This statement: JULY

Mr R. Thomas
42 Blackburn Street
FAIRBURN NSW 2631

Account No. 88634
Sheet No. 94

Name of account

R. THOMAS

Date	Particulars	Debit	Credit	Balance
19XX				
1 JULY	BROUGHT FORWARD			14 439.00 CR
5 JULY	C/C		167.00	14 606.00 CR
8 JULY		20794 1 100.00		13 506.00 CR
	FEE	4.80		13 501.20 CR
10 JULY		20797 25.00		13 476.20 CR
		20798 1 175.00		12 301.20 CR
14 JULY	C/C		832.00	13 133.20 CR
16 JULY		20799 123.72		13 009.48 CR
		20796 12 505.00		504.48 CR
17 JULY		20802 77.00		427.48 CR
18 JULY	C/C		130.00	557.48 CR
		20800 1 340.00		782.52 DR
	TFR — T. Green		1300.00	517.48 CR
22 JULY	RTD — R. Peters	50.00		467.48 CR
24 JULY		20801 80.00		387.48 CR
26 JULY	CHQ BK	3.00		384.48 CR
	STATE GOVT TAX ON WITHDRAWALS	15.50		368.98 CR
	STATE GOVT TAX ON DEPOSITS	4.70		364.28 CR

CASH RECEIPTS BOOK OF R. THOMAS

Date	Rec. no.	Particulars	Fol.	Discount allowed	Trade debtors	Sales	Sales tax	General	Bank
19XX									
July 1		Balance	b/f						14 439.00
3	CRR	Sales				31.45	5.55		
	201	T. Andrews		10.00	130.00				167.00
12	CRR	Sales				127.50	22.50		
	202	R. Peters			50.00				
	203	F. Browne			132.00				
	204	Capital						500.00	832.00
17	CRR	Sales				110.50	19.50		130.00
28	205	R. Turner		5.00	75.00				
	206	T. Andrews			140.00				215.00

CASH PAYMENTS BOOK OF R. THOMAS

Date	Chq. no.	Particulars	Fol.	Discount received	Trade creditors	General	Bank
19XX							
July 2	794	Wages				1 100.00	1 100.00
	795	F. Saunders		3.00	66.00		66.00
5	796	Motor Vehicles				12 505.00	12 505.00
	797	Advertising				25.00	25.00
10	798	Purchases				75.00	75.00
		Wages				1 100.00	1 100.00
12	799	A. Black			123.72		123.72
16	800	Wages				1 340.00	1 340.00
20	801	Office Equipment				80.00	80.00
24	802	T. Smith		4.50	77.00		77.00
	803	Stationery				14.50	14.50

EXERCISE 5.10 D. Luciano

The cash book extracts and bank statement for D. Luciano for January 19XX are on pages 379–380. You are required to carry out the following.
1. Compare the cash book with the bank statement for January.
2. Adjust the cash book by adding items that are in the bank statement but not in the cash book.
3. Balance the cash book at the end of January.
4. Prepare a bank reconciliation statement as at 31 January 19XX. This must agree with the cash book balance.

Statement of Account

Westpac Banking Corporation
STRATHVILLE NSW

SPECIMEN ONLY

This statement: **JANUARY**

Mr D. Luciano
163 Drummond Road
STRATHVILLE NSW 2456

Account No. **11024**
Sheet No. **72**

Name of account: **D. LUCIANO**

Date	Particulars	Debit	Credit	Balance
19XX				
1 JAN	BROUGHT FORWARD			1740.00 CR
2 JAN	C/C		420.00	2160.00 CR
10 JAN	C/C		490.00	2650.00 CR
	32175	70.00		2580.00 CR
12 JAN	D/D — T. Frawley		120.00	2700.00 CR
15 JAN	INTEREST ON C'TH BONDS		100.00	2800.00 CR
20 JAN	CHQ BK	35.00		2765.00 CR
	C/C		240.00	3005.00 CR
	32177	160.00		2845.00 CR
26 JAN	STATE GOVT TAX ON WITHDRAWALS	1.20		2843.80 CR
	STATE GOVT TAX ON DEPOSITS	0.85		2842.95 CR
	32178	130.00		2712.95 CR
29 JAN	RTD — K. Powell	380.00		2332.95 CR

CASH RECEIPTS BOOK OF D. LUCIANO

Date	Rec. no.	Particulars	Fol.	Discount allowed	Trade debtors	Sales	Sales tax	General	Bank
19XX Jan. 1		Balance	b/f						1740.00
2	CRR	Sales				346.50	73.50		420.00
10	82	E. Mayne		10.00	120.00				
	CRR	Sales				305.25	64.75		490.00
20	CRR	Sales				198.00	42.00		240.00
31	82	K. Powell			380.00				
	CRR	Sales				82.50	17.50		
	84	Office Furniture						25.00	505.00

CASH PAYMENTS BOOK OF D. LUCIANO

Date	Chq. no.	Particulars	Fol.	Discount received	Trade creditors	General	Bank
19XX							
Jan. 4	175	A. Jones			70.00		70.00
5	176	D. Brown		5.00	50.00		50.00
12	177	Petty Cash Reimbursement					
		General Expenses				50.00	
		Entertainment				49.00	
		Travel				30.00	
		Postage				31.00	160.00
19	178	Purchases				130.00	130.00
24	179	Purchases				90.00	90.00

Including information from previous month's bank reconciliation statement

When the balance at the beginning of the month in the cash book and the opening balance in the bank statement do not agree, it is necessary to go to the previous month's bank reconciliation statement and tick items which appear in the bank statement and the previous month's bank reconciliation statement.

The unpresented cheques and outstanding deposits in the previous month's bank reconciliation statement are those entries which appeared in the cash book the previous month but did not appear on the bank statement for that month.

Any unticked items in the previous month's bank reconciliation statement will go into the current month's bank reconciliation statement and continue to do so until the bank's accounting records have 'caught up' with these transactions.

For exercises 5.11 and 5.12 use copies of the blank cash book masters provided on pages 561–562. Use your own stationery to prepare the bank reconciliation statement.

EXERCISE 5.11 E. Egan

The bank statement and cash book extracts for E. Egan for July 19XX, together with the bank reconciliation statement as at 30 June 19XX are shown on pages 381–382. You are required to compare the records and carry out the following.

1. Adjust the cash book by adding items that are in the bank statement but not in the cash book.
2. Balance the cash book at the end of July.
3. Prepare a bank reconciliation statement as at 31 July 19XX. The balance on this statement must agree with the cash book balance.

BANK RECONCILIATION STATEMENT OF E. EGAN
as at 30 June 19XX

Credit balance as per bank statement				$4641.00
Add: Outstanding deposits				302.00
				4943.00
Less: Unpresented cheques	32401	73.00		
	32406	120.00		193.00
Debit balance as per cash book				$4750.00

Statement of Account
Westpac Banking Corporation
GUNNENDORE NSW

SPECIMEN ONLY

This statement: **JULY**

Mr E. Egan
38 Saleyards Road
GUNNENDORE NSW 2842

Account No. **77864**
Sheet No. **163**

Name of account: **E. EGAN**

Date	Particulars	Debit	Credit	Balance
19XX				
1 JULY	BROUGHT FORWARD			4641.00 CR
2 JULY	C/C		302.00	4943.00 CR
4 JULY	C/C		947.00	5890.00 CR
8 JULY	32401	73.00		5817.00 CR
	32406	120.00		5697.00 CR
	C/C		321.00	6018.00 CR
12 JULY	C/C		3000.00	9018.00 CR
	32407	94.00		8924.00 CR
	32408	1185.00		7739.00 CR
13 JULY	PP — Walton Motors	1000.00		6739.00 CR
15 JULY	32410	1290.00		5449.00 CR
	C/C		453.00	5902.00 CR
16 JULY	32409	190.00		5712.00 CR
20 JULY	C/C		175.50	5887.50 CR
	DD — E. Allen		256.00	6143.50 CR
25 JULY	CHQ BK	40.00		6103.50 CR
29 JULY	32414	1310.00		4793.50 CR
	32413	190.00		4603.50 CR
	STATE GOVT TAX ON WITHDRAWALS	1.75		4601.75 CR
	STATE GOVT TAX ON DEPOSITS	1.35		4600.40 CR
	RTD — B. James	202.00		4398.40 CR

CASH RECEIPTS BOOK OF E. EGAN

Date	Rec. no.	Particulars	Fol.	Discount allowed	Trade debtors	Sales	Sales tax	General	Bank
19XX									
July 1		Balance	b/f						4750.00
2	271	W. Field		3.50	164.00				
	CRR	Sales				685.12	97.88		947.00
8	272	B. James			202.00				
	CRR	Sales				104.12	14.88		321.00
12	273	Capital						3000.00	3000.00
15	CRR	Sales				396.37	56.63		453.00
19	274	L. Wallis		5.00	125.50				
	275	Office Equipment						50.00	175.50
31	CRR	Sales				217.00	31.00		248.00

CASH PAYMENTS BOOK OF E. EGAN

Date	Chq. no.	Particulars	Fol.	Discount received	Trade creditors	General	Bank
19XX							
July 2	407	Comco Pty Ltd			94.00		94.00
6	408	Wages				1185.00	1185.00
8	409	Office Rent				190.00	190.00
13	410	Wages				1290.00	1290.00
19	411	Repairs				46.00	46.00
20	412	Wages				1290.00	1290.00
22	413	Office Rent				190.00	190.00
27	414	Wages				1310.00	1310.00
	415	P. Blundell		7.50	126.00		126.00
29	416	Davis & Co.		7.60	135.00		135.00

EXERCISE 5.12 *Phuong Trading Co.*

The bank statement and cash book extracts for Phuong Trading Co. for November 19XX, together with the bank reconciliation statement as at 31 October 19XX are shown on pages 383–384. You are required to compare the records and carry out the following.

1. Adjust the cash book by adding items that are in the bank statement but not in the cash book.
2. Balance the cash book at the end of November.
3. Prepare a bank reconciliation statement as at 30 November 19XX. This must agree with the cash book balance.

BANK RECONCILIATION STATEMENT OF PHUONG TRADING CO.
as at 31 October 19XX

Credit balance as per bank statement			$6890.50
Add: Outstanding deposits			1460.00
			8350.50
Less: Unpresented cheques	11268	220.00	
	11271	184.00	404.00
Debit balance as per cash book			$7946.50

Statement of Account
Westpac Banking Corporation
ALBANY   NSW

This statement: **NOVEMBER**

Phuong Trading Co.
73 Milstead Road
ALBANY NSW 2825

Account No. **48637**
Sheet No. **253**

SPECIMEN ONLY

Name of account: **PHUONG TRADING CO.**

Date	Particulars		Debit	Credit	Balance
19XX					
1 NOV	BROUGHT FORWARD				6 890.50 CR
	C/C			1460.00	8 350.50 CR
2 NOV	C/C			210.00	8 560.50 CR
4 NOV		11268	220.00		8 340.50 CR
6 NOV	C/C			280.00	8 620.50 CR
10 NOV	INTEREST ON C'TH BONDS			520.00	9 140.50 CR
		11272	170.00		8 970.50 CR
12 NOV		11271	184.00		8 786.50 CR
		11273	236.00		8 550.50 CR
15 NOV	C/C			525.00	9 075.50 CR
17 NOV		11274	115.00		8 960.50 CR
	C/C			1540.00	10 500.50 CR
20 NOV	C/C			4630.00	15 130.50 CR
	DD — K. Boyle			150.00	15 280.50 CR
27 NOV		11276	548.00		14 732.50 CR
	STATE GOVT TAX ON WITHDRAWALS		2.20		14 730.30 CR
	STATE GOVT TAX ON DEPOSITS		2.75		14 727.55 CR
	CHQ BK		45.00		14 682.55 CR
30 NOV	INTEREST ON MORTGAGE		480.00		14 202.55 CR
	RTD — M. Martin		285.00		13 917.55 CR
		11277	90.00		13 827.55 CR
		11279	25.00		13 802.55 CR

CASH RECEIPTS BOOK OF PHUONG TRADING CO.

Date	Rec. no.	Particulars	Fol.	Discount allowed	Trade debtors	Sales	Sales tax	General	Bank
19XX Nov. 1		Balance	b/f						7946.50
	CRR	Sales				178.50	31.50		210.00
6	240	L. Lee		4.50	160.00				
	CRR	Sales				102.00	18.00		280.00
15	241	M. Martin			285.00				
	242	Rent Received						240.00	525.00
17	CRR	Sales				1309.00	231.00		1540.00
20	243	Capital						4050.00	
	244	R. Jakes		10.50	580.00				4630.00
30	CRR	Sales				657.05	115.95		773.00

CASH PAYMENTS BOOK OF PHUONG TRADING CO.

Date	Chq. no.	Particulars	Fol.	Discount received	Trade creditors	General	Bank
19XX Nov. 2	272	Purchases				170.00	170.00
4	273	S. Santiago		5.50	236.00		236.00
14	274	Petty Cash Reimbursement					
		Stationery				50.00	
		Postage				65.00	115.00
	275	Rent				400.00	400.00
15	276	Purchases				548.00	548.00
21	277	Advertising				90.00	90.00
27	278	B. Barton			70.00		70.00
	279	Purchases				25.00	25.00
30	280	D. Le Tran		9.50	315.50		315.50

When the business owes money to the bank

When the final balance on the bank statement is a debit balance (DR), the business owes money to the bank. When this situation occurs, the bank reconciliation statement is set out as shown on page 385.

BANK RECONCILIATION STATEMENT OF J. MASON
as at 31 March 19XX

Debit balance as per bank statement				$1463.00
Add: Unpresented cheques	094	270.00		
	098	102.00		
	099	410.00		782.00
				2245.00
Less: Outstanding deposits				310.00
Credit balance as per cash book				$1935.00

In the above example, the business begins the period owing money to the bank (bank overdraft). The unpresented cheques are added, which increases the amount the business owes to the bank. The outstanding deposits are then deducted and the amount owing to the bank is decreased.

In the cash book, the balance is shown brought down (b/d) on the cash payments side (that is, the cash payments book) as follows. (*Note*: This is a simplified example.)

CASH BOOK OF J. MASON

Cash receipts				Cash payments			
Date	Particulars		Bank	Date	Particulars		Bank
Mar. 1	Balance	b/d	5 320.00				
2–28	Various receipts		3 306.00	Mar. 2–28	Various payments		10 561.00
28	Balance	c/d	1 935.00				
			10 561.00				10 561.00
				Apr. 1	Balance	b/d	1 935.00

For exercises 5.13 and 5.14, use copies of the blank cash book masters provided on pages 561–562. Use your own stationery to prepare the bank reconciliation statements.

EXERCISE 5.13 *H. Rossey*

The bank statement and cash book extracts for H. Rossey for May 19XX are shown on pages 386–387. You are required to carry out the following.
1. Compare the cash book with the bank statement for May.
2. Adjust the cash book by adding items that are in the bank statement but not in the cash book.
3. Balance the cash book at the end of May.
4. Prepare a bank reconciliation statement as at 31 May 19XX. This must agree with the cash book balance.

Statement of Account

Westpac Banking Corporation
OLDCASTLE NSW

SPECIMEN ONLY

This statement: **MAY**

Mr H. Rossey
194 Midlothian Street
OLDCASTLE NSW 2642

Account No.: **23486**
Sheet No.: **73**

Name of account: **H. ROSSEY**

Date	Particulars		Debit	Credit	Balance
19XX					
1 MAY	BROUGHT FORWARD				1507.17 DR
3 MAY		20514	1780.00		3287.17 DR
4 MAY		20515	80.00		3367.17 DR
6 MAY	C/C			180.12	3187.05 DR
9 MAY		20517	156.12		3343.17 DR
11 MAY		20518	138.16		3481.33 DR
12 MAY	C/C			286.15	3195.18 DR
14 MAY	C/C			198.00	2997.18 DR
15 MAY	INTEREST ON C'TH BONDS			45.10	2952.08 DR
17 MAY		20520	1790.00		4742.08 DR
	CHQ BK		7.50		4749.58 DR
18 MAY	C/C			1436.50	3313.08 DR
21 MAY	FEE		6.20		3319.28 DR
24 MAY	TFR — L. Morris			164.10	3155.18 DR
	TFR — M. Smith			137.20	3017.98 DR
31 MAY		20516	200.00		3217.98 DR
	C/C			198.20	3019.78 DR
	STATE GOVT TAX ON WITHDRAWALS		5.00		3024.78 DR
	STATE GOVT TAX ON DEPOSITS		3.70		3028.48 DR

CASH RECEIPTS BOOK OF H. ROSSEY

Date	Rec. no.	Particulars	Fol.	Discount allowed	Trade debtors	Sales	Sales tax	General	Bank
19XX									
May 5	21	Ridge & Co.		5.50	180.12				180.12
10	22	S. Lisle			136.15				
	CRR	Sales				131.25	18.75		286.15
12	23	T. Carr			198.00				198.00
16	24	M. Raye		4.80	136.50				
	CRR	Sales				262.50	37.50		
	25	Capital						1000.00	1436.50
24	26	M. Haynes			198.20				198.20
30	CRR	Sales				406.85	58.15		
	27	Lornet Ltd			162.10				627.10

CASH PAYMENTS BOOK OF H. ROSSEY

Date	Chq. no.	Particulars	Fol.	Discount received	Trade creditors	General	Bank
19XX							
May 1		Balance	c/d				$1507.17
3	514	Wages				1780.00	1780.00
4	515	Petty Cash Reimbursement					
		Postage				60.00	
		Stationery				20.00	80.00
5	516	Drawings				200.00	200.00
	517	J. James		3.50	156.12		156.12
6	518	R. Gray			138.16		138.16
10	519	C. Falls		2.10	236.00		236.00
17	520	Wages				1790.00	1790.00
24	521	A. Bray			122.10		122.10
28	522	Purchases				536.60	536.60
30	523	Advertising				110.15	110.15

EXERCISE 5.14   R. Wheeler & Co.

The bank statement and cash book extracts for R. Wheeler & Co. for April 19XX, together with the bank reconciliation statement as at 31 March 19XX are shown below and on pages 388–389. You are required to carry out the following.

1. Compare the cash book with the bank statement for April.
2. Adjust the cash book by adding items that are in the bank statement but not in the cash book.
3. Balance the cash book at the end of April.
4. Prepare a bank reconciliation statement as at 30 April 19XX. This must agree with the cash book balance.

BANK RECONCILIATION STATEMENT OF R. WHEELER & CO.
as at 31 March 19XX

Debit balance as per bank statement				$5830.00
Add: Unpresented cheques		619	323.00	
		621	128.00	451.00
				6281.00
Less: Outstanding deposits				425.00
Credit balance as per cash book				$5856.00

Statement of Account
Westpac Banking Corporation
STURTSVILLE NSW

SPECIMEN ONLY

This statement: **APRIL**

R. Wheeler & Co.
133 Bradfield Highway
STURTSVILLE NSW 2751

Account No. **46709**
Sheet No. **82**

Name of account: **R. WHEELER & CO.**

Date	Particulars	Debit		Credit	Balance
19XX					
1 APR	BROUGHT FORWARD				5 830.00 DR
	C/C			425.00	5 405.00 DR
3 APR	C/C			242.50	5 162.50 DR
8 APR		80619	323.00		5 485.50 DR
		80621	128.00		5 613.50 DR
10 APR	C/C			102.10	5 511.40 DR
		80623	2963.00		8 474.40 DR
12 APR	INTEREST ON OVERDRAFT		155.00		8 629.40 DR
15 APR	C/C			1199.00	7 430.40 DR
		80624	82.00		7 512.40 DR
20 APR	C/C			28.00	7 484.40 DR
	DD — N. Hodgson			363.50	7 120.90 DR
24 APR	C/C			2087.00	5 033.90 DR
		80626	3010.00		8 043.90 DR
		80622	460.00		8 503.90 DR
28 APR	INTEREST ON C'TH BONDS			300.00	8 203.90 DR
		80627	9765.00		17 968.90 DR
		80628	175.00		18 143.90 DR
30 APR	RTD — J. Woods		28.00		18 171.90 DR
	CHQ BK		25.00		18 196.90 DR
	STATE GOVT TAX ON WITHDRAWALS		2.50		18 199.40 DR
	STATE GOVT TAX ON DEPOSITS		2.65		18 202.05 DR

CASH RECEIPTS BOOK OF R. WHEELER & CO.

Date	Rec. no.	Particulars	Fol.	Discount allowed	Trade debtors	Sales	Sales Tax	General	Bank
19XX Apr. 3	CRR	Sales				212.19	30.31		242.50
10	108	A. Luxon		4.50	102.10				102.10
15	109	A. R. Johnson		11.00	583.00				
	110	Rent Revenue						520.00	
	CRR	Sales				84.00	12.00		1199.00
20	111	J. Woods			28.00				28.00
24	112	Motor Vehicles						2020.00	
	CRR	Sales				58.62	8.38		2087.00
31	113	J. Raymond		4.00	182.00				
	CRR	Sales				206.50	29.50		418.00

CASH PAYMENTS BOOK OF R. WHEELER & CO.

Date	Chq. no.	Particulars	Fol.	Discount received	Trade creditors	General	Bank
19XX			b/d				
Apr. 1		Balance					5856.00
2	622	R. Preston		9.20	460.00		460.00
7	623	Wages				2963.00	2963.00
	624	Purchases				82.00	82.00
15	625	M. Hayes			36.50		36.50
21	626	Wages				3010.00	3010.00
24	627	Motor Vehicles				9765.00	9765.00
	628	L. Hastings		4.75	175.00		175.00
30	629	Petty Cash Reimbursement					
		Postage				55.00	
		General Expenses				28.00	83.00
	630	Advertising				207.50	207.50

When both the bank statement and the cash book show a credit balance

A bank statement can show a credit balance, indicating that the business has money in its bank account. However, when outstanding deposits are added and the unpresented cheques deducted, the business may owe money to the bank (that is, the account is temporarily overdrawn). Interest is charged on the overdrawn amount and shown on the next bank statement.

When the bank statement shows a credit balance, the bank reconciliation statement is set out as shown below.

BANK RECONCILIATION STATEMENT OF J. MASON
as at 31 August 19XX

Credit balance as per bank statement				$4375.00
Add: Outstanding deposits				100.00
				4475.00
Less: Unpresented cheques		430	1195.00	
		436	500.00	
		441	5000.00	6695.00
Credit balance as per cash book				$2220.00

For exercises 5.15 and 5.16, use copies of the blank cash book masters provided on pages 561–562. Use your own stationery to prepare the bank reconciliation statements.

EXERCISE 5.15 B. Camilleri & Sons

The bank statement and cash book extracts for B. Camilleri & Sons for July 19XX, together with the bank reconciliation statement as at 30 June 19XX are on pages 390–391. You are required to carry out the following.
1. Compare the records.
2. Adjust the cash book by adding items that are in the bank statement but not in the cash book.

3. Balance the cash book at the end of July.
4. Prepare a bank reconciliation statement as at 31 July 19XX. This must agree with the cash book balance.

BANK RECONCILIATION STATEMENT OF B. CAMILLERI & SONS
as at 30 June 19XX

Credit balance as per bank statement				$1430.00
Add: Outstanding deposits				245.00
				1675.00
Less: Unpresented cheques	89	137.00		
	91	96.50		233.50
Debit balance as per cash book				$1441.50

Statement of Account

Westpac Banking Corporation
NORMA NSW

SPECIMEN ONLY

This statement: JULY

B. Camilleri & Sons
42 Highgate Road
NORMA NSW 2716

Account No. 56789
Sheet No. 124

Name of account: B. CAMILLERI & SONS

Date	Particulars		Debit	Credit	Balance
19XX					
1 JULY	BROUGHT FORWARD				1430.00 CR
	C/C			245.00	1675.00 CR
3 JULY		23091	96.50		1578.50 CR
4 JULY	C/C			160.00	1738.50 CR
5 JULY	INTEREST ON MORTGAGE		265.00		1473.50 CR
		23089	137.00		1336.50 CR
9 JULY	C/C			210.00	1546.50 CR
13 JULY	CHQ BK		25.00		1521.50 CR
	DD — S. Carson			280.00	1801.50 CR
14 JULY	C/C			70.00	1871.50 CR
		23092	120.00		1751.50 CR
		23093	110.00		1641.50 CR
16 JULY	PP — Insurance		150.00		1491.50 CR
24 JULY	C/C			280.00	1771.50 CR
29 JULY	C/C			130.00	1901.50 CR
		23094	140.00		1761.50 CR
30 JULY	STATE GOVT TAX ON WITHDRAWALS		0.98		1760.52 CR
	STATE GOVT TAX ON DEPOSITS		1.02		1759.50 CR
		23096	130.00		1629.50 CR
	RTD — L. Moss		100.00		1529.50 CR
		23097	82.00		1447.50 CR

CASH RECEIPTS BOOK OF B. CAMILLERI & SONS

Date	Rec. no.	Particulars	Fol.	Discount allowed	Trade debtors	Sales	Sales Tax	General	Bank
19XX July 1		Balance	b/f						1441.50
4	412	A. Harper		3.00	160.00				160.00
9	CRR	Sales				183.75	26.25		210.00
14	413	Commission Revenue						70.00	70.00
24	414	L. Moss			100.00				
	CRR	Sales				157.50	22.50		280.00
29	415	G. Gray		2.25	130.00				130.00
30	416	B. Rowe			60.00				
	CRR	Sales				192.50	27.50		280.00

CASH PAYMENTS BOOK OF B. CAMILLERI & SONS

Date	Chq. no.	Particulars	Fol.	Discount received	Trade creditors	General	Bank
19XX July 6	092	A. Briggs		2.75	120.00		120.00
12	093	Petty Cash Reimbursement					
		Stationery				40.50	
		General Expenses				69.50	110.00
14	094	Purchases				140.00	140.00
21	095	L. Davis		3.50	162.00		162.00
	096	P. Newsom			130.00		130.00
26	097	Repairs				82.00	82.00
30	098	B. Rogers		12.50	716.50		716.50
	099	Office Equipment				2510.00	2510.00

EXERCISE 5.16   G. Abbott

The bank statement and cash book extracts for G. Abbott for March 19XX, together with the bank reconciliation statement as at 28 February 19XX are on pages 392–393. You are required to carry out the following.

1. Compare the records.
2. Adjust the cash book by adding items that are in the bank statement but not in the cash book.
3. Balance the cash book at the end of March.
4. Prepare a bank reconciliation statement as at 31 March 19XX. This must agree with the cash book balance.

BANK RECONCILIATION STATEMENT OF G. ABBOTT
as at 28 February 19XX

Credit balance as per bank statement				$5832.55
Add: Outstanding deposits				196.00
				6028.55
Less: Unpresented cheques	410	397.00		
	411	260.00		657.00
Debit balance as per cash book				$5371.55

Statement of Account

Westpac Banking Corporation
EASTBOURNE VIC

SPECIMEN ONLY

This statement: MARCH

Mr G. Abbott
195 Valley Road
EASTBOURNE VIC 3821

Account No. 98750
Sheet No. 128

Name of account: G. ABBOTT

Date	Particulars		Debit	Credit	Balance
19XX					
1 MAR	BROUGHT FORWARD				5832.55 CR
	C/C			196.00	6028.55 CR
3 MAR	C/C			210.50	6239.05 CR
		56410	397.00		5842.05 CR
6 MAR	INTEREST ON MORTGAGE		120.00		5722.05 CR
	C/C			384.00	6106.05 CR
8 MAR		56411	260.00		5846.05 CR
		56412	482.00		5364.05 CR
12 MAR	C/C			184.00	5548.05 CR
	CHQ BK		30.00		5518.05 CR
	STATE GOVT TAX ON WITHDRAWALS		0.57		5517.48 CR
	STATE GOVT TAX ON DEPOSITS		1.12		5516.36 CR
16 MAR	C/C			313.00	5829.36 CR
		56413	500.00		5329.36 CR
		56414	198.00		5131.36 CR
		56415	3682.00		1449.36 CR
20 MAR	C/C			314.10	1763.46 CR
	DD — P. Franks			251.00	2014.46 CR
25 MAR	C/C			241.50	2255.96 CR
		56416	142.00		2113.96 CR
27 MAR	RTD — M. Keene		184.00		1929.96 CR

CASH RECEIPTS BOOK OF G. ABBOTT

Date	Rec. no.	Particulars	Fol.	Discount allowed	Trade debtors	Sales	Sales tax	General	Bank
19XX Mar. 1		Balance	b/f						5371.55
3	922	R. Hoyle		7.80	210.50				210.50
6	923	F. O'Neale		5.50	156.00				
	CRR	Sales				188.10	39.90		384.00
12	924	M. Keene			184.00				184.00
15	925	B. Salter		8.20	263.00				
	926	Office Furniture						50.00	313.00
20	CRR	Sales				259.14	54.96		314.10
25	927	L. Moffatt			78.50				
	CRR	Sales				134.47	28.53		241.50
31	928	W. Fisher		11.00	384.75				
	CRR	Sales				193.05	40.95		618.75

CASH PAYMENTS BOOK OF G. ABBOTT

Date	Chq. no.	Particulars	Fol.	Discount received	Trade creditors	General	Bank
19XX Mar. 3	412	F. Fitzpatrick			482.00		482.00
7	413	Drawings				500.00	500.00
10	414	Purchases				198.00	198.00
	415	Wages				3682.00	3682.00
16	416	Electricity				142.00	142.00
20	417	C. Darke		12.50	362.00		362.00
24	418	D. Priam		15.00	493.50		493.50
30	419	General Expenses				28.50	28.50
	420	Office Equipment				2550.00	2550.00

When both the bank statement and the cash book show a debit balance

A bank statement can show a debit balance, indicating that the business owes money to the bank. However, when the unpresented cheques are added and the outstanding deposits deducted, the business may have money in the bank (that is, a debit balance in the cash book).

When the bank statement shows a debit balance, the bank reconciliation statement is set out as shown below.

BANK RECONCILIATION STATEMENT OF J. MASON
as at 31 March 19XX

Debit balance as per bank statement				$2365.00
Add: Unpresented cheques	501	120.00		
	512	60.00		180.00
				2545.00
Less: Outstanding deposits				3600.00
Debit balance as per cash book				$1055.00

For exercises 5.17 and 5.18, use copies of the blank cash book masters provided on pages 561–562. Use your own stationery to prepare the bank reconciliation statements.

EXERCISE 5.17 Thuan Importing Co.

The bank statement and cash book extracts for Thuan Importing Co. for April 19XX, together with the bank reconciliation statement as at 31 March 19XX are shown below and on pages 395–396. You are required to carry out the following.

1. Compare the records.
2. Adjust the cash book by adding items that are in the bank statement but not in the cash book.
3. Balance the cash book at the end of April.
4. Prepare a bank reconciliation statement as at 30 April 19XX. This must agree with the cash book balance.

BANK RECONCILIATION STATEMENT OF THUAN IMPORTING CO.
as at 31 March 19XX

Debit balance as per bank statement			$4076.00
Add: Unpresented cheques	160	230.00	
	162	315.10	545.10
			4621.10
Less: Outstanding deposits			480.00
Credit balance as per cash book			$4141.10

Statement of Account

Westpac Banking Corporation
OLDCASTLE NSW

SPECIMEN ONLY

This statement: **APRIL**

Thuan Importing Co.
363 Main Highway
OLDCASTLE NSW 2642

Account No.: **22256**
Sheet No.: **45**

Name of account: **THUAN IMPORTING CO.**

Date	Particulars		Debit	Credit	Balance
19XX					
1 APR	BROUGHT FORWARD				4076.00 DR
2 APR	C/C			480.00	3596.00 DR
4 APR	C/C			147.50	3448.50 CR
8 APR	INTEREST ON MORTGAGE		250.00		3698.50 DR
		61160	230.00		3928.50 DR
		61162	315.10		4243.60 DR
10 APR	C/C			1456.00	2787.60 DR
12 APR		61163	95.00		2882.60 DR
15 APR	C/C			136.50	2746.10 DR
	FEE		10.00		2756.10 DR
	CHQ BK		15.00		2771.10 DR
20 APR	C/C			377.50	2393.60 DR
		61165	72.00		2465.60 DR
24 APR	C/C			1189.00	1276.60 DR
		61166	172.00		1448.60 DR
	DD — Rent			200.00	1248.60 DR
	PP — R. Williams		120.00		1368.60 DR
28 APR	C/C			276.50	1092.10 DR
		61167	180.00		1272.10 DR
30 APR		61168	427.00		1699.10 DR
		61169	203.50		1902.60 DR
	STATE GOVT TAX ON WITHDRAWALS		0.98		1903.58 DR
	STATE GOVT TAX ON DEPOSITS		1.06		1904.64 DR

CASH RECEIPTS BOOK OF THUAN IMPORTING CO.

Date	Rec. no.	Particulars	Fol.	Discount allowed	Trade debtors	Sales	Sales tax	General	Bank
19XX Apr. 4	476	M. Anderson		8.00	147.50				147.50
10	477 CRR	P. Elliott Sales		14.50	236.00	1037.00	183.00		1456.00
15	478	R. Archer			136.50				136.50
20	479 CRR	B. Carua Sales		18.90	329.00	41.22	7.28		377.50
24	480	G. Nguyen		33.00	1189.00				1189.00
28	CRR	Sales				235.02	41.48		276.50
30	481 482	G. Ingram Capital			750.00			5000.00	5750.00

CASH PAYMENTS BOOK OF THUAN IMPORTING CO.

Date	Chq. no.	Particulars	Fol.	Discount received	Trade creditors	General	Bank
19XX Apr. 1		Balance	b/d				4141.10
3	163	V. Morrison		3.00	95.00		95.00
10	164	Purchases				49.50	49.50
	165	Advertising				72.00	72.00
15	166	S. Huong			172.00		172.00
18	167	Electricity				180.00	180.00
20	168	Rates				427.00	427.00
24	169	T. Buckley		6.50	203.50		203.50
28	170	A. Guthrie			46.75		46.75
	171	Office Equipment				133.00	133.00

EXERCISE 5.18 T. Moslowski

The bank statement and cash book extracts for T. Moslowski for June 19XX, together with the bank reconciliation statement as at 31 May 19XX are on pages 397–398. You are required to carry out the following.

1. Compare the records.
2. Adjust the cash book by adding items that are in the bank statement but not in the cash book.
3. Balance the cash book at the end of June.
4. Prepare a bank reconciliation statement as at 30 June 19XX. This must agree with the cash book balance.

BANK RECONCILIATION STATEMENT OF T. MOSLOWSKI
as at 31 May 19XX

Credit balance as per bank statement				$5631.50
Add: Outstanding deposits				1843.00
				7474.50
Less: Unpresented cheques		555	482.40	
		558	113.00	
		559	26.50	621.90
Debit balance as per cash book				$6852.60

Statement of Account
Westpac Banking Corporation
NORTH CITY   NSW

SPECIMEN ONLY

This statement: JUNE

Mr T. Moslowski
128 Harbourside Drive
NORTH CITY NSW 2421

Account No. 96873
Sheet No. 87

Name of account: T. MOSLOWSKI

Date	Particulars		Debit	Credit	Balance
19XX					
1 JUNE	BROUGHT FORWARD				5631.50 CR
	C/C			1843.00	7474.50 CR
3 JUNE	C/C			102.00	7576.50 CR
		40555	482.40		7094.10 CR
6 JUNE		40559	26.50		7067.60 CR
10 JUNE	C/C			471.60	7539.20 CR
	PP — R. Klein		52.80		7486.40 CR
		40558	113.00		7373.40 CR
15 JUNE	C/C			1000.00	8373.40 CR
		40560	198.00		8175.40 CR
18 JUNE	C/C			186.70	8362.10 CR
		40561	4623.00		3739.10 CR
		40563	50.00		3689.10 CR
21 JUNE	C/C			216.15	3905.25 CR
	DD — S. Miller			283.00	4188.25 CR
24 JUNE	C/C			242.35	4430.60 CR
		40564	147.50		4283.10 CR
28 JUNE		40565	4230.00		53.10 CR
		40567	208.00		154.90 DR
30 JUNE	CHQ BK		12.50		167.40 DR
	STATE GOVT TAX ON WITHDRAWALS		1.12		168.52 DR
	STATE GOVT TAX ON DEPOSITS		1.06		169.58 DR
	RTD — G. Seale		148.55		318.13 DR
		40566	212.00		530.13 DR
		40568	162.50		692.63 DR

CASH RECEIPTS BOOK OF T. MOSLOWSKI

Date	Rec. no.	Particulars	Fol.	Discount allowed	Trade debtors	Sales	Sales tax	General	Bank
19XX June 1		Balance	b/f						6852.60
3	092	C. Perkins		4.50	102.00				102.00
10	093	E. Harris			89.60				
	CRR	Sales				334.25	47.75		471.60
15	094	Capital						1000.00	1000.00
18	095	R. Clements			72.10				
	CRR	Sales				100.27	14.33		186.70
21	096	K. Ross		9.50	216.15				216.15
24	097	G. Seale			148.55				
	CRR	Sales				82.07	11.73		242.35
30	098	L. Newton		33.40	1846.00				
	099	C. Denning		38.00	2065.00				
	CRR	Sales				1440.12	205.73		5556.85

CASH PAYMENTS BOOK OF T. MOSLOWSKI

Date	Chq. no.	Particulars	Fol.	Discount received	Trade creditors	General	Bank
19XX June 4	560	F. Cheong		5.00	198.00		198.00
10	561	Wages				4623.00	4623.00
12	562	R. Crawford		5.85	275.80		275.80
	563	Drawings				50.00	50.00
18	564	F. Lewis			147.50		147.50
	565	Wages				4230.00	4230.00
	566	F. Giotti		5.60	212.00		212.00
	567	Electricity				208.00	208.00
26	568	Advertising				162.50	162.50
30	569	N. Laine				26.70	26.70
	570	M. Carnegie				103.60	103.60

Putting it together

Exercises 5A and 5B cover two consecutive periods. These exercises highlight the importance of constantly checking the current month's bank statement against the previous month's bank reconciliation statement as well as against the current month's records. For exercises 5A and 5B, use copies of the blank cash book masters provided on pages 561–562. Use your own stationery to prepare the bank reconciliation statements.

5A P. Poulos & Sons

The bank statement and cash book extracts of P. Poulos & Sons for March 19XX, together with the bank reconciliation statement as at 28 February 19XX are on pages 399–400. You are required to carry out the following.

1. Compare the records.
2. Adjust the cash book by adding items that are in the bank statement but not in the cash book.
3. Balance the cash book at the end of March.
4. Prepare a bank reconciliation statement as at 31 March 19XX. This must agree with the cash book balance.

BANK RECONCILIATION STATEMENT OF P. POULOS & SONS
as at 28 February 19XX

Credit balance as per bank statement				$7447.90
Add: Outstanding deposits				728.60
				8176.50
Less: Unpresented cheques	181	420.50		
	182	156.00		576.50
Debit balance as per cash book				$7600.00

Statement of Account

Westpac Banking Corporation
GREENLEIGH NSW

SPECIMEN ONLY

This statement: MARCH

P. Poulos & Sons
281 Marine Parade
GREENLEIGH NSW 2472

Account No. 7264
Sheet No. 31

Name of account: P. POULOS & SONS

Date	Particulars	Debit	Credit	Balance
19XX				
1 MAR	BROUGHT FORWARD			7447.90 CR
3 MAR	C/C		728.60	8176.50 CR
4 MAR	32181	420.50		7756.00 CR
5 MAR	32182	156.00		7600.00 CR
6 MAR	C/C		260.00	7860.00 CR
	32183	312.00		7548.00 CR
13 MAR	C/C		330.00	7878.00 CR
	32184	72.00		7806.00 CR
	32185	407.50		7398.50 CR
18 MAR	C/C		98.00	7496.50 CR
	32186	85.00		7411.50 CR
19 MAR	DD — R. Atkins		69.50	7481.00 CR
20 MAR	32187	113.00		7368.00 CR
22 MAR	C/C		503.00	7871.00 CR
27 MAR	32189	160.00		7711.00 CR
	CHQ BK	25.00		7686.00 CR
28 MAR	STATE GOVT TAX ON WITHDRAWALS	10.20		7675.80 CR
	STATE GOVT TAX ON DEPOSITS	5.70		7670.10 CR

CASH RECEIPTS BOOK OF P. POULOS & SONS

Date	Rec. no.	Particulars	Fol.	Discount allowed	Trade debtors	Sales	Sales tax	General	Bank
19XX Mar. 1		Balance	b/f						7600.00
3	CRR	Sales				221.00	39.00		260.00
10	208	B. Modini		4.00	146.00				
	CRR	Sales				156.40	27.60		330.00
15	209	R. Cole			98.00				98.00
20	210	J. Vincent		5.00	175.00				
	CRR	Sales				278.80	49.20		503.00
30	211	R. Rossini		6.00	234.00				234.00

CASH PAYMENTS BOOK OF P. POULOS & SONS

Date	Chq. no.	Particulars	Fol.	Discount received	Trade creditors	General	Bank
19XX Mar. 3	183	V. Angelo		8.00	312.00		312.00
10	184	Purchases				72.00	72.00
	185	Star Trading Co.		10.50	407.50		407.50
15	186	Advertising				85.00	85.00
18	187	L. Cheong			113.00		113.00
20	188	A. Denton			236.00		236.00
24	189	Rates				160.00	160.00
28	190	D. Harrison		2.75	107.25		107.25

Once you have completed the above procedures, you are required to carry out the following.
(a) Enter the balance b/d in the cash book for 1 April 19XX.
(b) Check that the information contained on the following source documents for April is correct, and correct any irregularities in accordance with guidelines set out in the firm's policies and procedures manual. If there are inconsistencies between the amounts in figures and the amounts in words, assume the amounts in figures are correct.
(c) After verification, enter details of documents into the cash book for April.
(d) Verify the entry of details of these document in the cash book by ticking each document against the cash book entry.
(e) Check the mathematical accuracy of figures entered in the cash book. Note and correct errors in accordance with guidelines set out in the firm's policies and procedures manual.
(f) Compare the cash book and the bank statement for April. Don't forget to check the previous month's bank reconciliation statement.
(g) Adjust the cash book by adding items that are in the bank statement but not in the cash book.
(h) Balance the cash book at the end of April 19XX.
(i) Prepare a bank reconciliation statement as at 30 April 19XX. This must agree with the cash book balance.

Duplicates of receipts

Rec. No. 212 Date: 3 April 19XX Rec'd from B. MODINI the sum of Two hundred dollars For: Payment of March Account Cash/Chq. $274.00 Discount 6.00 Amt Owing $280.00	Rec. No. 213 Date: 6 April 19XX Rec'd from STARK REALTY the sum of One hundred and eighty-five dollars For: Rent revenue Cash/Chq. $185.00	Rec. No. 214 Date: 10 April 19XX Rec'd from J. VINCENT the sum of One hundred and seventy-five dollars fifty cents For: Payment of March Account Cash/Chq. $175.50 Discount 4.50 Amt Owing $180.00
Rec. No. 215 Date: 17 April 19XX Rec'd from D. JENKINS the sum of One hundred and twenty-five dollars For: Payment on Account Cash/Chq. $125.00	Rec. No. 216 Date: 23 April 19XX Rec'd from R. COLE the sum of Three hundred and two dollars For: Payment of April Account Cash/Chq. $312.00 Discount 8.00 Amt Owing $320.00	

Cash register records

Cash Register Record 10 April 19XX Sales $243.10 Sales Tax 42.90 Total Sales $286.00	Cash Register Record 19 April 19XX Sales $268.60 Sales Tax 47.40 Total Sales $316.00	Cash Register Record 28 April 19XX Sales $156.40 Sales Tax 27.60 Total Sales $184.00

Cheque butts

Cheque No. 191 Date: 2 April 19XX To: PACIFIC POWER For: Electricity This cheque: $237.00	Cheque No. 192 Date: 3 April 19XX To: V. ANGELO For: Payment of March Account This cheque: $234.00 Discount: 6.00	Cheque No. 193 Date: 9 April 19XX To: STAR TRADING CO. For: Payment of March Account This cheque: $351.00 Discount: 9.00

Cheque No. 194	Cheque No. 195	Cheque No. 196
Date: *18 April 19XX*	Date: *26 April 19XX*	Date: *29 April 19XX*
To: GREEN ADVOCATE	To: D. HARRISON	To: CASH
For: Advertising	For: Payment of Account	For: Petty Cash Reimbursement
		Postage $18.00
		Stationery 45.00
This cheque: $76.00	This cheque: $165.75	This cheque: $63.00
	Discount: 4.25	

Statement of Account
Westpac Banking Corporation
GREENLEIGH NSW

SPECIMEN ONLY

This statement: **APRIL**

P. Poulos & Sons
281 Marine Parade
GREENLEIGH NSW 2472

Account No.: **7264**
Sheet No.: **32**

Name of account: **P. POULOS & SONS**

Date	Particulars	Debit	Credit	Balance
19XX				
1 APR	BROUGHT FORWARD			7670.10 CR
2 APR	C/C		234.00	7904.10 CR
3 APR	32188	236.00		7668.10 CR
4 APR	32190	107.25		7560.85 CR
5 APR	C/C		274.00	7834.85 CR
	32191	237.00		7597.85 CR
6 APR	DD — R. Slavin		178.00	7775.85 CR
	32192	234.00		7541.85 CR
10 APR	C/C		185.00	7726.85 CR
12 APR	32193	351.00		7375.85 CR
	CHQ BK	15.00		7360.85 CR
13 APR	C/C		461.50	7822.35 CR
19 APR	C/C		125.00	7947.35 CR
20 APR	32194	76.00		7871.35 CR
21 APR	C/C		316.00	8187.35 CR
26 APR	C/C		312.00	8499.35 CR
29 APR	STATE GOVT TAX ON WITHDRAWALS	5.20		8494.15 CR
	STATE GOVT TAX ON DEPOSITS	6.50		8487.65 CR
30 APR	RTD — B. Modini	274.00		8213.65 CR

5B *Green Bay Electrics*

The cash book of Green Bay Electrics shows a debit balance of $6712.00 on 1 May 19XX.

The duplicates of receipts, cash register records, cheque butts for receipts and payments made during May 19XX, the bank statement for May and the bank reconciliation statement as at 30 April 19XX are on pages 403–407. You are required to carry out the following.

(a) Verify and enter details of the following source documents into the cash book for May. If there are inconsistencies between the amounts in figures and the amounts in words, assume the amounts in figures are correct.
(b) Compare the cash book and the bank statement for May. Don't forget to check the previous month's bank reconciliation statement.
(c) Adjust the cash book by adding items that are in the bank statement but not in the cash book.
(d) Balance the cash book at the end of May 19XX.
(e) Prepare a bank reconciliation statement as at 31 May 19XX. This must agree with the cash book balance.

BANK RECONCILIATION STATEMENT OF GREEN BAY ELECTRICS
as at 30 April 19XX

Credit balance as per bank statement				$6733.00
Add: Outstanding deposits				192.00
				6925.00
Less: Unpresented cheques		099	64.00	
		103	149.00	213.00
Debit balance as per cash book				$6712.00

Duplicates of receipts

Rec. No. 231	Rec. No. 232	Rec. No. 233
Date: 6 May 19XX	Date: 17 May 19XX	Date: 20 May 19XX
Rec'd from A. MELTON the sum of *Two hundred and forty-seven dollars sixty-five cents*	Rec'd from T. RANDALL the sum of *One hundred and twenty-nine dollars*	Rec'd from P. JENNINGS the sum of *Eighty-one dollars and ninety cents*
For: Payment of April Account	For: Payment on Account	For: Payment of April Account
Cash/Chq. $247.65 Discount 6.35 Amt Owing $254.00	Cash/Chq. $192.00	Cash/Chq. $81.90 Discount 2.10 Amt Owing $84.00

Cash register records

Cash Register Record 4/5/19XX	Cash Register Record 17/5/19XX	Cash Register Record 28/5/19XX
Sales $181.05 Sales Tax 31.95 Total Sales $213.00	Sales $156.40 Sales Tax 27.60 Total Sales $184.00	Sales $66.30 Sales Tax 11.70 Total Sales $78.00

Cash Register Record 29/5/19XX
Sales $137.70 Sales Tax   24.30 Total Sales $162.00

Cheque butts

Cheque No. 98105 Date: *2 May 19XX* To: *CITY REAL ESTATE* For: *Rent* This cheque: $230.00	Cheque No. 98106 Date: *7 May 19XX* To: *P. WILSON* For: *Payment of April Account* This cheque: $224.25 Discount: 5.75	Cheque No. 98107 Date: *16 May 19XX* To: *CASH* For: *Wages* This cheque: $500.00

Cheque No. 98108
Date: *21 May 19XX*
 	
To: *M. KHAYAT*
For: *Payment on Account*
 	
This cheque: $128.00
	Cheque No. 98109
	Date: *25 May 19XX*
	
	To: *CASH*
	For: *Wages*
	
	This cheque: $500.00
		Cheque No. 98110
		Date: *29 May 19XX*
		
		To: *CASH*
		For: *Petty Cash Reimbursement*
		  Postage $ 9.00
		  Travel 15.00
		
		This cheque: $24.00

Statement of Account

Westpac Banking Corporation
GREEN BAY   NSW

SPECIMEN ONLY

This statement: **MAY**

Green Bay Electrics
72 Wattle Road
GREEN BAY NSW 2821

Account No.: **48-623**
Sheet No.: **61**

Name of account: **GREEN BAY ELECTRICS**

Date	Particulars		Debit	Credit	Balance
19XX					
1 MAY	BROUGHT FORWARD				6733.00 CR
2 MAY	C/C			192.00	6925.00 CR
4 MAY		98099	64.00		6861.00 CR
		98103	149.00		6712.00 CR
6 MAY	C/C			213.00	6925.00 CR
		98105	230.00		6695.00 CR
8 MAY	C/C			247.65	6942.65 CR
18 MAY		98107	500.00		6442.65 CR
19 MAY	C/C			376.00	6818.65 CR
22 MAY	C/C			81.90	6900.55 CR
27 MAY		98109	500.00		6400.55 CR
29 MAY	DD — K. Lewis			280.45	6681.00 CR
	C/C			78.00	6759.00 CR
30 MAY	STATE GOVT TAX ON WITHDRAWALS		7.20		6751.80 CR
	STATE GOVT TAX ON DEPOSITS		4.80		6747.00 CR
		98110	24.00		6723.00 CR
	CHQ BK		25.00		6698.00 CR

Once you have completed these procedures, you are required to carry out the following.

(a) Enter the balance b/d in the cash book for 1 June 19XX.
(b) Check that the information contained on the following source documents for June is correct, and correct any irregularities in accordance with guidelines set out in the firm's policies and procedures manual. If there are inconsistencies between the amounts in figures and the amounts in words, assume the amounts in figures are correct.
(c) After verification, enter details of documents into the cash book for June.
(d) Verify the entry of details from these documents in the cash book by ticking each document against the cash book entry.
(e) Check the mathematical accuracy of figures entered in the cash book. Note and correct errors in accordance with organisational policies and procedures.
(f) Compare the cash book and the bank statement for June. Don't forget to check the previous month's bank reconciliation statement.
(g) Adjust the cash book by adding items that are in the bank statement but not in the cash book.
(h) Balance the cash book at the end of June 19XX.
(i) Prepare a bank reconciliation statement as at 30 June 19XX. This must agree with the cash book balance.

Duplicates of receipts

Rec. No. 234	Rec. No. 235	Rec. No. 236
Date: *3 June 19XX*	Date: *10 June 19XX*	Date: *20 June 19XX*
Rec'd from CENTRAL REALTY the sum of *Three hundred and five dollars*	Rec'd from *E. NAGY* the sum of *Two hundred and seventeen dollars*	Rec'd from *A. MELTON* the sum of *Two hundred and eighteen dollars*
For: *Rent Received*	For: *Payment on Account*	For: *Payment of May Account*
Cash/Chq. $315.00	Cash/Chq. $217.00	Cash/Chq. $218.40 Discount 5.60 Amt Owing $224.00

Rec. No. 237
Date: 26 June 19XX

Rec'd from P. JENNINGS the sum of One hundred and fifty-nine dollars ninety cents

For: Payment of May Account

Cash/Chq.	$159.90
Discount	4.10
Amt Owing	$164.00

Cash register records

Cash Register Record 3/6/19XX	
Sales	$367.20
Sales Tax	64.80
Total Sales	$432.00

Cash Register Record 12/6/19XX	
Sales	$319.18
Sales Tax	56.32
Total Sales	$375.50

Cash Register Record 20/6/19XX	
Sales	$251.60
Sales Tax	44.40
Total Sales	$296.00

Cash Register Record 25/6/19XX	
Sales	$715.91
Sales Tax	126.34
Total Sales	$842.25

Cheque butts

Cheque No. 98111
Date: 4 June 19XX

To: P. WILSON
For: Payment of May Account

This cheque:	$319.80
Discount:	8.20

Cheque No. 98112
Date: 12 June 19XX

To: CASH
For: Wages

This cheque: $500.00

Cheque No. 98113
Date: 16 June 19XX

To: CITY REAL ESTATE
For: Rent

This cheque: $230.00

Cheque No. 98114
Date: 21 June 19XX

To: M. KHAYAT
For: Payment on Account

This cheque: $180.00

Cheque No. 98115
Date: 26 June 19XX

To: CASH
For: Wages

This cheque: $500.00

Cheque No. 98116
Date: 28 June 19XX

To: GENERAL POWER CO.
For: Electricity

This cheque: $260.00

Statement of Account

Westpac Banking Corporation
GREEN BAY NSW

SPECIMEN ONLY

This statement: **JUNE**

Green Bay Electrics
72 Wattle Road
GREEN BAY NSW 2821

Account No. **48-623**
Sheet No. **62**

Name of account: **GREEN BAY ELECTRICS**

Date	Particulars		Debit	Credit	Balance
19XX					
1 JUNE	BROUGHT FORWARD				6698.00 CR
2 JUNE	C/C			162.00	6860.00 CR
3 JUNE		98106	224.25		6635.75 CR
5 JUNE	C/C			747.00	7382.75 CR
		98108	128.00		7254.75 CR
7 JUNE		98111	319.80		6934.95 CR
12 JUNE	C/C			217.00	7151.95 CR
	CHQ BK		25.00		7126.95 CR
14 JUNE	C/C			375.50	7502.45 CR
		98112	500.00		7002.45 CR
22 JUNE	C/C			514.40	7516.85 CR
		98114	180.00		7336.85 CR
28 JUNE	C/C			842.25	8179.10 CR
		98115	500.00		7679.10 CR
29 JUNE	DD — K. Lewis			280.45	7959.55 CR
	STATE GOVT TAX ON WITHDRAWALS		7.40		7952.15 CR
	STATE GOVT TAX ON DEPOSITS		6.80		7945.35 CR
	RTD — E. Nagy		217.00		7728.35 CR

CHAPTER 6

Cash control

WHEN you have studied this chapter and completed the exercises, you should be competent in the following skills. Tick each skill when you have completed the relevant section.

LEARNING OUTCOMES

1. Maintain a petty cash system by recording and balancing petty cash transactions according to organisational procedures.
   - Check petty cash claims for accuracy and authenticity.
   - Record petty cash transactions in petty cash book and balance and reimburse fund at designated times or when applicable.
   - Present petty cash records to appropriate authority for checking within designated times.
   - Observe organisational policies and procedures for accountability, security and control of cash when maintaining petty cash system.

2. Prepare cash received daily for banking and complete appropriate banking documents.
   - Check record of day's takings against cash book entries.
   - Prepare cash, cheques and credit card summary for banking according to receiving bank's guidelines.
   - Accurately record details of cash, cheques and credit card transactions on bank deposit forms according to receiving bank's guidelines.

3. Reconcile cash records and prepare a bank reconciliation statement.
   - Adjust cash book for dishonoured cheques, bank charges and direct bank debits; total and balance cash book.
   - Identify and rectify discrepancies by comparing cash book with bank statement, identifying errors and taking appropriate action or referring to appropriate authority for rectification.

MAINTAINING A PETTY CASH SYSTEM

What is petty cash?

As part of a firm's 'cash secure' policy, it is normal business practice for all payments to be made by cheque. This is because cash is easy to misappropriate, whereas cheques provide written records of amounts paid out in both the company's and the bank's records.

However, cash is needed to pay for small day-to-day expenses involved in a business, such as tea and coffee, magazines and newspapers, flowers, parking fees, postage and bus and train fares. For this purpose, businesses operate a petty cash system.

The imprest petty cash system

The petty cash system is commonly managed by use of the **imprest system**. An initial sum of money is withdrawn from the bank by cheque. The amount will vary according to the needs and policy of the business — but is usually between $50 and $300. This is kept in the petty cash box or tin and is called the 'petty cash float'.

A member of staff, sometimes called the **petty cashier**, is put in charge of this petty cash float. This person is responsible for:
- the security of this money
- making payments when necessary
- writing up and balancing the petty cash book (which is the record of money advanced, payments made, and amounts received to reimburse the petty cash float)
- replenishing the petty cash float
- ensuring that funds are used for nominated petty cash items according to organisational policies and procedures.

The following is a simple illustration of the imprest system.

Imprest amount	$200
less amount spent (as per vouchers)	150
Cash (or balance) on hand	50
plus reimbursement cheque	150
Fund restored to original amount	**$200**
less amount spent (as per vouchers)	180
Cash on hand	20
plus reimbursement cheque	180
Fund restored to original amount	**$200**
and so on	

From the previous example, you will see that no matter how many times this cycle is repeated, the following formulae remain constant.

During the period, Imprest amount = Cash on hand + Expenditure (total of vouchers).

After balancing, Imprest amount = Cash on hand + Reimbursement amount.

To make a claim for money spent, the member of staff who spends the money must complete a petty cash voucher. If possible, a receipt for the amount spent should be attached to the petty cash voucher. The voucher is signed by the person claiming the payment. In some instances, the claim must also be signed by the claimant's supervisor authorising the payment.

Example
On 1 May 19XX, R. Miller spends $14.50 for tea and coffee for staff morning teas. An example of a completed petty cash voucher is shown below, followed by an explanation of the information contained in a petty cash voucher.

```
                                        NO. 1  ①
            Petty Cash Voucher
                      ② Date... 1 May 19XX

       ③ DEBIT      Sundry expenses

       ④ Particulars   Tea and coffee

       ⑤ Received   R. Miller   ⑥ $   14.50
```

A petty cash voucher includes the following information:
① a number, usually preprinted sequentially, to avoid misappropriation of funds
② the date on which the money was spent
③ the column in the petty cash book in which the amount is recorded (this is also the name of the account to which the item is charged in the firm's accounting system — tea and coffee is usually charged to 'Sundry or Miscellaneous Expenses' but may also be categorised as 'Staff Amenities')
④ a brief description of the purchase
⑤ the signature of the person receiving the money
⑥ the amount of the purchase.

A receipt for the purchase should be attached to the petty cash voucher. The receipt is proof that money was actually spent and includes written receipts, cash register receipts, cash sale dockets and credit card sales vouchers.

It is the responsibility of the petty cashier to check the accuracy and authenticity of petty cash claims before processing to ensure that:

- each claim is valid and has been incurred in accordance with organisational policies and procedures
- details on each voucher are correct and accurate, for example, the amount on the voucher is the same as the amount on the receipt
- expenditure has been authorised by the appropriate person
- each claim is supported by a receipt.

Some firms also require that a staff member receive an authorisation slip from a supervisor approving the petty cash claim. This approval is attached to the voucher and receipt and sighted by the petty cash fund cashier before payment is made from the petty cash fund. When the petty cashier is satisfied that all is in order, the cash is paid to the recipient who signs the voucher. The voucher is then placed in the petty cash tin.

EXERCISE 6.1 — R. Jagger & Co.

You are employed as petty cashier for R. Jagger & Co. During the first week of May, the following petty cash claims were made.

May 1   R. Miller spent $14.50 on tea and coffee
    2   K. Lyons spent $35.60 on a parcel to J. Timms, England
    3   F. Richards spent $20.00 on parking fees
    3   W. Peters spent $13.20 on six shorthand notebooks
    4   M. Watters spent $25.00 on flowers for the office
    5   B. Norman spent $15.50 on sandwiches for a sales meeting

Complete petty cash vouchers for these transactions. Use copies of the blank petty cash voucher on page 563 for this exercise and exercises 62–64. Remember to number each voucher sequentially. The following are the general ledger accounts to which these transactions will be debited:
- stationery
- postage
- travel expenses
- sundry expenses.

EXERCISE 6.2 M. Norman & Sons

You are employed by M. Norman & Sons as petty cashier. You are required to complete petty cash vouchers for the following. (Use the same four general ledger accounts as for exercise 6.1.)

April	7	L. Quinn spent $12.40 on tea and coffee
	8	G. Ford spent $28.00 on postage for a parcel to the United States
	10	M. Murray spent $48.00 on printing advertising handouts
	11	S. Hunter spent $15.50 on light globes
		F. Davies spent $4.00 on newspapers
	12	E. Owens spent $5.20 on bus fares

EXERCISE 6.3 Scientific Software

You are employed by Scientific Software as petty cashier. You are required to complete petty cash vouchers for the following, using the same general ledger accounts as in the previous exercises.

Sept.	9	S. Edwards spent $13.90 on magazines for reception area
	10	K. Abdullah spent $15.20 on taxi fares
	11	E. Huan spent $24.50 on copy paper
	14	S. Edwards spent $12.65 on tea and coffee
	16	E. Huan spent $18.00 on postage stamps
	17	K. Abdullah spent $1.70 on newspapers

EXERCISE 6.4 Snappy Photographers

You are employed by Snappy Photographers as petty cashier. You are required to complete petty cash vouchers for the following, using the same general ledger accounts as in the previous exercises.

Dec.	3	D. Garner spent $26.30 on printing of flyers
	4	E. Conway spent $18.20 on tea and coffee
	6	L. Rossi spent $22.40 on printer ribbons
	7	D. Garner spent $14.50 on taxi fares
	10	E. Conway spent $8.60 on cutting keys
	12	V. Chong spent $9.20 on parcel post

Recording petty cash transactions

The initial amount withdrawn to start the petty cash system is recorded in the cash payments book as 'Petty cash imprest' or **'Petty cash advance'**.

Example

On 1 May 19XX, R. Jagger & Co. commenced a petty cash float by drawing a cheque for the imprest amount of $300 made payable to 'Cash', cashing it at the bank and placing the $300 cash in the petty cash tin. An example of a cheque drawn to establish the petty cash imprest system is shown below.

1 May 19XX		
To Cash	**Westpac** Banking Corporation — SUNNY HILLS WA	First Bank in Australia
For Petty Cash — Imprest amount	Pay to Cash	1 / May /19 XX or bearer
	the sum of Three hundred dollars only — — — — — — —	$ 300.00
		R. JAGGER & CO.
$ 300.00	Cheque No. Branch BSB No. Account No.	SPECIMEN ONLY
8891432	⑈8891432 ⑈076⑈046⑈ 36⑈9439⑈	

As it would not be practical to have three $100 notes in the petty cash tin when paying out cash for small purchases, a change slip will need to be prepared and presented at the bank. This is a request that the cash received is made up of a number of smaller denominations of notes and coins.

The imprest cheque is recorded on the cash payments page of the cash book, as shown below. The cash book is usually set up so that receipts are shown on the left-hand page and payments are shown on the right-hand page. We will refer to these as the 'cash receipts book' and the 'cash payments book'.

CASH PAYMENTS BOOK OF R. JAGGER & CO.

Date	Chq. no.	Particulars	Fol.	Discount received	Sundry creditors	Purchases	Wages	General	Bank*
19XX May 1	432	Petty Cash Imprest						300.00	300.00

* The 'Bank' column records the total amount of each cheque.

Petty cash book

After the cheque is cashed and the money is placed in the petty cash tin, the amount is entered into the petty cash book. The petty cash book may be in the form of a book or ledger, ruled in columns to allow for the recording of:
- date
- amount received
- particulars, in other words, the reason for expenditure
- voucher number
- total amount shown on voucher
- dissection columns for expenditure.

The petty cash system may also be maintained electronically. It may form part of a sophisticated accounting software package, or it may be as simple as a spreadsheet model into which the petty cashier enters details from the petty cash vouchers. Usually the accounting software is protected and the petty cashier may have to enter a specified code or security number to gain access.

Example

Set out below is the manually maintained petty cash book of R. Jagger & Co. into which the imprest amount has been recorded.

PETTY CASH BOOK OF R. JAGGER & CO.

Amount received	Date	Particulars	Voucher no.	Total	Stationery	Postage	Travel expenses	Sundry expenses
300.00	19XX May 1	Imprest cheque						

At the end of the period selected (for example, weekly or monthly) or, in some cases, when the petty cash float is low, the petty cashier is required to write up and balance the petty cash book. It is decided by R. Jagger & Co. that the petty cash float will be replenished on a weekly basis.

To record petty cash transactions, the following steps are required.
1. Enter the transactions into the petty cash book from details on the petty cash vouchers.
2. Total the expenditure (amount spent) in the book.
3. Count the cash remaining in the petty cash tin.
4. The total expenditure for the period plus the cash on hand should equal the original petty cash advance (imprest amount).
5. Request that a cheque be drawn to reimburse (or replenish) the petty cash tin for the amount spent.
6. The amount of the reimbursement cheque plus the cash on hand should equal the original petty cash advance (imprest amount).

Example

After checking the following claims for accuracy and authenticity (as explained on page 411), the petty cashier for R. Jagger & Co. records the details in the petty cash book as shown.

	NO. 1
PETTY CASH VOUCHER	
DATE:	1 May 19XX
DEBIT:	SUNDRY EXPENSES
Particulars:	Tea and coffee
$14.50	Signed: *R. Miller*

	NO. 2
PETTY CASH VOUCHER	
DATE:	2 May 19XX
DEBIT:	POSTAGE
Particulars:	Parcel to England
$35.60	Signed: *K. Lyons*

	NO. 3
PETTY CASH VOUCHER	
DATE:	3 May 19XX
DEBIT:	TRAVEL EXPENSES
Particulars:	Parking fees
$20.00	Signed: *J. Richards*

	NO. 4
PETTY CASH VOUCHER	
DATE:	3 May 19XX
DEBIT:	STATIONERY
Particulars:	6 shorthand notebooks
$13.20	Signed: *W. Peters*

	NO. 5
PETTY CASH VOUCHER	
DATE:	4 May 19XX
DEBIT:	SUNDRY EXPENSES
Particulars:	Flowers for office
$25.00	Signed: *M. Watters*

	NO. 6
PETTY CASH VOUCHER	
DATE:	5 May 19XX
DEBIT:	SUNDRY EXPENSES
Particulars:	Sandwiches — meeting
$15.50	Signed: *B. Norman*

PETTY CASH BOOK OF R. JAGGER & CO.

Amount received	Date	Particulars	Voucher no.	Total	Stationery	Postage	Travel expenses	Sundry expenses
300.00	19XX May 1	Imprest (Chq. No. 1432)						
		Tea and coffee	1	14.50				14.50
	2	Parcel — J. Timms	2	35.60		35.60		
	3	Parking fees	3	20.00			20.00	
		Shorthand notebooks	4	13.20	13.20			
	4	Flowers — office	5	25.00				25.00
	5	Sandwiches — meeting	6	15.50				15.50

Balancing the petty cash book

To balance the petty cash book you need to ascertain:
- the amount spent
- the amount of cash on hand
- the reimbursement amount.

Amount spent

To ascertain the amount spent, total all the expenditure columns. The 'Total' column should equal the sum of the 'dissection' columns (Stationery, Postage, Travel expenses and Sundry expenses). Rule off the 'dissection' columns as shown below.

PETTY CASH BOOK OF R. JAGGER & CO.

Amount received	Date	Particulars	Voucher no.	Total	Stationery	Postage	Travel expenses	Sundry expenses
300.00	19XX May 1	Imprest (Chq. No. 1432)						
		Tea and coffee	1	14.50				14.50
	2	Parcel — J. Timms	2	35.60		35.60		
	3	Parking fees	3	20.00			20.00	
		Shorthand notebooks	4	13.20	13.20			
	4	Flowers — office	5	25.00				25.00
	5	Sandwiches — meeting	6	15.50				15.50
				123.80	= 13.20	+ 35.60	+ 20.00	+ 55.00

Amount of cash on hand

All the cash remaining in the tin is then counted. The amount of cash on hand is recorded in the petty cash book, as shown below. The amount spent (as per vouchers) plus the cash on hand equals the original imprest amount.

Both the 'Amount received' and 'Total' columns are totalled and ruled off. The amount of cash on hand is then shown (b/d) in the 'Amount received' column.

PETTY CASH BOOK OF R. JAGGER & CO.

Amount received	Date	Particulars	Voucher no.	Total	Stationery	Postage	Travel expenses	Sundry expenses
300.00	19XX May 1	Imprest (Chq. No. 1432)						
		Tea and coffee	1	14.50				14.50
	2	Parcel — J. Timms	2	35.60		35.60		
	3	Parking fees	3	20.00			20.00	
		Shorthand notebooks	4	13.20	13.20			
	4	Flowers — office	5	25.00				25.00
	5	Sandwiches — meeting	6	15.50				15.50
				123.80	13.20	35.60	20.00	55.00
	8	Cash on hand	c/d	176.20				
300.00				300.00				
176.20		Cash on hand	b/d					

Reimbursement amount

The reimbursement cheque is equal to the amount spent during the period. The reimbursement cheque is drawn and cashed and the cash is placed in the petty cash tin to bring the total amount of cash back to the amount of the original petty cash advance.

The amount of the reimbursement cheque is entered below 'Cash on hand' in the 'Amount received' column. The cash on hand plus the reimbursement amount equals the original imprest amount. Additional petty cash transactions may now be entered in the usual way, as follows.

PETTY CASH BOOK OF R. JAGGER & CO.

Amount received	Date	Particulars	Voucher no.	Total	Stationery	Postage	Travel expenses	Sundry expenses
300.00	19XX May 1	Imprest cheque	1432					
		Tea and coffee	1	14.50				14.50
	2	Parcel — J. Timms	2	35.60		35.60		
	3	Parking fees	3	20.00			20.00	
		Shorthand notebooks	4	13.20	13.20			
	4	Flowers — office	5	25.00				25.00
	5	Sandwiches — meeting	6	15.50				15.50
				①123.80	13.20	35.60	20.00	55.00
	8	Cash on hand	c/d	②176.20				
300.00				300.00				
② 176.20		Cash on hand	b/d					
③ 123.80		Reimbursement cheque	1448					
	9	Taxi fares	7	28.00			28.00	
	10	Tea/Coffee	8	14.50				14.50

Petty cash book		**Petty cash tin**
① Total amount spent (expenditure)	=	Total value of vouchers in tin
② Balance (cash on hand)	=	Cash remaining in tin. (This amount must agree with the money left in the petty cash tin. It represents the imprest amount *less* the amount spent.)
③ Reimbursement cheque amount	=	Amount of cash needed to replenish the petty cash float back to the amount of the initial advance (imprest amount *less* cash on hand).

In maintaining the petty cash system, it is helpful to be aware that during the period:

Cash on hand + Total value of vouchers = Original imprest amount.

After balancing:

Cash on hand + Amount of reimbursement cheque = Original imprest amount.

As part of the internal controls of the business, spot checks are often done to ensure that no fraudulent activity occurs.

An example of a petty cash reimbursement cheque is set out below, listing on the cheque butt the amount to be charged to the relevant expense accounts in the bookkeeping system. Usually the accountant checks that the petty cash has balanced and draws the cheque for the reimbursement. In a small business, the petty cash fund cashier may be called upon to fill in the required details on the cheque and present it to the appropriate person (or persons) for signature.

8 May 19XX		
To Cash	**Westpac** Banking Corporation	First Bank in Australia
	SUNNY HILLS WA	8 / May /19 XX
For Petty Cash	Pay to Cash	or bearer
Reimbursement	the sum of One hundred and twenty-three dollars	
Stationery $13.20	80 cents —	$ 123.80
Postage 35.60		R. JAGGER & CO.
Travel expenses 20.00		
Sundry expenses 55.00	Cheque No. Branch BSB No. Account No.	SPECIMEN ONLY
$ 123.80	⑈8891448 ⑈076⑈046⑉ 36⑈9439⑈	
8891448		

The reimbursement cheque is recorded in the cash payments book as follows.

CASH PAYMENTS BOOK OF R. JAGGER & CO.

Date	Chq. no.	Particulars	Fol.	Discount received	Sundry creditors	Purchases	Wages	General	Bank
19XX May 1	432	Petty Cash (imprest)						300.00	300.00
7	448	Petty Cash Reimbursement							
		Stationery						13.20	
		Postage						35.60	
		Travel expenses						20.00	
		Sundry expenses						55.00	123.80

The amounts listed in the expenditure break-up on the cheque butt are charged to the appropriate expense accounts in the bookkeeping system. They are recorded in the cash payments book and posted to the relevant accounts in the general ledger.

The only time that a posting is made to the petty cash imprest account in the general ledger is for the amount of the initial petty cash advance. The only exception to this is when the imprest amount — the amount of the original advance — needs to be increased or decreased.

Example

Let us assume that R. Jagger & Co. finds that $300 is insufficient funds for the imprest petty cash system and decides to increase that amount to $400 when the petty cash book is next balanced. On 14 May, the reimbursement amount needed to replenish the fund is $280, plus $100 to increase the imprest amount to $400. This is recorded on the reimbursement cheque as follows.

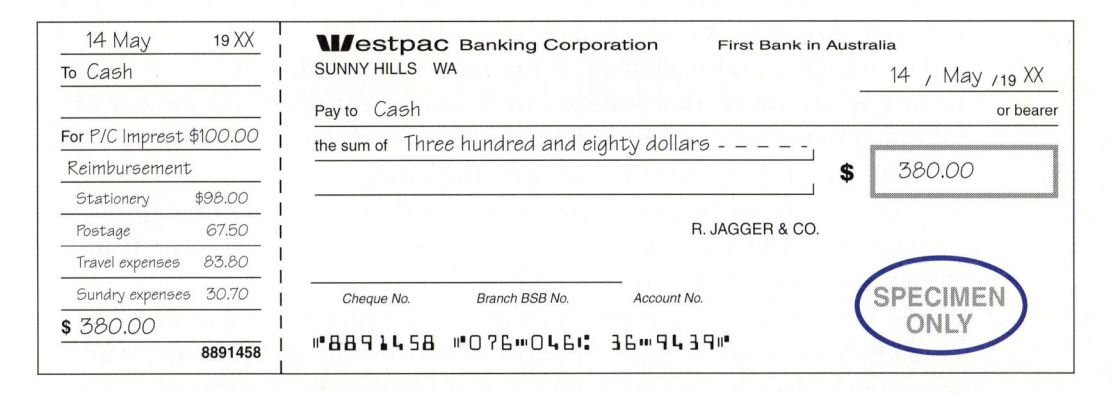

14 May 19XX		Westpac Banking Corporation — First Bank in Australia
To Cash		SUNNY HILLS WA
For P/C Imprest $100.00		14 / May / 19 XX
Reimbursement		Pay to Cash — or bearer
Stationery $98.00		the sum of Three hundred and eighty dollars - - - - - $ 380.00
Postage 67.50		R. JAGGER & CO.
Travel expenses 83.80		
Sundry expenses 30.70		Cheque No. Branch BSB No. Account No.
$ 380.00		SPECIMEN ONLY
8891458		⑊8891458 ⑊076⑊0461: 36⑊9439⑊

The details are entered into the cash book in the following way.

CASH PAYMENTS BOOK OF R. JAGGER & CO.

Date	Chq. no.	Particulars	Fol.	Discount received	Trade creditors	General	Bank
19XX							
May 1	432	Petty Cash (imprest)				300.00	300.00
7	448	Petty Cash Reimbursement					
		Stationery				13.20	
		Postage				35.60	
		Travel expenses				20.00	
		Sundry expenses				55.00	123.80
14	458	Petty Cash (imprest)				100.00	
		Petty Cash Reimbursement					
		Stationery				98.00	
		Postage				67.50	
		Travel expenses				83.80	
		Sundry expenses				30.70	380.00

Regardless of when a firm balances its petty cash system, it is important that the petty cash book is balanced and the fund replenished on the last day of the reporting period. If this is not done at the balance date, the expenses represented by the vouchers in the petty cash tin will not be included in the expense section of the Profit and Loss account, thus understating the expenses for the period under review.

Manual versus computerised petty cash systems

We have discussed in detail the recording, balancing and replenishing of the imprest petty cash system. As you have seen, performing this manually can be very time-consuming. By computerising the petty cash process, however, some of the steps in the manual recording are performed automatically. For example, a code may be keyed in so that when the amount of the voucher is entered into the 'Total' column, it is automatically entered into the appropriate 'dissection' column.

The totalling and balancing of the petty cash book is an automatic procedure in an accounting software package. In a spreadsheet model, when all the amounts are entered, the calculation is done automatically to provide the amount needed to reimburse the fund.

It should always be remembered that, although a computer processes data speedily and accurately, it cannot calculate the correct answers unless the operator enters the correct information.

The benefits for a business of using a computerised accounting system are largely in terms of time and ease of processing. If a business wants to computerise its accounting system, it can employ the services of a consultant who is experienced in setting up systems to suit the specific needs of particular businesses or it can purchase a commercial accounting package, such as Attaché and MYOB.

EXERCISE 6.5 T. Giananey & Co.

T. Giananey & Co. commences an imprest petty cash system on 1 June 19XX with $250. Petty cash is used six times during the following week, as shown on the petty cash vouchers on page 421. As petty cashier you are required to carry out the following. Use the blank forms that follow on pages 421–422 to complete this exercise.

1. Prepare a cheque ready for signature for the original imprest amount. (Note: In a real-life situation, of course, the cheque would be cashed and the money placed in the tin *before* any vouchers were written and paid.)
2. Enter the imprest amount in the petty cash book.
3. Check petty cash claims for accuracy and authenticity and record them in the petty cash book.
4. Balance the book on 7 June.
5. Prepare a cheque ready for signature to reimburse the petty cash tin for the amount spent.

CHAPTER 6: CASH CONTROL | 421

NO. 1	NO. 2	NO. 3
PETTY CASH VOUCHER	**PETTY CASH VOUCHER**	**PETTY CASH VOUCHER**
DATE: *1 June 19XX*	DATE: *2 June 19XX*	DATE: *4 June 19XX*
DEBIT: *SUNDRY EXPENSES*	DEBIT: *POSTAGE*	DEBIT: *TRAVEL EXPENSES*
Particulars: *Tea and coffee*	Particulars: *Stamps*	Particulars: *Parking fees*
$ 6.70 Signed: *J. Willis*	$28.50 Signed: *R. Patel*	$12.00 Signed: *L. Boian*

NO. 4	NO. 5	NO. 6
PETTY CASH VOUCHER	**PETTY CASH VOUCHER**	**PETTY CASH VOUCHER**
DATE: *4 June 19XX*	DATE: *4 June 19XX*	DATE: *7 June 19XX*
DEBIT: *STATIONERY*	DEBIT: *SUNDRY EXPENSES*	DEBIT: *SUNDRY EXPENSES*
Particulars: *Printer paper*	Particulars: *Newspapers*	Particulars: *Tin of paint*
$28.20 Signed: *P. Chai*	$ 8.00 Signed: *A. Dennis*	$ 7.25 Signed: *M. East*

19 XX

Westpac Banking Corporation   First Bank in Australia
FOREST VALLEY   TAS

To _____   /   /19
                 Pay to   or bearer
For _____
                 the sum of
                                                         $

                             T. GIANANEY & CO.

$ _____   SPECIMEN ONLY
   1103276   Cheque No.   Branch BSB No.   Account No.
                 ⑈1103276 ⑈032⑈076⑉ 65⑈4321⑈

PETTY CASH BOOK OF T. GIANANEY & CO.

Amount received	Date	Particulars	Voucher no.	Total	Stationery	Postage	Travel expenses	Sundry expenses
				c/f				

EXERCISE 6.6 M. Da Silva & Sons

M. Da Silva & Sons commences a petty cash imprest system on 1 July 19XX with $350. As petty cashier you made the payments shown below and on page 423 for vouchers received. You are required to carry out the following.

1. Complete a cheque for the imprest amount.
2. Enter the imprest amount and transactions in the petty cash book.
3. Balance the book on 7 July.
4. Complete a cheque to reimburse the petty cash tin for the amount spent.

Use the blank forms on pages 423–424 to complete this exercise.

NO. 1
PETTY CASH VOUCHER
DATE: *1 July 19XX*
DEBIT: *POSTAGE*
Particulars: *Stamps*
$32.00   Signed: *A. Hines*

NO. 2
PETTY CASH VOUCHER
DATE: *2 July 19XX*
DEBIT: *TRAVEL EXPENSES*
Particulars: *Bus fares*
$ 5.20   Signed: *C. Starr*

NO. 3
PETTY CASH VOUCHER
DATE: *3 July 19XX*
DEBIT: *SUNDRY EXPENSES*
Particulars: *Flowers*
$18.00   Signed: *G. Byrne*

NO. 4
PETTY CASH VOUCHER
DATE: *4 July 19XX*
DEBIT: *STATIONERY*
Particulars: *Printer ribbons*
$48.20   Signed: *L. Ho*

NO. 5
PETTY CASH VOUCHER
DATE: *4 July 19XX*
DEBIT: *SUNDRY EXPENSES*
Particulars: *Newspapers*
$ 8.00   Signed: *J. James*

NO. 6
PETTY CASH VOUCHER
DATE: *7 July 19XX*
DEBIT: *STATIONERY*
Particulars: *2 dozen biros*
$20.80   Signed: *B. Firenze*

CHAPTER 6: CASH CONTROL | 423

NO. 7
PETTY CASH VOUCHER
DATE: *7 July 19XX*
DEBIT: *SUNDRY EXPENSES*
Particulars: *Duplicate keys*
$29.00   Signed: *J. James*

NO. 8
PETTY CASH VOUCHER
DATE: *8 July 19XX*
DEBIT: *POSTAGE*
Particulars: *Airmail packages*
$45.30   Signed: *B. Firenze*

NO. 9
PETTY CASH VOUCHER
DATE: *10 July 19XX*
DEBIT: *TRAVEL EXPENSES*
Particulars: *Parking fees*
$22.00   Signed: *T. Jason*

PETTY CASH BOOK OF M. DA SILVA & SONS

Amount received	Date	Particulars	Voucher no.	Total	Stationery	Postage	Travel expenses	Sundry expenses
			c/f					

---

19 XX

To _____
For _____
_____
_____
$ _____
3742613

Westpac Banking Corporation   First Bank in Australia
MT GAMBIER   SA
                                    /   /19
Pay to _____ or bearer
the sum of _____
_____ $ [   ]
                              M. DA SILVA & SONS

Cheque No.   Branch BSB No.   Account No.
⑈ 3 7 4 2 6 1 3 ⑈ 0 4 1 ⋯ 3 4 2 ⑈:   9 8 ⋯ 7 6 5 4 ⑈

SPECIMEN ONLY

Cheque 1

Westpac Banking Corporation — First Bank in Australia
MT GAMBIER SA

19 XX
To _____
For _____

Pay to _____ or bearer
the sum of _____
$ _____

M. DA SILVA & SONS

Cheque No. 3742626 Branch BSB No. 041-342 Account No. 98-7654

SPECIMEN ONLY

EXERCISE 6.7 — P. Georgiou & Co.

P. Georgiou & Co. commences an imprest petty cash system on 1 August 19XX with $100. As petty cashier you authorised the payments shown below for vouchers received. You are required to carry out the following.

1. Complete a cheque for the imprest amount.
2. Enter the imprest amount and transactions in the petty cash book.
3. Balance the petty cash book on 8 August.
4. Complete a cheque to reimburse the petty cash tin for the amount spent.

Use the blank form below and on page 425 to complete this exercise.

Aug. 1	Post-it Notes, $3.60
	Bus fares, $4.80
2	Tea and coffee, $5.60
	Airmail postage, $4.20
3	File folders, $7.60
	Taxi fare, $9.20
4	Cleaning materials, $8.50
	Postage stamps, $9.00
5	Newspapers, $6.00

Cheque 2

Westpac Banking Corporation — First Bank in Australia
WHITE PLAINS NSW

19 XX
To _____
For _____

Pay to _____ or bearer
the sum of _____
$ _____

P. GEORGIOU & CO.

Cheque No. 4967321 Branch BSB No. 012-156 Account No. 98-3498

SPECIMEN ONLY

CHAPTER 6: CASH CONTROL | 425

	19 XX	**W**estpac Banking Corporation	First Bank in Australia
To		WHITE PLAINS NSW	/ /19
		Pay to	or bearer
For		the sum of	
			$
		for and on behalf of P. GEORGIOU & CO.	
$		Cheque No. Branch BSB No. Account No.	SPECIMEN ONLY
	4967329	⑈4967329⑈ ⑆012⑈156⑆ 98⑈3498⑈	

PETTY CASH BOOK OF P. GEORGIOU & CO.

Amount received	Date	Particulars	Voucher no.	Total	Stationery	Postage	Travel expenses	Sundry expenses
				c/f				

EXERCISE 6.8 Suregrow Seedling Co.

You are employed as petty cashier for Suregrow Seedling Co. and it is your responsibility to set up the petty cash fund. On 1 May 19XX, you cash the imprest cheque for $100, place the cash in the petty cash tin and make the payments shown below for vouchers received. Using a copy of the blank petty cash book master provided on page 564, carry out the following.

1. Record the imprest amount and the petty cash transactions in the petty cash book.
2. Balance the petty cash book at the end of the month, carry down the cash on hand and cash reimbursement cheque and record the amount ready for the recording of next month's vouchers.

Date		Voucher no.	Particulars	Amount ($)
May	1	128	Air mail postage	4.90
	4	129	Postage stamps	5.25
	7	130	Post-it Notes	2.40
	8	131	Printer ribbons	15.60
	12	132	Taxi fares	8.50
	14	133	Tea and coffee	5.80
	20	134	Fineline pens	4.80
	22	135	Light bulbs	2.37
	27	136	Postage	7.60
	31	137	Repairs to lock	12.40

EXERCISE 6.9 Napoli Furniture Co.

You are employed as petty cashier for Napoli Furniture Co. and it is your responsibility to set up the petty cash fund. On 1 September 19XX, you cash the imprest cheque for $150, place the cash in the petty cash tin and make the payments shown on page 427 for vouchers received. Using a copy of the blank petty cash book master provided on page 564, carry out the following.

1. Record the imprest amount and petty cash transactions in the petty cash book.
2. Balance the petty cash book at the end of the month, carry down the cash on hand and cash reimbursement cheque and record the amount ready for the recording of next month's vouchers.

Date	Voucher no.	Particulars	Amount ($)
Sept. 2	111	Shorthand pads	3.94
5	112	Postage stamps	9.00
7	113	Taxi fare	8.60
8	114	Parcel post	2.30
10	115	Tea and coffee	8.80
13	116	Window cleaning	25.00
18	117	Notepads	7.20
21	118	Staples	4.50
28	119	Flowers for reception	15.00
30	120	Ink cartridge for printer	49.95

EXERCISE 6.10   Kiddiworld Toy Co.

You are employed as petty cashier for Kiddiworld Toy Co. and it is your responsibility to set up the petty cash fund. On 1 August 19XX, you cash the imprest cheque for $80, place the cash in the petty cash tin and make the payments shown below for vouchers received. Using a copy of the blank petty cash book master provided on page 564, carry out the following.

1. Record the imprest amount and petty cash transactions in the petty cash book.
2. Balance the petty cash book at the end of the month, carry down the cash on hand and cash reimbursement cheque and record the amount ready for the recording of the next month's vouchers.

Date	Voucher no.	Particulars	Amount ($)
Aug. 2	263	Air mail postage	4.20
5	264	File folders	7.60
7	265	Taxi fare	9.20
8	266	Cleaning material	8.50
10	267	Postage stamps	9.00
13	268	Newspapers	6.00
18	269	Stamp pad ink	3.60
21	270	Bus fares	4.80
28	271	Tea and coffee	5.75
31	272	Printer ribbon	15.60

Note: The following exercises contain an additional dissection category for 'Repairs and maintenance'. (You will need to add this heading to the master on page 564.)

EXERCISE 6.11 Mitchell Engineering Ltd

You are employed by Mitchell Engineering Ltd and take over the duties of petty cashier on 1 May 19XX. The petty cash fund was established with a petty cash advance of $150 and was balanced at the end of April.

You pay the amounts shown below during May. Using a copy of the blank petty cash book master provided on page 564, carry out the following.
1. Record the vouchers in the petty cash book.
2. Balance the petty cash book at the end of the month, carry down cash on hand and cash reimbursement cheque and record the amount ready for the recording of next month's vouchers.

Date	Voucher no.	Particulars	Amount ($)
May 1	161	Air mail postage	4.90
2	162	Postage stamps	5.25
5	163	Post-it Notes	2.40
8	164	Printer ribbons	15.60
10	165	Taxi fare	8.50
13	166	Tea and coffee	5.80
15	167	Biro pens and pencils	10.50
18	168	Light bulbs	2.37
	169	Postage	7.60
21	170	Repairs to lock	15.00
23	171	Paper towels	5.30
25	172	Milk and biscuits	3.20
27	173	Flowers — office	10.00
29	174	Parking fees	6.00
31	175	Bus fares	4.80

EXERCISE 6.12 Porter Art Supplies

You are employed by Porter Art Supplies and take over the duties of petty cashier on 1 July 19XX. The petty cash fund was established with a petty cash advance of $80 and has been balanced at the end of June.

You pay the amounts shown on page 429 during July. Using a copy of the blank petty cash book master provided on page 564, carry out the following.
1. Record the vouchers in the petty cash book.
2. Balance the petty cash book at the end of the month, carry down the cash on hand and cash reimbursement cheque and record the amount ready for the recording of next month's vouchers.

Date	Voucher no.	Particulars	Amount ($)
July 2	92	Shorthand notebooks	3.94
5	93	Postage stamps	9.00
8	94	Taxi fare	8.60
10	95	Postage — air mail	2.30
15	96	Tea and coffee	8.80
21	97	Repair broken lock	13.50
25	98	Notepads	7.20
28	99	Staples	4.50
31	100	Flowers for reception	15.00

EXERCISE 6.13 B-Jay Cookware

You are employed by B-Jay Cookware and take over the duties of petty cashier on 1 October 19XX. The petty cash fund was established with a petty cash advance of $150 and has been balanced at the end of September.

You pay the amounts shown below during October. Using the blank petty cash book master provided on page 564, carry out the following.

1. Record the vouchers in the petty cash book.
2. Balance the petty cash book at the end of the month, carry down the cash on hand and cash reimbursement cheque and record the amount ready for the recording of next month's vouchers.

Date	Voucher no.	Particulars	Amount ($)
Oct. 1	62	Paperclips, staples	6.20
3	63	Taxi fare	4.80
5	64	Manila folders	2.30
8	65	Light bulbs	3.25
12	66	Postage stamps	9.00
	67	Repair light switch	19.50
16	68	Copy paper	14.60
18	69	Post-it Notes	7.40
21	70	Tea and coffee	4.60
23	71	Ink for stamp pad	2.60
25	72	Repair door lock	16.80
26	73	Taxi fare	13.70
	74	Biro pens	15.60
28	75	Flowers for office	18.40
31	76	Parking fees	6.00

Note: The following exercises run for two or more balancing periods. Dissections used in these exercises are: Stationery, Postage, Travel expenses, Sundry expenses.

EXERCISE 6.14 Cornelli Design Studio

Cornelli Design Studio decides to operate an imprest petty cash system to cater for its daily incidental expenses. You are appointed as petty cashier. It is your responsibility to set up and maintain the system, as follows.

1. You commence the petty cash fund on 1 July by cashing the imprest cheque for $100 and placing the cash in the petty cash tin. Record the imprest amount in the petty cash book, using a copy of the blank petty cash book master provided on page 564.
2. At the end of the first week, the following claims have been made and you have checked them for accuracy and authenticity.

Date	Voucher no.	Particulars	Amount ($)
July 1	1	Tea and coffee	8.50
	2	File folders	6.25
2	3	Newspaper	1.20
3	4	Postage stamps	9.00
6	5	Taxi fares	12.50
7	6	Duplicate keys cut	8.20
8	7	Light bulbs	4.20

Record these transactions in the petty cash book and balance and reimburse the fund on 8 July 19XX.

3. Continue to record the following transactions in the petty cash book.

Date	Voucher no.	Particulars	Amount ($)
July 8	8	Flowers for office	18.60
9	9	Newspaper	1.20
	10	Taxi fares	16.50
10	11	4 Fineline pens	8.00
	12	Parcel post	17.80
13	13	Parking fees	4.00
	14	Photocopy paper	12.30
14	15	Postage stamps	9.00
15	16	Biscuits for morning tea	2.80

4. As cash is running very low, the petty cash book is balanced at this stage. When reimbursing the fund, it is decided to increase the imprest amount by an additional $50, making the total imprest amount $150. In the 'Amount received' column, record the imprest amount of $50, then record the reimbursement amount in the usual manner.

5. Continue to record the following transactions and, when completed, balance the petty cash book and reimburse the petty cash fund to the new petty cash imprest amount.

Date	Voucher no.	Particulars	Amount ($)
July 15	17	Flowers for office	18.00
16	18	Newspaper	2.40
	19	Parking fees	6.80
17	20	Staples	5.40
	21	Taxi fares	7.20
20	22	Postage stamps	18.00
	23	Shorthand notebooks	5.20
21	24	Tea and coffee	8.50

EXERCISE 6.15 Martin & Viveras

Use a copy of the blank petty cash book master provided on page 564 to complete this exercise.

Martin & Viveras, Solicitors, have employed you as petty cashier and you commence your duties on 1 April 19XX. The petty cash system has an imprest amount of $150 and all records are balanced at the above date and placed in your care. Over the next month the following petty cash expenditure is incurred.

Date	Voucher no.	Particulars	Amount ($)
Apr. 1	128	Newspapers	1.70
	129	Taxi fare	9.25
2	130	Light globes	5.40
	131	Postage stamps	9.00
5	132	Tea and milk	8.40
8	133	Parking meters	16.00
9	134	Window cleaning	22.50
10	135	Biscuits	6.30
15	136	File folders	8.80
19	137	Cartage	28.20

As the amount of cash in the tin is running low, you must balance the petty cash book. The reimbursement cheque is then drawn, cashed and placed in the tin. You record the petty cash expenses shown on page 432, after verification according to organisational policies and procedures.

Date	Voucher no.	Particulars	Amount ($)
Apr. 20	138	Advertising flyers	18.30
21	139	Fineline pens	24.00
	140	Newspapers	1.70
23	141	Taxi fares	17.50
24	142	Copy paper	32.40
25	143	Parcel postage	16.30
26	144	Flowers for office	18.00
29	145	Magazines for office	6.95
30	146	Tea and coffee	13.40

EXERCISE 6.16 S. Jetson & Sons

Use a copy of the blank petty cash book master provided on page 564 to complete this exercise.

S. Jetson & Sons has employed you as petty cashier and you commence your duties on 1 August 19XX. The petty cash system has an imprest amount of $150 and all records are balanced at the above date and placed in your care. Over the next month, the following petty cash expenditure is incurred.

Date	Voucher no.	Particulars	Amount ($)
Aug. 1	502	Magazines for reception	12.90
2	503	Parking fees	6.00
5	504	Tea and sugar	8.20
7	505	Copy paper	17.85
8	506	Postage — parcel	8.00
	507	Window cleaning	30.00
11	508	Light globes	4.50
12	509	Double adaptor	1.20
14	510	Postage stamps	18.00
16	511	Parking fees	8.00
19	512	Biro pens	12.60

As the amount of cash in the tin is running low, you must balance the petty cash book. The reimbursement cheque is then drawn, cashed and placed in the tin. Now record the petty cash expenses shown on page 433, after verification according to organisational policies and procedures.

Date	Voucher no.	Particulars	Amount ($)
Aug. 20	513	Bus fares	4.60
21	514	Donation	5.00
	515	Taxi fare	12.50
23	516	Staples	6.15
	517	Window cleaning	30.00
24	518	File folders	16.00
26	519	Coffee and tea	12.20
	520	Postage stamps	18.00
27	521	Newspapers	1.70
29	522	Milk and sugar	4.30
30	523	Postage — parcel	9.20
31	524	Parking fee	18.00

EXERCISE 6.17 — H. Singh & Co.

Use a copy of the blank petty cash book master provided on page 564 to complete this exercise.

H. Singh & Co., Importers, has employed you as petty cashier and you commence your duties on 1 February 19XX. The petty cash system has an imprest amount of $100 and all records are balanced at the above date and placed in your care. Over the next few days, the following petty cash expenditure is incurred.

Date	Voucher no.	Particulars	Amount ($)
Feb. 1	311	Copy paper	27.60
2	312	Taxi fare	18.30
5	313	Window cleaning	25.00
6	314	Tea and sugar	8.30

As the amount of cash in the tin is running low, you must balance the petty cash book. The reimbursement cheque is then drawn, cashed and placed in the tin. Now record the following petty cash expenses, after verification according to organisational policies and procedures.

Date	Voucher no.	Particulars	Amount ($)
Feb. 8	315	Magazines for reception	21.60
10	316	Taxi fares	16.50
12	317	Coffee and biscuits	8.50
13	318	Newspapers	1.70
15	319	Parking meter	8.00
18	320	Postage stamps	26.00

As the petty cash fund needs replenishing, you must balance the petty cash book on 18 February, cash the reimbursement cheque and record the following payments after verification.

Date	Voucher no.	Particulars	Amount ($)
Feb. 19	321	Fineline pens	24.00
22	322	Postage — parcel	10.20
24	323	Tea and sugar	8.30
26	324	Copy paper	27.30
27	325	Window cleaning	25.00
28	326	Light globes	4.90

EXERCISE 6.18 V. Pappas & Sons

Use a copy of the blank petty cash book master provided on page 564 to complete this exercise.

V. Pappas & Sons has employed you as petty cashier and you commence your duties on 1 May 19XX. The petty cash system has an imprest amount of $150 and all records are balanced at the above date and placed in your care. Over the next few days, the following petty cash expenditure is incurred.

Date	Voucher no.	Particulars	Amount ($)
May 1	81	Tea and coffee	12.60
3	82	Express post — parcel	28.20
5	83	Parking fees	18.50
8	84	Notepads	15.00
9	85	Flowers for office	20.00
11	86	Repairs to lock	25.00
12	87	Parcel post	18.20

As the amount of cash in the tin is running low, you must balance the petty cash book. The reimbursement cheque is drawn, cashed and placed in the tin. Now record the following petty cash expenses, after verification according to organisational policies and procedures.

Date	Voucher no.	Particulars	Amount ($)
May 15	88	Taxi fares	16.40
16	89	Staples and paper-clips	6.20
	90	Donation	5.00
17	91	Postage stamps	18.00
18	92	Cleaning items	19.40
19	93	Inkjet cartridge (printer)	49.95
22	94	Copy paper	22.36
23	95	File folders	11.20

The petty cash float is running low again. Balance the petty cash book, draw and cash the reimbursement cheque and place the money in the tin.

At the end of the month, balance the petty cash book by drawing and cashing the reimbursement cheque, record the amount of reimbursement in the petty cash book and place the cash in the tin. Details of vouchers for the amounts spent up to the end of the month are as follows.

Date	Voucher no.	Particulars	Amount ($)
May 24	96	Postage — airmail	26.80
25	97	Notepads	13.20
	98	Fineline pens	19.80
26	99	Tea and coffee	13.10
29	100	Window cleaning	30.00
30	101	Light globes	8.60
	102	Magazines for reception	13.95
31	103	Flowers for office	20.00

Checking petty cash records

As part of the internal control system of the business, spot checks or audits of all the cash records are carried out. If employees are aware that their records may be checked at any time, the temptation to misappropriate funds is avoided.

It is important that company policy and procedures are adhered to and that all records of petty cash transactions, together with the petty cash tin containing cash and vouchers, are presented to the appropriate person for checking. This is usually done at regular intervals, as organised by the accounts manager through the petty cashier's supervisor.

Dealing with errors and irregularities

Part of the responsibility of the petty cashier is to be aware of irregularities and errors and to know how to handle them. Sometimes the cash may be short because of an honest mistake. At other times the petty cash book may not balance. Whatever the problem, check your work thoroughly as follows.
- Check vouchers for accuracy and authenticity before entering.
- Check that all vouchers are correctly entered.
- Check that amounts have been extended to the correct dissection columns.
- Check all additions, making sure that the total of the dissection columns is equal to the total of the 'Total' column.
- Count and re-count the cash carefully.

Security of petty cash

The following controls are implemented for the safeguarding of petty cash.
- One person, usually the petty cashier, is responsible for the administration of the petty cash fund.
- Access to the petty cash is restricted to the petty cashier. Another nominated person should be authorised to take over the petty cash if the petty cashier is ill or on holidays.
- All transactions are recorded as soon as possible. Any cash taken from the petty cash tin is replaced with a completed petty cash voucher plus a receipt (proof of purchase).
- Receipts should be marked as cancelled after reimbursement so they cannot be taken from the petty cash tin and re-submitted for payment.
- The petty cash tin is kept in a secure place during business hours and locked away in the safe overnight.

EXERCISE 6.19 Nguyen & Lee

Use a copy of the blank petty cash book master provided on page 564 to complete this exercise.

You have been employed as petty cashier for Nguyen & Lee, Importers, which established its petty cash system with $150. The recording of the petty cash expenses should be done weekly on the first day of the week. The petty cash book was balanced at the end of August (see opposite) but since then has been neglected. You are required to carry out the following.
1. In a real situation you would check the accuracy and authenticity of petty cash claims in accordance with the company's policies and procedures.
2. Record all vouchers to bring the petty cash book up to date, balance the book after recording transactions for 5 September and request a reimbursement cheque.

Date		Voucher no.	Particulars	Amount ($)
Sept.	1	38	Copy paper	11.20
	2	39	Taxi fare	14.50
		40	Staples	4.80
	3	41	Tea and coffee	9.70
		42	Postage stamps	13.50
	4	43	Cleaning items	11.52
		44	Newspaper	1.20
	5	45	Post-it Notes	6.25

PETTY CASH BOOK OF NGUYEN & LEE, IMPORTERS

Amount received	Date	Particulars	Voucher no.	Total	Stationery	Postage	Travel expenses	Sundry expenses
150.00	19XX Aug. 26 27 29	 Tea and coffee Parking fees Printer ribbons	b/f 35 36 37	86.00 13.60 7.00 34.00	26.00 34.00	9.00	8.60 7.00	42.40 13.60
				140.60	60.00	9.00	15.60	56.00
	31	Cash on hand	c/d	9.40				
150.00				150.00				
9.40 140.60	Sept. 1	Cash on hand Reimbursement cheque	b/d					
			c/f					

3. When the reimbursement cheque has been cashed and the cash placed in the petty cash tin, you must record the following transactions.

Date	Voucher no.	Particulars	Amount ($)
Sept. 8	46	Manila folders	2.50
9	47	Light globes	1.50
10	48	Fineline pens	20.00
12	49	Parcel post	25.00
13	50	Taxi fares	32.00
14	51	Repairs to window	28.00

4. Balance the petty cash book at this date, carry down the cash on hand, cash the reimbursement cheque and place the cash in the petty cash tin.

EXERCISE 6.20 — Oriental Supply Co.

The petty cash book of Oriental Supply Co. is incorrect. The fund is operated with an imprest amount of $100. The amounts in the 'Total' column are correct. You are required to carry out the following.

1. Check the work thoroughly, paying particular attention to extended figures and additions.
2. Correct errors by ruling a line neatly through the incorrect entry and writing the correct figure above it.
3. Balance the petty cash book and request a reimbursement cheque to be cashed to restore the fund to the imprest amount of $100. Use a copy of the blank petty cash book master on page 564 to complete this exercise.

PETTY CASH BOOK OF ORIENTAL SUPPLY CO.

Amount received	Date	Particulars	Voucher no.	Total	Stationery	Postage	Travel expenses	Sundry expenses
100.00	Mar. 8		b/f	19.00	4.00	10.00		5.00
		Taxi fares	38	14.50			15.40	
	9	Light bulbs	39	6.20				6.20
		Flowers for office	40	11.50				
	10	Newspapers	41	2.40				2.40
		Staples	42	6.20	6.20			
	11	Postage stamps	43	18.00		8.00		
		Parking fees	44	11.00			11.00	
	12	Cleaning items	45	9.20				9.60
				98.00	10.20	18.00	26.40	23.20
	8	Cash on hand	c/d	2.00				
			c/f					

EXERCISE 6.21 — Theory

Complete the following sentences.

1. It is considered good business practice for all amounts, except for small day-to-day expenses, to be paid by _____.

2. A common system for handling small day-to-day expenses to be paid in cash, and for which the vouchers should always add up to the initial amount, is called the _____ petty cash system.

3. The amount with which this system is commenced is called the _____.

4. The person in charge of the petty cash is sometimes called the _____.

5. The person in charge of the petty cash is responsible for:

    (a) _____

    (b) _____

    (c) _____

    (d) _____.

6. The amount unspent in the petty cash tin is called _____.

7. When a member of staff wishes to claim money from the petty cash float, a _____ must be completed.

8. Total expenditure for period plus _____ should equal _____.

9. The cheque drawn to replenish the petty cash float is called _____.

10. After balancing, _____ plus _____ is equal to the original imprest amount.

PREPARING AND VALIDATING DOCUMENTS FOR BANKING

Cash is the most 'liquid' asset of any business. It is easily transferred between people and therefore is easily misappropriated. The advent of electronic banking and funds transfer is eliminating the need for cash to change hands (there is more discussion of electronic banking and sales on pages 458–460). However, it is still necessary, as part of a business's 'cash secure' policy, that all money that comes into the business is banked intact daily. Apart from a cash reserve kept on the premises for petty cash, all payments of the business are made by cheque. No payments are made from the daily cash takings.

At the end of each day, all cash receipts are banked into the firm's bank account. Cash received daily may consist of:
- cheques received by mail from debtors (persons who owe money to the business)
- daily takings in the cash register from cash sales, including notes and coins, cheques and credit card vouchers.

Record of takings

Cheques received

All cheques received by mail are checked against the remittance advice attached to them and any discrepancy is noted. The details of each cheque are recorded in a cheque register and passed to the accounts clerk for receipts to be written and posted to debtors.

Cash received

Receipts for cash sales are issued to customers at the time of the sale. These are usually in the form of a cash register receipt. The cash register records and provides control over the cash received over the counter. The following procedures should be observed.
- Customers should be able to see the amount entered in the cash register.
- Receipts should be issued for *every* sale and recorded in the register.
- The cash register drawer should open only when an amount is keyed in.
- Staff who work with the cash register should not be able to access the internal cash register roll.

Cash registers keep a record of all cash transactions on a roll or tape inside the register. At the end of the day, cash sales are determined by 'balancing' the cash register roll against the day's takings in the cash register drawer.

Handwritten receipts can also be made out from the firm's receipt book. The original is handed to the customer and the duplicate remains in the book as a record of the cash received.

Cash receipts book

Cash receipts are recorded daily into the cash receipts book. It is the responsibility of the accounts clerk to check the record of daily takings (duplicate receipts) against the entries in the cash receipts book. Receipts should be ticked or crossed through as they are confirmed as recorded in the cash receipts book.

Example

The following receipts of Westwood Stereo Equipment have been checked against the cash receipts book. They are ticked as confirmation that they have been entered correctly into the cash receipts book (see page 442).

Duplicate copies of receipts

Rec. No. 342 ✓	Rec. No. 343 ✓	Rec. No. 344 ✓
Date: 11/8/19XX	Date: 12/8/19XX	Date: 12/8/19XX
Rec'd from M. PRIOR & CO. the sum of Two hundred and forty-one dollars eighty cents	Rec'd from ROSS REAL ESTATE the sum of Five hundred dollars	Rec'd from T. JACKSON the sum of Three hundred and seventy-six dollars
For: Payment of Account	For: Rent revenue	For: Payment on Account
Cash/Chq. $241.80 Discount 6.20 Amt. Owing $248.00	Cash/Chq. $500.00	Cash/Chq. $376.00

Rec. No. 345 ✓	Rec. No. 346 ✓	Rec. No. 347 ✓
Date: 13/8/19XX	Date: 14/8/19XX	Date: 15/8/19XX
Rec'd from G. BYRNE & CO. the sum of Four hundred and thirty-eight dollars seventy-five cents	Rec'd from ULTRA CAR SALES the sum of Eight thousand five hundred dollars	Rec'd from B. COUSENS the sum of One hundred and fifty dollars
For: Payment of Account	For: Motor vehicles (Car sold for cash)	For: Payment on Account
Cash/Chq. $438.75 Discount 11.25 Amt Owing $450.00	Cash/Chq. $8500.00	Cash/Chq. $150.00

Cash register records

Cash Register Record 11/8/19XX ✓	Cash Register Record 12/8/19XX ✓	Cash Register Record 13/8/19XX ✓
Sales $1076.80 Sales Tax 269.20	Sales $2016.00 Sales Tax 504.00	Sales $3056.00 Sales Tax 764.00
Total Sales $1346.00	Total Sales $2520.00	Total Sales $3820.00

```
┌─────────────────────────────┐  ┌─────────────────────────────┐
│    Cash Register Record     │  │    Cash Register Record     │
│         14/8/19XX           │  │         15/8/19XX           │
│                      ✓      │  │                      ✓      │
│                             │  │                             │
│   Sales        $4624.48     │  │   Sales        $3405.48     │
│   Sales Tax     1156.12     │  │   Sales Tax      851.37     │
│                             │  │                             │
│   Total Sales  $5780.60     │  │   Total Sales  $4256.85     │
└─────────────────────────────┘  └─────────────────────────────┘
```

Following is the cash receipts book of Westwood Stereo Equipment. The entries for cash receipts for the week ended 15 August 19XX have been checked against receipts and verified as being correct.

CASH RECEIPTS BOOK OF WESTWOOD STEREO EQUIPMENT

Date	Rec. no.	Particulars	Fol.	Discount allowed	Trade debtors	Sales	Sales tax	General	Bank
19XX									
Aug. 1		Balance	b/d						12 562.00
Aug. 11	342	M. Prior & Co. ✓		6.20	241.80				
	CRR	Sales ✓				1 076.80	269.20		1 587.80
12	343	Rent Revenue ✓						500.00	
	344	T. Jackson ✓			376.00				
	CRR	Sales ✓				2 016.00	504.00		3 396.00
13	345	G. Byrne & Co. ✓		11.25	438.75				
	CRR	Sales ✓				3 056.00	764.00		4 258.75
14	346	Motor Vehicles ✓						8500.00	
	CRR	Sales ✓				4 624.48	1156.12		14 280.60
15	347	B. Cousens ✓			150.00				
	CRR	Sales ✓				3 405.48	851.37		4 406.85
				17.45	1206.55	14 178.76	3544.69	9000.00	40 492.00

The above cash receipts book shows that cash received for the week included cheques received in the mail from debtors for which the firm's official receipts have been issued. The record in the cash receipts book is entered from the duplicate copy of these receipts.

Cash receipts for the week also include the daily cash takings of the firm. These are recorded from the internal cash register record — the cash register roll or tape. Cash received from cash sales may consist of:
- notes and coins
- cheques
- credit card sales vouchers (less any returns as per credit card credit vouchers).

The above cash receipts book also shows that the names of people to whom cash sales are made are not given — these are grouped under the heading 'Sales'. This is because the transactions have been completed, they do not owe money to the firm so their names are not required in the accounting records.

EXERCISE 6.22 J. Mason

You are employed as accounts clerk for J. Mason, clothing manufacturers. Apart from cheques received by mail from debtors, J. Mason runs a factory shop where discount clothing is sold on a cash-only basis. Cheques or credit cards are not accepted.

You are required to carry out the following.

1. Check the receipts below against the cash receipts book on page 444 to ensure that all cash received has been recorded.
2. As you confirm that a receipt has been recorded, place a tick in the top right-hand corner of the receipt.

Duplicate receipts

Rec. No. 21	Rec. No. 22	Rec. No. 23
Date: 5 April 19XX	Date: 7 April 19XX	Date: 9 April 19XX
Rec'd from TROPICAL TRENDS the sum of Three hundred and twelve dollars	Rec'd from TOP END FASHIONS the sum of Five hundred and forty-six dollars	Rec'd from TEVEN LEISUREWEAR the sum of Two hundred and eighty-six dollars sixty cents
For: Payment of March Account	For: Payment of March Account	For: Payment on Account
Cash/Chq. $312.00 Discount 8.00 Amt Owing $320.00	Cash/Chq. $546.00 Discount 14.00 Amt Owing $560.00	Cash/Chq. $288.60 Discount 7.40 Amt Owing $296.00

Cash register records

Cash Register Record 5/4/19XX	Cash Register Record 6/4/19XX	Cash Register Record 7/4/19XX
Sales $244.00 Sales Tax 36.00 Total Sales $280.00	Sales $344.60 Sales Tax 55.40 Total Sales $400.00	Sales $217.00 Sales Tax 31.00 Total Sales $248.00

Cash Register Record 8/4/19XX	Cash Register Record 9/4/19XX
Sales $132.60 Sales Tax 23.40 Total Sales $156.00	Sales $477.70 Sales Tax 84.30 Total Sales $562.00

CASH RECEIPTS BOOK OF J. MASON

Date	Rec. no.	Particulars	Fol.	Discount allowed	Sundry debtors	Sales	Sales tax	General	Bank
19XX Apr. 1		Balance	b/d						5882.00
5	21	Tropical Trends		8.00	312.00				
	CRR	Sales				244.00	36.00		592.00
6	CRR	Sales				344.60	55.40		400.00
7	22	Top End Fashions		14.00	546.00				
	CRR	Sales				217.00	31.00		794.00
8	CRR	Sales				132.60	23.40		156.00
9	23	Teven Leisurewear		7.40	288.60				
	CRR	Sales				477.70	84.30		850.60
				29.40	1 146.60	1 415.90	230.10		8 674.60

EXERCISE 6.23 — R. & L. Camping Supplies

You are employed as accounts clerk for R. & L. Camping Supplies. You are required to carry out the following.

1. Check the receipts below against the cash receipts book on page 445 to ensure that all cash received has been recorded.
2. As you confirm that a receipt has been recorded, place a tick in the top right-hand corner of the receipt.

Duplicate receipts

Rec. No. 426
Date: *8 January 19XX*

Rec'd from *ADVENTURES INCORPORATED*
the sum of *Two hundred and eighty dollars eighty cents*

For: *Payment of Dec. Account*

Cash/Chq. $280.80
Discount   7.20
Amt Owing $288.00

Rec. No. 427
Date: *18 January 19XX*

Rec'd from *SAFARI SHOP*
the sum of *One hundred and fifty-six dollars*

For: *Payment on Account*

Cash/Chq. $156.00

Rec. No. 428
Date: *28 January 19XX*

Rec'd from *GREAT OUTDOORS*
the sum of *Two hundred and four dollars seventy five cents*

For: *Payment Inv. no. 526*

Cash/Chq. $204.75
Discount   5.25
Amt Owing $210.00

Cash register records

Cash Register Record 7/1/19XX	
Sales	$142.80
Sales Tax	25.20
Total Sales	$168.00

Cash Register Record 16/1/19XX	
Sales	$232.90
Sales Tax	41.10
Total Sales	$274.00

Cash Register Record 24/1/19XX	
Sales	$309.40
Sales Tax	54.60
Total Sales	$364.00

CASH RECEIPTS BOOK OF R. & L. CAMPING SUPPLIES

Date	Rec. no.	Particulars	Fol.	Discount allowed	Sundry debtors	Sales	Sales tax	General	Bank
19XX Jan. 1		Balance	b/d						2561.00
7	CRR	Sales				142.80	25.20		168.00
8	426	Adventures Inc.		7.20	280.80				280.80
16	CRR	Sales				232.90	41.10		274.00
18	427	Safari Shop			156.00				156.00
24	CRR	Sales				309.40	54.60		364.00
28	428	Great Outdoors		5.25	204.75				204.75
				12.45	641.55	685.10	120.90		4008.55

EXERCISE 6.24 *Bluewater Marine Spares*

You are employed as accounts clerk for Bluewater Marine Spares. You are required to carry out the following.
1. Check the receipts below against the cash receipts book that follows to ensure that all cash received has been recorded.
2. As you confirm that a receipt has been recorded, place a tick in the top right-hand corner of the receipt. Circle any receipts not recorded.

Duplicate receipts

Rec. No. 156	
Date: *10 November 19XX*	
Rec'd from *BLUE BAY MARINA* the sum of *Three hundred and fifty-one dollars*	
For: *Payment of Oct. Account*	
Cash/Chq.	$351.00
Discount	9.00
Amt Owing	$360.00

Rec. No. 157	
Date: *12 November 19XX*	
Rec'd from *RITZY RUNABOUTS* the sum of *One hundred and sixty-eight dollars*	
For: *Payment on Account*	
Cash/Chq.	$168.00

Rec. No. 158	
Date: *22 November 19XX*	
Rec'd from *STAR REALTY* the sum of *Three hundred and twenty-five dollars*	
For: *Rent received*	
Cash/Chq.	$325.00

Cash register records

Cash Register Record 5/11/19XX	
Sales	$162.75
Sales Tax	23.25
Total Sales	$186.00

Cash Register Record 12/11/19XX	
Sales	$200.60
Sales Tax	35.40
Total Sales	$236.00

Cash Register Record 25/11/19XX	
Sales	$319.25
Sales Tax	48.75
Total Sales	$368.00

CASH RECEIPTS BOOK OF BLUEWATER MARINE SPARES

Date	Rec. no.	Particulars	Fol.	Discount allowed	Sundry debtors	Sales	Sales tax	General	Bank
19XX Nov. 1		Balance	b/d						3582.90
5	CRR	Sales				162.75	23.25		186.00
10	156	Blue Bay Marina		9.00	351.00				351.00
12	157	Ritzy Runabouts			168.00				
	CRR	Sales				200.60	35.40		404.00
22	158	Rent Revenue						325.00	325.00
25	CRR	Sales				319.25	48.75		368.00
				9.00	519.00	682.60	107.40	325.00	5216.90

Sorting cash ready for banking

All money that comes into the firm is banked intact daily. All cash, cheques and credit card vouchers should be collated and totalled daily and presented for banking according to accepted banking procedures. Some banks have special preferences regarding the way the cash is organised and presented.

Notes

Notes are sorted according to their denominations in bundles of ten, for example, ten $10 notes, ten $5 notes, and so on. Place the notes face up so that you are able to see:
- the signature
- the denomination of the note in words.

Fold each bundle of ten notes so that you can see the signature and the dollar amount (5, 10, 20 etc.) is showing in the top right-hand corner. Secure the bundles with elastic bands.

For the new polymer notes, however, leave them flat and place an elastic band around the middle of each bundle of ten notes.

When the bank counts notes, it groups them into 'flats', 'sections' and 'bundles' using the following method.

1. Ten notes of the same denomination are laid flat with the signature and the denomination of the note in words showing. This is called a 'flat'.

    10 notes = one 'flat' = 10 × $5 notes = $50.

2. Ten bundles of 'flats' are placed one on top of the other with an elastic band around each end of the group of notes. This is called a 'section'. The elastic bands around each end indicate that it is a 'section'.

    10 'flats' = one 'section' = 100 × $5 notes = $500.

3. Ten of these 'sections' put together are called a 'bundle'. An elastic band on either end of the bundle keeps it together.

    10 'sections' = one 'bundle' = 1000 × $5 notes = $5000.

Loose notes

Any loose notes, in other words those left over and not making up a complete bundle, should be laid flat (if polymer) or folded with the dollar amount inwards. Organise the notes from highest to lowest denomination. Secure them together with elastic bands.

Coins

Coin is usually placed either in a re-usable plastic bag, imprinted with a specified amount of coin, or wrapped (rolled) in special wrappers. Both the bags and wrappers may be obtained from the bank. Some banks have a preference for one or the other and your deposit should be prepared according to your bank's procedures.

You must place the correct denomination and value in the bags or wrappers according to the following tables.

Bagged coin

Denomination	No. of coins	Bag value
$2.00	25	$50.00
$1.00	20	$20.00
$0.50	20	$10.00
$0.20	50	$10.00
$0.10	100	$10.00
$0.05	40	$ 2.00

Rolled coin

Denomination	No. of coins	Roll value
$2.00	25	$50.00
$1.00	20	$20.00
$0.50	20	$10.00
$0.20	20	$ 4.00
$0.10	40	$ 4.00
$0.05	40	$ 2.00

Loose coin

Loose coin is placed in a plastic bag with the amount clearly marked on the front.

Although they are no longer issued, 1 cent and 2 cent coins are still legal tender and can be deposited. However, all business transactions are rounded off to the nearest 5 cent or 10 cent amount.
- 1c and 2c amounts are rounded *down* (12c becomes 10c)
- 3c and 4c amounts are rounded *up* (34c becomes 35c)
- 6c and 7c amounts are rounded *down* (26c becomes 25c)
- 8c and 9c amounts are rounded *up* (78c becomes 80c)

Counting cash

When counting notes and coin, record your cash totals on a cash break-up or cash summary slip.

When counting, remember to:
- count cash for value (for example, if counting $10 notes, count '10, 20, 30', not '1, 2, 3')
- count cash face up (so that you can see the signatures and amounts in words).

CASH SUMMARY SLIP

Cash register no.:   Date:

Denomination	Number	Amount
Notes: $100		
$ 50		
$ 20		
$ 10		
$ 5		
TOTAL NOTES		
Coin: $2.00		
$1.00		
$0.50		
$0.20		
$0.10		
$0.05		
TOTAL COIN		
TOTAL CASH		

The cash count should always be carried out in a secure environment and validated by at least two people.

Organising and counting cheques for banking

Cheques should be validated by checking that:
- the date on the cheque is valid and the cheque is not post-dated (with a future date) or stale (with a date more than 12 months old)
- the payee name is correct and the cheque is made out to the firm banking it
- the amount of the cheque is given in both words and figures and the amount in words agrees with the amount in figures
- the cheque is signed — an unsigned cheque is not valid and cannot be banked, so it should be returned to the drawer for signature.

Cheques are then sorted according to the firm's cash handling policies, and entered on a bank deposit slip according to the receiving bank's accepted procedures, listing:
- name of drawer — the firm or person on whose account the cheque is drawn
- name of drawee — the bank and branch on which the cheque is drawn
- amount of the cheque.

Organising credit card sales for banking

Many transactions are carried out using credit cards. The credit card supplier (for example, Bankcard, MasterCard, Visa, American Express or Diners Club) derives income from commission charged on the sales made using its credit card.

Credit card sales vouchers

When a credit card sale is made, the merchant (the seller of the goods) records the sale on a sales voucher (see below), the original or processor copy of which is banked with the daily takings or forwarded to the credit card supplier, depending on whether the card has been supplied by a bank or other credit provider.

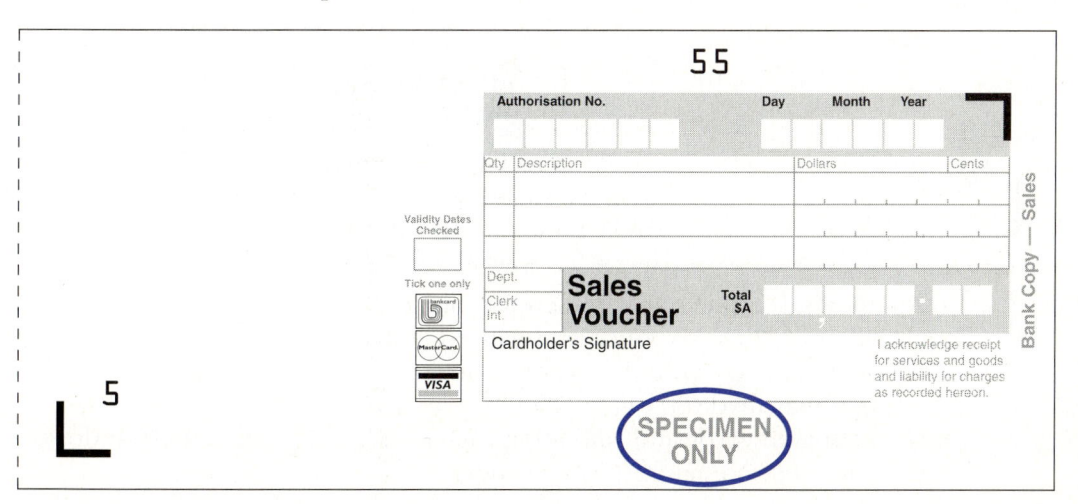

Credit card credit voucher

When goods that have been purchased with a credit card are returned by the customer as faulty or unwanted, the customer presents the credit card and a credit voucher (see below) is made out. This is processed to reduce the amount that the customer owes to the credit card supplier.

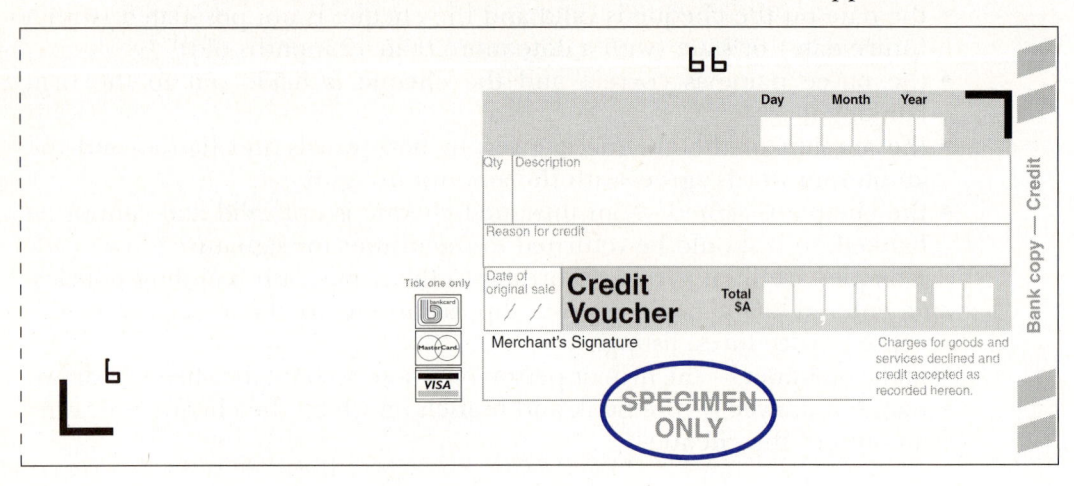

Credit card merchant summary

Details of all credit card transactions should be listed on a merchant summary slip (below). The original sales vouchers, as well as the originals of any credit card credit vouchers, are attached to this summary slip and banked with all other cash receipts for that day to be credited to the account of the merchant.

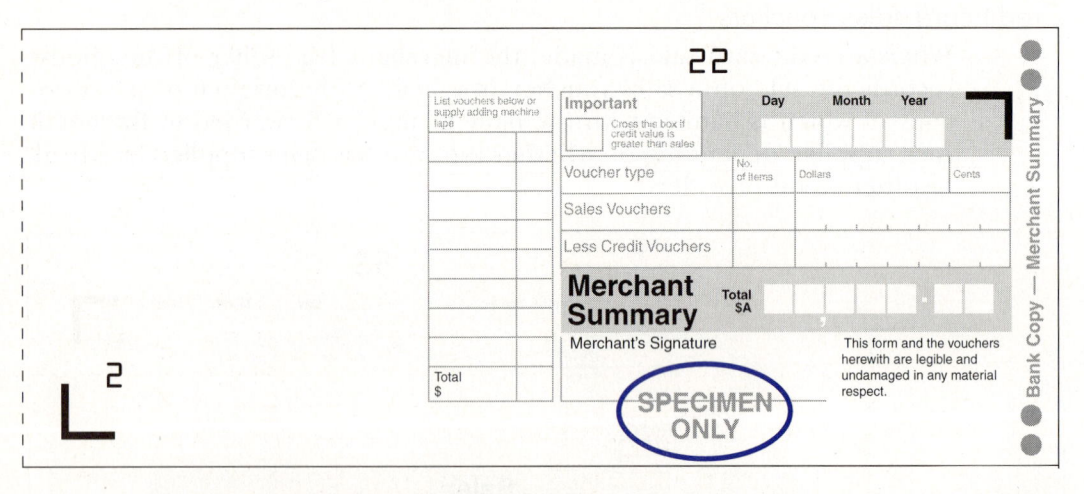

Always double-check that the credit card merchant summary agrees with the total of credit sales vouchers received. Make any amendments or verify their accuracy according to organisational policies and procedures of your firm. This may involve:
- correcting an error and initialling the correction, if authorised to do so
- referring a discrepancy to your supervisor.

Finally, you must check all of the above with entries in the receipts section of the cash book.

Preparing the bank deposit

The bank deposit is prepared by listing cash and cheques on a bank deposit form in accordance with the banking institution's guidelines.

When a firm's bank account is first opened, the firm is issued with a deposit book. This deposit book may be made up of deposit slips, with butts to be retained by the customer, similar to cheque butts. This type of deposit form has a section for cheque details on the reverse side (an example appears on pages 454–455). Other deposit books have a top section of the page for deposit details and a lower section of the page for cheque listings (see the example on page 452). This is especially useful for firms that have large volumes of cheques.

All deposit books have space for the following information:

- date on which the money is banked
- account name, which may be pre-printed by the bank or may be entered by hand (it must be entered exactly as recorded by the bank)
- deposit details, for which space is provided to record the notes, coin, cheques and credit card transactions. (If specific space is not provided for credit card transactions, record amount with cash and list details below cheque details.)
- signature of depositor or another person authorised to validate the deposit
- number of cheques, which the teller counts and ticks the appropriate box if correct. (The teller also checks the payee name to ensure that the cheque is being banked to the correct account, but does not check any other aspect of the cheque — this is done when the cheque is processed by the bank.)
- teller's initials and the bank's date stamp — this is the firm's only record that the deposit was carried out and must appear on the deposit book butt or the duplicate copy.

It should be noted that large deposit books are generally not pre-printed with an account name and number, which should be recorded by the customer. However, to allow for computer processing, a pre-encoded credit summary slip is prepared to accompany the deposit. This is similar in appearance to a normal bank deposit slip, with a tear-off butt, but contains only pre-encoded account details (that is, the account name and number and the BSB number) with a space being provided for entry of the total deposit amount. This slip is retained by the bank with the deposit. The butt, after being initialled and stamped by the teller, is returned to the customer with the deposit book to be retained as a record of the deposit.

452 MODERN ACCOUNTING PRACTICE — A MODULAR APPROACH

Deposit for account at

Westpac Banking Corporation   ARBN 007 457 141

Where this deposit is lodged at a bank or branch other than shown below it will be transferred under the Bank's internal procedures. The Bank is not to be responsible for delays in transmission to branch or transfer to nominated bank. Proceeds of cheques etc. will not be available till cleared.

Branch *(where account is held)*	
Paid in by *(Signature)*	
Credit A/c name & no.	

100	
50	
20	
10	
5	
Total notes	
Coin	
Cash total	

Teller	Comm.	No. of chqs

CREDIT

Date	/ /
Cash	
Cheques	
Bankcard/ MasterCard	
Less Charges	
Total $	

Particulars of cheques, etc., to be completed by depositor

	Drawer	Bank	Branch	Amount
1				
2				
3				
4				
5				
6				
7				
8				
9				
10				
11				
12				
13				
14				
15				
16				
17				
18				
19				
20				
21				
22				
23			SPECIMEN ONLY	
24				
			Carried forward	

ABLMDUP/38059 (9/94)

Example

The cashier for Westwood Stereo Equipment is required to prepare the bank deposit for 11 August 19XX. The following tasks are carried out to prepare the deposit ready for banking.

1. Count and organise the cash — notes and coin — according to the bank's procedures and list the details on the cash summary slip at right.

CASH SUMMARY SLIP		
Cash register no.: 1		**Date:** 11 Aug. 19XX
Denomination	Number	Amount
Notes: $100	2	200.00
$50	7	350.00
$20	4	80.00
$10	2	20.00
$5	1	5.00
TOTAL NOTES		$655.00
Coin: $2.00	14	28.00
$1.00	5	5.00
$0.50	8	4.00
$0.20	15	3.00
$0.10	4	.40
$0.05	12	.60
TOTAL COIN		$41.00
TOTAL CASH		$696.00

2. Complete the cash register summary slip for the day's takings, as follows.

CASH REGISTER SUMMARY SLIP	
Date	11/08/19XX
Register no.	1
Cash	$696.00
Cheques	$350.00
Credit card — Bankcard	$180.60
— MasterCard	—
— Visa	$119.40
Total sales	$1346.00
Checked: Cashier	*S. Britten*
Supervisor	*V. Aboud*

3. Check that the total on the cash register summary slip agrees with the cash register record of the day's takings on the cash register roll (internal cash register master tape). The amount in the cash register drawer less the amount of the daily change float should agree with the total on the cash register roll. (The change float is the amount of cash that was held in the cash register at the beginning of the day to provide change for early customers.)
4. Collate and total the cheques received in the mail from debtors: one cheque was received from M. Prior & Co. for $241.80 drawn on ANZ Perth.
5. Collate and total the cheques included with the day's takings: one cheque was received from J. Miller for $350.00 drawn on Westpac Geraldton, WA.
6. Collate the credit card transactions (both sales and credit vouchers) and record the details on the merchant summary slip (below). Original copies of sales and credit vouchers should be attached to the merchant summary slip. (There were credit sales vouchers for Bankcard, $180.60, and Visa, $119.40.)
7. All the details are then entered on the bank deposit slip.

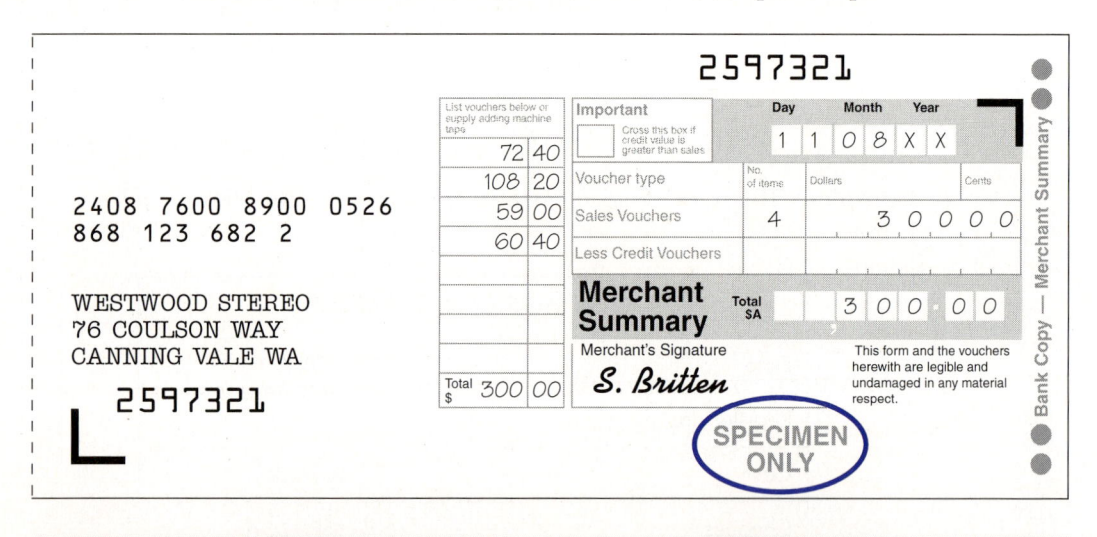

Reverse side

Bank Use Only — Third party cheque explanation				Bank use only		Details of Cheques
Details of Cheques *(Proceeds will not be available until cleared)*				100		
Drawer (i.e. Account Name on Cheque)	Bank	Branch	Amount	50		
J. MILLER	WPAC	Geraldton	350.00	20		
M. PRIOR	ANZ	Perth	241.80	10		
BANKCARD 180.60				5		
VISA 119.40				Coin		
Note: This deposit will be transferred under the Bank's internal procedures. The Bank will not be held responsible for delays in transmission.		Total $	591.80	Cash Total		

SPECIMEN ONLY

EXERCISE 6.25 — Westwood Stereo Equipment

As cashier for Westwood Stereo Equipment, you are required to prepare the bank deposit for 15 August 19XX. Use a copy of the blank deposit master provided on page 565. The branch name is Perth and the account name is Westwood Stereo Equipment.

The daily cash takings are made up as follows.
- Cash: Notes $2655.00
          Coin $99.05
- Cheques: $248.00 — M. Riley, ANZ, Mandurah, WA
            $172.00 — R. Bolton, Westpac, Clarendon, SA
            $210.00 — P. Gold, Commonwealth Bank, Albany, WA
- Credit card transactions: Bankcard $210.60
                              MasterCard $376.40
                              Visa $285.40

A cheque was also received in the mail from debtor B. Cousens for $150.00, drawn on National Australia Bank, Burwood, Victoria. (A receipt has been forwarded to the debtor.)

EXERCISE 6.26 — B-Jay Cookware

You are required to prepare the daily bank deposit for B-Jay Cookware on 18 November 19XX. Use a copy of the blank deposit master provided on page 565. The branch name is Brisbane and the account name is B-Jay Cookware.

The daily takings are made up as follows.
(a) Two cheques were received by mail from:
  - C. Eastall, drawn on Westpac, Coolangatta, Qld, for $263.75
  - B. Wayne, drawn on National Australia Bank, Maroochydore, Qld, for $185.50.

(b) The cash register summary slip has been completed and shows the following.
- Cash $631.80 (Notes $520.00, Coin $111.80 as per cash breakdown slip)
- Cheques P. Agnew, drawn on ANZ Balmain, NSW, for $142.20
            S. Patel, drawn on Westpac, Mosman, NSW, for $237.80
            L. Gomez, drawn on NAB, Pymble, NSW, for $162.40
- Credit card transactions   Bankcard $85.95
                              MasterCard $102.45
                              Visa $76.20

EXERCISE 6.27 Central Medical Equipment

As cashier for Central Medical Equipment you are required to prepare the bank deposit for 27 September 19XX. Use a copy of the blank deposit master provided on page 565. The branch name is Brisbane and the account name is Central Medical Equipment. Included in the deposit are the following.

(a) Cheques have been received by mail from debtors for which receipts have been prepared and despatched:
- $237.60   L. van Heusen, ANZ, Townsville, Qld
- $416.80   J. Partridge, Westpac, Cairns, Qld
- $384.30   M. Benedetto, Commonwealth, Rockhampton, Qld.

(b) The cash register summary slip for the day's takings has been completed and shows the following:
- Cash Notes $985.00
        Coin $72.20
- Cheques $82.90 V. Tonkin, Westpac, Southport, Qld
           $75.50 M. Tindall, ANZ, Brisbane, Qld
           $59.80 B. McGregor, Commonwealth, Ipswich, Qld
- Credit card transactions   Bankcard $142.80
                              MasterCard $103.30
                              Visa $96.70.

EXERCISE 6.28 Patel & Singh Importing

As cashier for Patel & Singh Importing, you are required to prepare the bank deposit for 23 June 19XX. Use a copy of the blank deposit master provided on page 565. The branch name is Shepparton and the account name is Patel & Singh Importing. Included in the deposit are the following.

(a) Cheques received by mail from debtors for which receipts have been prepared and despatched:
- $382.70   G. Henderson, ANZ, Strathmerton, Vic.
- $434.80   M. Picone, NAB, Numurkah, Vic.
- $296.40   K. Torresan, Westpac, Shepparton, Vic.

(b) The cash register summary slip for the day's takings has been completed and shows the following:
- Cash $838.00 (Notes $680.00, Coin $158.00 as per cash summary slip)
- Cheques $62.20 M. Sugden, NAB, Benalla, Vic.
  $39.80 P. Onorati, Commonwealth, Kyabram, Vic.
  $86.50 D. Miguel, Westpac, Shepparton, Vic.
- Credit card transactions   Bankcard $126.30
  MasterCard $92.20
  Visa $66.70.

BALANCING AND VALIDATING CASH RECEIPTS — A SUMMARY

In most businesses, cash is received over the counter and cheques are received through the mail. Businesses have established policies and procedures for ensuring that all cash and cheques received are balanced and validated.

Cash

The cash register records and provides control over the cash received over the counter. The following procedures should be observed.
- Customers should be able to see the amount entered in the cash register.
- Receipts should be issued for every sale and recorded in the register.
- The cash register drawer should open only when an amount is keyed in.
- Staff who work with the cash register should not be able to access the internal cash register roll.

Cash registers keep a record of all cash transactions on a roll or tape inside the register. At the end of the day, cash sales are determined by 'balancing' the cash register roll against the day's takings. The cash register is closed off and totalled. The amount recorded on the cash register roll for the day should equal the sum of the cash in the drawer (notes and coin), cheques and credit vouchers *less* the amount of the daily change float (the money that was in the drawer at the start of the day's business).

If the amounts disagree, the takings should be counted again and the supervisor notified. Most firms have particular procedures to be followed in case of a deficiency or a surplus.

Cheques

Incoming mail should be opened by the mail clerk who compares the cheques against their remittance advices and lists the details. This list is passed on to the accounts section. Cheques are then passed on to the cashier, who:
- ensures that the cheques are valid
- makes out receipts for the cheques (usually from debtors)
- records the cheque details on the bank deposit form
- sorts and includes the cheques with the daily bank deposit.

Validating bank deposits

After the bank deposit has been prepared, it should be validated as follows.
- Check the amount of cash and cheques against the cash register roll and daily receipt duplicates.
- Cross-check that the amount of the deposit agrees with the cash receipts for the day in the cash book.
- Ensure that the procedures for handling and counting cash, as outlined in the organisation's policies and procedures, have been adhered to, for example:
  — cash should be counted in a secure environment
  — the cash count should be verified by at least two people
  — the bank deposit must be transported to the bank in accordance with the firm's 'secure cash' policy
  — the firm's copy of the deposit book or butt (date stamped and initialled by teller) must be checked against the receipts section of the cash book.

Details of all the daily bank deposits are recorded on the bank statement which the bank sends to the business at the end of the month. This should also be checked and validated against the business's own records for the month and any discrepancies notified immediately.

ELECTRONIC BANKING PROCESSES

Electronic transfer of funds

As in all aspects of business, computers are used widely in the banking industry. A business can arrange with its bank to process payments, for example, lease payments, electronically to a nominated account on a specific date. This is called a 'periodic payment' and is shown as 'PP' on the bank statement.

Deposits to a firm's bank account can also be received electronically, for example, rent received monthly for rented premises. This is called a 'direct deposit' and is shown as 'DD' on the bank statement.

Amounts may also be transferred between accounts held in the same name, shown as 'TFR' on the bank statement. These processes are known as 'electronic transfer of funds'.

Electronic processing eliminates the need to complete cheques and deposit forms.

Automatic teller machine (ATM) transactions

If you operate an account with a bank, transactions can be carried out electronically using an automatic teller machine (ATM). These are usually situated outside the bank and operate on a 24-hour basis for the customers' convenience. Without needing to complete any forms, the ATM allows you to:
- withdraw money
- transfer money between accounts.

Deposits can also be made electronically, providing a deposit slip is completed and accompanies the deposit into the machine.

From ATMs, customers can also access information about their bank accounts, for example:
- account balance
- cheques paid
- deposits made.

Electronic funds transfer at point of sale (EFTPOS)

Many businesses provide this service to customers, particularly retail stores, supermarkets and service stations. This facility enables funds to be transferred from the customer's account to the business's bank account electronically when goods or services are being purchased.

The customer's credit card is passed through the EFTPOS machine at the sales counter and the customer enters his or her personal identification number (PIN). The amount of the transaction is then entered and the funds are transferred electronically from the customer's account to that of the business. The customer's bank account is debited and the business's account is credited by the amount of the sale, without the need for cash to change hands. The cash register prints an external receipt for the customer, as well as recording the details internally.

The electronic transfer of funds reduces the cost of processing cash transactions because it reduces the time involved and the amount of documentation traditionally required for a transaction. However, source documents provide security for cash transactions. Without this documentation, the people who design and set up computer systems need to ensure that a high degree of security and control are built in to protect computerised transactions. Some Internet access suppliers have already experienced problems with regard to security of customers' credit card transactions. Some problems have been rectified, but there is still a need to provide safeguards to prevent such problems recurring.

Telephone banking

Many bank customers can now use the telephone to conduct simple banking procedures. The bank allocates a specific access code to the customer. Then, using a telephone equipped with tone dialling (touchtone), it is possible for customers to access their own bank accounts to:
- obtain account balances
- transfer funds between accounts held in the one name
- obtain transaction details since their last statement
- pay certain bills, such as telephone, water rates, gas, council rates and insurance payments.

For a monthly fee, this same information may be accessed using a computer and a modem. Most banks offer this on-line banking service for customers which may also include business information, such as interest rates, foreign exchange rates, market forecasts, insurance information and investment opportunities. An additional advantage of an on-line service is that it allows you to view and print out account details or a list of transactions since the last statement was issued.

A time will come when banks will offer customers the facility to make payments electronically to any account in Australia. Instead of the bank handling these electronic transfers, customers will use their own computers to access their accounts and transfer funds to an account belonging to another person or business. Because financial data can be processed so quickly, access to this facility will enable a business to monitor its cash position more efficiently.

The main benefit of computerised operations in all areas of accounting is that many mundane tasks are performed automatically. This allows the accountants more time to analyse the information that systems produce and help management to evaluate past performances and plan for future operations. This information also gives rise to the accounting reports which satisfy the main aim of accounting — to provide economic information to enable users to make informed decisions about the allocation of their financial resources.

CHAPTER 7

Payroll

WHEN you have studied this chapter and completed the exercises, you should be competent in the following skills. Tick each skill when you have completed the relevant section.

LEARNING OUTCOMES

1. Calculate the weekly net pay for between three and six employees, for one pay period, taking into account the following:
   - starting and finishing times each day
   - overtime
   - paid leave
   - unpaid leave
   - employee deductions (PAYE tax, superannuation, medical insurance, union fees).

2. Calculate, accurately, payment due to individual employees from time sheet information.
   - Identify details of and calculate gross pay.
   - Calculate, accurately, net pay.
   - Prepare payment voucher, advice/pay slips and coinage analysis, detailing net pay, gross wages, PAYE tax and employee deductions.
   - Prepare coinage analysis for weekly pay packets.

3. Prepare payment vouchers for payment of monthly balances of PAYE tax and employee deduction suspense accounts created from the month's payroll payment vouchers.

▼

The payroll system forms part of the overall accounting system and accounts for what is known collectively as 'employee entitlements'. Employee entitlements cover the cost of labour and related **fringe benefits** and constitute a major expense for a business. The payroll system incorporates the calculation, preparation and payment of salaries and wages to employees.

Prior to 1994, there were no generally accepted principles for accounting for employee entitlements. In 1994, the Australian Accounting Research Foundation issued AAS 30 'Accounting for Employee Entitlements', which applies to all reporting entities that are not companies. Also, the Australian Accounting Standards Board issued AASB 1028, also entitled 'Accounting for Employee Entitlements', which was to apply to all companies that are reporting entities. These standards applied from the first reporting period following 30 June 1995 and define the following:

- *employer* — an entity which consumes the services of employees in exchange for providing employee entitlements
- *employee* — a person appointed or engaged under a contract of service, on a full-time, part-time, permanent, casual or temporary basis
- *employee entitlements* — benefit entitlements which employees accumulate as a result of rendering their services to an employer up to the reporting date, and include, but are not limited to, wages and **salaries** (including fringe benefits and non-monetary benefits), **leave** such as **annual leave**, **sick leave**, **long service leave** and superannuation, together with other post-employment benefits.

Additionally, Commonwealth and State government legislation requires that employers:

- maintain payroll records for each employee
- collect taxes on behalf of employees to be forwarded to the Australian Taxation Office
- comply with minimum standards governing amount of wages and salaries paid and hours worked
- comply with legislative requirements regarding superannuation and fringe benefits
- comply with payroll tax requirements levied by all State governments on gross wages and salaries of employees
- maintain a sound system of internal control to prevent errors and fraudulent activities.

INTERNAL CONTROL

Internal control is an important aspect of an employee entitlement (payroll) system, as payroll fraud is often experienced by businesses. Some examples of fraudulent activities are:

- overpaying employees
- making payments to fictitious employees
- continuing to pay employees after they have ceased to be employed
- overstating deductions.

Features of a sound internal control system with respect to payroll are as follows.
- separation of the operations of the following duties:
  (a) hiring employees
  (b) timekeeping
  (c) maintaining records
  (d) preparing payments
  (e) distributing cash or cheques to employees
  (f) making payments to employees' bank accounts
- accurate employer records maintained by the human resources (personnel) department, for example:
  (a) notice of employment
  (b) employee history records
  (c) job description
  (d) hours worked
  (e) rate of pay
  (f) authorisation for deductions (signed by employee)
  (g) details of any changes in (a) to (f) above as they occur, together with a record of notification of the payroll department
- the monitoring of timekeeping procedures, for example:
  (a) using a time clock to record hours worked daily for employees paid at an hourly rate
  (b) keeping a record of hours worked (either fortnightly or monthly) for salaried employees (kept by a supervisor) and, after being verified for accuracy, forwarding this to the payroll department at the end of each pay period.

ORGANISATIONAL POLICIES AND PROCEDURES

An important aspect of internal control in a business is that of employees' strict adherence to the firm's organisational policies and procedures which outline the company's policy on all aspects of the running of the business. Company policy with regard to payroll may outline the following:
- strict observance of conditions set out in relevant employment awards
- compliance with legislative requirements regarding payroll
- means to ensure that payments to employees are both timely and accurate
- maintenance of confidentiality at all times regarding payroll details and employees' personal details.

While the person in charge of the payroll department (for example, the financial controller) may be responsible for the processing of the weekly payroll, members of payroll staff, as well as staff from other areas, may have particular responsibilities. For example, the human resources (personnel) department may be required to deliver the employees' weekly time sheets and any relevant leave applications on a specific date, while maintaining security of payroll details and confidentiality of employees' personal details.

The payroll clerk is responsible for calculating the payroll, making necessary deductions, preparing vouchers to pay deducted monies to the appropriate authority and expediting the processing of employees' pay slips and payment of wages, either in cash or by cheque.

PAYMENT FOR LABOUR

Payment for labour (the payroll) includes:
1. Wages paid to employees on the following bases.
   - *Full time.* The employee is paid a salary or wage and is entitled to sick and holiday pay.
   - *Part time.* The employee is paid on an hourly basis, usually on a set schedule of hours and is not entitled to sick and holiday pay.
   - *Permanent part time.* The employee is paid on an hourly basis and is entitled to sick and holiday pay.
   - *Casual.* The employee is paid on an hourly basis and called upon when required.
   - *Piecework.* The employee is paid for the work produced; for example, in the garment industry on the number of garments produced, or in the fruit picking industry on the amount of fruit picked.
2. Commission payable to salesmen
3. Bonuses and allowances
4. Holiday pay, long service leave, superannuation and other fringe benefits.

SALARIES AND WAGES

An employee may be paid either a wage or a salary. A wage is paid on a periodical (usually weekly or fortnightly) basis, on a fixed number of hours. Time beyond the normal hours worked (for example, 40 hours per week) is paid as overtime. For example, a wage of $17.50 per hour would correspond to a wage for a 40-hour week of $700 ($17.50 × 40).

A salary is calculated on a yearly basis and paid either weekly, fortnightly or monthly as a fraction of the yearly salary; for example, $45 760 per annum, paid on a fortnightly basis, would be $45 760 ÷ 26 = $1760.00 per fortnight, or $880.00 weekly. Management and administrative staff are usually paid a salary, but are less likely to be paid overtime for excess hours worked.

The amount of wages paid is generally governed by an **industrial award**, **workplace agreement**, or **enterprise bargaining agreement** (that is, an **employment contract** between an employer and employees which is enforceable by law) and covers such items as:
- hours of work
- rate of pay
- rebates
- **paid leave** (for example, sick pay, holiday leave entitlements, **maternity leave**)
- unpaid leave (for example, **unpaid sick leave** and **unpaid maternity leave**)

- long service leave entitlements
- overtime
- superannuation (both employer and employee contributions)
- workers' compensation
- special allowances (for example, meal allowances, travel allowances, site allowances)
- clothing allowances, shift allowances.

PAYROLL SYSTEMS

The payroll system used within any one business will vary according to the size and complexity of the payroll. In a small firm, the payroll may be processed manually — a time-consuming task. Most firms, even small ones, use a computer to process their daily work. A simple self-calculating spreadsheet system may be used to process payroll information and print out pay slips. Some firms call in a consultant who specialises in this activity to set up a system designed specifically for the firm's needs, while others elect to purchase a payroll software package which will process the payroll on the firm's own computer. A large number of firms choose to use a non-computerised commercial payroll system.

Commercial payroll systems

Commercial payroll systems are designed to make the task of processing the payroll easier and incorporate preprinted documentation to suit the particular needs of the business. An example of a payroll system is the Kalamazoo, one-write system which consists of a series of carbon impregnated forms which are positioned, one on top of the other, on a special copy holder. These forms are positioned in such a way that, when the top form is completed, the details are recorded simultaneously, in the correct position, on every form in the copy holder. This enables the individual pay record (employee's earnings), payroll register (wages sheet) and pay advice (pay slip) to be completed at the one time.

One of the main advantages of a one-write system is the elimination of transposition errors which commonly occur when information is being copied from one place to another. The obvious disadvantage of the one-write system is that only one person can work on the payroll records at any one time.

Regardless of the system used, the same basic steps are followed when preparing the payroll, namely:
- calculate hours worked
- calculate gross pay
- calculate deductions/allowances
- calculate net pay.

Calculating hours worked

Where a small business has only two or three employees, it is not difficult to know the employees' starting and finishing times and to be aware of

absenteeism and holidays taken. However, in larger organisations, it is necessary to keep a record of these details. A record of the hours worked by each employee can be kept:
- on time cards or time sheets, or in a time book
- on bundy cards, whereby employees insert a card into a clocking machine on arrival each day and again on departure. The times of arrival and departure are automatically recorded on the card.

An example of a typical employee's time card is shown below.

EMPLOYEE TIME CARD

Week ending _____

DEPARTMENT _____   CLASSIFICATION _____

EMPLOYEE'S NAME _____   Payroll No. _____

DAY	TIME COMMENCED	TIME FINISHED	NORMAL HOURS WORKED	OVERTIME HOURS WORKED
Thursday				
Friday				
Saturday				
Sunday				
Monday				
Tuesday				
Wednesday				
		TOTAL HOURS		

Calculating gross pay

The gross pay or **gross earnings** of an employee are calculated by the employer using the hours worked as shown on the time card. Gross earnings represent the amount earned by an employee (including any bonuses, loadings, commissions and fringe benefits) before any deductions are made.

Overtime

Under the various awards, an employee is entitled to be paid overtime at the rate of at least one-and-a-half times (time-and-a-half) the regular rate for every hour worked in excess of 40 hours. For hours worked at weekends and on public holidays, most awards provide an overtime rate of twice the regular rate (double time), with some industries paying three times the regular rate (triple time) for hours worked on public holidays. However, executive and administrative staff, who are paid a salary, are usually exempt from overtime payment.

EXERCISE 7.1 Paige Industries Ltd

Throughout this exercise, the following will apply.
- When calculating time worked each day, allow for a one-hour lunch break; for example, an employee working from 8.00 a.m. to 5.00 p.m. works an eight-hour day, namely 8.00 a.m. to 12 noon (four hours) and 1.00 p.m. to 5 p.m. (four hours).
- Overtime is paid at:
  (a) time-and-a-half, for hours worked on week days and on Saturday mornings
  (b) double time, for hours worked on Saturday afternoons
  (c) triple time for hours worked on Sundays.
- Wages are paid from Thursday to the next Wednesday.
- Unpaid sick leave is deducted from the normal weekly wage. This occurs when a staff member's sick leave entitlement has been exhausted.

PAIGE INDUSTRIES LTD — EMPLOYEE INFORMATION

Name	Karmel, John	Mathias, Michael	Lee, Andrew	Erickson, Peta	Kingston, John
Address	6 May Road Penrith 2750	18 Tuna Place St Clair 2759	23 Rhodes Ave Smithfield 2164	8 Carter Road Auburn 2144	44 Wells St Burwood 2134
Date of birth	18.02.57	23.11.66	05.10.56	22.05.73	17.08.69
Payroll No.	7324	6987	6274	4367	4381
Department	Manufacturing	Sales	Manufacturing	Administration	
Classification	Fitter	Salesperson	Supervisor	WP operator	Salesperson
F/T or P/T	F/T	F/T	F/T	F/T	P/T
Weekly hours	40	40	40	37.5	N/A
Rate of pay	$8.00/h	$15.00/h	$10.50/h	$11.20/h	$25.00/h
Commenced	15.03.72	22.10.85	24.03.77	18.04.90	23.07.91
Tax File No.	123 456 789	123 456 790	124 567 890	125 666 887	Not supplied
Declaration form supplied	Yes	Yes	Yes	Yes	Yes
Tax-free threshold	No	Yes	Yes	No	No
Claim for dependants	No	Yes — spouse	Yes — sole parent	No	No
Deductions	Super — $10.00 Medical — $14.00 Union — $3.50	Super — $33.00 Savings — $25.00	Super — $12.60 Medical — $4.00 Union — $3.00	Super — $13.45 Medical — $3.50 Savings — $20.00	Nil

The following employee time card shows how a completed card should look.

	EMPLOYEE TIME CARD			
Week ending	Wednesday, 3 March 19XX			
DEPARTMENT	Manufacturing	CLASSIFICATION	Fitter	
EMPLOYEE'S NAME	JOHN KARMEL	Payroll No.	7324	
DAY	TIME COMMENCED	TIME FINISHED	NORMAL HOURS WORKED	OVERTIME HOURS WORKED
Thursday	8.00	5.00	8.0	
Friday	8.00	5.00	8.0	
Saturday	8.00	12.00		4.0
Sunday	9.00	11.00		2.0
Monday	8.00	5.00	8.0	
Tuesday	7.00	5.30	8.0	1.5
Wednesday	8.00	5.30	8.0	0.5
		TOTAL HOURS	40.0	8.0

John Karmel's gross wage is calculated as follows:

Normal time (40 hours) × hourly rate ($8) = $320.00
Overtime is calculated:
  6 hours @ $1\frac{1}{2}$ = 9 normal hours
  2 hours @ 3 = 6 normal hours
  Total overtime = 15 normal hours

Overtime (15 hours) × hourly rate ($8) = 120.00
Gross wage = $440.00

From the employee time cards below and the information given in the employee information sheet, calculate the gross wage for:
- Michael Mathias
- Andrew Lee
- Peta Erickson
- John Kingston.

EMPLOYEE TIME CARD

Week ending: Wednesday, 3 March 19XX
DEPARTMENT: Sales   CLASSIFICATION: Salesperson
EMPLOYEE'S NAME: MICHAEL MATHIAS   Payroll No. 6987

DAY	TIME COMMENCED	TIME FINISHED	NORMAL HOURS WORKED	OVERTIME HOURS WORKED
Thursday	8.00	6.00	8.0	1.0
Friday	8.00	5.00	8.0	
Saturday	8.00	12.00		4.0
Sunday	9.00	12.00		3.0
Monday	8.00	5.00	8.0	
Tuesday	7.00	5.00	8.0	1.0
Wednesday	8.00	5.00	8.0	
		TOTAL HOURS	40.0	9.0

EMPLOYEE TIME CARD

Week ending: Wednesday, 3 March 19XX
DEPARTMENT: Manufacturing   CLASSIFICATION: Supervisor
EMPLOYEE'S NAME: ANDREW LEE   Payroll No. 6274

DAY	TIME COMMENCED	TIME FINISHED	NORMAL HOURS WORKED	OVERTIME HOURS WORKED
Thursday	8.00	5.00	8.0	
Friday	8.00	6.00	8.0	1.0
Saturday	8.00	12.00		4.0
Sunday				
Monday	7.00	6.00	8.0	2.0
Tuesday	UNPAID SICK LEAVE*			
Wednesday	7.30	5.30	8.0	1.0
		TOTAL HOURS	32.0	8.0

* As Andrew Lee has used all his sick pay, he will be paid for only four days' work.

EMPLOYEE TIME CARD

Week ending: Wednesday, 3 March 19XX
DEPARTMENT: Administration
CLASSIFICATION: WP Operator
EMPLOYEE'S NAME: PETA ERICKSON
Payroll No.: 4367

DAY	TIME COMMENCED	TIME FINISHED	NORMAL HOURS WORKED	OVERTIME HOURS WORKED
Thursday	9.00	5.30	7.5	
Friday	8.00	5.30	7.5	1.0
Saturday	9.00	3.00		5.0
Sunday				
Monday	PAID SICK LEAVE		7.5	
Tuesday	9.00	6.30	7.5	1.0
Wednesday	9.00	5.30	7.5	
		TOTAL HOURS	37.5	7.0

EMPLOYEE TIME CARD

Week ending: Wednesday, 3 March 19XX
DEPARTMENT: Sales
CLASSIFICATION: Salesperson (P/T)
EMPLOYEE'S NAME: JOHN KINGSTON
Payroll no.: 4381

DAY	TIME COMMENCED	TIME FINISHED	NORMAL HOURS WORKED	OVERTIME HOURS WORKED
Thursday				
Friday				
Saturday	8.00	5.00	8.0	
Sunday				
Monday				
Tuesday				
Wednesday				
		TOTAL HOURS	8.0	

Calculating net pay

Employees are taxed under the Australian Government's **PAYE** (Pay as You Earn) **tax** scheme. To calculate the amount of taxation payable, it is necessary to obtain a copy of the Income Tax Instalments Weekly Rates Incorporating Medicare Levy schedule from the Australian Taxation Office. This schedule is also available at post offices.

DEDUCTIONS

Deductions which may be made are PAYE tax, superannuation, union fees, hospital and medical benefits, and savings plan contributions.

Income tax deductions

Under the *Income Tax Assessment Act 1936* (Cwlth), tax is levied on the income of wage and salary earners on a PAYE principle. This means that the income tax is paid as it is earned. It is the employer's responsibility to deduct the prescribed amount of tax from the employee's wage or salary. To determine the amount of income tax to be deducted, it is necessary to refer to the instalment schedule, an extract of which is reproduced on pages 472–475. The schedule lists the weekly earnings and the alternative amounts of tax which must be deducted.

The amount of tax payable is that determined from the schedule, less any adjustment for dependant and/or zone allowance. There are three levels of deduction provided in the schedule. These depend on whether or not the employee has furnished a **Tax File Number** and provided the employer with a completed employment declaration form, and whether the employee is claiming any dependant rebate.

Deductions authorised by the employee

An employee may authorise the employer to make other deductions from his or her wages or salary. The employee must sign an authority to enable these deductions to be made. Examples of such deductions are medical insurance, superannuation, union dues, savings plan contributions, payments to a credit union and a social club.

Allowances and payments

Broadly speaking, there are three types of allowances:
- those which compensate for specific working conditions; for example, zone allowances where rebates are available to people who live in remote areas of Australia
- those which are paid for special qualifications, overtime or higher duties
- those paid to cover expenses expected to be incurred by an employee in the course of his or her work (for example, tool allowance, uniform allowance, travel allowance and meal allowance (other than overtime meal allowance)).

DEPENDANT AND ZONE REBATE READY RECKONER

Rebate claimed	Instalment value	Rebate claimed	Instalment value	Rebate claimed	Instalment value	Rebate claimed	Instalment value	Rebate claimed	Instalment value	Rebate claimed	Instalment value	Rebate claimed	Instalment value	Rebate claimed	Instalment value
$	$	$	$	$	$	$	$	$	$	$	$	$	$	$	$
1	0.05	7	0.15	40	0.75	90	1.70	500	9.50	1000	19.00	1241	23.60	1700	32.30
2	0.05	8	0.15	50	0.95	100	1.90	558	10.60	1100	20.90	1300	24.70	1800	34.20
3	0.05	9	0.15	57	1.10	200	3.80	600	11.40	1116	21.20	1400	26.60	1900	36.10
4	0.10	10	0.20	60	1.15	300	5.70	700	13.30	1165	22.15	1488	28.25	2000	38.00
5	0.10	20	0.40	70	1.35	338	6.40	800	15.20	1173	22.30	1500	28.50	2500	47.50
6	0.10	30	0.55	80	1.50	400	7.60	900	17.10	1200	22.80	1600	30.40	3000	57.00

If the exact rebate claimed is not shown in the ready reckoner add the instalment values for an appropriate combination of rebates. Example: Rebate of $422 claimed. Add instalment values for rebates of $400, $20, and $2 = $7.60 + $0.40 + $0.05 = $8.05. Reduce the instalment shown in column 2 by $8.05.

INSTALMENT SCHEDULE

Weekly earnings	With tax free threshold	No tax free threshold	No tax file number	Weekly earnings	With tax free threshold	No tax free threshold	No tax file number	Weekly earnings	With tax free threshold	No tax free threshold	No tax file number	Weekly earnings	With tax free threshold	No tax free threshold	No tax file number
1	-	0.20	0.50	66	-	14.20	32.00	131	6.60	31.55	63.55	196	19.80	54.65	95.05
2	-	0.45	0.95	67	-	14.40	32.50	132	6.80	31.90	64.00	197	20.00	55.00	95.55
3	-	0.65	1.45	68	-	14.60	33.00	133	7.00	32.25	64.50	198	20.20	55.35	96.05
4	-	0.85	1.95	69	-	14.85	33.45	134	7.25	32.65	65.00	199	20.45	55.70	96.50
5	-	1.05	2.40	70	-	15.05	33.95	135	7.45	33.00	65.45	200	20.65	56.05	97.00
6	-	1.30	2.90	71	-	15.25	34.45	136	7.65	33.35	65.95	201	20.85	56.40	97.50
7	-	1.50	3.40	72	-	15.50	34.90	137	7.85	33.70	66.45	202	21.05	56.75	97.95
8	-	1.70	3.90	73	-	15.70	35.40	138	8.05	34.05	66.95	203	21.25	57.10	98.45
9	-	1.95	4.35	74	-	15.90	35.90	139	8.25	34.40	67.40	204	21.45	57.50	98.95
10	-	2.15	4.85	75	-	16.10	36.35	140	8.45	34.75	67.90	205	21.65	57.85	99.40
11	-	2.35	5.35	76	-	16.35	36.85	141	8.65	35.10	68.40	206	21.85	58.20	99.90
12	-	2.60	5.80	77	-	16.55	37.35	142	8.85	35.45	68.85	207	22.05	58.55	100.40
13	-	2.80	6.30	78	-	16.75	37.85	143	9.05	35.80	69.35	208	22.25	58.90	100.90
14	-	3.00	6.80	79	-	17.00	38.30	144	9.25	36.20	69.85	209	22.45	59.25	101.35
15	-	3.20	7.25	80	-	17.20	38.80	145	9.45	36.55	70.30	210	22.65	59.60	101.85
16	-	3.45	7.75	81	-	17.40	39.30	146	9.65	36.90	70.80	211	22.85	59.95	102.35
17	-	3.65	8.25	82	-	17.65	39.75	147	9.85	37.25	71.30	212	23.05	60.30	102.80
18	-	3.85	8.75	83	-	17.85	40.25	148	10.05	37.60	71.80	213	23.25	60.65	103.30
19	-	4.10	9.20	84	-	18.05	40.75	149	10.25	37.95	72.25	214	23.45	61.05	103.80
20	-	4.30	9.70	85	-	18.25	41.20	150	10.50	38.30	72.75	215	23.70	61.40	104.25
21	-	4.50	10.20	86	-	18.50	41.70	151	10.70	38.65	73.25	216	23.90	61.75	104.75
22	-	4.75	10.65	87	-	18.70	42.20	152	10.90	39.00	73.70	217	24.10	62.10	105.25
23	-	4.95	11.15	88	-	18.90	42.70	153	11.10	39.35	74.20	218	24.30	62.45	105.75
24	-	5.15	11.65	89	-	19.15	43.15	154	11.30	39.75	74.70	219	24.50	62.80	106.20
25	-	5.35	12.10	90	-	19.35	43.65	155	11.50	40.10	75.15	220	24.70	63.15	106.70
26	-	5.60	12.60	91	-	19.55	44.15	156	11.70	40.45	75.65	221	24.90	63.50	107.20
27	-	5.80	13.10	92	-	19.80	44.60	157	11.90	40.80	76.15	222	25.10	63.85	107.65
28	-	6.00	13.60	93	-	20.00	45.10	158	12.10	41.15	76.65	223	25.30	64.20	108.15
29	-	6.25	14.05	94	-	20.20	45.60	159	12.30	41.50	77.10	224	25.50	64.60	108.65
30	-	6.45	14.55	95	-	20.40	46.05	160	12.50	41.85	77.60	225	25.70	64.95	109.10
31	-	6.65	15.05	96	-	20.65	46.55	161	12.70	42.20	78.10	226	25.90	65.30	109.60
32	-	6.90	15.50	97	-	20.85	47.05	162	12.90	42.55	78.55	227	26.10	65.65	110.10
33	-	7.10	16.00	98	-	21.05	47.55	163	13.10	42.90	79.05	228	26.30	66.00	110.60
34	-	7.30	16.50	99	0.10	21.30	48.00	164	13.30	43.30	79.55	229	26.50	66.35	111.05
35	-	7.50	16.95	100	0.30	21.50	48.50	165	13.50	43.65	80.00	230	26.70	66.70	111.55
36	-	7.75	17.45	101	0.50	21.70	49.00	166	13.75	44.00	80.50	231	26.95	67.05	112.05
37	-	7.95	17.95	102	0.75	21.95	49.45	167	13.95	44.35	81.00	232	27.15	67.40	112.50
38	-	8.15	18.45	103	0.95	22.15	49.95	168	14.15	44.70	81.50	233	27.35	67.75	113.00
39	-	8.40	18.90	104	1.15	22.35	50.45	169	14.35	45.05	81.95	234	27.55	68.15	113.50
40	-	8.60	19.40	105	1.35	22.55	50.90	170	14.55	45.40	82.45	235	27.75	68.50	113.95
41	-	8.80	19.90	106	1.55	22.80	51.40	171	14.75	45.75	82.95	236	27.95	68.85	114.45
42	-	9.05	20.35	107	1.75	23.05	51.90	172	14.95	46.10	83.40	237	28.15	69.20	114.95
43	-	9.25	20.85	108	1.95	23.40	52.40	173	15.15	46.45	83.90	238	28.35	69.55	115.45
44	-	9.45	21.35	109	2.15	23.75	52.85	174	15.35	46.85	84.40	239	28.55	69.90	115.90
45	-	9.65	21.80	110	2.35	24.10	53.35	175	15.55	47.20	84.85	240	28.75	70.25	116.40
46	-	9.90	22.30	111	2.55	24.45	53.85	176	15.75	47.55	85.35	241	28.95	70.60	116.90
47	-	10.10	22.80	112	2.75	24.80	54.30	177	15.95	47.90	85.85	242	29.15	70.95	117.35
48	-	10.30	23.30	113	2.95	25.15	54.80	178	16.15	48.25	86.35	243	29.40	71.30	117.85
49	-	10.55	23.75	114	3.15	25.55	55.30	179	16.35	48.60	86.80	244	29.80	71.70	118.35
50	-	10.75	24.25	115	3.35	25.90	55.75	180	16.55	48.95	87.30	245	30.25	72.05	118.80
51	-	10.95	24.75	116	3.55	26.25	56.25	181	16.75	49.30	87.80	246	30.65	72.40	119.30
52	-	11.20	25.20	117	3.75	26.60	56.70	182	17.00	49.65	88.25	247	31.05	72.75	119.80
53	-	11.40	25.70	118	4.00	26.95	57.25	183	17.20	50.00	88.75	248	31.45	73.10	120.30
54	-	11.60	26.20	119	4.20	27.30	57.70	184	17.40	50.40	89.25	249	31.85	73.45	120.75
55	-	11.80	26.65	120	4.40	27.65	58.20	185	17.60	50.75	89.70	250	32.25	73.80	121.25
56	-	12.05	27.15	121	4.60	28.00	58.70	186	17.80	51.10	90.20	251	32.65	74.15	121.75
57	-	12.25	27.65	122	4.80	28.35	59.15	187	18.00	51.45	90.70	252	33.05	74.50	122.20
58	-	12.45	28.15	123	5.00	28.70	59.65	188	18.20	51.80	91.20	253	33.50	74.85	122.70
59	-	12.70	28.60	124	5.20	29.10	60.15	189	18.40	52.15	91.65	254	33.90	75.25	123.20
60	-	12.90	29.10	125	5.40	29.45	60.60	190	18.60	52.50	92.15	255	34.30	75.60	123.65
61	-	13.10	29.60	126	5.60	29.80	61.10	191	18.80	52.85	92.65	256	34.70	75.95	124.15
62	-	13.35	30.05	127	5.80	30.15	61.60	192	19.00	53.20	93.10	257	35.10	76.30	124.65
63	-	13.55	30.55	128	6.00	30.50	62.10	193	19.20	53.55	93.60	258	35.50	76.65	125.15
64	-	13.75	31.05	129	6.20	30.85	62.55	194	19.40	53.95	94.10	259	35.90	77.00	125.60
65	-	13.95	31.50	130	6.40	31.20	63.05	195	19.60	54.30	94.55	260	36.30	77.35	126.10

Figure 7.1: Sample extract from the Weekly Rates of Income Incorporating Medicare Levy Schedule

INSTALMENT SCHEDULE

Weekly earnings	With tax free threshold	No tax free threshold	No tax file number	Weekly earnings	With tax free threshold	No tax free threshold	No tax file number	Weekly earnings	With tax free threshold	No tax free threshold	No tax file number	Weekly earnings	With tax free threshold	No tax free threshold	No tax file number
1 $	2 $	3 $	4 $	1 $	2 $	3 $	4 $	1 $	2 $	3 $	4 $	1 $	2 $	3 $	4 $
261	36.75	77.70	126.60	341	54.45	106.10	165.40	421	76.05	134.50	204.20	501	104.45	168.45	243.00
262	37.15	78.05	127.05	342	54.70	106.45	165.85	422	76.40	134.85	204.65	502	104.80	168.90	243.45
263	37.45	78.40	127.55	343	54.90	106.80	166.35	423	76.75	135.20	205.15	503	105.15	169.35	243.95
264	37.65	78.80	128.05	344	55.10	107.20	166.85	424	77.10	135.60	205.65	504	105.50	169.80	244.45
265	37.90	79.15	128.50	345	55.35	107.55	167.30	425	77.45	135.95	206.10	505	105.85	170.25	244.90
266	38.10	79.50	129.00	346	55.55	107.90	167.80	426	77.80	136.30	206.60	506	106.20	170.70	245.40
267	38.30	79.85	129.50	347	55.80	108.25	168.30	427	78.15	136.65	207.10	507	106.55	171.15	245.90
268	38.55	80.20	130.00	348	56.00	108.60	168.80	428	78.50	137.00	207.60	508	106.90	171.55	246.40
269	38.75	80.55	130.45	349	56.20	108.95	169.25	429	78.85	137.35	208.05	509	107.25	172.00	246.85
270	38.95	80.90	130.95	350	56.45	109.30	169.75	430	79.25	137.70	208.55	510	107.65	172.45	247.35
271	39.20	81.25	131.45	351	56.65	109.65	170.25	431	79.60	138.05	209.05	511	108.00	172.90	247.85
272	39.40	81.60	131.90	352	56.85	110.00	170.70	432	79.95	138.40	209.50	512	108.35	173.35	248.30
273	39.65	81.95	132.40	353	57.10	110.35	171.20	433	80.30	138.75	210.00	513	108.70	173.80	248.80
274	39.85	82.35	132.90	354	57.30	110.75	171.70	434	80.65	139.15	210.50	514	109.05	174.25	249.30
275	40.05	82.70	133.35	355	57.55	111.10	172.15	435	81.00	139.50	210.95	515	109.40	174.70	249.75
276	40.30	83.05	133.85	356	57.75	111.45	172.65	436	81.35	139.85	211.45	516	109.75	175.15	250.25
277	40.50	83.40	134.35	357	57.95	111.80	173.15	437	81.70	140.20	211.95	517	110.10	175.60	250.75
278	40.70	83.75	134.85	358	58.20	112.15	173.65	438	82.05	140.55	212.45	518	110.45	176.00	251.25
279	40.95	84.10	135.30	359	58.40	112.50	174.10	439	82.40	140.90	212.90	519	110.80	176.45	251.70
280	41.15	84.45	135.80	360	58.60	112.85	174.60	440	82.80	141.30	213.40	520	111.20	176.90	252.20
281	41.35	84.80	136.30	361	58.85	113.20	175.10	441	83.15	141.75	213.90	521	111.55	177.35	252.70
282	41.60	85.15	136.75	362	59.05	113.55	175.55	442	83.50	142.20	214.35	522	111.90	177.80	253.15
283	41.80	85.50	137.25	363	59.25	113.90	176.05	443	83.85	142.65	214.85	523	112.25	178.25	253.65
284	42.05	85.90	137.75	364	59.50	114.30	176.55	444	84.20	143.10	215.35	524	112.60	178.70	254.15
285	42.25	86.25	138.20	365	59.70	114.65	177.00	445	84.55	143.55	215.80	525	112.95	179.15	254.60
286	42.45	86.60	138.70	366	59.95	115.00	177.50	446	84.90	144.00	216.30	526	113.30	179.60	255.10
287	42.70	86.95	139.20	367	60.15	115.35	178.00	447	85.25	144.45	216.80	527	113.65	180.05	255.60
288	42.90	87.30	139.70	368	60.35	115.70	178.50	448	85.60	144.85	217.30	528	114.00	180.45	256.10
289	43.10	87.65	140.15	369	60.60	116.05	178.95	449	85.95	145.30	217.75	529	114.35	180.90	256.55
290	43.35	88.00	140.65	370	60.80	116.40	179.45	450	86.35	145.75	218.25	530	114.75	181.35	257.05
291	43.55	88.35	141.15	371	61.00	116.75	179.95	451	86.70	146.20	218.75	531	115.10	181.80	257.55
292	43.75	88.70	141.60	372	61.25	117.10	180.40	452	87.05	146.65	219.20	532	115.45	182.25	258.00
293	44.00	89.05	142.10	373	61.45	117.45	180.90	453	87.40	147.10	219.70	533	115.80	182.70	258.50
294	44.20	89.45	142.60	374	61.65	117.85	181.40	454	87.75	147.55	220.20	534	116.15	183.15	259.00
295	44.45	89.80	143.05	375	61.90	118.20	181.85	455	88.10	148.00	220.65	535	116.50	183.60	259.45
296	44.65	90.15	143.55	376	62.10	118.55	182.35	456	88.45	148.45	221.15	536	116.85	184.05	259.95
297	44.85	90.50	144.05	377	62.35	118.90	182.85	457	88.80	148.90	221.65	537	117.20	184.50	260.45
298	45.10	90.85	144.55	378	62.55	119.25	183.35	458	89.15	149.30	222.15	538	117.55	184.90	260.95
299	45.30	91.20	145.00	379	62.75	119.60	183.80	459	89.50	149.75	222.60	539	117.90	185.35	261.40
300	45.50	91.55	145.50	380	63.00	119.95	184.30	460	89.90	150.20	223.10	540	118.30	185.80	261.90
301	45.75	91.90	146.00	381	63.20	120.30	184.80	461	90.25	150.65	223.60	541	118.65	186.25	262.40
302	45.95	92.25	146.45	382	63.40	120.65	185.25	462	90.60	151.10	224.05	542	119.00	186.70	262.85
303	46.15	92.60	146.95	383	63.65	121.00	185.75	463	90.95	151.55	224.55	543	119.35	187.15	263.35
304	46.40	93.00	147.45	384	63.85	121.40	186.25	464	91.30	152.00	225.05	544	119.70	187.60	263.85
305	46.60	93.35	147.90	385	64.10	121.75	186.70	465	91.65	152.45	225.50	545	120.05	188.05	264.30
306	46.85	93.70	148.40	386	64.30	122.10	187.20	466	92.00	152.90	226.00	546	120.40	188.50	264.80
307	47.05	94.05	148.90	387	64.50	122.45	187.70	467	92.05	153.35	226.50	547	120.75	188.95	265.30
308	47.25	94.40	149.40	388	64.75	122.80	188.20	468	92.70	153.75	227.00	548	121.10	189.35	265.80
309	47.50	94.75	149.85	389	64.95	123.15	188.65	469	93.05	154.20	227.45	549	121.45	189.80	266.25
310	47.70	95.10	150.35	390	65.15	123.50	189.15	470	93.45	154.65	227.95	550	121.85	190.25	266.75
311	47.90	95.45	150.85	391	65.40	123.85	189.65	471	93.80	155.10	228.45	551	122.20	190.70	267.25
312	48.15	95.80	151.30	392	65.75	124.20	190.10	472	94.15	155.55	228.90	552	122.55	191.15	267.70
313	48.35	96.15	151.80	393	66.10	124.55	190.60	473	94.50	156.00	229.40	553	122.90	191.60	268.20
314	48.60	96.55	152.30	394	66.45	124.95	191.10	474	94.85	156.45	229.90	554	123.25	192.05	268.70
315	48.80	96.90	152.75	395	66.80	125.30	191.55	475	95.20	156.90	230.35	555	123.60	192.50	269.15
316	49.00	97.25	153.25	396	67.15	125.65	192.05	476	95.55	157.35	230.85	556	123.95	192.95	269.65
317	49.25	97.60	153.75	397	67.50	126.00	192.55	477	95.90	157.80	231.35	557	124.30	193.40	270.15
318	49.45	97.95	154.25	398	67.85	126.35	193.05	478	96.25	158.20	231.85	558	124.65	193.80	270.65
319	49.65	98.30	154.70	399	68.20	126.70	193.50	479	96.60	158.65	232.30	559	125.00	194.25	271.10
320	49.90	98.65	155.20	400	68.60	127.05	194.00	480	97.00	159.10	232.80	560	125.40	194.70	271.60
321	50.10	99.00	155.70	401	68.95	127.40	194.50	481	97.35	159.55	233.30	561	125.75	195.15	272.10
322	50.30	99.35	156.15	402	69.30	127.75	194.95	482	97.70	160.00	233.75	562	126.10	195.60	272.55
323	50.55	99.70	156.65	403	69.65	128.10	195.45	483	98.05	160.45	234.25	563	126.45	196.05	273.05
324	50.75	100.10	157.15	404	70.00	128.50	195.95	484	98.40	160.90	234.75	564	126.80	196.50	273.55
325	51.00	100.45	157.60	405	70.35	128.85	196.40	485	98.75	161.35	235.20	565	127.15	196.95	274.00
326	51.20	100.80	158.10	406	70.70	129.20	196.90	486	99.10	161.80	235.70	566	127.50	197.40	274.50
327	51.40	101.15	158.60	407	71.05	129.55	197.40	487	99.45	162.25	236.20	567	127.85	197.85	275.00
328	51.65	101.50	159.10	408	71.40	129.90	197.90	488	99.80	162.65	236.70	568	128.20	198.25	275.50
329	51.85	101.85	159.55	409	71.75	130.25	198.35	489	100.15	163.10	237.15	569	128.55	198.70	275.95
330	52.05	102.20	160.05	410	72.15	130.60	198.85	490	100.55	163.55	237.65	570	128.95	199.15	276.45
331	52.30	102.55	160.55	411	72.50	130.95	199.35	491	100.90	164.00	238.15	571	129.30	199.60	276.95
332	52.50	102.90	161.00	412	72.85	131.30	199.80	492	101.25	164.45	238.60	572	129.65	200.05	277.40
333	52.70	103.25	161.50	413	73.20	131.65	200.30	493	101.60	164.90	239.10	573	130.00	200.50	277.90
334	52.95	103.65	162.00	414	73.55	132.05	200.80	494	101.95	165.35	239.60	574	130.35	200.95	278.40
335	53.15	104.00	162.45	415	73.90	132.40	201.25	495	102.30	165.80	240.05	575	130.70	201.40	278.85
336	53.40	104.35	162.95	416	74.25	132.75	201.75	496	102.65	166.25	240.55	576	131.05	201.85	279.35
337	53.60	104.70	163.45	417	74.60	133.10	202.25	497	103.00	166.70	241.05	577	131.40	202.30	279.85
338	53.80	105.05	163.95	418	74.95	133.45	202.75	498	103.35	167.10	241.55	578	131.75	202.70	280.35
339	54.05	105.40	164.40	419	75.30	133.80	203.20	499	103.70	167.55	242.00	579	132.10	203.15	280.80
340	54.25	105.75	164.90	420	75.70	134.15	203.70	500	104.10	168.00	242.50	580	132.50	203.60	281.30

Figure 7.1 (continued)

INSTALMENT SCHEDULE

Weekly earnings	With tax free threshold	No tax free threshold	No tax file number	Weekly earnings	With tax free threshold	No tax free threshold	No tax file number	Weekly earnings	With tax free threshold	No tax free threshold	No tax file number	Weekly earnings	With tax free threshold	No tax free threshold	No tax file number
1 $	2 $	3 $	4 $	1 $	2 $	3 $	4 $	1 $	2 $	3 $	4 $	1 $	2 $	3 $	4 $
581	132.85	204.05	281.80	661	161.25	239.65	320.60	741	191.20	278.10	359.40	821	226.80	316.90	398.20
582	133.20	204.50	282.25	662	161.60	240.10	321.05	742	191.65	278.60	359.85	822	227.25	317.40	398.65
583	133.55	204.95	282.75	663	161.95	240.55	321.55	743	192.10	279.05	360.35	823	227.70	317.85	399.15
584	133.90	205.40	283.25	664	162.30	241.00	322.05	744	192.55	279.55	360.85	824	228.15	318.35	399.65
585	134.25	205.85	283.70	665	162.65	241.45	322.50	745	193.00	280.05	361.30	825	228.60	318.85	400.10
586	134.60	206.30	284.20	666	163.00	241.90	323.00	746	193.40	280.50	361.80	826	229.00	319.30	400.60
587	134.95	206.75	284.70	667	163.35	242.35	323.50	747	193.85	281.00	362.30	827	229.45	319.80	401.10
588	135.30	207.15	285.20	668	163.70	242.75	324.00	748	194.30	281.50	362.80	828	229.90	320.30	401.60
589	135.65	207.60	285.65	669	164.05	243.20	324.45	749	194.75	281.95	363.25	829	230.35	320.75	402.05
590	136.05	208.05	286.15	670	164.45	243.65	324.95	750	195.20	282.45	363.75	830	230.80	321.25	402.55
591	136.40	208.50	286.65	671	164.80	244.15	325.45	751	195.65	282.95	364.25	831	231.25	321.75	403.05
592	136.75	208.95	287.10	672	165.15	244.65	325.90	752	196.10	283.45	364.70	832	231.70	322.25	403.50
593	137.10	209.40	287.60	673	165.50	245.10	326.40	753	196.55	283.90	365.20	833	232.15	322.70	404.00
594	137.45	209.85	288.10	674	165.85	245.60	326.90	754	197.00	284.40	365.70	834	232.60	323.20	404.50
595	137.80	210.30	288.55	675	166.20	246.10	327.35	755	197.45	284.90	366.15	835	233.05	323.70	404.95
596	138.15	210.75	289.05	676	166.55	246.55	327.85	756	197.85	285.35	366.65	836	233.45	324.15	405.45
597	138.50	211.20	289.55	677	166.90	247.05	328.35	757	198.30	285.85	367.15	837	233.90	324.65	405.95
598	138.85	211.60	290.05	678	167.25	247.55	328.85	758	198.75	286.35	367.65	838	234.35	325.15	406.45
599	139.20	212.05	290.50	679	167.60	248.00	329.30	759	199.20	286.80	368.10	839	234.80	325.60	406.90
600	139.60	212.50	291.00	680	168.00	248.50	329.80	760	199.65	287.30	368.60	840	235.25	326.10	407.40
601	139.95	212.95	291.50	681	168.35	249.00	330.30	761	200.10	287.80	369.10	841	235.70	326.60	407.90
602	140.30	213.40	291.95	682	168.70	249.50	330.75	762	200.55	288.30	369.55	842	236.15	327.10	408.35
603	140.65	213.85	292.45	683	169.05	249.95	331.25	763	201.00	288.75	370.05	843	236.60	327.55	408.85
604	141.00	214.30	292.95	684	169.40	250.45	331.75	764	201.45	289.25	370.55	844	237.05	328.05	409.35
605	141.35	214.75	293.40	685	169.75	250.95	332.20	765	201.90	289.75	371.00	845	237.50	328.55	409.80
606	141.70	215.20	293.90	686	170.10	251.40	332.70	766	202.30	290.20	371.50	846	237.90	329.00	410.30
607	142.05	215.65	294.40	687	170.45	251.90	333.20	767	202.75	290.70	372.00	847	238.35	329.50	410.80
608	142.40	216.05	294.90	688	170.80	252.40	333.70	768	203.20	291.20	372.50	848	238.80	330.00	411.30
609	142.75	216.50	295.35	689	171.15	252.85	334.15	769	203.65	291.65	372.95	849	239.25	330.45	411.75
610	143.15	216.95	295.85	690	171.55	253.35	334.65	770	204.10	292.15	373.45	850	239.70	330.95	412.25
611	143.50	217.40	296.35	691	171.90	253.85	335.15	771	204.55	292.65	373.95	851	240.15	331.45	412.75
612	143.85	217.85	296.80	692	172.25	254.35	335.60	772	205.00	293.15	374.40	852	240.60	331.95	413.20
613	144.20	218.30	297.30	693	172.60	254.80	336.10	773	205.45	293.60	374.90	853	241.05	332.40	413.70
614	144.55	218.75	297.80	694	172.95	255.30	336.60	774	205.90	294.10	375.40	854	241.50	332.90	414.20
615	144.90	219.20	298.25	695	173.30	255.80	337.05	775	206.35	294.60	375.85	855	241.95	333.40	414.65
616	145.25	219.65	298.75	696	173.65	256.25	337.55	776	206.75	295.05	376.35	856	242.35	333.85	415.15
617	145.60	220.10	299.25	697	174.00	256.75	338.05	777	207.20	295.55	376.85	857	242.80	334.35	415.65
618	145.95	220.50	299.75	698	174.35	257.25	338.55	778	207.65	296.05	377.35	858	243.25	334.85	416.15
619	146.30	220.95	300.20	699	174.70	257.70	339.00	779	208.10	296.50	377.80	859	243.70	335.30	416.60
620	146.70	221.40	300.70	700	175.10	258.20	339.50	780	208.55	297.00	378.30	860	244.15	335.80	417.10
621	147.05	221.85	301.20	701	175.45	258.70	340.00	781	209.00	297.50	378.80	861	244.60	336.30	417.60
622	147.40	222.30	301.65	702	175.80	259.20	340.45	782	209.45	298.00	379.25	862	245.05	336.80	418.05
623	147.75	222.75	302.15	703	176.15	259.65	340.95	783	209.90	298.45	379.75	863	245.50	337.25	418.55
624	148.10	223.20	302.65	704	176.50	260.15	341.45	784	210.35	298.95	380.25	864	245.95	337.75	419.05
625	148.45	223.65	303.10	705	176.85	260.65	341.90	785	210.80	299.45	380.70	865	246.40	338.25	419.50
626	148.80	224.10	303.60	706	177.20	261.10	342.40	786	211.20	299.90	381.20	866	246.80	338.70	420.00
627	149.15	224.55	304.10	707	177.55	261.60	342.90	787	211.65	300.40	381.70	867	247.25	339.20	420.50
628	149.50	224.95	304.60	708	177.90	262.10	343.40	788	212.10	300.90	382.20	868	247.70	339.70	421.00
629	149.85	225.40	305.05	709	178.25	262.55	343.85	789	212.55	301.35	382.65	869	248.15	340.15	421.45
630	150.25	225.85	305.55	710	178.65	263.05	344.35	790	213.00	301.85	383.15	870	248.60	340.65	421.95
631	150.60	226.30	306.05	711	179.00	263.55	344.85	791	213.45	302.35	383.65	871	249.05	341.15	422.45
632	150.95	226.75	306.50	712	179.35	264.05	345.30	792	213.90	302.85	384.10	872	249.50	341.65	422.90
633	151.30	227.20	307.00	713	179.70	264.50	345.80	793	214.35	303.30	384.60	873	249.95	342.10	423.40
634	151.65	227.65	307.50	714	180.05	265.00	346.30	794	214.80	303.80	385.10	874	250.40	342.60	423.90
635	152.00	228.10	307.95	715	180.40	265.50	346.75	795	215.25	304.30	385.55	875	250.85	343.10	424.35
636	152.35	228.55	308.45	716	180.75	265.95	347.25	796	215.65	304.75	386.05	876	251.25	343.55	424.85
637	152.70	229.00	308.95	717	181.10	266.45	347.75	797	216.10	305.25	386.55	877	251.70	344.05	425.35
638	153.05	229.40	309.45	718	181.45	266.95	348.25	798	216.55	305.75	387.05	878	252.15	344.55	425.85
639	153.40	229.85	309.90	719	181.80	267.40	348.70	799	217.00	306.20	387.50	879	252.60	345.00	426.30
640	153.80	230.30	310.40	720	182.20	267.90	349.20	800	217.45	306.70	388.00	880	253.05	345.50	426.80
641	154.15	230.75	310.90	721	182.55	268.40	349.70	801	217.90	307.20	388.50	881	253.50	346.00	427.30
642	154.50	231.20	311.35	722	182.90	268.90	350.15	802	218.35	307.70	388.95	882	253.95	346.50	427.75
643	154.85	231.65	311.85	723	183.25	269.35	350.65	803	218.80	308.15	389.45	883	254.40	346.95	428.25
644	155.20	232.10	312.35	724	183.65	269.85	351.15	804	219.25	308.65	389.95	884	254.85	347.45	428.75
645	155.55	232.55	312.80	725	184.10	270.35	351.60	805	219.70	309.15	390.40	885	255.30	347.95	429.20
646	155.90	233.00	313.30	726	184.50	270.80	352.10	806	220.10	309.60	390.90	886	255.70	348.40	429.70
647	156.25	233.45	313.80	727	184.95	271.30	352.60	807	220.55	310.10	391.40	887	256.15	348.90	430.20
648	156.60	233.85	314.30	728	185.40	271.80	353.10	808	221.00	310.60	391.90	888	256.60	349.40	430.70
649	156.95	234.30	314.75	729	185.85	272.25	353.55	809	221.45	311.05	392.35	889	257.05	349.85	431.15
650	157.35	234.75	315.25	730	186.30	272.75	354.05	810	221.90	311.55	392.85	890	257.50	350.35	431.65
651	157.70	235.20	315.75	731	186.75	273.25	354.55	811	222.35	312.05	393.35	891	257.95	350.85	432.15
652	158.05	235.65	316.20	732	187.20	273.75	355.00	812	222.80	312.55	393.80	892	258.40	351.35	432.60
653	158.40	236.10	316.70	733	187.65	274.20	355.50	813	223.25	313.00	394.30	893	258.85	351.80	433.10
654	158.75	236.55	317.20	734	188.10	274.70	356.00	814	223.70	313.50	394.80	894	259.30	352.30	433.60
655	159.10	237.00	317.65	735	188.55	275.20	356.45	815	224.15	314.00	395.25	895	259.75	352.80	434.05
656	159.45	237.45	318.15	736	188.95	275.65	356.95	816	224.55	314.45	395.75	896	260.15	353.25	434.55
657	159.80	237.90	318.65	737	189.40	276.15	357.45	817	225.00	314.95	396.25	897	260.60	353.75	435.05
658	160.15	238.30	319.15	738	189.85	276.65	357.95	818	225.45	315.45	396.75	898	261.05	354.25	435.55
659	160.50	238.75	319.60	739	190.30	277.10	358.40	819	225.90	315.90	397.20	899	261.50	354.70	436.00
660	160.90	239.20	320.10	740	190.75	277.60	358.90	820	226.35	316.40	397.70	900	261.95	355.20	436.50

Figure 7.1 *(continued)*

INSTALMENT SCHEDULE

Weekly earnings	Instalment With tax free threshold	Instalment No tax free threshold	Instalment No tax file number	Weekly earnings	Instalment With tax free threshold	Instalment No tax free threshold	Instalment No tax file number	Weekly earnings	Instalment With tax free threshold	Instalment No tax free threshold	Instalment No tax file number	Weekly earnings	Instalment With tax free threshold	Instalment No tax free threshold	Instalment No tax file number
1 $	2 $	3 $	4 $	1 $	2 $	3 $	4 $	1 $	2 $	3 $	4 $	1 $	2 $	3 $	4 $
901	262.40	355.70	437.00	976	296.65	392.05	473.35	1051	333.00	428.45	509.75	1126	369.40	464.80	546.10
902	262.85	356.20	437.45	977	297.10	392.55	473.85	1052	333.50	428.95	510.20	1127	369.85	465.30	546.60
903	263.30	356.65	437.95	978	297.60	393.05	474.35	1053	334.00	429.40	510.70	1128	370.35	465.80	547.10
904	263.75	357.15	438.45	979	298.10	393.50	474.80	1054	334.45	429.90	511.20	1129	370.85	466.25	547.55
905	264.20	357.65	438.90	980	298.60	394.00	475.30	1055	334.95	430.40	511.65	1130	371.35	466.75	548.05
906	264.60	358.10	439.40	981	299.05	394.50	475.80	1056	335.45	430.85	512.15	1131	371.80	467.25	548.55
907	265.05	358.60	439.90	982	299.55	395.00	476.25	1057	335.90	431.35	512.65	1132	372.30	467.75	549.00
908	265.50	359.10	440.40	983	300.05	395.45	476.75	1058	336.40	431.85	513.15	1133	372.80	468.20	549.50
909	265.95	359.55	440.85	984	300.50	395.95	477.25	1059	336.90	432.30	513.60	1134	373.25	468.70	550.00
910	266.40	360.05	441.35	985	301.00	396.45	477.70	1060	337.40	432.80	514.10	1135	373.75	469.20	550.45
911	266.85	360.55	441.85	986	301.50	396.90	478.20	1061	337.85	433.30	514.60	1136	374.25	469.65	550.95
912	267.30	361.05	442.30	987	301.95	397.40	478.70	1062	338.35	433.80	515.05	1137	374.70	470.15	551.45
913	267.75	361.50	442.80	988	302.45	397.90	479.20	1063	338.85	434.25	515.55	1138	375.20	470.65	551.95
914	268.20	362.00	443.30	989	302.95	398.35	479.65	1064	339.30	434.75	516.05	1139	375.70	471.10	552.40
915	268.65	362.50	443.75	990	303.45	398.85	480.15	1065	339.80	435.25	516.50	1140	376.20	471.60	552.90
916	269.05	362.95	444.25	991	303.90	399.35	480.65	1066	340.30	435.70	517.00	1141	376.65	472.10	553.40
917	269.50	363.45	444.75	992	304.40	399.85	481.10	1067	340.75	436.20	517.50	1142	377.15	472.60	553.85
918	269.95	363.95	445.25	993	304.90	400.30	481.60	1068	341.25	436.70	518.00	1143	377.65	473.05	554.35
919	270.40	364.40	445.70	994	305.35	400.80	482.10	1069	341.75	437.15	518.45	1144	378.10	473.55	554.85
920	270.85	364.90	446.20	995	305.85	401.30	482.55	1070	342.25	437.65	518.95	1145	378.60	474.05	555.30
921	271.30	365.40	446.70	996	306.35	401.75	483.05	1071	342.70	438.15	519.45	1146	379.10	474.50	555.80
922	271.75	365.90	447.15	997	306.80	402.25	483.55	1072	343.20	438.65	519.90	1147	379.55	475.00	556.30
923	272.20	366.35	447.65	998	307.30	402.75	484.05	1073	343.70	439.10	520.40	1148	380.05	475.50	556.80
924	272.65	366.85	448.15	999	307.80	403.20	484.50	1074	344.15	439.60	520.90	1149	380.55	475.95	557.25
925	273.10	367.35	448.60	1000	308.30	403.70	485.00	1075	344.65	440.10	521.35	1150	381.05	476.45	557.75
926	273.50	367.80	449.10	1001	308.75	404.20	485.50	1076	345.15	440.55	521.85	1151	381.50	476.95	558.25
927	273.95	368.30	449.60	1002	309.25	404.70	485.95	1077	345.60	441.05	522.35	1152	382.00	477.45	558.70
928	274.40	368.80	450.10	1003	309.75	405.15	486.45	1078	346.10	441.55	522.85	1153	382.50	477.90	559.20
929	274.85	369.25	450.55	1004	310.20	405.65	486.95	1079	346.60	442.00	523.30	1154	382.95	478.40	559.70
930	275.30	369.75	451.05	1005	310.70	406.15	487.40	1080	347.10	442.50	523.80	1155	383.45	478.90	560.15
931	275.75	370.25	451.55	1006	311.20	406.60	487.90	1081	347.55	443.00	524.30	1156	383.95	479.35	560.65
932	276.20	370.75	452.00	1007	311.65	407.10	488.40	1082	348.05	443.50	524.75	1157	384.40	479.85	561.15
933	276.65	371.20	452.50	1008	312.15	407.60	488.90	1083	348.55	443.95	525.25	1158	384.90	480.35	561.65
934	277.10	371.70	453.00	1009	312.65	408.05	489.35	1084	349.00	444.45	525.75	1159	385.40	480.80	562.10
935	277.55	372.20	453.45	1010	313.15	408.55	489.85	1085	349.50	444.95	526.20	1160	385.90	481.30	562.60
936	277.95	372.65	453.95	1011	313.60	409.05	490.35	1086	350.00	445.40	526.70	1161	386.35	481.80	563.10
937	278.40	373.15	454.45	1012	314.10	409.55	490.80	1087	350.45	445.90	527.20	1162	386.85	482.30	563.55
938	278.85	373.65	454.95	1013	314.60	410.00	491.30	1088	350.95	446.40	527.70	1163	387.35	482.75	564.05
939	279.30	374.10	455.40	1014	315.05	410.50	491.80	1089	351.45	446.85	528.15	1164	387.80	483.25	564.55
940	279.75	374.60	455.90	1015	315.55	411.00	492.25	1090	351.95	447.35	528.65	1165	388.30	483.75	565.00
941	280.20	375.10	456.40	1016	316.05	411.45	492.75	1091	352.40	447.85	529.15	1166	388.80	484.20	565.50
942	280.65	375.60	456.85	1017	316.50	411.95	493.25	1092	352.90	448.35	529.60	1167	389.25	484.70	566.00
943	281.10	376.05	457.35	1018	317.00	412.45	493.75	1093	353.40	448.80	530.10	1168	389.75	485.20	566.50
944	281.55	376.55	457.85	1019	317.50	412.90	494.20	1094	353.85	449.30	530.60	1169	390.25	485.65	566.95
945	282.00	377.05	458.30	1020	318.00	413.40	494.70	1095	354.35	449.80	531.05	1170	390.75	486.15	567.45
946	282.40	377.50	458.80	1021	318.45	413.90	495.20	1096	354.85	450.25	531.55	1171	391.20	486.65	567.95
947	282.85	378.00	459.30	1022	318.95	414.40	495.65	1097	355.30	450.75	532.05	1172	391.70	487.15	568.40
948	283.30	378.50	459.80	1023	319.45	414.85	496.15	1098	355.80	451.25	532.55	1173	392.20	487.60	568.90
949	283.75	378.95	460.25	1024	319.90	415.35	496.65	1099	356.30	451.70	533.00	1174	392.65	488.10	569.40
950	284.20	379.45	460.75	1025	320.40	415.85	497.10	1100	356.80	452.20	533.50	1175	393.15	488.60	569.85
951	284.65	379.95	461.25	1026	320.90	416.30	497.60	1101	357.25	452.70	534.00	1176	393.65	489.05	570.35
952	285.10	380.45	461.70	1027	321.35	416.80	498.10	1102	357.75	453.20	534.45	1177	394.10	489.55	570.85
953	285.55	380.90	462.20	1028	321.85	417.30	498.60	1103	358.25	453.65	534.95	1178	394.60	490.05	571.35
954	286.00	381.40	462.70	1029	322.35	417.75	499.05	1104	358.70	454.15	535.45	1179	395.10	490.50	571.80
955	286.45	381.90	463.15	1030	322.85	418.25	499.55	1105	359.20	454.65	535.90	1180	395.60	491.00	572.30
956	286.95	382.35	463.65	1031	323.30	418.75	500.05	1106	359.70	455.10	536.40	1181	396.05	491.50	572.80
957	287.40	382.85	464.15	1032	323.80	419.25	500.50	1107	360.15	455.60	536.90	1182	396.55	492.00	573.25
958	287.90	383.35	464.65	1033	324.30	419.70	501.00	1108	360.65	456.10	537.40	1183	397.05	492.45	573.75
959	288.40	383.80	465.10	1034	324.75	420.20	501.50	1109	361.15	456.55	537.85	1184	397.50	492.95	574.25
960	288.90	384.30	465.60	1035	325.25	420.70	501.95	1110	361.65	457.05	538.35	1185	398.00	493.45	574.70
961	289.35	384.80	466.10	1036	325.75	421.15	502.45	1111	362.10	457.55	538.85	1186	398.50	493.90	575.20
962	289.85	385.30	466.55	1037	326.20	421.65	502.95	1112	362.60	458.05	539.30	1187	398.95	494.40	575.70
963	290.35	385.75	467.05	1038	326.70	422.15	503.45	1113	363.10	458.50	539.80	1188	399.45	494.90	576.20
964	290.80	386.25	467.55	1039	327.20	422.60	503.90	1114	363.55	459.00	540.30	1189	399.95	495.35	576.65
965	291.30	386.75	468.00	1040	327.70	423.10	504.40	1115	364.05	459.50	540.75	1190	400.45	495.85	577.15
966	291.80	387.20	468.50	1041	328.15	423.60	504.90	1116	364.55	459.95	541.25	1191	400.90	496.35	577.65
967	292.25	387.70	469.00	1042	328.65	424.10	505.35	1117	365.00	460.45	541.75	1192	401.40	496.85	578.10
968	292.75	388.20	469.50	1043	329.15	424.55	505.85	1118	365.50	460.95	542.25	1193	401.90	497.30	578.60
969	293.25	388.65	469.95	1044	329.60	425.05	506.35	1119	366.00	461.40	542.70	1194	402.35	497.80	579.10
970	293.75	389.15	470.45	1045	330.10	425.55	506.80	1120	366.50	461.90	543.20	1195	402.85	498.30	579.55
971	294.20	389.65	470.95	1046	330.60	426.00	507.30	1121	366.95	462.40	543.70	1196	403.35	498.75	580.05
972	294.70	390.15	471.40	1047	331.05	426.50	507.80	1122	367.45	462.90	544.15	1197	403.80	499.25	580.55
973	295.20	390.60	471.90	1048	331.55	427.00	508.30	1123	367.95	463.35	544.65	1198	404.30	499.75	581.05
974	295.65	391.10	472.40	1049	332.05	427.45	508.75	1124	368.40	463.85	545.15	1199	404.80	500.20	581.50
975	296.15	391.60	472.85	1050	332.55	427.95	509.25	1125	368.90	464.35	545.60	1200	405.30	500.70	582.00

NOTE: Where employee's earn more than $1200, the weekly instalment is calculated as follows:
- Where the general exemption is claimed: $405.276 plus 48.50 cents for each $1 of earnings in excess of $1200
- Where the general exemption is NOT claimed: $500.707 plus 48.50 cents for each $1 of earnings in excess of $1200
- Where the income tax file number is NOT shown on the Employment Declaration: $581.995 plus 48.50 cents for each $1 of earnings in excess of $1200
Amounts so calculated should be rounded to the nearest 5 cents.

Figure 7.1 (*General information pages of schedule are found on pages 587–8*)

Allowances are added to the employee's normal weekly earnings and tax instalments are based on the whole amount. At the end of the financial year, the total amounts of various allowances are shown on the **group certificate**.

Overtime meal allowance paid to an employee is stipulated in the industrial award or employment contract under which the employee is employed, and is tax free. It is not shown on the group certificate at the end of the financial year.

Medicare Levy

As an amount for the Medicare Levy is included in the scheduled rate of deductions. Most employees will pay the levy as part of their normal tax instalment deductions.

Superannuation Guarantee

To overcome the problem of an ageing population with inadequate income for their old age, the Superannuation Guarantee Scheme was commenced in 1992. It provides a minimum level of superannuation payment or pensions on retirement and also allows for the accumulation of a pool of funds that may be used by Australian investors. The employers make these superannuation contributions for their employees' retirement. These contributions are allowed as a tax deduction for employers but *not* for employees.

The **superannuation guarantee levy** applies to all employers and covers most employees including full-time, part-time and casual staff and applies from 1992. All employers are required to provide superannuation support for employees. If the employer does not make these payments, he or she must pay the Superannuation Guarantee Charge. This charge is equal to the shortfall in superannuation contributions *plus* additional fees and charges. This charge is *not* tax deductible.

Tax File Number

In 1988 a Tax File Number was introduced by the Australian Taxation Office. In that year, all persons currently in employment completed a new employment declaration to inform their employers of their Tax File Number. An employee must quote his or her Tax File Number every time he or she commences a new job or changes a current job. If an employee fails to declare his or her Tax File Number, the employer is required to deduct tax at the highest marginal rate.

Employment Declaration form

Completing an **Employment Declaration form** (see figure 7.2 opposite) allows employees to take advantage of the tax-free threshold on income (that is, the amount of money which can be earned before the employee starts paying tax) and claim rebates for dependants. What employees state on the Employment Declaration form determines the amount of PAYE tax instalments to be deducted from the employee's gross wage or salary.

Figure 7.2: Sample Employment Declaration form

The completed Employment Declaration form shows:
- the employee's Tax File Number
- an application for tax-free threshold
- an application for dependant rebates.

To be eligible for any rebates, an employee must supply an Employment Declaration form and Tax File Number to his or her employer and must also claim the tax-free threshold. This tax-free threshold may also be claimed by low-income earners. If an employee does not complete the Employment Declaration form or does not provide his or her Tax File Number to the employer, the employer must deduct tax from the employee's wages at the top marginal rate as set out in column 4 of the instalment schedule (see pages 472–475).

Because the Employment Declaration form identifies individuals under the tax system, legislation has been passed to safeguard privacy and prevent Tax File Numbers being misused. It is therefore important that Employment Declaration forms be filed in a secure manner.

An Employment Declaration Form should be completed for *every* employer. The general exemption, and any rebates for which an employee may be eligible, can only be claimed from one employer. It is best to claim these from the employer with whom the most money is earned (the main employer). If an employee has more than one job, they must answer 'No' to question 9 on the Employment Declarations filled out for all employers except the main one.

Tax is levied on an employee's gross weekly wage or salary. To calculate tax for employees, you will need to have at hand:
- employee time cards
- employee information (or history)
- tax instalment schedule (current).

The gross weekly wage is calculated as follows.
1. To the normal weekly wage (including overtime):
   - add any allowances and irregular payments that are to be included in the week's pay to the employee's normal pay — disregard any cents in the total amount.
2. From the instalment schedule:
   - use the following information to calculate income tax to be deducted from the employee's gross wage.

1.	Weekly earnings	In column 1, find employee's total weekly income (disregarding cents).
2.	Deductions	Read off corresponding tax instalment from appropriate column: • column 2 (tax-free threshold is claimed) • column 3 (tax-free threshold *not* claimed) or • column 4 (employee has *not* supplied a Tax File Number).
3.	Rebates	If employee has claimed any rebates: • determine the weekly amount by using tables 2 and 3 and Dependant Zone Rebate Ready Reckoner • subtract weekly rebate from tax found in step 2.

The Dependant Rebate table as at 1 July 1995 is:

	Full rebate for year ($)	Weekly instalment value ($)
Spouse with *no* dependent child/student	$1241	$23.60
Sole parent	1165	22.15
Parent or parent-in-law	1116	21.20
Invalid relative	558	10.60

Example 1
Lorraine Costello's gross salary for a week is $286.50. She has no dependants and has lodged an Employment Declaration form, supplied a Tax File Number and is claiming the tax-free threshold. Her tax is calculated in the following manner:

    Column 1   Salary $286
    Column 2   Tax instalment: $42.45 (tax-free threshold claimed).

Example 2
Peter Cheong's gross salary for a week is $343.75. A Tax File Number and Employment Declaration form have been supplied. He is not claiming the tax-free threshold. His tax deduction is calculated as follows:

    Column 1   Salary $343
    Column 3   Tax instalment: $106.80 (tax-free threshold *not* claimed).

Example 3
Alexander Le Brun's gross salary for a week is $478. No Tax File Number has been lodged. His tax deduction is calculated in the following way:

    Column 1   Salary $478
    Column 4   Tax instalment: $231.85 (Tax File Number *not* supplied).

Example 4
Maria Luciano's gross salary for a week is $502. She has a dependent mother. Maria has lodged an Employment Declaration form, supplied a Tax File Number and is claiming the tax-free threshold. Her tax instalment is calculated as follows:

    Column 1   Salary $502
    Column 2   Tax instalment (with tax-free threshold) $ 104.80
                Less: Dependant rebate   21.20
                Tax deducted $ 83.60

If the employee is entitled to an adjustment for Medicare Levy, subtract the value of the adjustment (the Weekly Medicare Levy Adjustment schedule is available from tax offices).

Two important points to remember are:
- If an employee does not supply the employer with a valid Employment Declaration form *and* a Tax File Number, tax should be deducted at the top marginal rate using column 4 (no Tax File Number).
- To be eligible for rebates, the employee must have supplied an Employment Declaration form and a Tax File Number and also *must* have claimed the tax-free threshold.

The amount of tax payable in the following example was calculated using the instalment schedules reproduced on pages 472–75. This is an extract from the ATO's Income Tax Instalments Weekly Rates incorporating Medicare levy, effective for payments made on or after 1 July 1995. Students should use this schedule to calculate tax payable for all exercises in this text.

The general information on pages 1 and 2 of the schedule is reproduced at the back of the text on pages 587–88, and the Dependant Rebate table as at 1 July 1995 is shown on page 479.

WAGES CALCULATION CARD				
NAME:				Payroll No.:
DEPARTMENT:				CLASSIFICATION:
WEEK ENDING:				WEEKLY/HOURLY RATE:
	Normal hours		Adjusted O/T hours	Amount ($)
Normal time				
Overtime $1\frac{1}{2}$				
2				
3				
Sick pay				
GROSS PAY				
Deductions:			Amount ($)	
Tax on gross wage				
Less Dependant rebate				
Superannuation				
Medical insurance				
Savings plan				
Union fees				
TOTAL DEDUCTIONS				
NET PAY				

Example:
Calculation of net wages for John Karmel is demonstrated below:

WAGES CALCULATION CARD			
NAME: JOHN KARMEL			Payroll No.: 7324
DEPARTMENT: MANUFACTURING			CLASSIFICATION: FITTER
WEEK ENDING: 3 MARCH 19XX			~~WEEKLY~~/HOURLY RATE: $8.00
	Normal hours	Adjusted O/T hours	Amount ($)
Normal time	40.0		320.00
Overtime $1\frac{1}{2}$	6.0	9.0	72.00
2			
3	2.0	6.0	48.00
Sick pay			
GROSS PAY			440.00
Deductions:		Amount ($)	
Tax on gross wage		141.30	
Less Dependant rebate			
Superannuation		10.00	
Medical insurance		14.00	
Savings plan			
Union fees		3.50	
TOTAL DEDUCTIONS			168.80
NET PAY			271.20

* This information is taken from the employee information sheet for John Karmel on page 467.

EXERCISE 7.2 *Calculating net wage*

Using copies of the blank wages calculation card provided on page 566, and the information given for Paige Industries Ltd on pages 467–470, calculate the net wage for the week ending 3 March 19XX for:

Michael Mathias   Peta Erickson
Andrew Lee   John Kingston.

PREPARE A MANUAL PAYROLL REGISTER

When net wages have been calculated, they are entered in the payroll register (also called a weekly wage sheet) or in a wages book when a manual payroll is being prepared. There are several commercial wages books available. Whatever system is used, the information entered is virtually the same. A sample of a payroll register prepared for Paige Industries Ltd is shown on page 482.

PAIGE INDUSTRIES LTD
PAYROLL REGISTER — Week ended 3 March 19XX

Name	Payroll No.	INCOME Ord.	INCOME O/T	INCOME Sick and hol.	GROSS PAY	Tax	Super.	DEDUCTIONS Medical insurance	Savings	Union fees	TOTAL D'DNS	NET PAY
Karmel, J.	7324	320.00	120.00		440.00	141.30	10.00	14.00		3.50	168.80	271.20
Mathias, M.	6987	600.00	270.00		870.00	225.00	33.00		25.00		283.00	587.00
Lee, A.	6274	336.00	126.00		462.00	68.45	12.60	4.00		3.00	88.05	373.95
Erickson, P.	4367	336.00	128.80	84.00	548.80	189.35	13.45	3.50	20.00		226.30	322.50
Kingston, J.	4381	200.00			200.00	97.00					97.00	103.00
		1792.00	644.80	84.00	2520.80	721.10	69.05	21.50	45.00	6.50	863.15	1657.65

To verify the correctness of the payroll register, it is necessary to cross-add the 'Income' columns to check the amount of gross pay, and to cross-add the 'Deductions' columns to check total deductions. The total deductions should then be subtracted from the total gross pay to check the total net pay.

EMPLOYEE EARNINGS RECORD

An **employee earnings record** is used to provide a detailed and cumulative record of each employee's hours worked, gross pay, deductions and net pay for year to date. The information is updated from the appropriate details from the payroll register as shown. At the end of each pay period this provides:
- a record of all earnings and deductions to date
- all necessary information for completion of a group certificate at the end of the financial year.

Shown on page 484 is a sample of an employee earnings record together with a copy of the payroll register, indicating the source of the figures entered on the employee earnings record. Cumulative figures are assumed.

GROUP CERTIFICATE

Employers act as unpaid collectors for the Australian Taxation Office and are registered as either group or non-group employers. An employer with more than 10 employees is required to register as a group employer. Group employers are required to:
- remit tax instalments collected from employees to the Australian Taxation Office each month
- issue each employee with a group certificate at the end of the financial year (or at the end of a period of employment).

A group certificate contains all details of the employee's earnings as well as the amount of tax instalments deducted for the year. It must be issued to each employee even if no tax instalments have been deducted from the employee's earnings. A terminating employee must receive his or her group certificate *within 7 days* of ceasing employment, and continuing employees before 14 July each year. Group certificates are prepared in quadruplicate and are distributed as follows:
- *original* (top copy) — to be given to the employee for inclusion in his or her income tax return
- *duplicate copy* — to be given to the employee
- *triplicate copy* — to be sent to the Australian Taxation Office before a specified date
- *quadruplicate copy* — to be retained by the group employer.

PAIGE INDUSTRIES LTD
PAYROLL REGISTER — Week ended 3 March 19XX

Name	Payroll No.	INCOME Ord.	INCOME O/T	INCOME Sick and hol.	INCOME GROSS PAY	DEDUCTIONS Tax	DEDUCTIONS Super.	DEDUCTIONS Medical insurance	DEDUCTIONS Savings	DEDUCTIONS Union fees	TOTAL D'DNS	NET PAY
Karmel, J.	7324	320.00	120.00		440.00	141.30	10.00	14.00		3.50	168.80	271.20
Mathias, M.	6987	600.00	270.00		870.00	225.00	33.00		25.00		283.00	587.00
Lee, A.	6274	336.00	126.00		462.00	68.45	12.60	4.00		3.00	88.05	373.95
Erickson, P.	4367	336.00	128.80	84.00	548.80	189.35	13.45	3.50	20.00		226.30	322.50
Kingston, J.	4381	200.00			200.00	97.00					97.00	103.00
		1792.00	644.80	84.00	2520.80	721.10	69.05	21.50	45.00	6.50	863.15	1657.65

EMPLOYEE EARNINGS RECORD

Name .... KARMEL, John
Address .... 5 May Road
Suburb .... PENRITH NSW 2750

Date commenced 15.03.72

Department .... MANUFACTURING
Classification .... FITTER
Payroll no. 7324

Date of birth	Rebates claimed	Employment Declaration form	Tax-free threshold claimed		Pay rate	Tax File No.
18-02-57	Nil	Yes ✓ / No ☐	Yes ☐ / No ✓		$8.00 p/h	123 456 789

Deductions

Week ending	Gross pay	Tax	Super	Medical	Savings	Union fees	Total	Net pay	Year to date Gross	Year to date Tax	Year to date Super	Year to date Medical	Year to date Savings	Year to date Union fees
25/02/XX	392.00	124.20	10.00	14.00		3.50	151.70	240.30	13 258.50	4122.45	293.00	410.80		102.70
03/03/XX	440.00	141.30	10.00	14.00		3.50	168.80	271.20	13 698.50	4263.75	303.00	424.80		106.20

An example of a completed group certificate for 1996 is shown below:

Figure 7.3: Sample group certificate for 1996

Non-group employers use tax stamps. The employer purchases tax stamps to the value of the tax instalments and affixes them to a special tax stamp sheet maintained on behalf of the employee. At the end of the financial year, the employee is given this sheet of stamps to include with his or her income tax return.

Other details found on a group certificate are deductions (such as superannuation payments, health insurance and union dues) which are authorised by the employee and which the employer collects and remits to the organisations concerned.

PREPARATION OF WAGE ENVELOPES (PAY PACKETS)

Payment of wages to employees is often made by electronic transfer from the bank account of the business directly to the employee's bank or building society account. In this case, the employee receives a pay advice slip which informs him or her of the amount paid into his or her account, as well as a list of deductions from his or her gross wage.

Employees may receive their weekly wage in the form of a cheque made payable to each employee, or even in cash. In both cases, the cheque or the cash is enclosed in a wage envelope (or pay packet).

Cash analysis sheet

When wages are paid in cash, a cash analysis sheet is made up so that the correct denomination of notes and coins can be obtained from the bank to make up the individual pay envelopes. It is important to remember that the amounts to be placed in the pay envelopes must be rounded off to the nearest five cents. An example of a cash analysis sheet for Paige Industries Ltd for the week ending 3 March 19XX is shown below.

CASH ANALYSIS SHEET												
Employee's name	Net wage	$100	$50	$20	$10	$5	$2	$1	50c	20c	10c	5c
Karmel, J.	271.20		250	20				1		0.20		
Mathias, M.	587.00		550	20	10	5	2					
Lee, A.	373.95		350	20			2	1	0.50	0.40		0.05
Erickson, P.	322.50		300	20			2		0.50			
Kingston, J.	103.00		100				2	1				
	1657.65		1550	80	10	5	8	3	1	0.60		0.05

To verify the correctness of the cash analysis, cross-add the totals of all notes and coin columns to make sure they agree with the total net wage.

If payment is made by cash, it is necessary to prepare a cheque for the total wages. This cheque is made out to cash. A **payment voucher** may need to be completed authorising the cheque. (You will learn how to prepare payment vouchers later in this chapter.)

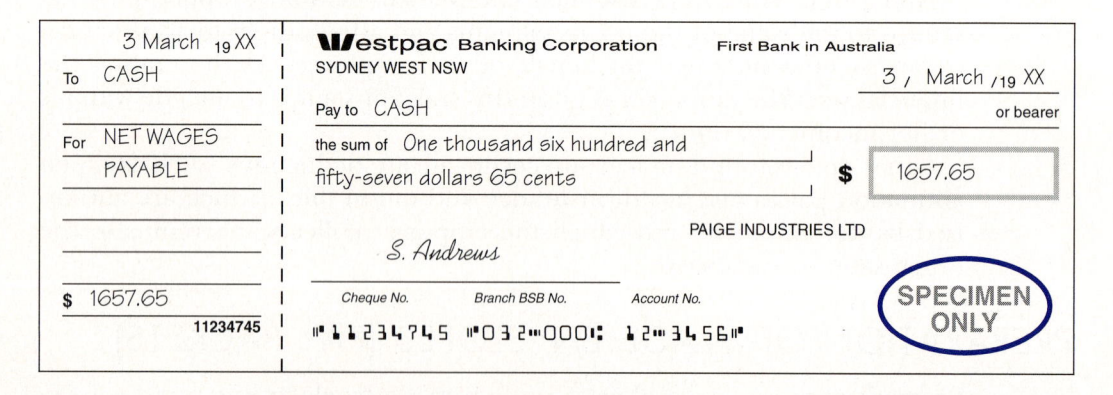

```
3 March 19XX        Westpac Banking Corporation    First Bank in Australia
To   CASH           SYDNEY WEST NSW                                3 / March /19 XX
                    Pay to  CASH                                        or bearer
For  NET WAGES      the sum of  One thousand six hundred and
     PAYABLE        fifty-seven dollars 65 cents              $   1657.65

                                                PAIGE INDUSTRIES LTD
                            S. Andrews
$ 1657.65           Cheque No.   Branch BSB No.   Account No.     SPECIMEN
       11234745     11234745     032 0000         12 3456          ONLY
```

A change docket, similar to the one shown on page 487, is then prepared to accompany the wages cheque, requesting the bank to pay the amount in the required notes and coins. The totals of the denominations are taken from the cash analysis sheet example above.

CHANGE DOCKET		
	$	c
$100		
$50	1550	00
$20	80	00
$10	10	00
$5	5	00
$2	8	00
$1	3	00
50c	1	00
20c		60
10c		
5c		05
TOTAL	1657	65

COMPLETING PAY SLIPS

A pay slip is completed, giving the employee the details of the pay enclosed in the pay envelope. Details of holiday pay are usually included on a separate pay slip in the same envelope. If an employee is paid by electronic transfer, a pay advice slip is completed and given to the employee. An example of a pay slip follows.

Example of pay slip

Name: Karmel, J.	Payroll no.: 7324
Week ending: 3 March 19XX	

Normal	$320.00
Overtime	120.00
Sick/Holiday	
GROSS PAY	$440.00
Deductions:	
Tax	141.30
Super	10.00
Medical	14.00
Savings	
Union	3.50
TOTAL DEDUCTIONS	168.80
NET PAY	$271.20

EXERCISE 7.3 *Preparing pay slips*

Prepare pay slips for M. Mathias, A. Lee, P. Erickson and J. Kingston for the week ended 3 March 19XX, using copies of the blank pay slip provided on page 570.

LEAVE

Depending upon the **award** under which they are employed, employees are entitled to various types of leave.

Paid leave

Under Australian awards, all employees are entitled to four weeks of paid annual leave each year, plus a leave loading of $17\frac{1}{2}$ per cent of the four weeks gross leave entitlement. (An exception to this is Victoria, where the holiday leave loading was abolished by the State government in October 1992.)

Annual leave accrues on a day-to-day basis. If an employee resigns, is dismissed or retrenched, the pro rata leave entitlement must be paid.

Where the annual leave loading payment for continuing employees exceeds $320, the employer is obliged to deduct tax, but only on *the amount exceeding $320*. However, the initial amount of $320 is not tax free as is frequently supposed, the tax payable on this amount being incorporated in the tax instalment schedule.

Other types of leave

There are a number of other types of leave.

- *Sick leave.* Australian awards provide for paid sick leave. The amount of paid sick leave for any employee varies, usually being 5–10 working days.
- **Bereavement leave.** This is paid leave granted on the death of a family member.
- **Long service leave.** This is leave paid to an employee when he or she works for an employer for a period of 10–15 years. Long service leave accrues from the time the employee commences employment but does not become payable until the end of the 10 or 15 years service.
- **Study leave.** Paid leave granted to an employee to pursue further study.
- *Maternity leave.* This is paid leave for a woman on the birth of a child.
- **Paternity leave.** This is paid leave for a man on the occasion of the birth of a child.

Unpaid leave

Unpaid leave includes the following.

- *Sick leave.* If an employee has exhausted his or her sick leave entitlement, unpaid sick leave must be taken if he or she has further illness.
- *Maternity leave.* This applies to a period following cessation of paid maternity leave.
- **Leave without pay.** If it becomes necessary for an employee to take time off in circumstances for which there is no paid leave entitlement, he or she may apply for leave without pay. This leave may be approved by an employer upon application from an employee for the stated reason. Approval is at the discretion of the employer.

CALCULATING HOLIDAY PAY

Annual leave is paid in advance. It is calculated and taxed on the basis of one week's normal pay and multiplied by the number of weeks leave to be taken. Some firms prepare two pay packets — one for the week worked and another for the holiday pay.

Example

In the following worked examples, the two employees have lodged their Tax File Numbers and completed Employment Declaration forms. Neither has claimed the tax-free threshold nor is claiming for a dependant. Both are continuing employees and will return to work after their holidays.

- *Employee 1*
  On 8 September 19XX, Kim Nguyen is taking four weeks' holiday.
  Normal time worked is 40 hours per week at $8.00 per hour. During the week prior to taking holiday leave, Kim did not work any overtime hours. Her normal weekly deductions are:
  - superannuation $15.00
  - medical insurance $7.00
  - union fees $3.50

  Kim's wages calculation card is shown on page 490. Note that a different form of the wages calculation card is used because Kim is taking annual leave.

- *Employee 2*
  On 8 September 19XX, Charles Brown is taking four weeks' holiday.
  Normal time worked is 40 hours per week at $15.00 per hour. No overtime hours were worked during the week prior to taking holidays. Charles's normal weekly deductions are:
  - superannuation $18.00
  - medical insurance $20.00
  - savings $15.00
  - union fees $4.00

  Charles's wages calculation card is shown on page 491.

WAGES CALCULATION CARD				
NAME: KIM NGUYEN				Payroll No.:
DEPARTMENT:				CLASSIFICATION:
WEEK ENDING: 8 SEPTEMBER 19XX				~~WEEKLY~~/HOURLY RATE: $8.00
	Normal hours		Adjusted O/T hours	Amount ($)
Normal time	40.0			320.00
Overtime $1\frac{1}{2}$				
2				
3				
Sick pay				
GROSS PAY				320.00
Deductions:			Amount ($)	
Tax on gross wage	98.65			
Less Dependant rebate	Nil		98.65	
Superannuation			15.00	
Medical insurance			7.00	
Savings plan				
Union fees			3.50	
TOTAL DEDUCTIONS				124.15
NET PAY				$195.85
GROSS HOLIDAY PAY	$320.00 × 4			1 280.00
Plus $17\frac{1}{2}$% leave loading				224.00
				1 504.00
Deductions:			Amount ($)	
Tax on normal wage of $320.00	$98.65 × 4		394.60	
Superannuation	$15.00 × 4		60.00	
Medical insurance	$7.00 × 4		28.00	
Savings plan				
Union fees	$3.50 × 4		14.00	
TOTAL DEDUCTIONS				496.60
NET HOLIDAY PAY				$1 007.40

WAGES CALCULATION CARD				
NAME: CHARLES BROWN		Payroll No.:	
DEPARTMENT:		CLASSIFICATION:	
WEEK ENDING: 8 SEPTEMBER 19XX		~~WEEKLY~~/HOURLY RATE: $15.00	
	Normal hours	Adjusted O/T hours	Amount ($)
Normal time	40.0		600.00
Overtime $1\frac{1}{2}$			
2			
3			
Sick pay			
*Excess on $17\frac{1}{2}$% leave loading ($420.00 − $320.00) = $100.00			100.00
GROSS PAY			700.00
Deductions:		Amount ($)	
Tax on gross weekly wage	258.20		
Less Dependant rebate	Nil	258.20	
Superannuation		18.00	
Medical insurance		20.00	
Savings plan		15.00	
Union fees		4.00	
TOTAL DEDUCTIONS			315.20
NET PAY			$384.80
GROSS HOLIDAY PAY	$600.00 × 4		2 400.00
Plus $17\frac{1}{2}$% leave loading		420.00	
Less Taxable excess above $320**		100.00	320.00
			2 720.00
Deductions:		Amount ($)	
Tax on normal wage of $600.00	$212.50 × 4	850.00	
Superannuation	$18.00 × 4	72.00	
Medical insurance	$20.00 × 4	80.00	
Savings plan	$15.00 × 4	60.00	
Union fees	$4.00 × 4	16.00	
TOTAL DEDUCTIONS			1 078.00
NET HOLIDAY PAY			$1642.00

* The tax schedule incorporates tax on the annual holiday leave loading up to $320. Where the holiday loading payment for continuing employees exceeds $320, only the amount over $320 is subject to tax. For PAYE purposes, this taxable excess is deducted from the total leave loading (see above**) and is included in the gross pay for the week just worked (see above *). The whole amount of the leave loading is regarded as income and is included in gross earnings on the group certificate.

EXERCISE 7.4 — Calculating holiday pay

Using copies of the blank wages calculation card provided on page 567, calculate the holiday pay for the following employees for the week ending 10 March 19XX. All employees have lodged their Tax File Number with their employer and completed the Employment Declaration form. None has claimed the tax-free threshold or claimed for a dependant.

Don't forget to calculate the $17\frac{1}{2}\%$ leave loading on the amount of holiday pay. If it exceeds $320, the difference between the tax free amount of $320 and the total leave loading is taxable. This amount is added to the normal weekly wage and tax applied to the total gross amount for the week. The holiday pay is calculated separately.

Students are required to look up the tax amount from the tax sheet printed in this book on pages 472–75.

1. Christine Hammond is taking three weeks' holiday.

   Normal time worked is 37.5 hours per week at $14.80 per hour. During the week ending 10 March, she worked two hours overtime at time-and-a-half.

   The following weekly deductions apply:
   - superannuation $16.65
   - medical insurance $3.70
   - savings plan $20.00

2. Mark Kramm is taking four weeks' holiday.

   Normal time worked is 40 hours per week at $15.60 per hour. During the week ending 10 March, he worked the following overtime:
   - six hours at time-and-a-half
   - four hours at double time.

   The following weekly deductions apply:
   - superannuation $18.75
   - medical insurance $5.00
   - union fees $3.75

3. Stephen Gordon is taking two weeks' holiday. Normal time worked is 40 hours per week at $17.30 per hour. During the week ending 10 March, he worked the following overtime:
   - five hours at time-and-a-half
   - four hours at triple time.

   The following weekly deductions apply:
   - superannuation $20.75
   - union fees $3.75

4. Jenny Talbot is taking four weeks' holiday. Normal rate is 37.5 hours per week at $15.50 per hour. She worked no overtime during the week ending 10 March. An amount of $17.45 is deducted weekly from Jenny's pay for superannuation.

EXERCISE 7.5 R. Frost & Co.

You are required to prepare the payroll for R. Frost & Co. for the week ended 10 March 19XX.

All employees have a one-hour lunch break from 12 noon to 1 p.m. and are paid overtime as follows:
- week days and on Saturday morning to noon — time-and-a-half
- Saturday afternoon — double time
- Sunday — triple time.

Sick pay entitlement is eight days per year and wages are paid from Thursday to the next Wednesday.

R. FROST & CO. — EMPLOYEE INFORMATION

Name	Garcia, Rosa	Bryson, Kevin	Cartier, Lisa	Fulford, Owen	Mischa, Tania
Address	14 Kent Street Narangba 4504	22 West Street Carindale 4152	91 Dart Road Annerley 4103	45 Simpson Ave Taringa 4068	103 Burton St Wynnum 4178
Date of birth	18.03.72	23.12.50	14.10.66	05.06.54	15.06.73
Payroll No.	1143	1190	1430	1448	2010
Department	Sales	Administration	Service	Service	Administration
Classification	Secretary	Accountant	WP operator	Serviceperson	Bookkeeper
F/T or P/T	F/T	F/T	F/T	F/T	F/T
Weekly hours	37.5	37.5	37.5	40.0	37.5
Rate of pay	$12.40/h	$720.00/week	$14.00/h	$16.70/h	$13.50/h
Commenced	24.02.89	27.06.90	05.07.90	12.10.91	14.06.93
Tax File No.	333 888 999	444 555 666	495 231 786	778 890 341	Not supplied
Declaration form supplied	Yes	Yes	Yes	Yes	Yes
Tax-free threshold	Yes	No	Yes	No	No
Claim for dependants	Invalid father	Nil	Sole parent	Nil	Nil
Deductions	Super — $18.60 Medical — $14.00 Savings — $30.00	Super — $25.48 Medical — $20.00	Super — $22.65 Savings — $20.00	Super — $34.75 Medical — $15.50 Union — $2.75	Super — $30.10

The information from the employees' time cards has been recorded on the employees' wages calculation cards. You are required to complete these and use them to prepare the following documentation, blank copies of which are provided on the pages indicated:
- payroll register (page 568)
- cash analysis sheet (page 569)
- change docket (page 570)
- cheque (page 544)
- pay slips for all employees (page 570).

Once you have completed the above, fill out the employee earnings records for all employees included on pages 498 to 500. (Complete the personal details for each employee from the employee information sheet on page 493.)

WAGES CALCULATION CARD				
NAME: ROSA GARCIA			Payroll No.: 1143	
DEPARTMENT: SALES			CLASSIFICATION: SECRETARY	
WEEK ENDING: 10 MARCH 19XX			~~WEEKLY~~/HOURLY RATE: $12.40	
	Normal hours	Adjusted O/T hours		Amount ($)
Normal time	37.5			$465.00
Overtime 1½	4.00	6.00		74.40
2	2.00	4.00		49.60
3				
Sick pay				
GROSS PAY				589.00
Deductions:		Amount ($)		
Tax on gross wage	?			
Less Dependant rebate	?	?		
Superannuation		18.60		
Medical insurance		14.00		
Savings plan		30.00		
Union fees				
TOTAL DEDUCTIONS				?
NET PAY				?

Kevin Bryson is taking 4 weeks' holiday from 17 March 19XX.

WAGES CALCULATION CARD			
NAME: KEVIN BRYSON			Payroll No.: 1190
DEPARTMENT: ADMINISTRATION			CLASSIFICATION: ACCOUNTANT
WEEK ENDING: 10 March 19XX			~~WEEKLY~~/HOURLY RATE: $720.00
	Normal hours	Adjusted O/T hours	Amount ($)
Normal time			720.00
Overtime $1\frac{1}{2}$			
2			
3			
Sick pay			
Excess on $17\frac{1}{2}$% leave loading* ($504.00 − $320.00)			?
GROSS PAY			?
Deductions:		Amount ($)	
Tax on gross wage	?		
Less Dependant rebate	Nil	?	
Superannuation		25.48	
Medical insurance		20.00	
Savings plan			
Union fees			
TOTAL DEDUCTIONS			?
NET PAY			?
GROSS HOLIDAY PAY	$720.00 × 4		2 880.00
Plus $17\frac{1}{2}$% leave loading		504.00	
Less Taxable excess over $320		?	320.00
			3 384.00
Deductions:		Amount ($)	
Tax on normal wage of $? (no dependant rebate)	? × 4	?	
Superannuation	$25.48 × 4	101.92	
Medical insurance	$20.00 × 4	80.00	
Savings plan			
Union fees			
TOTAL DEDUCTIONS			?
NET HOLIDAY PAY			?

* When the annual leave loading payment for continuing employees exceeds $320, only the amount over $320 is subject to tax. For PAYE purposes, this taxable excess is added to the gross pay for the week just worked and tax is applied on this figure. The taxable excess is deducted from the leave loading and only $320 is included in the gross holiday pay.

WAGES CALCULATION CARD

NAME: LISA CARTIER		Payroll No.: 1430	
DEPARTMENT: SERVICE		CLASSIFICATION: WP OPERATOR	
WEEK ENDING: 10 MARCH 19XX		~~WEEKLY~~/HOURLY RATE: $14.00	
	Normal hours	Adjusted O/T hours	Amount ($)
Normal time	30.0		$420.00
Overtime $1\frac{1}{2}$	2.0	3.0	42.00
2			
3			
Sick pay (1 DAY)	7.50		105.00
GROSS PAY			567.00
Deductions:		Amount ($)	
Tax on gross wage		?	
Less Dependant rebate		?	?
Superannuation		22.65	
Medical insurance			
Savings plan		20.00	
Union fees			
TOTAL DEDUCTIONS			?
NET PAY			?

WAGES CALCULATION CARD

NAME: OWEN FULFORD		Payroll No.: 1448	
DEPARTMENT: SERVICE		CLASSIFICATION: SERVICEPERSON	
WEEK ENDING: 10 MARCH 19XX		~~WEEKLY~~/HOURLY RATE: $16.70	
	Normal hours	Adjusted O/T hours	Amount ($)
Normal time	40.0		$668.00
Overtime $1\frac{1}{2}$	6.0	9.0	150.30
2	2.0	4.0	66.80
3			
Sick pay			
GROSS PAY			885.10

WAGES CALCULATION CARD (continued)			
GROSS PAY (from previous page)			885.10
Deductions:		Amount ($)	
Tax on gross wage		?	
Less Dependant rebate			
Superannuation		34.75	
Medical insurance		15.50	
Savings plan			
Union fees		2.75	
TOTAL DEDUCTIONS			?
NET PAY			?

WAGES CALCULATION CARD			
NAME: TANIA MISCHA			Payroll No.: 2010
DEPARTMENT: ADMINISTRATION			CLASSIFICATION: BOOKKEEPER
WEEK ENDING: 10 MARCH 19XX			~~WEEKLY~~/HOURLY RATE: $13.50
	Normal hours	Adjusted O/T hours	Amount ($)
Normal time	22.5		$303.75
Overtime $1\frac{1}{2}$			
2			
3			
Sick pay (2 DAYS)	15.0		202.50
GROSS PAY			506.25
Deductions:		Amount ($)	
Tax on gross wage			
Less Dependant rebate		?	
Superannuation		30.10	
Medical insurance			
Savings plan			
Union fees			
TOTAL DEDUCTIONS			?
NET PAY			?

EMPLOYEE EARNINGS RECORD

Name ......GARCIA, Rosa...... Date commenced ...... Department ......
Address ...... Classification ......
Suburb ...... Payroll No. ......

Date of birth ...... Rebates claimed ...... Employment Declaration form: Yes ☐ No ☐ Tax-free threshold claimed: Yes ☐ No ☐ Pay rate ...... Tax File No. ......

Week ending	Gross pay	Tax	Super	Medical	Deductions Savings	Union fees	Total	Net pay	Gross	Tax	Year to date Super	Medical	Savings	Union fees
3.03.XX	465.00	70.45	18.60	14.00	30.00		133.05	331.95	16740.00	4723.92	669.60	504.00	1080.00	

EMPLOYEE EARNINGS RECORD

Name ......BRYSON, Kevin...... Date commenced ...... Department ......
Address ...... Classification ......
Suburb ...... Payroll No. ......

Date of birth ...... Rebates claimed ...... Employment Declaration form: Yes ☐ No ☐ Tax-free threshold claimed: Yes ☐ No ☐ Pay rate ...... Tax File No. ......

Week ending	Gross pay	Tax	Super	Medical	Deductions Savings	Union fees	Total	Net pay	Gross	Tax	Year to date Super	Medical	Savings	Union fees
3.03.XX	720.00	267.90	25.48	20.00			313.38	406.62	26092.80	9727.85	917.28	720.00		

EMPLOYEE EARNINGS RECORD

Name: CARTIER, Lisa
Address: ....
Suburb: ....

Date of birth: ....

Department: ....
Classification: ....
Payroll No.: ....

Date commenced: ....

Rebates claimed: ....

Employment Declaration form: Yes ☐ No ☐

Tax-free threshold claimed: Yes ☐ No ☐

Pay rate: ....

Tax File No.: ....

Week ending	Gross pay	Tax	Super	Medical	Deductions Savings	Union fees	Total	Net pay	Gross	Tax	Year to date Super	Medical	Savings	Union fees
3.03.XX	525.00	90.80	22.65		20.00		133.45	391.55	18 900.00	6368.20	815.40		720.00	

EMPLOYEE EARNINGS RECORD

Name: FULFORD, Owen
Address: ....
Suburb: ....

Date of birth: ....

Department: ....
Classification: ....
Payroll No.: ....

Date commenced: ....

Rebates claimed: ....

Employment Declaration form: Yes ☐ No ☐

Tax-free threshold claimed: Yes ☐ No ☐

Pay rate: ....

Tax File No.: ....

Week ending	Gross pay	Tax	Super	Medical	Deductions Savings	Union fees	Total	Net pay	Gross	Tax	Year to date Super	Medical	Savings	Union fees
3.03.XX	668.00	242.75	34.75	15.50		2.75	295.75	372.25	24 048.00	8739.00	1251.00	558.00		99.00

EMPLOYEE EARNINGS RECORD

Name ..... MISCHA, Tania
Address .....
Suburb .....

Department .....
Classification .....
Payroll No. .....

Date commenced .....
Pay rate .....
Tax File No. .....

Date of birth	Rebates claimed	Employment Declaration form	Tax-free threshold claimed
		Yes ☐ No ☐	Yes ☐ No ☐

| Week ending | Gross pay | Deductions ||||| Total | Net pay |
		Tax	Super	Medical	Savings	Union fees		
3.03.XX	546.75		30.10					

Year to date

Gross	Tax	Super	Medical	Savings	Union fees
18 225.00	6145.20	1083.60			

EXERCISE 7.6 M. Diego & Co.

Using the employee information sheet below, the time sheets on pages 502–504 and copies of the blank wages calculation cards (provided on pages 566 and 567), the payroll register (provided on page 568), the cash analysis sheet (provided on page 569), the change docket (provided on page 570), the pay slip (provided on page 570) and the cheque (provided on page 544), you are required to carry out the following.

1. Calculate the hours worked for the week ending 8 May 19XX.
2. Prepare the wages calculation cards.
3. Prepare the payroll register.
4. Prepare the cheque for the payroll.
5. Prepare the cash analysis sheet and change docket.
6. Prepare pay slips for all employees.

Additional information:
- Employees are paid sick leave for eight days per year.
- Pay weeks are from Thursday to the following Wednesday.
- Overtime is paid at time-and-a-half on week days and on Saturday mornings; double time is paid on Saturday afternoons and triple time on Sundays and public holidays.

M. DIEGO & CO. — EMPLOYEE INFORMATION SHEET

Name	Martoub, L.	Ramsid, B.	Essex, F.	Fox, J.	Kemp, L.
Address	18 Mark Rd Auburn 2144	2 Castle Cres. Castle Hill 2154	99 Oaks Rd Parramatta 2150	23 Dundas St Ermington 2115	5 Dunne St Petersham 2049
Date of birth	20.03.45	05.11.51	18.02.52	02.12.63	21.04.66
Payroll No.	236	367	390	420	434
Department	Manufacturing	Administration	Manufacturing	Administration	Manufacturing
Classification	Carpenter	Supervisor	Turner	Exec. assistant	Fitter
F/T or P/T	F/T	F/T	F/T	F/T	F/T
Weekly hours	40	37.5	40	37.50	40
Rate of pay	$18.00 p/h	$800.00 p/week	$13.50 p/h	$17.80 p/h	$13.50 p/h
Commenced	02.03.80	12.12.82	14.05.85	16.12.87	20.02.90
Tax File No.	233 445 667	332 111 998	302 202 102	945 787 655	368 900 241
Declaration form supplied	Yes	Yes	Yes	Yes	Yes
Tax-free threshold	Yes	Yes	No	Yes	No
Claim for dependants	Spouse	Parent	No	Sole parent	No
Deductions	Super — $48.70 Medical — $12.00	Super — $48.00 Savings — $30.00	Super — $16.20 Union — $4.90	Super — $20.00 Medical — $15.00	Super — $16.56 Union — $4.90

EMPLOYEE TIME CARD

Week ending: Wednesday, 8 May 19XX
DEPARTMENT: Manufacturing   CLASSIFICATION: Carpenter
EMPLOYEE'S NAME: LEN MARTOUB   Payroll No. 236

DAY	TIME COMMENCED	TIME FINISHED	NORMAL HOURS WORKED	OVERTIME HOURS WORKED
Thursday	8.00	5.00	8.0	
Friday	8.00	5.00	8.0	
Saturday	8.00	12.00		4.0
Sunday				
Monday	PAID SICK LEAVE			
Tuesday	8.00	6.00	8.0	1.0
Wednesday	8.00	5.00	8.0	
		TOTAL HOURS	32.0	5.0

EMPLOYEE TIME CARD

Week ending: Wednesday, 8 May 19XX
DEPARTMENT: Administration   CLASSIFICATION: Supervisor
EMPLOYEE'S NAME: BAYAB RAMSID   Payroll No. 367

DAY	TIME COMMENCED	TIME FINISHED	NORMAL HOURS WORKED	OVERTIME HOURS WORKED
Thursday	9.00	5.30	7.5	
Friday	9.00	5.30	7.5	
Saturday				
Sunday				
Monday	9.00	5.30	7.5	
Tuesday	9.00	5.30	7.5	
Wednesday	9.00	5.30	7.5	
		TOTAL HOURS	37.5	

You are required to calculate holiday pay for B. Ramsid, who commences three weeks' holidays on 15 May 19XX.

EMPLOYEE TIME CARD

Week ending: Wednesday 8 May 19XX
DEPARTMENT: Manufacturing
CLASSIFICATION: Turner
EMPLOYEE'S NAME: FRANK ESSEX
Payroll No.: 390

DAY	TIME COMMENCED	TIME FINISHED	NORMAL HOURS WORKED	OVERTIME HOURS WORKED
Thursday	7.00	6.00	8.0	2.0
Friday	8.00	5.00	8.0	
Saturday	8.00	5.00		8.0
Sunday	8.00	10.00		2.0
Monday	7.00	5.00	8.0	1.0
Tuesday	8.00	5.00	8.0	
Wednesday	8.00	5.00	8.0	
		TOTAL HOURS	40.0	13.0

EMPLOYEE TIME CARD

Week ending: Wednesday, 8 May 19XX
DEPARTMENT: Administration
CLASSIFICATION: Executive assistant
EMPLOYEE'S NAME: JANETTE FOX
Payroll no.: 420

DAY	TIME COMMENCED	TIME FINISHED	NORMAL HOURS WORKED	OVERTIME HOURS WORKED
Thursday	9.00	6.30	7.5	1.0
Friday	9.00	5.30	7.5	
Saturday	9.00	11.00		2.0
Sunday				
Monday	PAID SICK LEAVE			
Tuesday	PAID SICK LEAVE			
Wednesday	9.00	5.30	7.5	
		TOTAL HOURS	22.5	3.0

EMPLOYEE TIME CARD

Week ending: Wednesday, 8 May 19XX

DEPARTMENT: Manufacturing   CLASSIFICATION: Fitter

EMPLOYEE'S NAME: LEO KEMP   Payroll No.: 434

DAY	TIME COMMENCED	TIME FINISHED	NORMAL HOURS WORKED	OVERTIME HOURS WORKED
Thursday	8.00	5.00	8.0	
Friday	8.00	5.00	8.0	
Saturday	8.00	11.00		3.0
Sunday				
Monday	8.00	6.00	8.0	1.0
Tuesday	8.00	5.00	8.0	
Wednesday	8.00	5.00	8.0	
		TOTAL HOURS	40.0	4.0

Leo Kemp commences 2 weeks' holiday on Wednesday 15 May 19XX. You are required to calculate his holiday pay.

EXERCISE 7.7 Forum Service Station

You are required to prepare the payroll for Forum Service Station for the week ended 3 July 19XX. You will need copies of the blank wages calculation cards (provided on pages 566 and 567), the payroll register (provided on page 568), the cash analysis sheet (provided on page 569), the change docket (provided on page 570), the pay slip (provided on page 570), and the cheque (provided on page 544).

Forum Service Station employs full-time and part-time employees. Full-time employees are paid overtime as follows:
- week days and Saturday mornings — time-and-a-half
- Saturday afternoons — double time
- Sunday — triple time.

Additional information:
- Employees are paid sick leave for five days per year.
- Full-time employees have a one-hour lunch break from 12 noon to 1 p.m.
- Wages are paid from Thursday to the next Wednesday.
- Part-time console operators are paid as follows:
  (a) A rate: Monday to Friday — $10 per hour
  (b) B rate: Evenings (after 5 p.m.) and Saturdays — $14 per hour
  (c) C rate: Sundays and public holidays — $18 per hour.

  Part-time console operators are allowed a half-hour meal break per shift.

FORUM SERVICE STATION — EMPLOYEE INFORMATION SHEET

Name	Vickers, M.	Schmidt, L.	Lambert, A.	Donetti, J.	Goh, P.
Address	18 Wells Rd Bondi 2026	8 Fitzroy St Paddington 2021	27 Timms Ave Randwick 2031	15 O'Hara Rd Maroubra 2035	97 Queen St Woollahra 2025
Date of birth	12.11.57	23.04.65	13.06.72	22.10.70	16.07.74
Payroll No.	234	278	290	301	325
Classification	Supervisor	Mechanic	Console operator	Console operator	Console operator
F/T or P/T	F/T	F/T	P/T	P/T	P/T
Weekly hours	40	40			
Rate of pay	$20 p/h	$18 p/h	A, B or C Rate	A, B or C Rate	A, B or C Rate
Commenced	23.04.88	05.06.89	10.12.92	06.08.93	11.09.93
Tax File No.	253 476 809	111 445 897	867 549 344	Not supplied	301 489 654
Declaration form supplied	Yes	Yes	Yes	Yes	Yes
Tax-free threshold	Yes	No	No	No	No
Claim for dependants	Spouse	No	No	No	No
Deductions	Super — $40.00 Medical — $16.00	Super — $36.00 Union — $5.00			

EMPLOYEE TIME CARD

Week ending: Wednesday, 3 July 19XX
DEPARTMENT: _____ CLASSIFICATION: Supervisor F/T
EMPLOYEE'S NAME: MAX VICKERS Payroll No.: 234

DAY	TIME COMMENCED	TIME FINISHED	NORMAL HOURS WORKED	OVERTIME HOURS WORKED
Thursday	7.30	4.30	8.0	
Friday	7.30	5.30	8.0	1.0
Saturday	7.30	12.00		4.5
Sunday				
Monday	7.30	5.30	8.0	1.0
Tuesday	8.00	6.00	8.0	1.0
Wednesday		SICK		
		TOTAL HOURS	32.0	7.5

M. Vickers is taking two weeks' holiday.

EMPLOYEE TIME CARD

Week ending: Wednesday, 3 July 19XX
DEPARTMENT: _____ CLASSIFICATION: Mechanic (F/T)
EMPLOYEE'S NAME: LEONARD SCHMIDT Payroll no.: 278

DAY	TIME COMMENCED	TIME FINISHED	NORMAL HOURS WORKED	OVERTIME HOURS WORKED
Thursday	7.30	5.30	8.0	1.0
Friday	7.30	4.30	8.0	
Saturday	8.00	4.00		8.0
Sunday				
Monday	UNPAID SICK LEAVE*			
Tuesday	7.30	5.30	8.0	1.0
Wednesday	7.30	4.30	8.0	
		TOTAL HOURS	32.0	10.0

* L. Schmidt has used up all his sick leave entitlement.

CHAPTER 7: PAYROLL 507

EMPLOYEE TIME CARD

Week ending __Wednesday, 3 July 19XX__

DEPARTMENT _____ CLASSIFICATION __Console operator (P/T)__

EMPLOYEE'S NAME __ALAN LAMBERT__ Payroll No. __290__

DAY	TIME COMMENCED	TIME FINISHED	NORMAL HOURS WORKED	OVERTIME HOURS WORKED
Thursday				
Friday				
Saturday	5.00 p.m.	12.00 a.m.	6.5	
Sunday	5.00 p.m.	12.00 a.m.	6.5	
Monday				
Tuesday				
Wednesday	5.00 p.m.	12.00 a.m.	6.5	
		TOTAL HOURS	19.5	

EMPLOYEE TIME CARD

Week ending __Wednesday, 3 July 19XX__

DEPARTMENT _____ CLASSIFICATION __Console operator (P/T)__

EMPLOYEE'S NAME __JEFF DONETTI__ Payroll No. __301__

DAY	TIME COMMENCED	TIME FINISHED	NORMAL HOURS WORKED	OVERTIME HOURS WORKED
Thursday	6.00 p.m.	3.00 a.m.	8.5	
Friday				
Saturday	1.00 p.m.	11.00 p.m.	9.5	
Sunday				
Monday	6.00 p.m.	3.00 a.m.	8.5	
Tuesday				
Wednesday				
		TOTAL HOURS	26.5	

	EMPLOYEE TIME CARD			

Week ending __Wednesday, 3 July 19XX__

DEPARTMENT _____ CLASSIFICATION __Console operator (P/T)__

EMPLOYEE'S NAME __PAUL GOH__   Payroll No. __325__

DAY	TIME COMMENCED	TIME FINISHED	NORMAL HOURS WORKED	OVERTIME HOURS WORKED
Thursday				
Friday	10.00 a.m.	5.00 p.m.	6.5	
Saturday				
Sunday				
Monday	10.00 p.m.	5.00 a.m.	6.5	
Tuesday				
Wednesday	8.00 p.m.	6.00 a.m.	9.0*	
		TOTAL HOURS	22.0	

* Two 30-minute meal breaks allowed

EXERCISE 7.8 — *Chase & Omara*

You are required to prepare the payroll for Chase & Omara for the week ended 5 October 19XX. You will need copies of the blank wages calculation cards (provided on pages 566 and 567), the payroll register (provided on page 568), the cash analysis sheet (provided on page 569), the change docket (provided on page 570), the payroll slip (page 570) and the cheque (provided on page 544).
- All employees have a one-hour lunch break.
- Overtime is paid as follows:
   (a) week days and Saturday (to noon) — time-and-a-half
   (b) Saturday afternoon — double time
   (b) Sundays and public holidays — triple time.
- Employees are paid sick leave for five days per year.
- Wages are paid from Thursday to the next Wednesday.

CHASE & OMARA — EMPLOYEE INFORMATION SHEET

Name	Guiness, P.	Cross, F.	Ernst, G.	Lord, P.	Rowell, K.
Address	22 Main St Gosford 2250	6 Seaview St Terrigal 2260	18 Ian St Gosford 2250	67 Byron St Woy Woy 2256	56 Pine Ave Gosford 2250
Date of birth	20.12.55	18.04.63	03.10.70	15.11.67	24.09.68
Payroll No.	440	490	501	535	567
Department	Electrical	Fashion	Fashion	Administration	Maintenance
Classification	Supervisor	Salesperson	Buyer	Telephonist	Cleaner
F/T or P/T	F/T	F/T	F/T	F/T	P/T
Weekly hours	37.5	37.5	37.5	37.5	20
Rate of pay	$14.50 p/h	$12.00 p/h	$19.50 p/h	$14.00 p/h	$10.50 p/h
Commenced	20.03.88	02.10.88	14.05.89	12.12.90	13.08.91
Tax File No.	235 678 900	340 301 405	112 568 902	224 598 765	Not supplied
Declaration form supplied	Yes	Yes	Yes	Yes	Yes
Tax-free threshold	Yes	Yes	No	No	No
Claim for dependants	Sole parent	Spouse	No	No	No
Deductions	Super — $21.75 Medical — $12.50	Super — $18.00	Super — $36.50 Medical — $11.00 Savings — $20.00	Super — $15.75	Union — $2.00

EMPLOYEE TIME CARD

Week ending __Wednesday, 5 October 19XX__

DEPARTMENT __ELECTRICAL__   CLASSIFICATION __Supervisor__

EMPLOYEE'S NAME __PATRICK GUINESS__   Payroll No. __440__

DAY	TIME COMMENCED	TIME FINISHED	NORMAL HOURS WORKED	OVERTIME HOURS WORKED
Thursday	8.30	7.00	7.5	2.0
Friday	UNPAID SICK LEAVE*			
Saturday	9.00	5.00		7.0
Sunday				
Monday	8.30	5.00	7.5	
Tuesday	8.30	5.00	7.5	
Wednesday	8.30	6.00	7.5	1.0
		TOTAL HOURS	30.0	10.0

* Patrick Guiness has used up his sick leave allowance.

EMPLOYEE TIME CARD

Week ending **Wednesday, 5 October 19XX**
DEPARTMENT **FASHION**   CLASSIFICATION **Salesperson**
EMPLOYEE'S NAME **FELICITY CROSS**   Payroll No. **490**

DAY	TIME COMMENCED	TIME FINISHED	NORMAL HOURS WORKED	OVERTIME HOURS WORKED
Thursday	9.00	7.30	7.5	2.0
Friday	9.00	5.30	7.5	
Saturday				
Sunday	9.00	3.00		5.0
Monday	PAID SICK LEAVE			
Tuesday	9.00	5.30	7.5	
Wednesday	9.00	5.30	7.5	
		TOTAL HOURS	30.0	7.0

Felicity Cross is taking two weeks' holiday from 5 October 19XX.

EMPLOYEE TIME CARD

Week ending **Wednesday, 5 October 19XX**
DEPARTMENT **FASHION**   CLASSIFICATION **Buyer**
EMPLOYEE'S NAME **GAI ERNST**   Payroll No. **501**

DAY	TIME COMMENCED	TIME FINISHED	NORMAL HOURS WORKED	OVERTIME HOURS WORKED
Thursday	9.00	5.30	7.5	
Friday	9.00	5.30	7.5	
Saturday	9.00	12.00		3.0
Sunday				
Monday	9.00	5.30	7.5	
Tuesday	9.00	5.30	7.5	
Wednesday	8.00	6.30	7.5	2.0
		TOTAL HOURS	37.5	5.0

EMPLOYEE TIME CARD

Week ending __Wednesday, 5 October 19XX__
DEPARTMENT __ADMINISTRATION__   CLASSIFICATION __Telephonist__
EMPLOYEE'S NAME __PATRICIA LORD__   Payroll No. __535__

DAY	TIME COMMENCED	TIME FINISHED	NORMAL HOURS WORKED	OVERTIME HOURS WORKED
Thursday	8.30	6.00	7.5	1.0
Friday	8.30	5.00	7.5	
Saturday	8.30	11.30		3.0
Sunday				
Monday	8.30	5.00	7.5	
Tuesday	8.30	5.00	7.5	
Wednesday	8.30	5.00	7.5	
		TOTAL HOURS	37.5	4.0

Patricia Lord is taking three weeks' holiday from 5 October 19XX.

EMPLOYEE TIME CARD

Week ending __Wednesday, 5 October 19XX__
DEPARTMENT __MAINTENANCE__   CLASSIFICATION __Cleaner__
EMPLOYEE'S NAME __KEVIN ROWELL__   Payroll No. __567__

DAY	TIME COMMENCED	TIME FINISHED	NORMAL HOURS WORKED	OVERTIME HOURS WORKED
Thursday	7.00	11.00	4.0	
Friday	7.00	11.00	4.0	
Saturday				
Sunday				
Monday	7.00	11.00	4.0	
Tuesday	7.00	11.00	4.0	
Wednesday	7.00	11.00	4.0	
		TOTAL HOURS	20.0	

RECORDING PAYROLL TRANSACTIONS IN THE ACCOUNTING SYSTEM

Accounting for **employee entitlements** involves preparation of journal entries to record details of the payroll and associated liabilities (i.e. details of gross wages, net wages and deductions for the pay period).

The payroll consists of gross wages, net wages and deductions, and these transactions are recorded in the appropriate journal.

Gross wages

The gross wages (or gross pay) represents the total wages expense of the payroll to the employer. It is a major expense to the business.

Net wages

The net wages payable (or net pay) represents that amount of the total payroll which is payable to the employees. This is a liability of the business.

Deductions

The **payroll deductions** represent the amounts collected by the employer on behalf of third parties. The major deduction is PAYE tax which is paid to the Australian Taxation Office on behalf of the employees. Other deductions consist of items such as medical insurance, superannuation and union fees, collected and paid on the authority of the employee.

As these amounts are payable to third parties, they represent a liability of the business and are held in suspense accounts until the end of the month when they are remitted to the appropriate organisations. When this money is paid out, the suspense accounts are cleared and the next month's deductions begin to accumulate.

Journal entries

To record payroll transactions in the accounting system, the following journal entries are required.

General journal

An entry is made in the general journal at the end of each payroll period to record the payroll transactions. The total wages expense (gross wage) represents a major expense to the business and as such is debited, while net wages payable to employees, income tax and other deductions, which are liabilities of the business (something owed), are credited. This is illustrated as:

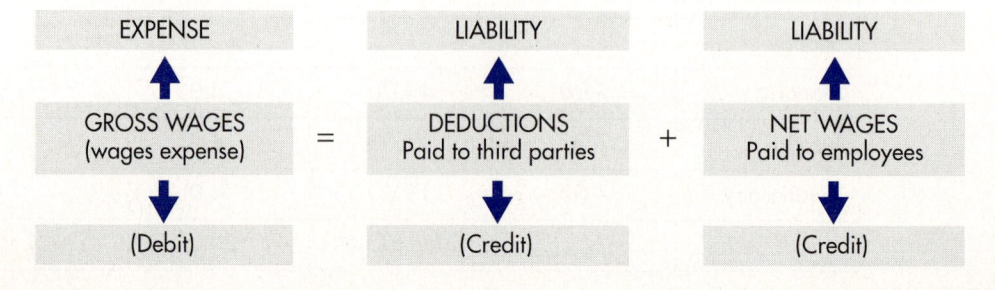

EXPENSE		LIABILITY		LIABILITY
↑		↑		↑
GROSS WAGES (wages expense)	=	DEDUCTIONS Paid to third parties	+	NET WAGES Paid to employees
↓		↓		↓
(Debit)		(Credit)		(Credit)

Example

Below are payroll details for Paige Industries Ltd for the month of March 19XX. The figures shown are assumed, in order to illustrate the recording of a full month of payroll activities and the subsequent remittance of amounts collected from employees' wages and salaries to the relevant organisations.

Note: As the exercise below and those that follow do not involve posting to the Accounts Receivable and Accounts Payable control accounts, the basic format for the general journal has been used. A blank master has been provided on page 573 for use in the exercises that follow.

PAIGE INDUSTRIES LTD
Payroll details for month of March 19XX

	Week ended 3/3/XX	Week ended 10/3/XX	Week ended 17/3/XX	Week ended 24/3/XX	Week ended 31/3/XX
WAGES EXPENSE (GROSS WAGES)	2520.80	2126.60	2321.20	2590.10	2242.40
Income Tax Payable	721.10	820.80	896.35	902.20	878.70
Superannuation Payable	69.05	69.05	69.05	69.05	69.05
Medical Insurance Payable	21.50	21.50	21.50	21.50	21.50
Group Savings Payable	45.00	45.00	45.00	45.00	45.00
Union Fees Payable	6.50	6.50	6.50	6.50	6.50
TOTAL DEDUCTIONS	(863.15)	(962.85)	(1038.40)	(1044.25)	(1020.75)
NET WAGES PAYABLE	1657.65	1163.75	1282.80	1545.85	1221.65

The general journal entry to record payroll details for the pay period ended 3 March 19XX is as follows:

EXTRACT OF GENERAL JOURNAL OF PAIGE INDUSTRIES LTD   Fol. GJ1

Date	Particulars	Fol.	Debit	Credit
19XX Mar. 3	Wages Expense (= Gross pay)		2520.80	
	Net Wages Payable (= Net pay)			1 657.65
	Group Tax Payable*			721.10
	Superannuation Payable			69.05
	Medical Insurance Payable			21.50
	Group Savings Payable			45.00
	Union Fees Payable			6.50
	Payroll and associated liabilities for week ending 3 March 19XX.			

* The amount of PAYE income tax deducted from the wages of employees and which the group employer remits to the Australian Taxation Office on a regular basis

The net wages payable to employees is recorded in the cash payments journal. However, to authorise the drawing of a cheque in a business, a payment voucher is usually completed.

Payment voucher

A payment voucher is a document authorising a payment of cash. Payment vouchers are used mainly in large organisations as a measure of control over cash payments. They are prepared by the accounting department and authorised by the financial controller (or other supervisory personnel).

A payment voucher includes the following details:
- voucher number
- payee
- due date
- date paid
- cheque number
- account debited
- account number
- amount of payment
- signature of person authorising payment.

Shown below is an example of a typical payment voucher which records details of a cheque drawn to pay net wages.

PAYMENT VOUCHER

	Account debited	Account no.	Amount
Voucher no. 451 **Payee** Cash **Cheque no.** 000745 **Due date** 9 March 19XX **Date paid** 3 March 19XX	Net Wages Payable	4.8	1657.65
Details of transaction	Net wages payable for pay period ended 3 March 19XX		
Authorised by			

In the above example, the employees are paid by cash. In this case, the cheque is made out to 'cash' for the total of the net wages payable. If the employees are paid by cheque, individual cheques are drawn, made out for each employee, with a payment voucher completed for each cheque drawn.

Cash payments journal

The net wages paid to employees are recorded in the cash payments journal. If the employees are paid in cash, the payroll cheque is cashed at the bank. If employees are paid by cheque, the individual cheques are listed in the cash payments journal.

Alternatively, where there are large numbers of cheques to be processed for employees, some firms prefer to open a special Wages' Payable account at the bank. The wages cheque is deposited into this account and employees' wages cheques are drawn against it. To record the net wages paid to employees in the cash payments journal, the following entry is made.

EXTRACT OF CASH PAYMENTS JOURNAL OF PAIGE INDUSTRIES LTD

Date	Chq. no.	Particulars (Account to be debited)	Fol.	Discount received	Trade creditors	General	Bank
19XX Mar. 3	745	Net Wages Payable				1657.65	1657.65

If the employees of Paige Industries Ltd are paid by cheque, the entry in the cash payments journal appears as follows:

EXTRACT OF CASH PAYMENTS JOURNAL OF PAIGE INDUSTRIES LTD

Date	Chq. no.	Particulars (Account to be debited)	Fol.	Discount received	Trade creditors	Net wages	General	Bank
19XX Mar. 3	745	J. Karmel				271.20		271.20
	746	M. Mathias				587.00		587.00
	747	A. Lee				373.95		373.95
	748	P. Erickson				322.50		322.50
	749	J. Kingston				103.00		103.00
						1657.65		1657.65

General ledger entries

The amounts in the general journal and cash payments journal are posted to the appropriate general ledger accounts.

The amount of gross wages represents the total expense of the payroll to the business and is recorded in the Wages Expense account. Wages expense is listed as an expense in the trial balance and is closed to the Profit and Loss account.

EXTRACT OF GENERAL LEDGER OF PAIGE INDUSTRIES LTD

Wages Expense (total expense to the business)   3.17

Date	Particulars	Fol.	Debit	Credit	Balance
19XX Mar. 3	Sundries	GJ1	2520.80		2520.80 Dr

Net Wages Payable (amounts paid to employees) 4.8

Date	Particulars	Fol.	Debit	Credit	Balance
19XX Mar. 3	Wages expense Cash payments	GJ1 CP1	 1657.65	1657.65 	1657.65 Cr 0.00

Group Tax Payable (amount owed to third party — Australian Taxation Office) 4.9

Date	Particulars	Fol.	Debit	Credit	Balance
19XX Mar. 3	Wages expense	GJ1		721.10	721.10 Cr

Superannuation Payable (amount owed to third party — Superannuation Fund) 4.10

Date	Particulars	Fol.	Debit	Credit	Balance
19XX Mar. 3	Wages expense	GJ1		69.05	69.05 Cr

Medical Insurance Payable (amount owed to third party — Medical Fund) 4.11

Date	Particulars	Fol.	Debit	Credit	Balance
19XX Mar. 3	Wages expense	GJ1		21.50	21.50 Cr

Group Savings Payable (amount owed to third party — Savings Bank) 4.12

Date	Particulars	Fol.	Debit	Credit	Balance
19XX Mar. 3	Wages expense	GJ1	45.00		45.00 Cr

Union Fees Payable (amount owed to third party — Workers' Union) 4.13

Date	Particulars	Fol.	Debit	Credit	Balance
19XX Mar. 3	Wages expense	GJ1		6.50	6.50 Cr

The above procedures are followed each week. Using the figures supplied in the payroll details for Paige Industries Ltd on page 513, at the end of the month the general journal, cash payments journal and general ledger entries appear as shown on pages 517–519.

EXTRACT OF GENERAL JOURNAL OF PAIGE INDUSTRIES LTD

Fol GJI

Date	Particulars	Fol.	Debit	Credit

19XX
Mar. 3
	Wages Expense
	  Net Wages Payable (= Net pay)
	  Group Tax Payable
	  Superannuation Payable
	  Medical Insurance Payable
	  Group Savings Payable
	  Union Fees Payable
	Payroll and associated liabilities for week ending 3 March.
		3.17
		4.9
		4.10
		4.11
		4.12
		4.13
		4.8
			2 520.80	
				1 657.65
				721.10
				69.05
				21.50
				45.00
				6.50

10	Wages expense
	  Net Wages Payable
	  Group Tax Payable
	  Superannuation Payable
	  Medical Insurance Payable
	  Group Savings Payable
	  Union Fees Payable
	Payroll and associated liabilities for week ending 10 March 19XX.
		3.17
		4.9
		4.10
		4.11
		4.12
		4.13
		4.8
			2 126.60	
				1 163.75
				820.80
				69.05
				21.50
				45.00
				6.50

17	Wages Expense
	  Net Wages Payable
	  Group Tax Payable
	  Superannuation Payable
	  Medical Insurance Payable
	  Group Savings Payable
	  Union Fees Payable
	Payroll and associated liabilities for week ending 17 March 19XX.
		3.17
		4.9
		4.10
		4.11
		4.12
		4.13
		4.8
			2 321.20	
				1 282.80
				896.35
				69.05
				21.50
				45.00
				6.50

24	Wages Expense
	  Net Wages Payable
	  Group Tax Payable
	  Superannuation Payable
	  Medical Insurance Payable
	  Group Savings Payable
	  Union Fees Payable
	Payroll and associated liabilities for week ending 24 March 19XX.
		3.17
		4.9
		4.10
		4.11
		4.12
		4.13
		4.8
			2 590.10	
				1 545.85
				902.20
				69.05
				21.50
				45.00
				6.50

31	Wages Expense
	  Net Wages Payable
	  Group Tax Payable
	  Superannuation Payable
	  Medical Insurance Payable
	  Group Savings Payable
	  Union Fees Payable
	Payroll and associated liabilities for week ending 31 March 19XX.
		3.17
		4.9
		4.10
		4.11
		4.12
		4.13
		4.8
			2 242.40	
				1 221.65
				878.70
				69.05
				21.50
				45.00
				6.50

EXTRACT OF CASH PAYMENTS JOURNAL OF PAIGE INDUSTRIES LTD

Date	Chq. no.	Particulars (Account to be debited)	Fol.	Discount received	Trade creditors	General	Bank
19XX							
Mar. 3	745	Net Wages Payable				1657.65	1657.65
10	759	Net Wages Payable				1163.75	1163.75
17	771	Net Wages Payable				1282.80	1282.80
24	789	Net Wages Payable				1545.85	1545.85
31	804	Net Wages Payable				1221.65	1221.65

EXTRACT OF GENERAL LEDGER OF PAIGE INDUSTRIES

Wages Expense 3.17

Date	Particulars	Fol.	Debit	Credit	Balance
19XX					
Mar. 3	Sundries	GJ1	2520.80		2 520.80 Dr
10	Sundries	GJ1	2126.60		4 647.40 Dr
17	Sundries	GJ1	2321.20		6 968.60 Dr
24	Sundries	GJ1	2590.10		9 558.70 Dr
31	Sundries	GJ1	2242.40		11 801.10 Dr

Net Wages Payable 4.8

Date	Particulars	Fol.	Debit	Credit	Balance
19XX					
Mar. 3	Wages expense	GJ1		1657.65	1657.65 Cr
	Cash payments	CP1	1657.65		0.00
10	Wages expense	GJ1		1163.75	1163.75 Cr
	Cash payments	CP1	1163.75		0.00
17	Wages expense	GJ1		1282.80	1282.80 Cr
	Cash payments	CP1	1282.80		0.00
24	Wages expense	GJ1		1545.85	1545.85 Cr
	Cash payments	CP1	1545.85		0.00
31	Wages expense	GJ1		1221.65	1221.65 Cr
	Cash payments	CP1	1221.65		0.00

Group Tax Payable 4.9

Date	Particulars	Fol.	Debit	Credit	Balance
19XX					
Mar. 3	Wages expense	GJ1		721.10	721.10 Cr
10	Wages expense	GJ1		820.80	1541.90 Cr
17	Wages expense	GJ2		896.35	2438.25 Cr
24	Wages expense	GJ2		902.20	3340.45 Cr
31	Wages expense	GJ3		878.70	4219.15 Cr

Superannuation Payable 4.10

Date	Particulars	Fol.	Debit	Credit	Balance
19XX					
Mar. 3	Wages expense	GJ1		69.05	69.05 Cr
10	Wages expense	GJ1		69.05	138.10 Cr
17	Wages expense	GJ2		69.05	207.15 Cr
24	Wages expense	GJ2		69.05	276.20 Cr
31	Wages expense	GJ3		69.05	345.25 Cr

Medical Insurance Payable 4.11

Date	Particulars	Fol.	Debit	Credit	Balance
19XX					
Mar. 3	Wages expense	GJ1		21.50	21.50 Cr
10	Wages expense	GJ1		21.50	43.00 Cr
17	Wages expense	GJ2		21.50	64.50 Cr
24	Wages expense	GJ2		21.50	86.00 Cr
31	Wages expense	GJ3		21.50	107.50 Cr

Group Savings Payable 4.12

Date	Particulars	Fol.	Debit	Credit	Balance
19XX					
Mar. 3	Wages expense	GJ1		45.00	45.00 Cr
10	Wages expense	GJ1		45.00	90.00 Cr
17	Wages expense	GJ2		45.00	135.00 Cr
24	Wages expense	GJ2		45.00	180.00 Cr
31	Wages expense	GJ3		45.00	225.00 Cr

Union Fees Payable 4.13

Date	Particulars	Fol.	Debit	Credit	Balance
19XX					
Mar. 3	Wages expense	GJ1		6.50	6.50 Cr
10	Wages expense	GJ1		6.50	13.00 Cr
17	Wages expense	GJ2		6.50	19.50 Cr
24	Wages expense	GJ2		6.50	26.00 Cr
31	Wages expense	GJ3		6.50	32.50 Cr

REMITTING DEDUCTIONS

PAYE tax and other deductions are recorded in the cash payments journal when they are paid to the organisations concerned (usually monthly), in accordance with agreements with these organisations. The payment of PAYE tax is made (either monthly or quarterly) in accordance with legislation passed by the federal government and must be paid to the Australian Taxation Office before the seventh day of the following month (or on the seventh day of the month following the end of the quarter), or fines apply.

These payments are recorded in the cash payments journal. Payment vouchers are prepared by the financial controller (or supervisor) authorising cheques to be drawn in favour of the various organisations to which the money is to be remitted. For the purposes of exercises in this chapter, assume that all payments are remitted on the first day of the next month, to the following organisations:

- Australian Taxation Office (Group Tax Payable)
- State Superannuation Fund (Superannuation Payable)
- Health Insurance Fund of Australia (Medical Insurance Payable)
- Nationwide Bank Ltd (Group Savings Payable)
- National Workers' Union (Union Fees Payable).

A payment voucher is prepared for each amount to be cleared from the suspense accounts each month. A completed payment voucher showing details for approval of payment of income tax to the Australian Taxation Office for the month of March for Paige Industries Ltd is set out below.

PAYMENT VOUCHER

	Account debited	Account no.	Amount
Voucher no. 452 **Payee:** Australian Taxation Office **Cheque no.** 000746 **Due date** 7 April 19XX **Date paid** 1 April 19XX	Group Tax Payable	4.9	4219.15
Details of transaction	Remittance of PAYE tax deducted for month of March 19XX.		
Authorised by			

The entries in the cash payments journal, to record remittance of funds held in the Wages Payable, Group Tax Payable, Superannuation Payable, Medical Insurance Payable, Group Savings Payable and Union Fees Payable suspense accounts to the relevant organisations are shown on pages 521–522.

EXTRACT OF CASH PAYMENTS JOURNAL OF PAIGE INDUSTRIES LTD

Date	Chq. no.	Particulars (Account to be debited)	Fol.	Discount received	Trade creditors	Wages	General	Bank
19XX Apr. 1	746	Group Tax Payable	4.9				4219.15	4219.15
	747	Superannuation Payable	4.10				345.25	345.25
	748	Medical Insurance Payable	4.11				107.50	107.50
	749	Group Savings Payable	4.12				225.00	225.00
	750	Union Fees Payable	4.13				32.50	32.50
							4929.40	4929.40

When the above entries are posted to the general ledger, the relevant accounts appear as follows:

Group Tax Payable

Date	Particulars	Fol.	Debit	Credit	Balance
19XX Mar. 3	Wages expense	GJ1		721.10	721.10 Cr
10	Wages expense	GJ1		820.80	1541.90 Cr
17	Wages expense	GJ2		896.35	2438.25 Cr
24	Wages expense	GJ2		902.20	3340.45 Cr
31	Wages expense	GJ3		878.70	4219.15 Cr
Apr. 1	Cash payments	CP2	4219.15		0.00

Superannuation Payable 4.10

Date	Particulars	Fol.	Debit	Credit	Balance
19XX Mar. 3	Wages expense	GJ1		69.05	69.05 Cr
10	Wages expense	GJ1		69.05	138.10 Cr
17	Wages expense	GJ2		69.05	207.15 Cr
24	Wages expense	GJ2		69.05	276.20 Cr
31	Wages expense	GJ3		69.05	345.25 Cr
Apr. 1	Cash payments	CP2	345.25		0.00

Medical Insurance Payable 4.11

Date	Particulars	Fol.	Debit	Credit	Balance
19XX Mar. 3	Wages expense	GJ1		21.50	21.50 Cr
10	Wages expense	GJ1		21.50	43.00 Cr
17	Wages expense	GJ2		21.50	64.50 Cr
24	Wages expense	GJ2		21.50	86.00 Cr
31	Wages expense	GJ3		21.50	107.50 Cr
Apr. 1	Cash payments	CP2	107.50		0.00

Group Savings Payable 4.12

Date	Particulars	Fol.	Debit	Credit	Balance
19XX					
Mar. 3	Wages expense	GJ1		45.00	45.00 Cr
10	Wages expense	GJ1		45.00	90.00 Cr
17	Wages expense	GJ2		45.00	135.00 Cr
24	Wages expense	GJ2		45.00	180.00 Cr
31	Wages expense	GJ3		45.00	225.00 Cr
Apr. 1	Cash payments	CP2	225.00		0.00

Union Fees Payable 4.13

Date	Particulars	Fol.	Debit	Credit	Balance
19XX					
Mar. 3	Wages expense	GJ1		6.50	6.50 Cr
10	Wages expense	GJ1		6.50	13.00 Cr
17	Wages expense	GJ2		6.50	19.50 Cr
24	Wages expense	GJ2		6.50	26.00 Cr
31	Wages expense	GJ3		6.50	32.50 Cr
Apr. 1	Cash payments	CP2	32.50		0.00

EXERCISE 7.9 R. Frost & Co.

Assume that the following are the payroll details of R. Frost & Co. for the month of March 19XX. Employees are paid in cash, and amounts deducted from employees' wages and salaries each month are remitted to the relevant organisations on the first day of the month following the payroll period.

R. FROST & CO.
Payroll details for month of March 19XX

	Week ended 3/3/XX	Week ended 10/3/XX	Week ended 17/3/XX	Week ended 24/3/XX	Week ended 31/3/XX
WAGES EXPENSE (GROSS WAGES)	3001.35	6835.35	3179.85	6296.74	3097.64
Group Tax Payable	1064.50	2242.25	1178.25	2333.17	1147.77
Superannuation Payable	131.58	233.50	131.58	270.58	133.58
Medical Insurance Payable	49.50	129.50	49.50	111.50	49.50
Group Savings Payable	50.00	50.00	50.00	110.00	50.00
Union Fees Payable	2.75	2.75	2.75	2.75	2.75
TOTAL DEDUCTIONS	(1298.33)	(2658.00)	(1412.08)	(2828.00)	(1383.60)
NET WAGES PAYABLE	1703.02	4177.35	1767.77	3468.74	1714.04

Using the information on page 522, you are required to carry out the following.
1. Prepare journal entries to record payroll and associated liabilities for each week.
2. Record payment of wages each week in the cash payments journal.
3. Complete payment vouchers to authorise remittance of monthly amount of deductions to the following organisations:
   (a) Australian Taxation Office
   (b) State Superannuation Fund
   (c) Health Insurance Fund of Australia
   (d) Nationwide Bank Ltd
   (e) National Workers' Union.
4. Record remittance of the above amounts in the cash payments journal.
5. Post all journals to the general ledger.

Use copies of the relevant blank masters provided at the back of this book to complete this exercise.

EXERCISE 7.10 M. Diego & Sons

Assume that the following are the payroll details of M. Diego & Sons for the month of May 19XX. Employees are paid in cash, and amounts deducted from employees' wages and salaries each month are remitted to the relevant organisations on 1 June 19XX.

M. DIEGO & SONS
Payroll details for month of May 19XX

	Week ended 1/5/XX	Week ended 8/5/XX	Week ended 15/5/XX	Week ended 22/5/XX	Week ended 29/5/XX
WAGES EXPENSE (GROSS WAGES)	5160.56	8083.35	4276.84	4106.28	3743.62
Group Tax Payable	1912.15	2153.65	1584.72	1521.53	1387.12
Superannuation Payable	245.06	326.58	149.46	149.46	149.46
Medical Insurance Payable	51.00	27.00	27.00	27.00	27.00
Group Savings Payable	30.00	120.00	30.00	30.00	30.00
Union Fees Payable	9.80	19.60	9.80	9.80	9.80
TOTAL DEDUCTIONS	(2248.01)	(2646.83)	(1800.98)	(1737.79)	(1603.38)
NET WAGES PAYABLE	2912.55	5436.52	2475.86	2368.49	2140.24

Using the information on page 523, on you are required to carry out the following.
1. Prepare journal entries to record payroll and associated liabilities for each week.
2. Record payments of wages each week in the cash payments journal.
3. Complete payment vouchers to authorise remittance of monthly amount of deductions to the following organisations:
   (a) Australian Taxation Office
   (b) State Superannuation Fund
   (c) Health Insurance Fund of Australia
   (d) Nationwide Bank Ltd
   (e) National Workers' Union.
4. Record remittance of the above amounts in the cash payments journal.
5. Post all journals to the general ledger.

Use copies of the relevant blank masters provided at the back of this book to complete this exercise.

EXERCISE 7.11 *Forum Service Station*

Assume that the following are the payroll details of Forum Service Station for the month of July 19XX. Employees are paid in cash, and amounts deducted from employees' wages and salaries each month are remitted to the relevant organisations on 1 August 19XX.

FORUM SERVICE STATION
Payroll details for month of July 19XX

	Week ended 3/7/XX	Week ended 10/7/XX	Week ended 17/7/XX	Week ended 24/7/XX	Week ended 31/7/XX
WAGES EXPENSE (GROSS WAGES)	4739.00	2856.00	3198.72	2943.48	3041.80
Group Tax Payable	1387.30	1058.23	1185.22	1090.64	1127.08
Superannuation Payable	156.00	116.00	116.00	116.00	116.00
Medical Insurance Payable	48.00	16.00	16.00	16.00	16.00
Union Fees Payable	5.00	5.00	5.00	5.00	5.00
TOTAL DEDUCTIONS	(1596.30)	(1195.23)	(1322.22)	(1227.64)	(1264.08)
NET WAGES PAYABLE	3142.70	1660.77	1876.50	1715.84	1777.72

Using the information on page 524, you are required to carry out the following.
1. Prepare journal entries to record payroll and associated liabilities for each week.
2. Record payments of wages each week in the cash payments journal.
3. Complete payment vouchers to authorise remittance of monthly amount of deductions to the following organisations:
   (a) Australian Taxation Office
   (b) State Superannuation Fund
   (c) Health Insurance Fund of Australia
   (d) Nationwide Bank Ltd
   (e) National Workers' Union.
4. Record remittance of the above amounts in the cash payments journal.
5. Post all journals to the general ledger.

Use copies of the relevant blank masters provided at the back of this book to complete this exercise.

EXERCISE 7.12 Chase & Omara

Assume that the following are the payroll details of Chase & Omara for the month of October 19XX. Employees are paid in cash, and amounts deducted from employees' wages and salaries each month are remitted to the relevant organisations on 1 November 19XX.

CHASE & OMARA
Payroll details for month of October 19XX

	Week ended 5/10/XX	Week ended 12/10/XX	Week ended 19/10/XX	Week ended 26/10/XX
WAGES EXPENSE (GROSS WAGES)	5952.13	3048.26	4216.90	3743.50
Group Tax Payable	1610.95	1038.02	1435.98	1274.77
Superannuation Payable	175.25	107.75	180.75	107.75
Medical Insurance Payable	23.50	23.50	45.50	23.50
Group Savings Payable	20.00	20.00	20.00	20.00
Union Fees Payable	2.00	2.00	2.00	2.00
TOTAL DEDUCTIONS	(1831.70)	(1191.27)	(1684.23)	(1428.02)
NET WAGES PAYABLE	4120.43	1856.99	2532.67	2315.48

Using the information on page 525, you are required to carry out the following.
1. Prepare journal entries to record payroll and associated liabilities for each week.
2. Record payments of wages each week in the cash payments journal.
3. Complete payment vouchers to authorise remittance of monthly amount of deductions to the following organisations:
   (a) Australian Taxation Office
   (b) State Superannuation Fund
   (c) Health Insurance Fund of Australia
   (d) Nationwide Bank Ltd
   (e) National Workers' Union.
4. Record remittance of the above amounts in the cash payments journal.
5. Post all journals to the general ledger.

Use copies of the relevant blank masters provided at the back of this book to complete this exercise.

Putting it together

For the following exercises (which involve preparing a manual payroll), you will need to copy the following blank forms provided at the back of this book:
- wages calculation cards (pages 566 and 567)
- payroll register (page 568)
- cheque (page 544)
- cash analysis sheet (page 569)
- change docket (page 570)
- pay slip (page 570)
- employee earnings record (page 571).

7A Playgym Equipment Co.

From the following employee information sheet and time sheets, you are required to carry out the following.
1. Calculate the hours worked for the week ending 16 September 19XX.
2. Prepare the wages calculation cards.
3. Prepare the payroll register.
4. Prepare the cheque for the payroll.
5. Prepare a cash analysis sheet and a change docket.
6. Prepare pay slips for all employees.
7. Complete the employee earnings record for Sondra Chevez. Her totals to date are: gross wage $9768.80, tax instalments $1758.30, superannuation $236.60, medical insurance $288.00.

PLAYGYM EQUIPMENT CO. — EMPLOYEE INFORMATION SHEET

Name	Chevez, Sondra	West, Adam	Carvin, Hilda	Kwan, Lee
Address	76 Moseley St Glenelg 5045	27 Torrens Rd Croydon 5008	56 Bayview Cr. Beaumont 5066	142 Greenhill Rd Eastwood 5063
Date of birth	12.02.72	26.10.64	23.06.59	13.09.79
Payroll No.	784	721	436	821
Department	Sales	Store	Administration	Store
Classification	Receptionist	Clerk	Secretary	Storeperson
F/T or P/T	F/T	F/T	F/T	F/T
Weekly hours	40	40	40	40
Rate of pay	$12 p/h	$18 p/h	$16.50 p/h	$10.50 p/h
Commenced	18.05.90	06.07.86	27.04.82	20.10.95
Tax File No.	763 216 992	837 321 764	921 363 541	Not supplied
Declaration form supplied	Yes	Yes	Yes	Yes
Tax-free threshold	Yes	Yes	No	No
Claim for dependants	Sole parent	Parent		
Deductions	Super — $18.20 Medical — $16.00	Super — $17.50 Savings — $5.00	Super — $25.60 Medical — $15.00 Union — $5.40	Super — $20.00 Medical — $15.00

Additional information:
- Employees are paid sick leave for eight days per year.
- A lunch break of one hour is allowed each day.
- Pay weeks are from Friday to the following Thursday.
- Overtime is paid at time-and-a-half on week days (in excess of eight hours) and on Saturday mornings until noon; double time is paid on Saturday afternoons and triple time on Sundays and public holidays.

EMPLOYEE TIME CARD

Week ending: Friday, 16 September 19XX

DEPARTMENT: SALES CLASSIFICATION: Receptionist

EMPLOYEE'S NAME: SONDRA CHEVEZ Payroll No. 784

DAY	TIME COMMENCED	TIME FINISHED	NORMAL HOURS WORKED	OVERTIME HOURS WORKED
Friday	8.00	7.00	8.0	2.0
Saturday				
Sunday				
Monday	8.00	5.00	8.0	
Tuesday	PAID SICK LEAVE			
Wednesday	8.00	5.00	8.0	
Thursday	8.00	5.00	8.0	
		TOTAL HOURS		

EMPLOYEE TIME CARD

Week ending: Friday, 16 September 19XX

DEPARTMENT: STORE CLASSIFICATION: Clerk

EMPLOYEE'S NAME: ADAM WEST Payroll No. 721

DAY	TIME COMMENCED	TIME FINISHED	NORMAL HOURS WORKED	OVERTIME HOURS WORKED
Friday	7.00	4.00	8.0	
Saturday				
Sunday				
Monday	7.00	4.00	8.0	
Tuesday	7.00	5.00	8.0	1.0
Wednesday	7.00	5.30	8.0	1.5
Thursday	7.00	4.30	8.0	0.5
		TOTAL HOURS		

EMPLOYEE TIME CARD

Week ending __Friday, 16 September 19XX__
DEPARTMENT __ADMINISTRATION__   CLASSIFICATION __Secretary__
EMPLOYEE'S NAME __HILDA CARVIN__   Payroll No. __436__

DAY	TIME COMMENCED	TIME FINISHED	NORMAL HOURS WORKED	OVERTIME HOURS WORKED
Friday	8.00	7.00	8.0	2.0
Saturday				
Sunday				
Monday	8.00	6.30	8.0	1.5
Tuesday	8.00	5.30	8.0	0.5
Wednesday	8.00	5.00	8.0	
Thursday	8.00	5.00	8.0	
		TOTAL HOURS		

Hilda is taking three weeks holiday commencing 17 September 19XX.

EMPLOYEE TIME CARD

Week ending __Friday, 16 September 19XX__
DEPARTMENT __STORE__   CLASSIFICATION __Storeperson__
EMPLOYEE'S NAME __LEE KWAN__   Payroll No. __821__

DAY	TIME COMMENCED	TIME FINISHED	NORMAL HOURS WORKED	OVERTIME HOURS WORKED
Friday	7.00	5.00	8.0	1.0
Saturday	9.00	4.00		6.0
Sunday				
Monday	7.00	4.30	8.0	0.5
Tuesday	UNPAID SICK LEAVE*			
Wednesday	7.00	4.00	8.0	
Thursday	7.00	4.30	8.0	0.5
		TOTAL HOURS		

* Lee has used all his sick pay.

7B Endeavour Supplies Ltd

From the following employee information sheet and the time sheets for Endeavour Supplies Ltd you are required to carry out the following.
1. Calculate the hours worked for the week ending 19 November 19XX.
2. Prepare the wages calculation cards.
3. Prepare the payroll register.
4. Prepare the cheque for the payroll.
5. Prepare a cash analysis sheet and a change docket.
6. Prepare pay slips for all employees.
7. Complete the employee earnings record for Donald Spencer. His totals to date are: gross wage $22 900, tax instalments $8734.90, superannuation $402.60, medical insurance $369.60, savings plan $220.

ENDEAVOUR SUPPLIES LTD — EMPLOYEE INFORMATION SHEET

Name	Nicolau, Angelo	Goradia, Maria	Spencer, Donald	Nelson, Michael
Address	42 Redgum Dr. Strathfield 2135	18 Hilltop Cr. Ryde 2112	121 Salisbury Rd Rose Bay 2029	89 Arden Street Randwick 2031
Date of birth	12.02.69	26.10.64	23.06.59	13.09.76
Payroll No.	476	522	333	589
Department	Maintenance	Administration	Administration	Store
Classification	Fitter	Receptionist	Supervisor	Storeperson
F/T or P/T	F/T	F/T	F/T	F/T
Weekly hours	40	40	40	40
Rate of pay	$14.50 p/h	$16.50 p/h	$860 p/week	$12.50 p/h
Commenced	16.08.88	28.03.92	13.10.86	22.11.94
Tax File No.	483 961 722	221 506 713	802 441 286	Not supplied
Declaration form supplied	Yes	Yes	Yes	Yes
Tax-free threshold	Yes	Yes	No	No
Claim for dependants	No	Sole parent	No	No
Deductions	Super — $15.00 Union — $6.50	Super — $13.50	Super — $18.30 Medical — $16.80 Savings — $10.00	Union — $6.50

Additional information:
- Employees are paid sick leave for seven days per year.
- General staff work from 7.30 a.m. to 4.30 p.m. (one-hour lunch break).
- Administrative staff work from 8.30 a.m. to 5.00 p.m. (30-minute lunch break).
- Pay weeks are from Friday to the following Thursday.

- Overtime is paid at time-and-a-half on week days (in excess of eight hours) and on Saturday mornings; double time is paid on Saturday after 12 noon and triple time on Sundays and public holidays.

EMPLOYEE TIME CARD

Week ending __Friday 8 December 19XX__
DEPARTMENT __MAINTENANCE__ CLASSIFICATION __Fitter__
EMPLOYEE'S NAME __ANGELO NICOLAU__ Payroll No. __476__

DAY	TIME COMMENCED	TIME FINISHED	NORMAL HOURS WORKED	OVERTIME HOURS WORKED
Friday	7.30	4.30	8.0	
Saturday	7.30	11.30		4.0
Sunday				
Monday	7.30	4.30	8.0	
Tuesday	7.30	5.00	8.0	0.5
Wednesday	7.30	5.00	8.0	0.5
Thursday	7.30	4.30	8.0	
		TOTAL HOURS		

EMPLOYEE TIME CARD

Week ending __Friday, 8 December 19XX__
DEPARTMENT __ADMINISTRATION__ CLASSIFICATION __Receptionist__
EMPLOYEE'S NAME __MARIA GORADIA__ Payroll No. __522__

DAY	TIME COMMENCED	TIME FINISHED	NORMAL HOURS WORKED	OVERTIME HOURS WORKED
Friday	8.30	6.00	8.0	1.0
Saturday				
Sunday				
Monday	8.30	5.00	8.0	
Tuesday	8.30	5.30	8.0	0.5
Wednesday	8.30	5.30	8.0	0.5
Thursday	8.30	5.00	8.0	
		TOTAL HOURS		

EMPLOYEE TIME CARD

Week ending: Friday, 8 December 19XX
DEPARTMENT: ADMINISTRATION
CLASSIFICATION: Supervisor
EMPLOYEE'S NAME: DONALD SPENCER
Payroll No.: 333

DAY	TIME COMMENCED	TIME FINISHED	NORMAL HOURS WORKED	OVERTIME HOURS WORKED
Friday	8.30	6.00	8.0	1.0
Saturday				
Sunday				
Monday	8.00	5.00	8.0	
Tuesday	8.00	6.00	8.0	1.0
Wednesday	8.00	6.00	8.0	1.0
Thursday	8.00	5.00	8.0	
		TOTAL HOURS		

Donald is taking two weeks' holiday commencing 9 December 19XX.

EMPLOYEE TIME CARD

Week ending: Friday, 8 December 19XX
DEPARTMENT: STORE
CLASSIFICATION: Storeperson
EMPLOYEE'S NAME: MICHAEL NELSON
Payroll No.: 589

DAY	TIME COMMENCED	TIME FINISHED	NORMAL HOURS WORKED	OVERTIME HOURS WORKED
Friday	7.30	4.30	8.0	
Saturday	8.00	4.00		7.0
Sunday				
Monday	7.30	4.30	8.0	
Tuesday	7.30	4.30	8.0	
Wednesday	7.30	4.30	8.0	
Thursday	7.00	4.30	8.0	
		TOTAL HOURS		

7C Global Press Ltd

From the following employee information sheet and the time sheets for Global Press Ltd you are required to carry out the following.
1. Calculate the hours worked for the week ending 28 May 19XX.
2. Prepare the wages calculation cards.
3. Prepare the payroll register.
4. Prepare the cheque for the payroll.
5. Prepare a cash analysis sheet and a change docket.
6. Prepare pay slips for all employees.
7. Complete the employee earnings record for Peter Seitawan. His totals to date are: gross wage $34 040, tax instalments $8754.60, superannuation $837.20, medical insurance $496.80, union fees $207.00.

GLOBAL PRESS LTD — EMPLOYEE INFORMATION SHEET

Name	Seitawan, Peter	Gee Kee, Lucy	Lloyd, Miranda
Address	46 Forest Drive Casuarina 6167	29 Epping Road Ballajura 6066	97 Western Ave Sorrento 6020
Date of birth	17.04.68	27.02.74	12.08.61
Payroll No.	148	291	122
Department	Accounts	Administration	Administration
Classification	Clerk	Clerk	WP operator
F/T or P/T	F/T	F/T	F/T
Weekly hours	40	40	40
Rate of pay	$17.50 p/h	$16.00 p/h	$800 p/week
Commenced	23.07.88	14.03.89	23.09.81
Tax File No.	811 218 924	921 459 336	376 814 202
Declaration form supplied	Yes	Yes	Yes
Tax-free threshold	Yes	Yes	No
Claim for dependants	No	Parent	No
Deductions	Super — $18.20 Medical — $10.00 Union — $4.50	Super — $15.50 Medical — $12.00 Savings — $10.00	Super — $22.30 Medical — $14.80 Savings — $15.00

Additional information:
- Employees are paid sick leave for eight days per year.
- General staff work from 7.30 a.m. to 4.30 p.m. (one-hour lunch break).
- Administrative staff work from 8.30 a.m. to 5.00 p.m. (one-hour lunch break).
- Pay weeks are from Friday to the following Thursday.

- Overtime is paid at time-and-a-half on week days (in excess of eight hours) and on Saturday mornings; double time is paid on Saturday after 12 noon and triple time on Sundays and public holidays.

		EMPLOYEE TIME CARD		
Week ending	Friday, 28 May 19XX			
DEPARTMENT	ACCOUNTS		CLASSIFICATION	Clerk
EMPLOYEE'S NAME	PETER SEITAWAN		Payroll No.	148

DAY	TIME COMMENCED	TIME FINISHED	NORMAL HOURS WORKED	OVERTIME HOURS WORKED
Friday	7.30	6.00	8.0	1.5
Saturday				
Sunday				
Monday	7.30	4.30	8.0	
Tuesday	7.30	5.00	8.0	0.5
Wednesday	7.30	4.30	8.0	
Thursday	UNPAID SICK LEAVE*			
		TOTAL HOURS		

* Peter has exhausted his sick leave entitlement.

		EMPLOYEE TIME CARD		
Week ending	Friday, 28 May 19XX			
DEPARTMENT	ADMINISTRATION		CLASSIFICATION	Clerk
EMPLOYEE'S NAME	LUCY GEE KEE		Payroll No.	291

DAY	TIME COMMENCED	TIME FINISHED	NORMAL HOURS WORKED	OVERTIME HOURS WORKED
Friday	8.30	6.30	8.0	1.0
Saturday				
Sunday				
Monday	8.30	5.30	8.0	
Tuesday	8.30	6.00	8.0	0.5
Wednesday	8.30	6.00	8.0	0.5
Thursday	8.30	5.30	8.0	
		TOTAL HOURS		

EMPLOYEE TIME CARD

Week ending __Friday, 28 May 19XX__
DEPARTMENT __ADMINISTRATION__   CLASSIFICATION __WP Operator__
EMPLOYEE'S NAME __MIRANDA LLOYD__   Payroll No. __122__

DAY	TIME COMMENCED	TIME FINISHED	NORMAL HOURS WORKED	OVERTIME HOURS WORKED
Friday	8.30	6.30	8.0	1.0
Saturday				
Sunday				
Monday	8.30	6.00	8.0	0.5
Tuesday	8.30	5.30	8.0	
Wednesday	8.30	6.00	8.0	0.5
Thursday	8.30	5.30	8.0	
		TOTAL HOURS		

Miranda is taking four weeks' holiday commencing 29 May 19XX.

7D Eastern Trading Co.

Exercises 7D to 7F (which involve entering payroll details in the accounting records) are to be prepared using copies of the relevant blank masters provided at the back of this book. Following are the payroll details of Eastern Trading Co. for the month of January 19XX. Employees are paid in cash, and amounts deducted from employees' wages and salaries each month are remitted to the relevant organisations on 5 February 19XX.

EASTERN TRADING CO.
Payroll details for month of January 19XX

	Week ended 7/01/XX	Week ended 14/01/XX	Week ended 21/01/XX	Week ended 28/01/XX
WAGES EXPENSE	5260.40	6180.20	5860.40	5592.60
Group Tax Payable	946.85	1112.46	1054.87	1006.66
Superannuation Payable	260.00	80.00	80.00	120.00
Medical Insurance Payable	154.00	116.00	116.00	124.00
Union Fees Payable	35.00	20.00	20.00	30.00
TOTAL DEDUCTIONS	(1395.85)	(1328.46)	(1270.87)	(1280.66)
NET WAGES PAYABLE	3864.55	4851.74	4589.53	4311.94

Using the information on page 535, you are required to carry out the following.
1. Prepare journal entries to record payroll and associated liabilities for each week.
2. Record payments of wages each week in the cash payments journal.
3. In the cash payments journal, record remittance of monthly amount of deductions to the following organisations:
   (a) Australian Taxation Office
   (b) State Superannuation Fund
   (c) Health Insurance Fund of Australia
   (d) National Workers' Union.
4. Post all journals to the general ledger.
5. Payment vouchers are not required for this exercise.

7E Northern Rivers Timber Co.

Following are the payroll details of Northern Rivers Timber Co. for the month of October 19XX. Employees are paid in cash, and amounts deducted from employees' wages and salaries each month are remitted to the relevant organisations on 5 November 19XX.

NORTHERN RIVERS TIMBER CO.
Payroll details for month of October 19XX

	Week ended 5/10/XX	Week ended 12/10/XX	Week ended 19/10/XX	Week ended 26/10/XX
WAGES EXPENSE	7242.80	6956.20	6842.60	7157.30
Group Tax Payable	1303.70	1252.15	1231.65	1288.25
Superannuation Payable	76.20	102.40	78.40	76.20
Union Dues Payable	28.60	42.80	28.60	28.60
TOTAL DEDUCTIONS	(1408.50)	(1397.35)	(1338.65)	(1393.05)
NET WAGES PAYABLE	5834.30	5558.85	5503.95	5764.25

Using the above information you are required to carry out the following.
1. Prepare journal entries to record payroll and associated liabilities for each week.
2. Record payments of wages each week in the cash payments journal.
3. In the cash payments journal, record remittance of monthly amount of deductions to the following organisations:
   (a) Australian Taxation Office
   (b) State Superannuation Fund
   (c) National Workers' Union.
4. Post all journals to the general ledger.
5. Payment vouchers are not required for this exercise.

7F Hardware Handi-Mart

Following are the payroll details of Hardware Handi-Mart for the month of August 19XX. Employees are paid in cash, and amounts deducted from employees' wages and salaries each month are remitted to the relevant organisations on 5 September 19XX.

HARDWARE HANDI-MART
Payroll details for month of August 19XX

	Week ended 6/08/XX	Week ended 13/08/XX	Week ended 20/08/XX	Week ended 27/08/XX
WAGES EXPENSE	8953.20	8679.30	8248.90	9176.20
Group Tax Payable	1611.50	1562.20	1484.65	1651.70
Superannuation Payable	84.60	68.40	66.20	68.40
Medical Insurance Payable	112.80	164.60	112.80	114.60
Union Dues Payable	32.80	28.40	28.40	28.20
TOTAL DEDUCTIONS	(1841.70)	(1823.60)	(1692.05)	(1862.90)
NET WAGES PAYABLE	7111.50	6855.70	6556.85	7313.30

Using the above information you are required to carry out the following.
1. Prepare journal entries to record payroll and associated liabilities for each week.
2. Record payments of wages each week in the cash payments journal.
3. Complete payment vouchers to authorise remittance of monthly amount of deductions to the following organisations:
   (a) Australian Taxation Office
   (b) State Superannuation Fund
   (c) Health Insurance Fund of Australia
   (d) Nationwide Bank Ltd
   (e) National Workers' Union.
4. Record remittance of above amounts in the cash payments journal.
5. Post all journals to the general ledger.

LIST OF MASTERS

Transaction analysis chart   539
General ledger   540
Purchase order   541
Batch control slip   541
Invoice   542
Delivery docket   542
Credit note   543
Cheques   544
Remittance advice   545
Receipt   546
Statement of Account   547
Credit card slips (sales voucher, credit voucher and merchant summary)   548
Deposit slip (front and back)   549
General journal — tabular format   550
Credit application form   551
Purchases journal   552
Purchases returns and allowances journal   552
Cash payments journal   553
Sales journal   554
Sales returns and allowances journal   555
Cash receipts journal   556
Trial balance   557
Accounts payable ledger   558
Accounts receivable ledger   559
Cash summary slip   560
Cash register summary slip   560
Cash receipts book   561
Cash payments book   562
Petty cash vouchers   563
Petty cash book   564
Deposit slip   565
Wages calculation card   566
Wages calculation card (including holiday pay)   567
Payroll register   568
Cash analysis sheet   569
Change docket   570
Pay slips   570
Employee earnings record   571
Payment voucher   572
General journal — basic format   573

TRANSACTION ANALYSIS CHART

Trans. no./ Date	Accounts affected	Type of account*	Inc. or dec.	Amount	Summary

* A = Asset, L = Liability, OE = Owner's Equity, R = Revenue, E = Expense

© S. Burden, H. Dunlop 1997   This page may be photocopied without record-keeping or payment of a fee.

GENERAL LEDGER OF .... Fol. ....

Date	Particulars	Fol.	Debit	Credit	Balance
19					

To:	No.:
	Date:
	Purchase Order

Please supply the goods listed below, quoting the above order number

QUANTITY	DESCRIPTION	APPROX. UNIT PRICE	ESTIMATED TOTAL

Deliver to:

Delivery required by:

Authorised by:

Batch Control Slip

Batch No.	
Type	
Date	From
To
No. of documents	
Batch total value	
Signed	
Checked	

Batch Control Slip

Batch No.	
Type	
Date	From
To
No. of documents	
Batch total value	
Signed	
Checked	

© S. Burden, H. Dunlop 1997 — This page may be photocopied without record-keeping or payment of a fee.

Invoice

Invoice No.:

Date:

Cust. Order No.:

QUANTITY	DESCRIPTION	UNIT PRICE	TOTAL

Terms: $2\frac{1}{2}$% 7 days or net 30 days 　　　No claims accepted after 7 days

E & O E

Date:　　　　　　　　　　　　　　　　　　　　No.:

Customer Order No.

To:

Delivery Docket

QUANTITY	DESCRIPTION	PRICE

The above-mentioned goods have been received in good order and condition.　　　　　　Received by:

		Credit Note No.:	
		Date:	
		Invoice No.:	
		Credit Note	

QUANTITY	DESCRIPTION	UNIT PRICE	TOTAL

Reason for return:

Terms: $2\frac{1}{2}$% 7 days, otherwise net 30 days   No claims accepted after 7 days

© S. Burden, H. Dunlop 1997

MASTERS

	19		**Westpac** Banking Corporation	First Bank in Australia
To				/ /19
			Pay to	or bearer
For			the sum of	
				$
$			Cheque No. Branch BSB No. Account No.	
	0000		⑊"0000 ⑊"032⑊"000⑊: 12⑊"3456⑊"	SPECIMEN ONLY

	19		**Westpac** Banking Corporation	First Bank in Australia
To				/ /19
			Pay to	or bearer
For			the sum of	
				$
$			Cheque No. Branch BSB No. Account No.	
	0000		⑊"0000 ⑊"032⑊"000⑊: 12⑊"3456⑊"	SPECIMEN ONLY

	19		**Westpac** Banking Corporation	First Bank in Australia
To				/ /19
			Pay to	or bearer
For			the sum of	
				$
$			Cheque No. Branch BSB No. Account No.	
	0000		⑊"0000 ⑊"032⑊"000⑊: 12⑊"3456⑊"	SPECIMEN ONLY

	19		**Westpac** Banking Corporation	First Bank in Australia
To				/ /19
			Pay to	or bearer
For			the sum of	
				$
$			Cheque no. Branch BSB no. Account no.	
	0000		⑊"0000 ⑊"032⑊"000⑊: 12⑊"3456⑊"	SPECIMEN ONLY

© S. Burden, H. Dunlop 1997   This page may be photocopied without record-keeping or payment of a fee.

Remittance Advice

Date:

To:

Date	Particulars	Ref.	Debit $	Credit $	Balance $

Details of payment

Balance owing
less Discount
Cheque amount

	No.
	Receipt

Date 19

RECEIVED from ....

the sum of .... dollars

and .... cents

being for .... of

	Cash/cheque		
	Discount		
	$		

Signed

	No.
	Receipt

Date 19

RECEIVED from ....

the sum of .... dollars

and .... cents

being for .... of

	Cash/cheque		
	Discount		
	$		

Signed

© S. Burden, H. Dunlop 1997   This page may be photocopied without record-keeping or payment of a fee.

Statement of Account

To:

for the month of

19

Date	Particulars	Ref.	Debit	Credit	Balance
19					

Current	30 days	60 days	90 days	Please pay final amount in this column

© S. Burden, H. Dunlop 1997 — This page may be photocopied without record-keeping or payment of a fee.

MASTERS

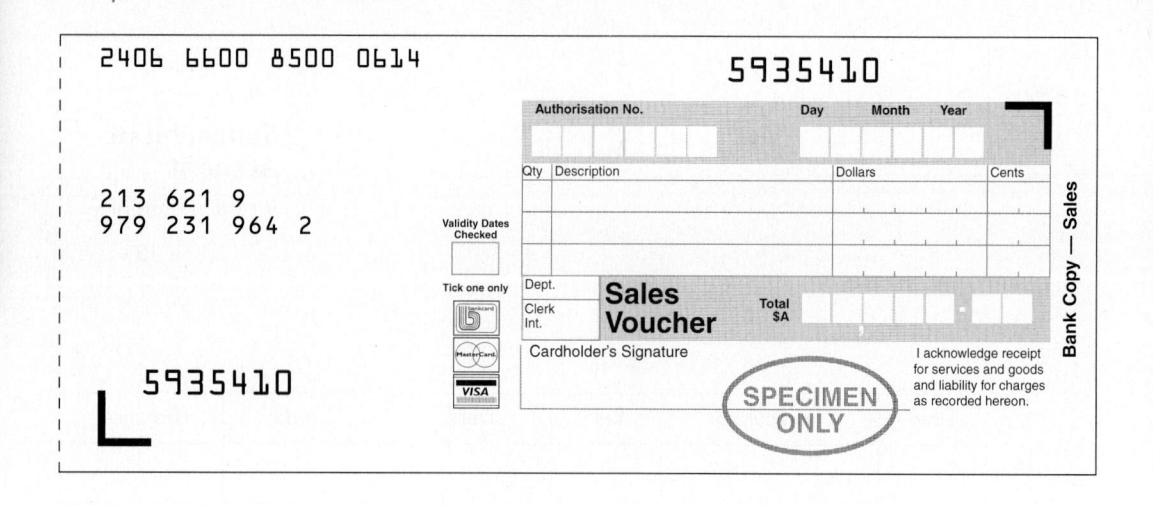

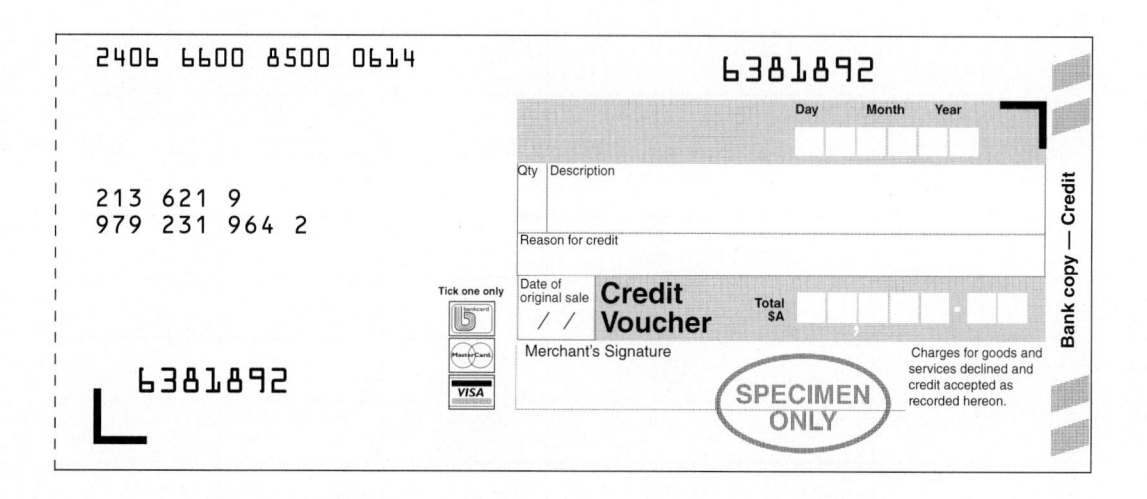

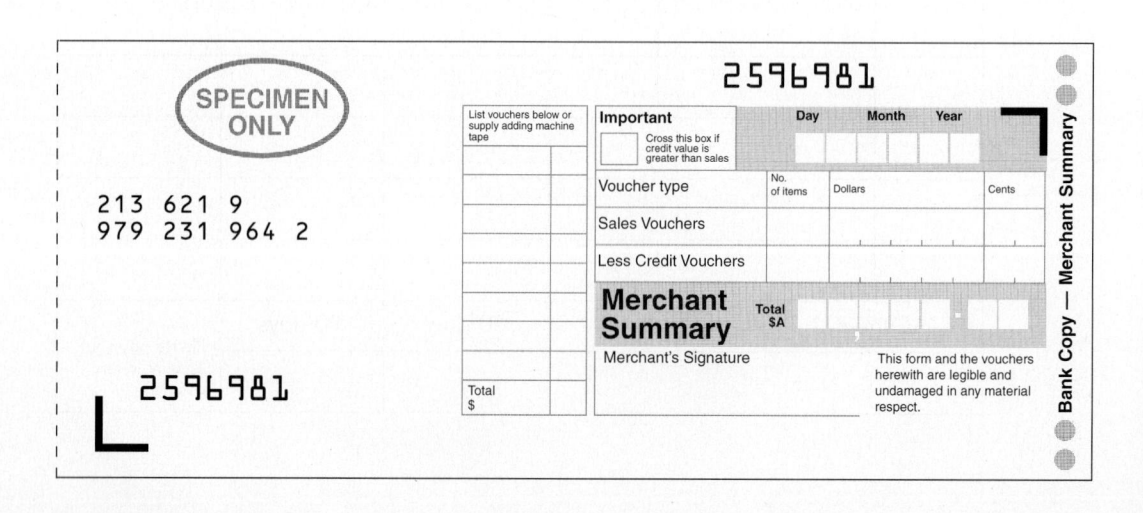

Bank Copy — Sales

2406 6600 8500 0614

5935410

213 621 9
979 231 964 2

5935410

Sales Voucher

SPECIMEN ONLY

Bank copy — Credit

2406 6600 8500 0614

6381892

213 621 9
979 231 964 2

6381892

Credit Voucher

SPECIMEN ONLY

Bank Copy — Merchant Summary

SPECIMEN ONLY

2596981

213 621 9
979 231 964 2

2596981

Merchant Summary

© S. Burden, H. Dunlop 1997 — This page may be photocopied without record-keeping or payment of a fee.

Westpac Banking Corporation

ARBN 007 457 141

Deposited for credit of

Date ___ / ___ / 19___

Deposited for credit of _____

Cash $ _____
Cheques $ _____
Total $ _____

Teller _____

Westpac Banking Corporation

DEPOSIT

Date ___ / ___ / 19___

Branch name _____

For CREDIT of _____

Paid in by (Signature) _____

Cash _____
Cheques See Reverse _____
TOTAL $ _____

No. chq's _____

SPECIMEN ONLY

⑈032⑈000: 12⑈3456⑈

Front

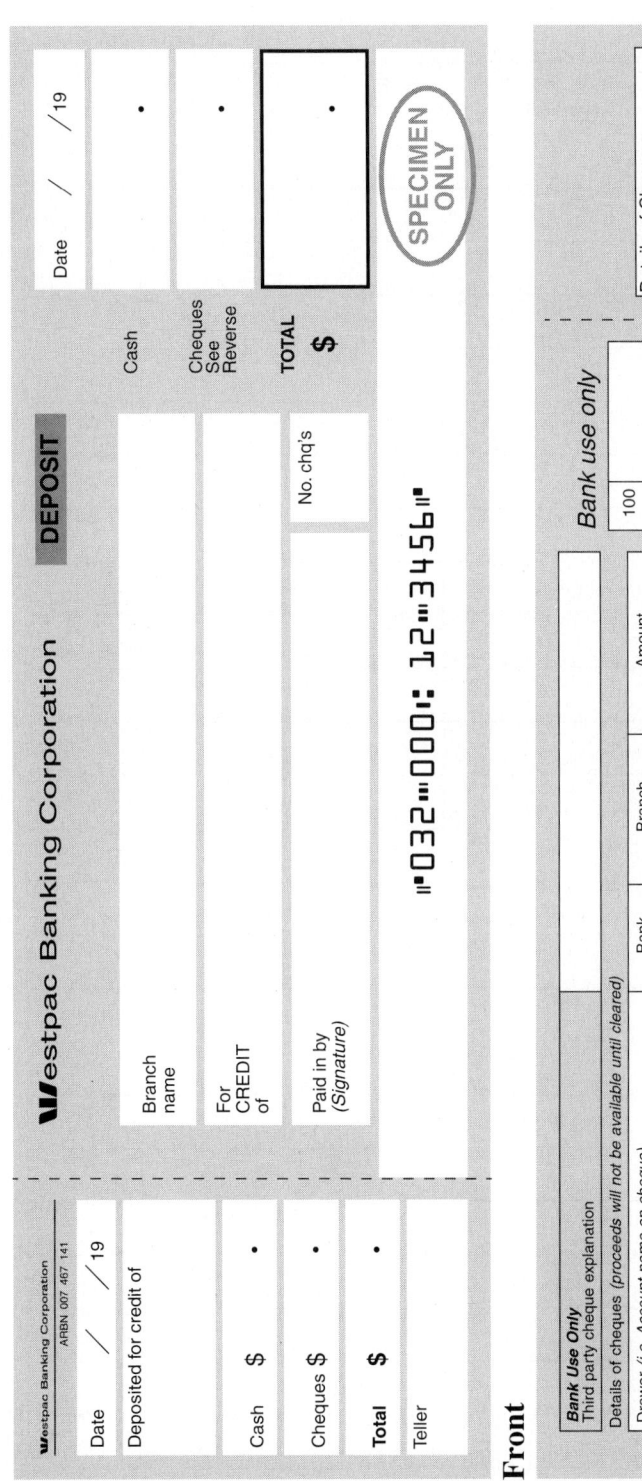

Bank Use Only
Third party cheque explanation
Details of cheques (proceeds will not be available until cleared)

Drawer (i.e. Account name on cheque)	Bank	Branch	Amount

Total $ _____

Note:
This deposit will be transferred under the Bank's internal procedures.
The Bank will not be held responsible for delays in transmission.

Details of Cheques

Bank use only

100				
50				
20				
10				
5				
Coin				
Cash Total				

SPECIMEN ONLY

Back

© S. Burden, H. Dunlop 1997   This page may be photocopied without record-keeping or payment of a fee.

GENERAL JOURNAL OF ....

DEBIT						CREDIT		Fol. ....
Accounts receivable	Accounts payable	General	Date	Particulars	Fol.	Accounts receivable	Accounts payable	General

© S. Burden, H. Dunlop 1997   This page may be photocopied without record-keeping or payment of a fee.

CREDIT APPLICATION FORM

NAME: ....

ADDRESS: ....

STATE: .... POSTCODE: ....

MONTHLY CREDIT REQUIRED ....

Credit Referees:

Company Name	Company Name	Company Name
Contact	Contact	Contact
Telephone No.	Telephone No.	Telephone No.
Fax No.	Fax No.	Fax No.

DECLARATION:

We the undersigned accept responsibility for any debts incurred by this firm jointly or severally:

Signed: .... Signed: ....

Position: .... Position: ....

PURCHASES JOURNAL OF .... Fol. ....

Date	Inv. no.	Particulars (Creditor's account to be credited)	Fol.	Amount	Monthly total

PURCHASES RETURNS AND ALLOWANCES JOURNAL OF .... Fol............

Date	CN no.	Particulars (Creditor's account to be debited)	Fol.	Amount	Monthly total

© S. Burden, H. Dunlop 1997   This page may be photocopied without record-keeping or payment of a fee.

CASH PAYMENTS JOURNAL OF.. Fol.................

Date	Chq. no.	Particulars (Account to be debited)	Fol.	Discount received	Trade creditors	General	Bank

© S. Burden, H. Dunlop 1997   This page may be photocopied without record-keeping or payment of a fee.

SALES JOURNAL OF .... Fol. ....

Date	Inv. no.	Particulars (Debtor's account to be debited)	Fol.	Sales	Sales tax	Debtors' total

© S. Burden, H. Dunlop 1997   This page may be photocopied without record-keeping or payment of a fee.

SALES RETURNS AND ALLOWANCES JOURNAL OF .... Fol. ....

Date	CN no.	Particulars (Debtor's account to be credited)	Fol.	Sales returns	Sales tax	Debtors' total

© S. Burden, H. Dunlop 1997   This page may be photocopied without record-keeping or payment of a fee.

CASH RECEIPTS JOURNAL OF .... Fol. ....

Date	Rec. no.	Particulars (Account to be credited)	Fol.	Discount allowed	Trade debtors	Sales	Sales tax	General	Bank

© S. Burden, H. Dunlop 1997 — This page may be photocopied without record-keeping or payment of a fee.

TRIAL BALANCE OF ....

as at ....

Account no.	Account name	Debit	Credit

© S. Burden, H. Dunlop 1997   This page may be photocopied without record-keeping or payment of a fee.

ACCOUNTS PAYABLE LEDGER OF .... Fol. ....

Date	Particulars	Fol.	Debit	Credit	Balance
19					

ACCOUNTS RECEIVABLE LEDGER OF .... Fol. ....

Date	Particulars	Fol.	Debit	Credit	Balance
19					

© S. Burden, H. Dunlop 1997 — This page may be photocopied without record-keeping or payment of a fee.

CASH SUMMARY SLIP		
Cash register no.:	Date:	
Denomination	Number	Amount
Notes: $100		
$50		
$20		
$10		
$5		
TOTAL NOTES		
Coin: $2.00		
$1.00		
$0.50		
$0.20		
$0.10		
$0.05		
TOTAL COIN		
TOTAL CASH		

CASH REGISTER SUMMARY SLIP	
Date	
Register no.	
Cash	
Cheques	
Credit card — Bankcard	
— MasterCard	
— Visa	
TOTAL	
Checked: Cashier	
Supervisor	

© S. Burden, H. Dunlop 1997 This page may be photocopied without record-keeping or payment of a fee.

CASH RECEIPTS BOOK OF ....

Date	Rec. no.	Particulars	Fol.	Discount allowed	Trade debtors	Sales	Sales tax	General	Bank
19									

CASH PAYMENTS BOOK OF ....

Date	Chq. no.	Particulars	Fol.	Discount received	Trade creditors	Purchases	Wages	General	Bank
19									

NO.	NO.
Petty Cash Voucher	**Petty Cash Voucher**
Date	Date ....
DEBIT	DEBIT ....
Particulars	Particulars ....
Received .... $ _____	Received .... $ _____
Petty Cash Voucher NO.	**Petty Cash Voucher** NO.
Date	Date ....
DEBIT	DEBIT ....
Particulars	Particulars ....
Received .... $ _____	Received .... $ _____
Petty Cash Voucher NO.	**Petty Cash Voucher** NO.
Date	Date ....
DEBIT	DEBIT ....
Particulars	Particulars ....
Received .... $ _____	Received .... $ _____

© S. Burden, H. Dunlop 1997   This page may be photocopied without record-keeping or payment of a fee.

PETTY CASH BOOK OF ....

Amount received	Date	Particulars	Voucher no.	Total	Stationery	Postage	Travel expenses	Sundry expenses	

© S. Burden, H. Dunlop 1997   This page may be photocopied without record-keeping or payment of a fee.

Deposit for account at

Westpac Banking Corporation ARBN 007 457 141

Where this deposit is lodged at a bank or branch other than shown below it will be transferred under the Bank's internal procedures. The Bank is not to be responsible for delays in transmission to branch or transfer to nominated bank. Proceeds of cheques etc. will not be available till cleared.

100	
50	
20	
10	
5	
Total notes	
Coin	
Cash total	

Teller	Comm.	No. of chqs

CREDIT

Date	/ /
Cash	
Cheques	
Bankcard/MasterCard	
Less Charges	
Total $	

Branch *(where account is held)*	
Paid in by *(Signature)*	
Credit A/c name & no.	

Particulars of cheques, etc., to be completed by depositor

	Drawer	Bank	Branch	Amount
1				
2				
3				
4				
5				
6				
7				
8				
9				
10				
11				
12				
13				
14				
15				
16				
17				
18				
19				
20				
21				
22				
23				
24				

ABLMDUP/38059 (9/94)

SPECIMEN ONLY

Carried forward

© S. Burden, H. Dunlop 1997   This page may be photocopied without record-keeping or payment of a fee.

WAGES CALCULATION CARD				
NAME:				Payroll No.:
DEPARTMENT:				CLASSIFICATION:
WEEK ENDING:				WEEKLY/HOURLY RATE:
	Normal hours		Adjusted O/T hours	Amount ($)
Normal time				
Overtime $1\frac{1}{2}$				
2				
3				
Sick pay				
GROSS PAY				
Deductions:		Amount ($)		
Tax on gross wage				
Less Dependant rebate				
Superannuation				
Medical insurance				
Savings plan				
Union fees				
TOTAL DEDUCTIONS				
NET PAY				

WAGES CALCULATION CARD				
NAME:			Payroll No.:	
DEPARTMENT:			CLASSIFICATION:	
WEEK ENDING:			WEEKLY/HOURLY RATE:	
	Normal hours		Adjusted O/T hours	Amount ($)
Normal time				
Overtime $1\frac{1}{2}$				
2				
3				
Sick pay				
Excess on $17\frac{1}{2}$% leave loading				
GROSS PAY				
Deductions:		Amount ($)		
Tax on gross wage				
Less Dependant rebate				
Superannuation				
Medical insurance				
Savings plan				
Union fees				
TOTAL DEDUCTIONS				
NET PAY				
GROSS HOLIDAY PAY				
Plus $17\frac{1}{2}$% leave loading				
Less Taxable excess above $320				
Deductions:		Amount ($)		
Tax on normal wage				
Superannuation				
Medical insurance				
Savings plan				
Union				
TOTAL DEDUCTIONS				
NET HOLIDAY PAY				

© S. Burden, H. Dunlop 1997   This page may be photocopied without record-keeping or payment of a fee.

568 MASTERS

PAYROLL REGISTER — Week ended

Name	Payroll No.	INCOME			GROSS PAY	DEDUCTIONS					TOTAL D'DNS	NET PAY
		Ord.	O/T	Sick and hol.		Tax	Super.	Medical insurance	Savings	Union fees		

© S. Burden, H. Dunlop 1997   This page may be photocopied without record-keeping or payment of a fee.

Employee's name	Net wage	$100	$50	$20	$10	$5	$2	$1	50c	20c	10c	5c

CASH ANALYSIS SHEET

© S. Burden, H. Dunlop 1997 This page may be photocopied without record-keeping or payment of a fee.

CHANGE DOCKET		
	$	c
$100		
$50		
$20		
$10		
$5		
$2		
$1		
50c		
20c		
10c		
5c		
TOTAL		

CHANGE DOCKET		
	$	c
$100		
$50		
$20		
$10		
$5		
$2		
$1		
50c		
20c		
10c		
5c		
TOTAL		

Name:	Payroll No.:	
Week ending:		
Normal		
Overtime		
Sick/Holiday		
GROSS PAY		
Deductions:		
Tax		
Super		
Medical		
Savings		
Union		
TOTAL DEDUCTIONS		
NET PAY		

Name:	Payroll No.:	
Week ending:		
Normal		
Overtime		
Sick/Holiday		
GROSS PAY		
Deductions:		
Tax		
Super		
Medical		
Savings		
Union		
TOTAL DEDUCTIONS		
NET PAY		

© S. Burden, H. Dunlop 1997

This page may be photocopied without record-keeping or payment of a fee.

EMPLOYEE EARNINGS RECORD

Name ....
Address ....
Suburb ....

Department ....
Classification ....
Payroll No. ....

Date commenced ....

Date of birth ....

Tax File No. ....

Rebates claimed ....

Employment Declaration form: Yes ☐ No ☐

Tax-free threshold claimed: Yes ☐ No ☐

Pay rate ....

Week ending	Gross pay	Tax	Deductions					Net pay	Year to date				
			Super	Medical	Savings	Union fees	Total		Gross	Tax	Super	Medical	Savings	Union fees

© S. Burden, H. Dunlop 1997   This page may be photocopied without record-keeping or payment of a fee.

PAYMENT VOUCHER

	Account debited	Account no.	Amount
Voucher no.			
Payee:			
Due date			
Cheque no.			
Date paid			
Details of transaction			
Authorised by			

PAYMENT VOUCHER

	Account debited	Account no.	Amount
Voucher no.			
Payee:			
Due date			
Cheque no.			
Date paid			
Details of transaction			
Authorised by			

© S. Burden, H. Dunlop 1997   This page may be photocopied without record-keeping or payment of a fee.

GENERAL JOURNAL OF .... Fol. ....

Date	Particulars	Folio	Debit	Credit
19				

GLOSSARY

AAS Standards AAS Standards are issued by the Australian Accounting Research Foundation (AARF) on behalf of the Institute of Chartered Accountants in Australia (ICA) and the Australian Society of Certified Practising Accountants (ASCPA).

AASB Standards AASB Standards are issued by the Australian Accounting Standards Board (AASB) and apply to corporate entities and have the legal backing of the Corporations Law.

Account The basic unit of the accounting system in which details of increases and decreases are recorded for assets, liabilities, revenue, expenses and owner's equity.

Account balance The difference between total debits and total credits in a particular account.

Accounting The process of recording, classifying and summarising financial information collected by bookkeepers for analysis and interpretation. It provides guidance in making business decisions and provides useful economic information to interested parties and users who depend on these results.

Accounting cycle The steps involved in the process of recording, classifying and summarising financial information.

Accounting entity For accounting purposes the business of a sole trader or a partnership is regarded as a separate accounting entity; that is, a being in its own right. Only the transactions of the business or the partnership are recorded. The personal financial dealings of the owners are completely separate to and distinct from those of the business.

Accounting equation This is based on the concept that at all times the total assets of the business are equal to the total liabilities and owner's equity. It is stated as: Assets = Liabilities + Owner's Equity.

Accounting period A time period, usually one year, over which business activity is measured. *See also* Reporting period.

Accounting Standard Accounting Standards provide specific rules on how particular types of financial transactions should be dealt with in the accounting records. They are backed by legislation.

Accounts payable This term refers to those persons or businesses from whom the business purchases trading goods on credit. As the business owes money to these persons or businesses, accounts payable are a liability of the business. *See also* Trade creditors.

Accounts payable ledger Contains detailed accounts of individuals or firms to whom the business owes money for goods or services received on credit. *See also* Creditors' ledger.

Accounts receivable Persons or firms to whom the business sells trading goods on credit. As these persons or businesses owe money to the business, accounts receivable are an asset of the business. *See also* Trade debtors.

Accounts receivable ledger Contains detailed accounts of amounts due from individuals or firms to whom the business has sold goods or services on credit. *See also* Debtors' ledger.

Ageing The process by which accounts receivable (amounts owing by trade debtors) are classified by the length of time they have been outstanding.

Alpha-numeric coding A method of coding ledger accounts for ease of reference, based on a combination of alphabetic characters and numbers.

Annual leave Under Australian awards, all employees are entitled to four weeks paid annual leave each year, plus (with the exception of Victoria) a leave loading of $17\frac{1}{2}\%$ of the four weeks gross leave entitlement. *See also* Paid leave.

Assets Assets are items of value owned by the business or owed to the business. SAC 4 defines assets as '... future economic benefits controlled by the entity as a result of past transactions or other past events'.

Audit The examination of financial accounts by an independent accountant (auditor) to ensure that they represent a true and fair view of the activities and financial position of the business.

Auditor Auditors have the responsibility of checking the accuracy of the financial information prepared by the accounting system. There are two types of auditors:
(a) external — who check the financial accounts and report to the shareholders
(b) internal — who are employed internally to check the quality and effectiveness of the accounting system that produces the information.

Award A determination by an industrial tribunal setting out working conditions, standard hours of work, salary scales, hourly wage rates and allowances such as overtime, to be paid to employees. *See also* Industrial award.

Bad debts Debts which prove to be irrecoverable and are written off in the accounting records. They are reported as losses in the expense section of the profit and loss statement.

Balance date The final day of the reporting period. This is when adjustments are made and accounts balanced. The expense and revenue accounts are closed off and final accounts prepared. Final accounts consist of the Trading Statement, Profit and Loss Statement and Balance Sheet.

Balance sheet A statement of assets, liabilities and owner's equity of a business *at a particular date*, usually at the last date of a designated trading period. It is a statement of what the business owns (or is owed) and what the business owes at a specific date.

Bank reconciliation statement A statement prepared to reconcile the balance shown on the bank statement with the balance in the Cash at Bank account in the general ledger.

Bank statement A statement issued by the bank which is a copy of the bank's record of deposits to and withdrawals from the customer's account with the bank.

Batch A collection of data to be processed at the one time, e.g. a batch of source documents.

Batching Also called batch processing. The method by which a collection of like data, e.g. a batch of source documents, is processed.

Bereavement leave Paid leave granted to an employee on the death of a family member.

Block coding A system of coding accounts in the ledger for ease of reference in which each category in the ledger is assigned a block of numbers.

Bookkeeping The detailed and accurate recording of all transactions which take place in a business. Bookkeeping records provide the information from which financial accounts are prepared.

Capital The amount a business owes to its owner(s). It represents the investment of the owner(s) in the business. It is the difference between the value of the assets and the value of the external liabilities of the business (*see* Accounting equation above). It is also known as proprietorship or owner's equity.

Cash Cash, cheques, and any other negotiable instrument which can be deposited in a bank account.

Cash register receipt A tear-off receipt from a cash register, handed to a customer as a receipt for a cash sale.

Cash register roll The record of daily cash sales from a cash register, including cash/cheques and credit card sales.

Cash sale docket A written receipt for a cash sale, used when a customer requires a more detailed receipt for a cash sale (sometimes issued in addition to the cash register receipt).

Change float The amount of cash held in a cash register at the beginning of the day to provide change for early customers.

Chart of accounts An index, map or guide to the location of accounts in the general ledger. Accounts are listed under their particular classification, e.g. current asset, current liability, expense, revenue, etc.

Cheque An order to the bank to pay, on demand, the amount of money written on the cheque, to the person named on the cheque.

Cheque butt Retained in the cheque book after the cheque is detached. It serves as a source document for the cash payments journal.

Company A business that has been structured so that it can be incorporated as a business entity governed by company legislation. When a company is formed, a separate legal entity is created.

Compensating error Occurs when the effects of two separate errors are cancelled out so that there is no difference in the trial balance.

Continuity of activity The business is regarded as an ongoing entity that will continue to operate in the future.

Contra entry A bookkeeping entry to 'set off' one account balance against another. Used for transfers between accounts, i.e. when a person or firm is both a creditor and a debtor. For example, when an amount due to a supplier in his or her role as a creditor of the business is reduced by the amount he or she owes as a debtor of the business.

Control account An account in the general ledger which represents 'in total' all the accounts in a subsidiary ledger, e.g. Accounts Receivable/Accounts Payable Control accounts represent 'in total' all the individual debtors'/creditors' accounts. These individual accounts are listed separately in the debtors'/creditors' ledgers.

Credit card credit voucher Records the credit card credit allowance to a customer for returns or overcharge.

Credit card merchant summary Summarises and is attached to daily credit card sales and returns and is banked with the daily deposit.

Credit card sales voucher Records credit card (e.g. Bankcard, MasterCard, Visa) sales to a customer.

Credit entry An entry on the right-hand side of a T-style ledger account or in the 'credit' column of a 3-column ledger account. Accounts which have a credit balance are liability, revenue and owner's equity accounts.

Credit note An adjustment note sent by a seller of trading goods to a purchaser when the purchaser returns faulty or damaged goods to the seller, and for other reasons such as overcharges or refunds on containers.

Creditor	A person or business to whom the business owes money for goods or services purchased on credit.
Creditors' ledger	Contains detailed accounts of individuals or firms to whom the business owes money for goods or services received on credit. *See also* Accounts payable ledger.
Cross-reference	When posting to the ledger from the journal, the page number of the journal is recorded alongside the ledger entry, and the ledger account number is recorded alongside the journal entry from which it has been posted.
Current assets	Assets which can be converted into cash or used up in the normal running of the business within one year of the balance date. Examples are stock, debtors, cash at bank, cash in hand.
Current liabilities	Those liabilities that will be paid within one year of the balance date, e.g. creditors.
Debit entry	An entry on the left-hand side of a T-style ledger account or in the 'debit' column of a 3-column ledger account. Accounts which have a debit balance are asset and expense accounts.
Debt	An amount owed by a debtor to a creditor.
Debtor	Individuals or firms to whom the business has sold goods or services on credit.
Debtors' ledger	Contains detailed accounts of individuals or firms to whom the business has sold goods or services on credit. *See also* Accounts receivable ledger.
Delivery docket	Accompanies the delivery of goods supplied on credit.
Discount allowed	The allowance *given by the business to trade debtors* for prompt settlement of accounts in full within the specified time as stated in the terms of trading of the business. Also known as settlement discount.
Discount received	Allowance *received by the business from trade creditors* for prompt settlement of accounts in full within the specified time as stated in the terms of trading of the business.
Dishonoured cheques	Cheques from customers which have been deposited in the firm's bank account but have not been paid for various reasons, e.g. insufficient funds in the customers' bank accounts.
Double entry	A system of recording transactions in terms of the accounting equation which is based on the concept that total debits are always equal to total credits, i.e. for every debit entry there is a corresponding credit entry and vice versa.
Drawee	The bank on which the cheque is drawn.
Drawer	The person who draws and signs the cheque. Note that the person who writes out or prepares the cheque may not necessarily be the person authorised to sign cheques on behalf of the business.

Drawings Goods or cash withdrawn from the business by the owner for personal use, and which may be in the form of cheques drawn on the business for cash, cheques drawn on the business for payment of personal accounts or goods taken from inventory. Drawings decrease owner's equity, i.e. the amount of capital that the owner has invested in the business.

Employee A person appointed or engaged under a contract of service, whether on a full-time, part-time, permanent, casual or temporary basis.

Employee earnings record Provides a detailed and cumulative record of each employee's hours worked, gross pay, deductions and net pay for year to date.

Employee entitlements A collective term for the cost of labour and related fringe benefits which constitute a major expense for a business. It includes annual leave, sick leave, long service leave, superannuation, and post-employment benefits.

Employer An entity which consumes the services of employees in exchange for providing employee entitlements.

Employment contract A contract between an employer and employee setting out conditions under which the employee works. It covers such items as hours of work, rate of pay etc., and is enforceable at law. *See also* Enterprise bargaining agreement, Workplace agreement.

Employment Declaration form A form completed by each employee to claim the general exemption and any rebates for which they are eligible. It can be lodged with only one employer.

Enterprise bargaining agreement A contract negotiated between an employer and employee, setting out the conditions under which the employee is employed, which is enforceable at law. *See also* Workplace agreement, Employment contract.

Expense The amount of assets a business uses up or consumes or the amount of costs a business incurs in the process of earning revenue in any one reporting period, e.g. purchases, rent, salaries, etc. Expenses decrease the owner's equity.

Expense recognition principle This principle states that expenses should be recorded in the accounting period in which the asset is used up or liability incurred in the process of earning revenue.

Folio number Page or reference number given to journals and to ledger accounts.

Fringe benefits Monetary or non-monetary benefits provided to employees as part of their salary package, e.g. provision of motor vehicle, low-interest loan, payment of educational expenses, subsidised housing.

General ledger Contains details of all of the accounts relating to the business, with the exception of the trade debtors' and trade creditors' individual accounts. The trade debtors' and trade creditors' accounts are represented 'in total' only in the general ledger by the Accounts Receivable Control account and the Accounts Payable Control account.

Gross earnings The amount earned by an employee (including any bonuses, loadings, commissions and fringe benefits) before any deductions are made. Also known as gross pay, gross wage.

Group certificate This certificate is issued to each employee at the end of the financial year (or at the end of a period of employment). The group certificate contains all of the details of an employee's earnings as well as the amount of tax instalments deducted for the year.

Historical cost All transactions are recorded as they occur and at the monetary value at that time, i.e. assets are recorded at their value (original cost) at the time of purchase.

Imprest petty cash system A system of administering the petty cash fund where the value of the original advance is always maintained, i.e. before balancing, cash on hand plus voucher is equal to original advance and, after balancing, cash on hand plus reimbursement cheque is equal to original advance.

Industrial award A determination by an industrial tribunal setting out working conditions, standard hours of work, salary scales, hourly wage rates and allowances such as overtime, to be paid to employees. *See also* Award.

Interest The expense incurred in borrowing money, i.e. the amount paid to the lender for the use of the money.

Internal controls The measures that a firm adopts to safeguard the assets, ensure accurate and reliable accounting records, promote operational efficiency and encourage adherence to the firm's organisational policies and procedures. The internal control system of a firm is composed of administrative and accounting controls.

Inventory Goods held for resale in the ordinary course of business in order to make a profit. *See also* Stock.

Invoice A source document issued by a supplier, providing details of charges to the customer for goods supplied on credit.

Journal A book of original entry used to record details of transactions from financial source documents.

Leave Employees are entitled to various types of leave, depending upon the award under which they are employed. Examples are sick leave and long service leave.

Leave without pay Leave approved by an employer upon application from the employee for a reason for which there is no leave entitlement. Approval is at the discretion of the employer.

Ledger A book of secondary entry, which classifies transactions under individual account headings.

Legal entity This status means that, in law, the company is treated as a separate 'person' or 'being' from the owners (the shareholders).

Liabilities The external equities of a business. They consist of amounts owed to persons or businesses other than the owner.

Limited liability In the case of shareholders in a company, liability is confined or limited to the amount (if any) unpaid on shares held.

Long service leave Leave paid to an employee when he or she works for the one employer for a period of 10–15 years. Long service leave accrues from the time the employee commences employment but does not become payable until the end of the 10 or 15 years service.

Maternity leave Paid leave for a woman upon the birth of a child.

Monetary convention All transactions of the business are recorded in money terms. A transaction is the exchange of goods or services for money.

Net loss Excess of *expenses over revenue* for a particular reporting period.

Net profit Excess of *revenue over expenses* for a particular reporting period.

Net wage The amount paid to an employee and calculated as: gross pay, less payroll deductions, plus any payroll allowances due to the employee.

Nominal accounts These record all details pertaining to revenue or expense accounts and include purchases, purchases returns, sales, sales returns, discount allowed, discount received, wages, rent, advertising, bad debts, etc.

Non-current assets (fixed assets): Business assets which have a useful life extending over more than one year. Examples are land, buildings, machinery, vehicles.

Numeric coding A method of coding ledger accounts for ease of reference. Each category in the ledger is assigned a number and the accounts numbered consecutively within the category.

Operating cycle The amount of time involved in purchasing inventory, selling it and receiving cash from its sale.

Owner's equity Owner's equity is the internal equity of the business and represents the amount of money that the business owes to the owner after deduction of its liabilities. *See also* Proprietorship.

Owner's equity accounts These record all details of the owner's investment in the business. Owner's equity accounts are Capital and Drawings.

Paid leave Under Australian awards, all employees are entitled to four weeks paid annual leave each year, plus (with the exception of Victoria) a leave loading of $17\frac{1}{2}\%$ of the four week gross leave entitlement. *See also* Annual leave.

Partnership A form of business structure where the business entity is owned by two or more people as partners, sharing profits and losses.

Paternity leave Paid leave for a man on the occasion of the birth of a child.

Payee The person to whom money is paid.

PAYE tax Tax is levied on the income of wage and salary earners under the *Income Tax Assessment Act 1936*, on a PAYE (pay as you earn) principle, i.e. the income tax is paid as it is earned and is deducted from the gross wage of employees in weekly instalments.

Payment voucher A document used to summarise and approve cash payments. They are used as source documents for some transactions, e.g. remitting payroll deductions to relevant organisations.

Payroll deductions Deductions which may be made are PAYE tax, superannuation, union fees, hospital and medical benefits, savings.

Personal accounts These record all details of persons or firms with whom the business deals on a credit basis, i.e. its debtors and creditors. These accounts carry the name of a person or firm.

Petty cash advance A specified amount of cash set aside to meet small day-to-day expenses. It is usually administered on the imprest system.

Petty cash system A system used to administer cash set aside for small cash payments for day-to-day expenses. *See also* Imprest petty cash system.

Petty cash voucher A form used to record purchases made from the petty cash fund. All payments made from the fund are supported by a petty cash voucher.

Petty cashier The person responsible for administration of the petty cash fund.

Posting The act of transferring the information from the journals to the relevant ledger accounts.

Private company A form of ownership suitable for small companies with a minimum of two and maximum of fifty shareholders. The words 'Pty Ltd' (Proprietary Limited) must appear in the company name.

Profit and loss statement An account which measures the performance of the business and determines whether the business has made a profit (or incurred a loss) for the reporting period.

Proprietor The owner of a business.

Proprietorship Proprietorship is the internal equity of the business and represents the amount of money that the business owes to the owner after deduction of its liabilities. For a sole trader, this represents the net investment of the proprietor in the business; that is, the amount of capital invested, plus any profits and less any losses or drawings by the proprietor. *See also* Owner's equity.

Public company A form of ownership chosen by very large companies. The word 'Ltd' (or Limited) must appear in the company name. Members of the public may buy shares in the company. The minimum number of shareholders is five, with the maximum number unlimited.

Purchase order A formal request for the supply of goods on credit, generated by the purchasing firm (customer) and sent to the supplier of the goods or services.

Purchase requisition An internal document from one department to another requesting the supply of goods.

Purchases invoice An invoice received from a supplier, providing details of goods purchased on credit.

Receipt Written acknowledgment of cash received.

Remittance advice Prepared and forwarded with a cheque, showing details of payment.

Reporting entity A business or firm in respect of which it is reasonable to expect that there are users who depend on the information in the firm's financial reports to make informed economic decisions about how to allocate their resources, e.g. shareholders — whether to invest.

Reporting period A time period over which business activity is measured; usually a year, but may be quarterly or even monthly. *See also* Accounting period.

Revenue The amount a business earns from the sale of goods or provision of services (both cash and credit transactions) plus any income received from investments during the reporting period under review. Revenue increases the owner's equity.

Revenue recognition principle This principle states that the revenue should be recorded in the accounting period in which it is earned rather than when the cash or asset is received.

SAC Statement of Accounting Concept. These are issued jointly by the Australian Accounting Research Foundation and the Australian Accounting Standards Board. Concepts statements are broad in scope and provide guidance on points that are not covered in the Standards. They are not mandatory.

Salary The amount paid either weekly, fortnightly or monthly to employees employed on an annual rate of pay in exchange for services rendered to their employer.

Sales invoice An invoice issued by a supplier, providing details of goods sold to trade debtors on credit.

Sales tax Tax levied by the government on various categories of trading goods. When applicable, it is collected by the seller of the goods and is payable to the Australian Taxation Office on or before a specified date, usually on a monthly basis.

Settlement discount An allowance made to a customer for prompt settlement of accounts in full. *See also* Discount allowed.

Sick leave Australian awards provide for paid sick leave. The amount of sick leave for any employee varies. It is usually between 5–10 working days in any one year.

Sole trader One who conducts a business for his or her own benefit and owns and controls the business.

Source document A business document prepared to record a transaction and which becomes a source of entry in the accounting records.

Statement of account The monthly account sent by the seller to the purchaser detailing all transactions which have taken place during the month and showing the total amount due at the end of the month.

Stock Goods held for resale in the ordinary course of business in order to make a profit. *See also* Inventory.

Study leave Paid leave granted to an employee to pursue further study.

Subsidiary ledger A group of individual accounts, the total value of which is represented by a related control account in the general ledger.

Sundry creditors Persons or businesses from whom the business purchases something, other than trading goods, e.g. a non-current asset such as a new computer for the business, on credit.

Sundry debtors Persons or firms to whom the business sells something, other than trading goods, e.g. a non-current asset such as a printer which has outlived its usefulness to the business, on credit.

Superannuation guarantee levy Applies to all employers and covers most employees including full-time, part-time and casual staff. It represents the minimum percentage of an employee's gross wage or salary which the employer must pay to a superannuation fund on behalf of the employee.

Tax File Number A number issued by the Australian Taxation Office to all persons currently in employment. If an employee fails to declare this Tax File Number, the employer is required to deduct tax at the highest marginal rate.

Terms of trading Trading conditions laid down by a creditor when a debtor commences purchasing goods or services on credit.

Trade creditors This term refers to those persons or businesses from whom the business purchases trading goods on credit. *See also* Accounts payable.

Trade debtors This term refers to those persons or businesses to whom the business sells trading goods on credit. *See also* Accounts receivable.

Trade discount The discount or allowance given by a manufacturer to a wholesaler, by a wholesaler to a creditor, to a buyer in the same trade, or when large quantities of goods are purchased.

Trading statement This is prepared to determine gross profit for the reporting period.

Transaction The exchange of money between two parties for equivalent goods or services.

Transposition errors Posting or recording errors in which digits are transposed, e.g. 84 instead of 48.

Trial balance A list of all debit and credit balances extracted from the general ledger *at a particular date*.

Unpaid maternity leave This applies to a period of leave following cessation of paid maternity leave.

Unpaid sick leave When an employee has used all his or her sick leave entitlement, unpaid sick leave must be taken if further illness develops.

Wages The amount paid to employees employed on an hourly rate of pay in exchange for labour.

Workplace agreement A contract negotiated between an employer and employee, setting out the conditions under which the employee is employed, which is enforceable at law. *See also* Enterprise bargaining agreement, Employment contract.

Income Tax Instalments
Weekly Rates
Incorporating Medicare Levy

Australian Taxation Office

Effective for payments made on or after
1 July 1995

This schedule should be read in conjunction with the *Group Employer's Payment Book*.

Who should use this schedule?
Use this schedule if you pay salaries and wages to employees on a weekly basis. Salaries and wages include directors fees and superannuation or other pensions, allowances, leave bonuses and lump sum payments.

The special circumstances of some employees may entitle them to use a different schedule for calculating tax instalments, ie shearers, fruit and vegetable harvesters, non-residents, employees in the entertainment industries and employees engaged on a daily basis. Ask at your local Tax Office for more information on the use of these special schedules.

Employment Declarations
These are forms that allow employees to take advantage of the tax free threshold (the 'general exemption') and to claim a reduction in tax instalments for dependant and zone rebates. Employees can claim the tax free threshold with *only* one employer, the employer who pays them the most.

Employment Declarations already lodged will remain in force after 1 July 1995. If employees' entitlements to rebates or the tax free threshold change, or they start work with a new employer, they must lodge a new *Employment Declaration*.

Tax File Numbers
If an employee does not give you a valid *Employment Declaration* AND Tax File Number, you must deduct tax at the top marginal rate using column 4 of this schedule, unless the employee:
- is under 16 years of age AND does not earn enough to pay tax; OR
- is receiving a pension from the Department of Social Security or a service pension from the Department of Veterans Affairs; OR
- has told you that a *Tax File Number Application/Enquiry* form has been lodged.

If a *Tax File Number Application/Enquiry* form has been lodged, the employee has 28 days to give you a Tax File Number. At the end of this time, if you are not notified otherwise by the Tax Office, you must deduct tax at the top marginal rate using column 4 of this schedule.

For employees who haven't given you a Tax File Number, you must deduct tax at the top marginal rate plus Medicare levy (currently 48.5%) from:
- the *whole* amount of leave bonus payments, whether paid on termination or not;
- payments on termination of employment, i.e. holiday pay, unused annual leave and long service leave; and
- the post June 1983 part of an eligible termination payment.

Employee does not usually live in Australia
Where an employee has answered NO to the question on the *Employment Declaration* "Are you an Australian resident for taxation purposes?", non-resident tax rates apply. Tax instalments on earnings (ignoring cents) should be calculated as follows:
- if the employee has NOT given you a valid Tax File Number, deduct 47 cents for each $1 of earnings, rounded to the nearest 5 cents;
- if the employee has given you a valid Tax File Number, deduct the amount calculated from Table 1 below, rounded to the nearest 5 cents.

TABLE 1   NON-RESIDENT TAX INSTALMENTS

Weekly earnings	Weekly tax instalment
$0 - $397	29 cents for each $1 of earnings
$398 - $729	$115.13 plus 34 cents for each $1 of earnings over $397
$730 - $960	$228.01 plus 43 cents for each $1 of earnings over $729
$961 & over	$327.34 plus 47 cents for each $1 of earnings over $960

Allowances
Allowances are to be added to the employee's normal weekly earnings, and tax instalments based on the whole amount. Allowances are to be taxed unless written approval has been given by the Tax Office. For more information, refer to the *Group Employer's Payment Book 1995-96*.

Annual leave bonus payments
- **Continuing employees**
  When a leave bonus payment exceeds $320, only the amount over $320 is subject to tax instalments. The whole amount of the payment is income and must be included in gross earnings on the group certificate.

- **Terminating employees**
  Refer to 'Lump sum payments on termination of employment' below.

Lump sum payments on termination of employment
- **Eligible termination payments**
  For more information on termination payments, refer to *ETPS - a guide for employers* which is available at your local Tax Office.

- **Unused annual leave, annual leave bonus and Long Service Leave (LSL) payments**

  - Bona fide redundancy, invalidity and early retirement scheme amounts

    All unused annual leave, all annual leave bonus over $320, 5% of LSL before 16 August 1978, and all LSL for the period after 15 August 1978, is subject to tax instalment deductions at the rate of 31.5%, rounded to the nearest 5 cents. Add this amount to the tax instalment for the employee's normal earnings and allowances.

How to calculate tax instalments
1. To the employee's normal weekly earnings, add any allowances and irregular payments that are to be included in this week's pay. Disregard any cents in the total amount.
2. Find the employee's total weekly income in column 1 of the schedule and read off the corresponding tax instalment in column 2 (tax free threshold is claimed), column 3 (tax free threshold NOT claimed), or column 4 (employee has NOT given you a Tax File Number).
3. If the employee has claimed any rebates, determine the weekly amount of the rebate by using Tables 2 and 3 and the Dependant and Zone Rebate Ready Reckoner. Subtract the weekly rebate from the tax found in Step 2.
4. If the employee is entitled to an adjustment for Medicare levy, subtract the value of the adjustment (as determined from the *Weekly Medicare Levy Adjustment* schedule which is available at Tax Offices) from the tax instalment found in Step 3.

NAT 1005 - 5.95

- **All other cases**

  5% of LSL before 16 August 1978, all LSL between 16 August 1978 and 17 August 1993 inclusive, and all unused annual leave and annual leave bonus accrued before 18 August 1993, is subject to tax instalment deductions at the rate of 31.5%, rounded to the nearest 5 cents. Add this amount to the tax instalment for the employee's normal earnings and allowances.

  All LSL, all unused annual leave and all annual leave bonus over $320 accrued after 17 August 1993, is subject to tax instalment deductions using either of the the methods outlined below.
  - If this post 17 August 1993 lump sum is less than $300, then tax instalments should be deducted at a rate of 35.5%.
  - Otherwise, divide the amount to be paid by 52 and add the result to the normal weekly gross earnings of the employee. Calculate the tax instalment on the 'new' gross figure. Take the difference between tax on the normal earnings and tax on the 'new' earnings, and multiply the result by 52. This amount is the total amount of tax instalments to be deducted from this part of the lump sum payment.

Rebates

Rebates reduce tax payable and are spread over the whole year in weekly instalments.

- **Dependant rebate**

  If the employee claims the full rebate at the 'Total rebates' question on the *Employment Declaration*, refer to Table 2 below for the weekly instalment value of the rebate. If a partial rebate is claimed, use the Dependant and Zone Rebate Ready Reckoner overleaf to find the weekly instalment value of the rebate. Deduct the rebate instalment value from the weekly tax instalment shown in column 2 of the schedule. NOTE: From 1 July 1995 the spouse rebate with dependant child/student can not be claimed through the tax instalment system.

  TABLE 2   DEPENDANT REBATE TABLE

	Full Rebate For Year $	Weekly Instalment Value $
Spouse with NO dependant child/student	1241	23.60
Sole parent	1165	22.15
Parent or parent in law	1116	21.20
Invalid relative	558	10.60

- **Zone rebate**

  If an employee claims a basic zone rebate at the 'Total rebates' question on the *Zone A and B Employment Declaration*, refer to Table 3 below for the weekly instalment value of the rebate. If other than the basic zone rebate is claimed, refer to the Dependant and Zone Rebate Ready Reckoner overleaf to determine the weekly instalment value of the rebate. Subtract the rebate instalment from the weekly tax instalment shown in column 2 of the schedule.

  TABLE 3   ZONE REBATE TABLE

	Basic Rebate For Year $	Weekly Instalment Value $
Zone B	57	1.10
Zone A	338	6.40
Special Zone	1173	22.30

Medicare levy variations

To claim the Medicare levy variation available to some low income earners with dependants, an employee must lodge a *Medicare Levy Variation Declaration* form along with their *Employment Declaration*. Current declarations will continue to apply after 1 July 1995. For instructions on the calculation of the Medicare levy adjustment, refer to the separate *Medicare Levy Adjustment* schedule available at Tax Offices.

Higher Education Contribution Scheme (HECS)

Since 1 July 1994 individuals with HECS debts may be required to have additional tax instalment deductions taken from their pay to cover these debts. Accordingly, the Tax Office publishes a Weekly HECS Supplement Schedule which is available from your local Tax Office.

Examples

- **No Tax File Number**

  The employee's weekly earnings are $300.90. Find $300 in column 1 and read off the corresponding tax instalment from column 4 of $145.50. *Do not allow any rebates or Medicare levy variation.*

- **Tax free threshold NOT claimed**

  The employee's weekly earnings are $563.50. Find $563 in column 1 and read off the corresponding tax instalment from column 3 of $196.05. *Do not allow any rebates or Medicare levy variation.*

- **Tax free threshold claimed**

  The employee's weekly earnings are $868.99. Find $868 in column 1 and read off the corresponding tax instalment from column 2 of $247.70.

  If the employee claims a spouse rebate of $1000 on the *Employment Declaration*, find this amount in the Dependant and Zone Rebate Ready Reckoner. Read off the corresponding tax instalment value of the rebate of $19.00. Subtract this from $247.70 and deduct the result ($228.70) for the tax instalment.

- **Employee does not usually live in Australia**

  The employee's weekly earnings are $503.60.
  - Where Tax File Number is provided, use Table 1 to calculate the tax instalment of $151.15 ($115.13 plus 34 cents for each dollar over $397 rounded to the nearest 5 cents).
  - Where Tax File Number is NOT provided, deduct 47 cents for each dollar of earnings. The tax instalment for this employee would be $236.40 (0.47 times $503 rounded to the nearest 5 cents). *Do not allow any rebates.*

- **Lump sum termination payment**

  An employee whose weekly wage is $500 voluntarily leaves his present employment and receives lump sum payments for unused LSL consisting of $800 for the period pre 16 August 1978, $5,000 for the period after 15 August 1978 and before 18 August 1993, and $600 for the period after 17 August 1993. The employee also receives unused annual leave of $400 and annual leave bonus of $100 accrued before 18 August 1993, and unused annual leave of $1,500 and annual leave bonus of $420 accrued after 17 August 1993.

  The tax instalments on the lump sum payments should be calculated as follows:
  - (5% of $800, plus $5000, plus $400, plus $100) times 31.5% = $1,745.10 (rounded to the nearest 5 cents); plus
  - the tax instalment on $542 ([$600 plus $1,500 plus ($420 minus $320)] divided by 52, plus $500, rounded to the next lower whole dollar amount) is $119.00. Subtract the instalment relating to the employee's normal earnings of $500 from this amount ($119.00 minus $104.10 = $14.90) and multiply the result by 52 ($774.80). The tax instalment to be deducted from the employee's lump sum payment is, therefore, $2,519.90 ($774.80 plus $1,745.10).

Enquiries

Any enquiries should be directed to the Withholding Taxes Enquiries section at your local Tax Office.

Calculation of instalments by formulae

The instalments shown in this schedule can be expressed in mathematical form. The relevant formulae are available from Tax Offices and may be of assistance to employers who make use of computers in the preparation of payrolls.

INDEX

AAS standards 5
AASB standards 5
accountability, of source documents 86
accounting
  function of 3–4
  what is it? 2
accounting conceptual framework 4–5
accounting controls 85
accounting cycle 48
  manual vs computerised system 94–5
accounting entity 4, 6
accounting equation 5, 6, 12–13
  balancing the 16–18
  transactions and 14–16
accounting period 5, 8
accounting standards 5
accounting system, recording payroll transactions in 512–22
accounts
  classification of 11–12, 40
  recording increases and decreases in 34
accounts payable 6, 81, 104
  source documents and journal entries 89–90, 106
accounts payable journals 97, 104–26
  posting to general ledger 182–8
    from cash payments journal 184
    from purchases journal 182–3
    from purchases returns and allowances journal 183–4
accounts payable ledger 205–37
  completed 214
  posting to 205–14
    from cash payments journal 212–14
    from general journal 206–9
    from purchases journal 209–11
    from purchases returns and allowances journal 211–12
  posting to incorrect creditor's account 160
accounts receivable 6, 81
  source documents and journal entries 89, 127
accounts receivable journals 97, 126–48
  posting to general ledger 189–96
    from cash receipts journal 190–1
    from sales journal 189–90
    from sales returns and allowances journal 190–1
accounts receivable ledger 237–85
  posting to 237–47
    from cash receipts journal 245–7
    from general journal 238–41
    from sales journal 241–3
    from sales returns and allowances journal 243–5
  posting to incorrect debtor's account 160–1
administrative controls 84–5
allowances and payments 471, 476
analysing transactions 37–45
annual leave 462, 489
annual leave loading 488
asset accounts 37, 40, 51
assets 2, 7, 11
auditing 4, 84
auditors 85
automatic teller machine (ATM) transactions 458–9

bad debts partly written off 155
bad debts recovered 155–6
bad debts write off 154–5
bagged coin 447
balance date 7
balance sheet 7, 25–6, 52
bank deposit books 451
bank deposit form 451, 452
bank deposit slip 79–80
bank deposits
  preparing 451–5
  validating 458
bank reconciliation procedures 286–337
bank reconciliation statement
  checking for errors 296, 374
  credit balance in both bank statement and Cash at Bank account 316
  credit balance in both bank statement and cash book 389
  debit balance in both bank statement and Cash at Bank account 320–1
  debit balance in both bank statement and cash book 393–4
  including information from previous month's statement 380
  preparation 291–325, 369–98
  reconciling over two consecutive periods 325–37, 398–407
  unpresented cheques and outstanding deposits 302
  when statement shows a credit balance 293–5, 371–4
  when statement shows a debit balance 309, 384–5
bank statement, dishonoured cheques recorded on 291, 355

589

INDEX

batching of source documents 86–90
bereavement leave 488
bookkeeping, what is it? 2–3
business documents 54–95
business ownership, types of 9–10

capital 2, 12
cash 339
  balancing and validating 457
  counting 448–9
  preparing and validating documents for banking 440–57
  security of 346–7
  sorting for banking 446–9
cash analysis sheet 486
cash book
  and bank reconciliation statement 369–98
  balancing 356–7
  checking accuracy of 358
  format 349–50
  maintenance 348–67
  recording receipts and payments 350–4
  types of 358–60
cash control 408–60
cash discount 61
cash payments, entry in cash book 351–2
cash payments journal 117–20, 184, 212–14
  dishonoured cheque entry 289–91
  payroll entries 514–15, 520–2
cash receipts
  balancing and validating 457–8
  entry in cash book 350–1
  entry in cash receipts book 440–1
cash receipts book 440–1
cash receipts journal 138–40, 245–7
  reversal entry for dishonoured cheque 289
cash received (takings) 440
cash records 339–407
  reconciling 286–91, 367–9
cash register receipt 70, 74, 345
cash register roll 70, 74, 89, 346, 457
cash register summary slip 341, 453
cash sale docket 70, 74, 345
cash sales 339–42
cash summary slip 341, 448, 453
cash transactions 14
change docket 486–7
change float 346
chart of accounts 7, 50, 51
cheque butt 66, 90
cheque coding details 66
cheque payment, for cash sales 344–5
cheque requisition form 67–8
cheques 65–6
  balancing and validating 457
  organising and counting for banking 449
cheques received (takings) 440
coin 447–8
columnar cash book 358
commercial cash book 359

commercial payroll systems 465
company 6, 9–10
contra entries 98, 156–7
control accounts 49
cooperative 10
correction of errors, general journal 157–61
counting cash 448–9
credit application 105
credit card credit voucher 75, 343, 450
credit card merchant summary 76, 343–4, 450
credit card sales 342–4
  organising for banking 449–51
credit card sales voucher 75, 343, 449
credit entry 7, 37
credit note 64–5, 89, 90
credit transactions 14
cross-references 174
'crossed' cheques 66–7

debit entry 7, 36
deductions 471–81, 512
  authorised by employee 471
  remitting 520–2
delivery docket 63
Dependant Rebate 479
deposit books 451
direct deposits 458
discount allowed 351
discount received 352
dishonoured cheques 288
  recording 286–91, 354–6
double-entry system 7, 36
drawings 12

EFTPOS sales 344, 459
electronic banking processes 458–60
electronic cash book 359–60
electronic funds transfer at point of sale *see* EFTPOS
electronic reporting systems 93–5
electronic transfer of funds 458
employee 462
employee earnings records 483, 484
employee entitlements 462, 512
employee time card 466
employer 462
employment contract 464
Employment Declaration form 476–80
enterprise bargaining agreement 464
error protection 93
ethics and accountability 347–8
expense accounts 38, 40, 51
expense recognition principle 7
expenses 7, 20

financial accounting 3
financial source documents 2, 49, 54–95
  accountability of 86
  batching of 86–90
  security of 86
  validity of 81–4
folio number 169

INDEX

folio references   172
franchise   10
fraud, payroll system   462
fringe benefits   462

general journal   49, 98–102
   basic format   170
   columnar (tabular) format   170–1
   correction of errors   157–61
   miscellaneous entries   149–62
   payroll entries   512–14
   posting from the   170–8
   posting to accounts payable ledger   206–9
   posting to accounts receivable ledger   238–41
   recording opening entries   101–2
general ledger   7, 49, 168–205
   completed   197–201
   postings from accounts payable journals   182–8
   postings from accounts receivable journals   189–96
   postings of payroll entries   515–19
   postings to   169
giving change   339–40
gross earnings   466
gross pay, calculating   466
gross wages   512
gross weekly wages, calculating   478–81
group certificate   483, 485
Group Savings Payable   520, 522
Group Tax Payable   520, 521

holiday pay, calculating   489–91
hours worked, calculating   465–6

imprest petty cash system   409–11
income tax deductions   471
Income Tax Instalments Weekly Rates Incorporating Medicare Levy   471, 472–5
industrial awards   464, 488
interest expense charged by creditors on overdue accounts   152–3
interest revenue (interest charged on overdue debtors' accounts)   153–4
internal controls   84–5, 347
payroll system   462–3
inventory (stock)   7
inventory (stock) drawings by owner   151–2
invoice   60, 89, 90

journals   2, 7, 49, 88
   what are they?   97–103
   see also specific journals

keeping a record of transactions   48–52

leave   462, 464–5, 488–9
leave without pay   489
ledger accounts, format   34–6
ledgers   2, 7, 49–51
   see also specific ledgers
legal entity   6

liabilities   2, 7, 12
liability accounts   37, 40, 51
long service leave   462, 488
loose coin   448
loose notes   447

management accounting   3
manual payroll register   481–3
maternity leave   464, 488, 489
Medical Insurance Payable   520, 521
Medicare Levy   471, 476, 479

net pay, calculating   471
net profit (or loss)   52
net wages   480–1, 512
non-current assets   98
   purchase on credit   149–50
   sale on credit   150–1
'not negotiable' cheque   66
notes (cash), sorting   446–7

outstanding deposits, bank reconciliation statement   302
overdraft   288, 369
overdue creditors' accounts, interest expense   152–3
overdue debtors' accounts, interest revenue   153–4
overtime   466
owner's equity   2, 7, 12
   and capital account   19–24
owner's equity accounts   37, 40, 51

paid leave   464, 488
partnership   9
paternity leave   488
pay packets, preparation   485–7
pay slips, completing   487–8
PAYE tax   471, 520
payment by cheque, for cash sales   344–5
payment for labour   464
payment voucher   486, 514, 520
payroll   462–537
   preparing the   465–71
payroll deductions   471–81, 512
payroll register, manual   481–3
payroll system
   internal control   462–3
   organisational policies and procedures   463–4
   types of   465
payroll transactions
   in the accounting system   512–19
   journal entries for   512–15
   remitting deductions   520–2
periodic payments   458
petty cash   69, 409
   security of   436
petty cash book   414–15
   amount of cash on hand   416
   amount spent   416
   balancing   415–19
   dealing with errors and irregularities   435–6
   reimbursement amount   417–19

petty cash records, checking 435
petty cash system 69
   maintenance 409–39
   manual vs computerised systems 420
petty cash transactions, recording 413
petty cash voucher 69, 410
petty cashier 409, 411
posting 93
   see also specific ledgers and journals
posting rules
   general journals to ledgers 267–8
   trading journals to ledgers 268–9
private company 10
profit 20
profit and loss statement 7, 24–5, 52
proprietary company 10
proprietor 8
proprietorship 2
public accounting 3
public company 10
public sector accounting 4
purchase and sale of non-current assets on credit 149–51
purchase order 58–60
purchase requisition 57–8
purchases journal 107–8, 182–3, 209–11
purchases returns and allowances journal 112–13, 183–4, 211–12

rebates 478–9
receipts 70–1, 89
   for cash sales 345–6
receiving and documenting payments/takings 339–46
receiving cash and giving change 339–40
reconciling
   bank statements 291–325
   cash records 286–91, 367–9
   invoices for payment to creditors 228
   over two consecutive periods 325–37
recording transactions 34–7
records of cash sales 73–4
remittance advice 68–9
remitting deductions 520–2
reporting period 3, 8
revenue accounts 37, 40, 51
revenue recognition principle 8
revenues 8, 20
rolled coin 448

salaries 462, 464–5
sales journal 127–9, 189–90, 241–3
sales returns and allowances journal 132–3, 190–1, 243–5
sales tax 60–1

schedule of creditors' balances 214–15
schedule of debtors' balances 247–8
security
   of cash 346–7
   of financial source documents 86
   of petty cash 436
sick leave 462, 488, 489
sole trader 4, 9
source documents *see* financial source documents
statement of account 73, 258–9
Statements of Accounting Concepts (SACs) 6, 7
study leave 488
subsidiary ledgers 49–50, 168–9
   reconciling with 205
sundry creditors 8
sundry debtors 8
superannuation guarantee levy 476
Superannuation Payable 520, 521

T-account 34–5
takings
   receiving and documenting 339–46
   record of 440–2
   verifying 346–8
Tax File Number 471, 476, 478
tax-free threshold 478
tax payable, calculating 480
tax stamps 485
taxation 471
telephone banking 459–60
terms of trading 61
3-column account 35–6
trade creditors *see* accounts payable
trade debtors *see* accounts receivable
trade discount 60
trading journal 49
trading statement 7
transaction analysis chart 18–19
transactions 2
transfers between accounts 98, 156–7
transposition errors 158–9, 201
trial balance 52, 201–2

Union Fees Payable 520, 522
unpaid leave 464, 489
unpresented cheques, bank reconciliation statement 302

validity of source documents 81–4
verifying the day's takings 346–9

wage envelopes, preparation 485–7
wages 464–5
wages calculation card 480–1, 490–1
workplace agreements 464